Taliban security personnel
stand guard along a road after
gunfire, 20 February 2023

Cont

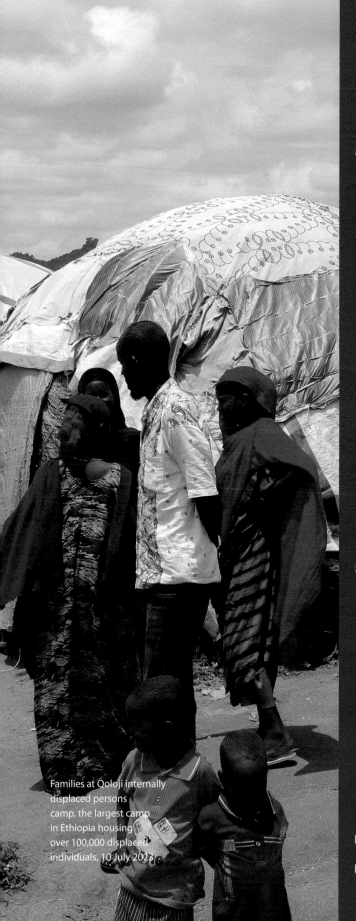

Families at Qoloji internally displaced persons camp, the largest camp in Ethiopia housing over 100,000 displaced individuals, 10 July 2023

THE
ARMED CONFLICT SURVEY

2023

The worldwide review of
political, military and humanitarian
trends in current conflicts

published by

Routledge
Taylor & Francis Group

for

The International Institute for Strategic Studies

The International Institute for Strategic Studies

Arundel House | 6 Temple Place | London | WC2R 2PG | UK

THE ARMED CONFLICT SURVEY 2023

First published December 2023 by **Routledge**
4 Park Square, Milton Park, Abingdon, Oxon, OX14 4RN

for **The International Institute for Strategic Studies**
Arundel House, 6 Temple Place, London, WC2R 2PG, UK

Simultaneously published in the USA and Canada by **Routledge**
52 Vanderbilt Avenue, New York, NY 10017

Routledge is an imprint of Taylor & Francis, an Informa business

© 2023 The International Institute for Strategic Studies

DIRECTOR-GENERAL AND CHIEF EXECUTIVE Dr Bastian Giegerich
EDITOR Dr Irene Mia
ASSISSTANT EDITOR Jana Phillips
CONTRIBUTING EDITOR FOR SUB-SAHARAN AFRICA Dr Benjamin Petrini
GRAPHICS COORDINATOR Christopher Harder
EDITORIAL Christopher Harder, Jack May, Adam Walters
DESIGN AND PRODUCTION Alessandra Beluffi, Ravi Gopar, Jade Panganiban, James Parker, Kelly Verity, Loraine Winter

CONFLICTS Adam Weinstein (Afghanistan and Pakistan), Dr Marcos Alan Ferreira and Dr Ryan Berg (Brazil), Grace Ellis and Mathijs Cazemier (Burkina Faso, Mali and Niger), Carlo Palleschi (Cameroon, Central African Republic and Mozambique), Ornella Moderan (Chad), Juan Pablo Medina Bikel (Colombia), Iris Madeline (Democratic Republic of the Congo, Rwanda and Uganda), Dr Umberto Profazio (Egypt and Libya), Marianne Richardson and Douglas Farah (El Salvador, Haiti, Honduras and Mexico), Dr Daniel Watson (Ethiopia, Nigeria, South Sudan and Sudan), Dr Alex Waterman (India and Kashmir), Dr Francesco Milan (Iraq, Somalia and Turkiye), Noor Hammad (Israel–Palestinian Territories), Morgan Michaels (Myanmar), Maximilian Hess (Nagorno-Karabakh and Russia–Ukraine), Michael Hart (Philippines and Thailand), Emile Hokayem (Syria), Dr Gregory Johnsen (Yemen)

REGIONAL ANALYSES Dr Irene Mia and Juan Pablo Medina Bickel (Americas), Adam Weinstein (Asia), Dr Nigel Gould-Davies (Europe and Eurasia), Dr Gregory Johnsen (Middle East and North Africa), Dr Benjamin Petrini (Sub-Saharan Africa)

REGIONAL SPOTLIGHTS Douglas Farah (Shifting Dynamics and New Conflict Zones in Latin America), Dr Bastian Giegerich and Dr Benjamin Petrini (The Looming Aftermath of War in Ukraine: Connecting Post-war Recovery, Security Guarantees and Domestic Defence Capabilities), Erica Pepe and Shiloh Fetzek (Weathering Converging Storms in North Africa: Climate, Political Instability and Food-system Resilience), Dr Alexandre Marc (From Global Jihad to Local Insurgencies: the Changing Nature of Sub-Saharan Jihadism), Antoine Levesques (The Re-emergence of the Tehrik-e-Taliban Pakistan and Implications for Regional Security)

THE CHART OF ARMED CONFLICT Erica Pepe, Juan Pablo Medina Bickel

RESEARCH CONTRIBUTIONS Matthew Bamber, Leo Cao, Henry Boyd, Karl Dewey, Birna Gudmundsdottir, Gauthier Lefevre, James Hackett, Emile Hokayem, Omar Rahim, Michael Tong

COVER IMAGES Getty

British Library Cataloguing in Publication Data
A catalogue record for this book is available from the British Library

Library of Congress Cataloguing in Publication Data

ISBN PAPERBACK: 978-1-032-73670-9
ISSN 2374-0973

Editor's Introduction

The Armed Conflict Survey 2023 continues to capture a world dominated by increasingly intractable conflicts and armed violence amid a proliferation of actors, complex and overlapping motives, global influences and accelerating climate change. The recent global shocks caused by the coronavirus pandemic and the ongoing war in Ukraine have added to the woes of fragile states and regions, reinforcing root causes of conflict while curtailing resources available to address or at least mitigate them. Moreover, Ukraine's unprecedented humanitarian and reconstruction needs are diverting ever more scarce international aid and development funding from other ongoing conflicts, which have been increasing in number over the last decade.[1] According to the United Nations Office for the Coordination of Humanitarian Affairs' Financial Tracking Service (FTS), the percentage of international humanitarian funding available to Yemen and Syria decreased from 11% and 9% respectively in 2021 to 7% and 6% in 2022, with Ukraine being the largest recipient globally that year at 10% (up from 0.6% in 2021).[2]

The accelerating climate crisis continues to act as a multiplier of both root causes of conflict and institutional weaknesses in fragile countries. Such countries are often very vulnerable to the effects of climate change, because they become trapped in a vicious circle where conflict erodes the state's ability to adapt and address climate impacts, while those same climate impacts contribute to conflict dynamics and governance failures.

At the global level, the intensity of conflict has also risen year on year in the reporting period of *The Armed Conflict Survey 2023* (1 May 2022–30 June 2023), with the number of fatalities and events increasing by 14% and 28% respectively.[3] This points to an increasingly problematic situation in many parts of the world in terms of humanitarian, stabilisation and reconstruction needs.

Conflict intractability and non-state armed groups

At the core of the grim outlook for conflict globally is the current complexity of contemporary wars, which often feature a large number of diverse non-state armed groups (NSAGs) as well as external interference. This, coupled with the diminished leverage of traditional resolution actors and processes, makes progress on their settlement a daunting task, contributing to their protractedness and resulting in little prospect for durable peace. The average duration of conflicts has increased over the last three decades amid an accelerated internationalisation of internal wars (which remain the most prevalent modality globally).[4]

Proliferating and ever-stronger NSAGs are among the main culprits of this situation. While their motivations, structures and modi operandi vary greatly within countries and globally, they share some common features. These include, notably, a universally growing importance as belligerent parties, political actors and providers of services and governance to the population under their control, as state legitimacy and reach deteriorate. They are also increasingly showing an unprecedented degree of fragmentation, with a myriad of small-scale groups competing for control and influence in Sub-Saharan Africa, Latin America and the Middle East, among others. Meanwhile, centralised insurgent movements have been largely disappearing or losing importance, contributing to the complexity of the conflict-actor landscape globally.

According to the International Committee of the Red Cross (ICRC), 459 armed groups of humanitarian concern were active globally as of June 2023, with around 195 million people living under their full or fluid control. Almost 80% of these groups provide some form of public services (including security, healthcare, education and social support) and/or extract taxes from the population under their control.[5] This phenomenon is of notable concern for Sub-Saharan Africa and the Middle East and North Africa, where a total of 295 groups operate, but it is also an issue in the rest of the world, with 83, 68 and 14 such groups active in Asia, the Americas, and Europe and Eurasia respectively. These actors are also becoming increasingly internationalised in terms of their presence, networks and operations amid continued support from and cooperation with third-party states, which often use them as proxies in internal conflicts of strategic importance to their foreign-policy goals. The ICRC estimates that 15% of armed groups globally give support to states, while 27% receive support from states.

Despite their crucial role in shaping and fuelling conflict dynamics, there is surprisingly little research and analysis devoted to capturing (and standardising) data on NSAGs' varying typologies and features. In an effort to fill this gap, *The Armed Conflict Survey* series provides standardised information on NSAGs active in each country covered, including their strength, areas of operation, organisational structure and leadership, resources, and domestic and external allies and opponents. The Regional Analysis chapters in *The Armed Conflict Survey 2023* also focus on the most important NSAGs per region, shedding light on their main characteristics, dynamics, and regional and global interlinkages.

Geopolitical competition further to the fore

Another driver of complexity, noted by *The Armed Conflict Survey* series since its inception in 2015, has been the increasing internationalisation of civil wars, through the intervention of a growing number and range of regional and global powers in pursuit of their strategic interests.[6] This accelerating trend of great-power (as well as emerging- and revisionist-power) competition resembles Cold War-style proxy wars, and Russia's full-scale invasion of Ukraine in February 2022 has escalated it to a new level. The invasion has not only ignited arguably the most important inter-state conflict since the Second World War, but it has also aggravated geopolitical divides between Western powers and those which do not completely subscribe to democratic principles and the prevalent rules-based international order.

The ascendence of these powers (China and Russia, but also Gulf countries, Iran and Turkiye, among others) has far-reaching repercussions for global stability and security. Their increased foreign-policy assertiveness is one of the main causes of the demise of traditional conflict-resolution and peacemaking processes, given that these powers often undermine or simply bypass existing institutions and forums (including the UN). It is also adding to an ongoing trend of democratic backsliding in many fragile regions of the world. By intervening with transactional approaches and an anti-Western bias, these powers often prop up authoritarian regimes and disregard fundamental principles of international humanitarian law, contributing to the weakening of democratic institutions, the militarisation of politics and *coups d'état*.

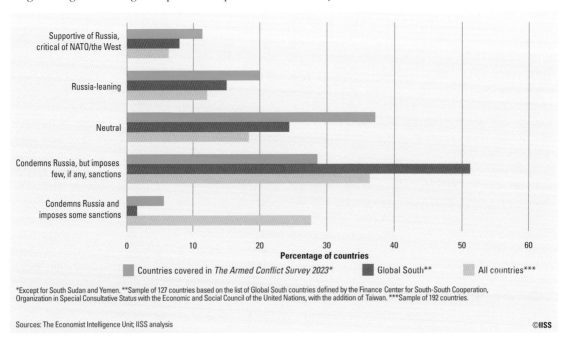

*Except for South Sudan and Yemen. **Sample of 127 countries based on the list of Global South countries defined by the Finance Center for South-South Cooperation, Organization in Special Consultative Status with the Economic and Social Council of the United Nations, with the addition of Taiwan. ***Sample of 192 countries.

Sources: The Economist Intelligence Unit; IISS analysis   ©IISS

Figure 1: Global stance towards Russia's invasion of Ukraine

Finally, their ascendence, coupled with years of perceived disengagement from the West in many fragile and conflict-affected countries, has led to increased geopolitical fragmentation in the Global South. The war in Ukraine has accelerated this trend, as the divide between Russia and Western powers has become unbridgeable and securing allies has become a strategic imperative (especially for the former). While Russia has faced widespread diplomatic isolation since the war began, many countries in the Global South have remained neutral or non-aligned despite Western powers' efforts (see Figure 1), highlighting the latter's diminishing influence and leverage in many parts of the world, including Sub-Saharan Africa and the Middle East. This has important consequences for geopolitical balances in most active conflicts.

Global energy-transition and climate-change-mitigation strategies are also becoming an increasingly important focus of geopolitical competition – a trend that is sure to continue in the coming decades. Disagreements over mitigation responsibilities and competition for control of critical resources and technologies for the green transition will become important sources of inter-state tensions and will exacerbate current geopolitical divides. Notably, control of critical minerals for the green transition might drive third-party intervention in civil wars in resource-rich, fragile countries, while amplifying (or creating new) sources of disputes among domestic conflict parties.

The International Institute for Strategic Studies' analysis filter for conflict has long added the geopolitical angle to the domestic dimension, in line with our global character and strategic research focus. Accordingly, *The Armed Conflict Survey* series has prominently featured regional and global drivers, interlinkages among conflicts across the world and international repercussions. Our Armed Conflict Global Relevance Indicator (ACGRI), now in its third edition, also benchmarks the global relevance of conflicts based on their geopolitical impact, as well as their intensity and human impact.

With geopolitics increasingly taking centre stage in the global conflict landscape, we have adopted a regional-focused approach for *The Armed Conflict Survey 2023*, with comprehensive Regional Analyses, as well as Regional Spotlight chapters on selected key regional trends. An increasing number of armed conflicts now have a consequential regional

dimension which needs to be ascertained to fully understand or address them. This approach allows us to provide our audience of experts, practitioners and policymakers with unique insights into the geopolitical and geo-economic threads linking conflicts across the world, as well as their interrelations with domestic dynamics (covered in synthetic profiles of conflict-affected countries).

Bringing conflict complexity to life

The data-rich analysis throughout *The Armed Conflict Survey 2023* is visually complemented by multiple graphic elements, including regional and conflict-specific maps, charts and tables. These illustrate core conflict trends during the reporting period and related data (including on military events, interventions, and humanitarian impacts and forced displacement), as well as regional and global links and spillovers. An exhaustive categorisation and analysis of conflict parties, together with regional timelines of key military/violent and political events for the reporting period, provide invaluable background information on the conflicts covered.

The accompanying Chart of Armed Conflict provides a visual snapshot of the global conflict landscape's complexity, with its proliferation of NSAGs and increasing external interventions. For each of the conflicts covered in *The Armed Conflict Survey 2023*, the Chart depicts involvements by foreign countries, deployments by major geopolitical powers, multilateral peace and stabilisation interventions, regional data on armed groups of humanitarian concern, total fatalities and the ACGRI's human-impact pillar.

Regional interlinkages and trends

The Armed Conflict Survey 2023 adopts an expanded regional focus compared to previous editions. This is in line with our efforts to offer a strategic assessment of the global conflict landscape, highlighting its most important drivers, trends and actors at any given time.

Each regional section includes an extended Regional Analysis chapter, providing an overview of the regional conflict trends, drivers and main actors (including coalitions, NSAGs and third-party interventions). The Regional Analyses also delve into the regional and international dimensions of the active conflicts and their future evolutions in each region, analysing prospects for peace and escalation, political risks and potential flashpoints to monitor at the regional level. This 'horizon scanning' exercise aims to provide forward-looking insights to inform the strategies of policymakers, practitioners and corporate actors operating in or near conflict-affected countries.

Regional Spotlights complement the Regional Analyses, covering trends of strategic importance for the region or the global conflict landscape. Trends highlighted and discussed include shifting drug-trafficking dynamics and new conflict zones in the Americas; the centrality of security guarantees in Ukraine's future reconstruction efforts; policy best practices to address overlapping climate, political and food-insecurity crises in North Africa; the changing nature of jihadism in Sub-Saharan Africa; and the re-emergence of the Tehrik-e-Taliban (TTP) in Pakistan and its implications for Asian security.

Americas
Armed conflict in the Americas remained mostly driven by criminal contestation over the control of lucrative illicit economies (notably drugs) in the reporting period, with multiple NSAGs fighting against one another and the state. These groups have, in time, also become political actors, infiltrating the state and challenging the latter's territorial control and governance. Their regional linkages along drug-supply chains in the Americas have been increasingly accompanied by global spillovers, as criminal groups progressively extend their international reach in response to shifting profit margins and trends in international demand.

The reconfiguration of drug routes and criminal networks continued during the reporting period, with outbreaks of violence and escalation in countries that were, until recently, considered relatively peaceful, including Argentina, Ecuador and Paraguay. Mexican criminal actors continued to diversify their portfolio into synthetic-drugs (including fentanyl) production and exports to the United States, heightening diplomatic friction between the two countries. Environmental crime was also on the rise, often converging with traditional drug-trafficking activities ('narcoecology'). Haiti's economic, political, security and humanitarian crises spiralled out of control, with violent events and fatalities registering a 22% and 100% increase (respectively) year on year and little hope for improvement amid timid steps towards external interventions to stabilise the country.[7]

The start of the 'total peace' process in Colombia (involving simultaneous peace negotiations with all active criminal groups in the country) and small steps towards the stabilisation of the Venezuela crisis (including the definition of a path towards fair elections in 2024) are reasons for hope for regional peace. However, the outlook remains fraught with risks, given the complexity of both processes and slow progress at the negotiating tables.

Europe and Eurasia
Conflict in the region continued to be linked to disagreements over borders between countries, as well as Russia's aspirations to restore dominance over the former countries of the Soviet Union and its position as a revisionist global power.

Tensions between Armenia and Azerbaijan over Nagorno-Karabakh built up in the reporting period, culminating in a third full-blown war on 19 September 2023 initiated by an Azerbaijani 'anti-terrorist operation' there. The war concluded in a matter of days with Azerbaijan's decisive victory. The ethnic Armenian government in Nagorno-Karabakh agreed to disband its army immediately and its institutions by the end of the year. The war triggered a mass exodus of the ethnic Armenian population, with more than 100,000 of its estimated 120,000 residents fleeing to Armenia by the end of September 2023. The latest dramatic developments were partly caused by unresolved issues regarding the region's final status after the 2020 war over Nagorno-Karabakh, which concluded without a final peace agreement between Armenia and Azerbaijan. In Central Asia, border tensions between Kyrgyzstan and Tajikistan, which had erupted in April 2021, continued to flare up episodically, while the conflict between Georgia and Russia remained frozen but of concern. The latter continues to occupy the regions of Abkhazia and South Ossetia following its 2008 war with the former.

The war in Ukraine has been and remains unpredictable. The diplomatic deadlock and military stalemate (i.e., the slow Ukrainian advance) point to a potentially protracted conflict. Meanwhile, instability has also begun to spread into Russia itself. Acts of sabotage and arson, carried out by Ukrainian operatives and dissident Russians, have increased. There are also domestic cracks within Russia's regime, exemplified by the Wagner Group mutiny in June 2023.

Ukraine has nevertheless begun planning for its post-war reconstruction with the support of the European Union, United Kingdom and US, among others, but this way forward will be challenging. In fact, the feasibility and sustainability of reconstruction will be inextricably linked to Kyiv obtaining meaningful security guarantees that ensure Ukraine's future territorial integrity against external aggression. Further, the emergence of a Ukrainian domestic military industry is a critical pillar going forward because security guarantees will likely not include NATO membership.

Middle East and North Africa

With the exception of the Israel–Palestinian Territories conflict, the reporting period saw a stalemate in conflicts across the region and a reluctant acceptance of the status quo by the international community, notably in Syria and Yemen – historically two of the region's most violent wars. The Arab League welcomed back Syrian President Bashar al-Assad to its annual summit in May 2023, more than a decade after it expelled the country due to Assad's conduct. Turkiye also started normalising relations with Assad. In Yemen, Saudi Arabia entered into direct negotiations with Ansarullah (the Houthi movement), putting the kingdom on a path that will likely result in recognition of Houthi rule over Sanaa and northern Yemen and the eventual partition of the country. The conflict in Libya remained at a stalemate, with the country divided between competing governments, while Iraq and Egypt both saw a decrease in fighting. Turkiye and the Kurdistan Workers' Party continued to clash, but with no significant loss of territory.

The Israel–Palestinian Territories conflict witnessed increased tensions and fighting, notably in the West Bank, where levels of violence have been at their highest since 2005. Israeli security services conducted an unprecedented number of deadly raids on Palestinian towns, while Palestinians continued lone-wolf violent assaults against civilians and the security sector. Violence was exacerbated by the Israeli extreme right-wing government, which continued settlement building and its attempts to strengthen the executive branch at the expense of the judiciary.

The spike in food prices has compounded the region's extreme climate-change vulnerability to create a major food-insecurity crisis, especially for import-dependent countries, notably in North Africa. The region's ability to tackle these multiple crises will have important implications for regional security dynamics as well as global energy security.

Sub-Saharan Africa

Sub-Saharan Africa continued to be the most conflict-affected region globally, with wars largely concentrated in four adjacent theatres – the Sahel, the Lake Chad Basin, the Great Lakes Region and East Africa – as well as the Central African Republic and Mozambique. Most conflicts there have internal, regional and international elements which contribute to their intractability.

Notable developments during the reporting period included the breakout of conflict in Sudan between the Sudan Armed Forces and the paramilitary Rapid Support Forces in April 2023, which engulfed Khartoum, other urban centres and peripheral regions, with critical regional implications; the end of the two-year civil war in Ethiopia with the signing of a peace agreement between the Ethiopian government and the Tigray People's Liberation Front in November 2022; the reignition of inter-state tensions between the Democratic Republic of the Congo and Rwanda; the end of France's *Operation Barkhane* and its pull-out from Mali and Burkina Faso; and the announced withdrawal of the UN Multidimensional Integrated Stabilization Mission in Mali, amid a wider drift towards military authoritarianism across the Sahel (with Niger being the latest country experiencing a military coup).

Although overall levels of violence in the region remained broadly unchanged year on year, jihadist violence markedly increased, especially in Somalia and the Sahel. Jihadist groups in the region have been evolving, becoming much more localised and intertwined with community and ethnic conflicts. Their international ties to the Islamic State (ISIS) and al-Qaeda have weakened, and connections between insurgent groups now appear to be limited to intra-regional collaborations.

Asia

Violence has significantly reduced in two of the three most consequential conflicts in Asia, those in Kashmir and Afghanistan, amid a continuation of the ceasefire brokered in February 2021 between India and Pakistan for the former and the consolidation of power and territorial control of the Afghan Taliban for the latter. On the other hand, the conflict in Myanmar between the military junta and a coalition of pro-democracy forces and ethnic armed organisations, following the former's coup in February 2021, continues despite sanctions imposed by the West on the State Administration Council (Myanmar armed forces or Tatmadaw) and the suspension of aid.

There is a risk that inter-state tensions between nuclear powers in the region could escalate into major conventional wars, including those between the US and China over the Taiwan Strait, between Pakistan and India along the Line of Control, and between China and India along the Line of Actual Control. Of these conflicts, the first two carry the highest risk of escalation.

The risks represented by the TTP to regional security and Pakistan's security and political stability have grown as the group has increased its activities in the region. Pakistan's deep political crisis and upcoming elections will make it difficult to reach a consensus around implementing an effective counter-terrorist strategy.

Notes

[1] The total number of conflicts as captured by the UCDP/PRIO Armed Conflict Dataset has been consistently on the rise since 2011, totalling 183 in 2022, the highest in three decades. UCDP disaggregates between state-based (i.e., at least one conflict party is a state) and non-state-based armed conflicts (i.e., conflict parties are exclusively NSAGs), and defines an armed conflict as the 'use of armed force between two parties' that 'results in at least 25 battle-related deaths in one calendar year'. Conflict 'parties' can be either state- or non-state-based depending on the type of conflict under consideration. Based on this definition, each country can have several different ongoing conflicts per year. This methodology explains the larger number of conflicts accounted for by UCDP compared to those identified in *The Armed Conflict Survey 2023*, which adopts the country as the primary unit of analysis. See UCDP/PRIO Armed Conflict Dataset Version 23.1 and UCDP Non-State Conflict Dataset Version 23.1. Nils Petter Gleditsch et al., 'Armed Conflict 1946–2001: A New Dataset', *Journal of Peace Research*, vol. 39, no. 5, 2002, pp. 615–37; Shawn Davies, Therese Pettersson and Magnus Öberg, 'Organized Violence 1989–2022 and the Return of Conflicts Between States?', *Journal of Peace Research*, vol. 60, no. 4, 2023; Ralph Sundberg, Kristine Eck and Joakim Kreutz, 'Introducing the UCDP Non-state Conflict Dataset', *Journal of Peace Research*, vol. 49, no. 2, 2012; and Uppsala Universitet, 'UCDP Definitions'.

[2] IISS calculations based on data reported as of 26 July 2023. This data refers to funding from multilateral organisations and governments only. See FTS, 'Total Reported Funding 2021'; and FTS, 'Total Reported Funding 2022'.

[3] IISS calculations based on data from the Armed Conflict Location & Event Data Project (ACLED), www.acleddata.com.

[4] For more details on both trends, see 'The Long Aftermath of Armed Conflicts', in IISS, *The Armed Conflict Survey 2021* (Abingdon: Routledge for the IISS, 2021), pp. 22–8.

[5] This data is drawn from the annual ICRC survey on armed groups completed in June 2023. The ICRC uses the generic term 'armed group' for a group that is not a state but has the capacity to cause violence that is of humanitarian concern. Armed groups also include those groups that qualify as conflict parties to a non-international armed conflict according to the Geneva Conventions, which the ICRC defines as 'non-state armed groups'. See Matthew Bamber-Zryd, 'ICRC Engagement with Armed Groups in 2023', ICRC Humanitarian Law & Policy, 20 October 2023.

[6] In regions like Sub-Saharan Africa, there are currently more armed conflicts with external intervention and regional dimensions than purely internal ones (i.e., confined within the borders of one country).

[7] IISS calculations based on data from the Armed Conflict Location & Event Data Project (ACLED), www.acleddata.com.

Notes on Methodology

The Armed Conflict Survey 2023 reviews and analyses developments, dynamics, trends and outlooks related to active armed conflicts around the world. We define an armed conflict as a sustained military confrontation between two or more organised actors making purposive use of armed force. The inclusion of a conflict in the book is based on this definition and the methodology detailed below.

Armed conflicts in 2022–23

The Armed Conflict Survey 2023 covers armed conflicts that were active between 1 May 2022 and 30 June 2023 (the 'reporting period') globally.[1] These are organised into 37 Country Profiles across five regional sections: the Americas, Europe and Eurasia, the Middle East and North Africa, Sub-Saharan Africa, and Asia. The analysis focuses on regional security dynamics, with Country Profiles providing an overview of each conflict. Each section is introduced by an in-depth Regional Analysis, which discusses the main regional trends, how different armed conflicts relate to and influence one another, the outlook of the conflicts in the region and political risks to monitor. The Regional Analysis is complemented by a Regional Spotlight, which offers a deep dive into a region-specific dynamic or trend. Country Profiles (which come in a shorter or longer form, depending on any given conflict's global relevance as assessed by IISS analysis) cover all active conflicts in each region and capture specific domestic dynamics as well as developments in the reporting period.

We have introduced several changes with respect to last year's edition to better capture regional and global conflict trends, while refining our methodology and ensuring timely coverage. We have restructured the regional sections to cover regional and cross-border trends and dynamics in more depth, and we have focused the country-specific analysis on key domestic trends and developments. The special-feature section covering global trends has been discontinued and replaced by Regional Spotlight chapters, which delve into emerging trends with both regional and global relevance.

Except for inter-state conflicts, *The Armed Conflict Survey 2023* uses the country as the unit of analysis – including for conflicts in Sub-Saharan Africa, some of which were bundled together in previous editions of *The Armed Conflict Survey* under the regional categories of the Sahel, the Lake Chad Basin and the Great Lakes Region. For Sub-Saharan Africa, this approach ensures a better coverage of domestic dynamics and developments than in previous editions, while retaining the regional focus through the expanded Regional Analysis chapter. In general, this approach allows for a more granular assessment and systematisation of the different conflicts active simultaneously in specific countries, for instance in India, Nigeria, Pakistan and Syria.

To reflect changes in the relative global relevance of conflicts in the reporting period, we have reduced and expanded the Haiti and Pakistan Country Profiles, respectively. We have also introduced new Country Profiles for Burkina Faso, Chad, the Democratic Republic of the Congo (DRC), Mali, Niger, Rwanda and Uganda.

Criteria for inclusion and removal

Defining armed conflict as a military or violent phenomenon means *The Armed Conflict Survey 2023* does not aim to determine the applicability of international humanitarian law to different conflict situations (as in the Geneva Conventions or the Rome Statute).

The Armed Conflict Survey 2023 includes armed confrontations that meet our thresholds in terms of **duration**, **intensity** and **organisation of the conflict parties**.

We require an armed conflict to run for three months at a minimum and feature violent incidents on a weekly or at least fortnightly basis.[2] The definition of armed conflict in *The Armed Conflict Survey 2023* does not involve a numerical threshold of battle-related deaths, contrary to conflict datasets such as the Uppsala Conflict Data Program. For wars between states – which feature substantial levels of military mobilisation, simultaneous and numerous armed clashes, or significant fatalities – the duration threshold may be relaxed.

The organisation of the conflict parties refers to their ability to plan and execute military operations or violent attacks. The scale of such attacks is not a factor in this determination – for the purpose of inclusion in *The Armed Conflict Survey 2023*, planting improvised explosive devices, for example, is equivalent to battlefield clashes. For armed conflicts that involve state parties, the deployment of armed forces or militarised (not regular) police is required. Non-state armed groups (NSAGs) must demonstrate some logistical and operational capacity, such as access to weapons and other military equipment, or an ability to devise strategies and carry out operations, coordinate activities, establish communication between members, and recruit and train personnel. Territorial control or a permanent base in an area is not necessary. *The Armed Conflict Survey 2023* does not require a specific type of organisational structure of armed groups to define the presence of a conflict. Not all NSAGs have a distinct and effective chain of command – for example, many of those operating in Sub-Saharan Africa do not – but can be highly decentralised, maintain an amorphous structure, rely on a transnational network or have a global reach. The lack of a hierarchical military structure is therefore not a reason for exclusion. In each Country Profile, the Conflict Parties section lists the main organisational capabilities of the actors involved.[3]

The Armed Conflict Survey 2023 excludes cases of protests and riots if they happen in isolation. Instances of government repression, ethnic cleansing or genocide that occur outside of a conflict situation are also not included, regardless of their scale, unless the population develops a capacity to fight back through an armed, organised resistance, or another state intervenes – as in the case of the Khmer Rouge regime in Cambodia when Vietnam invaded in 1979.

Given the increasingly complex nature of contemporary conflicts, our definition does not discriminate based on the nature of their drivers. *The Armed Conflict Survey 2023* includes conflicts motivated by political, socio-economic, ideological, religious and criminal reasons – or a combination of these elements. This approach allows us to cover conflicts in the Americas, which are mostly driven by criminal contestation over the control of illicit economies and involve actors with elusive political or ideological motives.

The Armed Conflict Survey 2023 applies two criteria for removal. Armed conflicts that have lost the above-defined characteristics for inclusion are removed after two years. An armed conflict terminated through a peace agreement also ceases to be included if it is followed by military demobilisation of all conflict parties.

Classification and categorisation of armed conflicts: scope and actors

The unit of analysis in *The Armed Conflict Survey 2023* is the country where the military or violent confrontation(s) that can be defined as armed conflict under our criteria takes place. In most cases, conflicts occur within the boundaries of a state and are therefore listed under that country's name. This applies for single conflicts but also for instances of overlapping distinct insurgencies occurring within the boundaries of a single country. Concomitant insurgencies ongoing in India, Iraq, Niger, Pakistan and the Philippines, to mention a few, are combined in one single Country Profile for the purpose of our analysis. Country Profiles identify and analyse the different conflicts within a country (and provide respective start dates and typologies) in instances of multiple confrontations. Conflicts that have elements of inter-state confrontation take the name of either the disputed region (i.e., Nagorno-Karabakh and Kashmir) or the parties involved (i.e., Russia–Ukraine and Israel–Palestinian Territories).

Conflicts may involve state or non-state actors. According to the types of actors involved and the interactions between them, armed conflicts have been grouped into one (or more) of the following four categories: inter-state conflicts, internal conflicts, transnational conflicts and internationalised-internal conflicts.[4]

An **inter-state** conflict involves two or more states (or a group of states) and takes place on the territory of one or several states, as well as in the global commons. This is the least common modality of conflict in the current landscape. However, inter-state conflicts are often among the most globally significant, as exemplified by the Russia–Ukraine war.

An **internal** conflict takes place in the territory of one state and is either fought by a government (and possibly allied armed groups) against one or more NSAGs, or between two or more NSAGs without the direct participation of state forces. Within this category, we include the sub-categories of localised insurgencies (such as the one ongoing in southern Thailand), intercommunal conflicts (such as the several conflicts in South Sudan) and organised crime (which applies to most of the conflicts in the Americas). However, these groupings are not necessarily mutually exclusive, and many internal conflicts feature characteristics of two or more sub-categories.

Transnational conflicts are those which take place across different countries or have important regional dimensions, such as many confrontations in Sub-Saharan Africa, including in the Sahel or in the Lake Chad Basin. In this type of conflict, armed actors may be active across countries that share borders, or national armed forces may join together to create a regional coalition.

Finally, **internationalised-internal** conflicts are confrontations in which the kernel of the dispute remains domestic, but which feature the military intervention of one or more external states. Such involvement may include training, equipping or providing military intelligence to a conflict party or participating in the hostilities, either directly or through local proxies and sponsored actors.

The Armed Conflict Global Relevance Indicator (ACGRI)

The Armed Conflict Survey 2023 features the third edition of our Armed Conflict Global Relevance Indicator (ACGRI) as an additional tool of analysis and prioritisation to complement internal qualitative expertise. The ACGRI assesses and benchmarks the global significance of conflicts across the world based on three pillars – or drivers – of significance, covering the following dimensions:

- The **human impact** of conflicts, in terms of human losses and hardship. The rationale for including this dimension stems from the nexus between conflict-related fatalities, forced displacement and further domestic social, economic and political instability with spillover effects on regional and global stability.
- The **incidence** of conflicts, as a measure of intensity and related security implications and potential negative externalities on neighbouring countries and beyond.
- The **geopolitical impact** of conflicts, measured by several variables we created to capture the

involvement of third parties and interventions by the international community, based on IISS proprietary data and other international sources. This year, this pillar includes the new 'humanitarian funding' variable, which captures the financial support provided by governments and multilateral organisations to address domestic humanitarian needs, including those resulting from armed conflicts.

The ACGRI uses the country in which a conflict occurs as the unit of analysis. This methodological choice is justified by the fact that most of the armed conflicts covered are internal (internationalised or not), meaning the conflict can be assimilated to the country in which it takes place. For cases in which multiple insurgencies are happening at once in a country, the country score encompasses all of them. However, the ACGRI is not able to assess the global significance of each domestic insurgency in isolation. Likewise, transnational conflicts are not given a regional score; global relevance is instead assessed at the level of each country involved.

In contrast, for the Nagorno-Karabakh and Israel–Palestinian Territories conflicts, the unit of analysis is the conflict itself. India and Pakistan are treated separately in the case of the conflict in Kashmir due to the presence of other localised insurgencies ongoing in both countries. For the Russia–Ukraine conflict, the indicator is calculated based on Ukraine data only, as the latter is the theatre of fighting. Geopolitical indicators relevant to Kashmir, such as the number of United Nations Security Council (UNSC) resolutions, are attributed to both countries to ensure that the final score reflects the geopolitical impact of the inter-state conflict, if applicable.

The indicator is composed of a total of nine variables (see Table 1), which are good proxies of the dimensions of global relevance we seek to cover, considering the availability of reliable data.

As a preliminary step to combine variable scores into pillar and ACGRI scores, data for each variable is normalised on a 0–10 scale, through the following approach:

Eq.1 (indicator data–0)/(y–0) × 10 = variable score

where the indicator data refers to continuous data, y refers to the maximum value from the target countries and 0 is used as the minimum value.[5]

Each pillar score is the arithmetic mean of the composing variable, multiplied by 10, giving a pillar score between 0 and 100.

The scores of the ACGRI composing pillars are displayed throughout the book in a continuous colour progression (using conditional formatting) in order to respect the cardinal (instead of ordinal) distance between countries and to reflect more precisely the differentiation of conflicts' global relevance based on the continuum of the ACGRI scores for the full sample.

Table 1: ACGRI pillars and variables

Pillar	Variable	Description	Source
Human impact	Fatalities	Number of fatalities due to violent events, by country, 1 May 2022–30 June 2023[6]	Armed Conflict Location & Event Data Project (ACLED), www.acleddata.com
	Refugees	Number of refugees (total), counted by country of origin, as of 31 December 2022	UN High Commissioner for Refugees, UN Relief and Works Agency for Palestine Refugees in the Near East
	Internally displaced persons (IDPs)	Number of IDPs (total), by country, as of 31 December 2022[7]	Internal Displacement Monitoring Centre
Incidence	Violent events	Number of violent events, by country, 1 May 2022–30 June 2023[8]	Armed Conflict Location & Event Data Project (ACLED), www.acleddata.com
Geopolitical impact	Foreign countries' involvement[9]	Number of foreign countries 'involved' in the conflict, by country, as of 30 June 2023[10]	IISS analysis, Military Balance+, Christoph Trebesch et al., 'The Ukraine Support Tracker: Which Countries Help Ukraine and How?', KIEL Working Paper, no. 2218, 2023
	Deployments by major geopolitical powers	Number of personnel deployed by major geopolitical powers in conflict-affected countries, by country, as of 30 June 2023[11]	Military Balance+
	UNSC resolutions	Number of UNSC resolutions concerning conflicts under review, by country, 1 May 2022–30 June 2023	UNSC
	Peacekeeping and other multilateral missions	Number of operational peacekeeping, special political and military missions and other multilateral missions concerning conflicts in countries under review, as of 30 June 2023[12]	Military Balance+, Stockholm International Peace Research Institute (SIPRI),[13] UN,[14] regional organisations, ad hoc coalitions
	Humanitarian funding	Total reported incoming funding from governments and multilateral organisations, by recipient country, in 2022[15]	UN Office for the Coordination of Humanitarian Affairs (UNOCHA) Financial Tracking Service (FTS)

Data for all the variables included in the ACGRI is listed in the Data Appendix, along with detailed source information, definition and the underlying calculation methodology for each variable.

Selected data from the ACGRI is also featured in the Key Conflict Statistics boxes in the Country Profiles, as well as other background variables relevant to the context under analysis, such as the Gini index, GDP per capita (based on purchasing power parity in constant prices–international dollars), the 'functioning of government' pillar of the Economist Intelligence Unit's Democracy Index and the Notre Dame Global Adaptation Initiative's climate-change 'vulnerability' score. Full data for all these background variables is also contained in the Data Appendix.

The Chart of Armed Conflict

The Chart of Armed Conflict provides relevant data and information for all active conflicts included in

The Armed Conflict Survey 2023. This year, the Chart depicts the increasing complexity of the contemporary conflict landscape, including the nexus between domestic and geopolitical dimensions and the multiplicity of actors involved. It includes the involvement of foreign countries in conflicts, deployments by major geopolitical powers and interventions by the international community through multilateral peace and stabilisation operations. The Chart also visualises insightful data on the number of armed groups of humanitarian concern, their territorial control and their provision of public services/extraction of taxes at the regional level. The human impact of conflict, as captured by the related ACGRI pillar, as well as fatalities are included for each country covered.

Data is from the IISS Military Balance+, the International Committee of the Red Cross, the official websites of the UN, regional multilateral organisations, ad hoc coalitions and other organisations.

Notes

[1] Although the reporting period for the conflicts included in *The Armed Conflict Survey 2023* ends on 30 June 2023, we have covered important developments that happened after this date to make the publication as timely as possible. Such developments include the *coup d'état* in Niger at the end of July 2023 and major events that occurred after the cut-off date in the conflicts in Ethiopia, Nagorno-Karabakh, Sudan and Ukraine. For all other cases, events after the end of June 2023 will be covered in *The Armed Conflict Survey 2024*.

[2] These numerical criteria may be overruled by a qualitative assessment in exceptional cases. For instance, we have decided to include Rwanda this year due to its overt support for the March 23 Movement's activities in the DRC and the consequent escalation in bilateral tensions, despite the country not fulfilling all the quantitative criteria for inclusion.

[3] Unless otherwise stated, all figures related to military strength and capability, defence economics and arms equipment in the Conflict Parties tables are taken from the Military Balance+.

[4] To reflect the significant changes in the nature of the conflicts in Afghanistan and Ukraine in recent years, *The Armed Conflict Survey 2022* made some adjustments that were retained this year. For Afghanistan, the typology of the conflict was revised to internal (localised insurgency and intercommunal) to take into account a new phase of the conflict (started in 2001), which began in 2021 with the full withdrawal of foreign troops and the Taliban's takeover. For Ukraine, we changed the name, typology of conflict and starting date to reflect the new reality of the conflict, which evolved from an internationalised-internal confrontation to a fully fledged inter-state conflict with Russia's full-scale invasion of Ukraine in February 2022.

[5] The normalisation formula is partially adjusted for the presence of outliers under the assumption of a normal distribution in the sample. An observation is treated as an outlier if it is three (3) standard deviations larger than the mean of the sample's distribution. The formula is as follows: $x_i > X + z_a S$, where x_i is the observation, X is the mean, z_a equals three (3) and S is the standard deviation of the sample. As a result, for all ACGRI variables except IDPs, UNSC resolutions, and peacekeeping and other multilateral missions, Ukraine is treated as an outlier and assigned the highest score, together with the country with the second-highest value in the sample.

[6] Conflict fatalities include those that result from battles, explosions/remote violence and violence against civilians.

[7] Most recent available data for Egypt was from 2020.

[8] Violent events include battles, explosions/remote violence and violence against civilians.

[9] Our methodology includes the following definition of 'involvement' for foreign countries in conflict. For internal conflicts, foreign countries are considered 'involved' if they are either present through the deployment of military capabilities (outside of a multilateral mission as defined in the ACGRI) or if they meet all the following criteria: presence of intelligence assets; provision of military financial support; role in an advisory or operational command-and-control capacity; and sale or transfer of military equipment. For inter-state conflicts, foreign countries are considered 'involved' if they are either present through the deployment of military capabilities (outside of a multilateral mission as defined in the ACGRI) or if they meet two or more of the following criteria: presence of intelligence assets; provision of military financial support; role in an advisory or operational command-and-control capacity; and sale or transfer of military equipment.

[10] Military aid to Ukraine only refers to aid worth more than US$1 billion in funding provided by over 30 countries between 24 January 2022 and 24 February 2023.

[11] This is calculated based on the number of military personnel deployed into conflict-affected countries by major geopolitical powers within the G20 (including unilaterally, as part of a combat coalition or as part of a mission under the aegis

of an international organisation organisation, but excluding deployments that are not conflict related).

[12] These include missions undertaken by the UN, regional organisations or ad hoc groups related to UN sanctions/UNSC resolutions or endorsed by the UN and other international organisations. Data refers to active missions as of 30 June 2023 that fulfil the following two criteria: objective (relating to multidimensional peace and conflict resolution) and geographical scope (relating to the analysed conflicts in the countries under review).

[13] SIPRI, 'SIPRI Map of Multilateral Peace Operations, 2023', May 2023.

[14] UN, 'UN Special Political Missions and Other Political Presences 2023', July 2023.

[15] This includes financial funding received by local governments, multilateral organisations, non-governmental organisations, pooled funds, private organisations, and Red Cross and Red Crescent organisations operating in the country under review. The data was retrieved from FTS on 26 July 2023. Figures are continuously updated, and later reports may differ from the data retrieved on the above date. FTS is a voluntary reporting mechanism in which the donor declares the value of the funding to FTS, which then oversees its curation, validation and processing in a centralised manner.

REGIONAL SECTIONS

A teenager sits next to his improvised bomb shelter made from wood, rice bags and sand in Kayah State, Myanmar, 13 May 2023

1 Americas

A group of 2,000 detainees are moved to the mega-prison Terrorism Confinement Centre, Tecoluca, El Salvador, 15 March 2023

Overview

Armed conflict in the Americas is internal in nature and mostly driven by criminal dynamics around the control of lucrative illicit economies (notably drugs), with multiple non-state armed groups (NSAGs) fighting against one another and the state. These groups, however, have been morphing into political actors in recent years, challenging the state's territorial control as well as its monopoly on the use of force and governance. They increasingly infiltrate governments at all levels to influence political decisions and policies in their favour through corruption, intimidation and/or the electoral votes that they control as bargaining chips. Exploiting states' weaknesses and low presence in territories under their control, NSAGs often provide basic services and

governance as well as economic opportunities to local populations, entrenching themselves in society and developing legitimacy.

National criminal groups are connected across the region along drug supply chains which stretch from production to final markets in the Americas (mostly the United States and Brazil, which are the largest and second-largest cocaine consumers globally). These domestic and regional dynamics have been increasingly accompanied by global spillovers, as criminal groups progressively extend their international reach, networks and operations in response to shifting profit margins and trends in international demand.

These factors, coupled with their high intensity and human impact (which continue to drive

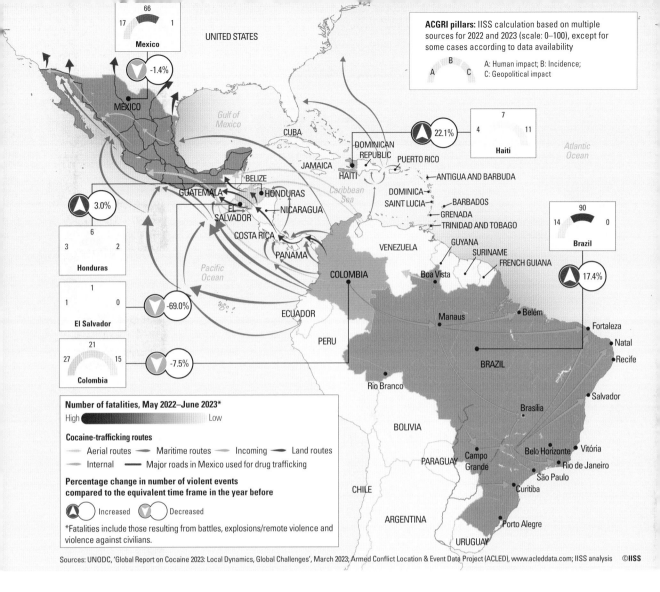

ACGRI pillars: IISS calculation based on multiple sources for 2022 and 2023 (scale: 0–100), except for some cases according to data availability

A: Human impact; B: Incidence; C: Geopolitical impact

Mexico — 66 — 17 — 1 — -1.4%

Haiti — 7 — 4 — 11 — 22.1%

Honduras — 6 — 3 — 2 — 3.0%

El Salvador — 1 — 1 — 0 — -69.0%

Colombia — 21 — 27 — 15 — -7.5%

Brazil — 90 — 14 — 0 — 17.4%

Number of fatalities, May 2022–June 2023*

High ———— Low

Cocaine-trafficking routes

- - - - Aerial routes   ——— Maritime routes   ——— Incoming   ■■■ Land routes
——— Internal   ■■■ Major roads in Mexico used for drug trafficking

Percentage change in number of violent events compared to the equivalent time frame in the year before

Increased   Decreased

*Fatalities include those resulting from battles, explosions/remote violence and violence against civilians.

Sources: UNODC, 'Global Report on Cocaine 2023: Local Dynamics, Global Challenges', March 2023; Armed Conflict Location & Event Data Project (ACLED), www.acleddata.com; IISS analysis   ©IISS

uncontrolled movements of people across the Americas), increase the importance of regional conflicts in the Americas for global security and stability. Conflicts in Colombia and Mexico are particularly relevant hotspots because of the crucial role played by the former in drug supply chains as a cocaine supplier and the strategic geographic position of the latter (close to the US), as well as the degree of internationalisation and sophistication of its drug-trafficking organisations (DTOs). Conflict in Brazil, once confined to urban areas and internal drug-supply dynamics, is also gaining increasing global relevance due to its growth across the country and the rapid internalisation and expansion of its criminal groups, which are now reaching into not only neighbouring South American countries but also Europe and lusophone Africa. Conflicts in

South America, including in Colombia and Brazil, also increasingly include environmental crimes, highlighting their relevance with respect to the protection of the Amazon and global climate mitigation.

Although not classified as a conflict according to *The Armed Conflict Survey* criteria, instability trends in Venezuela have far-reaching repercussions for regional security trends and beyond. The role played by the country in perpetuating conflict in Colombia in recent years; its links to controversial geopolitical powers (including Russia and Iran) and international criminal networks; and the major migrant crisis caused by its instability all underpin its global relevance. Lastly, although Haiti's violence dynamics remain largely localised, the unstoppable collapse of the state and increasingly powerful gangs in the country serve as a warning of the worst-case scenario that can result from governance flaws and institutional weaknesses.

The reporting period was marked by a further reconfiguration of drug routes and criminal networks, with outbreaks of violence and escalation in countries that, until recently, had been relatively spared from conflict, including Argentina, Ecuador and Paraguay. Mexican DTOs' increasing diversification into synthetic drugs (including fentanyl) production and exports to the US drove peaks of violence in some Mexican states along these drug-trafficking routes, as well as heightened diplomatic friction between the two countries. The introduction of a bill in the US Congress to designate Mexican DTOs as foreign terrorist organisations and calls for the US Army to be sent to Mexico to combat cartels in March 2023 highlighted the extent of bilateral acrimony.[1] In El Salvador, the state of exception and suspension of constitutional rights imposed by the government of Nayib Bukele since March 2022 slashed violence levels and gangs' power, prompting Honduras to adopt the same approach and engendering praise across Latin America. However, such an approach may prove unsustainable in the medium to long term given its high economic and human-rights costs.

The commencement of the 'total peace' process in Colombia involving simultaneous peace negotiations with all active criminal groups in the country, and timid steps towards the stabilisation of the Venezuela crisis and the definition of a path towards fair elections there in 2024, were positive developments which could potentially boost regional prospects for peace. Yet this outlook is fraught with risks amid repeated broken ceasefires in Colombia and little progress at the negotiating table for both processes.

Conflict Drivers

Political and institutional
State weakness and corruption
Institutional flaws exacerbated by widespread corruption have created a conducive environment for the establishment (and expansion) of NSAGs across the Americas. The weak rule of law across rural territories in Colombia, marginalised neighbourhoods in Central America and Brazil, and both rural and urban territories in Mexico has opened the way for criminal governance dynamics and illicit economies. Institutional fragility is further fuelled by deeply flawed criminal systems, with Latin America possessing some of the least-effective criminal-investigation systems globally.[2] This sustains a culture of impunity, which, in turn, greatly reduces the risks and repercussions for committing crimes. In Mexico alone, over 93% of crimes remain unreported and thus unsolved.[3] Moreover, inefficient penitentiary systems, with overcrowded jails and few rehabilitation programmes, perpetuate violence trends. Prison occupancy in the region is greater than what the system can hold, with particularly high levels (in descending order) in Haiti, Guatemala, Bolivia and El Salvador.[4]

The largest criminal groups in Brazil, El Salvador and Honduras use prisons as headquarters for their operations. High levels of incarceration and overcrowding also provide criminal groups with fertile ground for recruitment (and indoctrination) of inmates.

Socio-economic
Entrenched inequalities
Widespread socio-economic inequality and poverty have been structural features of Latin America's recent history, facilitating the emergence and persistence of instability flashpoints. Latin America is one of the most unequal regions in the world in terms of income, and the most unequal for capital concentration, with 10% of the population controlling 77% of the total household wealth.[5] In 2022, 32.1% of the region's population lived in poverty and 13.1% in extreme poverty.[6]

These factors amplify the attractiveness of highly profitable illicit economies, especially for young people, who are often among the most vulnerable segments of the population with some of the highest unemployment levels in the world.[7] Violence, including that caused by organised crime, is the main cause of death for people under 24 in Latin America.[8]

Security and military
Drug trafficking
Since the 1990s, drug trafficking has become the core of criminal violence and illicit economies. Proceeds

from narco-trafficking, mostly of cocaine, sustain the increasing military capability of criminal groups (including through weapons smuggled from the US to Mexico) to confront state forces and fight one another for control over drug production and lucrative drug routes across the region and to the main markets.

War on drugs
The adoption of hardline security policies – spearheaded by the US and centred around increased militarisation, the eradication of illicit crops and drugs interdiction – combined with the United States' liberal policies on firearms possession, which provides easy access to weapons for criminal organisations across the border, has further fuelled conflict in the region. Despite some successes in the form of increased drug seizures (mostly of cocaine) and the capture of a few major drug lords, including Mexico's Sinaloa Cartel drug lord Joaquín Guzmán (alias 'El Chapo') in 2016 and Colombia's Gulf Clan's Dairo Antonio Úsuga David (alias 'Otoniel') in 2021, the so-called 'war on drugs' approach has not curbed drug production or trafficking in any meaningful way.[9] Meanwhile, it has also had the unintended consequence of reinforcing the military power of criminal groups by prompting them to develop a higher retaliatory capacity to confront the state and increasing criminal actors' fragmentation.

The latter, in turn, has resulted in increased criminal contestation and the establishment of new trafficking routes within and across countries.[10] The strategy has also led to multiple instances of human-rights violations by state forces, including massacres in Brazil and Colombia.[11]

This 'war on drugs' approach is embedded in the international drug-control regime of the United Nations, which prioritises the reduction of the drug supply through security efforts. By abiding by the global legal system, governments have historically been constrained in adopting alternative responses to the ever-expanding drug business, including approaches focused on drug demand and root causes of violence.

Geopolitical
The Venezuela crisis
The political crisis in Venezuela continues to drive regional instability. The involvement of the regime of Nicolás Maduro in regional drug trafficking and its cooperation with Colombian NSAGs have made Venezuela a key node for cocaine trafficking from Colombia to Central America, Mexico, Brazil and Europe. These dynamics have notably strengthened Colombia's NSAGs, undermining that country's domestic security and conflict-resolution efforts.

Conflict Parties

Coalitions
The regional security agenda revolves around combatting drug trafficking, especially airborne and seaborne cocaine-trafficking routes. Despite not being directly involved as a conflict party, the US has traditionally played a leading role in the design and execution of security strategies against drug trafficking in Latin America. This is due to its strategic interest in the region's stability and in curbing cocaine flows into its own territory, as the US remains the largest consumption market for cocaine. Colombia, the largest cocaine producer globally, is another important actor in regional cooperation.

Over the past two decades, the US has cemented key security agreements in the region, with Colombia and Mexico as the main recipients of foreign military financial aid and training. The Mexico–US Bicentennial Framework for

Security, Public Health, and Safe Communities is currently the most important bilateral security agreement. Based on a shared responsibility to address security threats, this framework seeks to combat transnational organised crime and violence, their related socio-economic effects on local communities, and governance flaws that exacerbate impunity. The plan replaces the US–Mexico Mérida Initiative (2008–21), which allocated over US$3.3 billion to curb drug smuggling across the border and reduce governance flaws in Mexico, among other things.[12] In a similar vein, the US has been a vital security partner for Colombia with initiatives such as Plan Colombia (2000–16), which allocated over US$12bn primarily to increase the Colombian armed forces' military capabilities to combat criminal and terrorist groups involved in cocaine production and trafficking.[13]

The above-mentioned strategies have been complemented by the operations of the US Southern Command headquartered in Florida. As one of the 11 Combatant Commands of the US Army globally, the Southern Command regularly holds security exercises, including ones focused on tackling transnational threats such as organised crime, with over 20 countries in Latin America and the Caribbean.[14]

With the support of the US and building on over four decades of learning and improvement in anti-narcotics efforts at the domestic level, Colombia is a key security actor in the region. The US–Colombia Action Plan on Regional Security Cooperation, a cooperation agreement signed at the 2012 Summit of the Americas, provides training on law-enforcement activities to partner nations in the region to combat transnational organised crime. Under this initiative, the Colombian Navy and police have trained over 17,000 officials in various armed forces in Central America and the Caribbean, and in 2023 alone it will conduct 500 trainings.[15] Other regional security partnerships in which the US provides training and strategic coordination include the Caribbean Basin Security Initiative to increase transnational drug interdiction and the Central America Regional Security Initiative to strengthen domestic law-enforcement programmes and to tackle drug trafficking, illegal migration and flawed criminal-justice systems.

Non-state armed groups

The presence and activities of NSAGs in the region are shaped by drug-supply and -trafficking dynamics. In Colombia, criminal actors control the production of cocaine, including coca bushes and cocaine laboratories in rural areas, fighting against other NSAGs and/or state armed forces to retain (or expand) their territory. NSAGs are also present in isolated, key border regions for trafficking cocaine into Brazil, Central America, Ecuador, Mexico and Venezuela. The most powerful groups, including the Gulf Clan, the National Liberation Army (ELN) and Revolutionary Armed Forces of Colombia (FARC) dissidents, comprise numerous units across the country connected by one common leadership.[16] Colombian NSAGs mostly sell cocaine to Mexican and Brazilian criminal groups and have been increasingly dealing directly with Italian and Balkan mafia-type organisations, which largely control the wholesale cocaine business in Europe.

NSAGs in countries that are part of cocaine-trafficking routes are mostly involved in airborne and seaborne trafficking operations from South America to Central America and Mexico and terrestrial smuggling into the US. In general terms, Mexican DTOs, particularly the Sinaloa Cartel and the Cartel Jalisco New Generation, purchase cocaine from South America to smuggle into the US, relying on the help of Central American criminal gangs.[17] Across the region, Mexican DTOs are the most professionally organised criminal groups, with departments in charge of military, financial (including money-laundering) and trafficking operations. They have strict hierarchical (and often family-centred) structures. They also outsource trafficking operations to smaller, local criminal organisations. As the consumption of cocaine in the US has declined over recent years, the production of methamphetamines and synthetic opioids, including fentanyl, has gained more importance in DTOs' operations.

In Central America, urban gangs, notably the Mara Salvatrucha (MS-13), oversee and protect international drug loads while controlling the domestic retail of drugs, including marijuana and cocaine, and imposing illegal taxes on local populations and businesses. They have started to cultivate coca as well, notably in Honduras, but production remains minimal compared to South America's levels.

With Brazil's increasing relevance as a transit country for South American cocaine trafficking to Europe, Africa and Asia, domestic NSAGs have continued to expand their national and international operations. Despite traditionally being urban and prison-based, they have increasingly stretched into rural areas in the northern and eastern states of Brazil as well as into Paraguay and Argentina to control trafficking routes from Bolivia, Colombia and Peru. The First Capital Command (PCC) and Red Command notably have strong business ties with Colombian organisations to buy and transport cocaine and marijuana through the Amazon rainforest. They have also strengthened links with European mafia-type organisations.

Regardless of the country of origin, extortion, robbery and kidnapping are common activities across all NSAGs in the region. They are especially important for Haitian gangs, which remain fairly detached from the regional drug-production and -trafficking supply chain. Moreover, environmental crimes (including illegal mining and logging) have increasingly become an alternative revenue stream for Brazilian, Colombian and Mexican criminal groups, together with human smuggling.

Third-party interventions

There are no active international missions with military personnel in Latin America, except for the UN Verification Mission in Colombia which oversees the demobilisation of the over 13,000 former FARC combatants who signed a peace deal with the Colombian government in 2016.[18]

Haiti's spiralling political, humanitarian and security crisis has prompted calls for international interventions to stabilise the country, through a UN mission or possibly special forces deployed by regional powers, including the US and Canada. However, there seems to be little appetite for this, given the shortcomings of past international efforts, including the most recent UN Stabilisation Mission in Haiti (MINUSTA, 2004–17). MINUSTA ended amid major scandals, including a cholera outbreak caused by a staff member and allegations of over 130 child sexual abuses committed by UN peacekeepers.[19]

Regional and International Dimensions

Armed conflicts in the Americas have a unique type of global relevance. Although none of them are inter-state in nature or feature 'boots on the ground' third-party interventions, they have important global interlinkages and repercussions. Their high human impact (notably in terms of fatalities) and intensity exacerbate entrenched domestic socio-economic woes and institutional fragilities, as well as sustain migration flows and forced displacement to North America and, increasingly, across Latin America.[20] By adding to the political and economic strains faced by transit and destination countries, offering new business opportunities to criminal groups (through people smuggling and forced labour, amongst others) and creating tensions among concerned governments (including the US), these trends drive instability and insecurity at the regional level and beyond. The situation is further aggravated by the high vulnerability (and little resilience) to accelerating climate change of some of the countries most affected by armed conflict in the region, notably Haiti and Central America's Northern Triangle.[21]

Another powerful driver of international significance is the increasingly transnational character of the illicit economies and criminal actors fuelling armed violence in the region. Drug trafficking has historically been a regional affair, with drug supply chains and routes stretching from Colombia to the main regional markets in the US and Brazil. More recently, however, criminal groups have been expanding their reach within the Americas and to the rest of the world to match demand trends and take advantage of more lucrative opportunities, globalising their supply chains, operations and networks. The Brazilian PCC's expansion into South America, Europe and lusophone Africa to cater to increasing cocaine demand and the growing presence of Mexican DTOs in Colombia are two of many examples. The threat this represents to global security is compounded by the increasing infiltration of criminal groups into politics and governments across the region. The most extreme reflection of this trend is the emergence of 'criminal states' where institutions and criminal interests are intertwined, with adverse implications for global efforts to fight illicit economies, including money laundering. Two recent glaring examples of this have been the extradition to the US of Honduran former president Juan Orlando Hernández in April 2022 for drug-trafficking and weapons offenses and the conviction in the US of Mexican former public security minister Genaro García Luna in February 2023 for protecting and colluding with the Sinaloa Cartel.

On a related note, the increasing influence of geopolitical players other than the US (including China and, to a lesser extent, Russia and Iran) and the ensuing great-power competition in Latin America also have important negative ramifications for regional and global security. These geopolitical players are more likely to support authoritarian regimes (which often collude with criminal groups and foment instability in the region, as in the case of Venezuela), and their involvement in the region has contributed to the weakening of governance standards and democratic institutions. In particular, China's prominent role in the regional information-technology infrastructure and providing surveillance technologies (through 'safe cities' projects) with access to related data and intelligence is a growing cause of concern for the US and has strained bilateral relations between the US and its Latin American partners.[22] China's position as a major provider of analogues and precursors for fentanyl produced and trafficked by Mexican DTOs to the US is another significant risk to regional security and a source of geopolitical frictions.

Besides the major role played by the US in security cooperation and responses to armed violence in Latin America, there are several other international programmes and institutions which aim to support Latin American states' security and counter narco-trafficking. These include the UN Office on Drugs and Crime (UNODC), which advises and informs members on policies to combat illicit trafficking; the Organization of American States' Hemispheric Plan of Action Against Transnational Organized Crime and its related activities; and the European Union's Europe Latin America Programme of Assistance against Transnational Organised Crime (EL PAcCTO), which fosters international cooperation across countries on police services, justice systems and law enforcement. EL PAcCTO also provides direct support to Ameripol (a network of police forces in the region).

Outlook

Prospects for peace

Progress towards peace in the region rests on the success of Colombian President Gustavo Petro's signature 'total peace' initiative and the partially related efforts to stabilise Venezuela. Petro's ambitious plan to pursue simultaneous peace negotiations with all active criminal groups in Colombia while addressing the root causes of conflict (including land-distribution inequalities) could be a game changer for regional security given the centrality of the country in international drug-trafficking dynamics. Likewise, his efforts to concomitantly normalise relations with Venezuela (including in security cooperation) and promote a democratic transition there, by pushing the Maduro government to negotiate with the opposition, will be important for both the success of his 'total peace' policy and the removal of a perennial instability flashpoint in the region. Negotiations, originally started in 2021, between Maduro and his political opposition for a path to free and fair elections in 2024 have been deadlocked since resuming in November 2022.[23] A summit called by Petro in April 2023 failed to unblock the situation, but it confirmed Colombia's commitment and strategic interest in solving the Venezuela crisis as well as US President Joe Biden's willingness to lift sanctions on the Maduro regime, subject to real steps towards free elections in Venezuela. Petro's grand plan, however, faces many headwinds on both the domestic and international fronts, including the approaching US general elections in November 2024, which may pull Biden's attention away from South America or altogether reverse his conciliatory stance on Venezuela.

In Central America, the Bukele government's crackdown on gangs in El Salvador since March 2022 seems to have achieved a fragile pacification of the country, with violence levels decreasing to record lows and the state regaining control of most of its territory from an increasingly subdued MS-13. The continuation of the state of exception, declared in March 2022 for 30 days and renewed every month since, and the opening of a new mega-prison suggest that Bukele's stance will not change in the short to medium term, despite ever-more-limited public fiscal resources. While the approach has no doubt been effective in curbing violence in the short term and has won many supporters in Central America and beyond, the suspension of constitutional rights and mass arrests have done little to curb democratic and institutional backsliding in the country. Furthermore, it has raised the more general

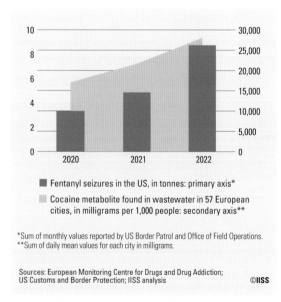

■ Fentanyl seizures in the US, in tonnes: primary axis*

▨ Cocaine metabolite found in wastewater in 57 European cities, in milligrams per 1,000 people: secondary axis**

*Sum of monthly values reported by US Border Patrol and Office of Field Operations.
**Sum of daily mean values for each city in milligrams.

Sources: European Monitoring Centre for Drugs and Drug Addiction; US Customs and Border Protection; IISS analysis   ©IISS

Figure 1: US fentanyl seizures and Europe cocaine consumption

question of whether undermining human rights is an acceptable trade-off for reduced insecurity.

Escalation potential and regional spillovers

The increasing globalisation of Latin American criminal groups, the opportunistic reconfiguration of such groups' activities and business portfolios, and the entry and establishment of European criminal actors in the region will continue to drive conflict and instability in the Americas (see Figure 1). As fully detailed in the Americas Regional Spotlight essay, 'Shifting Dynamics and New Conflict Zones in Latin America', growing drug demand in Europe and South America is fuelling conflict over the control of new drug-trafficking and -smuggling routes (including key ports). This trend is likely to remain strong in the short to medium term, with violence continuing to spread into previously peaceful countries, including Ecuador and, to a lesser extent, Argentina, Bolivia, Paraguay and Uruguay.

In North America, Mexican DTOs' ongoing efforts to refocus their portfolios on the fentanyl business will continue to cause spikes in localised violence in Mexican states linked to its production and trafficking, including Michoacán and Colima, home to Mexico's largest and second-largest ports, Lázaro Cárdenas and Manzanillo. It will also increasingly strain diplomatic and security relations with the US, where the fentanyl epidemic and related health emergency is rapidly becoming a national-security issue. Without major changes in current anti-narcotics approaches on both sides of the border and an improvement in the United States' relations with China, the fentanyl business will continue to flourish, driving increased overdose deaths, violence in Mexico and bilateral tensions.[24]

It is unlikely that any meaningful progress will be made on solving the major political, economic and security crisis in Haiti in the near term, as there is little international interest in intervention. Escalating gang violence and collapsing state structures in the country will probably result in more migration and instability spillovers into neighbouring countries (notably the Dominican Republic) and the Americas as a whole.

Against the backdrop of restrictive immigration policies in the US, rising migration flows driven by instability in Venezuela, Central America and the Caribbean (including Haiti and Cuba) will continue to make people smuggling an attractive venture. Old and new criminal groups (including the Venezuelan Tren de Aragua gang) will become involved in the business, spreading violence to countries traditionally regarded as very safe, such as Chile.

Meanwhile, as human trafficking gains prominence in criminal portfolios, environmental crimes (including illegal mining and logging) will continue to represent lucrative opportunities for criminal groups in the Amazon and beyond, although conditions may be less favourable under the careful watch of environmental champion and President of Brazil Luiz Inácio Lula da Silva.

Strategic implications and global influences

The progressive reconfiguration of the region's geopolitical order into a multipolar one, with the US competing with China for predominance and Venezuela as the fulcrum of great-power competition, will continue to influence security trends in the region.

Domestic drug-consumption developments have the potential to refocus the United States' attention on North America's security imperatives (notably addressing the fentanyl crisis), with less time and resources dedicated to drug dynamics in South America. In turn, the growing importance of European markets and criminal groups in the cocaine business will likely prompt the EU to assume an increasingly active role in security cooperation with the region, possibly providing momentum for exploring alternatives to the 'war on drugs' approach long sponsored by the US. This would chime with increasing calls from regional leaders (including Petro) to overhaul drug policies in order to take into consideration the demand side of the issue and the root causes of drugs trafficking.

At the same time, because of fentanyl's potency – which means that only very small quantities need to be produced and trafficked – the current militarised approaches that are exclusively focused on the supply side are not effective. This may also push the US to revise its anti-narcotics policies to place a greater emphasis on targeting domestic demand factors. The Bicentennial Framework's attention to public-health issues is a promising overture in this regard. The necessity of enlisting Mexico's support in the fight against fentanyl trafficking may also highlight the need to address the free movement of firearms across the border, a long-standing cause of tension between the two countries. While adopting more restrictive firearms policies domestically is not likely to be an option for the foreseeable future in the US, a greater focus could be put on exploring creative strategies to limit trafficking into Mexico.

REGIONAL KEY EVENTS

POLITICAL EVENTS

 COLOMBIA

19 June 2022

Petro, from the leftist Historical Pact coalition, wins Colombia's presidential run-off election.

 HAITI

October

Haiti's Prime Minister Ariel Henry and the UN secretary-general appeal for the deployment of an international force to help the Haitian National Police combat gangs.

 BRAZIL

30 October

Lula, from the leftist Workers' Party, is elected president of Brazil following a bitterly fought campaign against incumbent right-wing populist Jair Bolsonaro.

 VENEZUELA

26 November

Maduro resumes talks with the opposition Unitary Platform coalition in Mexico as the US eases some oil sanctions on Venezuela.

MILITARY/VIOLENT EVENTS

 ECUADOR

10 May 2022

At least 44 inmates are killed in Ecuador's Santo Domingo prison in a fight between gangs.

 PARAGUAY

11 May

Paraguay's special prosecutor against organised crime, Marcelo Pecci, is assassinated while on his honeymoon in Colombia.

 BRAZIL

24 May

At least 23 people are killed in the Vila Cruzeiro *favela* in Rio de Janeiro during a police raid.

 BRAZIL

21 July

At least 18 people are killed in the Alemão *favela* complex in Rio de Janeiro during a police raid.

 HAITI

September

The G9 gang takes control of the main fuel terminal in Haiti and seizes key highways.

 MEXICO

13 October

Mexico's congress votes to extend the army's public-security duties until 2028.

Americas

 HONDURAS

6 December

Honduras's President Xiomara Castro announces a state of exception in 162 neighbourhoods in San Pedro Sula and Tegucigalpa. The state of exception is renewed for a third time on 6 April 2023.

 BRAZIL

1 January 2023

Lula revokes a series of Bolsonaro's decrees, notably restricting access to firearms in Brazil.

 BRAZIL

21 January

Lula fires the head of the Brazilian army, Gen. Júlio Cesar de Arruda, for allegedly protecting the rioters who stormed government buildings in Brasília from arrest.

 HAITI

30 January

Just weeks after the last ten elected senators' terms expire, Steven Irvenson Benoit, the Montana Accord's prime minister-designate for Haiti, resigns from the High Transition Council (HTC), a body created following a breakthrough agreement between Henry and members of the Montana Accord.

 HAITI

6 February

The HTC is installed to plan general elections, with a new government entering into force in February 2024.

 MEXICO

21 February

Luna, Mexico's former director of the Federal Investigation Agency and public security minister, is convicted in the US for protecting and colluding with the Sinaloa Cartel.

 COLOMBIA

1 January 2023

Petro declares a bilateral ceasefire with the country's five largest NSAGs as part of his 'total peace' policy.

 MEXICO

5 January

A police operation to arrest Ovidio Guzmán López, son of drug lord 'El Chapo' and one of the leaders of the Sinaloa Cartel, prompts mayhem in Culiacán and results in at least 29 deaths.

 BRAZIL

8 January

Bolsonaro supporters storm Brazil's congress, Supreme Court and presidential palace in Brasília to protest the election results.

 MEXICO

14 February

The Mexican army seizes over 600,000 fentanyl pills in Sinaloa State in a raid on the largest synthetic-drug lab found in the country to that date.

 EL SALVADOR

25 February

The first 2,000 inmates are transferred to El Salvador's new mega-prison under Bukele's gang-crackdown policy.

MEXICO

8 March

A bill to designate Mexican DTOs as foreign terrorist organisations is introduced in the US Congress.

 MEXICO

18 April

Mexico's Supreme Court reverses the government's decision from September 2022 to move the National Guard under the Secretariat of National Defence's control.

 COLOMBIA

25 April

Petro holds a one-day conference with representatives of 19 countries and the EU to discuss the political situation in Venezuela.

HAITI

14–19 April

Clashes between gangs in Haiti's capital result in the deaths of at least 70 civilians.

 EL SALVADOR

11 May

El Salvador's government claims that there have been 365 days without homicides across the country since Bukele took office in 2019.

COLOMBIA

22 May

The Colombian government suspends its bilateral ceasefire with FARC dissident group Central General Staff after the former recruited and killed four indigenous children.

COLOMBIA

9 June

The Colombian government and ELN guerrillas agree to a 180-day bilateral ceasefire to start on 3 August 2023.

HAITI

11–13 June

Henry and Haitian political and civic leaders fail to reach any further substantial agreement during negotiations held in Jamaica and backed by the Caribbean Community.

HONDURAS

20 June

A prison riot in the Centro Femenino de Adaptación Social women's prison results in 41 dead as gangs lead an attack in response to the government's crackdown on corruption in prison facilities.

Notes

1   Eric Garcia, 'GOP Calls for Military Intervention in Response to Murdered American Tourists in Mexico', *Independent*, 7 March 2023.

2   This refers to 2022 data. World Justice Project, 'WJP Rule of Law Index'.

3   Ena Aguilar Peláez, 'Impunity in Mexico: 93% of Crimes Go Unreported', *Global Press Journal*, 5 April 2023.

4   Haiti's prisons are the second-most overcrowded out of a ranking of 207 countries, followed quite closely by prisons in Guatemala (9th), Bolivia (12th) and El Salvador (17th). Across the Americas (excluding the Caribbean islands, other than Haiti), only the US (133rd), Chile (142nd) and Belize (196th) have fewer prisoners than the official capacity that their prison system can hold. See World Prison Brief, 'Highest

to Lowest – Occupancy Level (Based on Official Capacity)', accessed 7 June 2023.

5   Lucas Chancel et al., 'World Inequality Report 2022', World Inequality Lab, 2022.

6   This represents an increase from the levels seen before the coronavirus pandemic: in 2019, 30.4% of the population lived in poverty and 11.4% in extreme poverty. For further detail see UN Economic Commission for Latin America and the Caribbean, *Social Panorama of Latin America and the Caribbean 2022* (Santiago: UN, 2022), p. 56.

7   Youth (people between the ages of 14 and 25) unemployment in Latin America in 2022 was 20.5%, compared to 24.8% in the Arab states and 29.2% in Northern Africa. See International Labour Organization, 'Global Employment Trends for Youth: Recovery in Youth Employment Is Still Lagging: Investing in Transforming Futures for Young People', 11 August 2022.

8   Pan American Health Organization, 'Half of All Deaths of Young People in the Americas Can Be Prevented', 5 March 2019.

9   Indeed, cocaine production (tons) and coca crops (hectares) reached record levels in 2021. See UN Office on Drugs and Crime, 'Global Report on Cocaine 2023', March 2023.

10 Peter Reuter, 'The Mobility of Drug Trafficking', in John Collins (ed.), *Ending the Drug Wars* (London: London School of Economics and Political Science, 2014), pp. 33–40.

11 Juan Albarracín, 'Crimen Organizado en América Latina' [Organised Crime in Latin America], Friedrich-Ebert-Stiftung, February 2023.

12 Congressional Research Service, 'Mexico: Evolution of the Mérida Initiative, FY2008–FY2021', IF10578, 20 September 2021.

13 June S. Beittel, 'Colombia: Background and U.S. Relations', R43813, Congressional Research Service, 16 December 2021.

14 The US Southern Command sponsors annual multinational security and military exercises in the region, including the *PANAMAX 2022* (August 2022) and *Fuerzas Comando 2023* (June 2023) with personnel from 22 Latin American and Caribbean security forces between the two events. See US Southern Command, 'Fuerzas Comando 2023'; US Southern Command, 'PANAMAX 2022'; and US Southern Command, 'Building Partner Capacity | Supporting Our Partners'.

15 US Department of State, 'Bureau of International Narcotics and Law Enforcement Affairs: Colombia Summary'; and US Embassy in Colombia, 'Cooperación entre Estados Unidos y Colombia hacen del país suramericano un líder en seguridad regional' [Cooperation Between the United States and Colombia Makes the South American Country a Leader in Regional Security], 4 May 2023.

16 Despite all having a national leadership, these groups adopt different organisational structures, including vertical structures (i.e., some FARC dissidents), horizontal structures (i.e., ELN guerrillas) and cooperation networks (i.e., the Gulf Clan).

17 According to the 2023 International Narcotics Control Strategy Report by the US Department of State, in 2022 cocaine trafficking via El Salvador was mostly seaborne, without entering into the country itself.

18 UN Verification Mission in Colombia, 'Secretary-general Stresses the Importance of Implementing the Peace Agreement and Advancing on Other Dialogues That Aim to Consolidate Peace', 10 April 2023.

19 Paisley Dodds, 'AP Exclusive: UN Child Sex Ring Left Victims but No Arrests', AP News, 12 April 2017.

20 For more information on changing migration patterns in the region see Inter-American Development Bank, Organization for Economic Cooperation and Development, 'Migration Flows in Latin America and the Caribbean: Statistics on Permits for Migrants', September 2021.

21 The latest ND-GAIN Country Index, which assesses countries' vulnerability to climate change together with their readiness to improve resilience, places Haiti, Honduras and El Salvador in the bottom part of its rankings at 169th, 142nd and 108th respectively out of 185 positions. Brazil (86th), Mexico (88th) and Colombia (97th) are doing slightly better but are still quite vulnerable. See ND-GAIN, 'ND-GAIN Country Index: Country Rankings', 2021.

22 Douglas Farah and Marianne Richardson, 'The PRC's Changing Strategic Priorities in Latin America: From Soft Power to Sharp Power Competition', Institute for National Strategic Studies *Strategic Perspectives*, no. 37, October 2021.

23 For more details on the negotiations see: Catherine Osborn, 'Petro Pushes to Restart Venezuela Talks', *Foreign Policy*, 28 April 2023.

24 See 'Fentanyl Trafficking Tests America's Foreign Policy', *The Economist*, 11 May 2023.

Americas

Shifting Dynamics and New Conflict Zones in Latin America

The cocaine trade has always been dynamic and opportunistic but for decades has primarily encompassed illicit enterprises in Colombia, Mexico and Central America. In the wake of the coronavirus pandemic, economic upheaval and political unrest across the continent, the trade is now rapidly expanding into new areas, involving new actors and including a more diversified portfolio of illicit products. Ecuador, traditionally peaceful, is now dealing with widespread violence due to fighting among European transnational criminal groups and regional cartels. Argentina's Rosario region is also seeing rising violence among new groups fighting for control of drug-trafficking and smuggling routes on the southern Atlantic coast. Brazil's First Capital Command (PCC), an emerging transnational criminal force, has extended its reach – and accompanying violence – to multiple countries through a diversified portfolio of illicit activities.

Evolving dynamics

Market forces and regional dynamics are driving the shifting flows of illicit products and violence south and east in South America. The dynamics of the cocaine trade are changing, both regionally and internationally. While American cocaine consumption has been dropping for more than a decade as the use of synthetic drugs grows, European consumption has expanded as the price has decreased and the purity has increased, making Europe a more attractive market with less risk of interdiction than the United States. Transnational criminal organisations are increasingly crossing the Atlantic, bypassing the US entirely.

At the same time, Argentina, Brazil, Chile and Uruguay have developed significant internal consumption markets, ranking among the top ten per capita consuming nations in the world.[1] These shifts toward expanding into different regional markets have opened the door for new supply-chain operators to move in. Supplying growing South American markets with cocaine and precursor chemicals to make cocaine carries lower cost

and risk than supplying European and US markets. While somewhat less profitable, the trade still generates hundreds of millions of US dollars each year, making it an attractive option.

As new, unsettled and unstable trafficking structures fight for territorial control, the geography of conflict is morphing. Across South America new actors such as Albanian organised crime, Turkish criminal groups and Italian Mafia-type groups like the 'Ndrangheta, which previously had been on the periphery of the South American cocaine trade, are emerging as significant players and are changing the dynamics of traditional cartels and criminalised state actors.[2] These groups are challenging current relationships and offering South American organisations new ways to expand profits through product and market diversification. Each group brings added prospects for the globalisation of products, money laundering and exchanges of lessons learned.

Ecuador as a new hotspot of criminal contestation

The ongoing violence and instability in once-tranquil Ecuador, focused on the port city of Guayaquil and the Ecuador–Colombia border region, is an example of the wide-ranging repercussions of transnational criminal organisations' escalating influence in this region. While these organisations have for years used Ecuador's coastal regions and porous borders, as well as the significant presence of the now-fragmented and violent dissident groups of the Revolutionary Armed Forces of Colombia (FARC), to facilitate the trafficking of cocaine, this long-standing dynamic is growing more complex, violent and widespread. Ecuador's relatively unsecured ports, many of which have long served as commercial fishing hubs, have become increasingly significant. The areas around the ports of Manta and Esmeraldas, for instance, have become key staging areas for cocaine produced on the Colombian side of the border and stored on the Ecuadorian side in *centros de acopio* (mega storage centres) near the Panama Canal. Meanwhile, Guayaquil, the nation's largest port and banking centre, has become a hub of violence for groups smuggling cocaine out on container ships and those seeking to exploit the nation's dollarised economy to launder the proceeds of illicit activities.[3]

Violence among criminal organisations is increasing and intensifying, and corruption probes continue to identify elite members of Ecuadorian law enforcement as parties to the drug trade.[4] The mayor of Guayaquil, in an open letter to President Guillermo Lasso, said criminal gangs 'have become a state within a state' there.[5] One key indicator is the skyrocketing homicide rate, which has quadrupled in the past six years. It grew from about six per 100,000 at the time of the peace agreement between the Colombian government and the FARC in 2016 to 26 per 100,000 in 2022.[6] More than half of the homicides in recent years have been concentrated in the Colombia border region, where Colombian, Ecuadorian, European and Mexican groups all vie for primacy.[7] Escalating prison violence driven by drug cartels is also leading to a dramatic increase in Ecuador's homicide rate. In 2019, there were 32 violent deaths in prisons; in 2020, there were 51, and in 2021, there were about 323.[8] The Lasso administration and Ecuadorian law enforcement attribute these developments to the growing power of drug-trafficking groups controlling many parts of the prison system.

There is an increasingly diverse group of actors involved in the violence, including Albanian organised crime. More than 991 Albanian nationals have arrived in Ecuador since 2016. They often arrive as investors and stay for short periods. The Ecuadorian press has documented at least six killings of Albanian nationals in the last three years.

Albanian national Dritan Rexhepi was arrested in Quito in 2014 and is currently serving a 13-year sentence for leading a criminal organisation that pioneered routes for moving cocaine from Ecuador to Italy and the rest of Europe.[9] Ergys Dashi, an Albanian national reportedly active in the drug trade, was shot to death in a restaurant in Guayaquil in late January 2022. Growing Albanian drug-trafficking networks reportedly also have alliances with the 'Ndrangheta.[10]

Rosario's growing relevance for cocaine trafficking

Rosario, the largest city in Argentina's Santa Fé province, has a homicide rate that is five times the national average and increasing: it jumped from 18.5 per 100,000 residents in 2021 to 22 per 100,000 in 2022.[11] The city straddles Route 34, one of the most important cocaine arteries of South America. The road cuts from Bolivia's southern border into the heart of Argentina, intersecting roads that carry illicit products south and east to Atlantic ports and west to Chile's Pacific coast. It is also home to the Port of Rosario on the Paraná River, a key stop on the riverine route used to move cocaine and other contraband products from Bolivia, Paraguay and Peru to regional and international markets.

While Rosario has been an important centre of convergence for multiple illicit economies, conflicts have spread beyond its borders as more cocaine flows south to satisfy regional markets and is intermixed with other contraband in transit. Police estimate that at least 70% of the murders are related to drug trafficking.[12] The violence is so widespread that gunmen even attacked a supermarket owned by the family of the Rosario native, international soccer superstar and national idol Lionel Messi and left a note saying, 'Messi, we are waiting for you', along with 14 bullet holes.[13]

Multiple criminal organisations are vying for control of Rosario. The city is home base for Los Monos, Argentina's most important cocaine-trafficking group. However, the group has reportedly fractured in recent months amid internal fighting, while at the same time waging a war of vendettas against rival gangs over stolen loads of cocaine. Because of this, according to law-enforcement and intelligence reports, Los Monos is now too weak to keep the Mexican Cartel Jalisco New Generation (CJNG) and Brazil's PCC from vying for a market share in Rosario. This is an example of the instability that often occurs with the weakening of a group that once had uncontested territorial control, allowing new groups and disputes to enter the fray.

The PCC's expansion and violence spillover

Few criminal groups have evolved or expanded more quickly than the PCC, which began as a prison-based gang in 1993 and 'in fewer than thirty years … has grown from a handful of prisoners into a powerful transnational criminal organisation' operating on three continents.[14] The group's centres of power are São Paulo and the Port of Santos, as well as Brazil's northeast, where thousands of members are held in prisons. It has also embedded a centre of operation in the Santa Cruz region of Bolivia, which shares an extensive border with Paraguay and is a major cocaine-shipment hub.[15]

The PCC excelled at planning and executing spectacular bank heists and jewellery-store robberies that raised tens of millions of US dollars for the group in Bolivia, Brazil and Paraguay. With those and other illicit funds, the PCC expanded into key parts of the cocaine supply chain that cater to Brazil's cities and are useful for moving illicit products to the broader international market. These key areas include the Port of Santos (the biggest port in the hemisphere to which the PCC now has extensive access); transit routes to and from Paraguay and Bolivia; and collection and distribution nodes in Africa (primarily the former Portuguese colonies Angola and Mozambique) and Europe (see Figure 1). The Brazilian police have also reported growing ties between the PCC and the 'Ndrangheta, with Domenico Pelle, one of the group's leaders, visiting São Paulo twice in 2018 to expand cocaine trafficking to Europe.[16]

This expansion has brought more conflict. Brazil's northeast has long been the epicentre of gang violence, with a series of bloody conflicts driven by territorial disputes with the Red Command (CV) gang – one of the PCC's biggest rivals – and other groups. These conflicts are usually centred around cocaine and weapons supply routes from Colombia and Venezuela and cocaine export routes to Europe.[17] The violence, however, has now spread to Paraguay, particularly in Ciudad del Este and other border zones, and Paraguayan prisons. While Paraguay's homicide rate is not as high as Brazil's, Paraguayan analysts estimate that, of the approximately 180 cases which involved hired killers in Paraguay in

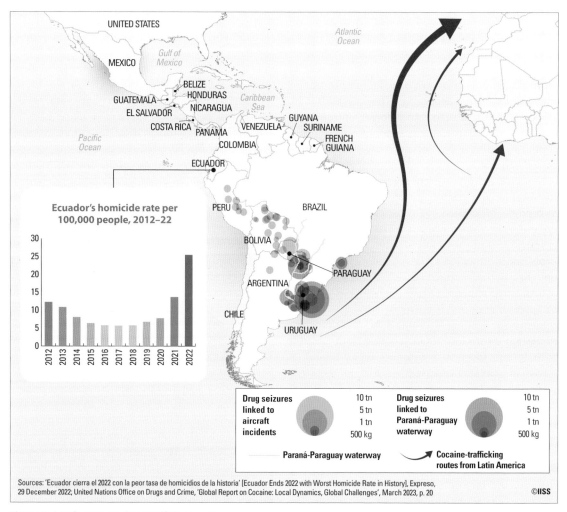

Sources: 'Ecuador cierra el 2022 con la peor tasa de homicidios de la historia' [Ecuador Ends 2022 with Worst Homicide Rate in History], Expreso, 29 December 2022; United Nations Office on Drugs and Crime, 'Global Report on Cocaine: Local Dynamics, Global Challenges', March 2023, p. 20 ©IISS

Figure 1: Southern Cone drug-trafficking routes

2021, at least a third were targeted assassinations carried out by hitmen on behalf of drug-trafficking cartels, of which the PCC was the most prominent.[18] In Bolivia as well, a series of assassinations of PCC members and other Brazilians appear to be the result of turf wars there.[19]

Not much hope for improvement

The rapid change in the conflicts and the illicit markets that drive violence in much of Latin America will probably continue for the foreseeable future, with cocaine likely remaining the dominant product, but with a possible increase in synthetic drugs as well. The current state of upheaval, with new players and groups entering the market by force and either taking root or being pushed out in a constant churn, could well be the new normal in the hemisphere. The 'total peace' initiative in Colombia will likely help push small, violent and less disciplined groups into the illicit markets, as it has in past stages when larger, stable trafficking organisations have withdrawn from the playing field after negotiating with the government and new, smaller groups (often factions of the main groups) have entered the market space. Historically, it takes years of intense violence before a more permanent hierarchy emerges.

Furthermore, the region has seen the spread of ideologically agnostic authoritarian governments that rely on transnational organised crime for revenue and corrupt gains. El Salvador serves as a prime example, where ideological foes during the country's 1980–92 civil war now jointly operate criminal enterprises under President Nayib Bukele's protection.[20] Even the much-publicised crackdown on gangs that has led to the arbitrary detention of over 60,000 people at the time of writing has

provided a financial windfall for prison directors and other government officials operating extorsion rackets for food, clothing and family visits under the government's protection.[21] These governments offer new opportunities for criminal groups to enter the fray, further feeding violent territorial disputes. In Central America's Northern Triangle, this government protection can lead to violence, particularly around elections, as various criminal groups back different candidates and coalitions.

Further south, Chile and Peru are facing the expansion of Venezuelan criminal groups like the Tren de Aragua, which sometimes operate through local franchises and are dominating the human-smuggling and -trafficking routes south of Venezuela and its environs. Meanwhile, Argentina, Paraguay and Uruguay are seeing the expansion of the Mexican CJNG into their national territories to take over lucrative Atlantic trafficking routes, further fragmenting the criminal world and dispersing the conflicts that ensue with territorial disputes. In these countries, the level of violence is rising sharply, particularly in terms of selective assassinations by criminal groups.[22]

Few countries in the hemisphere are prepared to effectively combat this new conflict landscape, and the decline of citizen security is one of the driving forces behind the new wave of authoritarian governments that are promising security while removing vital parts of the rule of law and democratic governance. Given the overall weakness of state institutions that are already struggling with post-coronavirus-pandemic economic recovery, endemic poverty and corruption, most states will grapple with these shifting paradigms with few resources and little understanding of the new reality.

Notes

[1] Douglas Farah and Marianne Richardson, 'Gangs No Longer: Reassessing Transnational Armed Groups in the Western Hemisphere', Institute for National Strategic Studies *Strategic Perspectives*, no. 38, May 2022.

[2] Author interviews with Italian intelligence officials in Santiago and Buenos Aires, March 2023.

[3] This information was obtained in author interviews in Quito and Manta Ecuador, October 2022.

[4] 'The "Narco Generals" Case in Ecuador', *Cuenca Dispatch*, 21 December 2021.

[5] International Crisis Group, 'Ecuador's High Tide of Drug Violence', 4 November 2022.

[6] Peter Appleby et al., 'InSight Crime's 2022 Homicide Round-up', InSight Crime, 8 February 2023; and David Gagne, 'InSight Crime's 2016 Homicide Round-up', InSight Crime, 16 January 2017.

[7] *Ibid.*

[8] Mario Alexis González, 'Ecuador cerrará 2021 con la peor crisis de seguridad de la década' [Ecuador Will End 2021 with the Worst Security Crisis in a Decade], *Primicias*, 27 December 2021.

9   James Marson and Giovanni Legorano, 'Drug Trail from Europe to Ecuador: Inside the Hunt for Elusive Narco Suspect', *Wall Street Journal*, 24 November 2021.

10 Alessandro Ford, 'Albanian Mafia Leaves Trail of Blood in Ecuador', InSight Crime, 5 January 2021.

11 Luis Bastús, 'Rosario crece: sube su tasa de homicidios' [Rosario Grows: Its Homicide Rate Rises], Página 12, 26 February 2023.

12 Gabrielle Gorder, 'Why Are Murders Spreading Across Argentina's Most Violent City?', InSight Crime, 8 November 2022.

13 Sebastian Fest, 'Messi and Rosario's Narco Wars: "We Are Waiting for You"', The Athletic, 12 March 2023.

14 InSight Crime and American University's Center for Latin American & Latino Studies, 'The Rise of the PCC: How South America's Most Powerful Prison Gang Is Spreading in Brazil and Beyond', CLALS Working Paper Series No. 30, December 2020, p. 5.

15 Leonardo Coutinho, 'The Evolution of the Most Lethal Criminal Organization in Brazil – the PCC', *PRISM*, vol. 8, no. 1, 19 February 2019.

16 Cecilia Anesi, Giulio Rubino and Luís Adorno, 'O PCC e a máfia italiana' [The PCC and the Italian Mafia], UOL Notícias, 5 December 2018.

17 Appleby et al., 'InSight Crime's 2022 Homicide Round-up'.

18 'Hay un crecimiento espectacular del sicariato en el Paraguay' [There Is a Spectacular Rise in Hitmen Assassinations in Paraguay], *Ultima Hora*, 6 February 2022.

19 'Hombre acribillado en San Matías tenía unos 17 procesos en Brasil' [Man Shot Down in San Matias Had 17 Criminal Cases in Brasil], *El Deber*, 20 January 2022.

20 Douglas Farah, 'How to Make a Billion Dollars Disappear: José Luis Merino, PDVSA, Alba Petróleos and the Bukele Administration's Enduring Ties to Transnational Criminal Structures', IBI Consultants, September 2020.

21 Héctor Silva Ávalos, 'Corrupción en las cárceles de Nayib Bukele: denuncian que cobran 1.500 dólares a los familiares para poder visitor a los presos' [Corruption in Nayib Bukele's Prisons: Family Members Denounce Being Charged 1,500 Dollars to Visit Family in Prison], *Infobae*, 19 March 2023.

22 This assessment is based on author interviews with law-enforcement officials in Argentina, Chile and Paraguay, June–December 2022.

MEXICO

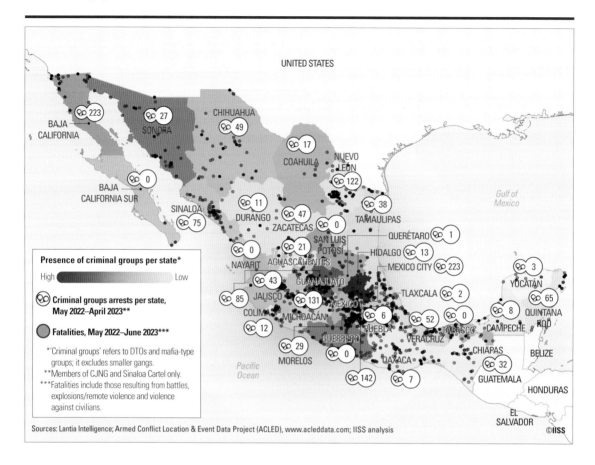

Sources: Lantia Intelligence; Armed Conflict Location & Event Data Project (ACLED), www.acleddata.com; IISS analysis

Conflict Overview

Mexican drug-trafficking organisations (DTOs) originated in the 1970s, trafficking cocaine from South America and marijuana crops from Mexico to the United States. The Guadalajara Cartel controlled this market until its leader's arrest in 1989, following the murder of a US Drug Enforcement Administration (DEA) agent in Guadalajara. After the arrest, the cartel divided its former territory to create the Sinaloa, Juárez, Tijuana and Sonora DTOs. This arrangement continued for decades as the DTOs took advantage of US narcotics demand, as well as the poverty, corruption, wide availability of firearms and lack of viable economic opportunities in many areas of Mexico.

In 2000, Mexico's dominant Institutional Revolutionary Party (PRI) lost national elections for the first time in 70 years. Political turnover at the state and local levels unravelled many unofficial pacts

between the cartels and government representatives, leading to an increase in cartel violence. In December 2006, then-president Felipe Calderón (2006–12) launched the war on drugs, which triggered a full-scale confrontation between state security forces and the DTOs. This seismic shift was followed by the Mérida Initiative in 2008, which provided greater funding for and collaboration between US and Mexican security forces to fight drug trafficking. In October 2021, the two governments adopted the Bicentennial Framework for Security, Public Health, and Safe Communities, which allows for even greater security and community-safety coordination and puts a larger focus on synthetic drugs.

To date, the Mexican government has identified 19 DTOs operating in Mexico: 11 operate in more than one state and two – the Sinaloa Cartel and the Cartel Jalisco

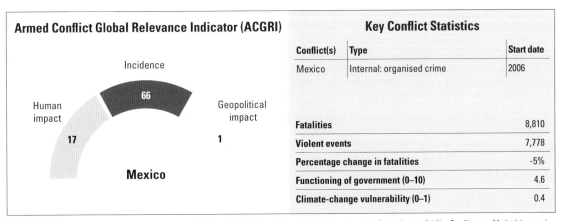

Armed Conflict Global Relevance Indicator (ACGRI)

Incidence

66

Human impact

Geopolitical impact

17

1

Mexico

Key Conflict Statistics

Conflict(s)	Type	Start date
Mexico	Internal: organised crime	2006
Fatalities		8,810
Violent events		7,778
Percentage change in fatalities		-5%
Functioning of government (0–10)		4.6
Climate-change vulnerability (0–1)		0.4

Americas

ACGRI pillars: IISS calculation based on multiple sources for 2022 and 2023 (scale: 0–100), except for some cases according to data availability. See Notes on Methodology and Data Appendix for all variables and further details on Key Conflict Statistics.

New Generation (CJNG) – are present in every state. The pattern of DTOs' territorial control is constantly changing, and the leadership is becoming increasingly fragmented. In 2019, authorities named the CJNG as the most prominent DTO in North America.[1] While the other DTOs do not have the same strength or influence as the Sinaloa Cartel or the CJNG, their large number and continued role in Mexico's diversifying criminal economy will likely continue to destabilise the state and drive sustained levels of local and regional violence.

Conflict Update

In 2022, Mexican authorities reported 31,915 homicides, or approximately 87 homicides per day. This amounts to 25.2 per 100,000 people a year.[2] While this is a slight decrease from 2021 (26 per 100,000), it represents the fifth consecutive year that homicides in Mexico surpassed 30,000.[3]

The CJNG is still the most powerful DTO in Mexico's criminal economy. It maintains economic operations in traditional illicit economies, such as drugs, kidnapping and extortion, as well as trafficking migrants. It has also expanded into new criminal economies, including fentanyl production and counterfeit pharmaceuticals, which take advantage of transnational networks to exploit regulatory gaps and weak law-enforcement capabilities. Furthermore, it has pursued new relationships with criminal networks in Asia.

The most significant change in the conflict between the DTOs and the state in 2022 was the renewed collaboration between the US and Mexico and the increased reliance on the Mexican military to provide public security. For instance, on 15 July 2022, Mexican authorities recaptured drug lord and fugitive Rafael Caro Quintero, who was wanted for the murder of US agent Enrique Camarena in 1985. This recapture was widely seen as a signal of warming US–Mexico relations regarding joint efforts to fight drug trafficking. Meanwhile, the increased reliance on the military represented a shift in President Andrés Manuel López Obrador's policies, as he pivoted away from addressing the root causes of violence through increased social spending and toward a more direct confrontation of the cartels' operations and territorial control. Thus, in September 2022, López Obrador reported that he had 'changed his mind' and his administration would be engaging directly in the fight for public security by using military force.[4]

The change in tactics followed a brutal and bloody summer in Mexico, during which there were repeated high-profile clashes between DTOs and state security forces that resulted in heavy losses on the state's side. On 26 June 2022, armed men attacked ten police officers, killing six and wounding two, near the town of Colombia, Nuevo León, about 15 kilometres from the US–Mexico border.[5] Federal troops were already providing public security in the area. In August 2022, organised crime also orchestrated coordinated attacks in five different states in Mexico.[6]

As the Mexican military took a more active role in public security, it faced repeated scandals. In August 2022, the Truth Commission investigating the disappearance of 43 students in 2014 called the event a 'state crime' for the first time and arrested dozens of current and former members of the military.[7] Furthermore, in February 2023, former secretary of public security Genaro García Luna was convicted in US federal court of taking millions of US dollars in bribes from the Sinaloa Cartel.[8] His trial provided a key example both of DTOs' entrenched position in the state and of the role that US bilateral relations with Mexico play in law enforcement.

Despite these and other scandals, according to a public-opinion survey, 80% of Mexican citizens want more military involvement in public security, particularly fighting organised crime.[9] On 13 October 2022, the Mexican congress voted for the military to remain publicly deployed in civilian areas to keep the peace until 2028.[10]

As these high-level strategic changes are implemented throughout Mexico's public-security infrastructure, cartels continue to take on the lowest and highest levels of government. On 5 January 2023, authorities arrested Ovidio Guzmán López, son of Joaquín 'El Chapo' Guzmán and one of the key leaders of the Sinaloa Cartel, in an operation that left 29 dead, 35 wounded and 21 arrested.[11] Then, on 14 February, the Mexican army raided a synthetic-drug lab controlled by the Sinaloa Cartel and seized almost 630,000 pills, about 128 kilograms of powdered fentanyl and about 100 kg of suspected methamphetamines.[12] Several months later, on 22 June, the mayor of Tijuana changed residences to a military base after receiving death threats, and soon after, on 27 June, 14 administrative employees of the Chiapas state security ministry were abducted (and then released) by an unknown criminal organisation.[13] Thus, even as the Mexican security apparatus achieves some successes against DTOs, they remain an evolving and ongoing threat that continues to challenge the state.

Conflict Parties

Secretariat of National Defence (SEDENA) – army and air force

Strength: 165,500.

Areas of operation: Nationwide but concentrated in the north and west Pacific states: Baja California, Chihuahua, Coahuila, Jalisco, Guerrero, Michoacán, Sonora and Tamaulipas.

Leadership: Gen. Luis Crecencio Sandoval (head of SEDENA) and Gen. Manuel de Jesús Hernández González (head of the air force).

Structure: Mexico's defence ministry has two sections: SEDENA and the Secretariat of the Navy (SEMAR). SEDENA comprises the army and the air force. The army is split into 12 military divisions and 46 zones. The air force has four divisions. The General Staff of National Defence is made up of eight divisions, of which the second and seventh divisions focus on DTOs.

History: The Ministry of War and the Navy was created in 1821 to supervise the army and the navy. In 1939, it was divided to create SEDENA and SEMAR.

Objectives: Provide internal security and fight drug trafficking.

Opponents: DTOs.

Affiliates/allies: SEMAR, the National Guard (GN) and special-forces combat group GAIN (Drug Trafficking Information Analysis Group), which is in charge of capturing DTO leaders. Also supported by the National Intelligence Centre (CNI) and the Attorney General's Office, as well as foreign governments, through cooperation programmes (e.g., the Bicentennial Framework for Security, Public Health, and Safe Communities with the US and, previously, the Mérida Initiative).

Resources/capabilities: Infantry, armoured vehicles and combat helicopters. 2022 budget: US$4 billion (MXN 81.1bn). 2023 budget: US$5.8bn (MXN 99.1bn).[14]

Secretariat of the Navy (SEMAR)

Strength: 50,500.

Areas of operation: Mexico's coasts, divided into the Pacific and the Gulf of Mexico–Caribbean zones.

Leadership: Adm. José Rafael Ojeda Durán.

Structure: Divided into General (70%) and Naval Infantry Corps (marines; 30%), which operate in eight naval regions and 18 naval zones (12 in the Pacific and six in the Gulf and Caribbean). The marines' special forces also combat criminal groups in Mexico's interior.

History: Created in 1821. SEMAR separated from SEDENA in 1939.

Objectives: Defend Mexico's coasts, strategic infrastructure (mainly oil platforms in the Gulf of Mexico) and the environment at sea, and fight piracy.

Opponents: DTOs, especially those that traffic people along the coasts, from South and Central America, and those that transport drugs via the sea from Colombia and Venezuela.

Affiliates/allies: SEDENA, GN and the CNI. Cooperates with US Coast Guard at the border.

Resources/capabilities: Fast vessels for interception, exploration and intelligence; supported by naval aviation. 2022 budget: US$1.6bn (MXN 32.5bn). 2023 budget: US$2.2bn (MXN 36.7bn).[15]

National Guard (GN)

Strength: 115,000.

Areas of operation: Across the whole country. The states of Guanajuato, Jalisco, Mexico, Michoacán, Oaxaca and Sinaloa had the highest number of GN units (referred to as 'operational control regions') at the end of 2022.

Leadership: Gen. (Retd) David Córdova Campos (commissioner).

Structure: The planned 266 coordination regions across the country are fully operational. In September 2022, SEDENA took full management control of the GN. However, in April 2023, Mexico's Supreme Court ruled that this move was unconstitutional.

History: Began operating in May 2019, by presidential order. The law gave GN personnel the authority to stop suspected criminals on the streets.

Objectives: Reduce the level of violence in the country and combat DTOs.

Opponents: DTOs and medium-sized criminal organisations.

Affiliates/allies: SEDENA, SEMAR, and local and municipal police.

Resources/capabilities: Acquired resources from the defunct Federal Police, including helicopter teams and equipment such as assault rifles. Relies on intelligence from SEDENA, SEMAR and the CNI.

Cartel Jalisco New Generation (CJNG)

Strength: Unknown.

Areas of operation: Headquartered in the state of Jalisco, with a presence in most states, particularly Colima, Guanajuato, Guerrero, Jalisco, Michoacán and Nayarit. It also controls the Pacific ports of Manzanillo and Lázaro Cárdenas, where chemicals from China enter Mexico. It has rapidly expanded in the US, where it is thought to have a presence in 35 states and Puerto Rico, and in South America, including Argentina, Colombia and Ecuador.

Leadership: The main leader is Nemesio Oseguera Cervantes, commonly known as 'El Mencho'.

Structure: El Mencho successfully co-opted all regional leaders of the Michoacán Family and the Knights Templar to control the laboratories in the Michoacán mountains.

History: Formed in 2011 in Guadalajara, Jalisco, the CJNG initially produced methamphetamine in rural laboratories in Jalisco and Michoacán. In 2012–13, it expanded to Veracruz. Since 2015–16, its influence has grown throughout the country, thanks in part to gaps left after the government successfully targeted other DTOs (such as the Michoacán Family, the Knights Templar, Los Zetas and the Sinaloa Cartel). It has also shifted to producing and trafficking synthetic drugs such as fentanyl and counterfeit pharmaceuticals, using precursor chemicals sourced from Asia.

Objectives: Maintain supremacy among Mexico's criminal networks.

Opponents: Other DTOs, particularly the Sinaloa Cartel. SEMAR, SEDENA's intelligence section and special forces. The US DEA and Defense Intelligence Agency (DIA).

Affiliates/allies: Demobilised members of the Michoacán Family and the Knights Templar, as well as large numbers of collaborating communities.

Resources/capabilities: Estimated capital of US$1bn from the sale of methamphetamine and fentanyl as well as the extortion of merchants and money-laundering activities in Guadalajara. Known to possess high-powered weapons including military-grade equipment and has used drones to attack government forces.

Sinaloa Cartel

Strength: Unknown.

Areas of operation: Headquartered in Culiacán, Sinaloa, but with a presence in all 32 states of Mexico and particularly in the Pacific (the cartel is also known as the Cartel del Pacífico or Cartel del Pacífico–Sinaloa). Outside Mexico, it is active in Asia, Canada, Central America and Europe. In the US, it has an important presence in California, Colorado, New York and Texas.

Leadership: Historical leader since the mid-1990s, Joaquín 'El Chapo' Guzman, was captured in 2016 and imprisoned for life in the US in 2019. His number two, Ismael 'El Mayo' Zambada García, is in a leadership struggle with El Chapo's son, Iván Archibaldo Guzmán Salazar. Ovidio Guzmán López, El Chapo's other powerful son, was arrested on 5 January 2023.

Structure: Hierarchical organisation, with three subdivisions: finance/business, logistics for drug transportation and military structures. In recent years, the cartel has associated with numerous smaller DTOs such as Los Salazar and Los Talibanes.

History: Preceded by the Guadalajara Cartel, co-founded in the late 1970s by leader Rafael Caro Quintero. In the 1990s, following the peace processes in Central America, the large-scale ground transit of cocaine began. In the mid-1990s, El Chapo became leader of the Sinaloa Cartel, opened routes from Guatemala to Mexico and the Tijuana route, and forged alliances with the Medellín Cartel in Colombia. Focused for 20 years on cocaine, but now diversifying into heroin, methamphetamine and fentanyl.

Objectives: Control all drug markets (for cocaine and methamphetamine, in particular), including production networks in Colombia, distribution in Central America and Mexico, and consumption in the US. Recover its position as the dominant DTO in Mexico.

Opponents: Other DTOs, particularly the CJNG. SEMAR, SEDENA's intelligence section and special forces. The US DEA and DIA.

Sinaloa Cartel

Affiliates/allies: Many subordinate medium-sized and small criminal organisations at the regional level, including cocaine-producing partners in Colombia. Partners with many corrupt Mexican government officials, particularly in its home state of Sinaloa and other regions where it operates.

Resources/capabilities: High-powered weapons, such as the Barrett M107 sniper rifle and anti-aircraft missiles, and a large fleet of drug-transport planes.

Los Zetas

Strength: Unknown. Hit hard by the government between 2012 and 2016.

Areas of operation: Tamaulipas State, mainly along the border with Texas, as well as Coahuila, Nuevo León, Veracruz, Tabasco and the area along the border with Guatemala.

Leadership: Founded by Heriberto Lazcano, former member of the Mexican army. Since 2013, 33 of its main leaders (including Lazcano) have been arrested or killed in combat by military forces. Its Cartel del Noreste splinter group is believed to be led by Juan Gerardo Treviño-Chávez 'El Huevo'.

Structure: Originally a horizontal, decentralised structure that worked as a large business with multiple criminal activities. Less successful at drug trafficking, its cells were involved in extortion, kidnapping, the collection of criminal taxes from businesses and migrant trafficking from Central America to Texas. Currently split into two main groups, Zetas Vieja

Escuela and the Cartel del Noreste. Another group known as Los Talibanes operates in north-central Mexico in association with the Sinaloa Cartel.

History: Began as the armed wing of the Gulf Cartel, drawing most of its members from the Mexican and Guatemalan armies. Notorious for perpetrating mass violence against the civilian population and migrants. Between 2010 and 2012, a major SEMAR offensive to dismantle the 'Gulf Corridor' weakened the group significantly. It is the DTO against which the Mexican government has been most successful.

Objectives: Control criminal activity in the Gulf of Mexico states.

Opponents: CJNG, Gulf Cartel and the special forces of SEMAR.

Affiliates/allies: Criminal networks in Tamaulipas State.

Resources/capabilities: Migrant smuggling and criminal taxes on merchants.

Gulf Cartel

Strength: Unknown.

Areas of operation: Operates and controls territory in Tamaulipas State, particularly the border area with Texas, including strategic border cities, such as Nuevo Laredo, Reynosa and Matamoros.

Leadership: The Gulf Cartel was led by Osiel Cárdenas Guillén at the peak of its power in the early 2000s but has suffered from high turnover of leadership since his capture in 2003. Numerous Gulf Cartel leaders have been arrested or killed by government forces in recent years.

Structure: Unstable, with fragmented leadership. Splinter groups include Los Ciclones, Los Metros, Panteras and Grupo Sombra.

History: The second-oldest DTO in the country, smuggling

alcohol, weapons and drugs across the US border since the 1940s. After forging a partnership with the Colombian Cali Cartel in the 1990s, the group focused on introducing cocaine to the US market. Los Zetas violently separated from the group in 2010.

Objectives: Smuggle drugs on the Texas–Tamaulipas border and control drug trafficking in northeast US.

Opponents: Los Zetas, CJNG and the special forces of SEMAR and SEDENA.

Affiliates/allies: Closely linked to Tamaulipas State's governors (three former governors have been charged in Texas) and criminal networks.

Resources/capabilities: Many Tamaulipas businessmen help the cartel to launder money.

Beltrán Leyva Organisation (BLO)

Strength: Unknown.

Areas of operation: Mainly in the states of Guerrero and Morelos, and the Mexico City–Acapulco highway. The group controls poppy production and the export of heroin from Iguala (Guerrero) to Chicago, IL.

Leadership: Founded by brothers Arturo, Alfredo, Carlos and Héctor Leyva. Arturo was killed in 2009 and the other three were imprisoned, with Héctor dying in 2018. The organisation is now split into various groups.

Structure: Based around vertically organised cells. After the death or imprisonment of the four brothers, it fragmented into different groups which primarily operate in the state of Guerrero. The two largest are Los Rojos and Guerreros

Unidos, the latter of which also traces its origins to splinter cells of the Knights Templar cartel. Both groups have been identified as being responsible for the 2014 Ayotzinapa massacre and are also believed to be in conflict with each other.

History: A breakaway group of the Sinaloa Cartel formed in 2008 in Sinaloa before moving to the South Pacific–Acapulco (Guerrero State), Morelos and Mexico State. The groups are among the most important DTOs operating in the highly violent region known as 'Tierra Caliente', which covers parts of the states of Guerrero, Michoacán and Mexico.

Objectives: Control heroin trafficking in the South Pacific and from Mexico to Chicago.

Beltrán Leyva Organisation (BLO)

Opponents: Sinaloa Cartel, CJNG and the special forces of SEDENA.

Affiliates/allies: An estimated 100,000 peasants who grow poppies in Guerrero.

Resources/capabilities: Profits from the sale of heroin in the US and from criminal activities such as extortion and kidnapping in Mexico.

Michoacán Family/Knights Templar (Cárteles Unidos)

Strength: Unknown.

Areas of operation: The surviving criminal cells moved to the states of Guanajuato, Guerrero and Mexico.

Leadership: Fragmented following the 2015 arrest of Servando Gómez Martínez. The current organisation, known as Cárteles Unidos, is led by Juan José Farías Álvarez 'El Abuelo'.

Structure: Organised into independent groups – including the Cartel del Abuelo and Los Viagras – that in recent years banded together under the name Cárteles Unidos. Many of these groups are notable for having begun as vigilante-style *autodefensa* (self-defence) groups but later branched out into criminal activities.

History: Gained power by producing methamphetamine, importing chemical precursors from China. Founded by Nazario Moreno Gonzalez in 2005, the organisation's initial recruitment was based on a religious discourse. Between 2006 and 2012, the group built a broad network of collaborators among the population, bribed many local politicians on the Pacific coast of Michoacán and ran methamphetamine laboratories in the mountains. However, the group was practically dismantled by Mexican government forces between 2013 and 2016. Following the capture of its first leaders, the Michoacán Family became the Knights Templar in 2013–14, under the leadership of Servando Gómez. The organisation known as Cárteles Unidos was created in 2019 as a response to CJNG activity in Michoacán.

Objectives: Control mining and agricultural production (of avocados for export to the US) in Michoacán State; control the port of Lázaro Cárdenas (for smuggling the chemical base for producing methamphetamine); and steal fuel in Guanajuato State.

Opponents: Sinaloa Cartel, CJNG and the special forces of SEDENA.

Affiliates/allies: A large number of collaborating peasants.

Resources/capabilities: The revenue from criminal taxes on many economic activities.

Tijuana Cartel (also known as Arellano Felix Family Organisation)

Strength: Exact numbers unknown, but thought to have regained some strength since 2018.

Areas of operation: A bi-national, cross-border organisation operating between Tijuana, Baja California and San Diego, CA, as well as in Los Angeles, CA.

Leadership: Its original leaders, Benjamin Arellano Felix and his brothers Ramón, Eduardo, Luis Fernando, Francisco, Carlos and Javier, are all imprisoned in Californian jails. The cartel is currently led by their sister, Enedina Arellano Felix.

Structure: Groups of young people become either gunmen or cocaine exporters (middle-class youth who have visas to cross the border). Their leaders are family members. A splinter group associated with the CJNG is known as the Cartel Tijuana New Generation.

History: During the 1980s and 1990s, the Arellano Felix brothers controlled the north of the country and transported drugs across the border using tunnels and people crossing the border, as well as migrants. The arrest of the Arellano Felix brothers led to the cartel's decline amid the Sinaloa Cartel's dominance in the region. However, the latter's troubles in recent years have led to a resurgence of the Tijuana Cartel.

Objectives: Control drug trafficking from Baja California to California, US.

Opponents: Sinaloa Cartel, the special forces of SEDENA and US intelligence services cooperating with Mexican authorities at the border.

Affiliates/allies: Many people cross the border daily with small amounts of drugs.

Resources/capabilities: Revenue from the cross-border cocaine trade.

Other relevant parties

There are several other significant DTOs operating in Mexico, including La Unión Tepito, the Santa Rosa de Lima Cartel and the Juárez Cartel.

Notes

1   South Carolina Department of Alcohol and Other Drug Abuse Services, 'Atlanta–Carolinas High Intensity Drug Trafficking Area's 2019 Threat Assessment', 16 December 2019.

2   Gobierno de México [Government of Mexico] '#ConferenciaPresidente | Martes 17 de enero de 2023' [#President'sConference | Tuesday, 17 January 2023], YouTube, 17 January 2023.

3   Gobierno de México [Government of Mexico], 'Informe Seguridad, Secretaria de Seguridad y Proteccion Ciudadana' [Security Report, Secretary of Security and Civilian Protection]; and Gobierno de México [Government of Mexico], '#ConferenciaPresidente | Jueves 20 de enero de 2022' [#President'sConference | Thursday, 20 January 2022], YouTube, 20 January 2022.

4   Reuters, '"Cambié de opinión": AMLO justifica militarización de seguridad pública en México' ['I Changed My Mind': AMLO Justifies Militarisation of Public Security in Mexico], *El Economista*, 6 September 2022.

5   Pablo Ferri, 'El asesinato de seis policías en Nuevo León pone de nuevo el foco en la frontera' [The Murder of Six Police Officers in Nuevo León Puts a Renewed Focus on the Border], *El País*, 27 June 2022.

6   Elena Reina, 'Eduardo Guerrero: "El narco mexicano no está debilitado, está más fuerte que nunca"' [Eduardo Guerrero: 'The Mexican Narco Is Not Weakened, It Is Stronger Than Ever'], *El País*, 21 August 2022.

7   Alejandro Santos Cid, 'Los familiares de los 43 de Ayotzinapa : "Desde un principio señalamos al Ejército y los policías que participaron en ese crimen de Estado"' [The Relatives of the 43 from Ayotzinapa: 'From the Beginning We Signalled to the Army and the Police That They Participated in This State Crime'], *El País*, 29 August 2022.

8   US Attorney's Office, Eastern District of New York, 'Ex-Mexican Secretary of Public Security Genaro Garcia Luna Convicted of Engaging in a Continuing Criminal Enterprise and Taking Millions in Cash Bribes from the Sinaloa Cartel', 21 February 2023.

9   Gabriel Moyssen, 'Mexicanos quieren más militares en seguridad; 80% está a favor, revela encuesta' [Mexicans Want More Military in Public Security; 80% Approve, a Survey Reveals], *El Universal*, 30 August 2022.

10   Vanessa Buschschlüter, 'Mexico Congress Votes to Keep Military on Streets', BBC News, 13 October 2022.

11   Redacción Animal Político [Editorial Staff, Animal Político], 'Operativo para detener a Ovidio Guzmán dejó 29 muertos, 35 heridos y 21 detenidos; descartan bajas civiles' [Operation to Detain Ovidio Guzman Leaves 29 Dead, 35 Wounded and 21 Detained; No Civilian Casualties], Animal Político, 6 January 2023.

12   'Mexican Soldiers Seize Nearly 630,000 Fentanyl Pills Inside "Highest-capacity Synthetic Drug Production Lab on Record"', CBS News, 16 February 2023.

13   'Armed Group Kidnaps 14 Security Ministry Staff in Mexico', Al-Jazeera, 28 June 2023.

14   Secretariat of the Treasury and Public Credit, 'Proyecto de presupuesto de egresos de la federación 2022: análisis de las funciones y subfunciones del gasto programable por destino del gasto' [Federal Expenditure Budget Project 2022: Analysis of the Functions and Sub-Functions of Programmable Expenditure by Expenditure Destination], September 2021; and Secretariat of the Treasury and Public Credit, 'Proyecto de presupuesto de egresos de la federación 2023: análisis de las funciones y subfunciones del gasto programable por destino del gasto' [Federal Expenditure Budget Project 2023: Analysis of the Functions and Sub-Functions of Programmable Expenditure by Expenditure Destination], September 2022.

15   *Ibid*.

COLOMBIA

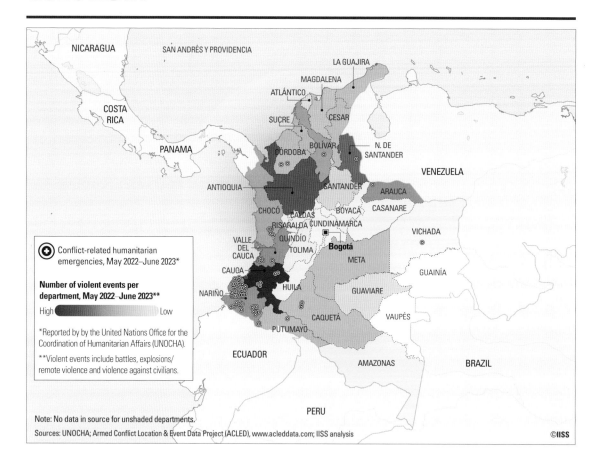

Conflict-related humanitarian emergencies, May 2022–June 2023*

Number of violent events per department, May 2022–June 2023**

High ⬤▬▬▬▬▬▬▬ Low

*Reported by by the United Nations Office for the Coordination of Humanitarian Affairs (UNOCHA).

**Violent events include battles, explosions/remote violence and violence against civilians.

Note: No data in source for unshaded departments.

Sources: UNOCHA; Armed Conflict Location & Event Data Project (ACLED), www.acleddata.com; IISS analysis   ©IISS

Conflict Overview

Colombia's internal armed conflict has been ongoing for nearly 60 years with an evolving landscape of actors and dynamics. Clashes started in the 1960s between state forces and guerrilla movements, which sought to reduce rural poverty and combat the political exclusion of socio-economic minorities, including left-wing political groups. The establishment in the 1980s of paramilitary groups to counter the expansion of guerrillas further intensified armed violence. At the same time, drug trafficking emerged as an increasingly important source of income for all non-state armed groups (NSAGs), and contestation over its control continues to exacerbate conflict patterns to this day. More recently, illegal mining (mostly gold), logging, cattle farming and ranching, as well as migrant smuggling and forced labour, are providing criminal groups with additional revenue streams.[1]

With support from the United States military through Plan Colombia (2000–16), the Colombian armed forces considerably increased their strength and capabilities, halting the territorial expansion of criminal groups, which by 2002 had an important presence in nearly half of the country.[2] Military gains were complemented by peace settlements with the United Self-Defense Forces of Colombia (AUC) paramilitaries (2002–06) and the Revolutionary Armed Forces of Colombia (FARC) guerrillas (2016), resulting in over 50,000 demobilisations.[3] However, flaws in the design and implementation of these processes led to spin-off groups taking up arms again and renewed violence dynamics.

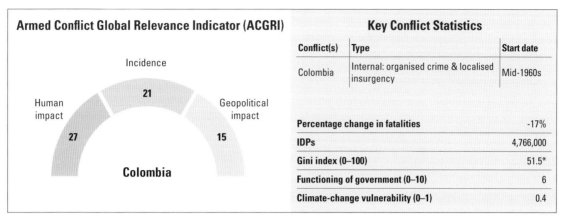

ACGRI pillars: IISS calculation based on multiple sources for 2022 and 2023 (scale: 0–100), except for some cases according to data availability. See Notes on Methodology and Data Appendix for all variables and further details on Key Conflict Statistics. *2021 as latest available data.

The current conflict landscape comprises combatants who either were not part of (or rejected) the political settlements or are new recruits. They are all driven by the ever-expanding and lucrative drug business, against a backdrop of limited (and often corrupt) state presence in rural areas and few opportunities in the legal economy. Three main NSAGs fuel armed violence. The most powerful (by territorial scope) is the Gulf Clan, a narco-paramilitary group linked to the demobilised AUC with a presence in 30% of the country. FARC dissidents, who opposed the 2016 peace agreement, and the National Liberation Army (ELN), which was not included in the peace agreement, have a presence in 14% of the territory each.[4] ELN and FARC dissidents, in particular, are also active in the western states of Venezuela along the border with Colombia.

Conflict Update

In August 2022, Gustavo Petro, a former member of the demobilised April 19th Movement guerrilla, was inaugurated as Colombia's first leftist president and embarked on his ambitious 'total peace' policy, seeking simultaneous peace negotiations with all active criminal groups. This new approach heralded important changes in security and conflict dynamics.

Unlike his predecessor's security policy, which primarily centred on military operations against criminal organisations' leaders, Petro's priority is to reach political agreements to reduce violence while also addressing its root causes. As part of this ambitious agenda, Petro restored diplomatic relations with Venezuela in August 2022, including security cooperation. Venezuela was designated as a guarantor of the Colombian government's peace talks with the ELN and hosted the first round of the talks in November–December 2022.

Meanwhile, with respect to anti-narcotics policy, Petro's aim is not to target the lower echelons of the drug-trafficking supply chain through forced eradication of coca crops by the military, as per the previous administration's approach. Instead, his efforts have been concentrated on voluntary eradication of coca crops, cocaine interdictions and financial measures against drug lords at the top of the cocaine-trafficking pyramid.

In parallel with the above policy changes, power struggles among NSAGs continued throughout the reporting period, with significant changes in relative territorial presence and military strength. While the number of municipalities with a presence of FARC dissidents and narco-paramilitaries increased by 14% and 4% respectively in the first half of 2022, those with an ELN presence shrank by 12%.[5] Territorial reconfiguration resulted in some deadly clashes, especially in border regions such as the southern department of Putumayo, where 18 FARC dissidents were killed in November 2022.[6] Contestation over territories along the Venezuelan border continued between the ELN and the Gulf Clan in municipalities such as Cúcuta in the Norte de Santander department. Clashes among NSAGs also took place in other departments such as Cauca, Choco and Nariño, exacerbating humanitarian crises. The number of Gulf Clan and ELN combatants increased substantially, reaching approximately 6,000 each in 2023.[7]

Initially, Petro seemed to be making quick progress with his 'total peace' policy. The Gulf Clan committed to a unilateral ceasefire as soon as Petro took office in August 2022, and ELN and FARC dissidents declared a unilateral ceasefire the following December. The initiative also prompted important adjustments in NSAGs' leadership and structure, such as higher coordination among Miguel Botache Santillana's (alias 'Gentil Duarte') FARC dissident units, which reorganised under the name of Central General Staff (EMC) and began exploratory peace negotiations with the government. Consequently, the overall number of violent events dropped from 2021–22. However, the number of internally displaced persons increased by a staggering 152% and the yearly count of murdered activists and human-rights defenders increased by 48%.[8]

Moreover, important setbacks followed in the first half of 2023. Less than a day after the government announced six-month bilateral ceasefire agreements with the ELN, the Gulf Clan, the FARC dissident groups Second Marquetalia and EMC, and the Conquering Self-Defence Forces of the Sierra on 1 January 2023, the ELN rejected the truce, alleging it had not been agreed at the negotiation table. Then, on 19 March 2023, the bilateral ceasefire with the Gulf Clan was suspended by Petro after the group infiltrated mining strikes in Antioquia department and conducted several attacks against civilian objectives. That same month, the government temporarily recalled its negotiators from the ELN peace talks after the murder of nine soldiers in Arauca (a department bordering Venezuela).[9] Similarly, on 22 May, the government lifted the bilateral ceasefire with the EMC in the departments of Caquetá, Guaviare, Meta and Putumayo after four indigenous children were killed by the group.[10] Nonetheless, negotiations with the ELN soon resumed, and a bilateral ceasefire was announced on 9 June, just a few days after the government established a new dialogue with several small narco-paramilitary urban gangs in Medellín.[11]

Despite the Petro administration's resolve to reach settlements with diverse criminal groups to reduce violence across the country, setbacks in ceasefires and the increasing territorial expansion and strength of NSAGs have made the situation very uncertain. The growing levels of coca-crop and cocaine production, and the profits stemming from drug trafficking, represent a major economic disincentive for criminal groups to hand over their arms.[12] By the end of the reporting period, the ELN was the only major conflict party that was part of formal negotiations with the government, but it had not yet reached any agreement.

Conflict Parties

Colombian armed forces

Strength: Army: 185,900; navy: 56,400; air force: 13,650; and National Police (PONAL): 165,800.[13]

Areas of operation: Across the country, but limited presence in some rural areas such as the Catatumbo, Urabá, Eastern Plains, Pacific coast regions and border areas.

Leadership: Gustavo Petro Urrego (commander-in-chief), Iván Velásquez Gómez (minister of defence) and Helder Fernán Giraldo Bonilla (general commander).

Structure: Army, navy and air force. PONAL oversees public and civil security. PONAL has been controlled and administered by the Ministry of National Defence and has included militarised units since 1953.

History: Originated in the late eighteenth century as the Liberating Army of the independence movement against the Spanish Empire. The military forces were formally created with the 1821 Cúcuta Constitution.

Objectives: Defend national sovereignty, militarily attack and defeat NSAGs, and maintain rule and order.

Opponents: ELN, FARC dissidents, Gulf Clan and other criminal organisations.

Affiliates/allies: PONAL.

Resources/capabilities: Defence budget of US$8.9 billion in 2022 and US$9.7bn in 2023.[14] Overall capabilities and professionalisation have improved in recent decades.

Gulf Clan (also known as Gaitanistas Self-Defence Forces of Colombia (AGC) or the Urabeños)

Strength: Approximately 6,000 members, though estimates vary.[15]

Areas of operation: Presence in at least 25 departments in Colombia, as well as in Panama and Venezuela.[16] The group is based in the Urabá region, in northwest Colombia, and has an

extensive presence in the city of Medellín and departments of Antioquia, Bolívar, Cesar, Chocó, Córdoba, La Guajira, Magdalena, Meta, Nariño, Norte de Santander, Santander, Sucre, Valle del Cauca and Vichada.

Gulf Clan (also known as Gaitanistas Self-Defence Forces of Colombia (AGC) or the Urabeños)

Leadership: Jobanis de Jesús Ávila Villadiego (alias 'Chiquito Malo') and José Gonzalo Sánchez Sánchez (alias 'Gonzalito'). Second-in-command Wilmer Antonio Giraldo Quiroz (alias 'Siopas') was killed in March 2023 amid internal vendettas.

Structure: Four main structures: 'Central Urabá' (the largest), 'Nelson Darío Hurtado', 'Roberto Vargas' and 'Jairo de Jesús Durango', with nine, six, five and four sub-structures respectively.[17]

History: Emerged from the demobilisation of AUC paramilitaries in 2006. Some of its leaders were either former Popular Liberation Army combatants who demobilised in 1991 or former FARC members who demobilised in the 2000s.

Objectives: Drug trafficking. Using the name Gaitanistas Self-Defence Forces is a way of legitimising itself as a group with political goals.

Opponents: Colombian armed forces; ELN in Antioquia, Bolívar, Chocó and Norte de Santander; and FARC dissidents in Antioquia, Nariño and Norte de Santander.

Affiliates/allies: Corrupt elements of the Colombian armed forces and state officials. It also works with Mexican drug-trafficking organisations, mainly the Sinaloa Cartel and the Cartel Jalisco New Generation (CJNG), as well as Italian (i.e., 'Ndrangheta and Cosa Nostra) and Balkan mafias.

Resources/capabilities: Financing mainly comes from transnational drug trafficking, providing services for independent drug traffickers and illegal mining. Multiple group members, including leaders, run their own international trafficking routes. The group also runs migrant smuggling in the Darién region on the border with Panama.

National Liberation Army (ELN)

Strength: Approximately 6,000 members in arms, including around 1,000 in Venezuela, and an unknown number of part-time militia members (though estimates vary).[18]

Areas of operation: Operates in at least 19 of Colombia's 32 departments and some cities, including Medellín, Cali, Cúcuta and very limitedly in Bogotá.[19] It retains a particularly strong presence along the border with Venezuela, especially in the departments of Arauca, Casanare and Norte de Santander, as well as, to a lesser extent, in Cesar, La Guajira and Vichada. It has also expanded within Venezuela, especially in Bolívar, Táchira and Zulia states.

Leadership: Eliécer Erlington Chamorro Acosta (alias 'Antonio García'; commander).

Structure: Organised into a federal structure. The Central Command directs the ELN's strategy and is composed of four publicly recognised commanders and a larger 30-person National Direction. The ELN has seven regional war fronts, including the Camilo Torres Restrepo National Urban War Front, and 75 sub-fronts.[20]

History: Founded in 1964 by a group of left-wing intellectuals and students embracing liberation theology, who directly studied the Cuban Revolution.

Objectives: On paper, overthrow the Colombian government and create a socialist state; operationally, local 'armed resistance'.

Opponents: Gulf Clan in Antioquia, Bolívar, Chocó and Norte de Santander; EMC in Arauca, Bolívar, Cauca and Norte de Santander departments and in Apure State, Venezuela; Second Marquetalia in parts of Nariño.

Affiliates/allies: Second Marquetalia politically and territorially in Cauca, Norte de Santander and Apure State, Venezuela; 33rd Front of the EMC in Norte de Santander; some members of the Venezuelan armed forces in Apure; and Sinaloa Cartel and CJNG in Mexico.

Resources/capabilities: Besides drug trafficking, extortion, illegal mining and gasoline trafficking are important sources of income. It imposes taxes on and regulates the drug trade in Cauca, Chocó and Norte de Santander.

FARC dissidents: Central General Staff (EMC)

Strength: 2,800–3,480 members, though estimates vary.[21]

Areas of operation: Presence in at least 15 of Colombia's 32 departments (Amazonas, Arauca, Bolívar, Caquetá, Casanare, Cauca, Guainía, Guaviare, Meta, Nariño, Norte de Santander, Putumayo, Valle del Cauca, Vaupés and Vichada), as well as in Apure and Amazonas states in Venezuela.

Leadership: Néstor Gregorio Vera Fernández (alias 'Iván Mordisco'; top commander and coordinator, and leader of the 1st Front), Alexander Díaz Mendoza (alias 'Calarcá'; second in command) and Omar Pardo Galeano (alias 'Antonio Medina'; third in command and leader of the 28th Front).

Structure: Replicates the former FARC operational structure with fronts and mobile columns. It is presently composed of over 20 units. However, leadership only coordinates how individual structures operate and peace dialogues with the government.

History: The EMC is the new name of Gentil Duarte's FARC dissidents, which they adopted after he was killed by the ELN in May 2022 in Venezuela. The group brings together multiple FARC units which rejected the 2016 peace agreement. In March 2023, for the purposes of 'total peace' negotiations, its new leader, Mordisco, ratified the coordination of actions across the group's units.

Objectives: Rebuild the old FARC, recover the areas of the old FARC, and fight the state.

Opponents: Colombian armed forces; Gulf Clan in Bolívar and Nariño; ELN in Arauca, Cauca and Bolívar; Second Marquetalia units in Cauca, Nariño and Putumayo; and the Venezuelan armed forces in Apure State, Venezuela.

Affiliates/allies: ELN in Catatumbo and Cauca; Mexican drug-trafficking organisations, mainly Sinaloa Cartel and CJNG; and First Capital Command (PCC) and Red Command in Brazil.

FARC dissidents: Central General Staff (EMC)

Resources/capabilities: Inherited FARC's former economic structures and rent-seeking activities (including extortion, drug trafficking and illegal mining). Generates income through drug trafficking or tax collection on drug distribution in its areas of influence.

FARC dissidents: Second Marquetalia

Strength: 1,646–1,800 members in arms, though figures vary.[22]

Areas of operation: At least ten departments, especially in border areas with Venezuela, mainly in Norte de Santander and Cesar, and border areas with Ecuador in Putumayo and Nariño. It also operates in Apure and Amazonas states in Venezuela.

Leadership: The main commanders include Luciano Marín Arango (alias 'Iván Márquez'), José Aldinever Sierra Sabogal (alias 'Zarco Aldinever'), José Vicente Lesmes (alias 'Walter Mendoza') and Géner García Molina (alias 'Jhon 40').

Structure: Has incorporated other groups under a claimed unified command. Its organisational structure includes a 'National Direction'.

History: Created in 2018 when a group of senior FARC commanders abandoned the reincorporation process and resumed fighting; its existence was publicly announced in August 2019.

Objectives: Recreate the original FARC, take over the state or initiate a new negotiation process.

Opponents: Colombian armed forces and EMC dissidents in Cauca, Nariño and Putumayo, as well as Apure State, Venezuela.

Affiliates/allies: ELN, especially on a political level, but also on a local level in Cauca department and Apure State, Venezuela. It also works with the Mexican CJNG and the Brazilian PCC.

Resources/capabilities: Its sources of financing include former undeclared assets of the FARC, drug trafficking and illegal gold mining. It also has renewed weaponry with more modern rifles.

Notes

[1] The Gulf Clan taxes migrant-smuggling activities in the Darién region between Colombia and Panama. In the areas bordering Venezuela in the departments of Norte de Santander and Arauca, groups such as the ELN recruit Venezuelan migrants and/or force them to work on coca farms.

[2] Under Plan Colombia, the United States provided more than US$10bn in financial assistance to the Colombian armed forces, mainly to fight terrorist groups and drug trafficking. In 2002, non-state armed groups were present in 561 out of 1,101 municipalities of the country. For more information, see June S. Beittel, 'Colombia: Background and U.S. Relations', R43813, Congressional Research Service, 16 December 2021; and Centro Nacional de Memoria Histórica [National Centre for History's Memory], ¡Basta Ya! Colombia: Memorias de guerra y dignidad [It is Enough! Colombia: Memories of War and Dignity] (Bogotá: National Printing House, 2013).

[3] National Reintegration Agency, 'ARN en cifras corte marzo 2023' [ARN in Data Cut-off March 2023], 27 April 2023.

[4] In the first half of 2022, the Gulf Clan operated in 326 municipalities, FARC dissident groups in 161 and the ELN in 162, out of 1,123 municipalities. Indepaz, 'Informe sobre presencia de grupos armados en Colombia 2021–2022 (1)' [Report of Presence of Armed Groups in Colombia 2021–2022 (1)], 22 February 2023.

[5] Ibid. Besides the Gulf Clan, there are other smaller narco-paramilitary groups including the Caparros, Oficina de Envigado, Pachely, Pachenca, Popular Liberation Army (EPL) and Rastrojos.

[6] Juan Esteban Lewin and Camila Osorio, '18 muertos por combates entre dos grupos disidentes en el Putumayo' [18 Dead in Clashes Between Two Dissident Groups in Putumayo], El País, 21 November 2022.

[7] 'Las cifras del aumento de la guerra en Colombia que reveló el propio comisionado' [The Figures of the Increase in Conflict Levels in Colombia Revealed by the Commissioner Himself], El Tiempo, 19 April 2023.

[8] IISS calculation using data from the International Displacement Monitoring Centre, 'Global Internal Displacement Database', May 2023; and 'Colombia Killings of Social Leaders Hit Record in 2022 – Ombudsman', Reuters, 23 January 2023.

[9] Richard Emblin, 'Colombia's Petro Recalls Peace Negotiators After ELN Kills Nine Soldiers', City Paper, 29 March 2023.

[10] Camilo Castillo, 'Estado Mayor Central le pide al Gobierno restablecer el cese al fuego bilateral' [Central General Staff Asks the Government to Restore the Bilateral Ceasefire], El Tiempo, 15 June 2023.

[11] The bilateral ceasefire refers to military clashes between the state forces and the ELN, but it does not include other criminal activities such as kidnapping and forced recruitment. Regarding the negotiations with criminal organisations held in Medellín, instead of agreeing to a political negotiation, the government offered a reduction of jail time (with a maximum of eight years) in exchange for ceasing criminal activities, mostly drug trafficking.

[12] According to the latest available data in the United Nations Office of Drugs and Crime 'World Drug Report 2023', in 2021 Colombia hit record highs in terms of cocaine manufacturing and hectares used for coca-bush cultivation since records began in 2005 and 1998, respectively.

[13] For PONAL figures, see Policia Nacional de Colombia, 'Cifras de personal' [Personnel Figures], 21 June 2023.

[14] 'Aprobado presupuesto 2023: ¿Qué cambió en comparación con el último cálculo del gobierno de Iván Duque?' [Approved Budget for 2023: What Changed Compared to the Last Calculation of the Government of Iván Duque?], *Cambio*, 19 October 2022. Calculation based on 18 October 2022 US dollar to Colombian peso exchange rate.

[15] State figures suggest up to 6,000 members, although independent estimates point at up to 9,000. 'Las cifras del aumento de la guerra en Colombia que reveló el propio comisionado' [The Figures of the Increase in Conflict Levels in Colombia Revealed by the Commissioner Himself], *El Tiempo*, 19 April 2023; and Méndez, 'Informe confidencial del Gobierno: en Venezuela hay 1.441 disidentes y elenos' [Government's Confidential Report: There Are 1,441 Dissidents and ELN Combatants in Venezuela].

[16] Indepaz, 'Informe sobre presencia de grupos armados en Colombia 2021–2022 (1)' [Report of Presence of Armed Groups in Colombia 2021–2022 (1)], p. 11.

[17] Méndez, 'Informe confidencial del Gobierno: en Venezuela hay 1.441 disidentes y elenos' [Government's Confidential Report: There Are 1,441 Dissidents and ELN Combatants in Venezuela].

[18] *Ibid*.

[19] Indepaz, 'Informe sobre presencia de grupos armados en Colombia 2021–2022 (1)' [Report of Presence of Armed Groups in Colombia 2021–2022 (1)], pp. 90–9.

[20] Alicia Liliana Méndez, 'Son 14.626 los integrantes de redes criminales que piden pista en la "paz total"' [There Are 14,626 Members of Criminal Networks That Ask to be Considered in the 'Total Peace'], 5 March 2023.

[21] 'Las cifras del aumento de la guerra en Colombia que reveló el propio comisionado' [The Figures of the Increase in Conflict Levels in Colombia Revealed by the Commissioner Himself]; and Méndez, 'Informe confidencial del Gobierno: en Venezuela hay 1.441 disidentes y elenos' [Government's Confidential Report: There Are 1,441 Dissidents and ELN Combatants in Venezuela].

[22] *Ibid*.

Americas

BRAZIL

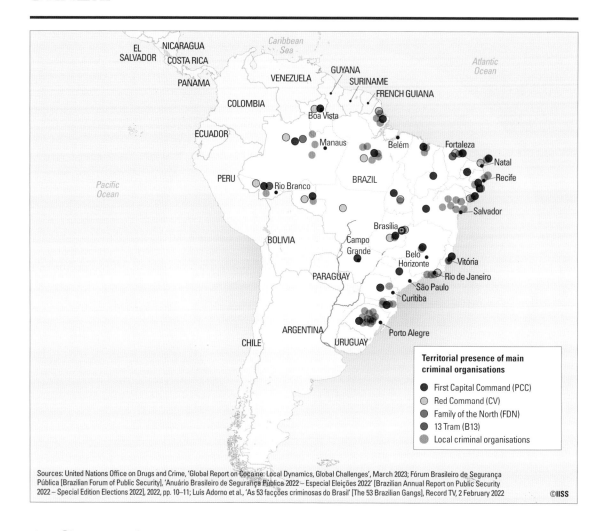

Territorial presence of main criminal organisations

- First Capital Command (PCC)
- Red Command (CV)
- Family of the North (FDN)
- 13 Tram (B13)
- Local criminal organisations

Sources: United Nations Office on Drugs and Crime, 'Global Report on Cocaine: Local Dynamics, Global Challenges', March 2023; Fórum Brasileiro de Segurança Pública [Brazilian Forum of Public Security], 'Anuário Brasileiro de Segurança Pública 2022 – Especial Eleições 2022' [Brazilian Annual Report on Public Security 2022 – Special Edition Elections 2022], 2022, pp. 10–11; Luís Adorno et al., 'As 53 facções criminosas do Brasil' [The 53 Brazilian Gangs], Record TV, 2 February 2022   ©IISS

Conflict Overview

Brazil has battled entrenched criminal organisations for decades, with the country's prison system facilitating the growth of such organisations and serving as their operational headquarters. The major factions vying for power are the First Capital Command (PCC), based in São Paulo; the Red Command (CV), headquartered in Rio de Janeiro; and the Family of the North (FDN), based in Manaus. Brazil's criminal landscape is also marked by an increasing number of smaller organisations that usually seek alliances with one of the major factions to control territory and drug routes. The proliferation of these smaller organisations has been punctuated by the presence of powerful militia groups in states like Rio de

Janeiro. These groups, comprised of police officers and members of former and current state security services, often operate in a similar fashion to other criminal organisations – controlling territory, extorting businesses and increasingly competing over the drug-trafficking business.

Intense criminal contestation, combined with profit-seeking motives, have driven the rapid internationalisation of Brazil's main criminal groups. The PCC, for instance, operates on at least three continents and has forged working relationships and alliances with other major international organisations, such as the Italian 'Ndrangheta and Serbian and Albanian criminal

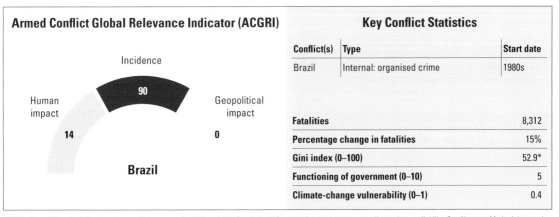

ACGRI pillars: IISS calculation based on multiple sources for 2022 and 2023 (scale: 0–100), except for some cases according to data availability. See Notes on Methodology and Data Appendix for all variables and further details on Key Conflict Statistics. *2021 as latest available data.

groups.[1] Its main international drug-trafficking routes involve moving product from Paraguay and Bolivia through Brazil to former Portuguese colonies in Africa (Angola and Mozambique) and eventually onwards to Europe. An alternative to this route involves shipping products directly from Brazil's northeast to Europe. Key to this international expansion has been the group's control of critical infrastructure, such as ports in Brazil (and other countries), to export illicit products. While drug trafficking has traditionally been the main illicit industry, other activities have gained momentum, including illegal mining, logging and wildlife trafficking, as well as highway theft involving truckloads of high-tech electronics (e.g., mobile phones and computers).

Geographically, the bulk of Brazil's violence has been concentrated in urban areas since the 1980s.[2] Recently, however, there has also been an increase in violence in Brazil's rural areas, fuelled by land-owners and illegal-mining and -logging groups allying with criminal organisations.[3]

Conflict Update

During the reporting period, Brazil continued to experience significant conflict. The country registered 39,519 homicides in 2022 (or 19.5 per 100,000), a less than 2% decrease compared to 2021.[4] Brazil invested more in public security, including in police intelligence in states such as Pernambuco and Paraíba and surveillance equipment in São Paulo State, which may have contributed to the modest decline in homicides. However, it could also be explained by a 'pax mafiosa' situation, with some criminal organisations having emerged victorious over their rivals and imposing an iron-fisted rule over parts of Amazonas, Mato Grosso, Mato Grosso do Sul and São Paulo states.[5] After the homicide rate peaked between 2017 and 2018, some of Brazil's major criminal organisations ceased fighting and a more stable hierarchy emerged. For instance, the CV has consolidated its position on the Solimões River route in the Amazon region, an uninterrupted riverine network stretching from the tri-border area with Colombia and Peru to the convergence of the Amazon River with the

Atlantic Ocean; the PCC controls parts of the stretch of largely uninhabited forest in the same area; and the FDN continues to have a strong presence in the city of Manaus, with alliances also in Ceará State.[6]

Rio de Janeiro State and the Amazon region remained epicentres of conflict, with other regions, such as Brazil's northeast, registering significant spikes in criminal violence. The latter is important to note because the northeast is home to several of the most significant embarkation points for drugs heading directly to Europe. This fuels violence in cocaine transport areas, borders with Paraguay and Bolivia, and especially in port cities, from which products exit Brazil after having transited through the country.

Contestation continued among the FDN, CV and PCC in the Amazon region over the drug corridor stretching from the Brazil–Colombia–Peru tri-border area, deep in the heart of the Amazon rainforest, to the mouth of the Amazon River. Notably, in this region, smaller criminal groups, such as the 13 Tram (B13) (Acre State), increased their influence in local illicit markets by moving product and forging alliances with larger groups.

In the central and southwest regions of Brazil, a key drug-trafficking route, referred to as the 'Caipira Route', has been consolidated by the PCC and plays a key role in the latter's profit-making and internationalisation strategy. After ferrying drugs from Paraguay and Bolivia, the PCC leverages its access to the Port of Santos to ship product to West Africa and Europe. Along this path, PCC competitors are often killed. Meanwhile, the PCC has sought greater control in the northeast part of Brazil to facilitate more direct shipping routes via the northern Atlantic Ocean, leading to clashes with local criminal organisations, especially the Crime Syndicate (SDC) (Rio Grande do Norte State) and the Guardians of the State (GDE) (Ceará State).[7]

Killings committed by police also remained an important driver of violence trends, as President Jair Bolsonaro, whose term expired at the end of 2022, favoured a hardline security approach to combat criminal organisations. From 2019–22, 184 out of 237 massacres (defined as involving three or more deaths) were conducted by police, which translates to roughly one massacre every eight days.[8] A notable example occurred on 24 May 2022 in the Vila Cruzeiro *favela*, which killed at least 23 people.[9] It was the most violent event in Rio de Janeiro since the raid on the Jacarezinho *favela* almost exactly one year before.

Another significant trend observed during the reporting period was the convergence of traditional drug-trafficking activities and environmental crime. Categorised as 'narcoecology', this criminal convergence unites '[drug] trafficking with the illegal logging market, with land grabbing and with mining on indigenous lands, especially in Roraima State'.[10] The PCC, for instance, has allied with illegal mining and logging groups to control territory, seeking to exploit Brazil's natural resources and facilitate drug trafficking to Europe and West Africa, with increasingly negative repercussions for indigenous communities.

In a major departure from Bolsonaro's hardline security policies and his apparent disregard for environmental crimes, his successor, President Luiz Inácio Lula da Silva, has moved to curb the military's increased political power, police killings and access to firearms for civilians. He is also seeking to fight illegal economies in the Amazon and to offer greater protection to environmental leaders.

All these developments occurred against the backdrop of increasing political polarisation, exacerbated by a presidential election in which Lula narrowly defeated Bolsonaro in October 2022. In response to the election outcome, Bolsonaro supporters overran the military police and stormed congress and the presidential palace on 8 January 2023.[11]

Conflict Parties

Military Police of Rio de Janeiro (PMERJ/PM)

Strength: About 41,000–43,000 members.[12]

Areas of operation: Rio de Janeiro State.

Leadership: Col. Luiz Henrique Marinho Pires (commander-in-chief).

Structure: Accountable to the Rio State government. Its hierarchy resembles that of the army and its members are reserves for the armed forces.

History: Created in May 1809; current structure introduced in July 1975.

Objectives: Fight organised-crime groups.

Opponents: Organised-crime groups and militias.

Affiliates/allies: Unofficially, some militias and Pure Third Command (TCP).

Resources/capabilities: Weapons currently used include the IMBEL *ParaFAL* 7.62mm battle rifle and the IMBEL IA2 assault rifle.

First Capital Command (PCC)

Strength: 20,000–30,000 members.[13]

Areas of operation: Based in São Paulo State but maintains operations throughout much of Brazil, especially in Amazon border regions. Also operates (independently or in cooperation with local gangs and mafias) in Argentina,

Bolivia, Colombia, Italy, Mozambique, the Netherlands, Paraguay, Peru, Portugal, South Africa and Venezuela.

Leadership: Marcos Willians Herbas Camacho (alias 'Marcola') took over the leadership in 2002, although he has

First Capital Command (PCC)

been imprisoned since 1999. Other important leaders are Valdeci Alves dos Santos (alias 'Colorido') and Geraldo dos Santos Filho.

Structure: Highly organised, with a CEO (Marcola) and strategic Deliberative Council, Board of Directors, Administrative Board, Legal Board, State Board, Economic Board, Institutional Relations Board, Human Resources and an intelligence branch. These groupings are referred to as *'sintonias'*. The structure on the street is comprised of 'managers', 'soldiers', 'scouts' and 'killers'.

History: Established in the early 1990s by eight inmates in Taubaté Prison, the group became well known after its attacks against state officers and institutions in São Paulo State. In May 2006, on the orders of PCC leaders, the group instigated around 50 prison rebellions and 251 attacks in one week, resulting in 453 dead and 53 wounded.[14] The group has since expanded to other Brazilian states and currently traffics drugs to West Africa and Europe.

Objectives: Deepen and entrench its position of power in Brazil and beyond.

Opponents: CV, FDN and GDE.

Affiliates/allies: In Brazil, local criminal organisations: First Command of Vitória, B13 and Ifara. Internationally: 'Ndrangheta and Albanian and Serbian mafia-type organisations.

Resources/capabilities: Revenue sources include drug trafficking, bank and cargo robbery, money laundering, illegal gambling and kidnapping for ransom. The PCC's average revenue is about US$200 million per year. The gang uses pistols, rifles, bazookas and grenades.

Red Command (CV)

Strength: Approximately 30,000 members.[15]

Areas of operation: Rio de Janeiro metropolitan area, with most important bases in Complexo do Alemão, Chapadão, Salgueiro complexes and the *favelas* of Chatuba, Antares and Rocinha. Since the 2000s, the CV has expanded into other states such as Amazonas, Acre, Ceará, Mato Grosso and Pará.[16]

Leadership: Most prominent leaders are Márcio Santos Nepomuceno (alias 'Marcinho VP') and Elias Pereira da Silva (alias 'Elias Maluco'). Gelson Lima Carnaúba (alias 'Gê'), one of the founders of the FDN, switched sides in 2018 and now leads the CV in Amazonas State.

Structure: Decentralised structure with 'area leaders' in charge of neighbourhoods and *favelas*, and 'managers' responsible for drug-dealing spots, which are secured by 'soldiers' who fend off threats by other dealers or the police. 'Scouts' keep watch for potential risks and warn 'soldiers'.

History: The oldest and second-largest criminal faction in the country, the CV emerged in 1979 in a prison on Ilha Grande, off the southern coast of Rio de Janeiro. Its first sources of income were bank and jewellery-store robberies, before it shifted to drug trafficking in the 1980s, importing cocaine from Colombia and exporting it to Europe. Its activity declined after a police pacification programme in the Alemão *favela* complex in November 2010, but the group has since regained prominence and spread throughout Brazil and beyond.

Objectives: Maintain and enlarge its operating area to other neighbourhoods in Rio de Janeiro and other Brazilian states to expand its drug-trafficking market and extortion practices.

Opponents: In Brazil, PCC and other local criminal organisations such as B13, GDE, SDC, Tocantis Mafia, Class A Command, 30 Tram and Northern Union.

Affiliates/allies: In Rio de Janeiro: None. In Brazil: First Group of Santa Catarina and regional CV affiliates in Pará, Amazonas and Mato Grosso states.

Resources/capabilities: Revenue sources include drug trafficking, extortion of small businesses, kidnapping for ransom and weapons smuggling. Members are equipped with large numbers of handguns, AK-47s, bazookas and grenades.

Friends of Friends (ADA)

Strength: Unknown. However, according to PMERJ intelligence, numbers have been waning for several years.

Areas of operation: Rio de Janeiro State.

Leadership: Celso Luis Rodrigues (alias 'Celsinho da Vila Vintém'), one of the gang's founders.

Structure: Decentralised structure with 'area leaders' in charge of neighbourhoods and *favelas*, and 'managers' responsible for drug-dealing spots, which are secured by 'soldiers' who fend off threats by other dealers or the police. 'Scouts' keep watch for potential risks and warn 'soldiers'.

History: Created in the late 1990s in the penitentiary system of Rio de Janeiro State, it has in recent years suffered heavy losses in clashes with the CV and, to a lesser extent, the TCP.

Objectives: Maintain its few areas of control in Rio de Janeiro city and expand operations to other neighbourhoods, especially outside the Rio de Janeiro metropolitan area where there is less competition.

Opponents: CV, TCP, militias and PMERJ.

Affiliates/allies: Unofficially, PCC.

Resources/capabilities: Main revenue source is drug trafficking. Weapons include guns, pistols, rifles, bazookas and grenades.

Militias (various)

Strength: Unknown.

Areas of operation: About 256 square kilometres (approximately 50%) of the Rio de Janeiro metropolitan area.[17]

Leadership: Gang of Zinho (formerly the Justice League), the largest and most organised of the Rio militias, is led by Luís

Militias (various)

Antônio da Silva Braga (alias 'Zinho').[18] Natalino Guimarães, the Justice League's founder, remains influential. The leadership of other smaller militia groups is unclear.

Structure: Similar structure to gangs, with 'area leaders', 'managers' and 'soldiers', although at a different scale. 'Area leaders' control more than one neighbourhood or region, while 'managers' are responsible for a region or neighbourhood. Unlike in drug groups, 'soldiers' operate from privileged positions (such as police stations). 'Killers' are responsible for executions.

History: Militias are comprised of former or current police officers, firefighters and other professionals in the area of public security. The militias claim to provide security but also traffic drugs and extort, abduct and kill locals. During the latest Rio de Janeiro administrations of governors Wilson Witzel and Cláudio Castro, militias expanded significantly.

Objectives: Expand control over licit and illicit business and gain political influence, including by directly holding public offices in municipalities.

Opponents: ADA, CV and occasionally PMERJ.

Affiliates/allies: TCP and corrupted state officials.

Resources/capabilities: Revenue sources include both licit and illicit business, such as drug trafficking, extortion, murder-for-hire operations, oil theft and sale, money laundering, real-estate transactions, and internet and TV services. Since militia members are often law-enforcement agents, they have access to the same weapons as those agencies, especially .40-calibre pistols and various types of rifles.

Family of the North (FDN)

Strength: Approximately 13,000 members, but numbers might be lower due to changes in leadership since 2018.[19]

Areas of operation: Amazonas, Acre, Ceará and Pará states.

Leadership: José Roberto Barbosa (alias 'Zé Roberto da Compensa').

Structure: Decentralised structure with 'area leaders' in charge of neighbourhoods and *favelas*, and 'managers' responsible for drug-dealing spots, which are secured by 'soldiers' who fend off threats by other dealers or the police. 'Scouts' keep watch for potential risks and warn 'soldiers'.

History: Created by Carnaúba (now in the CV) and Barbosa between 2006 and 2007, it became widely known after prison massacres in Manaus in 2015. That year, the FDN, together with the CV, carried out murders of PCC leaders; efforts by the state to broker a truce failed. The FDN competes for the treasured 'Solimões route', used to transport cocaine produced in Colombia and Peru through rivers in the Amazon region, towards strategic ports and airports in Bahia, Ceará, Pará and Pernambuco states.

Objectives: Expand and consolidate control of drug-trafficking routes in the Amazon region; survive the onslaught from the CV and PCC in Amazonas State.

Opponents: PCC, CV and B13.

Affiliates/allies: GDE.[20]

Resources/capabilities: Revenue sources include drug trafficking and money laundering. Members use pistols, rifles, bazookas and grenades.

Pure Third Command (TCP)

Strength: Unknown.

Areas of operation: Rio de Janeiro State.

Leadership: Bruno da Silva Loureiro (alias 'Coronel') and Alvaro Malaquias Santa Rosa (alias 'Peixão').

Structure: Decentralised structure with 'area leaders' in charge of neighbourhoods and *favelas*, and 'managers' responsible for drug-dealing spots, which are secured by 'soldiers' who fend off threats by other dealers or the police. 'Scouts' keep watch for potential risks and warn 'soldiers'.

History: Created from the 2002 union of dissidents from ADA and the now-defunct Third Command (formed in the 1980s) after the death of Ernaldo Pinto de Medeiros (alias Uê) and the arrest of Celsinho da Vila Vintém (head of ADA). It has acquired partial control over several *favelas* since 2016, establishing itself as the second-most powerful criminal organisation in Rio after the CV (excluding the vigilante militias). During 2017 and 2018, the rapid decline of ADA led many of its members to switch their allegiance to the TCP. The TCP's evangelical Christian members have been known to attack and expel followers of Afro-Brazilian religions from their areas.

Objectives: Maintain areas currently under its control and expand its operating area to other neighbourhoods in Rio de Janeiro and other states.

Opponents: CV, ADA and PMERJ.

Affiliates/allies: Militias, in some areas.

Resources/capabilities: Revenue sources include drug trafficking and extortion. Weapons include pistols, rifles, bazookas and grenades.

Other relevant parties

There are many other relevant criminal organisations whose territory is more circumscribed, such as the B13 and Ifara. These groups became more relevant throughout 2022 by allying themselves with Brazil's largest criminal organisations and playing an active role in achieving territorial expansion. Like their larger allies, they are mostly prison-based criminal organisations.[21]

Notes

1   Information collected in an interview with a public attorney in São Paulo State, April 2023.

2   Alba Zaluar, 'Turf War in Rio de Janeiro: Youth, Drug Traffic, Guns and Hyper-masculinity', in Vania Ceccato (ed), *The Urban Fabric of Crime and Fear* (Dordrecht: Springer, 2012), pp. 217–37.

3   Roberta H. Maschietto and Marcos A. Ferreira, 'Limitations of the State Bias in the Analysis of Violence in Peace and Conflict Studies: Reflections from the Northeast of Brazil', paper presented to the conference 'IV Encontro Brasileiro de Estudos para a Paz' [IV Brazilian Meeting of Peace Studies], Uberlândia, Brazil, 22–24 November 2022; and Centro de Documentação Dom Tomás Balduíno (CPT), *Conflitos no Campo – Brasil 2021* [Conflicts in Rural Areas – Brazil 2021] (Goiânia: CPT, 2022).

4   '17º Anuário Brasileiro de Segurança' [17th Brazilian Security Report], Fórum Brasileiro de Segurança Pública, 2023.

5   Ciro Biderman et al., '*Pax Monopolista* and Crime: The Case of the Emergence of the *Primeiro Comando da Capital* in São Paulo', *Journal of Quantitative Criminology*, vol. 35, September 2019, pp. 573–605; and Marcos Alan Ferreira and Oliver P. Richmond, 'Blockages to Peace Formation in Latin America: The Role of Criminal Governance', *Journal of Intervention and Statebuilding*, vol. 15, no. 2, February 2021, pp. 161–80.

6   Interview with a Federal Police officer who served as an intelligence liaison for Amazonas State, 10 April 2023; see also Ryan C. Berg, 'Tussle for the Amazon: New Frontiers in Brazil's Organized Crime Landscape', Florida International University, October 2021.

7   Information collected in fieldwork in Fortaleza, Ceará State, January 2023.

8   'Brasil: Alteração nas rotas internacionais do tráfico de drogas "pioram" cenário de violência no país' [Brazil: Change in International Drug Trafficking Routes 'Worsens' Setting of Violence in the Country], e-GLOBAL, 23 February 2023.

9   Lívia Torres, 'Operação da Vila Cruzeiro deixa 23 mortos, diz Polícia Civil' [Operation in Vila Cruzeiro Leaves 23 Dead, Says Civil Police], G1, 26 May 2022.

10 Aiala Colares Couto, cited in Leandro Machado, 'Facções controlam tráfico e financiam crimes ambientais na Amazônia, diz pesquisador' [Gangs Control Trafficking and Finance Environmental Crimes in the Amazon, Says Researcher], BBC News, 15 March 2023.

11 Rob Picheta, 'The Violent Attack on Brazil's Government Was Months in the Making. Here's What You Need to Know', CNN, 9 January 2023.

12 'Sem Concurso, PMERJ Tem 30 Mil Soldados a Menos que Previsto em Lei' [Without Competition, PMERJ Has 30 Thousand Fewer Soldiers than Provided for by Law], Folha Dirigida, 7 October 2019.

13 Marcos Alan S.V. Ferreira, 'Brazilian Criminal Organizations as Transnational Violent Non-state Actors: A Case Study of the Primeiro Comando da Capital (PCC)', *Trends in Organized Crime*, vol. 22, 2019, pp. 148–65; and 'Crime e poder: PCC movimenta R$ 1 bilhão e tem "batizados" fora do país' [Crime and Power: PCC Moves R$1 Billion and Has Members Outside the Country], UOL, 9 January 2023.

14 Ferreira, 'Brazilian Criminal Organizations as Transnational Violent Non-state Actors: A Case Study of the Primeiro Comando da Capital (PCC)'.

15 Robson Bonin, 'Comando Vermelho vira preocupação do governo Bolsonaro – entenda' [Red Command Is a Concern in Bolsonaro's Administration – Understand], *Veja*, 22 August 2020.

16 Luís Adorno et al., 'As 53 facções criminosas do Brasil' [The 53 Brazilian Gangs], Record TV, 2 February 2022.

17 Daniel Hirata and Maria Isabel Couto, 'Mapa Histórico dos Grupos Armados do Rio de Janeiro' [Historical Map of Armed Groups in Rio de Janeiro], Grupo de Estudos dos Novos Ilegalismos/Instituto Fogo Cruzado, September 2022.

18 Marcela Lemos, 'Como Liga da Justiça se transformou no Bonde do Zinho, maior milícia do RJ' [How Justice League Transformed into Gang of Zinho, Most Powerful Militia in Rio], UOL, 26 August 2022.

19 'PCC', *Americas Quarterly*; and InSight Crime and American University's Center for Latin American & Latino Studies, 'The Rise of the PCC: How South America's Most Powerful Prison Gang Is Spreading in Brazil and Beyond', CLALS Working Paper Series No. 30, 6 December 2020, p. 23.

20 Cadu Freitas, 'GDE tem mais de 25 mil membros e domina maioria dos bairros de Fortaleza, diz PC' [GDE Has 25 Thousand Members and Dominates Most of Fortaleza's Neighborhoods, Says PC], *Diário do Nordeste*, 18 January 2021.

21 These organisations are (by state): Acre: Bonde dos 13 (13 Tram, B13), Ifara; Amapá: Família Terror do Amapá, Amigos para Sempre, União do Crime do Amapá; Amazonas: Revolucionários do Amazonas, Crias da Tríplice; Bahia: Katiara, Comando da Paz, Caveira, Bonde do Maluco, Mercado do Povo Atitude, Ordem e Progresso, Bonde do Ajeita; Ceará: Guardiões do Estado (Guardians of the State, GDE); Distrito Federal: Comboio do Cão; Espírito Santo: Primeiro Comando de Vitória, Trem Bala; Goiás: Família Monstro; Maranhão: Bonde dos 40, PCM; Minas Gerais: Família Monstro; Pará: Comando Classe A (Class A Command), Bonde dos 30, União do Norte (Northern Union), Equipe Rex, Equipe Real; Paraíba: Okaida, Estados Unidos; Paraná: Máfia Paranaense; Pernambuco: Okaida; Rio Grande do Norte: Sindicato do Crime (Crime Syndicate, SDC); Rio Grande do Sul: Abertos, Bala na Cara, Os Manos, Comando Pelo Certo, Farrapos, Unidos pela Paz, Os Tauras, Vândalos, Mata rindo, Grupo K2, Cebolas, PCI; Rondônia: Primeiro Comando do Panda; Santa Catarina: Primeiro Grupo Catarinense (First Group of Santa Catarina), CVSC, Força Revolucionária Catarinense, Primeiro Crime Revolucionário Catarinense; Sergipe: Bonde dos Maluco; Tocantins: Máfia Tocantinense (Tocantins Mafia).

HAITI

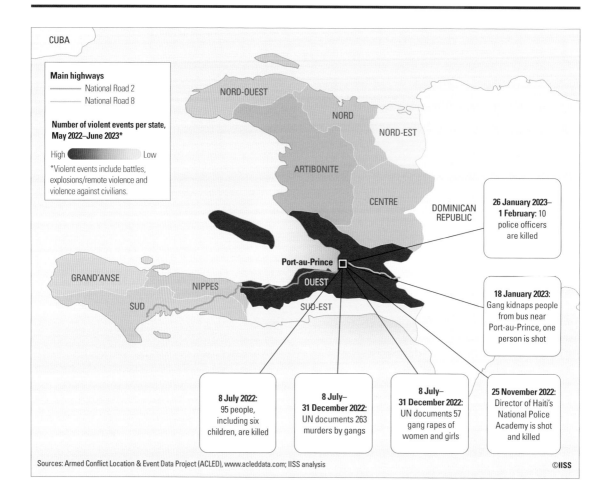

Main highways
National Road 2
National Road 8

Number of violent events per state, May 2022–June 2023*

High   Low

*Violent events include battles, explosions/remote violence and violence against civilians.

CUBA

NORD-OUEST

NORD

NORD-EST

ARTIBONITE

CENTRE

DOMINICAN REPUBLIC

GRAND'ANSE

NIPPES

SUD

OUEST

SUD-EST

Port-au-Prince

26 January 2023– 1 February: 10 police officers are killed

18 January 2023: Gang kidnaps people from bus near Port-au-Prince, one person is shot

8 July 2022: 95 people, including six children, are killed

8 July– 31 December 2022: UN documents 263 murders by gangs

8 July– 31 December 2022: UN documents 57 gang rapes of women and girls

25 November 2022: Director of Haiti's National Police Academy is shot and killed

Sources: Armed Conflict Location & Event Data Project (ACLED), www.acleddata.com; IISS analysis

©IISS

Conflict Overview

Following the overthrow in 1986 of the Duvalier family dictatorship, which had been in power for almost 30 years, Haiti has experienced a long succession of *coups d'états*, political violence, contested elections and interim governments. During this period, there has been only one smooth transition of power, when René Préval (1996–2001; 2006–11) handed over the presidency to an elected successor in 2001. More recently, the assassination of president Jovenel Moïse on 7 July 2021 precipitated an ongoing political and electoral impasse that has resulted in an unprecedented constitutional crisis.[1] The current government is led by acting Prime Minister Ariel Henry and has little legitimacy. As of June 2023, the country also had no president and no elected representatives in parliament, amid continued delays in organising new elections. Despite attempts by some politicians and civil-society actors to design a road map out of the political crisis, such as the Montana Accord, little progress has been made toward political stability, with security conditions continuing to deteriorate and the population still reeling from the devastating earthquake that hit southern Haiti in August 2021. Organised armed gangs now control much of the capital of Port-au-Prince and surrounding areas, challenging state function and legitimacy.

Armed Conflict Global Relevance Indicator (ACGRI)

Incidence

7

Human
impact

Geopolitical
impact

4

11

Haiti

Key Conflict Statistics

Conflict(s)	Type	Start date
Haiti	Internal: organised crime	2021

Fatalities	1,728
Percentage change in fatalities	100%
GDP per capita, PPP (constant international $)	2,677
Functioning of government (0–10)	0
Climate-change vulnerability (0–1)	0.5

ACGRI pillars: IISS calculation based on multiple sources for 2022 and 2023 (scale: 0–100), except for some cases according to data availability. See Notes on Methodology and Data Appendix for all variables and further details on Key Conflict Statistics.

Conflict Update

During the reporting period, the situation in Haiti continued to degenerate amid dire humanitarian conditions (about five million people face acute hunger) and spiralling gang violence, with unprecedented homicide and kidnapping rates.[2] Armed groups continued to expand their territorial control and challenge (and infiltrate) the state. A notable example was the capture of Port-au-Prince's main fuel terminal and major highways in September 2022, which severely impacted the functioning of hospitals, businesses and schools, among others. On the political front, the remaining ten elected senators' terms expired in January 2022, leaving the country with no elected officials and no scheduled elections, despite Henry's appointment of a transition council to guarantee that general elections would be held.[3] Meanwhile, only one of the 11 people arrested and charged for Moïse's

assassination (Rudolph Jaar, the mastermind of the plot) has been convicted thus far.

Haitian leaders inside and outside Haiti have called for foreign involvement to help stabilise the country. However, due to the history of many failed foreign interventions in Haiti in the twentieth century, the international community remains reluctant to send troops or volunteer United Nations peacekeeping forces. Regional partner countries such as the United States, Canada and other Caribbean nations have been seeking ways to help without sending military forces. For instance, the US imposed sanctions on Haitian criminal businesses, and the US and Canada sent equipment to the Haitian National Police. Canada began hosting working groups in September 2022 to discuss regional support for Haiti, and in January 2023, Jamaica expressed a willingness to deploy soldiers and police to secure the country.

Conflict Parties

Haitian National Police (PNH)

Strength: About 9,500 members, but exact strength unknown.[4]

Areas of operation: Nationwide.

Leadership: Frantz Elbé (director general).

Structure: Several branches including:
■ Central Directorate of the Administration and General Services (DCASG)
■ Central Directorate of the Administrative Police Force (DCPA)
■ Intervention and Maintenance of Order Corps (CIMO)
■ General Security Unit of the National Palace (USGPN)
■ Departmental Operation and Intervention Brigade (BOID)
■ Central Directorate of the Judicial Police (DCPJ)

■ Controlling of Narcotics Trafficking Brigade (BLTS)
Each of Haiti's ten administrative departments also has its own police force.

History: Created in June 1995 after the Haitian army was demobilised in April that year.

Objectives: The PNH is the main law-enforcement body in Haiti. Its branches are tasked with a wide range of security duties, including guarding the president, drug interdiction and protecting the environment.

Opponents: Grand Ravine *baz* ('base' in Creole), 5 Segonn in Village de Dieu and 400 Mawozo, among other gangs.

Haitian National Police (PNH)

Affiliates/allies: Some elements of the PNH are believed to have a modus vivendi with the G9 gang coalition headed by Jimmy Chérizier (alias 'Barbecue') and especially the Baz Pilate.

Resources/capabilities: The PNH's firepower is believed to be met, if not exceeded, by that of the various armed groups operating in the Port-au-Prince metropolitan area.

G9 Family and Allies (G9)

Strength: Unknown, but at least several hundred.[5]

Areas of operation: The extent of its reach is unknown, but it is reportedly heavily concentrated in Port-au-Prince, with various affiliate gangs controlling different neighbourhoods. It is known to occupy the Port-au-Prince neighbourhood Belekou Cité Soleil district, as well as Chancerelles, Delmas, La Saline, Martissant and Pont Rouge. It also reportedly controls Village de Dieu and the Grand-Ravine commune, and its operational headquarters is in Waf Jérémie.

Leadership: Jimmy Chérizier (alias 'Barbecue'), a former officer in the PNH's Department Unit for Maintenance of Order (UDMO). He went rogue following a November 2017 PNH raid against a gang in the Grand Ravine slum, in which at least two police officers and ten civilians died.

Structure: The extent of its structure and relationships between member groups is largely unknown. As of latest reporting, the G9 is a confederation of gangs controlled from Port-au-Prince's lower Delmas region. In addition to Chérizier's cadre, the G9 also claims the armed groups in the following areas as its members:
- The Boston section of Cité Soleil, currently led by Mathias Saintil
- The Belekou section of Cité Soleil, currently led by Andrice Iscard (alias 'Iska')
- The neighbourhood of La Saline, currently led by Serge Alectis (alias 'Ti Junior')
- Most of the neighbourhood of Bel Air north of the National Palace; the group is allied with the Krache Dife (Fire Spitters) gang led by James Alexander (alias 'Sonson')
- The Ti Bois section of the Martissant neighbourhood in the capital's south, currently led by Chery Christ-Roi (alias 'Cristla')
- The Champs de Mars neighbourhood (the administrative zone of the government) and the Ti Bois neighbourhood, with increasing influence in cities in northern Haiti. The gang in these areas, known as the Baz Pilate, is believed to have close links to the police. Its leadership is unclear.

History: In June 2020, Chérizier, alongside dozens of armed, masked men, announced the existence of the G9 in a videotaped address, saying a 'major revolution' was beginning in Haiti.

Objectives: Some G9 groups have used political rhetoric at times, but it is unclear whether this is part of a genuine attempt to begin encroaching on political power.

Opponents: Village de Dieu gang and Grand Ravine *baz*.

Affiliates/allies: Some elements of the PNH are believed to be sympathetic or affiliated.

Resources/capabilities: Extensive resources due to its control over several docks in the Port-au-Prince metropolitan area and the looting of stores and businesses.

400 Mawozo

Strength: Unknown, but reportedly the largest criminal group in Haiti. As of March 2022, it had 1,000 members scattered around Port-au-Prince and was said to have a waiting list of potential recruits.[6]

Areas of operation: Outskirts of Port-au-Prince, namely the Croix-des-Bouquets municipality. Its presence has been reported in the Ganthier, Thomazeau and Fonds-Verettes municipalities. It reportedly also operates along the Dominican border, and it controls a wide swathe of territory in eastern Haiti.

Leadership: Joseph Wilson (alias 'Lanmò San Jou').

Structure: Leadership is thought to be based in the Croix-des-Bouquets municipality, with other cells operating east and north of Port-au-Prince.

History: Founded by Germine 'Yonyon' Jolly, who led 400 Mawozo from prison until he was deported to the US in May 2022.

Objectives: Generate income through extensive kidnapping activities.

Opponents: The PNH, G9 and Chen Mechann.

Affiliates/allies: Smaller gangs in Canaan, Tabarre and Tirobu areas.

Resources/capabilities: Likely millions of US dollars from kidnapping.

5 Segonn

Strength: Unknown.

Areas of operation: Village de Dieu neighbourhood of Port-au-Prince. It successfully took over the Palace of Justice, where the Haitian court system is located, in June 2022.

Leadership: Izo.

Structure: Izo is assisted by several deputies and foot soldiers.

History: Emerged in its current formation after the killing of former Village de Dieu gang leader Arnel Joseph in February 2021.

Objectives: Beyond criminal enrichment, unclear.

Opponents: Ti Bois *baz* and the PNH.

5 Segonn

Affiliates/allies: As of last reporting, allied with the Grand Ravine *baz*.

Resources/capabilities: Extensive, mostly derived from kidnapping.

Grand Ravine *baz*

Strength: Unknown.

Areas of operation: Rue Bolosse 4ème and 5ème Avenue, Pont Breya and the area commonly known as *zòn pwojè*.

Leadership: Renel Destina (alias 'Ti Lapli').

Structure: Ti Lapli is assisted by several subordinates, including aliases 'Bougoy' and 'Killy'. The current structure is uncertain due to fighting between these three leaders in April 2021.

History: Grand Ravine has been an armed-groups stronghold for much of the last 26 years. The current iteration, with Ti Lapli as leader, has existed since about 2018.

Objectives: Increase income through kidnapping, hijacking trucks and other criminal activities.

Opponents: Ti Bois *baz* and the PNH.

Affiliates/allies: 5 Segonn.

Resources/capabilities: Extensive kidnapping network.

Ti Bois *baz*

Strength: Unknown.

Areas of operation: Area of Martissant demarcated by Fontamara 23, Martissant 7 and the *zone denwi*.

Leadership: Chery Crist-Roi (alias 'Cristla').

Structure: Cristla is assisted by several deputies.

History: Emerged in its current arrangement under the leadership of Cristla about 21 years ago.

Objectives: Retain control of its area of Martissant.

Opponents: Grand Ravine *baz* and 5 Segonn.

Affiliates/allies: The Ti Bois *baz* is part of the G9 coalition of gangs.

Resources/capabilities: Generates income through taxes on trucks bringing supplies to and from the mountainous areas and quarries within its section of Martissant, as well as nightclubs, bars, restaurants and various other businesses. Despite being outnumbered by other groups in the area, the Ti Bois *baz* has defended its territory for many years.

Baz Pilate

Strength: Unknown.

Areas of operation: Reportedly controls large sections of Port-au-Prince, namely the Champs de Mars neighbourhood (the administrative zone of the government) and the Ti Bois neighbourhood, with increasing influence in cities in northern Haiti.

Leadership: Ezeckiel Alexandre.

Structure: Unknown.

History: Unknown.

Objectives: Unknown.

Opponents: Unknown.

Affiliates/allies: Reportedly allied with the G9.

Resources/capabilities: Members are thought to be current and former police officers, namely those who served in special-weapons and tactics or riot units and use notoriously brutal methods. It generates revenue from drug trafficking, burglary, racketeering and targeted killings. It reportedly controls the Port-au-Prince administration, has influence in the justice system and is developing a role as a security partner for select economic groups.

Notes

1 A dispute between president Moïse and the opposition over the termination of Moïse's five-year term resulted in the former dissolving parliament in early 2020 and ruling by decree until his death. Moïse had also proposed controversial constitutional changes, including allowing two consecutive presidential five-year terms.

2 UN Meetings Coverage and Press Releases, 'Key Political Developments, Sanctions Offer Hope to Haiti's Recovery if Supported by International Community, Special Representative Tells Security Council', 24 January 2023.

3 Evens Sanon, 'Haiti Appoints Council amid Push to Hold General Elections', AP News, 6 February 2023.

4 Luke Taylor, 'Haitian Cops Are Poorly Paid and Outgunned – and Part of the Problem', *Guardian*, 2 February 2023.

5 Dánica Coto, 'Haitian Gang Alliance Makes Demands in Contest with Government over Power', PBS, 14 October 2023; and Etant Dupain and Hande Atay Alam, 'Critical Haiti Gas Terminal Freed After Weeks of Talks with G9 Gang Leader', CNN, 6 November 2022.

6 InSight Crime, '400 Mawozo', 23 March 2022.

EL SALVADOR

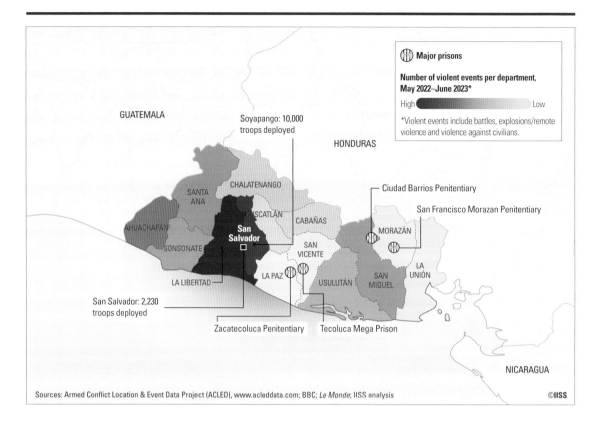

Sources: Armed Conflict Location & Event Data Project (ACLED), www.acleddata.com; BBC; *Le Monde*; IISS analysis   ©IISS

Conflict Overview

From 2003 onwards, the Salvadoran state has been enmeshed in a prolonged battle with the Mara Salvatrucha (MS-13) gang for territorial control, political legitimacy and economic resources. The MS-13 was established in El Salvador in the mid-1990s by members deported from prisons in California, and by the early 2000s it had evolved into a considerable military force, capable of challenging the state. Over several decades, the MS-13 recruited veterans from El Salvador's civil war (1979–92), as well as consolidated territorial control and developed revenue streams from extortion, kidnapping, assassinations, and the sale of marijuana, crack cocaine and cocaine. The MS-13 thrived amidst El Salvador's widespread poverty, socio-economic challenges and weak governance, benefiting from the country's strategic position between Mexico and South American drug suppliers.

Successive political administrations tried various repressive strategies that failed to halt the gang's expansion. By 2012, the MS-13 had over 12,000 members and its main rival, the Barrio 18 gang, had 8,000–10,000 members.[1] Furthermore, El Salvador's homicide rate was among the highest in the world. These facts induced the government to formally negotiate with the gangs, and a 'truce' was enacted in 2012, in which the government offered the gangs concessions and payments in return for reducing visible homicides. However, this agreement also showed the gangs the true scope of their political leverage, and the pact collapsed in 2014. The MS-13 has since grown its military capabilities, using spikes in violence as leverage in negotiations with the government. Meanwhile, Barrio 18 has suffered from territorial losses and internal divisions.

Nayib Bukele, a political outsider, won El Salvador's 2019 general elections with campaign promises to end

Armed Conflict Global Relevance Indicator (ACGRI)

Incidence

1

Human impact

1

Geopolitical impact

0

El Salvador

Key Conflict Statistics

Conflict(s)	Type	Start date
El Salvador	Internal: organised crime	2003

Percentage change in fatalities	-71%
GDP per capita, PPP (constant international $)	9,307
Gini index (0–100)	39*
Functioning of government (0–10)	3.6
Climate-change vulnerability (0–1)	0.4

ACGRI pillars: IISS calculation based on multiple sources for 2022 and 2023 (scale: 0–100), except for some cases according to data availability. See Notes on Methodology and Data Appendix for all variables and further details on Key Conflict Statistics. *2021 as latest available data.

corruption and insecurity. While he publicly continued the government's long-standing *mano dura* (firm hand) zero-tolerance policy against gang activity, he also quietly continued negotiations with the MS-13.

Conflict Update

In early 2022, the Bukele administration achieved another fragile peace in which the MS-13 enjoyed certain privileges and protections for key members in exchange for reducing visible homicides. However, in March 2022, a spike in gang-related violence resulted in the deaths of more than 80 people in one weekend, prompting Bukele to declare a state of exception for 30 days, suspending constitutional rights and ordering mass arrests.[2] A year later, the state of exception still defines El Salvador's internal-security policy. The National Assembly has renewed the decree every month after it was enacted (as of June 2023), and more than 64,000 people have been arrested.[3]

The combined impact of these policies has damaged the MS-13's strategic position, effectively challenging much of its control in El Salvador and substantially reducing violence levels.[4] However, it is questionable whether this curtailing of violence and of the M-13's power will be sustainable in the long run, as many concerns have been raised by civil-society organisations regarding the state of exception's impact on democracy, the rule of law and human rights in El Salvador.

Conflict Parties

El Salvador armed forces

Strength: 24,500 troops.

Areas of operation: Throughout El Salvador.

Leadership: René Francis Merino Monroy (minister of defence).

Structure: Six brigades across the country; three infantry battalions; one special military-security brigade with two military-police and two border-security battalions; one artillery brigade; one mechanised cavalry regiment; a special-forces command with one special-operations group; and an anti-terrorist command.

History: The armed forces held long-standing control over the government, to the detriment of El Salvador's democracy, which contributed to the outbreak of the 1979–92 civil war.

The 1992 Chapultepec Peace Accords introduced key reforms to the relationship between the military and civil society, establishing civilian oversight of the military and creating a civilian police force.

Objectives: Responsible for defence against external threats. The armed forces also work with the police for internal-security purposes, including fighting the MS-13 and Barrio 18. They play a primary role in counter-narcotics operations and continue to play a law-enforcement role alongside the police (despite this being ruled unconstitutional by the Supreme Court in 2020).

Opponents: MS-13, Barrio 18, cocaine-transport groups and other smaller criminal groups in El Salvador.

Americas

El Salvador armed forces

Affiliates/allies: The National Civil Police (PNC) and some civilian paramilitary groups.

Resources/capabilities: Special-operations command, high-mobility multi-purpose wheeled vehicles, light armoured vehicles, multiple other armoured vehicles, eight UH-1H helicopters, two UH-1M helicopters and assorted other helicopters.

National Civil Police (PNC)

Strength: About 26,000.

Areas of operation: Throughout El Salvador.

Leadership: Mauricio Antonio Arriaza Chicas (director general).

Structure: The security force tasked with countering the MS-13 comprises three anti-gang units of approximately 600 special-forces troops and 400 PNC officers.[5] This force is separate from the PNC's counter-narcotics and organised-crime units.

History: Founded by the 1992 Chapultepec Peace Accords to repair civil society's relationship with the security forces. The PNC has faced significant challenges since its formation, most notably organised crime led by the MS-13 and other groups.

Objectives: Confront internal threats, including combatting gangs, organised crime and drug trafficking. Anti-gang units are tasked with targeting non-incarcerated leaders of the MS-13 and restricting the communications capabilities of the leadership in prison.

Opponents: MS-13, Barrio 18, cocaine-transport groups and other smaller criminal groups in El Salvador.

Affiliates/allies: El Salvador's armed forces, particularly under Bukele's administration.

Resources/capabilities: Specialised units combine the use of helicopters, armoured vehicles and assault rifles, which partially offsets the PNC's lack of heavy weapons.

Mara Salvatrucha (MS-13)

Strength: About 30,000 operating in El Salvador.[6]

Areas of operation: Following the mass arrests of supposed gang members under the state of exception during the summer of 2022, the MS-13's current territorial control is unclear but seems to have been reduced. Before the state of exception, it was estimated to operate in 93% of El Salvador's municipalities (247 of 262), and each member was part of a network of at least six people.[7]

Leadership: Vladimir Antonio Arevalo-Chavez (alias 'Vampiro de Montserrat Criminales'), Walter Yovani Hernandez-Rivera (alias 'Baxter de Park View') and Marlon Antonio Menjivar-Portillo (alias 'Rojo de Park View'), who were arrested by United States authorities. Others remain free, including Jose Wilfredo Ayala-Alcantara (alias 'Indio de Hollywood'), Jorge Alexander De La Cruz (alias 'Cruger de Peatonales'), Juan Antonio Martínez-Abrego (alias 'Mary Jane de Hollywood') and Francisco Javier Román-Bardales (alias 'Veterano de Tribus').[8]

Structure: Run by the *ranfla histórica* (national leadership), which sets the overall policies and strategies from prisons in El Salvador. Due to internal fragmentation, the *ranfla histórica* has devolved some decision-making power to the *ranfla libre* (gang leadership not in prison). Below them are the *palabreros* (those who delegate orders) and *programas* (groups of highly compartmentalised street-level units, known as *clicas*), with semi-autonomous leadership across multiple neighbourhoods and the *clicas*.

History: Founded in the 1980s in poor and marginalised neighbourhoods of Los Angeles, CA. In the 1990s, US authorities deported many incarcerated Salvadoran MS-13 members. They arrived in El Salvador with limited community and country ties at a time when El Salvador was emerging from its civil war with experienced combat veterans, weak institutions and widely available weapons.

Objectives: Control territory in which it can exercise its own laws and authority. The group does not want to overthrow the national government. Rather, it aims to displace traditional, entrenched cocaine-transport groups (such as the Cartel de Texis, Los Perrones and others) for financial gain. As the group gained greater political legitimacy, its strategy likely shifted to include embedding members within the state structure to facilitate the systemic extortion of entire government agencies rather than just targeting individuals. It is unclear whether the group is still pursuing this strategy following the state of exception.

Opponents: Barrio 18 and state security forces.

Affiliates/allies: MS-13 structures in Honduras and Guatemala, as well as parts of the Sinaloa Cartel and Cartel Jalisco New Generation in Mexico. It is occasionally a tactical partner of state security forces.

Resources/capabilities: Financial resources derived from extortion, protecting cocaine loads for other groups, kidnapping, human smuggling, murder-for-hire and money laundering. This income is not evenly distributed among MS-13's *clicas*. Groups that control key cocaine-trafficking routes or beach areas for sea-transported loads are better off. Some centralised redistribution exists but inequality among groups is a constant source of tension. The MS-13 possesses a growing number of new weapons, including Dragunov sniper rifles, Uzis, rocket-propelled grenades and a small number of light anti-tank weapons.

Barrio 18

Strength: Unknown, but much smaller than the MS-13.

Areas of operation: Select neighbourhoods in San Salvador and surrounding areas. Much less extensive than the MS-13's territorial control.

Leadership: Run by *palabreros* (leaders) who are largely incarcerated. They control criminal activities.

Structure: Organised into *canchas*, which are units of territorial control that may or may not represent municipalities. Each *cancha* has a number of *tribus* (tribes), which are small social units. Beyond *tribus*, there are also collaborators who work with the gang but are not officially members. The gang is divided into two rival factions, the Revolutionaries and the Sureños.

History: Grew under the same conditions that benefited the MS-13 but did not achieve the same level of territorial control or diversification. Still nominally present in El Salvador but with a much more reduced profile than before.

Objectives: Control territory and generate revenue from illicit activities such as extortion and drug trafficking.

Opponents: MS-13 and state security forces.

Affiliates/allies: The Mexican Mafia, networks of lawyers, taxi drivers and mechanics.

Resources/capabilities: Revenue from extortion.

Americas

Notes

[1] United Nations Office on Drugs and Crime, 'Transnational Organized Crime in Central America and the Caribbean: A Threat Assessment', September 2012, p. 27.

[2] Anna-Cat Brigida, 'Surge in Gang Killings Spurs Fear, Uncertainty in El Salvador', Al-Jazeera, 28 March 2022; and Marcos Alemán, 'El Salvador aprueba nueva prórroga a estado de excepción' [El Salvador Approves a New Extension to the State of Exception], *Los Angeles Times*, 14 February 2023.

[3] Anna-Cat Brigida, 'El Salvador Prisoner "Rearrests" Fuel New Concerns', Al-Jazeera, 17 February 2023.

[4] Parker Asmann and Carlos Garcia, 'MS-13's Mexico Program Key to El Salvador Gang Negotiations', InSight Crime, 1 March 2023.

[5] Jeannette Aguilar, 'Las políticas de seguridad pública en El Salvador 2003–2018' [Public Security Policies in El Salvador 2003–2018], National Civil Police, 10 March 2021, p. 61.

[6] Kylie Madry, 'El Salvador Boosts Jail Time for Gang Members After Rash of Murders', Reuters, 31 March 2022.

[7] Human Rights Watch, 'World Report 2020', 2020, p. 187; and Douglas Farah and Kathryn Babineau, 'The Evolution of MS 13 in El Salvador and Honduras', *PRISM*, vol. 7, no. 1, 2017.

[8] US Attorney's Office, Eastern District of New York, 'Three of the Highest-ranking MS-13 Leaders in the World Arrested on Terrorism and Racketeering Charges', 23 February 2023.

HONDURAS

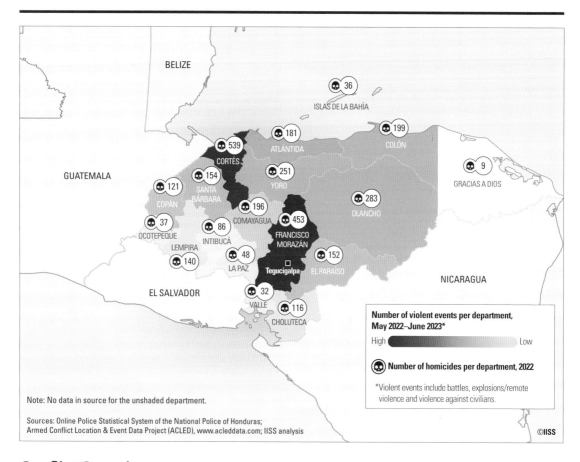

BELIZE

ISLAS DE LA BAHÍA · 36

CORTÉS · 539

ATLÁNTIDA · 181

COLÓN · 199

GUATEMALA

SANTA BÁRBARA · 154

YORO · 251

GRACIAS A DIOS · 9

COPÁN · 121

OCOTEPEQUE · 37

COMAYAGUA · 196

OLANCHO · 283

LEMPIRA

INTIBUCÁ · 86

FRANCISCO MORAZÁN · 453

EL PARAÍSO · 152

140

LA PAZ · 48

Tegucigalpa

NICARAGUA

EL SALVADOR

VALLE · 32

CHOLUTECA · 116

Number of violent events per department, May 2022–June 2023*

High ▬▬▬▬▬▬ Low

☠ **Number of homicides per department, 2022**

*Violent events include battles, explosions/remote violence and violence against civilians.

Note: No data in source for the unshaded department.

Sources: Online Police Statistical System of the National Police of Honduras; Armed Conflict Location & Event Data Project (ACLED), www.acleddata.com; IISS analysis

©IISS

Conflict Overview

Insecurity in Honduras is driven largely by the expansion of the Mara Salvatrucha (MS-13) gang, which is fighting with the state and other criminal elements as it seeks to expand its drug-trafficking structure and territory. Like in El Salvador and Guatemala, the MS-13 in Honduras was established by group members who were deported from California in the late 1990s. The gang initially specialised in cocaine-transportation and production, before expanding into other drugs and achieving a near-monopoly on Honduras's internal drug market. This lucrative drug income eventually enabled the group to stop extorting local businesses and instead gain significant political goodwill from communities in its areas of control, which helped push out competing criminal groups.

These developments progressed against a continued backdrop of rampant poverty, economic stagnation and engrained corruption in Honduras. The indictment and extradition to the United States of former president Juan Orlando Hernández (2014–22) on drug-trafficking and weapons charges is a case in point. In recent years, the MS-13 expanded its criminal, political and economic operations, collaborating as an independent partner with Mexican drug-trafficking organisations to ship cocaine from Colombia and Venezuela to Mexico and increasing its control of cocaine-processing laboratories in Honduras. The group also learned how to use encrypted apps for communications; the dark web and cyber currency for financial transactions; and drones for reconnaissance operations. These advances present direct threats to already fragile state institutions.

Armed Conflict Global Relevance Indicator (ACGRI)	**Key Conflict Statistics**

Armed Conflict Global Relevance Indicator (ACGRI)

Incidence

6

Human impact   Geopolitical impact

3   **2**

Honduras

Key Conflict Statistics

Conflict(s)	Type	Start date
Honduras	Internal: organised crime	2003

Percentage change in fatalities	10%
GDP per capita, PPP (constant international $)	5,786
Gini index (0–100)	48.2*
Functioning of government (0–10)	3.9
Climate-change vulnerability (0–1)	0.5

Americas

ACGRI pillars: IISS calculation based on multiple sources for 2022 and 2023 (scale: 0–100), except for some cases according to data availability. See Notes on Methodology and Data Appendix for all variables and further details on Key Conflict Statistics. *2019 as latest available data.

Conflict Update

Honduras continued to grapple with high homicide and extortion rates in the reporting period as the MS-13 further consolidated control over internal markets and drug-trafficking routes. Honduras's homicide rate in 2022 was 35.8 per 100,000, the highest in Latin America.[1]

The assassination of three police officers near Trujillo in the department of Colón and other confrontations led to an environment of instability in many densely populated areas of the country.[2] In December 2022, following the example of President Nayib Bukele in El Salvador, President Xiomara Castro announced a state of exception in 162 city neighbourhoods, allowing the army to police these areas.[3] On 6 April 2023, the Honduran government renewed the state of exception for a third time.[4]

While the state of exception in El Salvador dealt a major blow to MS-13's power in the country, it remains to be seen how the MS-13 in Honduras will respond to a similar approach. Given Castro's campaign promises to reinforce the rule of law and democratic fundamentals, the suspension of constitutional rights for suspected gang affiliates may also prove politically unsustainable.

Conflict Parties

Military Police of Public Order (PMOP) and National Anti-Gang Force (FNAMP)

Strength: About 4,000 PMOP officers and 500 FNAMP members.[5]

Areas of operation: Throughout Honduras, with a focus on areas with high gang and drug-trafficking presences, usually major urban centres or locations with formal or informal border crossings such as Tegucigalpa, San Pedro Sula, Palmerola and the Guatemala–Honduras border centred in Copán (land) and Omoa (sea).

Leadership: Infantry Col. Rosbel Leonel Hernández Aguilar (PMOP leader) and Lt-Col. Amílcar Hernández (FNAMP leader).

Structure: The PMOP has eight combat battalions and one canine battalion and reports to the Ministry of Defence. The FNAMP reports to the PMOP but has not publicly defined its operational structure.

History: The PMOP was created by congress in 2013 to address the increasing presence of organised criminal groups in Honduras, despite concerns about a militarised police force. FNAMP was formed in July 2018 as a special unit to combat organised crime.

Objectives: Retake territory from the MS-13 and dismantle its operational structures, as well as combat transnational organised crime and drug trafficking.

Opponents: MS-13, other smaller gangs, and local and transnational drug-trafficking organisations.

Affiliates/allies: Parts of the Anti-Gang Unit of the National Police, the TIGRES special-forces unit of the police, the military of Honduras and US military/police trainers.

Resources/capabilities: Honduras' total defence budget for 2022 was US$379 million. The total defence budget for 2023 is US$425.2m.

Mara Salvatrucha (MS-13)

Strength: 9,000–15,000 full members, as well as about 40,000 recruits training to be lookouts and messengers waiting to be formally initiated into the gang.

Areas of operation: Throughout Honduras, with territorial control concentrated in the cities of San Pedro Sula, Puerto Cortés and Omoa, and in the department of Copán along the border with Guatemala.

Leadership: Senior MS-13 leaders in Honduras are largely in prison, though few have been identified.

Structure: Compartmentalised leadership structure with numerous *clicas* (highly compartmentalised units at street level) forming *programas* (groups of *clicas*), which report to the *ranfla* (prison-based senior leadership).

History: Founded in the 1980s in poor and marginalised neighbourhoods of Los Angeles, CA. In the 1990s, US authorities deported many incarcerated Honduran MS-13 members. They arrived in Honduras with weak community and country ties and established cells for their own protection.

Objectives: Diversify its criminal portfolio by controlling key cocaine-trafficking nodes, selling krispy (a synthetic version of marijuana) and expanding its control of migrant-smuggling routes. Its primary objective is to become a vertically integrated transnational criminal structure allied with Mexican drug-trafficking groups and to control multiple criminal revenue streams.

Opponents: Sectors of the state security forces not involved in corruption practices; smaller gangs (such as Barrio 18, the Chirizos and Ponce); extra-judicial paramilitary groups; and rival criminal groups involved in cocaine trafficking.

Affiliates/allies: The MS-13 structures in El Salvador and Guatemala; the Sinaloa Cartel and the Cartel Jalisco New Generation in Mexico; and Venezuelan and Colombian cocaine suppliers.

Resources/capabilities: Proceeds from cocaine shipment and migrant smuggling, as well as controlling local drug markets, provide the group with a yearly income of tens of millions of US dollars. Other localised revenue sources include investments in motels, car lots, private-security firms, buses and public transportation. Advanced tunnelling techniques, cocaine-laboratory operation and expanding territorial control have allowed the gang to protect its operations, store products and increase revenues.

Notes

[1] Secretaria de Estado en el Despacho de Seguridad, Gobierno de Honduras [Secretary of State in the Security Bureau, Government of Honduras], 'Situacion Comparativa de Casos de Homicidios a Nivel Nacional (Datos Preliminares)' [Comparative Situation of National Homicide Cases (Preliminary Data)], 2022; and Peter Appleby et al., 'InSight Crime's 2022 Homicide Round-up', InSight Crime, 8 February 2023.

[2] US Embassy Tegucigalpa, 'Security Alert: Department of Colón and Areas Near Trujillo', US Embassy in Honduras, 25 April 2022.

[3] Jeff Ernst, 'Honduras Declares War Against Gangs – and for Control of Popular Narrative', *Guardian*, 4 January 2023.

[4] 'Honduras Extends, Expands State of Emergency for Second Time', Reuters, 21 February 2023.

[5] 'Honduras dispuso el estado de excepción en su guerra contra las pandillas y desplegó cientos de policías en las calles' [Honduras Deploys the State of Exception in Its War Against the Gangs, Sending Hundreds of Police to the Streets], *Infobae*, 7 December 2022.

2 Europe and Eurasia

A military vehicle with a Ukrainian flag stands in front of a destroyed building, Borodianka, Ukraine, 4 August 2022

Overview

The consequences of the break-up of the Soviet Union in 1991 continue to reverberate across the region and beyond. Security relations between, and governance arrangements within, the 15 successor states that were created by this geopolitical 'big bang' have not uniformly stabilised into orderly and mutually secure relationships. Instead, a variety of conflicts continue to bring instability and violence to the region.

The causes of these conflicts vary. Unlike most contemporary conflicts globally, the majority in this region are inter-state wars involving regular armed or security forces. If there is a factor common to most of them, it is that borders – primarily international ones between countries, but also administrative ones within them – are not accepted as legitimate by all parties.

However, conflict is not simply a legacy of the Soviet Union's break-up; it involves specific choices by political leaders. This is especially true of Russia's war in Ukraine, where Russian President Vladimir Putin rejected a legitimate, internationally recognised border – one that Russia itself had hitherto recognised – and has sought to annex Ukrainian territory into Russia and, in the longer term, dominate the country.

During the reporting period, there were two active conflicts in the post-Soviet region according to *The Armed Conflict Survey 2023* criteria: the Russia–Ukraine war and the Armenian–Azerbaijani conflict over Nagorno-Karabakh.[1] Other instability hotspots included flare-ups between Kyrgyzstan and Tajikistan and an episode of civil unrest in Uzbekistan.

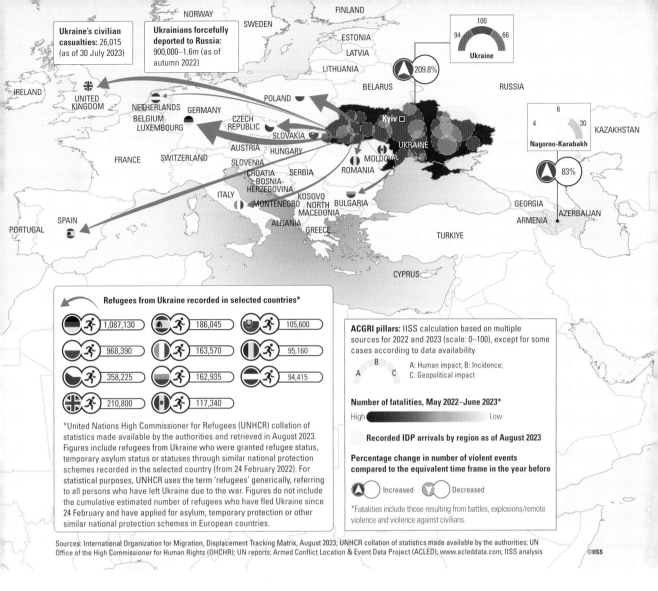

By far the most significant conflict was the Russia–Ukraine war, which escalated dramatically with Russia's full-scale invasion in February 2022.[2] This has had profound consequences not only for the region but for the world. It is the biggest war in Europe since 1945 and has already led to hundreds of thousands of casualties. It continues to generate severe humanitarian, economic and environmental consequences and could escalate further. By violating state sovereignty, it challenges a basic principle of the international order. Meanwhile, its impact on commodities prices has put pressure on fragile economies. The West, China, India and many countries in the Global South have expressed their deep alarm at the war. It remains the most acute geopolitical crisis worldwide.

The war has been and continues to be unpredictable.[3] Instability has also begun to spread into Russia itself. Acts of sabotage and arson, carried out by Ukrainian operatives and dissident Russians, have increased. From January–May 2023 alone, there were at least 57 publicly reported cases, most of them attacks on railways, military-enlistment centres and energy assets.[4] Maxim Fomin (better known as Vladlen Tatarsky), a prominent Russian military blogger, and Darya Dugina, daughter of the extreme nationalist Alexander Dugin, were killed. In March, May and June, far-right Russian nationalist forces fighting against the Russian state carried out armed incursions from Ukrainian territory into Bryansk and Belgorod regions, which border Ukraine. Uninhabited aerial vehicles, believed to be Ukrainian in origin, carried out several attacks deep into European Russia, including on Moscow.

Most seriously of all, domestic tensions fuelled by Russia's poor performance in the war escalated into an armed mutiny by several thousand troops from the Wagner Group, a Russian paramilitary organisation closely linked to the Kremlin and Russian military intelligence. The group first occupied Rostov-on-Don, the headquarters of the Southern Military District and a major planning centre for Russia's war in Ukraine, before marching towards Moscow. Wagner forces reportedly got within 200 kilometres of the Russian capital before the crisis was defused by an agreement between Putin and the group's head Yevgeny Prigozhin, with Belarus's leader Alyaksandr Lukashenka playing a mediating role.[5] Two months later, Prigozhin and other senior Wagner figures were killed in a plane crash, which was widely seen as Putin's revenge for the mutiny.

Tensions between Armenia and Azerbaijan, meanwhile, reflect issues that remain unresolved following their war in late 2020 over Nagorno-Karabakh, the ethnic Armenian-majority enclave within Azerbaijan. The war ended in November 2020 with Azerbaijan's victory, but without a peace agreement or final resolution of the issues that have caused regional instability since the late 1980s. Peace talks began in late 2021, but sporadic military clashes resumed in early 2022 as Azerbaijan increased pressure for a final settlement. In the most serious of such episodes, in September 2022, Azerbaijani forces made incursions into Armenian territory, leading to nearly 300 deaths.[6] In December, environmental activists, widely seen as acting at the Azerbaijani government's behest, obstructed the Lachin corridor connecting Armenia with Nagorno-Karabakh, effectively blockading the enclave. In April 2023, Azerbaijan set up a checkpoint on the Lachin corridor, and in July it even barred the provision of humanitarian supplies by the International Committee of the Red Cross. As of June 2023, over 400 combatants and civilians had been killed since the 2020 ceasefire.[7]

In Central Asia, border tensions between Kyrgyzstan and Tajikistan, which had erupted in April

Figure 1: Russian military deployment in Europe and Eurasia*

	Personnel
Ukraine	175,000
Georgia (Abkhazia & South Ossetia)	4,000
Armenia	3,000
Tajikistan	3,000
Azerbaijan (Nagorno-Karabakh)	2,000
Belarus	2,000
Moldova (Transnistria)	1,500
Kyrgystan	500
Grand total	191,000

Sources: Military Balance+; IISS analysis
*As of August 2023, not under the aegis of an international organisation.

2021 with the loss of over 50 lives, continued to flare up episodically.[8] The most serious incident, in September 2022, saw the use of heavy armour and at least one laser-guided bomb. At least 37 people were killed, and over 130,000 Kyrgyz civilians were reportedly evacuated.[9] On 1 July 2022, protests erupted in Nukus, the capital of Karakalpakstan, which is the only autonomous province in Uzbekistan (and one of only two in Central Asia). These were triggered by proposed constitutional amendments to remove Karakalpakstan's autonomous status. The government suppressed the protests, including with small arms and grenades. The constitutional amendments were withdrawn. Government sources state that 21 people died, including four members of the security forces, and over 270 were injured.[10] Some unofficial sources give higher figures.

One further conflict, between Georgia and Russia, remained frozen but still of concern. Russia continues to occupy the regions of Abkhazia and South Ossetia following its 2008 war with Georgia. Although Russia has been forced to redeploy some forces it had based there to fight in Ukraine – reportedly reducing deployments by around 3,000 personnel – there are recurring concerns that its remaining forces are periodically advancing their positions by stealth further into Georgia (see Figure 1).

Conflict Drivers

Political and institutional drivers
Absence of accepted borders
The lack of accepted, legitimate borders by the countries that share them has been a recurring driver of conflict in the region. In the case of the Kyrgyzstan–Tajikistan conflict, this is because only half of their border has been demarcated since the Soviet Union broke up. Disputes over access

to shared water sources also exacerbate tensions. In the case of the unrest in Uzbekistan, the issue is internal borders. Conflict was triggered by Tashkent's decision to withdraw, without effective consultation, the constitutional autonomy that Karakalpakstan had enjoyed.

In the case of the Russia–Ukraine war, the inter-state border was accepted as legitimate by both countries. Indeed, Russia signed many inter-state agreements with Ukraine, as well as the 1994 Budapest Memorandum with the United States and United Kingdom, in which it committed to respecting Ukraine's territorial integrity. Two decades later, however, Russia abruptly revised its position and ceased to respect this international border. In violation of international law, its first invasion in February 2014 led to its occupation of Crimea and to gaining effective control, through puppet administrations, over the Donbas region in eastern Ukraine. Its second, full-scale invasion in February 2022 sought to occupy almost all the country and to forcibly replace the elected government in Kyiv. As of June 2023, Russia occupied about 18% of Ukraine.[11] In September 2022, Russia declared sovereignty over four further regions (Kharkiv, Kherson, Luhansk and Zaporizhzhia), amending its constitution to incorporate them into its territory, and has since sought to administer them as subjects of the Russian Federation. Almost no other country recognises these annexations, nor the 2014 annexation of Crimea.

Geopolitical drivers
Russia's ambitions
The rejection by Russia of international borders that it had previously accepted points to another major cause of instability in the region: the growth of Russia's power and, with it, aspirations to restore influence and dominance over the former countries of the Soviet Union (a region it describes as the 'near abroad') as well as restore its position as a revisionist global power. This led it to occupy Abkhazia and South Ossetia after its war with Georgia in 2008 and then to carry out its two invasions of Ukraine in 2014 and 2022. The victory that Putin hoped to achieve with the full-scale invasion of Ukraine in 2022 was also aimed at projecting Russian power into Europe to press for a major revision of the European security order. This would entail, in particular, a de facto reversal of the post-Cold War enlargement of NATO. Two proposed treaties with the US and NATO, drafted by the Russian Ministry of Foreign Affairs at Putin's behest in December 2021, reflected these ambitions.

Conflict Parties

Coalitions
Russia and Ukraine are each supported indirectly by other countries. Ukraine is now dependent on military equipment, ammunition and logistical support from Western countries and their partners under the auspices of the Ukraine Defense Contact Group. This includes air defence, heavy armour and long-range artillery and missile systems. Some countries are also providing military training and intelligence. Meanwhile, Western financial help is sustaining the war-torn Ukrainian economy.

Russia receives weapons systems and ammunition from Belarus, Iran and North Korea. Since the start of the war, Russia has deployed forces on, and launched ground and air attacks from, Belarusian territory. While China is not known to have provided weapons systems to Russia, it is believed to have increased its supply of militarily useful components and equipment.

Turkiye's military support for Azerbaijan, which includes equipment and training, has been key to Azerbaijan's strides in Nagorno-Karabakh.

Non-state armed groups
Russia's full-scale invasion was initially led by its regular armed forces (comprising professional personnel), with other security organisations and militias from the so-called Donetsk People's Republic and Luhansk People's Republic playing a secondary role. Heavy losses suffered by these forces resulted in an increasing reliance on other sources of personnel, such as mobilised reservists and so-called 'private security companies'. The latter organisations are illegal under Russian law, but in reality are state-linked paramilitary forces. The largest and

most significant is the Wagner Group. This is state-funded and retains close links to Russian military intelligence. Its forces comprise former regular soldiers and special forces, volunteers, and convicted criminals who have been offered their freedom in return for fighting in Ukraine. Smaller paramilitary forces, such as Potok, created by state gas company Gazprom, and Redut, linked to the Ministry of Defence, are also engaged in combat. Following the June 2023 insurrection by a part of the Wagner Group under Prigozhin, and Prigozhin's subsequent death in an August 2023 plane crash, the future of these forces appears uncertain.

Russia has recruited some foreign fighters, especially from the Middle East and Africa, and has also sought to recruit from Serbia. The head of Chechnya, Ramzan Kadyrov, has sent part of the substantial Chechen armed forces loyal to him to fight in Ukraine, though with uncertain efficacy.

An International Legion comprising foreign fighters, mostly from Western countries, fights in support of Ukraine, as do a small number of Belarusians who oppose their leader, Lukashenka. In addition, at least two Russian nationalist groups, the Russian Volunteer Corps and the Freedom of Russia Legion, made armed incursions into Russia in March, May and June 2023.

Regional and International Dimensions

The Russia–Ukraine war is reshaping the regional and global security and economic order. As of June 2023, several hundred thousand troops have been killed or wounded, and over 9,000 Ukrainian civilians have been killed, with the true total likely far higher.[12] Over 5.6 million Ukrainian civilians have left the country, with a further 5.9m internally displaced.[13] Ukraine's national income has fallen by a third. A March 2023 World Bank report estimated that Ukraine would require US$411 billion over the next ten years to recover and rebuild after the war.[14]

The war continues to spread alarm and uncertainty in the region. Belarus remains a co-belligerent but not a co-combatant, providing extensive assistance to Russia – including the use of its territory to base Russian forces and launch attacks – without directly intervening with its own military assets. In March 2023, Putin announced that Russia would deploy tactical nuclear weapons in Belarus, and in June he claimed that deployment had begun. If confirmed, this would be the first time that Russia has deployed nuclear weapons outside its territory. However, Western sources have indicated that there is no evidence this has gone ahead.

Moldova, which shares a 1,200 km border with Ukraine, continues to suffer disruption from the war, such as the overflight of Russian missiles. Russia, which controls the Transnistria region of Moldova and bases troops there, has been trying to destabilise the country, including through energy-supply cuts and price rises. In February 2023, the Moldovan prime minister Natalia Gavrilita resigned, citing the 'multiple crises' that Russia's actions had caused.

President Maia Sandu announced that Russia was planning to overthrow the government by orchestrating violent protests.

The war is transforming Western security thinking and organisation. At its June 2022 summit in Madrid, NATO adopted a new Strategic Concept and invited Finland and Sweden to join the Alliance. Finland has since done so, and all NATO member countries have signed the Accession Protocol for Sweden. At the 2023 Vilnius Summit, NATO members committed further support to Ukraine, created a new NATO–Ukraine Council, and agreed that they would 'be in a position to extend an invitation to Ukraine to join the alliance when allies agree and conditions are met'.[15]

Russia's invasion has evoked wider concern that it sets a precedent for the violation of basic norms of state sovereignty and international order. Some Asian states, in particular, have drawn parallels between this war and a possible future conflict involving China. Repeated Russian threats and hints that it could resort to nuclear weapons have heightened such concerns.

The war has had major economic consequences, as well as security ones. For much of 2022, it stoked energy price rises. Restrictions on Ukrainian exports due to Russia's control of the Black Sea, despite an agreement to allow some shipments to global markets, continued to inflate food prices. Russia's decision in July 2023 not to renew the Black Sea Grain Initiative led to an immediate rise in prices and threatened to put poorer societies under further strain.

The war is also transforming economic state-craft. The West and its allies have imposed the most severe sanctions and export controls on a major power in peacetime, including new measures, such as the G7 price cap imposed on Russian crude-oil exports in December 2022 and on oil products in February 2023. More recent measures, notably the European Union's 11th sanctions package, adopted in June 2023, focus on hindering Russia's circumvention of sanctions, especially by closing import routes through third countries. The latter thus face greater scrutiny and potentially sanctions.

Russia has seen substantial diplomatic isolation since the war began. One hundred forty-one countries in the United Nations General Assembly voted to condemn Russia's invasion of Ukraine on its first anniversary in February 2023. Russia and the West are engaging in diplomatic competition to attract the sizeable number of states that have abstained in UN votes on the war. Russia's 2023 Foreign Policy Concept, its first since 2016, formalised its war-induced turn towards the Global South, especially Africa and the Islamic world. The second Russia–Africa Summit in St Petersburg in July 2023 reflected its efforts to deepen ties with these countries.

Even major states that abstained in such voting, in particular China and India, expressed their concern about the war, notably at the Samarkand Summit of the Shanghai Cooperation Organisation in September 2022. From late 2022, however, there were signs that China was moving closer to Russia. Chinese President Xi Jinping's state visit to Moscow in March 2023 appeared to confirm this, as did reports that China was stepping up its supply of militarily useful goods and components (though not weapons) to Russia.

The war has driven further international changes. In March 2022, Russia was expelled from the Council of Europe. In November, the UN General Assembly approved a resolution calling for the establishment of a 'register of damage for Ukraine as [a] first step towards an international compensation mechanism for victims of Russian aggression'.[16] In March 2023, the International Criminal Court issued arrest warrants for Putin and Maria Lvova-Belova, the Russian Commissioner for Children's Rights, for the alleged unlawful deportation and transfer of children from Ukraine.

Several external actors have devised peace plans to end the war. The two most significant are those proposed by China in February 2023 and a group of African states in June. Both Russia and Ukraine rejected these plans.

The Nagorno-Karabakh conflict also has regional and global dimensions. The EU and US have sought to mediate Armenian–Azerbaijani talks to achieve a peace settlement and avert another war. EU president Charles Michel and US Secretary of State Antony Blinken have both hosted talks. After the September 2022 escalation in fighting, the EU proposed a two-year monitoring mission, which formally began in February 2023. Talks reportedly made 'tangible progress' in 2023, but by summer 2023, the deepening humanitarian crisis caused by the blockade of Nagorno-Karabakh, whose residents suffered shortages of food, medicine and other basic goods, evoked grave concern.

Under the terms of the 2020 ceasefire, Russia deployed around 2,000 peacekeepers to the Armenia–Azerbaijan border for a five-year period.

Outlook

Prospects for peace
An early end to the Russia–Ukraine war appears unlikely. The two sides remain far apart on any possible peace terms. Russia demands that Ukraine accept the 'new territorial reality' of its current occupation as a precondition of peace negotiations, while Ukraine insists on the return of all land within its internationally recognised borders. In addition, there is no indication that Russia has abandoned the initial primary goal of its invasion, namely the subjugation of Ukraine. There is thus no assurance that a peace agreement that recognised Russia's control of the areas it currently occupies would represent a stable outcome, rather than a prelude to further aggression.

Moreover, a genuine end to the war, rather than a temporary ceasefire, would require a host of wider political, legal, economic and security issues to be resolved. These include the question of security guarantees and reparation payments for

Ukraine, accountability for war crimes, the return of Ukrainian citizens deported to Russia, and the terms under which sanctions on Russia would be lifted. A post-war settlement would therefore require a complex diplomatic process.

Escalation potential and regional spillovers

There are at least three ways that the war could escalate. Firstly, its intensity could increase if Russia turns more of its human and material potential into a useable military force. Thus far, the regime has calibrated its mobilisation of resources with the need to maintain domestic control, and it has sought to avoid imposing excessive strains on elites and the wider public, which might threaten stability. As the June 2023 Wagner Group revolt showed, security hardliners are pressing for an intensification of the war effort. If they got their way, Russia would mobilise much more fully, but would also likely impose even more severe domestic repression and possibly close Russia's borders to prevent the flight of citizens avoiding conscription. The countries that are supporting Ukraine would then be faced with the choice of whether to escalate military assistance in response.

Secondly, Russia could escalate horizontally through attacks on Western assets. A series of still-unexplained attacks on subsea infrastructure have heightened this concern. There are worries, too, that Russia could test NATO's resolve by probing borders with NATO members. In July 2023, Belarusian helicopters violated Polish airspace amid reports that Belarus was preparing to send an influx of migrants across the border, as it did in 2021. In early August 2023, Russia attacked Ukrainian grain facilities on the Danube within a few hundred metres of the Romanian border.[17]

Thirdly, Russia could escalate vertically by using weapons of mass destruction, especially tactical nuclear weapons, as it has threatened since the start of its invasion. Given the risks to Russia of doing so, the probability of such use is low, but it cannot be fully discounted. There is also concern that Russia might resort to a smaller, but still very serious, nuclear option by destroying the Zaporizhzhia Nuclear Power Plant, which it currently occupies, potentially leading to the irradiation of the surrounding territory.

The relationship between Armenia and Azerbaijan remains volatile and strained. The two countries are continuing to negotiate a peace treaty.

Strategic implications and global influences

The course of the war in Ukraine will also depend on the wider contest of resolve between Russia and the West and its allies. The latter, which provide essential support to Ukraine, far exceed Russia in economic strength and thus deliverable military supplies. While they have steadily escalated their support, it remains unclear how far, and at what rate, they will sustain this.

China's policy is another key variable. On the one hand, China's material resources could mitigate the disadvantage Russia faces with respect to the West and thus help it sustain its war effort. On the other hand, if Chinese fears of escalation grow, its diplomacy could conceivably help pressure Russia to end the war on terms acceptable to Ukraine and its supporters.

REGIONAL KEY EVENTS

POLITICAL EVENTS

MILITARY/VIOLENT EVENTS

 **RUSSIA–UKRAINE**

17 May 2022
Ukrainian soldiers surrender in Mariupol. Russia takes the city after weeks of fighting.

UZBEKISTAN

1–2 July

Protests erupt in Karakalpakstan – over a constitutional amendment to remove the province's autonomous status – and are violently suppressed by Uzbek security forces.

RUSSIA–UKRAINE

4 July

Russia captures the Luhansk region (half of the Donbas), making up a large territorial loss for Ukraine.

NAGORNO-KARABAKH

3 August

The Azerbaijani government launches drone strikes as retaliation against Armenian incursions into Azerbaijani territory.

RUSSIA–UKRAINE

29 August

Ukraine initiates its first major counter-offensive against Russian forces in the south, aiming to capture the Kherson region.

RUSSIA–UKRAINE

5 September

Taking Moscow by surprise, Ukrainian forces launch a counter-offensive in the Kharkiv region.

NAGORNO-KARABAKH

13 September

Following a Russian-negotiated ceasefire, Azerbaijan accuses Armenia of violating agreements and retaliates with force.

KYRGYZSTAN, TAJIKISTAN

14–16 September

Border tensions between Kyrgyzstan and Tajikistan flare up again.

RUSSIA–UKRAINE

22 July 2022

Russia and Ukraine sign separate agreements with Turkiye and the UN permitting the export of millions of tonnes of Ukrainian grain, alongside Russian grain and fertiliser.

NAGORNO-KARABAKH

14 September

With 155 dead due to a flare-up in the conflict, Armenia and Azerbaijan agree to a new ceasefire (more favourable for Azerbaijan).

NAGORNO-KARABAKH

19 September

US Secretary of State Blinken hosts a trilateral meeting with the Armenian and Azerbaijani foreign ministers on the sidelines of the UN General Assembly.

RUSSIA–UKRAINE

21 September

Putin declares a partial mobilisation of reservists, sparking protests that lead to nearly 1,200 arrests.

Europe and Eurasia

RUSSIA–UKRAINE

30 September

Putin announces the annexation of Donetsk, Luhansk, Kherson and Zaporizhzhia regions after 'referendums' claim up to 99% of residents are in favour of annexation.

 RUSSIA–UKRAINE

November

The European Parliament designates Russia as a state sponsor of terrorism and the UN General Assembly demands Russia pay reparations to Ukraine for damages.

 NAGORNO-KARABAKH

12–15 December

Azerbaijan blockades the Lachin corridor, a key road linking Armenia and the Nagorno-Karabakh region, and Russia expresses concern over rising tensions between the two countries.

 RUSSIA–UKRAINE

21 December

Ukrainian President Volodymyr Zelenskyy visits US President Joe Biden at the White House, following a nearly US$2bn aid package to Ukraine.

 NAGORNO-KARABAKH

10 January 2023

Armenia refuses to host military drills as part of the Collective Security Treaty Organisation due to Russia's inaction against the Lachin corridor blockade.

 RUSSIA–UKRAINE

Early February

The EU, US, G7 and other allies declare a global price cap on Russian refined oil, while the EU bans all Russian refined oil products.

 RUSSIA–UKRAINE

20 February

Biden meets with Zelenskyy and US embassy staff in Ukraine, declaring that 'Kyiv stands'.

 NAGORNO-KARABAKH

22 February

In a 13-to-two ruling, the International Court of Justice demands an end to the Azerbaijani blockade of the Lachin corridor.

 RUSSIA–UKRAINE

9 November

Russian forces retreat from Kherson after months of fighting the Ukrainian counter-offensive.

 RUSSIA–UKRAINE

31 December

Ukraine strikes a building in Donetsk in a surprise New Year's Eve attack. Over 63 Russian soldiers are killed.

NAGORNO-KARABAKH

23 February

Ruben Vardanyan, prime minister of Artsakh (Nagorno-Karabakh), is removed after just four months in office by President of Artsakh Arayik Harutyunyan.

 RUSSIA–UKRAINE

26 April

Zelenskyy has his first phone call with Chinese President Xi since Russia's 2022 invasion. Xi promises to send a delegation for peace talks.

 RUSSIA–UKRAINE

14–15 May

Following his visit to Germany, Zelenskyy makes surprise visits to Paris and London, securing new military-aid packages from all three nations.

 NAGORNO-KARABAKH

25 May

Pashinyan and Aliyev meet Putin in Moscow to discuss widening the Lachin corridor. Putin claims only 'technical' issues remain unresolved.

 NAGORNO-KARABAKH

11 May 2023

While negotiations continue in Brussels, fighting resumes in the Sotk region, with both sides accusing the other of violating the ceasefire.

 RUSSIA–UKRAINE

Early June

Ukraine begins new counter-offensive operations, with major fighting along the Zaporizhzhia front and around Bakhmut.

 RUSSIA–UKRAINE, BELARUS

17 June

Putin confirms that the first batch of tactical nuclear weapons have been stationed in Belarus.

 RUSSIA–UKRAINE

23 June

The Wagner Group takes control of Rostov-on-Don and marches to Moscow. The mutiny fails one day later, and leader Yevgeny Prigozhin is exiled. Prigozhin subsequently dies in a plane crash in August 2023.

 NAGORNO-KARABAKH

19–20 September

Azerbaijan launches an 'anti-terrorist' offensive in Nagorno-Karabakh, reclaiming full control of the region and triggering a large exodus of ethnic Armenians amid fears of persecution.

Notes

1   The dramatic developments in Nagorno-Karabakh in September 2023, which culminated with Azerbaijan successfully reclaiming the disputed region after a short military offensive, are not covered in the Regional Analysis. See the addendum to the Nagorno-Karabakh chapter for a brief analysis of these developments.

2   This was Russia's second invasion of Ukraine, following the first invasion in February 2014.

3   See the Ukraine Country Profile for more details.

4   'Sabotage Acts in Russia More Than Double in 2023', *Moscow Times*, 15 May 2023.

5   'Rebel Russian Mercenaries Turn Back Short of Moscow "to Avoid Bloodshed"', Reuters, 24 June 2023.

6   Jakub Przetacznik, Sebastian Clapp and Angelos Delivorias, 'Question Time: Heightening Tensions Between Armenia and Azerbaijan', European Parliamentary Research Service, October 2022.

7   International Crisis Group, 'The Nagorno-Karabakh Conflict: A Visual Explainer', 1 August 2023.

8   'Upheaval in Central Asia: What Is Driving Change in Eurasia's Heartland?', in IISS, *Strategic Survey 2022* (Abingdon: Routledge for the IISS, 2022), p. 255.

9   Human Rights Watch, 'Kyrgyzstan/Tajikistan: Apparent War Crimes in Border Conflict', 2 May 2023.

10 Human Rights Watch, 'Uzbekistan: Police Abuses in Autonomous Region Protests', 7 November 2022.

11 See, for example, Scott Reinhard, 'Ukraine Has Reclaimed More Than Half the Territory Russia Has Taken This Year', *New York Times*, 14 November 2022.

12 OHCHR, 'Ukraine: Civilian Casualty Update 31 July 2023', 31 July 2023.

13 UN Human Rights Council (UNHRC), 'Situation Operational Data Portal: Ukraine Refugee Situation', updated 8 August 2023; and USA for UNHRC, 'Ukraine Emergency', 2023.

14 'World Bank Says $411bn Cost to Rebuild War-torn Ukraine', Al-Jazeera, 23 March 2023.

15 'Russia–Ukraine War: List of Key Events, Day 504', Al-Jazeera, 12 July 2023.

16 Council of Europe, 'Council of Europe Summit Creates Register of Damage for Ukraine as First Step Towards an International Compensation Mechanism for Victims of Russian Aggression', 17 May 2023.

17 Matthew Mpoke Bigg et al., 'Russia Strikes Danube Port, Escalating Attacks on Ukraine Grain Routes', *New York Times*, 24 July 2023.

The Looming Aftermath of War in Ukraine: Connecting Post-war Recovery, Security Guarantees and Domestic Defence Capabilities

Russia's full-scale invasion of Ukraine in February 2022 has caused extensive human suffering and massive destruction. There is a long list of post-war reconstruction priorities, from physical infrastructure and addressing war traumas to economic recovery and defence capabilities, among others. Within one year of the war, needs assessments put the estimate of the recovery cost for Ukraine at US$411 billion – a staggering figure that is equivalent to about two times the country's GDP in 2021.[1] As the war rages on, the exercise of estimating costs and planning for reconstruction is largely speculative, because the actual efforts and resources needed will become clear only once major military operations are over. Nonetheless, Ukraine's government has already launched a National Recovery Plan (NRP), and high-level discussions among donors have been taking place regarding the country's post-war needs in terms of capital to be mobilised and which sectors should be prioritised (see Figure 1).

Tenets of post-war reconstruction in Ukraine against standard practices

The transition from war to peace is by no means a modern phenomenon. The term 'reconstruction', associated with the aftermath of war, can be traced back to the American Civil War. Subsequently, it was embedded in the post-Second World War order through the establishment of the International Bank for Reconstruction and Development (i.e., the World Bank). However, it is in the post-Cold War era that efforts to prevent or mitigate the incidence of wars (in particular, intra-state ones) and to facilitate post-war reconstruction became mainstream.

In the aftermath of the Cold War, intractable civil wars from the Balkans to Central America to Sub-Saharan Africa to East Asia were resolved, and a reconstruction 'industry' was spearheaded by an international community of states that was eager to expand both the tenets of liberal democracy and the prosperity promised by the market economy. In the last two decades, post-war recovery and stabilisation have increasingly started while countries were still suffering from violence (e.g., Afghanistan between 2001 and 2021 and Colombia before the 2016 peace agreement), although the bulk of reconstruction can only be achieved when peace and security are restored.[2]

The case of Ukraine, however, is remarkably different than past examples and reverting to the 'science' of post-conflict reconstruction could be inappropriate. Unlike post-Cold War reconstruction cases, which were by and large related to civil wars, Ukraine is suffering from an external invasion and war of aggression initiated by a permanent member of the United Nations Security Council. The fact that this is a full-blown, state-on-state war alters the post-war security conditions that both domestic and international actors must consider. Domestically, while war-torn countries are usually characterised by a sovereignty deficit, with weak and fragmented institutions, the government of Ukraine is not in this same position. Though it has grappled with corruption and other governance challenges since regaining independence in 1991, the Ukrainian government now exhibits strength, cohesion and the resolution to take charge of its reconstruction trajectory.

Framing Kyiv's external security guarantees

Unusually, the discourse on reconstruction needs and recovery opportunities proceeds somewhat disjointedly from Ukraine's quest for security guarantees. As a matter of fact, the feasibility of the former depends a lot on the success of the latter: security guarantees for Ukraine are the *sine qua non* of post-war recovery. It will be very difficult for meaningful reconstruction to start, or for foreign investments to be mobilised effectively, in the absence of agreements and frameworks that contemplate Ukraine's future security. Twin goals for Ukraine should be to set up binding external commitments and to enable the development of credible domestic defence capabilities, the combination of which would deter any future potential threat to Ukrainian sovereignty

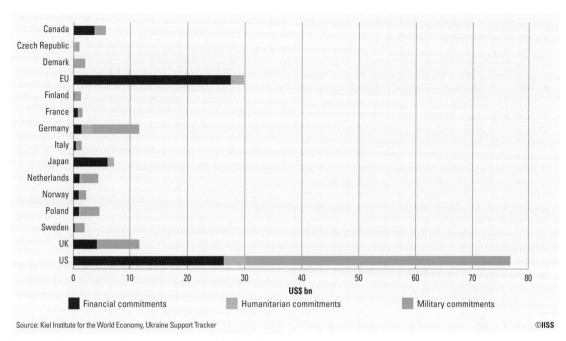

Source: Kiel Institute for the World Economy, Ukraine Support Tracker   ©IISS

Figure 1: Aid support to Ukraine, 24 January 2022–31 May 2023

and territorial integrity coming from Russia (or any other foreign power).

Historic precedents play an important role in influencing how potential future security guarantees are seen in Kyiv. The 1994 Budapest Memorandum in which Ukraine relinquished its nuclear arsenal in exchange for political-security assurances from Russia, the United Kingdom and the United States was first violated in 2014 with Russia's annexation of Crimea and the opening of a front in eastern Ukraine. It was then definitely buried with Russia's 2022 full-scale invasion. Further, in 2008, NATO's commitment to Ukraine's (and Georgia's) membership was not followed up by a timeline or a NATO Membership Action Plan (MAP), in part because a few NATO members were worried about Russia's reaction if Ukraine and Georgia were put on a formal path to membership. In addition, political commitment to and public support for NATO membership in Ukraine were fragile at the time, which was another factor in the decision-making of some NATO member states around the Alliance's 2008 Bucharest Summit.[3]

With these precedents in mind, as well as a Ukrainian electorate and government now firmly united in their desire to join NATO (and the European Union), and a permanent 'no-trust-in-Russia' policy in place for the foreseeable future,

Ukrainian officials have repeatedly asserted that future agreements guaranteeing Ukraine's security must be legally binding. Both NATO and EU membership are ultimate goals for Ukraine because both organisations have treaty-based collective-defence clauses.[4] Moreover, NATO's collective defence is backed by the US, which is still the pre-eminent military power in the world, while the EU has a track record of mobilising enormous resources to aid the economic transformation of its member states.

Achieving membership in one or both of these organisations will remain difficult in the short term. At a NATO summit in Vilnius held from 11–12 July, NATO leaders stated that 'Ukraine's future is in NATO', set up a NATO–Ukraine Council and waived the requirement for a MAP, but they also rather vaguely declared that NATO 'will be in a position to extend an invitation to Ukraine to join the Alliance when Allies agree and conditions are met'.[5] On the margins of the NATO summit, G7 nations announced that they would begin negotiating formal security commitments to Ukraine, which underpin guarantees. EU membership, on the other hand, must be preceded by accession talks, which represent a lengthy and costly process that has countrywide implications in terms of designing regulations that are in line with the EU's body of laws and reforming political and economic governance more widely – a challenging proposition while Ukraine is at war. The European Council conclusions from 30 June 2023 reiterated:

> The European Council acknowledges Ukraine's commitment and substantial efforts to meet the required conditions in its EU accession process. It encourages Ukraine to continue on its path of reforms. The European Union will continue to work closely with Ukraine and support its efforts to fully meet all conditions.[6]

Kyiv must navigate many complexities as part of its accession to both organisations. One of these is to avoid giving Russia an effective veto on accession by prolonging the war and thus preventing the conditions for Ukraine to join NATO and the EU.

The need for domestic defence capabilities as a pillar of security guarantees

The fact that sustainable peace and reconstruction will require massive investment in military capabilities and defence capacity-building is the second area in which the case of Ukraine will challenge the assumptions and mandates of the reconstruction industry. Given Ukraine's experience with previous security guarantees and the challenges of generating meaningful and legally binding ones in the current context, it is unsurprising that Ukraine will want to invest in its future ability to generate credible military capabilities that effectively underpin its national deterrence and defence efforts vis-à-vis Russia.

As Swedish Minister for Defence Pål Jonson argued at the 20th IISS Shangri-La Dialogue in June 2023, a key driver of Sweden's decision to apply for NATO membership was the realisation brought about by Russia's aggression that 'NATO supports its partners, but it defends its allies'.[7] As long as Ukraine is not a NATO member state, the conclusion in Kyiv must be that Ukraine needs to be able to defend itself, which requires a degree of self-sufficiency in defence-industrial terms (which, incidentally, Sweden also pursued before it applied for NATO membership). For this reason, Ukraine's NRP highlights the domestic defence-industrial sector as critical and a 'strategic imperative' for national security.[8]

While defence-industrial sites have been targeted by Russia's military and some are in occupied territory, Ukraine's indigenous defence-industrial base continues to deliver munitions and weapons to the Armed Forces of Ukraine. To some extent, this reflects Ukraine's history as an important part of the Soviet Union's defence-industrial base, building naval vessels, ballistic missiles and aircraft engines, among other things. However, it is also the result of Ukraine's early attempts to disperse production sites, relocate facilities to friendly neighbouring countries, and put Ukroboronprom, the state-owned arms manufacturer, on a 24-hour, seven-day-a-week schedule. While there are limitations to what Ukraine can produce, especially in current circumstances, notable successes include the RK-360MC *Neptun* anti-ship missile system developed by Luch Design Bureau, which allegedly sank the Russian cruiser *Moskva* in 2022; the 2S22 *Bohdana* self-propelled howitzer, firing NATO-calibre 155-millimetre rounds, which may have entered production in 2023; and certain types of locally developed and produced uninhabited aerial vehicles. Ukraine's ability to produce artillery munitions for use with Soviet-era systems is notable as well.

The successful sustained prosecution of Kyiv's campaign to evict Russian forces from Ukrainian territory depends on the steady supply of Western armaments. However, the existing defence-industrial base and the inventiveness bred by the necessity to defend against armed aggression give Ukraine options for the future. During the reconstruction phase, Ukraine will be a customer of the Western defence industry, purchasing defence equipment with a priority likely placed on availability and speed, followed by requirement and price. Ukraine will also pursue a strategy of inviting Western companies to consider co-production and technology-sharing arrangements to meet military-capability needs. Rheinmetall, one of Germany's premier land-systems producers, signed an agreement with Ukroboronprom in May 2023 to establish a joint venture which will focus initially on maintenance and repair for German-produced armoured vehicles provided to Ukraine, but is meant to later expand into technology transfer and joint production of Rheinmetall products in Ukraine. In the same month, Ukrainian President Volodymyr Zelenskyy announced that BAE Systems is pursuing a similar path that might start with service provisions to Ukraine and later include a production element. Finally, there will be areas in which Ukraine may rely on indigenous production. It is likely that a basic trade-off will drive Ukrainian ambitions: the less convincing that the security guarantees provided by Western powers are, the more self-sufficient Ukraine will strive to be in defence-industry terms.

Four broad challenges will need to be addressed as Ukraine considers the defence-industry dimension of its reconstruction. Firstly, there is security itself. While the war continues, many international defence companies are reluctant to move beyond assisting their own governments in either replenishing national stocks or delivering equipment for transfer to Ukraine. Given that any new defence-industry site in Ukraine is liable to become a target, protecting against that risk – either with military assets, for example, in the form of air defence, or financially through war-risk insurance that is hard to come by – will matter to company leaders. Secondly, there are governance concerns given Ukraine's poor record in this area in which layers of complicated bureaucracy, including in military-industrial matters, provide opportunity for graft. Reforming and modernising Ukroboronprom will be in the Ukrainian government's interest if it wants to consider wide-ranging defence-industrial partnerships. At the same time, there is now an opportunity to set up technology accelerators and defence-innovation hubs to promote and enable defence-technology-focused start-ups that have sprung up in Ukraine. Thirdly, Western governments maintain export-control and non-proliferation mechanisms that might set limits on what Ukraine can hope to access, both as a customer and in terms of technology transfer. Finally, some defence-industry players might wonder whether a partnership arrangement will ultimately only serve to turn Ukraine's defence industry into a future competitor.

Notes

[1] The World Bank, 'Updated Ukraine Recovery and Reconstruction Needs Assessment', 2023/ECA/82, 23 March 2023.

[2] Benjamin Petrini, 'The Long Aftermath of Armed Conflicts', in IISS, *The Armed Conflict Survey 2021* (Abingdon: Routledge for the International Institute for Strategic Studies, 2021).

[3] See NATO, 'NATO Decisions on Open-door Policy', 3 April 2008 (updated 4 April 2008).

[4] In NATO, this is Article 5; in the EU, it is Article 42.7 TEU. According to the Treaty of Lisbon (2007), EU members benefit from a mutual defence arrangement.

[5] NATO, 'Vilnius Summit Communiqué', 11 July 2023 (updated 19 July 2023).

[6] European Council, 'European Council Meeting (29 and 30 June 2023) – Conclusions', EUCO 7/23, 30 June 2023.

[7] IISS, '20th Asia Security Summit, the Shangri-La Dialogue: Fourth Plenary Session, Saturday 3 June 2023: Dr Pål Jonson, Minister for Defence, Sweden', June 2023.

[8] National Recovery Council, 'Ukraine's National Recovery Plan', July 2022.

RUSSIA–UKRAINE

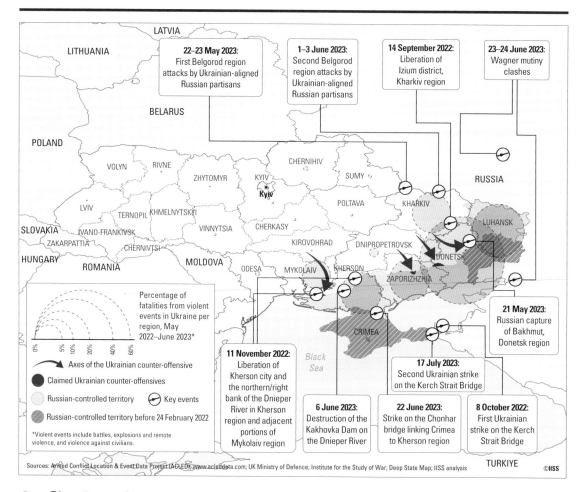

22–23 May 2023: First Belgorod region attacks by Ukrainian-aligned Russian partisans

1–3 June 2023: Second Belgorod region attacks by Ukrainian-aligned Russian partisans

14 September 2022: Liberation of Izium district, Kharkiv region

23–24 June 2023: Wagner mutiny clashes

21 May 2023: Russian capture of Bakhmut, Donetsk region

11 November 2022: Liberation of Kherson city and the northern/right bank of the Dnieper River in Kherson region and adjacent portions of Mykolaiv region

17 July 2023: Second Ukrainian strike on the Kerch Strait Bridge

6 June 2023: Destruction of the Kakhovka Dam on the Dnieper River

22 June 2023: Strike on the Chonhar bridge linking Crimea to Kherson region

8 October 2022: First Ukrainian strike on the Kerch Strait Bridge

Percentage of fatalities from violent events in Ukraine per region, May 2022–June 2023*

0%   5%   10%   20%   40%   60%

→ Axes of the Ukrainian counter-offensive

● Claimed Ukrainian counter-offensives

Russian-controlled territory   ⊘ Key events

Russian-controlled territory before 24 February 2022

*Violent events include battles, explosions and remote violence, and violence against civilians.

Sources: Armed Conflict Location & Event Data Project (ACLED), www.acleddata.com; UK Ministry of Defence; Institute for the Study of War; Deep State Map; IISS analysis   ©IISS

Conflict Overview

Russia's full-scale invasion of Ukraine, launched on 24 February 2022, built upon eight years of aggression by the Kremlin towards Kyiv, beginning with the invasion and subsequent annexation of Crimea in February–March 2014 in the aftermath of Ukraine's pro-Western Revolution of Dignity. The Kremlin subsequently stoked conflict across Ukraine's easternmost Donetsk and Luhansk regions. It armed and financially supported breakaway forces, as well as ordered its troops to intervene directly in major clashes in 2014 and 2015, even after signing the Minsk II agreement ostensibly aimed at ending active clashes in February 2015. Russian President Vladimir Putin, despite long denying Russia's direct involvement in the conflict, increasingly fixated on disagreements with the post-Revolution of Dignity governments of Ukraine. He also promoted a narrative around a supposed historical unity of the Russian and Ukrainian nations, as well as allegations that Kyiv was discriminating against Russian speakers.

In the lead-up to the full-scale invasion, Putin argued that Ukraine's attempts to move closer to NATO were a threat to Russian security, although, at that time, Kyiv had not made any formal progress towards its desired accession to the Alliance. The invasion revealed that Putin ultimately aimed to replace the Ukrainian government, as well as to seize all of Ukraine east of the Dnieper River and along the Black Sea coast. Russia was swiftly forced to withdraw from much of northern Ukraine in the face

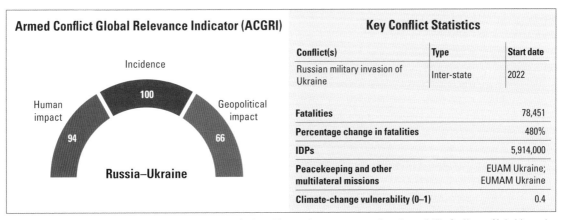

Conflict(s)	Type	Start date
Russian military invasion of Ukraine	Inter-state	2022

Fatalities	78,451
Percentage change in fatalities	480%
IDPs	5,914,000
Peacekeeping and other multilateral missions	EUAM Ukraine; EUMAM Ukraine
Climate-change vulnerability (0–1)	0.4

ACGRI pillars: IISS calculation based on multiple sources for 2022 and 2023 (scale: 0–100), except for some cases according to data availability. See Notes on Methodology and Data Appendix for all variables and further details on Key Conflict Statistics.

of fierce resistance and failed in efforts to advance towards Ukraine's southwestern Odesa region. Yet, in September 2022, the Kremlin claimed that it was annexing all of the eastern and southern regions of Donetsk, Luhansk, Kherson and Zaporizhzhia, despite never occupying the entirety of any of them.

Ukraine has since had several successful counter-offensives, but the conflict – already Europe's largest and deadliest since the Second World War – continues unabated. As yet, no formal peace process has been agreed upon, nor is one likely to be agreed upon in the foreseeable future. Precise military casualties remain unknown, but one estimate disclosed to journalists in August 2023 by United States government officials suggested that Russia may have suffered nearly 300,000 total casualties and Ukraine nearly 200,000.[1] The United Nations has reported at least 9,117 civilian deaths following the full-scale invasion to 30 June 2023, though it warns that it 'believes that the actual figures are considerably higher'.[2] The UN has also reported that the conflict has resulted in over 5.6 million refugees – although it stipulates that this too is likely an undercount – and has left nearly 6m people internally displaced.[3] The war's ramifications have already reshaped security paradigms and postures across the continent and around the world, including by prompting an unprecedented level of Western cohesion regarding sanctions and military support, as well as the accession of Finland, and soon Sweden, to the NATO Alliance.

Conflict Update

Russia's invasion of Ukraine did not make any significant progress over the reporting period. The conflict continued to rage along several fronts in Ukraine's south and east, with Russian drone and missile strikes threatening cities and infrastructure across Ukraine.

The northernmost front is located along the borders between Russia's Bryansk, Kursk and Belgorod regions and Ukraine's Sumy, Chernihiv and Kharkiv regions. Although Russian forces were pushed out of the former two Ukrainian regions in April 2022 and much of Kharkiv region in September 2022, daily cross-border shelling continued. Russian forces also continued to occupy roughly 5% of Kharkiv region's northeast, where clashes were ongoing daily. To the east, fighting continued around the lines of control near the Oskil River, where Ukrainian forces retained a foothold in western Luhansk region. Kyiv does not formally comment on shelling in Russian territory but has emphasised that it retains the right to return fire. There were two cross-border incursions by Russian partisan groups aligned with Ukraine on 22–23 May and 1–3 June into Belgorod region.

Fighting also occurred along the border between Luhansk and Donetsk regions, centred on the Serebrianka forest and around Ukrainian-held Bilohorivka in the south of Luhansk region, although the most intense clashes in northern Donetsk region were around the town of Bakhmut. Russian forces took Bakhmut after ten months of attacks on 21 May 2023, but Ukrainian forces have since retaken some territory on its outskirts. Daily clashes also continued around the city of Donetsk, which has been under Russian occupation since 2014, but there was little change to the lines of control there.

Ukraine's latest counter-offensive, which began in early June 2023, has been focused on areas further south in Donetsk region around the Mokri Yaly River and across the line of control that runs through Zaporizhzhia region. While some settlements have been retaken, progress has been slow and Ukrainian officials have publicly acknowledged that they face significant challenges without sufficient air cover. Although the US and other Western allies announced on 20 May 2023 that they were prepared to train Ukrainian forces on and deliver F-16 *Fighting Falcon* combat aircraft for this purpose, no concrete timeline was established.

West of Zaporizhzhia region Ukrainian forces recorded their largest success in terms of territory retaken with an offensive from late August–November 2022 that ultimately forced Russian forces to withdraw from the right bank of the Dnieper River, resulting in the liberation of occupied portions north of the river and the Mykolaiv-Buh Gulf at its mouth in Mykolaiv and Kherson regions, including the city of Kherson. Shelling across the river remained intense, however, and the region also saw the destruction of the Kakhovka Dam on the Dnieper River on 6 June 2023, which resulted in devastating flooding downstream. There were concerns about the security of the Russian-occupied Zaporizhzhia Nuclear Power Plant further upstream on the Dnieper River outside Enerhodar, due to continuous shelling and the draining of the Kakhovka Reservoir following the dam's destruction.

Russian missile and drone strikes have targeted cities across Ukraine. Although Kyiv and Zaporizhzhia have been the most frequently targeted, attacks occurred as far west as Lviv. Russia launched regular attacks on crucial Ukrainian power and water infrastructure in October 2022, which have continued unabated since then. These have taken on a new dimension following Russia's withdrawal from the Black Sea Grain Initiative on 17 July 2023, which the Kremlin followed with repeated strikes against agricultural and port infrastructure in Odesa region. Ukrainian forces have also targeted infrastructure used by Russia in its invasion, most notably through two attacks on the Kerch Strait Bridge linking Russia's Krasnodar Krai

with occupied Crimea on 8 October 2022 and 17 July 2023. The overwhelming majority of Ukraine's attacks behind the front have targeted Russian military positions, largely with drones and occasional saboteur attacks. However, there have also been a number of drone strikes on oil-storage facilities in both occupied territory and Russia itself, as well as a handful of attacks against Russian military and occupation officials and propagandists.

The war has had major political ramifications, both in Ukraine and Russia and internationally. Ukraine has received over US$70 billion in military aid from its Western allies, notably from the European Union, United Kingdom and US (with well over double that pledged), and it has received additional aid from other countries including Australia, Japan and South Korea.[4] Furthermore, the war has led to the expansion of NATO, with Finland joining the Alliance on 4 April 2023, and neighbouring Sweden expected to join in the latter half of 2023. The countries supporting Ukraine have also enforced the largest coordinated international sanctions regime in modern history, targeting the Kremlin and its affiliated elites, military supplies and ability to continue to bankroll the war. Nevertheless, the Kremlin has shown no intention of halting the conflict and has responded by weaponising energy supplies. Moreover, the conflict may still lead to new forms of non-military inter-state tensions, including escalating cyber attacks and sabotage against infrastructure internationally, as evidenced by the 26 September 2022 Nord Stream pipelines explosions in the North Sea. Investigations into those blasts are ongoing, and blame has not formally been assigned. However, the Kremlin has been suspected of involvement in other sabotage efforts as well, including against ammunition depots in NATO member state Bulgaria.

Within Russia itself, the war has led to the first mass mobilisation in the country's post-Soviet history, which in turn has resulted in the largest exodus of Russian nationals since the Soviet Union's collapse and tensions among the elite. The latter was exemplified by the revolt led by Yevgeny Prigozhin on 23–24 June 2023, when forces under his Wagner Group briefly occupied large swathes of the cities of Voronezh and Rostov-on-Don on the Ukrainian border and marched towards Moscow, before agreeing to put down arms. The Wagner Group was established by the Kremlin in 2014 to give it plausible deniability, at least in state-run and state-friendly news outlets, regarding military and intelligence operations and commercial activities abroad. It has led many of the Kremlin's interventions in African countries such as the Central African Republic and Mali in the years since then, and it took a prominent role in the war in Ukraine, including leading the siege of Bakhmut. Prigozhin claimed that his rebellion was aimed at replacing Russia's military leadership rather than targeting Putin. However, the incident, and the reported deaths of Prigozhin and other senior Wagner Group leaders in a subsequent August 2023 plane crash widely blamed on the Kremlin, highlighted how the war in Ukraine also threatens Russia's own internal stability.

Conflict Parties

Armed Forces of Ukraine

Strength: 650,000 active military personnel, 250,000 active gendarmerie and paramilitary, and 400,000 reserve military, although the vast majority are conscripts and volunteers who have joined since the full-scale invasion began on 24 February 2022 (up from 196,600 active military personnel at that time).

Areas of operation: Across Ukraine, with active combat against Russia's invasion in Donetsk, Kharkiv, Kherson, Luhansk and Zaporizhzhia regions. Ukrainian military intelligence is suspected of organising and supporting attacks in Russian territory, although Kyiv does not formally comment on such incidents.[5]

Leadership: President Volodymyr Zelenskyy (supreme commander-in-chief), Valerii Zaluzhnyi (commander-in-chief) and Oleksii Reznikov (defence minister).

Structure: The Ukrainian armed forces include the army, navy and air force, as well as separate Special Operations Forces, Airborne Assault Forces and Territorial Defence Forces. There are also several volunteer groups fighting alongside the armed forces with varying degrees of integration into the military command structure.

History: The Armed Forces of Ukraine were formally founded following the Soviet Union's dissolution in 1991. Since then, they have undergone several substantial transformations, first in the aftermath of Russia's initial invasion in February 2014 and again after the full-scale invasion began in February 2022. After February 2022, Ukraine mobilised its reserve and territorial forces and received substantial donations of military equipment and training support from partner nations.

Objectives: Defence of Ukraine and liberation of Russian-occupied territory.

Opponents: Armed Forces of the Russian Federation, Wagner Group and other Russian state-backed paramilitary organisations.

Affiliates/allies: NATO member states have provided Ukraine with military supplies. Since 2020, Ukraine has been a NATO Enhanced Opportunities Partner.

Resources/capabilities: Ukraine's stand-alone capabilities have been greatly degraded by the Russian invasion, but Kyiv is regularly supplied by its Western allies, which have provided significant military equipment and materiel since February 2022 and have pledged further continued supplies. These supplies have included the provision of main battle tanks, other armoured vehicles, air-defence systems, drones, artillery, armoured vehicles and ammunition, as well as legacy Soviet aircraft and parts. The US and numerous European partners have also agreed to supply and train Ukrainian pilots on F-16 combat aircraft. Ukraine's defence budget was US$3.6bn for 2022 (budget released prior to Russia's invasion) and is US$30.9bn for 2023.

Armed Forces of the Russian Federation

Strength: 1,150,000 active military, 550,000 active gendarmerie and paramilitary, and 1,500,000 reserve military personnel. Russian men aged 18–27 (from 2024, 18–30) are required to do a year of military service and are thereafter placed in the reserves. At least 300,000 Russians have been mobilised since September 2022.[6] In December 2022, Russia's Ministry of Defence announced it would aim to reach 1.5m active personnel.[7] Russia has also integrated conscripted and volunteer forces from its former proxy entities in eastern Ukraine, the so-called Luhansk People's Republic and Donetsk People's Republic.

Areas of operation: Ground operations take place in occupied Crimea and Donetsk, Luhansk, Kharkiv, Kherson and Zaporizhzhia regions. Over the reporting period, Russia also attacked Ukraine's Chernihiv, Kyiv, Mykolaiv, Sumy and Zhytomyr regions, though it has since been repulsed from these. Drone and missile strikes continue across Ukraine.

Leadership: President Vladimir Putin (commander-in-chief), Gen. Sergei Shoigu (defence minister) and Gen. Valery Gerasimov (chief of the general staff).

Structure: Russia's military includes a separate army, air force and navy, as well as Airborne Forces and Strategic Rocket Forces.

History: The Armed Forces of the Russian Federation were founded in 1991 and took over most of the Soviet Army's stock and assets, including bases outside of the Russian Federation. Their command and operational structures have been reformed under Putin, but they retain many inherited Soviet-era military practices. Over the last decade, the Russian armed forces have also undertaken a substantial re-equipment and modernisation programme.

Objectives: Defence of Russia and annexation of Ukrainian territory.

Armed Forces of the Russian Federation

Opponents: Armed Forces of Ukraine.

Affiliates/allies: Armed Forces of Belarus (Russia uses Belarusian bases for launching operations against Ukraine) and private security companies.

Resources/capabilities: Russia has extensive military capabilities and one of the world's largest defence industries. Western sanctions have targeted Russia's military supply chain and, in particular, computer and microchip technology that Russia does not produce domestically. Thus far, these have not significantly impacted Russia's military capabilities, though this may be due to its large weapons stockpiles. NATO officials claim that such sanctions have at least caused issues for Russia in producing new weaponry. Russia's defence budget for 2022 was $68.5bn. In the first half of 2023 alone, leaked Russian government documents show that the country spent more than 5.6 trillion roubles (US$57.4bn) on defence, 12.0% more than allocated, and the Kremlin plans to spend more than US$100bn under its 2023 budget (one-third of public expenditure).[8]

Wagner Group

Strength: 25,000 as of late June 2023, according to its leadership.[9]

Areas of operation: Belarus, Ukraine and formerly Russia's Voronezh and Rostov regions. The group announced on 18 July that it had left its facility in Molkino, Krasnodar Krai, which had long been its primary base. Its headquarters in St Petersburg were also shuttered.

Leadership: Unclear after the group's chief Yevgeny Prigozhin and commander Dmitry Utkin were killed in an aeroplane crash on 23 August 2023.

Structure: The company was established by businessman Prigozhin. Its structure is not well documented.

History: The Wagner Group is a Russian security organisation closely linked to the Kremlin, Russian military intelligence and Russia's Ministry of Defence. It is used by Russia to carry out a range of officially deniable military and intelligence operations and commercial activities abroad, including in the Middle East and Africa. The group was established in 2014, and it and other private military companies proliferated following Russia's involvement in the 2015 war in Syria, where they played an active role. The Wagner Group also operates extensively in Africa, where it is contracted to provide security for governments and is involved in profitable resource extraction. It took a leading role in the siege of Bakhmut in Donetsk region from August 2022–May 2023, which raised its public profile significantly in Russia. However, its status is currently in limbo. Following an abortive mutiny led by Prigozhin on 23–24 June 2023, a major part of the Wagner Group's forces was deployed in Belarus. The death of Prigozhin and other senior Wagner Group figures in August 2023 has deepened uncertainty about the group's future. After the mutiny, Putin acknowledged that the group was directly funded by the Russian state and noted the lack of any Russian legislation allowing such private military groups. At the end of July, Russia advanced legislation enabling regional governors to create military companies, and this could lead to further significant changes in their form and function.

Objectives: In the reporting period, the group has primarily served to provide the Armed Forces of the Russian Federation with a force-multiplication capability and also to recruit prisoners and others seen as undesirable by the formal military leadership, often for use in high-casualty infantry attacks.

Opponents: Armed Forces of Ukraine.

Affiliates/allies: Armed Forces of the Russian Federation. However, the Wagner Group's erstwhile leadership was opposed to the current military leadership of the Russian armed forces and engaged in clashes with the regular Russian army on 23–24 June 2023.

Resources/capabilities: The group has been directly armed and supplied by the Armed Forces of the Russian Federation, and even received military aircraft during the height of its activity in Ukraine.

Other relevant parties

While Wanger is by far Russia's best-known, ostensibly 'private' military company, there are several other smaller such groups (including Shchit, Patriot, Redut and RSB-Group, among others). In the aftermath of the Wagner Group's June 2023 mutiny, and the deaths of Prigozhin and Utkin, it is unclear if some of its operations in Ukraine may be handed over to these groups. The majority of these Russian private military companies began operations around the time of the Russian intervention in Syria in 2015, although some have operated in Africa both before and since then.

Belarus is also involved in the war as a co-belligerent (though not a direct co-combatant). Russian forces have used Belarusian territory for deployments to and attacks on Ukraine. Belarus has provided a range of other services as well, including equipment, logistics and training.

Notes

1   Helene Cooper et al., 'Troop Deaths and Injuries in Ukraine War Near 500,000, U.S. Officials Say', *New York Times*, 18 August 2023; and 'Troop Deaths, Injuries in Ukraine War Nearing 500,000 – NYT Citing US Officials', Reuters, 18 August 2023.

2   UN Office of the High Commissioner for Human Rights, 'Civilian Casualties in Ukraine from 24 February 2022 to 30 June 2023', 7 July 2023; and UN Office of the High Commissioner for Human Rights, 'Ukraine: Civilian Casualty Update', 17 July 2023.

3   UN Human Rights Council (UNHRC), 'Situation Operational Data Portal: Ukraine Refugee Situation', updated 8 August 2023; and USA for UNHRC, 'Ukraine Emergency', 2023.

4   The figure for Western military aid is as of April 2023. Hanna Arhirova, 'With No Peace in Sight, NATO Countries Eye More Ukraine Help', 3 April 2023. See also Paola Tamma, 'EU Plans up to €72 Billion in Aid for Ukraine', Politico, 14 June 2023; and Jonathan Masters and William Merrow, 'How Much Aid Has the U.S. Sent Ukraine? Here Are Six Charts', Council on Foreign Relations, 10 July 2023.

5   See Julian E. Barnes et al., 'U.S. Believes Ukrainians Were Behind an Assassination in Russia', *New York Times*, 5 October 2022; Natasha Bertrand, Zachary Cohen and Kylie Atwood, 'Exclusive: Ukraine Has Cultivated Sabotage Agents Inside Russia and Is Giving Them Drones to Stage Attacks, Sources Say', CNN, 5 June 2023; and Natasha Bertrand and Zachary Cohen, 'US Intelligence Indicates Ukrainians May Have Launched Drone Attack on Kremlin', CNN, 25 May 2023.

6   See 'Russia Says Over 200,000 Drafted into Army Since Putin's Decree', Reuters, 4 October 2022; 'As Putin Signs New Law on Draft, Russia Says Spring Call-up Is Running as Planned', Reuters, 15 April 2023; and Uliana Pavlova, 'Putin Signs Law to Mobilize Russian Citizens Convicted of Serious Crimes', CNN, 5 November 2023.

7   'Russian Defense Minister Calls for Increasing Army to 1.5 Million Troops and Raising Draft Age from 18 to 21', Meduza, 21 December 2022.

8   Reuters, 'Russia Doubles 2023 Defense Spending Plan as War Costs Soar', 4 August 2023.

9   Torreddo, 'Новое сообщение Пригожина. 25000 идут на Москву' [Prigozhin's New Message. 25000 Go to Moscow], YouTube, 23 June 2023.

Europe and Eurasia

NAGORNO-KARABAKH

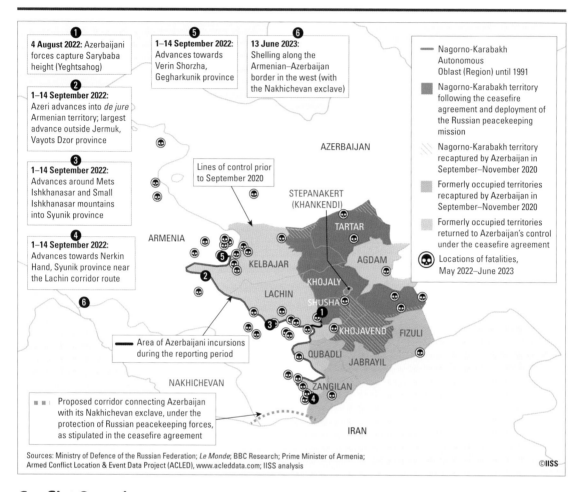

❶ 4 August 2022: Azerbaijani forces capture Sarybaba height (Yeghtsahog)

❷ 1–14 September 2022: Azeri advances into *de jure* Armenian territory; largest advance outside Jermuk, Vayots Dzor province

❸ 1–14 September 2022: Advances around Mets Ishkhanasar and Small Ishkhanasar mountains into Syunik province

❹ 1–14 September 2022: Advances towards Nerkin Hand, Syunik province near the Lachin corridor route

❺ 1–14 September 2022: Advances towards Verin Shorzha, Gegharkunik province

❻ 13 June 2023: Shelling along the Armenian–Azerbaijan border in the west (with the Nakhichevan exclave)

— Nagorno-Karabakh Autonomous Oblast (Region) until 1991

Nagorno-Karabakh territory following the ceasefire agreement and deployment of the Russian peacekeeping mission

Nagorno-Karabakh territory recaptured by Azerbaijan in September–November 2020

Formerly occupied territories recaptured by Azerbaijan in September–November 2020

Formerly occupied territories returned to Azerbaijan's control under the ceasefire agreement

Locations of fatalities, May 2022–June 2023

Lines of control prior to September 2020

AZERBAIJAN

STEPANAKERT (KHANKENDI)

TARTAR

AGDAM

ARMENIA

KELBAJAR

KHOJALY

LACHIN

SHUSHA

KHOJAVEND

FIZULI

QUBADLI

JABRAYIL

—— Area of Azerbaijani incursions during the reporting period

NAKHICHEVAN

ZANGILAN

▪ ▪ ▪ Proposed corridor connecting Azerbaijan with its Nakhichevan exclave, under the protection of Russian peacekeeping forces, as stipulated in the ceasefire agreement

IRAN

Sources: Ministry of Defence of the Russian Federation; *Le Monde*; BBC Research; Prime Minister of Armenia; Armed Conflict Location & Event Data Project (ACLED), www.acleddata.com; IISS analysis

©IISS

Conflict Overview

The conflict over Nagorno-Karabakh has been ongoing since 1988, when the ethnic-Armenian-led regional legislature in the Soviet Union's Nagorno-Karabakh Autonomous Oblast (NKAO) voted to unify with the Armenian Soviet Socialist Republic. In subsequent years, tensions between ethnic Armenians and Azerbaijanis intensified across the two territories amid the Soviet Union's collapse, leading to the First Nagorno-Karabakh War, which ended in 1994 with ethnic-Armenian forces controlling all of the former NKAO as well as a number of other surrounding districts. The lines of control remained broadly static until the Second Nagorno-Karabakh War from September to November 2020, which culminated with a ceasefire that saw ethnic-Armenian forces withdraw from all territory outside the former NKAO and roughly 40% of the former NKAO itself.[1] The ceasefire was mediated by Russia and included a provision for the deployment of Russian forces as peacekeepers into Nagorno-Karabakh and the Lachin corridor (the sole remaining geographical link to Armenia) until 2025. The ceasefire has proven tenuous, with regular clashes along the lines of control and the *de jure* Armenia–Azerbaijan border and with Azerbaijani forces occupying parts of *de jure* Armenian territory over the last two years. There have also been various incidents along Armenia's western border with Azerbaijan's Nakhichevan exclave.

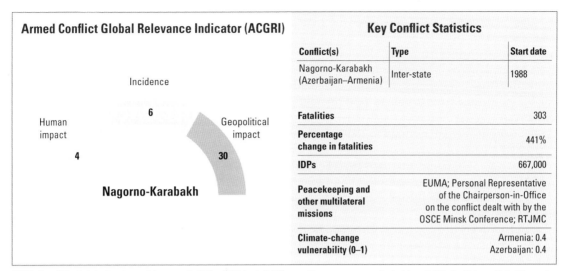

Conflict(s)	Type	Start date
Nagorno-Karabakh (Azerbaijan–Armenia)	Inter-state	1988

Fatalities	303
Percentage change in fatalities	441%
IDPs	667,000
Peacekeeping and other multilateral missions	EUMA; Personal Representative of the Chairperson-in-Office on the conflict dealt with by the OSCE Minsk Conference; RTJMC
Climate-change vulnerability (0–1)	Armenia: 0.4 Azerbaijan: 0.4

ACGRI pillars: IISS calculation based on multiple sources for 2022 and 2023 (scale: 0–100), except for some cases according to data availability. See Notes on Methodology and Data Appendix for all variables and further details on Key Conflict Statistics.

The conflict has a notable geopolitical component, with Turkiye supporting Azerbaijan as a key arms supplier and Russia offering security guarantees for Armenia under the Collective Security Treaty Organisation (CSTO) – although both have sought to avoid overt, direct involvement in the fighting. The Organization for Security and Co-operation in Europe (OSCE) also has a separate process that is meant to bring together the European Union, United States and Russia. However, it was already ineffective before Russia's 2022 full-scale invasion of Ukraine and has since all but collapsed, though the parties remain involved in separate diplomatic channels with Armenia and Azerbaijan.

Conflict Update

In the reporting period, the conflict was marked by clashes along the *de jure* border between Azerbaijan and Armenia as well as confrontations along the lines of control around the ethnic-Armenian-controlled portion of the Nagorno-Karabakh territory. The Armenian forces in Nagorno-Karabakh are distinct from Armenia's military, although the government of Azerbaijan does not recognise this. There were deadly clashes between the Azerbaijani military and both the Armenian military and the armed forces of Nagorno-Karabakh, with two brief, but significant, primary periods of conflict.

Firstly, on 3–4 August 2022, clashes along the lines of control in Nagorno-Karabakh and the Lachin corridor resulted in Azerbaijani forces capturing the Sarybaba height (Yeghtsahogh in Armenian) north of the Lachin corridor. The corridor is the key overland route connecting ethnic-Armenian-inhabited areas of Nagorno-Karabakh with Armenia and is supposed to be secured by Russian observers as part of the November 2020 ceasefire agreement.

Secondly, on 13–14 September 2022, Azerbaijani forces launched an attack across the Armenia–Azerbaijan border, which included artillery and drone strikes. The two sides subsequently resumed talks, but Azerbaijan has since retained control of several strategic positions in Armenia's Gegharkunik, Vayots Dzor and Syunik provinces. According to Armenia, the fighting left Azerbaijan with control of approximately 140 square kilometres of its territory.[2] There have continued to be clashes since the attack, including claims by the ethnic-Armenian authorities in Nagorno-Karabakh of shelling by Azerbaijani forces and artillery exchanges on the Armenia–Azerbaijan border, the former most recently on 5 July 2023 and the latter on 11 May 2023. The deadliest reported incident occurred on 27–28 June: Azerbaijan's military claimed that one of its soldiers was shot, and Armenian authorities in Nagorno-Karabakh subsequently claimed that four of its soldiers were killed by shelling.[3]

The September 2022 incursions arguably had the most significant geopolitical impact as thereafter Armenian Prime Minister Nikol Pashinyan triggered mutual-defence clauses under the Russian-dominated CSTO. Although the Kremlin called for a halt to hostilities, the Armenian request was effectively ignored, and Armenian officials later admitted that they had discussed potentially withdrawing from the bloc in response. Although Russian peacekeepers remained in place during the reporting period, Russia's inaction emboldened Baku as the war in Ukraine absorbed Russia's military capabilities and weakened its geostrategic clout in the region. Furthermore, though Russian-Armenian businessman Ruben Vardanyan, who is seen as close to the Kremlin, was installed as state minister of Nagorno-Karabakh self-declared authorities in November 2022, Baku insisted on his removal and he was ousted in February 2023. Armenia's diplomatic approach has increasingly drifted away from Russia and towards the EU and US, and Yerevan has also sought to improve relations with Turkiye, a key supplier of arms to Azerbaijan. On 27 December 2022, the Armenian government invited the EU to establish a civilian monitoring mission. The EU Mission in Armenia (EUMA) formally began on 20 February 2023.[4]

These sporadic clashes and the shifting influence of regional power have affected diplomatic discussions between Armenia and Azerbaijan, but Armenian officials have nevertheless said, as recently as 4 June 2023, that they could envisage a settlement by the end of the year. Two months prior, Pashinyan had made one of the most significant concessions to date, stating that he could accept Azerbaijan retaining formal sovereignty over all of Nagorno-Karabakh. However, Baku has refused to engage in direct negotiations with the ethnic-Armenian authorities in the region. A de facto blockade of Nagorno-Karabakh has been in place since 12 December 2022, when alleged activists began obstructing the corridor. Although the government of Azerbaijan denied that it was involved, it established new positions in March 2023 which were seen as enforcing the blockade. On 11 July, Azerbaijan's State Border Service began barring International Committee of the Red Cross vehicles, which had been the only vehicles allowed to pass the blockade for the preceding seven months. The de facto blockade amid ongoing bilateral talks with Azerbaijan has prompted tensions between the ethnic-Armenian authorities in Nagorno-Karabakh and Pashinyan's government. It has also incited protests within Armenia itself, and further moves towards a settlement could prove destabilising for the country.

Conflict Parties

Armenian armed forces

Strength: 42,900 active military personnel, 4,300 active gendarmerie and paramilitary personnel, and an additional 210,000 reservists, many of whom have recent combat experience from the 2020 Second Nagorno-Karabakh War. Military service is mandatory for Armenian men aged 18–27 and lasts 24 months.

Areas of operation: Armenia, mainly deployed along the international border with Azerbaijan.

Leadership: Prime Minister Nikol Pashinyan (commander-in-chief), Suren Papikyan (defence minister) and Edvard Asryan (chief of the general staff).

Structure: Consists of four army corps as well as separate air and air-defence forces.

History: Established in 1991 following the Soviet Union's collapse and subsequently amalgamated with former Soviet and volunteer paramilitary forces which had participated in the First Nagorno-Karabakh War.

Objectives: Defence of Armenia and deterrence in relation to Nagorno-Karabakh.

Opponents: Azerbaijani armed forces.

Affiliates/allies: Coordinates with the Nagorno-Karabakh Defence Army (NKDA). The alliance with Russia through the CSTO is strained, but Moscow retains a base that houses around 2,500 soldiers in Gyumri in northern Armenia, with another 500 personnel at an air base near Yerevan.[5] Russia is believed to have drawn down forces in Gyumri and rotated out experienced officers since its full-scale invasion of Ukraine began in February 2022.

Resources/capabilities: Armenia has announced a US$1.2 billion defence budget for 2023, a 53.6% increase from 2022 (US$781 million). Significant amounts of Soviet-era military equipment are still in use. While Russia has historically been Armenia's primary source of new military equipment, no major sales have been announced over the last year. Instead, Yerevan reportedly reached an agreement with India in late 2022 for the supply of new artillery and anti-tank systems.[6]

Azerbaijani armed forces

Strength: 64,050 active military personnel, 15,000 active gendarmerie and paramilitary personnel, and 300,000 reservists, with conscription mandatory for men aged 18–35. Service is 18 months for conscripts, though a 12-month exception is possible for university graduates.

Areas of operation: Across Azerbaijan, including along the lines of control separating it from areas of Nagorno-Karabakh controlled by ethnic-Armenian forces and in the western exclave of Nakhichevan. Since 2021, Armenian officials have claimed that the Azerbaijani armed forces have also occupied territory within *de jure* Armenia.[7]

Leadership: President Ilham Aliyev (commander-in-chief), Col.-Gen. Zakir Hasanov (defence minister) and Col.-Gen. Karim Valiyev (chief of the general staff).

Structure: Comprises three services: the army, air force and navy, the latter of which operates in the Caspian Sea. The army includes four corps, with a separate Combined Arms Army based in the Nakhichevan exclave.

History: The Azerbaijani military was initially created in 1991 following the collapse of the Soviet Union but had a difficult beginning amid political infighting and some Soviet-era forces aligning with ethnic-Armenian forces. It was significantly reconstituted following the First Nagorno-Karabakh War and has been a priority for government investment ever since.

Objectives: Retaking Nagorno-Karabakh and the defence of Azerbaijan.

Opponents: NKDA and Armenian armed forces.

Affiliates/allies: Turkiye.

Resources/capabilities: Azerbaijan budgeted US$3.1bn for national security and defence in 2023 (compared to US$2.6 in 2022). Its annual defence spending significantly exceeds that of Armenia. Azerbaijan has established supply relationships with Israel, Pakistan, Russia and Turkiye. Furthermore, in June 2023, it announced a landmark deal to purchase Italian-manufactured military transport aircraft, despite a long-standing request from the OSCE that European countries refrain from arms sales to parties in the conflict.

Nagorno-Karabakh Defence Army (NKDA)

Strength: Estimated 12,000 active-duty personnel, though the authorities of the unrecognised Nagorno-Karabakh Republic do not formally disclose personnel figures. Armenian officials have estimated as many as 25,000–30,000 when including reserves.[8]

Areas of operation: Personnel are stationed along the lines of control and in major population centres, and they patrol strategic locations. The NKDA's operational area has been significantly curtailed since the Second Nagorno-Karabakh War.

Leadership: Arayik Harutyunyan, president of Artsakh (Nagorno-Karabakh) (commander-in-chief), and Lt-Gen. Kamo Vardanyan (defence minister).

Structure: Single branch (ground forces), supported by volunteers and informal fighters.

History: Established in 1992 following the region's unrecognised declaration of independence. Operational control was in part separated from Armenia following the 2020 Second Nagorno-Karabakh War.

Objectives: Self-defence.

Opponents: Azerbaijani armed forces.

Affiliates/allies: Armenian armed forces.

Resources/capabilities: Legacy stock, much of which was sourced from Armenia until 2020, in addition to Soviet-era stock. The provision of new weaponry and ammunition remains unclear but is understood to be highly restricted since the Second Nagorno-Karabakh War.

Armed Forces of the Russian Federation

Strength: 1,960 peacekeepers.[9] The force is restricted to a five-year term, which is due to end in November 2025 and will be renewed automatically unless either Azerbaijan or Armenia demands the force's withdrawal. Russia also has roughly 3,000 military personnel at its leased bases in Gyumri and Erebuni in Armenia.

Areas of operation: Most Russian peacekeepers are deployed along the Lachin corridor and in the eastern and southern areas of Nagorno-Karabakh not recaptured by Azerbaijan in 2020. Russia maintains a military presence including several bases in Armenia, and it also operates several outposts in southern Armenia near the border with Azerbaijan.

Leadership: President Vladimir Putin (commander-in-chief), Gen. Sergei Shoigu (defence minister), Gen. Valery Gerasimov (chief of the general staff), Col.-Gen. Alexsander Lentsov (Nagorno-Karabakh peacekeeping contingent) and Col. Konstantin Gaponenko (102nd Military Base).

Structure: Most peacekeeping units currently stationed in Nagorno-Karabakh belong to the 15th Motor Rifle Brigade of the Central Military District (Russian Ground Forces). Russia's leased Armenian base in Gyumri (the 102nd Military Base) is formally assigned to Russia's Southern Military District and is also the operational parent of the air base at Erebuni outside Yerevan.

History: Russia has formally leased the 102nd Military Base since 1995, and the separate peacekeeping contingent in Nagorno-Karabakh was established as part of the November 2020 ceasefire.

Objectives: Ceasefire monitoring in Nagorno-Karabakh for a minimum of five years, subject to renewal. The 2020 ceasefire agreement also instructs Federal Security Service border guards to guarantee transport links between Azerbaijan and its Nakhichevan exclave, although such transport has not begun.

Europe and Eurasia

Armed Forces of the Russian Federation

Opponents: N/A.

Affiliates/allies: Russia's CSTO obligations to Armenia do not extend to Nagorno-Karabakh and the Kremlin has ignored Armenian requests for assistance and support with regard to Azerbaijani occupation of *de jure* Armenian territory. The force does enable Russia to exert influence on the conflict participants, but this is seen as waning.

Resources/capabilities: Russian peacekeepers in Nagorno-Karabakh have light weapons and around 90 medium and light armoured vehicles at their disposal. At Gyumri, the 102nd Military Base hosts a motor-rifle brigade-equivalent, along with mobile air-defence systems. The air base at Erebuni comprises a single fixed-wing squadron with MiG-29 *Fulcrum* fighter aircraft, as well as a mixed helicopter squadron with Ka-52, Mi-24 and Mi-8 variants. Some of the latter are forward deployed to Stepanakert (Khankendi) with the peacekeeping contingent.[10]

Nagorno-Karabakh Country Profile – October 2023 Addendum

The conflict in Nagorno-Karabakh erupted into a third full-blown war on 19 September 2023. It was swiftly concluded, with the government of Azerbaijan achieving a decisive victory. The ethnic Armenian government in Nagorno-Karabakh sued for peace a day later, subsequently agreeing to disband its army immediately and its institutions by the end of the year.[11]

The conflict began after Azerbaijan claimed that two highway department employees and four soldiers had been killed in two mine incidents along the lines of control in Nagorno-Karabakh and launched an 'anti-terrorist operation'.[12] Although tensions had been building in the preceding weeks, the launch of a major attack came as US and European officials were continuing efforts to mediate talks between Azerbaijan and the government of Armenia. The president of the self-declared Nagorno-Karabakh Republic had resigned at the end of August as part of an effort to reach a settlement with the central government in Baku, as Nagorno-Karabakh had been under siege for nine months.[13]

Azerbaijani forces far outnumbered those of the NKDA. Despite the swift conclusion to the fighting, both sides reported significant casualties. Baku stated that 192 of its soldiers were killed, while officials from the Nagorno-Karabakh Republic announced that at least 190 soldiers were killed and more than 400 wounded.[14] The total civilian death toll remains unknown, and there have been unconfirmed reports that civilians were intentionally targeted. Azerbaijan's victory triggered a mass exodus of the ethnic Armenian population, with more than 100,000 of Nagorno-Karabakh's estimated 120,000 residents fleeing for Armenia by the end of September.[15] The deadliest single incident occurred during the exodus when an estimated 170 civilians were killed after an explosion at a petrol station outside Stepanakert (Khankendi) on 25 September.[16]

The ramifications of the conflict will be significant not only for the future of Nagorno-Karabakh and wider Azerbaijan but also for relations between Azerbaijan and Armenia. The war's impact on Armenia risks triggering political instability in the country. While Armenia refrained from direct involvement in the war – recognising that such action would likely have been futile following its defeat in the Second Nagorno-Karabakh War in 2020 – the Azerbaijani armed forces continue to occupy positions within Armenia seized in the intervening years. On 30 September 2023, Azerbaijan reported that one of its soldiers had been killed by Armenian sniper fire near the border with Armenia's Syunik province, though Yerevan denied this.[17] Tensions over the area will remain high given Baku's demand for a corridor to its Nakhichevan exclave west of Armenia.

Notes

1   See Common Space, 'Document: Full Text of the Agreement Between the Leaders of Russia, Armenia and Azerbaijan', 10 November 2020.

2   Ministry of Foreign Affairs of the Republic of Armenia, 'Minister of Foreign Affairs Ararat Mirzoyan's Remarks at the 29th OSCE Ministerial Council', 1 December 2022.

3   RFE/RL's Armenian Service, 'Azerbaijan, Armenia Exchange Deadly Fire in Nagorno-Karabakh as Peace Talks Get Under Way', Radio Free Europe/Radio Liberty, 28 June 2023.

4   See Press and Information Team of EUMA, 'EU Mission in Armenia (EUMA)', EU External Action, 28 February 2023.

5   See Reuters Staff, 'Armenia Seeks Bigger Russian Military Presence on Its Territory', Reuters, 22 February 2021.

6   Manu Pubby, 'Arming Armenia: India to Export Missiles, Rockets and Ammunition', *Economic Times*, 6 October 2022; and Vakkas Dagantekin, 'Armenia Reportedly Buys Weapons from India Worth $245M', Anadolu Agency, 30 September 2022.

7   See Ministry of Foreign Affairs of the Republic of Armenia, 'Minister of Foreign Affairs Ararat Mirzoyan's Remarks at the 29th OSCE Ministerial Council'.

8   'Армия обороны Арцаха будет выступать гарантом суверенитета Арцаха, а по переговорам формируется новая повестка – Пашинян' [Pashinyan: The National Defence Army of Artsakh Will Act as a Guarantor of the Sovereignty of Artsakh, and a New Agenda Is Being Formed as a Result of Negotiations], ARKA News Agency, 16 November 2020.

9   'Russia Sends Nearly 2,000 Peacekeepers to Nagorno-Karabakh, Defense Ministry Says', TASS, 10 November 2020. The International Crisis Group subsequently reported a total of 'some 4,000 Russian soldiers and emergency services staff'. See International Crisis Group, 'Post-war Prospects for Nagorno-Karabakh', Report no. 264, 9 June 2021, p. i.

10   'Вопрос выживания: 25 лет назад Россия создала военную базу в Армении' [A Question of Endurance: Russia Established Its Military Base in Armenia 25 Years Ago], Gazeta.ru, 16 March 2020.

11   Pjotr Sauer, 'Nagorno-Karabakh's Breakaway Government Says It Will Dissolve Itself', *Guardian*, 28 September 2023.

12   Associated Press, 'Azerbaijan Announces an "Anti-Terrorist Operation" Targeting Armenian Positions in Nagorno-Karabakh', VOA, 19 September 2023.

13   Author's sources.

14   Avet Demourian, 'Azerbaijan Arrests the Former Head of Separatist Government After Recapturing Nagorno-Karabakh', AP News, 27 September 2023.

15   George Wright, 'Nagorno-Karabakh: Armenia Says 100,000 Refugees Flee Region', BBC News, 30 September 2023.

16   Lenta, 'Ostanki pogibshix pri vzryve v Nagornom Karabakhe vyevezut v Armeniyu' [The Bodies of Those Killed in the Explosion in Nagorno-Karabakh Are Taken to Armenia], 29 September 2023.

17   Agence France-Presse, 'Azerbaijan Says Soldier Killed by Sniper on Armenian Border', Barron's, 30 September 2023.

3 Middle East and North Africa

A Palestinian youth holds a flag next to burning tyres during a protest by the border fence with Israel east of Gaza, 3 July 2023

Overview

The reporting period continued to be marked by stalemates in most conflicts across the region with, in some cases, a grudging acceptance of the status quo. This was most notably the case in Syria and Yemen – historically two of the region's most violent conflicts and ones of greatest humanitarian concern (see Figure 1). The Arab League welcomed back Syrian President Bashar al-Assad to its annual summit in May 2023, more than a decade after it expelled the country due to Assad's failure to end brutal government crackdowns on pro-democracy protesters during the early days of the conflict there. Turkiye's President Recep Tayyip Erdoğan also broached normalising relations with Assad. In Yemen, Saudi Arabia entered into direct negotiations with the Houthis, putting the kingdom on a

path that will likely result in recognition of Houthi rule over Sanaa and north Yemen and the eventual partition of the country.

In Syria and Yemen, the international community is beginning to recognise what has long been obvious to most observers: Assad and the Houthis are not going to be militarily defeated by the current configuration of forces opposing them and are unwilling to give away at the bargaining table what they have won on the battlefield. As a result – and despite Western pressure and pleas – Syria's neighbours have reached a grudging acceptance that Assad is not going anywhere. In turn, this realisation has presented them with a stark choice: either recognise and re-establish relations with Syria and Assad – without any guarantee of significant reciprocation

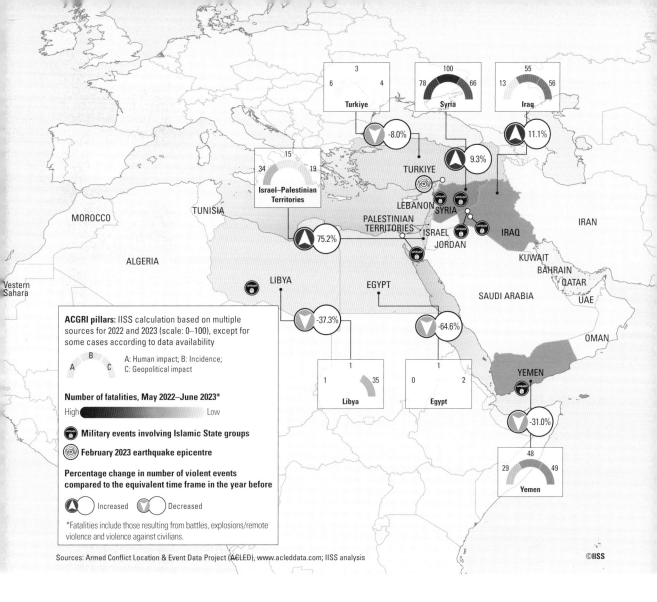

ACGRI pillars: IISS calculation based on multiple sources for 2022 and 2023 (scale: 0–100), except for some cases according to data availability

A: Human impact; B: Incidence;
C: Geopolitical impact

Number of fatalities, May 2022–June 2023*

High ————————— Low

⊘ Military events involving Islamic State groups

◎ February 2023 earthquake epicentre

Percentage change in number of violent events compared to the equivalent time frame in the year before

▲ Increased   ▼ Decreased

*Fatalities include those resulting from battles, explosions/remote violence and violence against civilians.

Sources: Armed Conflict Location & Event Data Project (ACLED), www.acleddata.com; IISS analysis   ©IISS

– or continue to freeze out his regime as part of a policy that has not produced the intended results despite more than a decade of trying.

Assad visited the United Arab Emirates (UAE) in March 2022, his first trip to an Arab state since the fighting in Syria began in 2011. He followed it up with trips to Oman in February 2023 and then back to the UAE in March, before visiting Saudi Arabia for the May Arab League summit, where he addressed his fellow leaders. Muhammad bin Salman, the crown prince of Saudi Arabia, said he hoped Syria's 'return to the Arab League leads to the end of its crisis'.[1]

In Yemen, following a Chinese-brokered agreement between Saudi Arabia and Iran to restore diplomatic relations between the two countries, a Saudi delegation flew to Sanaa to begin negotiations on a Saudi withdrawal and an end to the war. Notably, representatives of the Presidential Leadership Council (PLC), Yemen's broad though fractious domestic anti-Houthi coalition, did not participate in the talks. It appears that – eager to withdraw – Riyadh is willing to leave the country even if it risks reigniting the civil war there.

As part of the Chinese-brokered deal, Iran pledged to end weapons shipments to the Houthis and pressure the group not to carry out cross-border missile attacks into Saudi Arabia. The latter now appears willing to exit the country, leaving the Houthis in control of Sanaa and much of northern Yemen. While a Saudi exit would likely end the international portion of the war, it is unclear if it would also end Yemen's civil war. The Houthis appear eager to take oil and gas fields in Marib and Shabwa, which would require more offensives post-Saudi withdrawal. At the same time, the anti-Houthi coalition is likely to devolve into infighting as the various groups in the PLC attempt to position themselves to rule the non-Houthi south.

Across the rest of the region, fighting either remained static or decreased. Libya remains in a political deadlock with the country divided between competing governments: the Government of National Unity (GNU) based in Tripoli, and the Government of National Stability centred on Benghazi and Sirte. The conflict between Turkiye and the Kurdistan Workers' Party (PKK) saw frequent clashes, although no significant loss of territory. Iraq and Egypt both saw a decrease in fighting, although northern Iraq witnessed a 30% spike in political violence associated with increased Turkish operations against the PKK.[2]

As in the previous year, only the Israeli–Palestinian conflict witnessed a marked escalation in tensions and fighting during the reporting period. Palestinian lone-wolf attacks increased, as well as Israeli settlers' violence, which increased for the sixth consecutive year in 2022, with fighting taking place primarily in the West Bank.[3] 2022 witnessed the worst violence in the West Bank since 2005, while the summer of 2023 was also extremely violent. Much of the violence in 2023 was exacerbated by the Israeli government led by Prime Minister Benjamin Netanyahu, which continued settlement building and its attempts to strengthen the executive branch at the expense of the judiciary. The government includes two parties that oppose Palestinian statehood (Religious Zionism and Jewish Power) and continues to face domestic protests for its attempts to assert the authority of Israel's high court.

Conflict Drivers

Political and institutional

Institutional fragility

Weak institutions have historically plagued the Middle East. But perhaps at no other point in recent history have regional institutions been as brittle as they have been over the past two decades. This fragility has, in turn, exacerbated and extended ongoing conflicts in the region.

In Yemen, for example, then-president Abd Rabbo Mansour Hadi's rash decision in 2016 to move Yemen's central bank from Sanaa, where it was under Houthi control, to Aden effectively split the bank into two competing institutions and laid the groundwork for two separate economies within Yemen. More than the outcome of any battle, it is this division that will likely result in the eventual partition of Yemen.

Similarly, in Libya, institutions that were hollowed out under the regime of Muammar Gadhafi fractured and fragmented after his death in 2011 and the fighting that followed. These institutions, particularly those controlling resources such as oil, have become political prizes that actors use to penalise and punish their enemies. Even Israel, where institutions have been traditionally viewed as fairly sound, has struggled to contain popular protests over the Netanyahu government's attempts to exert more authority over the judiciary.

Socio-economic

Sectarian divisions

Ethnic and sectarian tensions remain significant drivers of regional conflicts and instability. In Iraq, sectarian issues continue to exacerbate insecurity within the country. This dynamic has been aggravated by the rising tensions within Iraq's Shia community, particularly between the followers of Muqtada al-Sadr, who withdrew from parliament in June 2022, and members of the Shi'ite Coordination Framework (SCF), which is backed by Iran and now controls the parliament and, to a certain extent, the judiciary. In August 2022, Sadr's followers breached the Green Zone and clashed with SCF elements; more than 30 people were killed in the fighting.[4]

In Syria and Yemen, Shia minorities – Alawis in the former and Zaydis in the latter – continue to fight against their more numerous Sunni neighbours. In both countries, sectarian identity largely determines one's politics. The conflict between Turkiye and the Kurds, and that between the Israelis and the Palestinians, remain at heart ethnic conflicts that have proven largely intractable for decades.

Food insecurity

Historically, food insecurity has been a structural driver of conflict in the region, contributing to the Syrian civil war, for example. More recently, food crisis in Libya was at least partly responsible for Libyan National Army leader Field Marshall Khalifa Haftar's July 2022 decision to block the country's oilfields and terminals. Similarly, in Yemen, many families are in a precarious position due to inflation and the fact that the national currency has lost much of its value since the start of the conflict. In the north, the Houthis have used the situation to their advantage, weaponising food aid by providing it to the families that contribute fighters to their cause and withholding it from those whose men do not fight.[5] To a much greater extent than their rivals, the Houthis have used food insecurity as leverage to recruit child soldiers,[6] while other increasingly desperate families sell off their young daughters to wealthy men in the Gulf as a way of trying to raise money.

Security and military
Non-state armed groups
Armed groups act as conflict drivers; this is unsurprising given the number and nature of conflicts in the region. It is most obviously the case in Yemen, where the number of armed groups has increased as the conflict has persisted. What started as a bifurcated conflict between then-president Hadi and the Houthis has morphed into a multi-sided affair. In 2017, after Hadi dismissed several government officials due to concerns they were becoming too popular, those same officials formed the Southern Transitional Council – with the stated goal of establishing an independent southern Yemen. The UAE, which withdrew its forces from Yemen in 2019, has offset its drawdown by funding, arming and training various armed groups throughout southern Yemen; some of these groups are aligned with one another, while others are not.

In Syria, infighting between jihadist groups, Kurdish forces and various other actors initially weakened the resistance to Assad's forces. Meanwhile, the SCF's growing control over Iraq's military and security agencies could spark future clashes – both with the Sadrists and with local Sunnis, who are wary of Iran's mounting influence in the country. In the Palestinian Territories, the ongoing dispute between Fatah and Hamas remains a potential flashpoint.

Geopolitical
Great-power competition
The growing and increasingly bellicose competition between the United States and China together with Russia's war on Ukraine have contributed to current conflict trajectories in the region. The impact is most evident in Syria, where Russia has moved to consolidate its forces and taken control of Wagner Group fighters in the country following the attempted mutiny in June 2023 by Yevgeny Prigozhin, then leader of the Russian private military company.[7] It is unclear what this will mean for Russian forces in Syria, or whether President Vladimir Putin will be able to absorb Wagner forces into the Russian military.

China is increasingly active on the diplomatic and economic fronts, leveraging development promises and economic might into political capital. In March 2023, China announced that it had brokered a deal between Saudi Arabia and Iran to restore diplomatic relations between the two countries, which many saw as a first step towards ending the war in Yemen. Reducing the tensions between Saudi Arabia and Iran may also help to stabilise the conflict in Syria. Beijing appears to want to offer countries in the region an alternative to the US; in doing so, President Xi Jinping believes that China will be in a stronger position vis-à-vis the US. China is particularly concerned with protecting its oil supplies from the Middle East.

Conflict Parties

Coalitions and third-party interventions
Perhaps the most important security coalition in the Middle East is the unacknowledged and unofficial coalition of Iran-backed groups. From Syria and Yemen to Iraq and the Palestinian Territories, Iran-backed actors have played a significant role in many of the region's wars. Moreover, at least currently, many of these groups appear to be winning. Over the past several years – and during some of the most intense periods of fighting – these groups have demonstrated a surprising degree of ideological unity. However, it is unclear if this unity of purpose will endure as the region's conflicts transition from a period of active fighting to one of consolidation.

In Yemen, the Houthis, who have diplomatic relations with only Iran and Syria and are heavily dependent on Iranian support, appear poised to maintain control over northern Yemen if not seize more territory in Marib and other oil- and gas-producing provinces. In Iraq, Iran-backed groups outmanoeuvred

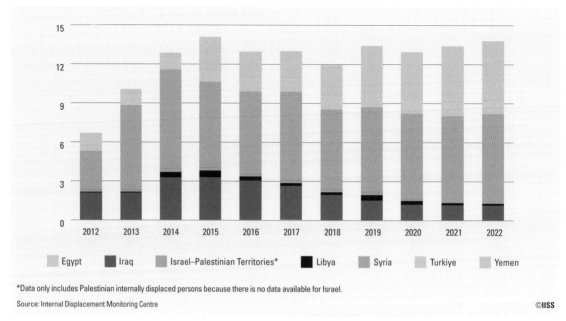

*Data only includes Palestinian internally displaced persons because there is no data available for Israel.

Source: Internal Displacement Monitoring Centre   ©IISS

Figure 1: Number (total) of internally displaced persons (by conflict and violence), in millions

their main Shia rival, Sadr, as well as Sunni groups and now control much of the government. The situation is similar in Syria, where Iran's support for Assad proved important in the early days of the war.

Iran's regional rival, Saudi Arabia, has also engaged in multiple conflicts in the region, albeit with much less success. Where Tehran utilised proxies and non-state actors beholden to Iran, Riyadh worked to cobble together international coalitions. The most developed of these was the Saudi-led coalition of ten countries that intervened in Yemen in March 2015. However, within a few years, many countries had withdrawn from the coalition, eventually leaving only Saudi Arabia and the UAE, which pursued vastly different goals in Yemen. Saudi Arabia and the UAE now appear suspicious and uncertain of each other's motives and interests throughout the region.

Non-state armed groups

Al-Qaeda franchises, such as al-Qaeda in the Arabian Peninsula (AQAP) in Yemen, and Islamic State (ISIS)-affiliated groups in Egypt, Iraq and Syria, continue to conduct low-level insurgencies. However, no terrorist group in the region currently appears capable of controlling and administering territory as they did a decade ago in Iraq, Syria and Yemen.

In Yemen, AQAP remains active and carries out small-scale attacks, mostly in the south. In Syria, Hayat Tahrir al-Sham, the main jihadist group in Idlib, spent much of the reporting period fighting the remnants of ISIS and other rival jihadist groups.[8] The US continued to target ISIS leadership in Iraq and Syria, killing one of the group's senior figures in April 2023. It also carried out a drone strike in May that the US initially reported had killed a senior al-Qaeda leader.[9]

Also in Syria, the PKK-linked Syrian Democratic Forces (SDF) continued to face Turkish pressure and airstrikes. President Erdoğan, who won a third term in May, increased pressure on the PKK by holding out the prospect of normalising relations with Assad, a development he hoped might help erode Kurdish autonomy in northern Syria.

Regional and International Dimensions

Although the majority of the region's conflicts have local roots and are primarily fought by local actors, many have international implications. For instance, the Turkiye–PKK conflict is intimately tied to the war in Syria, as well as NATO expansion, which is in turn linked to Russia's war on Ukraine.

In November and December 2022, following a bombing in Istanbul that Turkiye blamed on the PKK, Erdoğan ordered weeks of airstrikes against Kurdish positions in northern Syria, killing more than 100 fighters. The SDF initially responded by ceasing all joint anti-ISIS operations with the US, although it later backtracked.[10] The SDF also administers the ISIS prison camp at al-Hol, which holds an estimated 12,000 ISIS prisoners and their families, including Europeans and foreign nationals.[11] Concurrently, Erdoğan is also seeking to repatriate the estimated 3.6 million Syrian refugees in Turkiye.[12]

Ankara has similarly tied Turkiye's conflict with the PKK to broader international issues, particularly Finland's and Sweden's efforts to join NATO in the wake of Russia's invasion of Ukraine. Throughout 2022, Turkiye warned Finland several times that it needed to take 'concrete steps' to curb the PKK's activities on its soil before Ankara would agree to support its application for NATO membership.[13] In late March 2023, Turkiye's parliament eventually voted to approve Finland's application, although Erdoğan has reiterated that Sweden must do more before Turkiye can agree to it joining the Alliance.[14]

China is also active in the region – increasingly so on the diplomatic front. The Chinese-brokered deal between Saudi Arabia and Iran to restore their relations will play an important role in de-escalating the conflict in Yemen. Meanwhile, Riyadh has made clear to Washington that establishing diplomatic relations with Israel would require US support for a Saudi Arabian nuclear programme, among other conditions.[15] While it is unlikely that the US would agree to these terms – Israel has stated that it would not allow the country to pursue a nuclear programme, while US President Joe Biden has his own baggage with Muhammad bin Salman – if such a deal were to materialise, it would have a significant impact on the Israeli–Palestinian conflict, as Saudi Arabia has long stated that it would not sign a peace deal with Israel until there is a Palestinian state. Should Saudi Arabia normalise relations with Israel prior to the formation of a recognised Palestinian state, it could result in an intensified Israeli settlement policy and lessen international pressure on Israel to deal with the Palestinians – particularly given that, post-Abraham Accords, Israel already has less incentive to strike a deal.

The United Nations has appointed special envoys (or representatives) for three of the region's conflicts – Yemen, Syria and Libya – with relatively little success. Sanctions also appear to have had minimal impact on the fighting on the ground. In Yemen, the asset freeze and travel ban have done little to discourage the Houthis – the only conflict party the UN Security Council has sanctioned – as they largely do not travel abroad or have assets outside Yemen. The UN has sanctioned only one person in Libya since 2018, while in Syria most of the sanctions are levied by the US or European countries rather than the UN, where Russia has often exercised its veto in defence of the Assad regime.

Outlook

Prospects for peace

The coming year is likely to see a further solidification of the status quo. In many of the region's conflicts, the result is likely to be less fighting but not necessarily peace. In Syria, Assad's return to the Arab League signalled the region's acceptance that he will remain president for the foreseeable future. Although Assad is unlikely to recover all of the territory that Syria held before the 2011 uprising, his regime may succeed in retaking some areas.

Libya is likely to remain a divided country with competing governments. Neither side has the forces, money or munitions to pressure the other to submit. Only in Yemen is there an opportunity for a true breakthrough. However, a peace deal between the Houthis and Riyadh, should it materialise, might end one part of the conflict – Saudi Arabia's involvement – while sparking renewed fighting in Yemen's civil war.

Escalation potential and regional spillovers

A Saudi withdrawal from Yemen and its recognition of the Houthis in the north would likely spark a two-front conflict on the ground. Firstly, the Houthis would push deeper into Marib and potentially even Shabwa and Hadramawt, although a previous Houthi incursion into Shabwa elicited a response from the UAE. Secondly, there would likely be infighting within the anti-Houthi alliance, as each element struggles to seize and hold as much territory as possible. In particular, the Southern Transitional Council, which continues to advocate for an independent southern state, may unilaterally declare independence, pushing out its rivals within the PLC while attempting to secure a unilateral deal with the Houthis.

The Israeli–Palestinian conflict and the Turkiye–PKK conflict are both ripe for escalation. In Israel, Netanyahu's narrow coalition includes anti-Palestinian groups that may continue to urge him to expand settlement-building projects. As Netanyahu's overall popularity decreases, he will likely lean more heavily on his right-wing allies. In Turkiye, Erdoğan's re-election as president and the concessions he has received from Sweden and Finland may embolden him to continue to use Turkish forces against Kurdish forces operating in Syria.

Strategic implications and global influences

China's involvement in brokering the restoration of diplomatic relations between Saudi Arabia and Iran was possibly the most important strategic event of early 2023. It remains to be seen whether China can leverage this diplomatic breakthrough to secure more advantages for itself as it pushes back against US competition. For instance, Beijing has long been pushing Riyadh to decouple from the US dollar and sell oil in yuan. China also has the highest number of outbound tourists in the world, and tourism is a key pillar of Muhammad bin Salman's economic plan for the kingdom.[16]

Whether China will be able to use its economic muscle within the Middle East to advance its interests – while blunting those of the US – will be a key question for late 2023 and early 2024. The Middle East will likely become an arena of intensified US–China competition in the years ahead, with significant consequences for the region's conflicts.

It is likely that the grind of Russia's war in Ukraine and the brief attempted mutiny in June by the late head of the Wagner Group will slowly erode Russia's footprint in the region, as it retracts to solidify support at home.

REGIONAL KEY EVENTS

POLITICAL EVENTS

 IRAQ

12 June 2022

Sadr and the Sadrist bloc withdraw from parliament; Sadr later announces his resignation from politics.

 LIBYA

12 July

The Tripoli-based GNU replaces the chief of the National Oil Corporation, Mustafa Sanalla, with Farhat Bengdara, in a political struggle over the oil sector.

MILITARY/VIOLENT EVENTS

YEMEN

July and August 2022

Two anti-Houthi factions – the Southern Transitional Council and al-Islah – clash in Shabwa province.

EGYPT

22 August

Aided by tribal fighters, Egyptian forces make gains against Sinai Province in Gilbana, near the Suez Canal.

 IRAQ

29 August

Sadr's followers clash with other Iran-affiliated Shia groups in Baghdad.

SYRIA

`19 October`

Russia withdraws ground troops and air-defence systems from Syria, a development that further bolsters Israel's position in the region.

 TURKIYE

`13 November`

A bomb explodes in Istanbul, killing eight people; Ankara blames the PKK.

 ISRAEL–PALESTINIAN TERRITORIES

`2–4 December`

After the shooting of Ammar Mufleh by an Israeli soldier on 2 December, Israel bombs Hamas targets in the Gaza Strip, while Hamas fires rockets into Israel.

 **ISRAEL–PALESTINIAN TERRITORIES**

`2 November`

Netanyahu wins the election to become Israel's prime minister.

 **SAUDI ARABIA, IRAN**

`7–10 December`

Xi Jinping visits Saudi Arabia; the trip prepares the ground for a diplomatic breakthrough between Saudi Arabia and Iran.

 YEMEN

`17 January 2023`

The Houthis resume talks with the Yemeni and Saudi governments via informal back channels to maintain the ongoing informal truce.

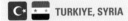 **TURKIYE, SYRIA**

`6 February`

A major earthquake strikes southern and central Turkiye and northern and western Syria, resulting in over 50,000 casualties.

 **EGYPT, TURKIYE, SYRIA**

`27 February`

Egypt's Foreign Minister Sameh Shoukry meets with Assad and Turkish Foreign Minister Mevlüt Çavuşoğlu during visits to Syria and Turkiye.

 YEMEN

`26 February 2023`

A US drone strike reportedly kills two AQAP operatives, including a media chief, in central Yemen.

 LIBYA

`2 March`

Libya's High Council of State votes for a constitutional amendment aimed at preparing for elections.

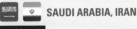 **SAUDI ARABIA, IRAN**

`11 March`

China brokers a deal to restore diplomatic relations between Saudi Arabia and Iran.

 SYRIA

`24 March`

The US conducts multiple airstrikes targeting Iran-aligned groups in eastern Syria, in retaliation for a drone attack that killed a US contractor and wounded five US soldiers.

Middle East and North Africa

IRAQ

27 March

Iraqi lawmakers pass a controversial amendment to Iraq's election laws that undermines smaller parties and independent candidates; hundreds protest in Baghdad as a result.

 TURKIYE

30 March

Turkiye drops its objections and approves Finland's application to join NATO.

 YEMEN

13 April

Saudi diplomats conclude face-to-face talks with the Houthis in Sanaa; they discuss ending Saudi involvement in the war in Yemen.

 SYRIA

4 April

US Central Command announces that US forces have killed Khalid Aydd Ahmad al-Jabouri, a senior ISIS leader.

 LIBYA

15 April

Civil war breaks out in Sudan, which may impact Libya as the Rapid Security Forces in Sudan were responsible for controlling the Sudanese side of the Libya–Sudan border.

 ISRAEL–PALESTINIAN TERRITORIES

May

Israeli troops and Palestinians clash in the Gaza Strip following the death of Palestinian Islamic Jihad leader Khader Adnan.

 SYRIA

19 May

Assad is welcomed back to the Arab League, more than a decade after Syria was expelled.

 TURKIYE

28 May

Erdoğan is re-elected as Turkiye's president.

 ISRAEL–PALESTINIAN TERRITORIES

13 June

China hosts Palestinian President Mahmoud Abbas in Beijing; he is the first Arab leader to be hosted by China in 2023.

 SYRIA

28 June

In the wake of the Wagner Group's attempted mutiny, Russia begins a takeover of the private military company, including its units in Syria.

 TURKIYE

13 June

The PKK declares an end to its unilateral ceasefire, citing escalating Turkish attacks against its forces in Syria and Iraq as well as the isolation of its imprisoned leader Abdullah Öcalan.

 LIBYA

30 June

The GNU reportedly launches air raids against a Wagner Group base southwest of Benghazi; the GNU denies being responsible for the attack.

Notes

1   'Assad Gets Warm Reception as Syria Welcomed Back into the Arab League', Al-Jazeera, 19 May 2023.

2   Timothy Lay, 'ACLED Year in Review: Global Disorder in 2022', The Armed Conflict Location & Event Data Project (ACLED), 31 January 2023.

3   United Nations Human Rights Office of the High Commissioner, 'Israel: UN Experts Condemn Record Year of Israeli Violence in the Occupied West Bank', 15 December 2022.

4   'Supporters of Iraq's al-Sadr Leave Green Zone After Violence', Al-Jazeera, 30 August 2022.

5   Samy Magdy, 'Groups: Both Sides Used Starvation as Tool in Yemen War', AP News, 1 September 2021.

6   United Nations Human Rights Council, 'Situation of Human Rights in Yemen, Including Violations and Abuses Since September 2014: Report of the Group of Eminent International and Regional Experts on Yemen', A/HRC/45/6, 28 September 2020, pp. 12–13.

7   Mona Yacoubian, 'Ukraine's Consequences Are Finally Spreading to Syria', War on the Rocks, 10 January 2023; and Benoit Faucon, Joe Parkinson and Drew Hinshaw, 'Putin Moves to Seize Control of Wagner's Global Empire', *Wall Street Journal*, 28 June 2023.

8   International Crisis Group, 'Containing Transnational Jihadists in Syria's North West', Report no. 239, 7 March 2023.

9   US Central Command, 'Helicopter Raid in Northern Syria Targets Senior ISIS Leader', 17 April 2023; and Oren Liebermann, 'US Set to Launch Formal Investigation into Disputed Syrian Drone Strike After Reports It Killed a Civilian, Defense Officials Say', CNN, 14 June 2023.

10 'SDF Says No More Anti-ISIL Operations After Turkish Attacks', Al-Jazeera, 2 December 2022.

11 Mona Yacoubian, 'Al-Hol: Displacement Crisis Is a Tinderbox that Could Ignite ISIS 2.0', United States Institute of Peace, 11 May 2022.

12 Eyyüp Demir, 'Despite Uncertainty, Syrian Refugees in Turkey Remain Hopeful', VOA, 28 June 2023.

13 Suzan Fraser, 'Turkey Remains Concerned by Alleged PKK Activity in Finland', AP News, 8 December 2022.

14 Ben Hubbard and Safak Timur, 'Talks in Turkey on Sweden's Bid to Join NATO End with No Progress Reported', *New York Times*, 14 June 2023.

15 Mark Mazzetti et al., 'Biden Administration Engages in Long-shot Attempt for Saudi–Israel Deal', *New York Times*, 17 June 2023.

16 Travel China Guide, 'China Outbound Tourism in 2017'.

Middle East and North Africa

Weathering Converging Storms in North Africa: Climate, Political Instability and Food-system Resilience

The war in Ukraine has had a devastating impact on food security in many import-dependent countries in North Africa, including Algeria, Egypt, Libya, Morocco and Tunisia. The global wheat- and energy-market crises resulting from the conflict have compounded the region's extreme vulnerability to accelerating climate change and triggered a dramatic increase in food prices. These developments have raised questions about North Africa's resilience to future trade disruptions, its climate-adaptation capacity and the lessons it learned regarding stabilising its food systems following the Arab Spring. The region's ability to tackle these multiple crises will have important repercussions for regional security dynamics and global geo-economic balances around energy security.

Climate vulnerability and food security

North Africa has long been one of the most food-insecure regions globally, with its vulnerability to the impacts of climate change representing a substantial challenge to agricultural productivity.[1] Rising temperatures, extreme heat events and increasingly erratic rainfall patterns have taken a significant toll on domestic food production, causing prices to spike and wheat availability to decrease. Severe food insecurity was on the rise in the 2020–22 period in all countries in the region (see Figure 1). Notably, in Libya, the proportion of the total population facing food insecurity has constantly increased during the last few years and reached a high of 39.8% in the 2020–22 period – compared to 30.9% in the 2015–17 period.[2] Meanwhile, Algeria experienced a 12.2% decline in food affordability between 2019 and 2022.[3] Morocco is also witnessing a deterioration in its food-security environment.[4] Its wheat production for the year 2022/23 is forecast to be well below historic averages due to drought conditions, which are consistent with projected climate changes for the region.[5]

At the same time, countries in the region have made only limited progress towards improving their climate-adaptation capacity, as highlighted by the minimal increases in their respective 'readiness' scores in the most recent Notre Dame Global Adaptation Initiative (ND-GAIN) Country Index.[6] In this context, Egypt, with its large and fast-growing population, is at significant risk.[7] Its wheat demand is rapidly outpacing domestic production, exposing the country to price fluctuations as one of the world's largest net importers. Moreover, agricultural production has likely already been maximised in the country, while many productive areas, particularly along the Nile and in the Nile Delta, are highly exposed to climate impacts, including rising sea levels and saline intrusion.

The war in Ukraine has added to COVID-19-pandemic-related supply-chain disruptions and further exacerbated these vulnerability trends, given North Africa's dependency on Ukrainian wheat. In fact, over the period 2020–23, Egypt,

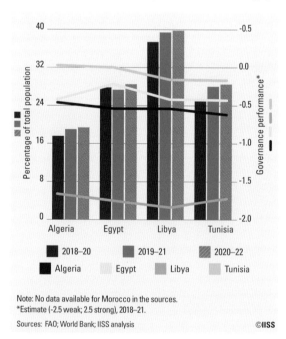

Note: No data available for Morocco in the sources.
*Estimate (-2.5 weak; 2.5 strong), 2018–21.

Sources: FAO; World Bank; IISS analysis   ©IISS

Figure 1: Government effectiveness and prevalence of moderate or severe food insecurity in the total population (percent, three-year average)

Libya, Morocco and Tunisia experienced increases in wheat prices of up to 50%.[8] Even Algeria, a net exporter of wheat, has not escaped the repercussions of the war due to its significant reliance on fertiliser imports from Russia.[9]

The United Nations' Black Sea Grain Initiative, launched in July 2022, managed to stabilise trade flows to and food prices in North Africa by facilitating Ukraine's exports.[10] UN data shows that over three million tonnes of food commodities were shipped to North African countries under the initiative, accounting for 10% of the total world shipping.[11] However, Russia's termination of the agreement in July 2023, and its subsequent targeting of Ukrainian export infrastructure, pose renewed threats to the region's food security. Egypt, the sixth-largest recipient globally under the Black Sea Grain Initiative, is particularly exposed to this risk.[12]

Food insecurity, political instability and geopolitical stressors

Food-price shocks not only threaten the livelihoods and well-being of millions but also often have significant negative effects on political stability, as exemplified by the many demonstrations that erupted worldwide in 2007 and 2008 amid surging food prices due to weather shocks and trade restrictions. The close nexus between food insecurity, social unrest and political upheaval has also been evident in North Africa in recent years. Most notably, high food costs and frustrations with governments' inability to control prices through subsidies were some of the main drivers behind the initial protests that led to the Arab Spring in the early 2010s.

Political instability in North Africa is not only a regional but also a global concern. One reason for this is the region's importance for Europe's energy security, especially in the current context of Europe's plans to decouple from Russia's energy supplies and import both fossil fuels and renewable energy from other sources. Ongoing great-power competition in North Africa adds to regional instability trends. The contentious relationship between Algeria and Morocco, for instance, is complicated by the former's historical ties with Russia – one of its major weapons suppliers. Likewise, Libya's domestic fragility is worsened by Russia's and China's involvement in the country, through arms deals and the deployment of private military and security contractors.

All this underscores the urgent need to implement comprehensive strategies to address immediate challenges arising from political and market volatility as well as prioritise investments in building climate resilience and economic stability. In response to the escalating food crisis in North Africa over the past few years, governments and the international community have implemented a range of measures to mitigate the situation in the short term. On the domestic side, governments have taken steps such as subsidising food prices, providing food aid and increasing food imports. Tunisia, for instance, has resorted to food rationing, a move that triggered protests and demands for the prime minister to resign in late 2022. On the international side, the Black Sea Grain Initiative promoted by the UN had a positive impact on trade flows and prices before being suspended.

Long-term planning: governance, resilience and lessons learnt

The above highlights that already vulnerable countries are often exposed in multiple ways to compounding stressors. The coming decades are likely to see increasingly dispersed but interconnected 'polycrises', resulting from varying combinations of trade disruptions, climate-change impacts, breadbasket failures, instability and conflict. These drivers will affect commodities markets and food and nutrition security, with acute vulnerabilities in many African and Middle Eastern countries.

Multiple interconnected vulnerabilities call for multifaceted solutions. Fundamentally, North African countries need to be shaping agricultural-, economic- and social-support policies to anticipate more frequent and severe supply disruptions and price spikes. Such interventions will need to be carefully calibrated to avoid distorting the market and further driving food-price inflation (export controls and panic buying, for example, could produce this negative result).

The current crisis has also highlighted the importance of regional and international cooperation and coordination in preparing for and managing these kinds of emergencies and disruptions. Such cooperation can enable monitoring, early warning and rapid response to food- and import-price volatility by strengthening and enabling information sharing and situational awareness. There are an array of tools available that can inform such analysis.[13] There are some examples already of information sharing and coordination including through platforms like the G20's Agricultural Market Information System and its Rapid Response Forum, which tries to understand trends in the market and provides a venue for policy coordination and strategy to avoid counterproductive responses that might lead to food-price spikes.

Managing vulnerability will also require adequate humanitarian funding, including well-tailored cash-support programmes, food-voucher programmes or, in extreme cases, direct food aid. For donors, the two former options are generally more efficient ways of providing aid than food distribution. Countries also need to be prepared to expand the eligibility criteria for such aid in times of crisis and to meet the needs of the most vulnerable among both urban and rural populations, including refugees, migrants and asylum seekers, while preventing subsidies from going to households with a greater capacity to absorb food-price increases. For example, although Egypt was affected by price spikes related to the war in Ukraine, the crisis was not as catastrophic as in the years prior to the Arab Spring. This is partially because, this time around, the country instituted some policies to reduce the impact on consumers. These included purchasing more wheat domestically, instituting a price cap on unsubsidised bread, and rolling out several economic policies like expanding cash-support programmes, tax reductions and salary rises to help households cope with food and fuel inflation. The government has learnt from past experience, but whether Egypt has the economic flexibility to insulate its population this way in the future will depend in part on its future climate resilience.

As part of mitigating the inflationary impact of supply shocks, it will be important to try to manage import dependencies. There are already some efforts under way to work on these issues, for example, under the direction of Egypt's General Authority for Supply Commodities. The recent crisis has also pushed countries to seek innovative solutions. For instance, Tunisia's national government is not able to secure international financing to purchase food on global markets or to institute subsidies. Therefore, Tunisia's Cereals Office, a public company overseen by the Ministry of Agriculture, Water Resources and Fisheries, approached international financial institutions directly in 2022 and secured a US$161m loan to buy wheat and build and renovate field and port silos as well as transportation infrastructure for grain.[14]

To reduce exposure on the supply side, agricultural policies should aim to improve domestic food production by continuing to address vulnerabilities to climate-change impacts like drought, pests and land degradation, while also promoting sustainability and climate resilience. Examples of such policies include supporting crop diversification, moving towards more drought-tolerant and nutritious alternatives to imported grains, and building efficient irrigation systems. Other technical measures can increase agricultural productivity and help reduce vulnerability, such as improving food-storage capacities or using data from satellites or other remote-sensing tools to inform farming practices regarding fertiliser use, pest management and disease. Measures to increase production will also need to promote sustainability – given the region's existing and projected water scarcity, limits on agricultural expansion and limits on climate adaptation – and address potential impacts on people or biodiversity. Otherwise, they may risk compounding vulnerability.

In all efforts, it will be necessary to try to avoid causing further problems. Excessive interference can destabilise the market and drive further inflation. Some non-governmental organisations, therefore, have suggested avoiding sanctioning food or fertiliser as a response to conflicts, arguing that near-term responses should not work against longer-term sustainability and food-system resilience.

More fundamentally, deep reforms to global food systems are needed to anticipate a future environment of recurrent and concurrent crises. External crisis drivers are unlikely to lessen, particularly given global reliance on relatively few breadbasket regions and the potential for climate anomalies to disrupt production, possibly leading to multiple breadbasket failures. North African countries will need to become more resilient and prepare for market volatility. They have experience with the role food-price spikes played in the Arab Spring. The latest food crisis linked to Russia's war in Ukraine should be a further motivator for governments to strengthen their capacities for crisis prevention and management, particularly given climate vulnerabilities, future demographics, growing food demand and geopolitical trends towards more complex crises that reverberate through global systems, including in food-commodities markets.

Notes

1   See Food and Agriculture Organization of the UN (FAO) et al., *Near East and North Africa: Regional Overview of Food Security and Nutrition 2022* (Cairo: FAO, 2023). See also the vulnerability score of the latest University of Notre Dame 'ND-GAIN Country Index', 2021. The 'vulnerability' score measures a country's exposure, sensitivity and ability to adapt to the negative impact of climate change. ND-GAIN calculates the overall vulnerability by considering vulnerability in six life-supporting sectors: food, water, health, ecosystem service, human habitat and infrastructure.

2   FAO et al., *Near East and North Africa: Regional Overview of Food Security and Nutrition 2022*; and FAOSTAT, 'Libya'. Refer to the chart entitled 'Prevalence of Moderate or Severe Food Insecurity (5) (3-year Average)'.

3   Food affordability refers to the composite indicator created by *The Economist* Impact team, which comprises several variables including change in average food costs, proportion of the population under the global poverty line, agricultural import tariffs and food safety-net programmes, among others. See *The Economist* Impact, 'Global Food Security Index 2022', 2022.

4   See *The Economist* Impact, 'Global Food Security Index 2022'. The overall score for each country (0–100, where 100 equals the best conditions) comprises four pillars: affordability, availability, quality and safety, and sustainability and adaptation. Morocco's scores for 2020 and 2022 were 64.9 and 63, respectively.

5   United States Department of Agriculture, the Foreign Agricultural Service, 'Grain and Feed Update: Morocco', 28 June 2023.

6   See the readiness score of the latest University of Notre Dame 'ND-GAIN Country Index', 2021. The 'readiness' score measures a country's ability to leverage investments and convert them to adaptation actions. ND-GAIN measures overall readiness by considering three components: economic readiness, governance readiness and social readiness. Data retrieved in August 2023.

7   Egypt's population exceeded 102m in 2022. UN Framework Convention on Climate Change, 'Egypt's Second Updated Nationally Determined Contributions', 26 June 2023.

8   IISS analysis based on FAO data. Specifically, Tunisia's average import prices of durum wheat in 2022 reached US$665 per tonne, up from US$435 in 2021, corresponding to about a 50% increase. Egypt's General Authority for Supply of Commodities purchased imported wheat at a cost of US$494 per tonne in April 2022, up from US$360 in January 2022, corresponding to about a 40% increase. In Libya, the median price for wheat flour increased by 50% in 2020. See FAO, 'GIEWS Country Brief: Tunisia', 27 July 2022; Jakob Rauschendorfer and Ekaterina Krivonos, *Implications of the War in Ukraine for Agrifood Trade and Food Security in the Southern and Eastern Mediterranean: Egypt, Jordan, Lebanon, Morocco and Tunisia* (Rome: FAO, 2022); and FAO, 'GIEWS Country Brief: Libya', 13 May 2020.

9   See FAO et al., *Near East and North Africa: Regional Overview of Food Security and Nutrition 2022*, p. 45.

10 The Black Sea Grain Initiative was an agreement reached by Russia, Turkiye and Ukraine as proposed by the UN secretary-general in July 2022 'to facilitate the safe navigation for the export of grain and related foodstuffs and fertilizers' from Ukrainian ports. UN, 'Initiative on the Safe Transportation of Grain and Foodstuffs from Ukrainian Ports', July 2022.

11 The sum of tonnes of food commodities received by North African countries under the Black Sea Grain Initiative from August 2022–July 2023 is as follows: Egypt 1.6m, Tunisia 0.7m, Libya 0.6m, Algeria 0.2m and Morocco 0.1m. UN Black Sea Grain Initiative Joint Coordination Centre (JCC), 'Vessel Movements', July 2023.

12 Egypt received 1.6m tn of food commodities under the Black Sea Grain Initiative from August 2022–July 2023, the highest tonnage after China (8m), Spain (6m), Turkiye (3.2m), Italy (2.1m) and the Netherlands (2m). UN Black Sea Grain Initiative JCC, 'Vessel Movements'.

13 These include, for example, the International Food Policy Research Institute's Food Security Portal.

14 Janel Siemplenski Lefort, 'Stocking Up for Resilience', European Investment Bank, 25 April 2023.

SYRIA

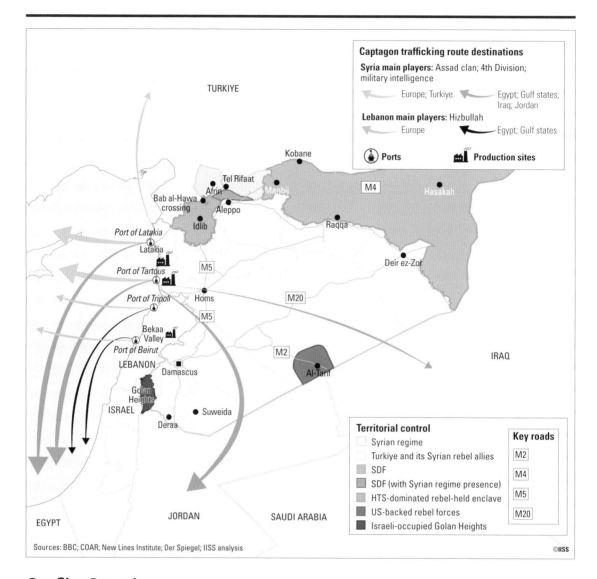

Captagon trafficking route destinations

Syria main players: Assad clan; 4th Division; military intelligence

→ Europe; Turkiye   → Egypt; Gulf states; Iraq; Jordan

Lebanon main players: Hizbullah

→ Europe   → Egypt; Gulf states

Ports   Production sites

Territorial control
- Syrian regime
- Turkiye and its Syrian rebel allies
- SDF
- SDF (with Syrian regime presence)
- HTS-dominated rebel-held enclave
- US-backed rebel forces
- Israeli-occupied Golan Heights

Key roads
- M2
- M4
- M5
- M20

Sources: BBC; COAR; New Lines Institute; Der Spiegel; IISS analysis   ©IISS

Conflict Overview

Due to Syria's central geographic position in the Middle East and its complex human terrain, the conflict there has local, regional and international drivers.

The Syrian uprising started in 2011 following decades of economic decline, widening social inequalities, systemic corruption and brutality by the government of Bashar Al-Assad, which allowed no space for political debate. Dominated by members of the Alawite minority but enjoying cross-confessional

support, the regime relied on loyal military units and security forces, as well as military partnerships with Iran and Russia.

Once the uprising was met by regime repression, Syria fractured along regional, ethnic, confessional and political lines. Its disintegration was fuelled by regional competition and transnational forces, including Salafi-jihadist groups, such as the Islamic State (ISIS) and al-Qaeda (which morphed into Hayat Tahrir al-Sham, HTS).

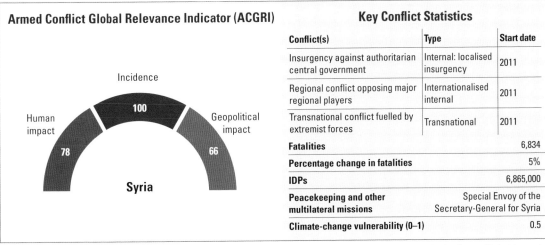

Conflict(s)	Type	Start date
Insurgency against authoritarian central government	Internal: localised insurgency	2011
Regional conflict opposing major regional players	Internationalised internal	2011
Transnational conflict fuelled by extremist forces	Transnational	2011
Fatalities		6,834
Percentage change in fatalities		5%
IDPs		6,865,000
Peacekeeping and other multilateral missions		Special Envoy of the Secretary-General for Syria
Climate-change vulnerability (0–1)		0.5

ACGRI pillars: IISS calculation based on multiple sources for 2022 and 2023 (scale: 0–100), except for some cases according to data availability. See Notes on Methodology and Data Appendix for all variables and further details on Key Conflict Statistics.

Russia's intervention in 2015 and the rapid drawdown of Western and Arab support for the rebellion tilted the balance decisively in favour of the Assad regime. Since 2017, Iran, Russia and Turkiye have shaped the battlefield and the conflict's politics. As a result, the Assad regime has extended its control to approximately 65% of the national territory and around 55% of the pre-war population. Its authority remains contested, its resources limited and its power base narrow. However, deprived of external sponsors, cohesion and sense of purpose, the rebellion and the remnants of the political opposition no longer constitute an existential challenge. The

Assad-led government rejects any power-sharing arrangement and has obstructed mediation efforts, illustrated by the fact that the last meeting of the United Nations track in Geneva took place in June 2022. The regime has benefitted from the development of a war economy and has allowed the proliferation of predatory loyalist militias.

Islamist extremism remains a powerful force in Syria, with several groups explicitly endorsing Salafi ideals. The most prominent is ISIS, which maintains an active presence in eastern and southern Syria and conducts an insurgency against regime and Kurdish forces.

Conflict Update

During the reporting period, the regime continued to benefit from regional fatigue and a trend towards de-escalation of rivalries. Two developments mollified regional attitudes towards Damascus: the Saudi–Iranian agreement of March 2023 and the detente between the Gulf states and Turkiye. Moreover, the devastating February earthquake triggered regional engagement, prompting a rapid Arab outreach to the Assad regime. Soon after, prominent Arab ministers visited the Syrian president, paving the way for the country's official re-entry into the Arab League in May. Assad attended the Arab League's annual summit in Riyadh, posing for the first time in the company of heads of state and government who had shunned him since 2011. At the summit, Arab governments expressed a preference for a political

settlement to the conflict and stated their intention to facilitate the return of Syrian refugees, halt drug trafficking and support Syrian humanitarian needs, without outlining a clear plan. Arab officials also lobbied Western governments to ease or lift sanctions and allow greater humanitarian assistance, recovery and investment efforts in Syria. However, Western governments seem committed to maintaining Assad's isolation, having concluded that engagement would be detrimental to Syria's stabilisation and refugee returns given the regime's lack of reciprocity and positive actions. In the United States, there was a congressional effort to resist normalisation and intensify the sanctions regime against Syria.

There is considerable evidence that the Assad regime is actively engaged in producing and exporting captagon, an amphetamine drug gaining popularity across the Middle East.[1] The 4th Division (a unit commanded by Maher al-Assad, the president's brother) and various security services control factories and smuggling routes. The revenues of the captagon trade – believed to amount to many times the value of Syria's legal trade – constitute a significant source of income for the regime.[2] Taming this activity is an explicit objective of the Arab states that facilitated Syria's return to the Arab League; these states have offered financial incentives but also threatened to use force to achieve this goal. Jordan has reportedly conducted several attacks inside Syria against trafficking networks. Western governments have imposed sanctions against Syrian and Lebanese individuals close to the regime for being involved in captagon production and trafficking.[3]

Turkiye has continued to view Syria as an immediate security problem and has threatened to conduct more interventions against Kurdish forces there due to their links with the Kurdistan Workers' Party (PKK). Western diplomacy and Russian pressure have dissuaded Ankara from expanding its

zone of control in Syria. The normalisation of ties between Turkiye and the Assad regime has proceeded more slowly than that between the latter and the Arab states – due to the personal animosity between Turkish President Recep Tayyip Erdoğan and Assad, as well as Turkiye's reluctance to agree to a withdrawal of its forces from areas it controls in Syria, which Damascus demands as a precondition for normalisation.

Syria continues to be an arena for the United States' (and Israel's) competition with Iran. The latter remained active across the country, reportedly flying in weaponry under the cover of humanitarian assistance during the aftermath of the earthquake.[4] Israel's air campaign to destroy Iranian assets in Syria maintained its intensity and momentum in 2022 and early 2023. However, Arab normalisation with Assad and Iranian–Russian rapprochement could reduce Israel's freedom to operate in Syria, or make it politically costlier. Iranian-backed groups have also harassed US bases in northeast Syria, leading to the death of at least one US contractor. These events have led to US retaliation against militias.[5]

Conflict Parties

Syrian Armed Forces/The Syrian Arab Army (SAF/SAA)

Strength: Unclear.

Areas of operation: Southern, coastal and central Syria and parts of northern Syria.

Leadership: Bashar al-Assad (commander-in-chief). Key elite units of the SAA, such as the Republican Guard and the 4th Division, fall under the command of Maher al-Assad, the president's brother. Other units are heavily influenced by Russian or Iranian commanders.

Structure: Consists of the army, navy, air force, intelligence services and the National Defence Forces. The SAA adopts a hybrid military structure that compensates for its shrinking military personnel with paramilitary militias and pro-regime fighters, including foreign fighters backed by Iran. Since 2017, with Russian support, efforts have focused on integrating or dissolving these militias and reorganising and equipping the command-and-control structure, with mixed results.

History: Since its establishment in 1945, the SAA has played a key role in Syrian politics. It was involved in bringing Hafez al-Assad and the Ba'athist-Alawite dynasty to power in 1970. The high percentage of Alawites in key positions in the SAA exacerbated sectarianism after the 2011 outbreak of war. The disproportionate reliance on Alawite manpower is a key vulnerability, necessitating interventions by Iran's Islamic Revolutionary Guard Corps (IRGC), Hizbullah (beginning in 2013) and Russia (2015) to mitigate the risk of military collapse.

Objectives: Regain military control over the entire Syrian territory.

Opponents: Israeli forces, Turkish forces, US forces, Syrian Democratic Forces/People's Protection Units (SDF/YPG), ISIS and al-Qaeda affiliates, and Syrian National Army (SNA).

Affiliates/allies: Iranian and Iranian-backed forces, Russian and Russian-backed forces, Hizbullah and other Shia militias.

Resources/capabilities: Benefits from significant Russian air, artillery and missile support and intelligence capabilities.

Hayat Tahrir al-Sham (HTS)

Strength: 12,000–15,000 (estimate).[6]

Areas of operation: Idlib province, northwestern Syria.

Leadership: Abu Mohamed al-Golani.

Structure: Maintains a joint military-operations room with other local rebels. The HTS-linked Syrian Salvation Government focuses on territorial control and on the provision of public services via a decentralised governance system and quasi-formal service-provision institutions.

Hayat Tahrir al-Sham (HTS)

History: Originally known as Jabhat Fatah al-Sham (formerly Jabhat al-Nusra or Al-Nusra Front) and linked to the Islamic State of Iraq, it broke away when the latter declared itself the Islamic State of Iraq and al-Sham (ISIS) in 2013 and later split from al-Qaeda in 2016. In 2017 it merged with several smaller factions and rebranded itself as HTS.

Objectives: Maintain control over Idlib in the short term, including through crushing remaining ISIS and al-Qaeda cells. In the long run, overthrow the Assad regime.

Opponents: SAF, Iranian and Iranian-backed forces, Russian forces, ISIS, and al-Qaeda and affiliates.

Affiliates/allies: Turkish forces around the mutual objective of deterring SAA offensives and uprooting radical cells affiliated to ISIS or al-Qaeda.

Resources/capabilities: Light weaponry, rocket launchers, anti-tank guided missiles as well as a small number of mechanised vehicles. It has seized weaponry from other rebel groups, including those equipped by Turkiye and Western governments. It also has used vehicle-borne improvised explosive devices and suicide bombings. It reportedly finances itself primarily through taxation in Idlib province.

(Turkiye-sponsored) Syrian National Army (SNA)

Strength: 80,000 (estimate).[7]

Areas of operation: Northern and northwestern Syria.

Leadership: SNA units are currently deployed alongside Turkish military forces and therefore operate under Turkish leadership.

Structure: A conglomerate of dozens of different militias, ranging vastly in size, affiliation and ideology, composed of Syrian militants, who are trained and equipped by Turkiye. The SNA is divided into seven main legions, each composed of a wide array of divisions and brigades.

History: Created as a splinter group of the Turkiye-backed Free Syrian Army. The SNA has been trained and equipped by the Turkish government since 2016. In 2019, the Idlib-based and Turkiye-sponsored National Front for Liberation was merged into the SNA.

Objectives: Take control of northern Syria.

Opponents: Syrian government forces, Iranian and Iranian-backed forces, SDF/YPG and ISIS.

Affiliates/allies: Turkish Armed Forces (TSK).

Resources/capabilities: While a handful of formations have received US-sponsored training and equipment, the SNA has been fully reliant on Turkiye's support since its creation. Turkiye has provided small arms as well as infantry vehicles, and SNA military operations have benefitted from the Turkish army's fire support via artillery and airstrikes.

Syrian Democratic Forces/People's Protection Units (SDF/YPG)

Strength: 40,000–60,000 (estimate).[8]

Areas of operation: Northern Syria.

Leadership: Mazloum Kobani Abdi, also known as Sahin Cilo (military commander). Abdi is a former senior member of the PKK.

Structure: Organised mainly along ethnic and territorial lines. Syrian Kurds lead the YPG and the Women's Protection Units (YPJ); both include a small component of international volunteers grouped into an international battalion. Other ethnic groups are organised under various military formations within the SDF, mainly as military councils.

History: Created in 2015 as a direct response to the advance of ISIS into northern Syria, building on various pre-existing alliances. Since then, it has fought against ISIS and the Turkish military.

Objectives: Control northern Syria.

Opponents: Turkish forces, SNA, ISIS, and al-Qaeda and affiliates.

Affiliates/allies: PKK, Russia, Syrian regime and US.

Resources/capabilities: While it built upon the experience of its militias, since its formal creation, the SDF has been equipped, trained and advised by the US. SDF units are equipped with small arms and some infantry vehicles.

Islamic State (ISIS)

Strength: Between 5,000 and 7,000 in Iraq and Syria, half of which are fighters.[9]

Areas of operation: Across eastern Syria, notably along the Euphrates and the Badiya desert as well as in the governorate of Homs in central Syria and along the M20 highway that runs between Palmyra and Deir ez-Zor.

Leadership: Abu al-Husain al-Husaini al-Qurashi (caliph and leader of ISIS since November 2022).

Structure: The presence of ISIS in Syria has changed considerably since the 2017 loss of Raqqa and its gradual territorial defeat. Its central command remains in place, but greater autonomy is granted to local cells across Syria and Iraq to generate resources and facilitate insurgent campaigns.

History: Originated in Iraq around 2003. It fought to establish a caliphate during the Syrian civil war. In the period 2014–17, ISIS controlled many territories in Iraq and Syria and governed more than eight million people. Since 2017 (in Iraq) and 2019 (in Syria), the group has lost control of all the territories it held.

Objectives: Regain territorial hold in Syria and Iraq.

Opponents: SAF; SNA; HTS; Russian, Turkish and US armed forces; Iranian and Iranian-backed and commanded militias; and SDF/YPG.

Islamic State (ISIS)

Affiliates/allies: ISIS fighters in other countries.

Resources/capabilities: Relies on guerrilla warfare, hit-and-run tactics and conventional asymmetrical operations, using light and small weaponry and deploying insurgent tactics including suicide bombings.

Armed Forces of the Russian Federation

Strength: 4,000 troops in Syria (estimate).

Areas of operation: Across Syria.

Leadership: President Vladimir Putin (commander-in-chief), Sergei Shoigu (defence minister) and Valery Gerasimov (chief of the general staff).

Structure: The Russian mission in Syria involves ground forces, special forces, attack aircraft and bombers, an air-defence component and military intelligence. Russian private military contractors operate in front-line roles together with conventional units.

History: Since 2015, Russia has shaped the Syrian battlefield, playing a crucial strategic and operational role to shore up and reorganise Syrian government forces and assist the Assad regime in capturing key areas.

Objectives: Reform the Syrian army, integrate irregular and rebel groups into the SAA and support capacity-building.

Opponents: US forces, SNA, HTS, ISIS, and al-Qaeda and affiliates.

Affiliates/allies: SAF, 5th Corps of SAA and Tiger Force.

Resources/capabilities: Has deployed significant air, artillery, missile, missile-defence and intelligence capabilities in Syria, testing new weapons and tactics.

Turkish Armed Forces (TSK)

Strength: 10,000–15,000 in Syria.[10]

Areas of operation: Northwestern and northern Syria.

Leadership: President Recep Tayyip Erdoğan (commander-in chief), Gen. (retd) Hulusi Akar (minister of national defence) and Gen. Yasar Guler (chief of general staff).

Structure: The TSK is present in Syria via ground forces, special forces, military intelligence and reconnaissance.

History: Involved in Syria since the conflict began in 2011. For the first five years, it primarily provided training and equipment to the Syrian armed opposition and humanitarian aid. Military operations increased beginning in 2016 following ISIS terrorist attacks in Turkiye and the YPG's territorial gains. Ankara intervened in 2020 to halt an SAF offensive into opposition-controlled Idlib and has maintained thousands of troops in Idlib ever since to deter further offensives.

Objectives: Destroy the PKK, including through eliminating key figures in northern Syria and rolling back territorial gains of its Syrian offshoot (YPG); secure Turkiye's border with Syria; limit refugee influx into Turkiye; and prevent military defeat of Syrian opposition allies.

Opponents: YPG, ISIS, al-Qaeda and affiliates, SAF, and Iranian and Iranian-backed and commanded militias.

Affiliates/allies: Relies extensively on the SNA as a local actor and support force in northern Syria.

Resources/capabilities: Turkiye's defence budget for 2022 was US$6.3 billion. Turkiye trains, equips and arms the SNA and deploys its own military mechanised infantry battalions on the ground, as well as F-16 fighter jets and ANKA-S uninhabited aerial vehicles (UAVs). Its military capabilities include air attack and intelligence, surveillance and reconnaissance assets, such as the F-16 and the *Bayraktar TB2* UAV, armoured tanks and special-forces units.

Iranian armed forces

Strength: 3,000 in Syria (estimate).

Areas of operation: Southern and eastern Syria, Damascus, Aleppo and some front lines in northwestern Syria.

Leadership: Brig.-Gen. Esmail Ghaani (military leader of the Quds Force, QF).

Structure: Iran operates militarily in the country through a number of military organisations and local and regional Shia militias. Its military operations in Syria are organised by the QF, the ground forces of the IRGC, and a smaller group of units drawn from the regular Iranian army, Artesh, that began to arrive in Syria in early 2016. The QF conducts external military operations in Syria, training and equipping pro-Iranian and regime militias from Afghanistan, Iraq, Lebanon, Pakistan and Syria. Iran maintains substantial influence within certain elements of the SAF, particularly militias nominally incorporated within the Local Defence Forces.

History: Active in Syria since 2011. In the conflict's early stages Tehran provided the Syrian regime with financial aid, arms shipments and communication-jamming equipment. With the gradual intensification of fighting, Iran sent several hundred senior QF and Hizbullah operatives as military advisers and planners, with significant escalation occurring in 2013 amid rebel gains and the weakening of the Assad regime. Iran has sent thousands of fighters from various military organisations to fight in Syria under Iranian leadership and deploys Iranian manpower mainly as battlefield commanders in key positions. Iranian and pro-Iranian forces fought leading battles in Homs (2012–14), Aleppo (2015–16), Deir ez-Zor (2017) and Deraa (2018).

Objectives: Preserve the Assad regime, shore up militia partners, build a military infrastructure inside Syria, contain Russian and Turkish influence, and deter Israel.

Iranian armed forces

Opponents: Israeli forces (airstrikes), HTS, ISIS and al-Qaeda affiliates, SNA and SDF/YPG.

Affiliates/allies: Hizbullah and other Shia militias in Afghanistan, Iraq, Lebanon, Pakistan and Syria; SAF; and Russian forces.

Resources/capabilities: Operates several military bases and camps inside Syria with entrenched strategic infrastructure throughout the country. Iran provides an array of weaponry to its allies, including anti-tank guided missiles and UAVs, but its main contributions are command and control along with mobilisation of foreign and militia fighters.

Combined Joint Task Force–*Operation Inherent Resolve* (CJTF–OIR)

Strength: 900 in Syria (estimate), including advisers, special forces, etc.

Areas of operation: Northeastern Syria areas under control of the SDF/YPG, and southern Syria in al-Tanf garrison near the Iraqi and Jordanian borders.

Leadership: Maj.-Gen. Matthew McFarlane.

Structure: The US leads the CJTF–OIR, which brings together over 20 coalition partners.

History: Created in October 2014 when the US Department of Defense formalised ongoing military operations against ISIS. In late 2015, the first US ground troops entered Syria to recruit, organise and advise Syrian Kurdish and Arab opposition fighters in the fight against ISIS. The developing partnership between the US and the SDF/YPG became a significant source of tension between the US and Turkiye.

In late 2019, under pressure from Ankara and via the unilateral decision of then-president Donald Trump, the US contingency withdrew more than half of its forces (then around 2,000 personnel) and narrowed its military presence to eastern areas of SDF-controlled territory (in addition to al-Tanf).

Objectives: Enable and support SDF counter-insurgency operations against ISIS, while shoring up local stability to deny ISIS opportunities to resurface and expand.

Opponents: ISIS, and al-Qaeda and affiliates.

Affiliates/allies: SDF/YPG.

Resources/capabilities: Airstrikes targeting ISIS, as well as special-forces support to SDF counter-insurgency operations. Armoured vehicles protect CJTF–OIR bases, including those adjacent to oilfields in northeastern Syria.

Middle East and North Africa

Notes

1   See 'Syria: Addicted to Captagon', BBC iPlayer, 26 June 2023; and Dr Karam Shaar and Caroline Rose, 'The Syrian Regime's Captagon Endgame', Newlines Institute for Strategy and Policy, 24 May 2023.

2   *Ibid*.

3   See, for example, US Department of the Treasury, 'Treasury Sanctions Syrian Regime and Lebanese Actors Involved in Illicit Drug Production and Trafficking', 8 July 2023.

4   Suleiman Al-Khalidi, James Mackenzie and Parisa Hafezi, 'Exclusive: Iran Exploits Earthquake Relief Mission to Fly Weapons to Syria', Reuters, 12 April 2023.

5   Jim Garamone, 'US Responds to Attack That Killed US Contractor in Syria', US Department of Defense, 24 March 2023.

6   United Nations Security Council, 'Twenty-fourth Report of the Analytical Support and Sanctions Monitoring Team Submitted

Pursuant to Resolution 2368 (2017) Concerning ISIL (Da'esh), Al-Qaida and Associated Individuals and Entities', S/2019/570, 30 August 2019.

7   Hassan Ibrahim, 'Poor Salaries and Frequent Delay: A Policy to Dissolve "National Army" or Gain Loyalty', Enab Baladi, 18 April 2023.

8   EU Agency for Asylum, '1.2. Syrian Democratic Forces and Asayish', September 2020.

9   UN Security Council, 'Thirty-first Report of the Analytical Support and Sanctions Monitoring Team Submitted Pursuant to Resolution 2610 (2021) Concerning ISIL (Da'esh), Al-Qaida and Associated Individuals and Entities', S/2023/95, 13 February 2023, p. 11.

10 'Turkey Has Evacuated Seven Syrian Military Posts', Reuters, 18 December 2020.

IRAQ

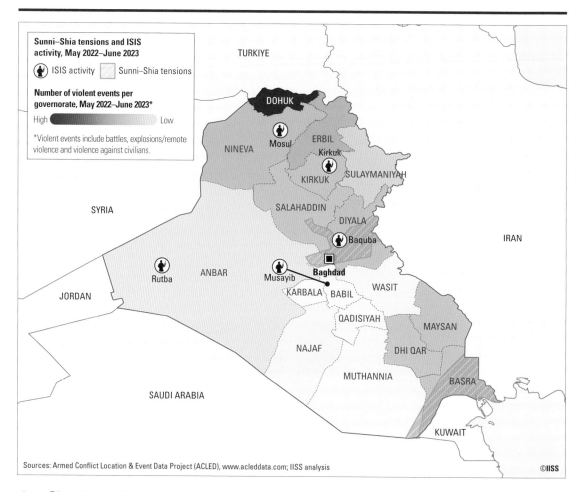

Sunni–Shia tensions and ISIS activity, May 2022–June 2023

ISIS activity   Sunni–Shia tensions

Number of violent events per governorate, May 2022–June 2023*

High ———————————— Low

*Violent events include battles, explosions/remote violence and violence against civilians.

Sources: Armed Conflict Location & Event Data Project (ACLED), www.acleddata.com; IISS analysis   ©IISS

Conflict Overview

Iraq continues to grapple with instability and political disunity, 20 years after the United States-led invasion of the country toppled Saddam Hussein and his regime. The primary sources of political and security tensions remain the Sunni–Shia divide, ongoing conflicts between the Kurdistan Regional Government (KRG) and Baghdad (as well as within the Iraqi Kurdish minority), and the Islamic State (ISIS) jihadist insurgency across the country.

The social and political divisions that resulted from the brutal rule of Hussein's Sunni Ba'ath Party – in a predominantly Shia country – were further aggravated by the US-backed 'de-Ba'athification' process, which barred individuals with any prior ties to the party from government-related positions.

Since party membership was a requirement for most public roles during Hussein's dictatorship, the de-Ba'athification process effectively excluded a substantial proportion of Iraqi society from positions of power, generating deep discontent among former Ba'ath members and the broader Sunni minority.

During the civil war that ensued, Shia cleric Muqtada al-Sadr and his Mahdi Army – a collection of militias that chiefly targeted US-led coalition forces deployed under *Operation Iraqi Freedom* – gained prominence among the Shia community. Meanwhile, Sunni armed militias emerged as a consequence of the de-Ba'athification process. Although the power vacuum presented an opening for Iran to expand its influence in Iraq, Tehran directed its

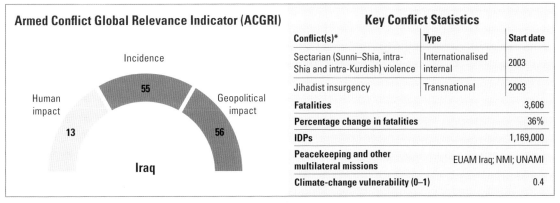

Conflict(s)*	Type	Start date
Sectarian (Sunni–Shia, intra-Shia and intra-Kurdish) violence	Internationalised internal	2003
Jihadist insurgency	Transnational	2003
Fatalities		3,606
Percentage change in fatalities		36%
IDPs		1,169,000
Peacekeeping and other multilateral missions		EUAM Iraq; NMI; UNAMI
Climate-change vulnerability (0–1)		0.4

ACGRI pillars: IISS calculation based on multiple sources for 2022 and 2023 (scale: 0–100), except for some cases according to data availability. See Notes on Methodology and Data Appendix for all variables and further details on Key Conflict Statistics. *See the Turkiye Country Profile for the transnational conflict involving Turkish security forces and the Kurdistan Workers' Party (PKK) in northern Iraq.

support primarily towards the Badr Brigades rather than Sadr's forces.

The emergence of ISIS as a significant threat in 2014 heightened Tehran's concerns, prompting an increased Iranian role in Iraq. Tehran's religious leadership called on the Shia community to take up arms against the group, which led to the formation of various armed militias across the country, under the umbrella of Popular Mobilisation Units (PMU). With the creation of the Shi'ite Coordination Framework (SCF) in late 2019, Iran-supported Shia actors in Iraq (including the PMU) grew in relevance and influence in the country.

Conflict Update

Alongside the battle against ISIS, political and violent clashes between and within Sunni and Shia groups remained a constant feature of political life in Iraq during the reporting period. Additionally, the presence of sectarian clientelism and corruption continued to exacerbate the feelings of neglect experienced by many communities that have endured 20 years of conflict. These groups complain about Baghdad's inaction, further feeding tensions between local authorities and the central government.

After almost a year of political deadlock following the October 2021 elections, Iraq managed to elect a new president, Abdul Latif Rashid, a veteran politician from Bafel Talabani's Patriotic Union of Kurdistan (PUK), who then appointed Mohammed Shia' al-Sudani as prime minister. Supported by the Shi'ite Coordination Framework, Sudani's nomination has been strongly opposed by Sadr's bloc, which came out of the 2021 elections with a relative majority of votes but failed to form a government and has consistently asked for the dissolution of the current parliament and a new round of elections.[1] Tensions peaked in August 2022 when Sadrist protesters and militias breached Baghdad's Green Zone and clashed with PMU elements. Thirty people were killed and hundreds were injured as a result of the clashes, which only ended after Sadr publicly called for the protesters to leave the Green Zone.[2]

Since becoming prime minister, Sudani has focused on lowering tensions between his government (particularly its SCF component) and the Sadrist movement. An ongoing replacement of key appointees across government, the civil service and local authorities – which Sudani has pursued in a gradual way – risks fuelling the Sadrist movement's frustration if scores of political figures close to Sadr, who have risen to influential positions over the years, are removed.

Another concern for Sudani stems from the widening political rift in the KRG, where the PUK has been accusing the ruling Kurdistan Democratic Party (KDP), led by Masoud Barzani, of marginalising its decision-makers and withholding financial resources earmarked for areas under PUK control. As a result of these tensions, the two parties' cohabitation in power is increasingly fragile.

During the reporting period, Iraq saw a sharp reduction in attacks carried out by ISIS and PMU-linked militias. The former's relative inactivity is likely explained by its inability to reorganise following several targeted killings of its senior leaders, coupled with an increase in the number of counter-terrorism operations conducted against it by Iraqi and partner security forces. The PMU's de-escalation seems to be a by-product of the SCF's growing influence in Baghdad, with violence becoming increasingly counterproductive and risking undermining political efforts at the governmental level. There was an uptick in tribal violence, however, with a significant number of security incidents taking place between Baghdad and the neighbouring Diyala governorate – a crossroads of Sunni–Shia grievances where the persistent presence of ISIS

elements compounds tensions. This area has been the focus of the majority of Iraqi forces' counter-terrorism operations.

Iraq's relations with the US are likely to dictate the success of the ongoing anti-ISIS campaign. In his first interview as prime minister, Sudani stressed the importance of a continued US military presence in Iraq, albeit in a training and support capacity. His position reflects a need to strike a balance between retaining international support and appeasing the SCF's significant pro-Iran component, which pushes for a swift and complete withdrawal of international military forces operating under the aegis of the Combined Joint Task Force – *Operation Inherent Resolve* (CJTF–OIR).

Conflict Parties

Iraqi Security Forces (ISF)

Strength: 193,000.

Areas of operation: All areas of Iraq excluding the Kurdistan Region of Iraq.

Leadership: Prime Minister Mohammed Shia' al-Sudani (commander-in-chief), Abdul Amir Rashid Yarallah (army chief of staff), Thabit al-Abassi (defence minister) and Abdul Amir al-Shammari (interior minister).

Structure: Consists of the army, air force and navy. In the fight against ISIS, the army has cooperated with the Federal Police and the Ministry of Interior (MoI) intelligence agency (the Federal Investigation and Intelligence Agency, Falcons Cell), the Counter-Terrorism Service (CTS), PMU and other intelligence organs. The army reports to the Ministry of Defence, the Federal Police to the MoI and the CTS to the Prime Minister's Office (PMO).

History: The capture of Tikrit and Mosul by ISIS in 2014 led to the partial disintegration of Iraqi forces. The forces have been rebuilt with the assistance of the US-led coalition but remain insufficiently equipped for counter-insurgency tasks.

Objectives: Defeat ISIS and ensure security across the country. Since the territorial defeat of ISIS, Iraqi forces have focused on eliminating remaining cells in rural areas. The armed forces also play a role in providing security in the provinces to tackle tribal fighting, protest-related violence and criminality.

Opponents: ISIS.

Affiliates/allies: Kurdish Peshmerga, CJTF–OIR, PMU and CTS.

Resources/capabilities: A range of conventional land, air and naval capabilities, including armoured fighting vehicles, anti-tank missile systems, artillery and fixed- and rotary-wing aircraft.

Popular Mobilisation Units (PMU)

Strength: Approximately 165,000.[3]

Areas of operation: Areas previously held by ISIS, including Anbar, Nineva, Diyala and Salahaddin provinces, and areas of southern Iraq, particularly Jurf al-Sakhar in Babil province, and shrine cities of Najaf, Karbala and Samarra in Salahaddin.

Leadership: The PMU has a distinct chain of command from the other Iraqi forces. Formally under the PMO and technically directly answerable to the prime minister, de facto leadership of the organisation had resided with the PMU Commission's chief of staff (formerly Abu Mahdi al-Muhandis). The latter's assassination in 2020 triggered a leadership struggle. Kataib Hizbullah commander Abdul-Aziz al-Muhammadawi (also known as Abu Fadak) was elevated to lead the organisation, although power is thought to operate more via a committee of senior figures. However, some PMU brigades loyal to Najaf-based Grand Ayatollah Ali al-Sistani split in practice from the

PMU Commission and re-formed as a separate entity answerable to the PMO, yet still technically part of the PMU. Moreover, various groups within the PMU have a high degree of operational autonomy, such as Saraya al-Salam, the Badr Organisation and Asa'ib Ahl al-Haq.

Structure: Approximately 40–60 paramilitary units under the umbrella organisation. Formally, the PMU is a branch of the Iraqi security apparatus. However, each unit is organised around an internal leader, influential figures and fighters.

History: Formed in 2014 when Grand Ayatollah Ali al-Sistani called upon Iraqi men to protect their homeland against ISIS, the PMU brought together new and pre-existing groups. In 2016, the units were formally recognised as a branch of the Iraqi security apparatus.

Objectives: Initially, to fight ISIS. Some units have evolved into hybrid entities seeking political power. The PMU also

Popular Mobilisation Units (PMU)

functions as an effective counter-protest force and seeks to use violence and coercion to intimidate political rivals. All groups are committed, at least nominally, to expelling US and foreign forces from Iraq. Rising tensions with Turkiye have also been noted, with a rocket attack on the Turkish military base near Mosul (Zilkan) in April 2021 being attributed to PMU groups.

Opponents: ISIS, US and allied forces, and Turkiye.

Affiliates/allies: SCF, ISF and Iranian Islamic Revolutionary Guard Corps (IRGC).

Resources/capabilities: Units receive state funds but the capabilities of the units differ. Those supported by Iran receive arms and training from the IRGC, including heavy weapons and small arms.

Islamic State (ISIS)

Strength: Between 5,000 and 7,000 in Iraq and Syria, half of which are fighters.[4]

Areas of operation: Active predominantly in Iraq's northern and central provinces in mountainous and desert areas. Most attacks in 2022–23 occurred in Baghdad and Diyala governorates.

Leadership: Abu al-Husain al-Husaini al-Qurashi (caliph and leader of ISIS since November 2022).

Structure: ISIS operates as a covert terrorist network across Iraq, using a largely autonomous sleeper-cell structure. The organisation continues to have meticulous bureaucratic structures, internal discipline, a strong online presence and robust financial systems.

History: Originated in Iraq around 2003 but proclaimed itself a separate group from al-Qaeda in Iraq, fighting to create a

caliphate, during the Syrian civil war. Between 2014 and 2017, ISIS controlled extensive territories and governed more than eight million people in Syria and Iraq. It has now lost all its territory, since 2017 in Iraq and since March 2019 in Syria.

Objectives: ISIS continues to fight and project ideological influence globally. In Iraq it operates through decentralised, guerrilla-style insurgent tactics, carrying out hit-and-run attacks, kidnappings and killings of civilians and local tribal and political leaders, and targeted assassinations of ISF members.

Opponents: ISF, Kurdish Peshmerga, PMU and CJTF–OIR forces.

Affiliates/allies: ISIS fighters in other countries.

Resources/capabilities: Carries out attacks through shootings and explosions, using small arms, cars, improvised explosive devices (IEDs), suicide-vest IEDs, suicide-vehicle-borne IEDs and mortar bombs.

Kurdish Peshmerga

Strength: Between 200,000 and 300,000.[5]

Areas of operation: KRG.

Leadership: Nechirvan Barzani (commander-in-chief), Shoresh Ismail Abdulla (minister of Peshmerga affairs) and Lt-Gen. Jamal Mohammad (Peshmerga chief of staff).

Structure: A Kurdish paramilitary force that acts as the military of the KRG and Iraqi Kurdistan. While remaining independent, it operates officially as part of the Kurdish military system. Peshmerga forces are divided between political factions, the most dominant being the KDP and the Patriotic Union of Kurdistan.

History: Began as a Kurdish nationalist movement in the 1920s and soon developed into a security organisation. Following the ISIS advance, the Peshmerga took disputed territories in June 2014 – including Kirkuk – which were retaken by the ISF in October 2017.

Objectives: Ensure security in the KRG, including by fighting ISIS.

Opponents: ISIS, PKK and PMU.

Affiliates/allies: CJTF–OIR and ISF.

Resources/capabilities: Poorly equipped, lacking heavy weapons, armoured vehicles and facilities. The US has provided some financial assistance and light weapons, such as rifles and machine guns.

Kurdistan Workers' Party (PKK)

Strength: 4,000–5,000 (estimate) in Turkiye and Iraq.[6]

Areas of operation: Sinjar, northern Iraq.

Leadership: Abdullah Öcalan (ideological leader, despite his imprisonment since 1999), Murat Karayilan (acting leader on the ground since Öcalan's capture) and Bahoz Erdal (military commander).

Structure: While operating under the same command and leadership, the PKK's armed wing is divided into the People's Defence Forces (HPG) and the Free Women's Unit (YJA-STAR).

History: Founded by Öcalan in 1978. The PKK has been engaged in an insurgency campaign against the Turkish Armed Forces (TSK) since 1984.

Objectives: Preserve its operational autonomy and capacity with a base of operation in Iraq to support its broader agenda in Turkiye.

Opponents: TSK and Kurdish Peshmerga.

Affiliates/allies: Sinjar Alliance in Iraq, PMU and the Syrian Democratic Forces/People's Protection Units (SDF/YPG) in Syria.

Resources/capabilities: Relies on money-laundering activities and drug trafficking to generate revenues, in addition to donations from the Kurdish community and diaspora and left-wing international supporters. The PKK relies on highly mobile units, using guerrilla tactics against Turkish military targets.

Middle East and North Africa

Turkish Armed Forces (TSK)

Strength: 4,000 personnel unilaterally deployed in Iraq, with over 86 under the aegis of NATO Mission Iraq.

Areas of operation: Northern Iraq, especially Dohuk and Nineva plains. The TSK is currently engaged in *Operation Claw-Tiger* against the PKK in the Haftanin region. It maintains Zilkan base in Nineva.

Leadership: President Recep Tayyip Erdoğan (commander-in-chief), Gen. (retd) Hulusi Akar (minister of national defence) and Gen. Yasar Guler (chief of general staff).

Structure: Turkish Army units operating under the Turkish Land Forces Command and squadrons carrying out airstrikes operating under the Air Force Command are subordinate to the Chief of General Staff. Gendarmerie units reporting to the Gendarmerie Command are subordinate to the Ministry of Interior.

History: Rebuilt after the collapse of the Ottoman Empire in 1922. The TSK was significantly restructured after the country joined NATO in 1951, to become NATO's second-largest armed force.

Objectives: Combat the PKK and its allied forces and prevent it from establishing safe havens and mobility corridors in northern Iraq; prevent the PMU from overrunning Sinjar and establishing a land corridor to Syria for Iran.

Opponents: PKK, Sinjar Alliance, PMU and YPG/SDF in Syria.

Affiliates/allies: Miscellaneous local militias, such as those connected to the Iraqi Turkmen Front, which received training from Turkish Special Forces from 2015.

Resources/capabilities: Turkiye's defence budget for 2022 was US$6.3 billion. Its military capabilities include air attack and intelligence, surveillance and reconnaissance assets such as the F-16 and the *Bayraktar* TB2 uninhabited aerial vehicle, armoured tanks and special-forces units.

Combined Joint Task Force–*Operation Inherent Resolve* (CJTF–OIR)

Strength: The exact number of coalition forces (including advisers, special forces, etc.) in Iraq is unknown. The US provides the largest component of the coalition (2,500 people) and has been repositioning its forces and handing over Iraqi bases to the Iraqi government. By December 2021, the CJTF–OIR had nominally shifted its role from combatant to advisory.

Areas of operation: Working in tandem with the ISF in areas previously held by ISIS, including Anbar, Diyala, Nineva and Salahaddin.

Leadership: Maj.-Gen. Matthew McFarlane.

Structure: The US leads the CJTF–OIR, which brings together over 20 coalition partners.

History: Established in October 2014 when the US Department of Defense formalised ongoing military operations against ISIS.

Objectives: Fight ISIS in Iraq and Syria, through airstrikes in support of Iraqi and Kurdish forces. Ground forces are deployed as trainers and advisers.

Opponents: ISIS and PMU.

Affiliates/allies: ISF and Kurdish Peshmerga.

Resources/capabilities: Air support (airstrikes complementing military operations by Iraqi armed forces) and artillery.

Notes

[1]   'Iraq's al-Sadr Demands Dissolution of Parliament, Early Elections', Al-Jazeera, 3 August 2022.

[2]   'Supporters of Iraq's al-Sadr Leave Green Zone After Violence', Al-Jazeera, 30 August 2022.

[3]   European Union Agency for Asylum, 'Country Guidance: Iraq', June 2022, p. 72.

[4]   United Nations Security Council, 'Thirty-first Report of the Analytical Support and Sanctions Monitoring Team Submitted Pursuant to Resolution 2610 (2021) Concerning ISIL (Da'esh), Al-Qaida and Associated Individuals and Entities', S/2023/95, 13 February 2023, p. 11.

[5]   Bilal Wahab, 'The Rise and Fall of Kurdish Power in Iraq', Washington Institute for Near East Policy, Spring 2023.

[6]   Bureau of Counterterrorism, US Department of State, 'Country Reports on Terrorism 2021', 2021, p. 300.

ISRAEL–PALESTINIAN TERRITORIES

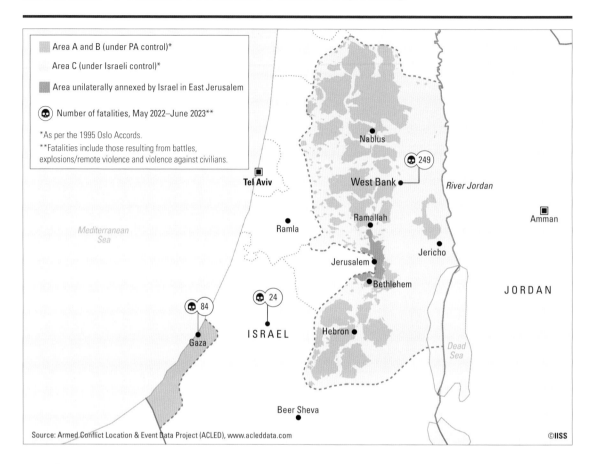

Source: Armed Conflict Location & Event Data Project (ACLED), www.acleddata.com   ©IISS

Conflict Overview

The Israel–Palestinian Territories conflict began in November 1947 with clashes in Mandatory Palestine between Arab Palestinian and Zionist groups. The outbreak of hostilities followed the United Nations General Assembly's adoption that year of Resolution 181, which called for the partition of the territory into two states along ethno-religious lines.

Upon the termination of the British Mandate of Palestine in May 1948, the Zionist leadership announced the creation of the state of Israel. An Arab intervention to support the Palestinians – who rejected the partition plan – was defeated. It was followed by the expansion of the Israeli state and the expulsion of approximately 750,000 Palestinians. The subsequent 1967 Six-Day War and the 1973 Yom Kippur War saw Israel triple the size of its territory by capturing East Jerusalem

and the West Bank from Jordan, the Gaza Strip and the Sinai Peninsula from Egypt, and the Golan Heights from Syria. In response, the UN Security Council called for an Israeli withdrawal from the occupied territories. East Jerusalem and the Golan Heights were permanently annexed in the early 1980s, while the Sinai Peninsula was returned to Egypt in 1979. Parts of the West Bank are currently governed by the Palestinian Authority (PA); the Gaza Strip, which Israel evacuated in 2005, is now ruled by Hamas.

Occupation, denial of rights and deteriorating socio-economic conditions sparked Palestinian intifadas in 1987–93 and 2000–05. Since 2020, armed groups have proliferated in the West Bank in the context of the PA's eroding legitimacy. Consequent Israeli incursions into the West Bank led the PA to

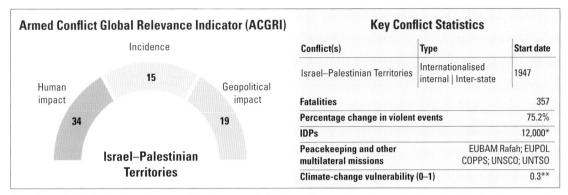

ACGRI pillars: IISS calculation based on multiple sources for 2022 and 2023 (scale: 0–100), except for some cases according to data availability. See Notes on Methodology and Data Appendix for all variables and further details on Key Conflict Statistics. *For Palestinian Territories only. **For Israel only.

suspend security coordination with Israel in January 2023, while Israeli authorities have since June 2022 withheld tax revenues collected on behalf of the PA, deepening the economic crisis there.

The 2020 US-brokered Abraham Accords – which established diplomatic relations between Israel and Bahrain, Morocco, Sudan and the United Arab Emirates – have failed to produce dividends for the Palestinians. Israeli settlement expansion has continued unabated, despite initial reports of a settlement freeze. With peace talks between the parties stalled since the 1993 Oslo Accords, violence has risen in recent years.[1] Settler violence towards Palestinians has increased dramatically, with recorded incidents in the first half of 2021 more than double the figure for the same period in 2020.[2] Moreover, an uptick in Palestinian attacks in Israel and against Israeli targets in the West Bank prompted the Israel Defense Forces (IDF) to launch *Operation Break the Wave* in March 2022.

Conflict Update

The establishment in late 2022 of what is widely viewed to be the most right-wing government in Israeli history has raised questions about Israel's short- and long-term outlook for the Israel–Palestinian Territories conflict. The coalition government of Benjamin Netanyahu includes Religious Zionism and Jewish Power, two parties that openly oppose Palestinian statehood and have made annexation of Palestinian land part of their platforms. The behaviour of senior Israeli officials has undermined perceptions that the government is committed to a negotiated peace settlement. Furthermore, the government has transferred oversight of civilian affairs in the West Bank from military to civilian authorities under Minister of Finance Bezalel Smotrich. This development, in effect, extends Israeli sovereignty into the West Bank and has been criticised as tantamount to annexation.[3]

This hardline approach coincides with widespread social unrest around the coalition's plan to overhaul the judicial system to give the executive branch more power over the judiciary. These convulsions have further diverted attention from the conflict.

On the Palestinian side, political infighting between the two main political parties – Fatah, which dominates the West Bank and the PA, and Hamas, which controls Gaza – has prevented the emergence of a unified political strategy for establishing a Palestinian state. With the legitimacy of the PA decreasing – due to a combination of authoritarian measures and rising criticism of its security cooperation with Israel – Palestinians are increasingly divided. A December 2022 poll found that should presidential elections be held, Hamas leader Ismail Haniyyeh would defeat PA President Mahmoud Abbas by 54% to 36%.[4] At the same time, many Palestinians have resorted to alternative tactics in the struggle against Israel. Armed groups such as the Palestinian Islamic Jihad (PIJ) and Hamas's military wing advocate armed struggle and remain influential in Palestinian society and politics. Popular frustration with the PA's poor and brutal leadership and Israel's continued military occupation have also led to the rise of new unaffiliated militant groups.[5]

Middle East and North Africa

There was an uptick in violent events during the reporting period. 2022 represented the 'sixth year of consecutive annual increase in the number of Israeli settler attacks in the occupied West Bank'.[6] Between May 2022 and March 2023, 235 Palestinian and 46 Israeli fatalities were recorded.[7] There was an increase in Palestinian lone-wolf attacks, as well as violent clashes between Palestinian civilians and fighters and Israeli security forces and civilian settlers. Israeli society was shocked by the heightened incidence of deadly shooting and car-ramming attacks in Israel, prompting Netanyahu to announce plans to loosen gun laws for Israelis. In light of the intensified violence, Israel detained 3,000 Palestinians between January and May 2023.[8]

The epicentre of violence has shifted away from Gaza towards the West Bank and Israel: 84% of Palestinian fatalities and 48% of Israeli fatalities between May 2022 and March 2023 happened in the West Bank.[9] Settlers attacked Palestinian villages with increasing frequency and violence. The political brinkmanship of the coalition has fuelled intercommunal violence. For example, Smotrich said that the 'village of Huwara needs to be wiped out' following a settler attack on the village that was reported to have injured 350 people.[10] The settler attack was triggered by the killing of two Israelis by a Palestinian a day earlier. Hate crimes by Jewish extremists against Palestinian Arabs were on the rise during the reporting period, with 838 such incidents recorded from January to the end of November 2022, compared to 446 in all of 2021.[11]

In August 2022, hostilities broke out in Gaza between the PIJ and the IDF amid rising tensions resulting from Israel's efforts to crack down on PIJ activities in the West Bank. Over 1,000 rockets were launched from Gaza into Israel and at least 20 major shooting attacks took place across Israel and the West Bank, resulting in 11 civilian deaths during the reporting period.[12] Israeli incursions into the West Bank as part of *Operation Break the Wave* were countered by new, unaffiliated and localised Palestinian groups, such as the Lion's Den and the Jenin Brigades. These armed groups are popular: a December 2022 survey found that 72% of Palestinians supported the formation of independent armed groups, such as the Lion's Den, and that 48% supported disbanding the PA.[13] These new cycles of violence in Israel and the occupied territories are prompting speculation of a third intifada.

Conflict Parties

Israel Defense Forces (IDF)	
Strength: 169,500 active military, 465,000 in reserve.	**Opponents:** Hamas, Hizbullah, Iran and Iran-backed groups.
Areas of operation: Gaza Strip, Iraq, Lebanon, Syria and the West Bank.	**Affiliates/allies:** Strong military ties with the United States.
Leadership: Lt-Gen. Herzi Halevi, appointed chief of staff in January 2023.	**Resources/capabilities:** The IDF boasts sophisticated equipment and training and has received military aid from the US. Israel has a highly capable defence industry, including aerospace; intelligence, surveillance and reconnaissance; and counter-rocket systems. It is also believed to have an operational nuclear-weapons capability, although estimates of the size of this arsenal vary. The IDF can operate simultaneously in the West Bank, Gaza, Lebanon, Syria and Iraq, though it favours a clandestine, incursive nature when operating outside the Palestinian Territories.
Structure: Three service branches consisting of air force, ground forces and navy.	
History: The IDF was founded in 1948 from the paramilitary organisation Haganah, which fought during the 1948 Arab–Israeli War.	
Objectives: Homeland defence.	

Hamas	
Strength: Hamas's military wing, the Izz al-Din al-Qassam Brigades (IDQ), is estimated to comprise 30,000 fighters, including 400 naval commandos.[14]	**Structure:** Hamas's international political leadership exercises ultimate authority; other wings and branches, such as the IDQ, observe the strategy and guidelines established by Hamas's Shura Council and Political Bureau, or Politburo.
Areas of operation: Gaza Strip, Israel and the West Bank.	
Leadership: Yahya Sinwar (head of Hamas) and Ismail Haniyyeh (chief of the Political Bureau).	**History:** Founded in 1987 by members of the Muslim Brotherhood in the Palestinian Territories, Hamas is the

Hamas

largest Palestinian militant Islamist group. Australia, Canada, the European Union, the United Kingdom and the US have designated it a terrorist group. However, many Palestinians view Hamas as a legitimate popular resistance group.

Objectives: The group's original charter called for the obliteration or dissolution of Israel and for the full liberation of Palestine, but Haniyyeh announced in 2008 that Hamas would accept a Palestinian state within the borders of the pre-1967 war. This position was confirmed in a new charter in 2017, in which the group agreed to concede to the national consensus regarding a political solution with Israel.

Opponents: Fatah-led PA, Israel, PIJ (periodically) and Salafi-jihadist groups.

Affiliates/allies: Iran.

Resources/capabilities: The IDQ's capabilities include artillery rockets, mortars and anti-tank systems. Israel's military actions have periodically degraded the command and physical infrastructure of Hamas but have seemingly had little effect on the IDQ's long-term ability to import and produce rockets and other weapons.

Palestinian Islamic Jihad (PIJ)

Strength: The PIJ's armed wing, the al-Quds Brigades, is estimated to comprise up to 8,000 fighters.[15]

Areas of operation: Gaza Strip and the West Bank.

Leadership: Ziad al-Nakhaleh.

Structure: Governed by a 15-member leadership council. In 2018, the PIJ council elected nine new members to represent its members in the West Bank, the Gaza Strip, Israeli prisons and abroad.

History: Established in 1979 by Fathi Shaqaqi and Abd al-Aziz Awda, who were members of the Egyptian Muslim Brotherhood until the late 1970s. Of the Gaza-based militant

groups, the PIJ poses the most significant challenge to Hamas's authority there, having derailed unofficial ceasefire agreements between Hamas and Israel in the past.

Objectives: Establish a sovereign, Islamic Palestinian state within the borders of pre-1948 Palestine.

Opponents: Israel and, periodically, Hamas.

Affiliates/allies: Iran, Syria and Hizbullah.

Resources/capabilities: The PIJ has expanded the size of its weapons cache by producing its own rockets. Before the August 2022 hostilities, the PIJ was estimated to have between 6,000 and 7,000 rockets.[16]

Other relevant parties

Several small armed resistance groups have emerged across the West Bank. These groups are very localised and are generally comprised of young men. The Lion's Den, the Nablus Brigade, and the Jenin Brigade are reportedly the largest of such groups. Unaffiliated with the traditional parties of the conflict, their political agendas are unclear. They conduct primarily defensive operations in response to Israeli raids and operations in the West Bank, although they have occasionally attacked Israeli military infrastructure and settlers.

Notes

1   Israeli settlements and outposts currently number 132 and 146, respectively, comprising almost 700,000 settlers in the West Bank and Jerusalem, in violation of Article 49 of the Fourth Geneva Convention. See Peace Now, 'Jerusalem'. Note on the calculation of the 700,000 figure: Peace Now estimates 465,400 settlers in the West Bank in 2021 (Peace Now, 'Population') plus a further 229,377 settlers in Jerusalem in 2021. A recent report puts the figure for settlers in the West Bank in January 2023 at 502,678. See 'Yesha Settler Umbrella Group Says Over Half a Million Israelis Live in West Bank', *Times of Israel*, 12 May 2023.

2   Human Rights Watch, 'World Report 2022: Events of 2021', 16 December 2021, p. 357.

3   '"Israel Practices Apartheid," Say Israeli Law Professors', Middle East Monitor, 30 March 2023.

4   Palestinian Center for Policy and Survey Research, 'Public Opinion Poll No (86)', 10 December 2022.

5   Human Rights Watch reports that the PA 'systematically arrests arbitrarily and tortures dissidents'. See Human Rights Watch, 'World Report 2022: Events of 2021', p. 354.

6   UN Office of the High Commissioner for Human Rights, 'Israel: UN Experts Condemn Record Year of Israeli Violence in the Occupied West Bank', 15 December 2022.

7   UN Office for the Coordination of Humanitarian Affairs (UNOCHA), 'Data on Casualties'.

8   'Israel Detained 3,000 Palestinians Since Start of 2023', Middle East Monitor, 30 May 2023.

9   UNOCHA, 'Data on Casualties'.

10   Loveday Morris and Sufian Taha, 'Six Killed in Israeli Raid on Jenin as Settlers Attack Palestinian Town Again', *Washington*

Post, 7 March 2023; and Bethan McKernan, '"Never Like This Before": Settler Violence in West Bank Escalates', *Guardian*, 27 February 2023.

11 Lilach Shoval, 'Israeli Security Agencies Concerned Over Rise in Settler Violence in West Bank', Al-Monitor, 5 December 2022.

12 See Israeli Security Agency (Shabak), 'Monthly Summary', August 2022; and Ministry of Foreign Affairs, 'Wave of Terror 2015–2023', 18 May 2023.

13 Palestinian Center for Policy and Survey Research, 'Public Opinion Poll No (86)', 13 December 2022.

14 'Senior IDF Commander Says Hamas Has 30,000 Men, 7,000 Rockets, Dozens of Drones', *Times of Israel*, 11 February 2021.

15 Australian National Security, 'Palestinian Islamic Jihad', 17 January 2022.

16 Shai Levy, '"עלות השחר": המ הבדל ןיב מבצע לום גה'יאד הזכל לום סאמחה?' ['Dawn': What Is the Difference Between an Operation Against Jihad and One Against Hamas?], Mako, 6 August 2022.

YEMEN

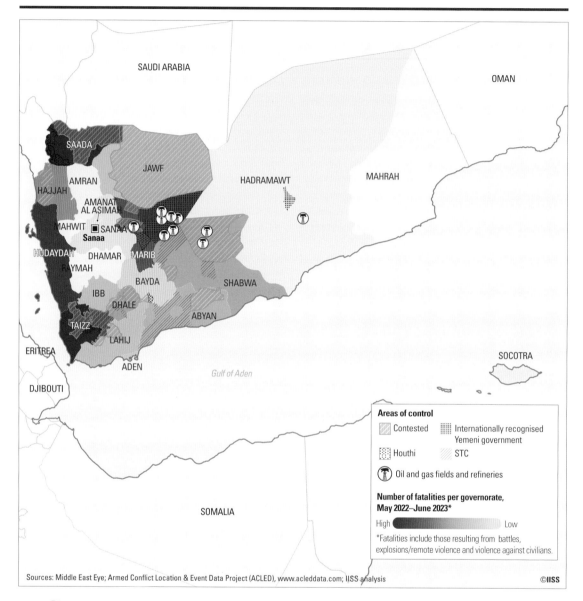

Areas of control

- Contested
- Houthi
- Internationally recognised Yemeni government
- STC
- Oil and gas fields and refineries

Number of fatalities per governorate,
May 2022–June 2023*

High ▬▬▬▬▬ Low

*Fatalities include those resulting from battles,
explosions/remote violence and violence against civilians.

Sources: Middle East Eye; Armed Conflict Location & Event Data Project (ACLED), www.acleddata.com; IISS analysis   ©IISS

Conflict Overview

Like most conflicts in Yemen, the current war has deep roots. In 1962, a coup within the military overthrew the Zaydi Imamate and, following an eight-year civil war, instituted a republic in northern Yemen. Zaydi *sayyids* – descendants of the Prophet Muhammad who had been at the top of Yemen's social pyramid – suddenly found themselves at the bottom and frequently suffered discrimination.

The Houthis – also known as Ansarullah ('Partisans of God') – grew out of Zaydi dissatisfaction with republican rule and a corresponding desire to protect and preserve traditional Zaydi teachings and theology in the late 1980s. From 2004–10, the Houthis fought six wars against the Yemeni government under then-president Ali Abdullah Saleh. Following the Arab Spring and Saleh's forced

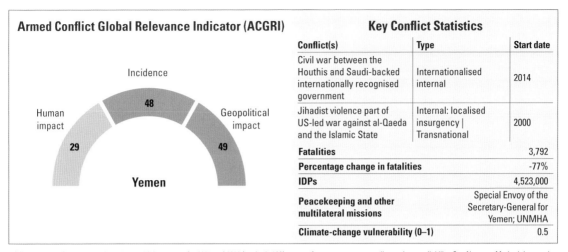

ACGRI pillars: IISS calculation based on multiple sources for 2022 and 2023 (scale: 0–100), except for some cases according to data availability. See Notes on Methodology and Data Appendix for all variables and further details on Key Conflict Statistics.

resignation in 2012, the Houthis began to consolidate control in their home province of Saada, eventually moving on Yemen's capital, Sanaa.

In September 2014 the Houthis took Sanaa, eventually placing the country's internationally recognised president, Abd Rabbo Mansour Hadi, under house arrest. In early 2015, Hadi escaped house arrest and travelled to Aden, where he asked Yemen's neighbours in the Gulf Cooperation Council to intervene militarily and restore him to power.[1] Saudi Arabia, which was concerned that the Houthis, a Zaydi–Shia revivalist group, might become a Hizbullah-like organisation on its southern border, put together a coalition to combat the movement. The Saudi-led coalition began airstrikes in March 2015.

The Saudi-led coalition has largely relied on airstrikes and local forces on the ground. The Houthis have benefitted from a growing alliance with Iran, which has smuggled ballistic-missile components into Yemen in violation of United Nations Security Council (UNSC) resolutions.[2] After more than eight years of fighting, the Houthis maintain control over much of northern Yemen, while it is unlikely that the group can be removed from Sanaa.

Conflict Update

In April 2022, the Houthis and the Saudi-led coalition agreed to a two-month nationwide ceasefire.[3] A week later, on 7 April, Saudi Arabia and the United Arab Emirates (UAE), which also has troops on the ground in Yemen, forced president Hadi to step down.[4]

Immediately prior to his resignation speech, Hadi removed from office then-vice president Ali Mohsen – who otherwise would have taken power – and instead handed executive authority to an eight-person Presidential Leadership Council (PLC). The latter, whose members were selected by Saudi Arabia and the UAE, was intended to present a common front and paper over the divisions that had hobbled the anti-Houthi alliance in recent years. Most notably, the PLC included representatives from the Southern Transitional Council (STC), which advocates for an independent south; the al-Islah political grouping; and prominent military figures, such as Tareq Saleh, who was allied with the Houthis until December 2017.

The nationwide truce between the Houthis and the Saudi-led coalition was extended twice, each time for two months, before expiring in October 2022.[5] However, a resumption of large-scale violence did not ensue; for the most part, the country settled into an unofficial truce.

With a few exceptions, the clashes that took place after the ceasefire's expiry were fought between the various parties of the PLC – particularly al-Islah and the STC. In July and August 2022, forces loyal to the STC fought against those affiliated with al-Islah in southern Shabwa province.[6] Although both groups are represented on the PLC, they have conflicting goals. The STC wants to create and head an independent southern Yemen. Al-Islah favours a reunified Yemen with a strong Muslim Brotherhood influence. Although these clashes eventually tapered off, the tensions and divisions within the PLC remained.

A significant breakthrough in peace discussions came in March 2023, when China brokered a deal between Saudi Arabia and Iran to restore their diplomatic relations.[7] Riyadh agreed to cut funding to Iran International, a satellite channel that Iran blamed for stoking domestic protests, while Tehran agreed to cease smuggling missile components to the Houthis and to pressure the group not to launch cross-border strikes into Saudi Arabia.[8] Weeks later, in April 2023, Saudi negotiators travelled to Sanaa to speak directly with the Houthis. Although these talks failed to produce a comprehensive settlement, they did appear to be a step in that direction. Immediately after the talks, nearly 900 prisoners were exchanged between the two sides, including several high-profile prisoners the Houthis had effectively held as human shields.[9] These developments highlight Saudi Arabia's increasing fatigue with the conflict and its willingness to accept Houthi control in the north as part of the price for its withdrawal. However, it is unclear whether the Houthis will be satisfied with only the north, or if they will attempt to take Marib and then advance into Shabwa and Hadramawt. These provinces contain the bulk of Yemen's oil and gas fields; the Houthis will need an economic base to maintain an independent state in the north.

Equally unclear is whether the PLC can hold together absent the support of Saudi Arabia and the UAE. Early signs suggest that its survival is unlikely, which may mean that a complete Saudi and UAE withdrawal from Yemen will bring the war full circle, transforming it from a regional rivalry back into a civil war between the Houthis and their rivals.

Conflict Parties

The Houthi movement (Ansarullah)

Strength: 200,000.

Areas of operation: The group holds much of northern Yemen, parts of the Red Sea coast in and around Hudaydah, and parts of Marib.

Leadership: Abdul Malik al-Houthi.

Structure: Abdul Malik al-Houthi is the supreme commander. However, the organisation has both an official branch of power – the Supreme Political Council, which is headed by President Mahdi al-Mashat – and a more informal group of 'supervisors', many of whom are appointed by Mohammad Ali al-Houthi, who heads the Supreme Revolutionary Council.

History: The Houthis began as a Zaydi revivalist movement in the late 1980s, fought six successive wars against the Yemeni government from 2004–10, and took control of Sanaa in 2014.

Objectives: To hold and govern at least northern Yemen, including the oil and gas fields in Marib province.

Opponents: The Saudi-led coalition, including the UAE, and the internationally recognised Yemeni government represented by the PLC.

Affiliates/allies: Iran and Hizbullah.

Resources/capabilities: Ballistic missiles and uninhabited aerial vehicles (UAVs) capable of reaching Riyadh and the UAE.

Southern Transitional Council (STC)

Strength: 55,000.

Areas of operation: Holds Aden, much of Lahij, Socotra and parts of Abyan and Shabwa; active in Hadramawt.

Leadership: Aidarous al-Zubaidi (president of the STC, member of the PLC).

Structure: The STC is led by a president and has a leadership council.

History: The STC was formed in 2017 after then-president Hadi dismissed al-Zubaidi and several other influential politicians from their positions.

Objectives: Establish an independent state in southern Yemen.

Opponents: The STC is nominally opposed to the Houthis, but within the anti-Houthi coalition they are opposed to al-Islah.

Affiliates/allies: UAE.

Resources/capabilities: Many – although not all – of the local actors that the UAE began establishing in early 2016, including the Security Belt Forces, form the STC's armed wing.

Joint Forces

Strength: 15,000.

Areas of operation: Red Sea coast and Taizz province.

Joint Forces

Leadership: Tareq Saleh, who is also a member of the PLC.

Structure: The group follows a traditional command-and-control military structure, although in 2021 it opened a political office.

History: Following the violent break-up of the Houthi–Saleh alliance in December 2017, Tareq Saleh and a group of former Republican Guard forces moved south and joined UAE troops in Mokha.

Objectives: Ensure a seat at the negotiating table for what remains of Ali Abdullah Saleh's network.

Opponents: Houthis.

Affiliates/allies: UAE.

Resources/capabilities: Small arms, light infantry vehicles, and some intelligence, surveillance and reconnaissance (ISR) capabilities. Much of the Joint Forces' resources are provided by the UAE.

Giants Brigades

Strength: 30,000–35,000.

Areas of operation: Primarily the Red Sea coast, although the group has been deployed to Shabwa previously.

Leadership: One of the commanders, Abdul al-Rahman al-Muharami (Abu Zara'a), is a member of the PLC.

Structure: Thirteen Brigades, backed by the UAE, and led by individual commanders.

History: The UAE established the Giants Brigades in 2016 along the southern Red Sea coast. Much of its initial training took place in and around the Horn of Africa.

Objectives: The Giants Brigades is largely comprised of Salafi fighters. Although largely pro-secession, the leadership until recently did not appear to support the STC. However, in May 2023 Abu Zara'a joined the STC.

Opponents: Houthis.

Affiliates/allies: UAE and increasingly STC.

Resources/capabilities: Backed and armed by the UAE, which provides small and light arms, infantry vehicles and some ISR capabilities.

Hadrami Elite Forces

Strength: 7,000.

Areas of operation: Hadramawt.

Leadership: Faraj al-Bahsani, a former governor of Hadramawt province, and STC vice president since May 2023.

Structure: Recruits from both coastal and Wadi Hadramawt and is organised along traditional military lines, with local commanders in charge of different units.

History: The UAE established the force in 2016 to expel al-Qaeda in the Arabian Peninsula (AQAP) from Mukalla.

Objectives: Ensure a degree of Hadhrami autonomy and security, and revenue capture from Yemen's resources.

Opponents: Houthis.

Affiliates/allies: UAE and increasingly STC.

Resources/capabilities: Backed and armed by the UAE, which provides small and light arms, light infantry vehicles and some ISR capabilities.

Al-Islah affiliated forces

Strength: 20,000.

Areas of operation: Red Sea coast, Taizz, Marib, Shabwa, Abyan and Hadramawt provinces.

Leadership: Muhammad al-Yadumi is the party's chairman, although Abdullah al-Alimi, the former director of president Hadi's office, is a member of the PLC.

Structure: Al-Islah is a political party that has many members serving in prominent positions within the Yemeni armed forces. Its affiliated forces do not have their own units or brigades and, instead, are spread throughout the Yemeni military, although they are concentrated primarily in Taizz, Marib and Wadi Hadramawt.

History: Al-Islah was formed in 1990. Under the Hadi government it cultivated ties with military officers and ensured that its members were promoted through Abdullah al-Alimi.

Objectives: Ensure that al-Islah has a prominent role in any Yemeni government, that the country remains united and, failing that, to ensure that the STC does not take unilateral control of the south.

Opponents: Houthis, UAE and STC.

Affiliates/allies: Saudi Arabia and some tribal support.

Resources/capabilities: Much of the military in Marib and Taizz provinces and in the 1st Military Zone are affiliated with al-Islah and, as such, have light and medium arms, armoured vehicles, missiles and some air capabilities.

Saudi Arabian armed forces

Strength: 15,000 estimated in Yemen and on the Yemeni border.

Areas of operation: Northern border areas, Marib, Aden, Hadramawt, Mahrah provinces and Socotra.

Middle East and North Africa

Saudi Arabian armed forces

Leadership: Muhammad bin Salman (crown prince and defence minister).

Structure: Units operating in Yemen are part of the kingdom's military and under the command of the Saudi defence ministry.

History: Saudi Arabia entered the war in 2015 as the leader of a ten-country coalition. Following the UAE's drawdown in

mid-2019, Saudi Arabia deployed more ground troops and took over the UAE base in Aden.

Objectives: Exit the war, without unduly strengthening an Iranian ally on its southern border.

Opponents: Houthis.

Affiliates/allies: UAE, PLC, Tareq Saleh and al-Islah.

Resources/capabilities: ISR assets (UAVs and satellites), fighter jets, air defences, small arms, light weapons and tanks.

UAE armed forces

Strength: 3,000 in Yemen (estimate).

Areas of operation: Mokha, Shabwa and throughout southern Yemen via UAE-backed local actors.

Leadership: Sheikh Muhammad bin Zayed Al Nahyan (the UAE's de facto ruler).

Structure: Following the UAE drawdown in mid-2019, the remaining forces largely function as advisers.

History: The UAE joined the Saudi-led coalition as its primary partner in 2015. It deployed a number of ground troops and took significant casualties. In mid-2019, as UAE-backed local actors took on greater security responsibilities, the UAE

drew down its forces. However, it retains a small presence in Yemen and is able to influence events through UAE-backed local actors.

Objectives: Maintain veto authority across southern Yemen, particularly along the coasts, to ensure the UAE's commercial and shipping interests.

Opponents: Houthis and al-Islah.

Affiliates/allies: Saudi Arabia, STC, Tareq Saleh, Giants Brigades and Hadrami Elite Forces.

Resources/capabilities: ISR assets (UAVs and satellites), fighter jets, air defences, small arms and light weapons.

Other relevant parties

Al-Qaeda in the Arabian Peninsula (AQAP) and an Islamic State (ISIS) affiliate are active in Yemen. AQAP, which numbers roughly 6,000 members, is active in Abyan, Bayda and parts of Shabwa. ISIS, which has fewer members than AQAP, is present in southern Yemen.

Notes

[1] UN Security Council (UNSC), 'Identical Letters Dated 26 March 2015 from the Permanent Representative of Qatar to the United Nations Addressed to the Secretary-General and the President of the Security Council', S/2015/217, 27 March 2015.

[2] See UNSC, 'Final Report of the Panel of Experts on Yemen', S/2018/594, 26 January 2018.

[3] 'UN Welcomes Announcement of Two-month Truce in Yemen', UN News, 1 April 2022.

[4] Summer Said and Stephen Kalin, 'Saudi Arabia Pushed Yemen's Elected President to Step Aside, Saudi and Yemeni Officials Say', Wall Street Journal, 17 April 2022.

[5] Mohammed Alghobari and Reyam Mokhashef, 'Yemen Truce Expires as UN Keeps Pushing for Broader Deal', Reuters, 4 October 2022.

[6] 'Tensions Between Islah- and STC-affiliated Forces in Shabwa Explode with Assassination Attempt', Yemen Review, Sana'a Center for Strategic Studies, 12 August 2022.

[7] Peter Baker, 'Iran–Saudi Pact Is Brokered by China, Leaving US on Sidelines', New York Times, 11 March 2023.

[8] Dion Nissenbaum, Summer Said and Benoit Faucon, 'Iran Agrees to Stop Arming Houthis in Yemen as Part of Pact with Saudi Arabia', Wall Street Journal, 16 March 2023.

[9] Aziz El Yaakoubi and Mohammed Alghobari, 'Houthi Official Says Yemen Peace Talks Made Progress, Further Rounds Planned', Reuters, 14 April 2023.

LIBYA

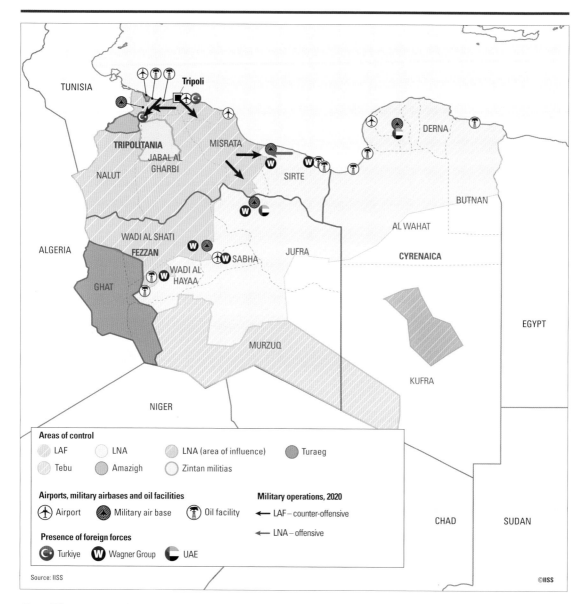

Source: IISS

©IISS

Conflict Overview

In 2011, large-scale protests against Muammar Gadhafi – who had been the de facto leader of Libya since 1969 – sparked a revolution that led to a civil war between the regime and the rebels. The NATO-led intervention informed by the Responsibility to Protect principle brought about a regime change that saw revolutionary forces take control of the country. In 2014, new divisions became apparent

that bore strong similarities to the regional divide between Islamist and secular forces that had become more visible in Egypt after its 2013 military coup. This second phase of the civil war quickened Libya's fragmentation and provided opportunities for terrorist organisations to proliferate.

In April 2019, Field Marshal Khalifa Haftar, whose Libyan National Army (LNA) had

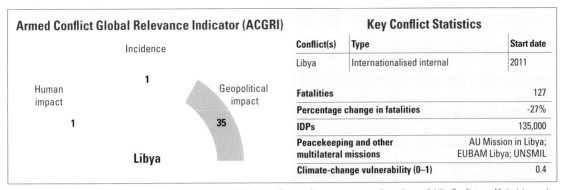

ACGRI pillars: IISS calculation based on multiple sources for 2022 and 2023 (scale: 0–100), except for some cases according to data availability. See Notes on Methodology and Data Appendix for all variables and further details on Key Conflict Statistics.

progressively taken control across Cyrenaica and Fezzan, launched *Operation Flood of Dignity* against the internationally recognised government in Tripoli (the Government of National Accord, GNA). It was a pivotal moment in the conflict, transforming it from low-intensity fighting into a major confrontation. Turkiye's direct military intervention in support of the Libyan Armed Forces (LAF, supporting the GNA) tilted the balance, forcing Haftar to withdraw the LNA from Tripoli. In turn, the risk of a rapid collapse of the LNA led Egypt (which had backed Haftar) to threaten a direct military intervention.

The military stalemate provided a window of opportunity, and a ceasefire agreement was signed in October 2020. Since then, Libya has remained in a state of frozen conflict despite the establishment of an interim Government of National Unity (GNU). The failure to hold elections in December 2021 led to renewed political polarisation, with the establishment of a rival Government of National Stability (GNS) headquartered between Benghazi and Sirte. The ensuing institutional split, which created parallel authorities, had an immediate impact on the oil industry following the resumption of an oil blockade in areas under the LNA's control in April 2022.

Conflict Update

The intractable nature of the conflict in Libya was confirmed by sporadic clashes in Tripoli during the reporting period. Simmering tensions between rival militias have escalated several times since the establishment of the GNS, whose prime minister – Fathi Bashagha – was sworn in by the House of Representatives (HoR) in March 2022. Since then, armed groups backing the GNS have attempted to take control of the capital several times. On 16 May 2022, Bashagha himself managed to enter Tripoli, albeit briefly, with the support of the Nawasi Brigade and the 166th Brigade. However, he was ultimately forced to leave following the mobilisation of rival groups.

The infighting in Tripoli escalated on 26 and 27 August 2022; 42 people were killed and 160 injured in the worst clashes since the October 2020 ceasefire. As a result, the Nawasi Brigade and Haitham Tajouri (a Libyan warlord and former leader of the influential Tripoli Revolutionaries Brigade) were ejected

from the capital – a development that highlighted the increasing clout of rival groups supporting the GNU, such as the Stability Support Apparatus and the 444th Brigade. These clashes consolidated the position of the GNU prime minister, Abdul Hamid Dbeibah, who remains in power despite the transitional nature of the GNU, which was established in 2021 by the United Nations-sponsored Libyan Political Dialogue Forum.

Despite temporarily neutralising the challenge posed by the GNS, Dbeibah has not been able to regain the upper hand in the whole of Libya.[1] Having failed to take Tripoli using Bashagha as a proxy, from April to July 2022 Haftar imposed an oil blockade on terminals and fields in areas under LNA control. This hybrid strategy, which fully leveraged the energy crisis that resulted from the Russian invasion of Ukraine in February 2022, underscored the LNA's confrontational stance. In April 2022, the LNA suspended its participation in the Joint Military

Council (also known as 5+5), a body created as part of the military track of the Libyan peace process.

Against the backdrop of the significant food crisis affecting North Africa, the weaponisation of oil exacerbated existing socio-economic grievances and led to widespread protests. These culminated in the July 2022 attack against the HoR building in Tobruk and the removal of Mustafa Sanalla from the chairmanship of the National Oil Corporation.[2] The latter was the primary request (together with the resignation of Dbeibah) of the tribesmen and protesters behind the oil blockade.

Sanalla was replaced by the former governor of the Central Bank of Libya, Farhat Bengdara, who is considered to be close to Haftar. The compromise, which prolonged the political longevity of Abdul Hamid Dbeibah, was reportedly negotiated in a meeting between Haftar's son Saddam (who is considered next in the line of succession for LNA leader) and Ibrahim Dbeibah, special adviser and nephew of the GNU prime minister. It was facilitated by the United Arab Emirates (UAE), which, though traditionally a supporter of the LNA, had recently adopted a new, pragmatic foreign-policy course that favoured detente with Abu Dhabi's regional rivals, including Turkiye.[3]

The rapprochement between Abu Dhabi and Ankara, however, widened the gap between the former and Egypt, which began to actively boycott the GNU. It has also not helped to de-escalate tensions in the Eastern Mediterranean between Egypt and Turkiye caused by the latter's military intervention in and delimitation of maritime boundaries with Tripoli in 2019. A new memorandum of understanding (MoU) on energy cooperation between the GNU and Turkiye in October 2022 further heightened tensions across the region.

On a more positive note, the deadlock over the appointment of a new UN special representative of the secretary-general for Libya has been resolved with the appointment of Abdoulaye Bathily, who presented a new road map in February 2023. Alongside the establishment of a 'high-level steering panel' for Libya that would presumably smooth the election process, Bathily's strategy seems to rely much more on the diplomatic activism of the African Union (AU). Energised by the appointment of the first African representative as the head of the UN Support Mission in Libya, the AU has been trying to promote national reconciliation as a preliminary step to renew the legitimacy of Libya's institutions.

Conflict Parties

Libyan Armed Forces (LAF)

Strength: Unclear. Given the undisclosed number of militias fighting on behalf of the LAF and the undefined relationship between these groups and the central command, it is impossible to determine its exact strength.	**Objectives:** The LAF's primary objective is to repel any offensive on the capital. Otherwise, it seeks to shore up support for the GNU and foil any attempt to unseat Dbeibah.
Areas of operation: After the ceasefire agreement of October 2020, the LAF remained in control of western Libya, including Misrata, Sabratha, Sorman, Tripoli and the Watiya air base.	**Opponents:** The LNA and its allies, and terrorist groups such as the Islamic State (ISIS) and al-Qaeda in the Islamic Maghreb (AQIM).
Leadership: As head of the Presidency Council, Mohammed al-Menfi is supreme commander of the LAF, while Maj.-Gen. Mohammed al-Haddad is chief of staff.	**Affiliates/allies:** Armed groups opposing the LNA's offensive in western and southern Libya. The LAF has received considerable military support from Turkiye.
Structure: Militias in the capital represent the backbone of the LAF, which also includes other militias from Misrata, Zawiya and Zintan.	**Resources/capabilities:** Turkiye has sent weapons, advisers and military equipment to shore up support for the GNA, including *Bayraktar* TB2 and ANKA S-1 uninhabited aerial vehicles, *Kirpi* armoured vehicles and air-defence systems.
History: In the aftermath of Haftar's attack on Tripoli in 2019 armed groups and militias in western Libya rallied in support of the GNA, which integrated most of these groups into the LAF.	

Libyan National Army (LNA) or the Libyan Arab Armed Forces (LAAF)

Strength: Around 25,000 fighters but the regular army is made up of some 7,000 troops. The 106th Brigade is the largest unit, exceeding 5,000 fighters.[4]	**Areas of operation:** Large swathes of Libya, including Cyrenaica and Fezzan, and Sirte.

Libyan National Army (LNA) or the Libyan Arab Armed Forces (LAAF)

Leadership: While HoR President Agila Saleh is supreme commander, Khalifa Haftar, appointed field marshal in 2016, holds the real power. Maj.-Gen. Abdul Razzaq al-Nazhuri is the chief of staff and Oun al-Furjani is chief of staff of Haftar's office.

Structure: The LNA includes the Al-Saiqa Special Forces, the 106th Brigade, the 166th Brigade and the 101st Brigade. The LNA also relies on co-opting local armed groups where the opportunity presents itself.

History: In 2014 Haftar launched *Operation Dignity*, targeting Islamist factions in Benghazi. In 2015, the HoR gave legitimacy to *Operation Dignity*, prompting the LNA's creation.

Objectives: Originally established to fight Islamist and terrorist groups responsible for attacks, the LNA gradually became instrumental in Haftar's project to seek absolute power and avoid civilian oversight.

Opponents: Islamist groups and terrorist organisations; revolutionary groups, such as the militias in Misrata, Tripoli and Zintan; Tebu armed groups; and Chadian rebel forces.

Affiliates/allies: Tribal militias mainly in eastern Libya but also in Tripolitania and Fezzan; Sudanese rebel forces and paramilitaries; mercenaries from Chad; and private security companies, such as the Wagner Group.

Resources/capabilities: Chinese-made *Wing Loong* II drones armed with *Blue Arrow* (BA7) air-to-surface missiles have allegedly been provided by the UAE, which has also deployed military personnel and transferred at least five types of military equipment to Libya, according to the UN Panel of Experts on Libya.

ISIS–Libya

Strength: Approximately 50 militants.[5]

Areas of operation: Southern areas, such as Murzuq, Sabha and Umm al-Aranib.

Leadership: Former emir Abu Moaz al-Tikrit, also known as Abdul Qader al-Najdi, was killed in September 2020 during clashes with the LNA in Sabha. Another top commander, Mohamed Miloud Ahmed, also known as Abu Omar, was arrested in a raid carried out by the LNA in Obari in March 2021.

Structure: Despite some distinction between regional branches, ISIS has maintained a centralised structure in Libya.

History: ISIS emerged in Libya in 2014–15, when it was able to gain a foothold in Derna and Sirte, threatening Misrata. In 2016, with the crucial support of US Africa Command, Misrata militias took control of Sirte, neutralising the threat.

Objectives: Derail the peace process and re-establish a presence in Libya, which was the most successful province of ISIS between 2014 and 2015.

Opponents: The GNU and affiliated militias; the LNA and its local allies; the Muslim Brotherhood and other moderate Islamist groups (including Sufi followers); and foreign powers engaged in the fight against terrorism (the United States in particular).

Affiliates/allies: The group has always taken a confrontational stance vis-à-vis other terrorist organisations in Libya. However, since its defeat in Sirte, reports suggest that ISIS is collaborating with other jihadist groups, including AQIM.

Resources/capabilities: ISIS militants have seized trucks carrying fuel and gained revenue from imposing taxes on human traffickers and arms smugglers. The group has also resorted to kidnapping for ransom.

Turkish Armed Forces (TSK)

Strength: Over 700 Turkish military advisers and intelligence officers (on Libyan soil).

Areas of operation: Southern Tripoli, Sabratha, Sorman and Tarhouna, extending to the outskirts of Jufra and Sirte. It has a reported presence at the Mitiga airport in Tripoli and the Watiya air base. Turkish troops have also been based at the Tripoli military port, the Khoms naval base, the Zuwara barracks and several bases in Misrata and Tripoli.

Leadership: President Recep Tayyip Erdoğan (commander-in-chief), Gen. (retd) Hulusi Akar (minister of national defence) and Gen. Yasar Guler (chief of general staff). The head of the Turkish military mission in Libya is Osman Aytac.

Structure: Turkish army units operating under the Turkish Land Forces Command – and squadrons carrying out airstrikes operating under the Air Force Command – are subordinate to the chief of general staff.

History: In November 2019, Turkiye signed an MoU with the GNA that provided for military assistance and training. In early 2020, Turkiye began to intervene militarily in support of the GNA, contributing significantly to repelling Haftar's offensive on Tripoli.

Objectives: Initially, prevent Haftar's forces from taking control of Tripoli. Following the collapse of the LNA offensive, its aim is to consolidate the GNA first and then the GNU, while also providing training to the LAF and carrying out demining operations.

Opponents: The LNA and its foreign backers, including Egypt, Russia and the UAE.

Affiliates/allies: GNU/LAF and Qatar. The TSK has deployed mercenaries and private security contractors in support of the authorities in Tripoli, including from SADAT, a security firm run by Anrar Tanriverdi, a close associate of Erdoğan.

Resources/capabilities: Turkiye has sent weapons, advisers and military equipment, including TB-2 *Bayraktar* and ANKA S-1 drones, *Kirpi* armoured vehicles and air-defence systems, such as *Hawk* air-defence missile batteries and 3D *Kalkan* radar to the Libyan theatre.

Wagner Group

Strength: Approximately 1,500–2,000 personnel on the ground in Libya.[6]

Areas of operation: Wagner operatives have been spotted at different air bases (Jufra, Brak al-Shati, Ghardabiya, Sabha and Waddan) and oilfields (Sharara and El Feel). Wagner operatives are also present at the Es-Sider oil terminal.

Leadership: Unclear after the group's chief Yevgeny Prigozhin and commander Dmitry Utkin were killed in an aeroplane crash on 23 August 2023.

Structure: The company was established by businessman Yevgeny Prigozhin. Its structure is not well documented.

History: The Wagner Group is a Russian security organisation closely linked to the Kremlin, Russian military intelligence and Russia's Ministry of Defence. It is used by Russia to carry out a range of officially deniable military and intelligence operations and commercial activities. The group was established in 2014, and it and other private military companies proliferated following Russia's involvement in the 2015 war in Syria, where they played an active role. Its status is currently in limbo. Following an abortive mutiny led by Prigozhin on 23–24 June 2023, a major part of the Wagner Group's forces was deployed in Belarus. The death of Prigozhin and other senior Wagner Group figures in August 2023 has deepened uncertainty about the group's future. After the mutiny, Putin acknowledged that the group was directly funded by the Russian state and noted the lack of any Russian legislation allowing such private military groups. At the end of July, Russia advanced legislation enabling regional governors to create military companies, and this could lead to further significant changes in their form and function.

Objectives: Since September 2019, Wagner has acted as a force multiplier for the LNA, providing tighter coordination, anti-drone capability, expert snipers and advanced equipment. After the collapse of the LNA offensive, it consolidated Haftar's position and reinforced his grip on critical infrastructures.

Opponents: GNA, TSK and US.

Affiliates/allies: The LNA and its foreign backers, including Egypt and the UAE. The Wagner Group reportedly recruited several thousand Syrian mercenaries to back the LNA in 2020. Most of them came from pro-Assad militias and paramilitary organisations affiliated with the Syrian Army.

Resources/capabilities: Throughout 2020 Russian military cargo aircraft, including Il-76s, supplied the Wagner Group with military armoured vehicles, SA-22 air-defence systems, fuel, ammunition and other supplies. In May 2020, at least 14 MiG-29 and SU-24 jets were deployed from Russia to Libya through Syria. The UAE reportedly provided financial assistance to the Wagner Group to deploy its mercenaries to Libya.

Notes

1   The GNS is effectively a front for Haftar given his influence over the executive. Close associates such as Ali al-Qatrani and Salem Maatouq al-Zedma (both deputy prime ministers), as well as Ihmeed Houma (defence minister), Khaled Massoud Abdrrabbu (justice minister) and Osama Hammad (finance minister), obtained relevant positions in the GNS. See Hazem Tharwat, 'Backdoor Deals Leave Haftar as Libya's Kingmaker in New Bashagha Government', Mada Masr, 3 March 2022.

2   Stephanie T. Williams, 'Two Years on from the Ceasefire Agreement, Libya Still Matters', *Policy Brief*, Brookings Institution, November 2022.

3   Emaddedin Badi, 'The UAE Is Making a Precarious Shift in Its Libya Policy. Here's Why', Atlantic Council, 27 October 2022.

4   Jason Pack, 'Kingdom of Militias: Libya's Second War of Post-Qadhafi Succession', Italian Institute for International Political Studies, May 2019; and Jalel Harchaoui and Mohamed-Essaïd Lazib, 'Proxy War Dynamics in Libya', Virginia Tech School of Public and International Affairs in Association with Virginia Tech Publishing, 2019.

5   'Twenty-ninth Report of the Analytical Support and Sanctions Monitoring Team Submitted Pursuant to Resolution 2368 (2017) Concerning ISIL (Da'esh), Al-Qaida and Associated Individuals and Entities', UN Security Council, S/2022/83, 3 February 2022, p. 11.

6   'Fonti "Nova": almeno 1.500 mercenari russi del gruppo Wagner ancora presenti in Libia' [Sources 'Nova': At Least 1,500 Russian Mercenaries of the Wagner Group Still Present in Libya], Nova News, 12 May 2022.

Middle East and
North Africa

EGYPT

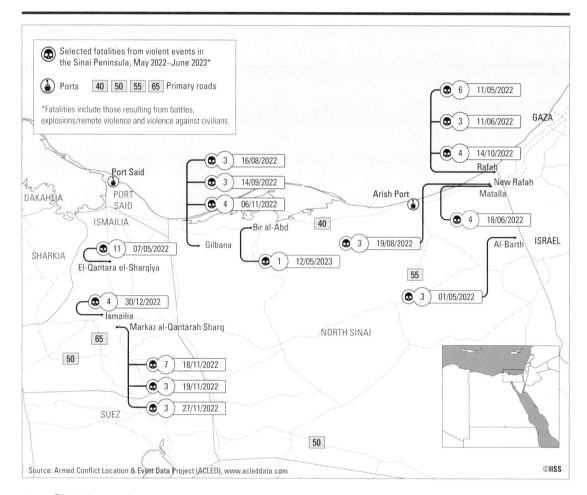

Selected fatalities from violent events in the Sinai Peninsula, May 2022–June 2023*

Ports   40 50 55 65   Primary roads

*Fatalities include those resulting from battles, explosions/remote violence and violence against civilians.

Source: Armed Conflict Location & Event Data Project (ACLED), www.acleddata.com   ©IISS

Conflict Overview

The conflicts between Arab states and Israel during the twentieth century significantly destabilised the impoverished border region of Sinai in Egypt. As a result of the 1978 Camp David Accords – brokered by the United States between Egypt and Israel – the peninsula became a demilitarised zone. Tribalism prospered there due to a lack of investment and the absence of state institutions. The rise of Islamist groups – after the 2011 revolution that toppled then-president Hosni Mubarak, and particularly following the 2013 military coup against his successor Muhammad Morsi – exacerbated pre-existing tensions, providing new opportunities for Sinai-based militants.

The most prominent threat has come from Sinai Province (Wilayat Sinai), formed in November 2014

after Ansar Beit Al Maqdis (ABM, a jihadist group) switched allegiance from al-Qaeda to the Islamic State (ISIS). The group has conducted frequent terror attacks focused on security and military outposts. It has also targeted civilians, as shown by the 2017 Bir al-Abed attack in which at least 311 people were killed and 122 injured.[1] With the support of its allies (including Israel and the US), in 2018 the Egyptian Armed Forces (EAF) launched a military campaign to retake the area. *Operation Sinai* was successful in degrading terrorist groups' capabilities but drew criticism from international human-rights groups and non-governmental organisations, which accused the EAF of war crimes and extrajudicial killings.[2]

Armed Conflict Global Relevance Indicator (ACGRI)

Incidence

1

Human
impact

Geopolitical
impact

0

2

Egypt

Key Conflict Statistics

Conflict(s)	Type	Start date
Sinai Peninsula	Internal: localised insurgency	2011

Fatalities	138
Percentage change in fatalities	-58%
IDPs	3,200*
Functioning of government (0–10)	3.2
Climate-change vulnerability (0–1)	0.4

ACGRI pillars: IISS calculation based on multiple sources for 2022 and 2023 (scale: 0–100), except for some cases according to data availability. See Notes on Methodology and Data Appendix for all variables and further details on Key Conflict Statistics. *2020 as latest available data.

Conflict Update

Jihadist militants continued to carry out attacks in the reporting period, targeting checkpoints, military facilities and critical infrastructure, such as gas pipelines. The trend saw a spike in May 2022. On 7 May an attack against a water pumping station in Qantara, Ismailia province, killed at least 11 EAF soldiers and injured five others.[3] Three days later, five soldiers were killed and two were injured in clashes between the EAF and Sinai Province in Rafah. Both attacks were claimed by ISIS, which, since the start of the insurgency, has found a safe haven along the border with Israel and the Palestinian Territories, where it has expanded its presence and found recruits. However, the EAF's destruction of smuggling tunnels along the Gaza Strip has significantly degraded the capabilities of militants in Sinai, who

have also suffered as a result of the improved relations between Cairo and Hamas.

For these reasons, jihadists have gradually moved their operations from northeast to northwest Sinai – demonstrated by the more frequent attacks in Ismailia governorate. The terrorist threat, which has so far been unable to impact navigation along the heavily guarded Suez Canal, has been mitigated by the state's co-optation of the Bedouin tribes, regrouped under the umbrella of the Sinai Tribes Union.[4]

Counter-terrorism operations have also benefitted from closer cooperation between Egypt and Israel, which has not only provided tactical air support to Cairo in its fight against Sinai Province but also allowed for a limited remilitarisation of the peninsula despite the terms of the 1978 peace treaty.

Conflict Parties

Egyptian Armed Forces (EAF)

Strength: 438,500 active armed personnel and 479,000 in reserve.

Areas of operation: North Sinai, South Sinai and Red Sea governorates, militarised triangle (Halayeb/Shalateen), Western Desert and Salloum border (Matrouh governorate – the western border with Libya).

Leadership: Supreme Council of the Armed Forces, led by Maj.-Gen. Mohamed Zaki (defence minister) and Maj.-Gen. Osama Askar (chief of staff of armed forces).

Structure: The EAF consists of the army, air force and navy; paramilitary forces are formed under the Ministry of Interior.

History: The first troop deployments into the Sinai Peninsula to fight the Islamic State began in 2014, triggered by the pledge of allegiance to the Islamic State by militants in the area.

Objectives: Control border security and address all national-security threats originating abroad. Since 2013 it has remilitarised the Sinai Peninsula, notably in North Sinai.

Opponents: Sinai Province, ABM and Muslim Brotherhood.

Affiliates/allies: France, Germany, Israel, Russia, United Arab Emirates, United Kingdom and US.

Resources/capabilities: In 2022, the EAF had an estimated budget of US$5.2 billion, or 1.1% of GDP. Egypt also receives around US$1.3bn in Foreign Military Assistance annually from the US.

Directorate of Military Intelligence (DMI)

Strength: Unclear, although the ascension of Abdel Fattah al-Sisi to Egypt's presidency in 2014 strengthened the DMI within the armed forces. Sisi was director of the DMI between 2010 and 2012.

Areas of operation: North Sinai governorate (train and assist programme with local Bedouin militias) and eastern Libya (train and assist programme with the Libyan National Army).

Leadership: Maj.-Gen. Khaled Megawer (director).

Structure: The DMI is part of the Ministry of Defense.

History: The DMI has been the main military actor in the peninsula since December 2018, following the deadly terror

attack in Bir al-Abed in 2017. The DMI works in conjunction with the EAF to conduct operations in the Sinai against the insurgency.

Objectives: Protect the state, DMI and Sisi from any attack; monitor foreign threats towards Egypt (alongside the General Intelligence Services); and lead on local intelligence gathering and community support in the Sinai Peninsula.

Opponents: Sinai Province.

Affiliates/allies: EAF and General Intelligence Services.

Resources/capabilities: Unclear.

Sinai Province (Wilayat Sinai)

Strength: Estimated 1,000 militants.[5] Since 2019 it includes small numbers of Palestinian militants and ISIS foreign fighters displaced from the conflicts in Iraq and Syria.

Areas of operation: North Sinai.

Leadership: In April 2022, the group's senior leader, Abu Omar al-Ansari, was killed in an airstrike reportedly carried out by Israeli jets.[6] Some evidence suggests that there are training camps in Sinai and the Gaza Strip.

Structure: Several jihadists are known to have travelled to Syria for training, suggesting that the ISIS leadership structure periodically plays a role in the Sinai insurgency.

History: First established in November 2014 with a pledge of allegiance by ABM fighters to then-ISIS leader Abu Bakr al-Baghdadi. Its activities reached a peak in 2017 with a series

of terror attacks in mainland Egypt as well as in the Sinai Peninsula. The group has never been able to seize significant territory in the peninsula but remains an active insurgency.

Objectives: Establish an Islamic state and fight the EAF.

Opponents: EAF, wider Egyptian security forces, Israel, non-Sunni Muslims and non-Muslims.

Affiliates/allies: Other terrorist groups affiliated with al-Qaeda and active in Sinai, like Jund al-Islam.

Resources/capabilities: Anecdotal evidence suggests most income is received via economic smuggling between the Sinai Peninsula and Gaza via tunnels. The group also benefits from an active weapons-smuggling war economy bringing weapons from Libya into Sinai.

Sinai Tribes Union (STU)

Strength: Unclear. In May 2022, local media reported that hundreds of tribe members had become involved.[7]

Areas of operation: North Sinai.

Leadership: Ibrahim al-Arjani.

Structure: The STU includes several Sinai tribes. Among the most prominent are the Armilat, the Sawarka and the Tarabin, the latter being the largest of the Sinai tribes.

History: Formed in 2015.

Objectives: Confront extremist organisations active in the Sinai Peninsula and provide support to the EAF.

Opponents: Sinai Province.

Affiliates/Allies: EAF and DMI.

Resources/capabilities: The EAF has provided the STU with arms and equipment.

Notes

1   Nour Youssef, 'Motives in Egypt's Deadliest Terrorist Attack: Religion and Revenge', *New York Times*, 1 December 2017.

2   In April 2019, Reuters published an investigation that cast a spotlight on the Egyptian security forces' counter-terrorism operations and accusations of extrajudicial killings. The investigation contradicted the official line of the Ministry of Interior, that the suspects neutralised during several operations were Islamist militants, drawing on the testimonies of the latter's relatives and family members, as well as forensic experts. See 'Special Report: Egypt Kills

Hundreds of Suspected Militants in Dispute Gun Battles', Reuters, 5 April 2019.

3   'Islamic State Claims Attack That Killed 11 Egyptian Troops', AP News, 8 May 2022.

4   'Egyptian Army Changes Strategy in War Against Terrorism in Sinai', Al-Monitor, 30 May 2022.

5   'Thirty-first Report of the Analytical Support and Sanctions Monitoring Team Submitted Pursuant to Resolution 2610 (2021) Concerning ISIL (Da'esh), Al-Qaida and Associated Individuals and Entities', UN Security Council, S/2023/95, 13 February 2023, p. 10.

6   Emanuel Fabian, 'Islamic State Accuses Israel of Slaying Jihadist Leader in Sinai Airstrike', *Times of Israel*, 1 May 2022.

7   'Meet the Newly Remade Union of Sinai Tribes, the Force Taking Over the Fight in Sinai', Mada Masr, 24 May 2022.

TURKIYE

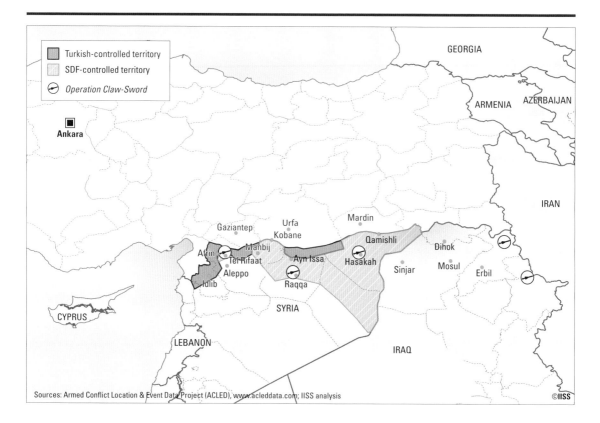

Sources: Armed Conflict Location & Event Data Project (ACLED), www.acleddata.com; IISS analysis   ©IISS

Conflict Overview

The conflict between Turkiye and the Kurdistan Workers' Party (PKK) – an organisation recognised as a terrorist group by the former, the European Union and the United States – has been ongoing for nearly 40 years. It has encompassed various actions, including PKK surprise attacks on Turkish military posts and patrols, and large-scale military and security operations aimed at the Kurdish organisation. The PKK was established in the late 1970s to advocate for the rights of Turkiye's Kurdish minority. It was driven initially by its imprisoned founder Abdullah Öcalan's desire for an independent Kurdish state. Over time, however, the organisation adjusted its objectives to focus on attaining political and cultural autonomy, alongside ethnic recognition, within Turkiye.

Historically, violent incidents occurred primarily in southeastern Turkiye, where the majority of the Turkish Kurdish minority resides, and in northern Iraq, where the PKK has established bases and training camps. However, in 2016, the conflict expanded into Syrian territory when Turkiye engaged in combat against the People's Protection Units (YPG), the Syrian Kurdish affiliate of the PKK, which forms the primary fighting force of the Syrian Democratic Forces (SDF). The clashes between Turkiye and Kurdish units significantly escalated in 2018 following the former's initiation of *Operation Olive Branch* in northern Syria; while the conflict is still active in Turkiye, Iraq and Syria, the epicentre of Turkiye–PKK clashes has shifted towards the latter, with both sides focusing their efforts on the Syrian front. Recurrent waves of major Turkish military operations against the SDF have failed to alter the balance of power in northern Syria.

Armed Conflict Global Relevance Indicator (ACGRI)

Incidence

3

Human
impact

Geopolitical
impact

6   4

Turkiye

Key Conflict Statistics

Conflict(s)	Type	Start date
Ethnic insurgency (Turkiye)	Internal: localised insurgency	1984
Fight between Turkish security forces and the PKK (Iraq)	Transnational	1984
Fight between Turkish security forces and the YPG (Syria)	Transnational	2016

Fatalities	300
Percentage change in fatalities	-15%
IDPs	1,099,000
Functioning of government (0–10)	5
Climate-change vulnerability (0–1)	0.4

ACGRI pillars: IISS calculation based on multiple sources for 2022 and 2023 (scale: 0–100), except for some cases according to data availability. See Notes on Methodology and Data Appendix for all variables and further details on Key Conflict Statistics.

Conflict Update

Tensions significantly increased after a bomb exploded in Istanbul in November 2022, killing eight civilians and injuring more than 80 others. Ankara accused the PKK of being responsible for the attack. Despite the latter denying any involvement, a military retaliation against PKK-affiliated targets in northern Syria followed. Soon after the bombing, the Turkish military launched *Operation Claw-Sword*, a week-long series of airstrikes into Syrian territory.[1]

The February 2023 earthquake brought immense devastation and loss of life to Turkiye and Syria. In response, senior PKK leader Cemil Bayik publicly asked all PKK units to refrain from any military activity within Turkish territory, initiating what has de facto become an indefinite, unilateral ceasefire for the PKK on Turkish soil.[2] In March, ahead of Turkiye's May general elections, the PKK leadership decided to further extend the ceasefire in recognition of the importance of the 2023 vote and the potential for leadership change.[3] While the PKK has claimed it has not initiated any military activity during the ceasefire, Turkiye has continued to conduct operations within and outside the country, leading to numerous violent incidents and deaths on both sides.

The re-election of President Recep Tayyip Erdoğan is likely to provide impetus to the ongoing Russia-brokered negotiations between Turkiye and Syria, which aim to re-establish constructive bilateral diplomatic relations. If successful, these talks may lead to the withdrawal of Turkish military forces from northern Syria – in exchange for the dismantling of Kurdish political autonomy and self-rule in the region, which would be a significant blow to the SDF.

Conflict Parties

Turkish Armed Forces (TSK)

Strength: 355,200 active military, 378,700 in reserve and 156,800 active gendarmerie and paramilitary.

Areas of operation: Southeastern Turkiye, northern and northwestern Iraq, and northern and northwestern Syria.

Leadership: President Recep Tayyip Erdoğan (commander-in-chief), Gen. (retd) Hulusi Akar (minister of national defence) and Gen. Yasar Guler (chief of general staff).

Structure: Turkish army units operating under the Turkish Land Forces Command and squadrons carrying out airstrikes operating under the Air Force Command are subordinate to the chief of general staff. Gendarmerie units reporting to the Gendarmerie Command are subordinate to the Ministry of Interior.

History: Rebuilt after the collapse of the Ottoman Empire in 1922. The TSK was significantly restructured after the country joined NATO in 1951, to become NATO's second-largest armed force.

Objectives: Eradicate the PKK and preserve national unity.

Opponents: The PKK and its affiliate organisations, particularly the YPG/SDF in Syria.

Middle East and North Africa

Turkish Armed Forces (TSK)

Affiliates/allies: Relies extensively on the Syrian National Army (SNA) as a support force in northern Syria.

Resources/capabilities: Turkiye's defence budget for 2022 was US$6.3 billion. Its military capabilities include air attack and intelligence, surveillance and reconnaissance assets such as the F-16 and the *Bayraktar* TB2 uninhabited aerial vehicle, armoured tanks and special-forces units.

Kurdistan Workers' Party (PKK)

Strength: 4,000–5,000 (estimate) in Turkiye and Iraq.[4]

Areas of operation: Southeastern Turkiye and northern Iraq.

Leadership: Abdullah Öcalan (ideological leader, despite his imprisonment since 1999), Murat Karayilan (acting leader on the ground since Öcalan's capture) and Bahoz Erdal (military commander).

Structure: While operating under the same command and leadership, the PKK's armed wing is divided into the People's Defence Forces (HPG) and the Free Women's Unit (YJA-STAR).

History: Founded by Öcalan in 1978. The PKK has been engaged in an insurgency campaign against the TSK since 1984.

Objectives: Political and cultural recognition of the Kurdish minority in Turkiye; adoption of a democratic federalist system of governance.

Opponents: TSK.

Affiliates/allies: YPG/SDF in Syria.

Resources/capabilities: Relies on money-laundering activities and drug trafficking to generate revenues, in addition to donations from the Kurdish community and diaspora and left-wing international supporters. The PKK relies on highly mobile units, using guerrilla tactics against Turkish military targets.

(Turkiye-sponsored) Syrian National Army (SNA)

Strength: 80,000 (estimate).[5]

Areas of operation: Northern Syria.

Leadership: SNA units are currently deployed alongside Turkish military forces and therefore operate under Turkish leadership.

Structure: A conglomerate of dozens of different militias, ranging vastly in size, affiliation and ideology, composed of Syrian militants, who are trained and equipped by Turkiye. The SNA is divided into seven main legions, each composed of a wide array of divisions and brigades.

History: Created as a splinter group of the Turkiye-backed Free Syrian Army. The SNA has been trained and equipped by the Turkish government since 2016. In 2019, the Idlib-based and Turkiye-sponsored National Front for Liberation was merged into the SNA.

Objectives: Take control of northern Syria.

Opponents: YPG/SDF.

Affiliates/allies: TSK.

Resources/capabilities: While a handful of formations have received US-sponsored training and equipment, the SNA has been fully reliant on Turkiye's support since its creation. Turkiye has provided small arms as well as infantry vehicles, and SNA military operations have benefitted from the Turkish army's fire support via artillery and airstrikes.

Syrian Democratic Forces/People's Protection Units (SDF/YPG)

Strength: 40,000–60,000.[6]

Areas of operation: Northern Syria.

Leadership: Mazloum Kobani Abdi, also known as Sahin Cilo (military commander). Abdi is a former senior PKK member.

Structure: Organised mainly along ethnic and territorial lines. Syrian Kurds lead the YPG and the Women's Protection Units (YPJ); both include a small component of international volunteers grouped into an international battalion. Other ethnic groups are organised under various military formations within the SDF, mainly as military councils.

History: Created in 2015 as a direct response to the advance of the Islamic State (ISIS) into northern Syria, building on various pre-existing alliances. Since then, it has fought against ISIS and the Turkish military.

Objectives: Control northern Syria.

Opponents: Turkiye and SNA.

Affiliates/allies: PKK.

Resources/capabilities: While it built upon the experience of its militias, since its formal creation the SDF has been equipped, trained and advised by the US. SDF units are equipped with small arms and some infantry vehicles.

Notes

1   'Turkey Kurdish Strikes: Operation Claw-Sword Targets Militant Bases', BBC News, 20 November 2022.

2   'Cemil Bayik: We Won't Carry Out Military Actions Unless the Turkish State Attacks Us', ANF News, 9 February 2023.

3   'PKK Extends Unilateral Ceasefire to Include Turkish Elections Period', Rudaw, 28 March 2023.

4   Bureau of Counterterrorism, US Department of State, 'Country Reports on Terrorism 2021', 2021, p. 300.

5   Hassan Ibrahim, 'Poor Salaries and Frequent Delay: A Policy to Dissolve "National Army" or Gain Loyalty', Enab Baladi, 18 April 2023.

6   EU Agency for Asylum, '1.2. Syrian Democratic Forces and Asayish', September 2020.

4 Sub-Saharan Africa

Fighters for the National Movement for the Liberation of Azawad pose for a picture, Mali, 28 August 2022

Overview

Sub-Saharan Africa continues to be the most conflict-affected region globally, with wars largely concentrated in four theatres – the Sahel, the Lake Chad Basin, the Great Lakes Region and Eastern Africa – as well as the Central African Republic (CAR) and Mozambique.[1] While conflicts in Sub-Saharan Africa are primarily internal in nature, they also include regional and international elements. This contributes to their complexity. *The Armed Conflict Survey 2023* identifies 15 conflict-affected countries in the region during the reporting period, 14 of which form an uninterrupted geographical block – a fact that reinforces the need for a regional cross-border perspective.

The levels of violence on the continent in 2022 – in terms of violent events and fatalities – only slightly increased compared to 2021.[2] There was a spike in jihadist violence in 2022 overall, especially in Somalia and the Sahelian countries of Burkina Faso and Mali, though several other countries were also affected.[3] In the 13-month reporting period, both violent events and fatalities increased in Chad, Mali, Somalia and Sudan compared to the previous 13 months, while they decreased in the CAR, the Democratic Republic of the Congo (DRC), Ethiopia, Mozambique, Nigeria, South Sudan and Uganda. Comparing the same two periods, the lethality of violence – defined as the ratio of fatalities over events – increased in Burkina Faso, Cameroon, CAR, Chad, the DRC, Mali and South Sudan, while it decreased in all the other conflict-affected countries on the continent.

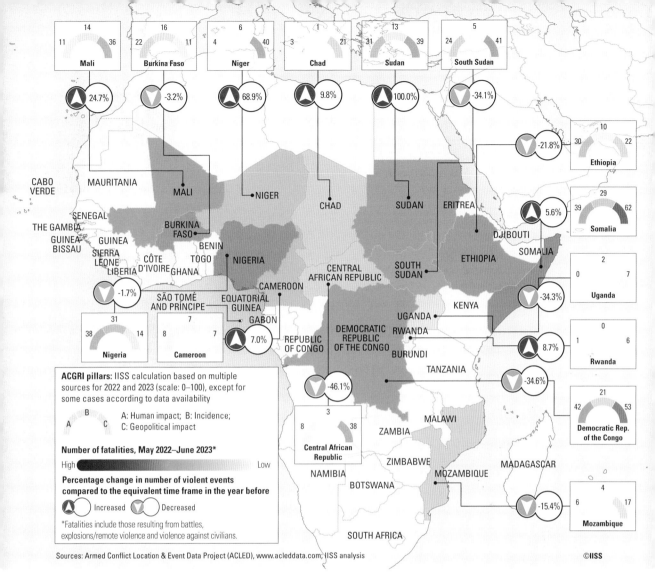

ACGRI pillars: IISS calculation based on multiple sources for 2022 and 2023 (scale: 0–100), except for some cases according to data availability

A: Human impact; B: Incidence; C: Geopolitical impact

Number of fatalities, May 2022–June 2023*

High — Low

Percentage change in number of violent events compared to the equivalent time frame in the year before

Increased   Decreased

*Fatalities include those resulting from battles, explosions/remote violence and violence against civilians.

Sources: Armed Conflict Location & Event Data Project (ACLED), www.acleddata.com; IISS analysis   ©IISS

Confirming a trend that started in the early 2010s, the most prevalent conflict type on the continent continues to be internationalised-internal conflicts, or civil wars with external interventions (i.e., the CAR, Ethiopia, Mali, Mozambique and Somalia, among others), which have become increasingly lethal. All conflicts on the continent, however, defy clear-cut categorisation, due to aspects such as the role of cyber warfare and the involvement of transnational non-state armed groups (NSAGs) and unaccountable third-party interventions (e.g., Russia via the Wagner Group).

Most internal conflicts today are fought on multiple levels, including locally (e.g., the DRC and Nigeria) and in national capitals through armed politics (e.g., Mali and Sudan), and they can involve both international (e.g., third-party states, multilateral stabilisation missions or peacekeeping missions) and transnational

actors (e.g., Salafi-jihadist groups). Conflicts can also play out in the cyber domain through disinformation campaigns (e.g., Burkina Faso). Another notable feature of conflicts in the region is the increasing proliferation of conflict parties, which highlights the fragmentation of armed violence and governance. Most conflict-affected countries feature some degree of violence between NSAGs – often communal conflicts in which the state is not a conflict party.

Throughout the reporting period, Sub-Saharan Africa's conflict-affected countries also remained some of the hardest hit by the global economic turmoil resulting from the coronavirus pandemic and the war in Ukraine. Alongside extreme weather events (e.g., drought in Somalia and floods in South Sudan), these dynamics either exacerbated or metastasised existing armed conflicts, contributing to their protractedness. In Sub-Saharan Africa, there were over 145 million people facing acute food insecurity in 2022, a remarkable increase compared to nearly 120m in 2021.[4] In terms of conflict-induced displacement, by the end of 2022, an estimated 108.4m individuals were forcibly displaced worldwide.[5] Out of this, Sub-Saharan Africa had 6.8m refugees and 27.5m internally displaced persons (IDPs) due to conflict and violence.[6]

The most important conflict developments in the reporting period include:

- the April 2023 breakout of internal conflict in Sudan between the Sudan Armed Forces (SAF) and the paramilitary Rapid Support Forces (RSF), which engulfed the capital Khartoum, other urban centres and peripheral regions, and has critical regional implications;
- the end of the two-year civil war in Ethiopia with the signing of the Agreement for Lasting Peace Through a Permanent Cessation of Hostilities between the Ethiopian government and the Tigray People's Liberation Front (TPLF) in November 2022;
- the reignition of inter-state tensions between the DRC and Rwanda as a result of the escalation of violent activities in Eastern Congo by the March 23 Movement (M23, an NSAG which Rwanda supports); and
- in the Sahel, the end of France's *Operation Barkhane* and its pull-out from Mali and Burkina Faso, as well as the announced withdrawal of the United Nations Multidimensional Integrated Stabilization Mission in Mali (MINUSMA), in parallel with a drift towards military authoritarianism in both countries.[7]

Conflict Drivers

Political and institutional

Institutional fragility

Deep-seated institutional fragility and governance gaps in service provision and the control of peripheral areas have driven the expansion of armed conflict during the last decade. Fragile states' chronic inability to build accountable institutions, uphold the rule of law, and provide adequate services and meaningful economic opportunities to citizens is compounded by the emergence and consolidation of NSAGs, which bring insecurity but also provide some form of governance at the local level. To different degrees, the resulting fragmentation of power and security renders some conflicts protracted and intractable, including in the CAR, the DRC, Mali and Nigeria.

Unresolved political transitions

In parallel, conflict-affected countries often suffer from failed political transitions and unstable political settlements (e.g., in Ethiopia and Sudan). More recently, the continent has experienced a decline in democratic norms and institutions. In 2020–22, the number of military overthrows of civilian governments (both failed and successful) was nearly at the level of the full preceding decade (2010–19). In the last three years alone, successful coups took place in Burkina Faso (twice), Chad, Guinea, Mali (twice) and Sudan, in addition to five failed overthrows in The Gambia, Guinea-Bissau, Niger, São Tomé and Príncipe, and Sudan again. After the end of the reporting period, a successful coup took place in Niger in July 2023. Coups' popularity in conflict-affected countries reflects the perceived failure of civilian governments to tackle rising insecurity and address their populations' demands.

Socio-economic

Weak social contracts

Historically, most Sub-Saharan countries have suffered from weak social contracts between rulers and citizens. This is manifested through the state's predatory use of the country's wealth (for example, in the DRC and Sudan) or through its failure to extend basic services to marginalised communities in peripheral regions, which results in the consolidation of parallel informal authorities and economies at the local level. In some cases, such as in Ethiopia, Mali and South Sudan, intercommunal violence around traditional patterns of competition for scarce resources intersects with a lack of state presence. These embedded dynamics provide the bedrock for insurgencies to form and proliferate (including transnational jihadist insurgencies).

Illicit economies

In those regions with high-valued commodities like minerals (e.g., the CAR and the eastern DRC), NSAGs oversee a system of local labour exploitation, violence and illicit trafficking, with either the participation or the complicity of economic and political elites, at both central and local levels. Thus, some conflicts are tightly linked to illicit markets, as NSAGs play the role of conflict entrepreneurs.

Security and military

Fragmentation of security and proliferation of armed actors

Countries with vast territories and chronic state absence from peripheries, like Mali and Mozambique, suffer from security fragmentation. This is one expression of the centre–periphery divide that characterises most conflict-affected countries in Sub-Saharan Africa. Armed forces and the security sector are traditionally deployed to defend the capital city, the most prosperous economic regions and the elites in power. In countries like the DRC and Sudan, for example, such dynamics have entailed a constant process of accommodating NSAGs at the local level. In fact, the proliferation of NSAGs is another major conflict driver that is common to all conflicts on the continent. These groups – with their diverse natures and goals – significantly contribute to making armed conflicts protracted and intractable. The use of pro-state militias by Sudan in Darfur and the support offered to NSAGs by competing neighbouring countries (e.g., Rwanda) in the DRC are two notable examples of fragmented security and the proliferation of armed actors.

Additionally, state security has sometimes used lethal force against unarmed civilians, including sexual violence, human-rights abuses and massacres. These episodes are common in the DRC, Ethiopia, Mali and South Sudan, among others. Because of a lack of accountability and justice, such episodes have exacerbated grievances and contributed to patterns of cyclical violence.

Geopolitical

Western involvement

In the last few years, geopolitical drivers of armed conflict in Sub-Saharan Africa have been augmented by a new phase of global geopolitical competition, which has led some to speak about a modern 'scramble for Africa'. The post-Cold War era has been characterised by Western countries dominating political, economic and security relations with the continent, and providing support to conflict-resolution, stabilisation and peace-keeping initiatives. However, such influence is currently waning.

Russia's and China's role

Russia has taken an increasing diplomatic and security role in Africa's conflict-affected countries over the last several years – a situation that by most accounts has exacerbated existing conflicts and led to higher levels of violence, notably in the CAR and Mali. Meanwhile, though China has taken on a strong economic role on the continent, including in extractive industries, it is currently unclear how this impacts conflict dynamics, if at all.

Conflict Parties

Coalitions

The transnational character of armed conflicts in West Africa and the Sahel (where jihadist extremist groups exploit porous borders) induces countries in the region to adopt coordinated and, at times, integrated responses. These ad hoc security initiatives differ substantially from peacekeeping operations.[8] Facing mounting insecurity in the Sahel, the governments of Burkina Faso, Chad, Mali, Mauritania and Niger created the G5 Sahel Joint Force (FC-G5S) with the goal of fostering military cooperation and joint operations, especially around shared borders. However, the coalition (operational since 2017) has

had no significant impact on improving security, and conflicts have worsened in the region. Following the establishment of a military regime, Mali withdrew from the FC-G5S in May 2022, further diminishing the coalition's legitimacy and effectiveness.

Another notable coalition, the Multinational Joint Task Force (MNJTF), was created in the 1990s to counteract crime and violence in the Lake Chad Basin. While it was inactive for several years, the coalition was revived in 2015 to fight Jama'atu Ahlis Sunna Lidda'awati wal-Jihad (JAS, popularly known as Boko Haram), and it currently includes 13,000 troops from Benin, Cameroon, Chad, Niger and Nigeria.[9] Countries participating in both the FC-G5S and the MNJTF have emphasised the military and intelligence components of their cooperation, while the underlying causes of violence have been left unaddressed. Thus, the limited success of these coalitions stems from the participating countries' inability to provide governance and economic-development responses, in addition to security interventions.

The threat of conflict and instability in the last decade resulted in the empowerment of regional economic communities (RECs) as instruments for intra-regional dialogue on conflict prevention and for cooperation on security issues. RECs do not retain a formal mandate on peace and security, but they act either under the mandate of, or in cooperation with, the African Union (AU). Several of these organisations, notably the Intergovernmental Authority on Development (IGAD) in East Africa and the Economic Community of West African States (ECOWAS), have played an increasing diplomatic role as well as a security one.

The most recent examples of RECs' engagement include the following. In mid-2021 the Southern African Development Community (SADC) established the SADC Standby Force Mission in Mozambique (SAMIM) to respond to the growing jihadist insurgency in Cabo Delgado. SANIM proved successful and security conditions improved throughout 2022. Likewise, the East African Community's (EAC) deployment in

the eastern DRC, after the latter became the EAC's seventh member in early 2022, exemplifies how some RECs have expanded their functions. This is the first time that the EAC has placed boots on the ground, with the goal of supporting the DRC in its fight against armed groups.

Non-state armed groups

Over the last decade, Sub-Saharan Africa has witnessed a proliferation of NSAGs that either battle the state or fight against other NSAGs, or both. The average number of conflicts between NSAGs per year between 1991 and 2011 was 22, while between 2012 and 2022 this figure rose to 36 (see Figure 1). In 2022, there were 42 non-state conflicts, down from a peak of 49 in 2020.[10] Furthermore, jihadist violent-extremist groups have consolidated their position in the region, turning Sub-Saharan Africa into the largest hotspot of Islamist terrorism globally.

Current NSAGs in Sub-Saharan Africa are increasingly varied in nature, and their complexity of goals and features defy clear categorisation. This is in contrast to the Cold War period when these actors tended to be ideologically driven and politically motivated, aiming to gain power and offer an alternative to corrupt and inefficient governments. Such groups include jihadist extremists, localised insurgencies and militias, and criminal organisations preoccupied with either rent extraction or trafficking, or both. The overlaps and ties between

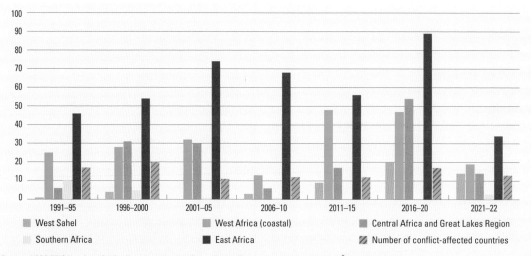

Sources: UCDP/PRIO Non-State Conflict Dataset version 23.1; Shawn Davies, Therese Pettersson and Magnus Öberg, 'Organized Violence 1989–2022 and the Return of Conflicts Between States?', *Journal of Peace Research*, vol. 60, no. 4, 2023; Ralph Sundberg, Kristine Eck and Joakim Kreutz, 'Introducing the UCDP Non-state Conflict Dataset', *Journal of Peace Research*, vol. 49, no. 2, 2012

©IISS

Figure 1: Number of non-state conflicts and conflict-affected countries in Sub-Saharan Africa, 1991–2022

these groups – for instance, the way that transnational jihadist extremist groups interact with local rebellions and exploit local grievances – has resulted in a complex NSAG landscape.

NSAGs' proliferation and fragmentation today are the main drivers of protracted and intractable conflicts and a major impediment to peace solutions, either because they do not want to negotiate or because they are content with attaining local goals. From the Sahel to the Lake Chad Basin to Eastern Congo, what NSAGs have in common is a seeming unwillingness to pursue and hold formal power: they are not after regime change, but rather pursue local power and enrichment through abusive and predatory behaviours vis-à-vis local populations.

Third-party interventions

Most of today's civil wars in Sub-Saharan Africa feature external military intervention, a factor that also underpins their intractability. Between 1991 and 2012 there were never more than five internal conflicts with external interventions per year. This number has skyrocketed since then, reaching a peak of 18 in 2020.[11]

Throughout the reporting period, external middle and great powers continued to intervene in internal conflicts on the continent, while the war in Ukraine further exacerbated tensions amongst external interveners (notably between Russia and Western state actors). The Sahel is the most visible example of this trend. After a decade-long and expanding conflict, Mali's civilian government was toppled in May 2021 by a military junta, which rose to power on an anti-French agenda. Bamako then experienced a deterioration of relations with several West African and Sahelian countries, and severed political and security ties with France, which had provided bilateral and regional security support via *Operation Barkhane* since 2014. In turn, Russia quickly filled the political and security void left by France by strengthening ties with the junta and approving the deployment of the Wagner Group in Mali.

This situation replicated what had happened not long before in the CAR, where Russia's political influence and security ties were cultivated at the expense of French ones. This poses a fundamental policy dilemma for Western actors regarding how to effectively support stabilisation at the regional level when conflicts and insecurity are worsening, democratic practices are backsliding, and their traditional diplomatic clout and political leverage are fading.

Russia views Sub-Saharan Africa as an ideal theatre for exercising influence and eroding Western presence and interests. Moscow uses covert political and security means that allow deniability to pursue its aims. The Wagner Group is the most notorious and infamous Russian private military contractor (PMC), but not the only one. Collectively, Russian PMCs have operated in 19 countries in Sub-Saharan Africa in the last decade.[12] Russia also operates in the cyber-warfare domain, as well as conducting disinformation campaigns.

Regional and International Dimensions

Most conflict-affected countries in Sub-Saharan Africa suffer simultaneously from two or more internal conflicts, which often take place near porous borders and in marginalised areas. The instability of one country thus affects the stability of its neighbours, resulting in complex, interlocking regional conflict dynamics. The armed conflicts in the Sahelian Liptako-Gourma tri-border region, the Lake Chad Basin and the Great Lakes Region are cases in point.

Some specific events and factors have caused the rising internationalisation of conflicts on the continent during the last decade. The fall of Libyan dictator Muammar Gadhafi in 2011 and the subsequent civil war in Libya prompted the opening of illicit-trafficking corridors of migrants and weapons, as well as the movement of various NSAGs on Gadhafi's payroll. These NSAGs brought havoc to Mali and the wider Sahel region.

The rise of the Islamic State (ISIS) in the Middle East also led to the establishment of franchises of ISIS in Sub-Saharan Africa. Transnationalism characterises current jihadist insurgencies. The operational and financial links between jihadist groups across countries and continents have never been fully ascertained. Nonetheless, ideological affinities, the indiscriminate use of violence and a complete disregard for internationally sanctioned borders underpin the transnational dimension of violent jihadist groups, including Al-Qaeda affiliates. According to the Critical

Threats Project, such groups are either active or present in 19 countries in Sub-Saharan Africa today, and four more countries are considered to be either transit zones for groups or at risk of jihadist attacks.[13]

Finally, there is an increasing trend of third-party countries intervening in civil wars on the continent by military means. From 2011–21, 27 so-called internationalised civil wars have taken place in Sub-Saharan Africa, compared to 12 in the preceding two decades combined (1991–2010). In 2022, there were 16 internationalised civil wars on the continent, while there were ten internal conflicts without external intervention.[14] The former used to be the exception until about 2011 but are now the norm.[15]

Currently, interventions are not limited to Western countries' counter-terrorism operations, like the United States in Somalia and France in selected West African countries, but instead include a host of emerging powers pursuing their strategic interests. In the Horn of Africa, for example, Qatar, Saudi Arabia, Türkiye and the United Arab Emirates have political influence and/or security ties in Ethiopia, Somalia and Sudan, among others. This trend is likely to increase, as indicated by frenetic activity on the diplomatic front. For instance, China, the European Union and Türkiye regularly hold forums with continental state actors, while Moscow convened the second Russia–Africa Summit in July 2023, which, however, did not repeat the success of its 2019 edition. For its part, in 2022, the administration of US President Joe Biden unveiled an Africa strategy and hosted its own US–Africa Leaders Summit, while Vice President Kamala Harris and Secretary of State Antony Blinken made high-profile visits on the continent in the first half of 2023. Competition for strategic influence in Africa now takes place in several domains, including extraction of natural resources, foreign direct investment, aid and debt relief, security provision, and military transfers.

Russia's war in Ukraine has exacerbated these drivers and the divisions on the continent. By negotiating over two dozen security agreements in the last few years alone, Moscow has been able to erode Western interests in several parts of Sub-Saharan Africa, notably in the CAR and Mali. Furthermore, African countries are divided on the question of Russia's invasion of Ukraine. Since 24 February 2022, the continent has split three times on key votes by the UN General Assembly condemning Russia's actions. One year after Russia's invasion, 23 countries in Africa did not vote on, abstained from voting on or voted against a UN resolution demanding Russia's withdrawal from Ukraine.[16]

Outlook

Prospects for peace

The trend of civil wars in Sub-Saharan Africa becoming increasingly internationalised will likely escalate in the years to come – a fact that negatively affects peace prospects and conflict-resolution efforts. The war in Ukraine and ongoing geopolitical competition will have negative implications for the continent. Great-power competition over economic interests and political influence in Sub-Saharan Africa now has security as one of its central features. Moreover, the war's effects on food security on the continent (and beyond) are alarming.

 The involvement of third parties makes settling armed conflicts on the continent a seemingly impossible task, as a delicate balance needs to be struck between national sovereign actors' regional interests and geopolitical considerations. A fundamental dilemma for the region is how to reconcile multilateral conflict-resolution processes (either international or regional) with the interests of third-party states.

Bleak prospects for peace are also driven by a trend of decreasing comprehensive peace agreements. National-level peace processes have become fragmented and fewer over time, while local security agreements, which are limited in scope, are on the rise.[17] Today, conflict parties are unable and often unwilling to reach comprehensive, inclusive and sustainable peace deals. There are many factors that account for this trend, including the proliferation of conflict parties (both domestic and international); the depoliticisation of conflict and institutionalisation of violence; national leaderships' lack of vision and political will; and the diminished leverage of conflict-resolution processes led by multilateral actors.

Escalation potential and regional spillovers

Regionally, the most consequential armed conflict is the civil war in Sudan. As of 30 June 2023, the outcome of the battle between the SAF and the RSF that extended to Khartoum and other urban centres remained uncertain. Further, the civil war has taken an ethnic dimension in western Sudan, in particular in Darfur. There, the conflict is escalating, and deep-seated latent tensions are turning violent again.

Regional instability is a major concern. Sudan sits at the centre of an extremely fragile and volatile region already affected by conflict and violence. To varying degrees, five out of the seven countries bordering Sudan (notably, the CAR, Chad, Ethiopia, Libya and South Sudan) currently experience some form of either armed conflict or a troubled war-to-peace transition period. Because of its recent history and its dependence on oil revenues from Khartoum, South Sudan is the country most directly affected by the fighting. Mass displacement from Sudan at its western border – at an even greater scale than witnessed thus far – could further strain the delicate domestic balance of power and weak coping mechanisms in the CAR and Chad, for example. A reactivation of the violent border dispute between Sudan and Ethiopia could also result in a larger regional crisis.

Other conflicts on the continent – especially the regional wars in the eastern DRC and the Sahel – have already escalated in the last few years. West Africa (including Benin, Togo and Côte d'Ivoire) has increasingly experienced jihadist violence in the last two years, although countries in the sub-region have been able to enact effective countermeasures to contain the threat. In the eastern DRC, an inter-state conflict between the country and Rwanda is at risk of escalating because of the role played by the latter in supporting the M23 insurgency in the DRC.

Strategic implications and global influences

The expanding political and security ties between some African countries and Russia indicates the potential for armed conflicts on the continent to become increasingly internationalised. Russia's model of co-opting undemocratic ruling elites proved successful in the CAR and Mali. This trend is enabled by the failing state of democratic standards across Africa. According to the Economist Intelligence Unit's (EIU) Democracy Index 2022, the majority of African conflict-affected countries suffer from different levels of authoritarianism.[18] Instances of incumbent rulers manipulating election results and/or extending constitutionally bound term limits have therefore been a further cause for concern. The rise of authoritarian powers at the global level (including China, Russia, Turkiye and Gulf countries) also has an impact on certain African countries and their respective political and economic elites.

REGIONAL KEY EVENTS

POLITICAL EVENTS

 SOMALIA

15 May 2022

Hassan Sheikh Mohamud wins Somalia's presidential election.

MILITARY/VIOLENT EVENTS

 CAMEROON

June 2022

Cameroon deploys several hundred soldiers to its northern border after over 40,000 civilians are displaced by JAS/Boko Haram attacks.

  **SOMALIA, ETHIOPIA**

Late July

Somalia-based al-Shabaab launches attacks across the border into Ethiopia.

Sub-Saharan Africa

CHAD

8 August

Chad signs a peace agreement in Doha with rebel and opposition groups, though some groups reject the terms of the deal.

 CAMEROON, NIGERIA

25 August

Governors from Cameroon and Nigeria initiate plans to reopen borders, rebuild schools and repair border regions where JAS/Boko Haram has been defeated.

 CAMEROON

13 September

The Interim Government of Ambazonia's long-time spokesperson Chris Anu declares himself president.

 MALI

24 September

The Malian government begins drafting a new constitution and prepares for elections in 2024 to restore civilian rule.

 BURKINA FASO

30 September

A coup in Burkina Faso sees Captain Ibrahim Traoré take power following months of instability under president Paul-Henri Damiba.

 CHAD

11 October

Chadian prime minister Albert Pahimi Padacke resigns amid the postponing of elections to 2024.

 ETHIOPIA

2 November

The Ethiopian government signs a peace agreement with the TPLF, ending the two-year civil war.

 THE DRC, RWANDA

4 August

UN experts state that there is 'solid evidence' of Rwandan armed-forces personnel fighting alongside M23 rebels in the DRC.

 MALI

15 August

The French-led *Operation Barkhane* in Mali completes its full withdrawal.

 ETHIOPIA

24 August

Violence returns to Tigray as the TPLF and the Ethiopian government blame each other for breaking the temporary peace.

 SOMALIA

18 September

A combined AU Transition Mission in Somalia and Somali forces offensive against al-Shabaab weakens the group's position in the Hiiraan region.

 BURKINA FASO

21–22 November

The International Conference on the Accra Initiative approves the launch of its Multinational Joint Task Force, with 2,000 troops to be deployed to Burkina Faso within the month.

SUDAN

`5 December`

The Sudanese military and political parties sign a deal to pave the way towards elections in 2024.

 THE DRC, RWANDA

`24 January 2023`

The DRC accuses Rwanda of an 'act of war' after Rwandan forces shoot down a Congolese fighter jet.

 NIGERIA

`1 March`

Bola Ahmed Tinubu wins Nigeria's presidential election, prompting calls for a recount due to concerns of voter disenfranchisement.

 ETHIOPIA

`9 April`

Protests erupt in Ethiopia's Amhara region against the government's dissolution of regional militias, with full-scale fighting breaking out in July 2023 and a state of emergency declared in August 2023.

 THE DRC, RWANDA

`23 May`

The DRC files a complaint with the International Criminal Court regarding Rwanda's support of the M23.

 THE CAR

`30 May`

President Faustin-Archange Touadéra announces a referendum on the CAR's constitution, with potential reforms including the elimination of term limits.

 THE CAR

`2 February 2023`

The Wagner Group sustains heavy casualties as part of the CAR's offensive against rebel forces.

 THE DRC

`11 March`

A ceasefire between the DRC and M23 rebels fails as each side accuses the other of violations.

 MALI

`12 April`

ISIS and its allies seize Mali's northeastern village of Tidermene, isolating the regional capital of Menaka.

 SUDAN

`15 April`

Civil war breaks out in Sudan between the SAF and the paramilitary RSF.

 NIGER, NIGERIA

`May`

Niger and Nigeria conduct a joint operation against the Islamic State West Africa Province stronghold in Arege (Lake Chad Basin).

 CAMEROON

`1 May`

Ambazonian separatists ambush a military outpost in Matouke, less than 40 kilometres from Douala, Cameroon's economic capital.

Sub-Saharan Africa

MALI

June

Mali requests the departure of the decade-long UN peacekeeping mission MINUSMA, and this is approved by the UN Security Council.

 SUDAN

3 June

Fighting resumes following the expiration of a ceasefire negotiated by Saudi Arabia and the US in Sudan.

 SOMALIA

19 June

Somalia's government announces the killing of 43 al-Shabaab militants, including two senior commanders, during airstrikes by the Somali National Army forces.

 NIGER

26 July

The presidential guard removes and detains President Mohamed Bazoum, suspends the constitution and installs General Abdourahmane Tchiani as head of state.

Notes

1   The countries that belong in each area can overlap in some cases (e.g., Chad). Some countries can be part of one of these areas but still have very distinct national drivers of conflict (e.g., Nigeria).

2   Timothy Lay, 'ACLED Year in Review: Global Disorder in 2022', Armed Conflict Location & Event Data Project (ACLED), January 2023.

3   For further information on jihadist insurgencies in Sub-Saharan Africa, see the Sub-Saharan Africa Regional Spotlight essay, 'From Global Jihad to Local Insurgencies: The Changing Nature of Sub-Saharan Jihadism' in this book. See also Africa Center for Strategic Studies, 'Fatalities from Militant Islamist Violence in Africa Surge by Nearly 50 Percent', 6 February 2023.

4   Global Network Against Food Crises and Food Security Information Network, 'Global Report on Food Crises 2023', 2023.

5   UN High Commissioner for Refugees (UNHCR), 'Global Trends: Forced Displacement in 2022', 14 June 2023.

6   UNHCR, 'Refugee Data Finder'; and Internal Displacement Monitoring Centre, 'Global Internal Displacement Database'. Data is as of 31 December 2022.

7   The military coup in Niger that took place in late July 2023 does not fall under the reporting period for *The Armed Conflict Survey 2023*. An analysis of its full implications will be included in next year's edition.

8   See Cedric de Coning and Andrew E. Yaw Tchie, 'Ad Hoc Initiatives Are Shaking Up African Security', London School of Economics, 8 February 2023.

9   Freedom Chukwudi Onuoha, Andrew E. Yaw Tchie and Mariana Llorens Zabala, *A Quest to Win the Hearts and Minds: Assessing the Effectiveness of the Multinational Joint Task Force* (Oslo: Norwegian Institute of International Affairs, 2023), p. 37. The MNJTF website puts this number at around 10,000 troops.

10 See Shawn Davies, Thérèse Pettersson and Magnus Öberg, 'Organized Violence 1989–2022 and the Return of Conflicts Between States?', *Journal of Peace Research*, vol. 60, no. 4, 2023; and Ralph Sundberg, Kristine Eck and Joakim Kreutz, 'Introducing the UCDP Non-state Conflict Dataset', *Journal of Peace Research*, vol. 49, no. 2, 2012. According to UCDP/PRIO, 'a state-based armed conflict is a contested incompatibility that concerns government and/or territory where the use of armed force between two parties, of which at least one is the government of a state, results in at least 25 battle-related deaths in one calendar year'. See Uppsala Universitet, 'UCDP Definitions'.

11 See Davies, Pettersson and Öberg, 'Organized Violence 1989–2022 and the Return of Conflicts Between States?'; and Nils Petter Gleditsch et al., 'Armed Conflict 1946–2001: A New Dataset', *Journal of Peace Research*, vol. 39, no. 5, 2002.

12 Brian Katz et al., 'The Expansion of Russian Private Military Companies', Center for Strategic & International Studies, September 2020.

13 See 'The Salafi-jihadi Movement in Africa: As of July 2023', map in Brian Carter et al., 'Salafi-jihadi Movement Weekly Update', Critical Threats, 5 July 2023.

[14] See Davies, Pettersson and Öberg, 'Organized Violence 1989–2022 and the Return of Conflicts Between States?'; and Gleditsch et al., 'Armed Conflict 1946–2001: A New Dataset', pp. 615–37.

[15] See 'Sub-Saharan Africa Regional Analysis', in IISS, *The Armed Conflict Survey 2022* (Abingdon: Routledge for the IISS, 2022), pp. 200–203.

[16] 'UN Tells Russia to Leave Ukraine: How Did Countries Vote?', Al-Jazeera, 24 February 2023.

[17] See Jan Pospisil, Laura Wise and Christine Bell, 'Untangling Conflict: Local Peace Agreements in Contemporary Armed Violence', Report no. 5, Austrian Study Centre for Peace and Conflict Resolution, 27 May 2020.

[18] Nigeria is the only Sub-Saharan African country among those assessed in this volume which is classified as a 'hybrid regime'. See EIU, 'Democracy Index 2022', 2022.

From Global Jihad to Local Insurgencies: the Changing Nature of Sub-Saharan Jihadism

For more than a decade the Islamist insurgency in Sub-Saharan Africa has seemed unstoppable. 2022 saw another uptick in jihadist violence across the continent. Fatalities increased by 48% compared to the previous year, while violent incidents increased by 22%.[1] The annual number of attacks in the region have doubled since 2016, and Sub-Saharan Africa is now the region with the greatest annual number of terrorist attacks globally (see Figure 1).[2] However, the jihadist insurrections in Sub-Saharan Africa are also evolving. They have become much more localised, building on local grievances and becoming intertwined with community and ethnic conflicts. The international dimension of jihadism has practically disappeared in the region and connections between insurgent groups remain limited to some sub-regional collaborations. Jihadist groups' increasing involvement in local conflicts and the protector role that they play for various communities have made them resilient and more popular than the government in some places. However, their increasing reliance on local funding (e.g., via extortion) often puts them at odds with the local population, as illustrated by the backlash against al-Shabaab in Somalia.

While Islamic militants are widespread across the continent in areas with Muslim populations, organised violent groups are concentrated in specific areas in the Sahel, Lake Chad Basin, Somalia, northern Mozambique and North Kivu province in the Democratic Republic of the Congo (DRC). Countries neighbouring these areas are also impacted by cross-border militant activities, including the use of their territories for recruitment and the smuggling of arms and other illicit goods for revenue-generating purposes. This is the case notably for Kenya, Tanzania and Uganda in East Africa and Benin, Côte d'Ivoire, Ghana and Togo in West Africa.

The state of play of Sub-Saharan jihadism

The Sahel

In the Sahel, jihadist insurgency impacts primarily Mali, Burkina Faso and, to a lesser extent, Niger. The epicentre of the conflict is the tri-border area between the three countries, the Liptako-Gourma region. However, central Mali and northern Burkina Faso are now seeing some of the worst violence following the departure of French troops from both countries. The Group to Support Islam and Muslims (JNIM) is the main jihadist group operating in this region. It is an association of five major organisations and smaller factions, and the leader is Iyad Ag Ghaly, a long-time Tuareg militant who fought the Malian government as one of the leaders of the 1990s Tuareg insurrection. He is also the leader of Ansar Dine, which is a movement principally comprised of Tuareg militants. However, the most active jihadist non-state armed group (NSAG) in Mali today is Katibat Macina (one of JNIM's factions), which is led by Amadou Koufa. The group is responsible for the insurrection in central Mali and for the main incursions into neighbouring countries. In Burkina Faso, the insurgency is now mainly in the hands of Ansarul Islam, a group very close to Katibat Macina. Islamic State Sahel Province is also increasing its activities in this region and is now in open conflict with JNIM.

Lake Chad Basin

The jihadist insurrection in the Lake Chad Basin is mostly centred on Nigeria, but Cameroon, Chad and Niger are also impacted. Ansaru and Islamic State West Africa Province (ISWAP) are the two dominant groups in the region. This insurrection began in 2009 and is now stable, with the number of terrorist events and fatalities in 2022 remaining largely the same as in 2021, but it is still very violent. In Nigeria, it is particularly affecting the states of Adamawa, Borno and Yabe. However, it is also increasingly mixed up with the activities of several non-jihadist militias that are involved in banditry, kidnapping and cattle rustling and local community conflicts that are currently active in most of northern Nigeria. These militias are now more lethal than jihadist groups.

Somalia

Somalia has experienced an increase in violence in the last year, essentially linked to a successful counter-offensive against the main jihadist group, al-Shabaab. The ongoing offensive is a well-coordinated effort by clan militias (who are leading the fight), the Somali National Army, federal and state forces, and the African Union Transition Mission in Somalia. They are also supported by special forces from Western countries. Despite important territorial gains made by militias and the government since the beginning of 2022, al-Shabaab's fighting capability is still considerable, and there are concerns that it maintains the ability to strike back. A critical issue is how to re-establish a state presence in newly liberated areas that have been controlled by the group for decades.

Mozambique

Northern Mozambique saw a recrudescence of militant activities in rural areas in 2022, after a decrease in violence following the 2021 separate interventions by Rwandan and South African troops, who managed to push out militants from major cities in the oil region of Cabo Delgado. The number of violent incidents linked to militant jihadists groups – mostly Ahlu al-Sunnah wal-Jamaah (ASJ, locally known as 'al-Shabaab'), which has claimed allegiance to the Islamic State (ISIS) – has increased. This has prompted concerns that the insurrection is expanding again in rural areas and to other regions.

Eastern Congo

Conflict has been spreading across the eastern DRC since 2022, and jihadist groups play a role in this new phase. The Allied Democratic Forces (ADF), a key actor in the conflict, started in Uganda as an ultra-conservative Muslim rebel movement. Later it was pushed out of Uganda by the national army and is now based in the Rwenzori Mountains in eastern DRC, collaborating with other Islamist insurgent groups in the region. The ADF pledged allegiance to ISIS in 2017. ISIS started claiming ADF attacks in 2019, and in 2020 the ADF adopted the name of Islamic State Central Africa Province, also known as Wilayat Wasat Afriqiyya.

Sub-Saharan jihadism: localised with diverse strategies

Claims of allegiance to al-Qaeda or ISIS hide the fact that insurgent groups in Sub-Saharan Africa are essentially local insurgencies, which receive little or no external support. In fact, while most jihadist groups claim a transnational allegiance, there is very little evidence that al-Qaeda or ISIS has any capacity to provide meaningful support to these self-proclaimed franchises. These jihadist groups are, instead, largely self-financed. Some collaboration exists at the sub-regional level; for example, the ADF allegedly helped train ASJ fighters in Mozambique. However, these networks of collaboration are now very limited compared to their previous strength.

Sub-Saharan jihadist groups have adopted somewhat different strategies in the use of violence against local populations. ISIS affiliates are remarkably violent and brutal, leading a war against what they consider apostate regimes and other Muslim sects, like the Shia. However, their use of terrorist tactics creates profound resentment and does not allow them to establish themselves in communities in a sustainable way. Al-Qaeda affiliates tend to be less violent and more pragmatic, especially now that they have abandoned international jihadism and are aiming to control territory by offering an alternative local governance system – one that is allegedly more in line with Islamic law and principles compared to the state's system. The group often collaborates tactically with non-religious armed movements and has indicated its willingness to negotiate with the state. Al-Qaeda affiliates' approaches increasingly resemble the strategy of the Taliban in Afghanistan during the later years of its insurrection. Most NSAGs remain loosely institutionalised and relatively fragmented, with many splinter groups operating with little direction from the leadership. ISIS and al-Qaeda franchises are also increasingly at odds with each other. Notoriously, an ISWAP splinter group is now fighting against JNIM and various other militias in northern Mali.

Jihadism and local grievances

Since most jihadist groups have largely abandoned international goals and connections, they have become increasingly involved in local conflicts and exploiting local tensions. Most of the conflicts in the regions where they operate are centred around access to and the management of natural resources, amid faltering governance responses by states.

Sub-Saharan Africa

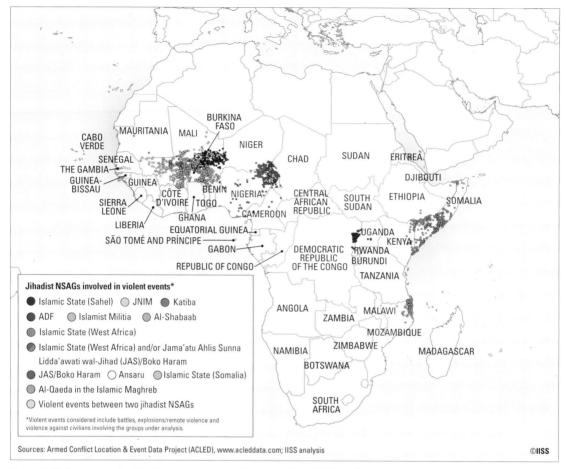

Figure 1: Violent events by jihadist non-state armed groups, 1 May 2022–30 June 2023

These conflicts have been exacerbated significantly by accelerating climate change.

In the Sahel, the pastoralist–agriculturalist divide has been traditionally and structurally adversarial. Many Fulani communities practise transhumance herding and must move southward due to droughts, which have become a constant occurrence in northern Sahel. At the same time, many agriculturists are moving into traditional grazing areas. Thus, the jihadist insurgency is building on decades of tensions over access to land. Agriculturists belong to ethnic groups that are also dominant among the urban and political elites, who have little incentive to resolve these tensions. For instance, some countries have introduced transhumance bans that have significantly worsened herders' plight. Salafi jihadists are sometimes viewed as protectors of the Fulani population and their traditional land rights, including in the areas bordering Benin, Côte d'Ivoire and Togo. This situation has been exacerbated in the Sahel by the creation of ethnic militias that have been responsible for massacres and perpetrated violence against certain ethnicities, such as the Fulani.

Jihadists are also involved in smaller intercommunal conflicts. In northern Ghana, for example, JNIM is an actor in the Mamprusi–Kusasi conflict (which is fuelled by long-standing tensions between different ethnic groups in the town of Bawku). In Somalia, al-Shabaab had originally garnered popular support by establishing an alternative governance system rooted in justice and conflict resolution, outside of clan rivalry. The group had promoted a narrative of equity that resonated with minor clans and youth who felt marginalised by major-clan leadership. In Mozambique, the ethnic component of the conflict in Cabo Delgado is key, as Muslim Mwani people have felt disfranchised since the country's independence. Large gas resources have been discovered in the north of the country, but the northern population has enjoyed no subsequent improvement in economic conditions. This has further fuelled grievances against the state.

To survive without external financing, insurgent groups have developed elaborate methods of local fundraising. For instance, Somalia's al-Shabaab has added to its traditional revenues from road taxes by managing sections of the charcoal trade and taxing cattle export and new building constructions throughout the country. It has also penetrated various state institutions, establishing an elaborate network of corruption. It is estimated that in 2022 al-Shabaab raised about US$100 million through taxes and extortion, compared to the US$250m in taxes officially collected by the government.[3] In the Sahel, JNIM revenues are derived from taxation on roads, kidnapping, the protection of gold mines, vehicle theft and diverse types of smuggling (especially now that the northern border is no longer controlled by French troops) as well as direct taxation of communities. The fact that insurgent groups are mostly dependent on local fundraising encourages them to adopt a strategy of territorial control in order to generate more opportunities to extract funds.

The above developments put NSAGs increasingly at odds with local populations, as communities perceive that the cost of supporting jihadists groups is higher than the benefits such groups provide. For instance, it is widely accepted that the revolt of local clan militias in Somalia was triggered by al-Shabaab's abuse of power and the pressure it placed on a population affected by a long-lasting and devastating drought. In the Sahel, more and more reports of abuse by militant groups are surfacing. The increasingly extractive nature of these movements is limiting their further territorial expansion as they are met with resistance from communities that see their protection as too costly. However, in some other areas, like northern Mali, abuses by national armed forces still generate popular appeal for jihadist groups, despite their increasing demands on the population.

Improved quality of governance as a way forward

As some jihadist groups try to base their legitimacy on protecting communities from the abuse of the state or other NSAGs, the effectiveness of states' responses to local populations' needs and demands is becoming central to the fight against jihadist groups. Across the continent, the ability of the state to project a positive response on the ground, alleviate tensions between communities, and maintain effective and accountable security services is essential to countering insurgencies. In Mali and Burkina Faso, inexperienced military juntas have proved incapable of addressing the spike in violence which followed the French armed forces' pull-out from both countries and the deployment of the Wagner Group in Mali. Many lessons can be learned from countries like Mauritania, which quelled a significant insurgency in the 2010s, and Niger, which has managed to keep violence levels under control despite many jihadist incursions in the west of the country.

The governance of the security sector is particularly important, given its prominence in the fight against extremists. Security forces must effectively protect the local population; be adequately trained and equipped; and be sufficiently flexible and rapid in their interventions. The examples of Mauritania and Niger show that security forces can be successful in pushing back insurgents if they are perceived as legitimate and enjoy the support of local communities. Niger, which was facing a rapidly progressing jihadist insurrection in 2021, has since drastically reassessed its approach in this sense, resulting in a significant drop in violent incidents.

Providing economic support to the population in areas that are at risk of insurgency is another important component for an effective prevention strategy. In all Sub-Saharan African countries affected by Salafi jihadism, efforts have been made by the international community to increase development aid. For instance, aid flow to Somalia increased by nearly 300% from 2000–20 and more than nine times for Niger during the same period.[4] However, the increase in aid can only have an impact over the long term for two main reasons. Firstly, the areas in which jihadists operate are often arid and far away from large urban centres. Prospects for improving the local economy and availability of jobs are therefore seriously constrained by geographical conditions. Secondly, the governance structure needed to implement projects in marginalised areas is often lacking.

Previous examples demonstrate that the most effective approach in fighting insurgencies is outreach by the government to local communities and traditional authorities, and even groups involved in illicit economies, to listen to their grievances and negotiate arrangements that can improve their lives within the boundaries of the law. This type of approach has been dramatically lacking in Mali. Conversely, Niger has established agencies for this purpose, such as the High Authority for the Consolidation of Peace, and Mauritania has carried out considerable outreach to local communities and religious authorities. Likewise, programmes targeted at young people vulnerable to recruitment by jihadist movements have been implemented with some success in Kenya, Mauritania and Somalia. These have involved negotiating with local community groups that have ties with jihadist movements and trying to address their grievances, so that community leaders can themselves convince their youth not to join extremist groups. Establishing communication channels with some of the less extreme militant groups has also been a successful strategy in places like Niger and Mauritania.

The experiences of countries which have been successful in combatting jihadist insurgencies show that finding an effective balance between providing security, supporting local development, and negotiating with communities and some armed groups is essential. This is, however, very difficult to achieve as it requires effective institutions and political leadership – things that need to be implemented by countries themselves. It is very challenging for foreign institutions to influence such processes.

Notes

[1]   Africa Center for Strategic Studies, 'Fatalities from Militant Islamist Violence in Africa Surge by Nearly 50 Percent', 6 February 2023.

[2]   United Nations Development Programme, 'Journey to Extremism in Africa: Pathways to Recruitment and Disengagement', 2023.

[3]   UN Security Council, 'Thirtieth Report of the Analytical Support and Sanctions Monitoring Team Submitted Pursuant to Resolution 2610 (2021) Concerning ISIL (Da'esh), Al-Qaida and Associated Individuals and Entities', S/22/547, 15 July 2022; and Wendy Williams, 'Reclaiming Al Shabaab's Revenue', defenceWeb, 5 April 2023.

[4]   World Bank, 'Net Official Development Assistance and Official Aid Received (Current US$) – Somalia'; and World Bank, 'Net Official Development Assistance and Official Aid Received (Current US$) – Niger'.

Sub-Saharan Africa

MALI

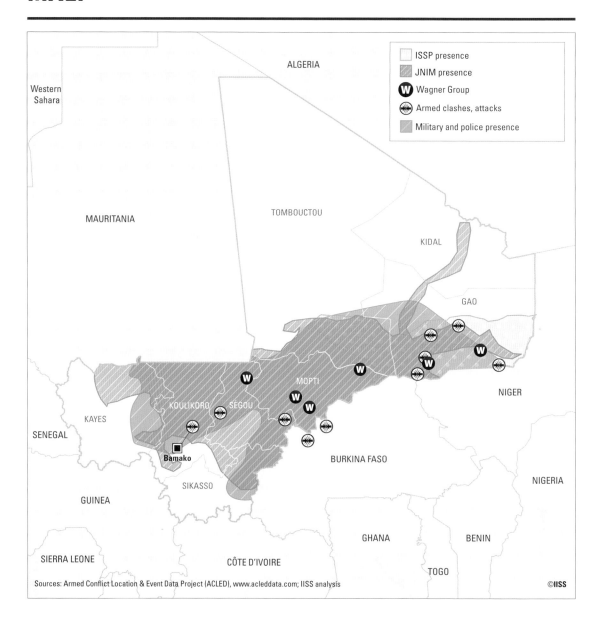

Sources: Armed Conflict Location & Event Data Project (ACLED), www.acleddata.com; IISS analysis ©IISS

Conflict Overview

The start of Mali's conflict is largely attributed to the 2011 fall of the Muammar Gadhafi regime in Libya, which resulted in regional instability, the proliferation of weapons in the Liptako-Gourma region (at the intersection of Burkina Faso, Mali and Niger) and the revival of a transnational Tuareg irredentism that led to rebellion in 2012. By 2013, the collapse of state authority in northern Mali prompted French military intervention through *Operation Serval*, which in 2014 became the trans-Sahelian *Operation Barkhane*. It also resulted in the deployment of the African-led International Support Mission in Mali (AFISMA), which was later taken over by the ongoing United Nations Multidimensional Integrated Stabilization Mission in Mali (MINUSMA).

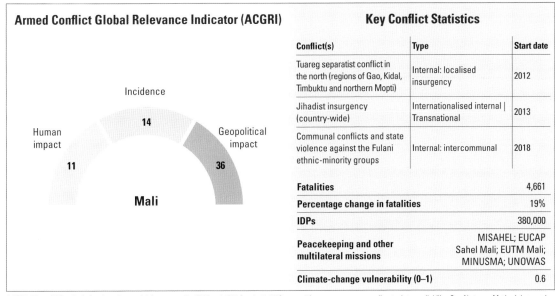

Conflict(s)	Type	Start date
Tuareg separatist conflict in the north (regions of Gao, Kidal, Timbuktu and northern Mopti)	Internal: localised insurgency	2012
Jihadist insurgency (country-wide)	Internationalised internal | Transnational	2013
Communal conflicts and state violence against the Fulani ethnic-minority groups	Internal: intercommunal	2018
Fatalities		4,661
Percentage change in fatalities		19%
IDPs		380,000
Peacekeeping and other multilateral missions		MISAHEL; EUCAP Sahel Mali; EUTM Mali; MINUSMA; UNOWAS
Climate-change vulnerability (0–1)		0.6

ACGRI pillars: IISS calculation based on multiple sources for 2022 and 2023 (scale: 0–100), except for some cases according to data availability. See Notes on Methodology and Data Appendix for all variables and further details on Key Conflict Statistics.

These interventions paved the way for a negotiated peace agreement in 2015 – the Algiers accord – between the pro-independence umbrella group the Coordination of Azawad Movements (CMA), pro-Bamako groups (the Platform and associated groups) and the state.

Despite important mediation efforts, the country has faced extreme instability since 2011. Protracted conflict has expanded towards the central and southern regions of Mali. Two competing violent extremist organisations (VEOs) are predominant: the Islamic State Sahel Province (ISSP), which emerged from a split within al-Mourabitoun in 2015, and the Group to Support Islam and Muslims (JNIM), created in 2017 as a coalition between al-Qaeda-affiliated groups. Violence is also perpetrated by several other actors, including local militias, self-defence forces and security forces, which all vie for greater power and control over resources.

The relentless spread of insecurity has resulted in unprecedented displacement rates, increased human-rights violations (including sexual violence) and a widened gap between those in power and their populations. The Malian crisis is not contained within its borders, as it poses significant challenges to peace and stability in the wider Sahel region. Insufficient or abusive state presence in Mali's border areas has facilitated the spread of VEOs to neighbouring Burkina Faso and Niger and further south to the coastal states of Benin, Côte d'Ivoire, Ghana and Togo, where an increasing number of attacks have been recorded.

Conflict Update

Over the last year, the international dimension of Mali's cutting ties with France and developing a relationship with Russia has overshadowed more nuanced considerations of the country's intersecting conflict dynamics. The reporting period was marked by a rupture in the multilateral security architecture which had come to dominate Mali's landscape over the past ten years. The official termination of the Defense Cooperation Treaty between Mali and France in May 2022 was perceived as one of the most consequential geopolitical shifts in the region since 2012. The decade-long French military intervention had grown increasingly unpopular due to its inability to effectively curtail violent extremism and its spread across the Sahel. Furthermore, the two successive military takeovers in Mali in August 2020 and May 2021 marked a reversing of the country's democratic practices.

Since the most recent coup, attempts by the military junta of Colonel Assimi Goita to do away with former regional and international partnerships highlight an ambition to revamp its counter-terrorism approach.

In June 2022, for instance, Mali withdrew from the G5 Sahel, the coalition of Sahelian states created in February 2014. Simultaneously, a number of nations – including Benin, Côte d'Ivoire, Germany and the United Kingdom – announced their intention to withdraw earlier than planned from MINUSMA. Then, the Malian Armed Forces (FAMa) reportedly established a partnership with the Russian private security organisation Wagner Group to address security challenges. Finally, the junta's request on 16 June 2023 for the full withdrawal of MINUSMA and the subsequent termination of its mandate was a key impetus for the further deterioration of relations between Mali and its partners. The vacuum left by the withdrawal of foreign forces and profound divisions within the African bloc have added a layer of unpredictability to the situation.

Another significant development during the reporting period was the worsening of relations between Malian authorities and the CMA. These tensions peaked in December 2022 when the three main armed movements constituting the CMA – the National Movement for the Liberation of Azawad (MNLA), the High Council for the Unity of Azawad (HCUA) and the Arab Movement of Azawad (MAA) – suspended their participation in the monitoring and implementation of the Algiers accord due to the government's purported disengagement from the peace agreement. In February 2023, the three groups merged their command structures in an attempt to increase their military capacity. While the implications of this are unclear, these events speak to the fragility of the peace deal. The reinvigoration of the Azawad independence cause is likely to harm Mali's attempt at mending national divisions.

By openly contesting and delegitimising symbols of the state – whether it be through active battles against the FAMa, targeting government officials or attacking state structures such as schools – jihadist armed groups operating in central Mali seek to present their alternative order as a viable option. Their approach is brutal, and growing competition between armed groups is deadly and protracted. Within the last year, ISSP pursued attacks in the Liptako-Gourma region to gain back control from JNIM and to return to areas that had traditionally been the group's stronghold. Notably, the increase in violence against civilians within the reporting period is attributed to both state and non-state actors. Hundreds of ethnic Fulanis are stigmatised for their alleged over-representation in armed groups and have been killed in counter-terrorism operations by the Malian army, self-defence groups and Wagner mercenaries. This prompted the UN to launch an investigation into potential human-rights violations following the murder of over 500 civilians allegedly by FAMa and Russian mercenaries in the village of Moura in 2022, while many similar but smaller-scale incidents have also occurred during counter-terrorism operations.[1]

Escalating violence has exacerbated the country's humanitarian crisis. An estimated 380,000 Malians remained internally displaced and faced food, shelter and healthcare shortages as of 30 April 2023, according to the UN High Commissioner for Refugees. An additional 64,000 people crossed borders – mostly from Burkina Faso – to seek refuge in Mali due to the intensification of conflicts in neighbouring states.[2]

Conflict Parties

Malian Armed Forces (FAMa)

Strength: Approximately 21,000 active military personnel (air force: 2,000; army: 19,000), as well as 6,000 national gendarmerie, 1,000 national police and 10,000 national-guard personnel.

Areas of operation: Northern, central and southern Mali, particularly in the tri-border Liptako-Gourma area near Burkina Faso and Niger.

Leadership: Col. Assimi Goita.

Structure: Consists of the air force, army, national gendarmerie, national police and the national guard.

History: Created at independence in 1960. Following years of underinvestment, FAMa has been significantly strengthened over the past decade, including through the European Union's military training mission from 2013–22.

Objectives: Counter-terrorism and territorial security.

Opponents: JNIM, CMA and ISSP.

Affiliates/allies: Burkina Faso, Economic Community of West African States (ECOWAS), EU, France (until May 2022), Niger, MINUSMA, United States, Russian private military contractors and Russia.

Resources/capabilities: The defence budget for 2022 was US$827 million, and it is projected to be US$1.1 billion for 2023.

Permanent Strategic Framework (CSP) (a coalition of Coordination of Azawad Movements (CMA) and Platform)

Strength: Unclear, but the number of CMA fighters was estimated to be 800–4,000 prior to the 2015 Algiers accord.[3] The number of Platform fighters is unknown.

Areas of operation: CMA and Platform are primarily active in northern Mali, including the regions of Gao, Kidal and Timbuktu.

Leadership:
CSP: Bilal Ag Acherif (president) and Fahad Ag Almahmoud (vice president).
CMA: Leadership of the coalition rotates among its members on a regular basis.
Platform: A loose alliance of autonomous non-state armed groups and self-defence militias.

Structure:
CSP: Born out of a merger between the CMA and Platform – the main armed movements in northern Mali and signatories of the Algiers accord.
CMA: A coalition including the MNLA, the HCUA and a CMA-affiliated faction of the MAA.
Platform: An umbrella organisation that includes the Imghad Tuareg Self-Defence Group and Allies, the MAA–Platform faction, the Coordination for the Movements and Fronts of Patriotic Resistance, and the Movement for the Salvation of Azawad-Daoussak.

History: Following the collapse of the Gadhafi regime and the 2012 Tuareg insurrection, in 2014 the MNLA came together with other rebellious factions in the region, including HCUA and MAA, to create the CMA. In 2021, CMA merged with

Platform – a coalition comprised of several groups in favour of Malian state authority – to form the CSP in an attempt to coordinate their actions and reconcile their interests. In the time since, the CSP has managed this to some extent, but challenges remain which prevent full unity in its actions.

Objectives:
CSP: Coordinate CMA and Platform efforts to implement the 2015 Algiers accord for peace and reconciliation, combat insecurity and take into account the aspirations of local populations.
CMA: A coalition of Azawad rebel groups originally fighting for self-determination. Independence is no longer an objective but may become so again due to friction in implementing the Algiers accord.
Platform: Formed in support of Mali's territorial integrity. However, its members have widely differing agendas and interests, with some engaging in local disputes while others support the security forces.

Opponents: ISSP and JNIM.

Affiliates/allies:
CMA: Formally cooperates with FAMa, MINUSMA and Platform but has previously cooperated with jihadist groups.
Platform: FAMa, MINUSMA and formerly *Operation Barkhane*.

Resources/capabilities: Small arms and light weaponry. For the CMA, remnants of the Libyan military arsenal left behind after the ousting of Gadhafi.

Group to Support Islam and Muslims (JNIM)

Strength: Unknown.

Areas of operation: Mostly active in northern and central Mali (with an expansion southward towards Bamako).

Leadership: Iyad Ag Ghaly, a long-time Tuareg militant who is also the leader of Ansar Dine, one of the main groups constituting JNIM.

Structure: Created as an alliance of equals.

History: JNIM was created in 2017 as a coalition between al-Qaeda-affiliated groups such as Ansar Dine, al-Mourabitoun, al-Qaeda in the Islamic Maghreb–Sahel, Katibat Macina and other smaller factions.

Objectives: Establish an Islamic state in the Sahel, replacing existing state structures and expelling foreign forces.

Opponents: FAMa, foreign forces, Russian private military contractors and ISSP.

Affiliates/allies: Al-Qaeda, al-Qaeda in the Islamic Maghreb–North Africa, Katibat Macina and Katibat Serma. Cooperates with Ansarul Islam, though their relationship is ambiguous.

Resources/capabilities: Heavy weaponry and improvised explosive devices (IEDs), including vehicle-borne IEDs and suicide-vehicle-borne IEDs.

Islamic State Sahel Province (ISSP)

Strength: Unknown.

Areas of operation: Gao, Menaka, Mopti and Timbuktu.

Leadership: Abdul Bara al-Sahrawi (also known as al-Ansari) and a cadre of local commanders.

Structure: Unclear.

History: ISSP emerged from a split within al-Mourabitoun in 2015 and was originally known as the Islamic State in the Greater Sahara (ISGS). ISGS pledged allegiance to the Islamic State (ISIS) in 2015, and in 2019 it became part of the Islamic

State West Africa Province (ISWAP). ISIS recognised the group as an independent *wilayat* (province) in March 2022 under the name ISSP.

Objectives: Establish an Islamic caliphate based on strict interpretation of the Koran and adherence to ISIS ideology.

Opponents: JNIM, FAMa, G5 Sahel Joint Force (FC-G5S) and MINUSMA.

Affiliates/allies: Katibat Salaheddine, ISIS, ISWAP and other smaller militias.

Resources/capabilities: IEDs and light weaponry.

Wagner Group

Strength: Around 1,000 troops.[4]

Areas of operation: Central Mali (Mopti and Ségou), and Timbuktu area.

Leadership: Unclear after the group's chief Yevgeny Prigozhin and commander Dmitry Utkin were killed in an aeroplane crash on 23 August 2023.

Structure: The company was established by businessman Yevgeny Prigozhin. Its structure is not well documented.

History: The Wagner Group is a Russian security organisation closely linked to the Kremlin, Russian military intelligence and Russia's Ministry of Defence. It is used by Russia to carry out a range of officially deniable military and intelligence operations and commercial activities. Since November 2020, the group has established ties with the military junta whilst increasing their power and access to resources. The group has since been involved in FAMa's counter-insurgency and civilian-protection efforts. The group was established in 2014, and it and other private military companies proliferated following Russia's involvement in the 2015 war in Syria, where they played an active role. The Wagner Group also operates extensively in Africa, where it is contracted to provide security for governments and is involved in profitable resource extraction. It took a leading role in the siege of Bakhmut in Donetsk region from August 2022–May 2023, which raised its public profile significantly in Russia. However, its status is currently in limbo. Following an abortive mutiny led by Prigozhin on 23–24 June 2023, a major part of the Wagner Group's forces was deployed in Belarus. The death of Prigozhin and other senior Wagner Group figures in August 2023 has deepened uncertainty about the group's future. After the mutiny, Putin acknowledged that the group was directly funded by the Russian state and noted the lack of any Russian legislation allowing such private military groups. At the end of July, Russia advanced legislation enabling regional governors to create military companies, and this could lead to further significant changes in their form and function.

Objectives: Support FAMa's security operations against jihadist groups.

Opponents: JNIM, CMA and ISSP.

Affiliates/allies: FAMa.

Resources/capabilities: The Malian government is paying Wagner US$10m a month for its services.[5]

G5 Sahel Joint Force (FC-G5S)

Strength: Between 5,000 and 10,000 troops provided by the four remaining member countries (Burkina Faso, Chad, Mauritania and Niger).[6] Although Mali decided to withdraw from the task force on 15 May 2022, Malian FC-G5S forces were still active domestically throughout the reporting period.

Areas of operation: Border regions between Mali and Mauritania, between Niger and Chad and in the Liptako-Gourma tri-border area.

Leadership: Eric Yemdaogo Tiare (executive secretary).

Structure: In January 2023, the defence ministers of the four member countries announced the operationalisation of 14 new battalions, including five in Burkina Faso, two in Chad, two in Mauritania and five in Niger.[7] However, as of 30 April 2023, the task force was still in the process of developing a new concept of operations.

History: While the G5 Sahel as an organisation was established in 2014 (comprising members Burkina Faso, Chad, Mali, Mauritania and Niger), the joint force was created in February 2017 with the support of France and the UN to address threats across the Sahel, such as terrorism and transnational organised crime, including the smuggling of goods and human trafficking.

Objectives: Strengthen security along the borders of member states through intelligence sharing and the deployment of joint patrols.

Opponents: JNIM and ISSP.

Affiliates/allies: Foreign and regional armed forces and MINUSMA.

Resources/capabilities: Suffers from underfunding and unpredictable financing. Troop deployment is slow due to a lack of logistical capacity and equipment.

United Nations Multidimensional Integrated Stabilization Mission in Mali (MINUSMA)

Strength: 13,289 military, 1,920 police and 1,792 civilian personnel (859 national, 754 international and 179 UN volunteers).[8]

Areas of operation: Countrywide, with a concentration of forces in the central and northern regions.

Leadership: El-Ghassim Wane (special representative of the secretary-general and head of MINUSMA).

Structure: Within the reporting period, 55 countries contributed to the military force and 26 countries to the police force.[9] However, during this same period, Côte d'Ivoire, Germany and the UK each announced their withdrawal from the operation.

History: Established in April 2013 by UN Security Council (UNSC) Resolution 2100 following the 2012 Tuareg rebellion. In the same year, ECOWAS's AFISMA was incorporated under MINUSMA's command. MINUSMA has seen the largest number of casualties among UN peacekeeping operations.[10] The 2022 early withdrawal of several key participating nations has damaged the capacity and legitimacy of the mission. On 30 June 2023, at the request of Mali's junta, the UNSC unanimously approved the complete withdrawal of MINUSMA forces within the last six months of the year.

Objectives: Support the implementation of the 2015 Algiers accord, including the protection of civilians in central and northern Mali.

Opponents: JNIM, CMA and ISSP.

Affiliates/allies: FAMa and FC-G5S.

Resources/capabilities: Budget of US$1.2bn for July 2022–June 2023.[11]

Notes

1   UN, 'Moura: Over 500 Killed by Malian Troops, Foreign Military Personnel in 2022 Operation', 12 May 2023.

2   UN Office for the Coordination of Humanitarian Affairs, 'Mali: Humanitarian Dashboard', 30 April 2023.

3   Baba Ahmed, 'Mali: le business du cantonnement?' [Mali: The Cantonment Business?], *Jeune Afrique*, 29 April 2016 (updated 5 September 2016); and Baba Ahmed and Christophe Boisbouvier, 'Nord-Mali: guerre à huis clos' [North Mali: War Behind Closed Doors], *Jeune Afrique*, 21 February 2012.

4   Global Initiative Against Transnational Organized Crime, 'The Grey Zone: Russia's Military, Mercenary and Criminal Engagement in Africa', 16 February 2023.

5   US Department of State, 'Potential Deployment of the Wagner Group in Mali', 15 December 2021.

6   UNSC, 'Peace and Security in Africa', S/2022/838, 16 November 2022.

7   A. Y. Barma, 'G5 Sahel: l'Etat-major de la Force conjointe ramené à Niamey, 14 bataillons bientôt opérationnels (Ministres de la Défense)' [G5 Sahel: Joint Force Headquarters Brought Back to Niamey, 14 Battalions Soon to Be Operational (Ministers of Defence)], ActuNiger, 12 January 2023.

8   MINUSMA, 'Personnel', June 2023.

9   MINUSMA, 'Personnel', December 2022.

10   MINUSMA, 'History'.

11   UNSC, 'Situation in Mali: Report of the Secretary-General', S/2023/402, 1 June 2023.

BURKINA FASO

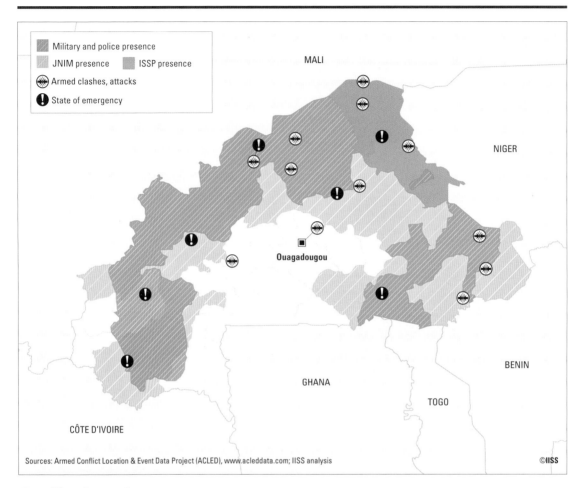

Sources: Armed Conflict Location & Event Data Project (ACLED), www.acleddata.com; IISS analysis   ©IISS

Conflict Overview

Burkina Faso is currently regarded as the epicentre of a regional and transnational conflict that began over ten years ago in Mali and has involved various local and foreign parties. Armed groups pursuing transnational politico-religious agendas have proliferated in recent years, benefitting from the lack of state presence along the border between Mali and Burkina Faso. A deadly January 2016 attack in the heart of Ouagadougou, claimed by al-Qaeda in the Islamic Maghreb (AQIM), marked the start of Burkina Faso's confrontation with violent extremist organisations (VEOs). A growing sentiment of social injustice, primarily among Fulani herders, then led to an uptick in violence by the Ansarul Islam militant group. From 2019 onwards, the activities of other VEOs

intensified, chiefly in northern and eastern provinces. These organisations included the al-Qaeda-affiliated Group to Support Islam and Muslims (JNIM) and its rival Islamic State Sahel Province (ISSP). By 2022, Burkina Faso faced its deadliest year on record, with terror-related deaths totalling 1,135.[1]

Conflict drivers in Burkina Faso are multi-faceted and violence is a symptom of much deeper, long-standing issues. Competing power structures keep the country fragmented and various centralised governments have done little to address pervasive fault lines between the government and local communities and between communities themselves. Within such a context, armed groups and criminal networks have proliferated and latched onto socio-political and

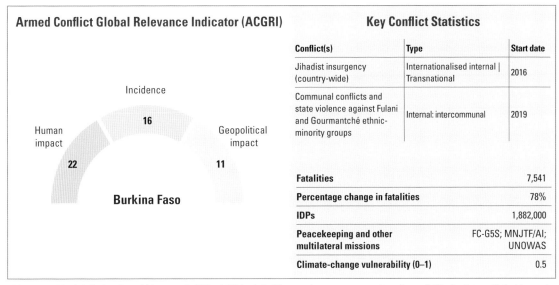

Armed Conflict Global Relevance Indicator (ACGRI)

Incidence
16

Human
impact

Geopolitical
impact

22   **11**

Burkina Faso

Key Conflict Statistics

Conflict(s)	Type	Start date
Jihadist insurgency (country-wide)	Internationalised internal | Transnational	2016
Communal conflicts and state violence against Fulani and Gourmantché ethnic-minority groups	Internal: intercommunal	2019

Fatalities	7,541
Percentage change in fatalities	78%
IDPs	1,882,000
Peacekeeping and other multilateral missions	FC-G5S; MNJTF/AI; UNOWAS
Climate-change vulnerability (0–1)	0.5

ACGRI pillars: IISS calculation based on multiple sources for 2022 and 2023 (scale: 0–100), except for some cases according to data availability. See Notes on Methodology and Data Appendix for all variables and further details on Key Conflict Statistics.

economic grievances. This demonstrates the army's inability to effectively tackle symmetric and asymmetric threats. Moreover, VEOs have exploited feelings of abandonment and dispossession to turn local communities – referred to as *cadets sociaux* (social juniors) – against the central state deemed responsible for their marginalisation. Due to an absence of formal mechanisms to express grievances, the use of violence has become an important tool of political leverage in local communities' relationship with state institutions.

Violence in Burkina Faso can be highly localised, but the transnational dimensions of this conflict make it complex to manage. The pursuit of jihadist groups across national borders means that Burkina Faso is encircled by instability. Conflicting approaches among the actors striving to bring an end to the conflict have resulted in little progress being made, while JNIM and ISSP continue to strengthen their footholds and social cleavages driven by insecurity continue to grow.

Conflict Update

Two successive military coups within nine months, the expansion of VEOs and a growing humanitarian crisis show the destabilising toll of the conflict in Burkina Faso over the reporting period. The state's legitimacy was contested at multiple levels and its governing capacity was stretched to a breaking point as spiralling insecurity took hold.

Initially confined to the borders with Niger and Mali (i.e., the Liptako Gourma tri-border area), the conflict spread during the reporting period. The epicentre may remain in the northeast, but the presence of JNIM has been recorded along the entire border with Mali. The period was marked by the intensification of armed violence, with JNIM killing hundreds of civilians in a series of coordinated attacks. Meanwhile, the influence

of ISSP in Burkina Faso was limited to the northern Sahel province.

An important shift toward a state-led approach to tackling the violence was also observed. Through vast military recruitment campaigns, the junta led by Captain Ibrahim Traoré increased the capacity of the Burkina Faso Armed Forces (FABF), as well as the Volunteers for the Defense of the Homeland (VDP), a civilian auxiliary group on which it now heavily relies for local vigilante counter-terrorism operations. The annual defence budget was increased by almost 50% from 2022 to 2023.[2] The junta enforced various security measures in the early months of 2023 to curtail the violence, such as imposing a state of emergency in 22 of Burkina Faso's 45 provinces.[3] As of June 2023, the government had signalled its intention to continue

Sub-Saharan Africa

on this trajectory and was looking at ways to further grow the size of the VDP.[4]

Reinforcing this focus on a state-led approach, transitional president Traoré ordered the withdrawal by February 2023 of French troops which had been assisting Burkinabe forces in conflict-ridden areas under *Operation Sabre*, accusing them of doing too little to re-establish security. This withdrawal allowed the Burkinabe authorities to assume greater responsibility for the internal handling of the security crisis. Despite speculation that mercenaries from the Russian Wagner Group may become active in Burkina Faso, as they have been in neighbouring Mali, there is no concrete evidence yet of their involvement in the country. As the manpower of state security forces has increased, so too have accusations of violence perpetrated by them. The most notable tragedy was a massacre in April 2023 in which armed men in uniform, allegedly members of the FABF and VDP, surrounded Karma village and killed more than 150 people.[5] Heavy-handed military operations, frequent attacks on civilians and high rates of displacement have catalysed Burkina Faso's worst humanitarian crisis in recorded history.

In Burkina Faso, the legacy of state-led marginalisation has an important ethnic component. Because of their perceived over-representation in VEOs, Fulani and Gourmantché communities have suffered more frequent attacks by the FABF. This has been notable in the Sahel, Centre-Nord, Est and Centre-Est regions, where they have historically been prominent. These attacks have become increasingly indiscriminate and have targeted other ethnic groups as well, most recently Mossi communities, who have long held political power.[6] This trend is exacerbating communal conflict, intra-state divisions and other local grievances. It also contributes to massive displacements of populations both internally and into neighbouring Mali and Niger.

Finally, the multiplication of areas besieged by armed groups has severely restricted local populations' access to food, medicine, water and other critical goods, and it has hindered humanitarian assistance to isolated communities. For instance, the northern town of Djibo has been under siege by JNIM for over a year, which has further aggravated food insecurity for the 370,000 people living in the area.[7] Frequent attacks along the roads leading to the town have prevented critical supplies from reaching the population. The unfolding humanitarian disaster only further underlines Burkina Faso's fragility and exposes the limitations of military-led approaches to overcoming the crisis.

Conflict Parties

Burkina Faso Armed Forces (FABF)

Strength: 11,200 active military personnel (air force: 600; army: 6,400; gendarmerie: 4,200), as well as an additional 250 active gendarmerie and paramilitary personnel.

Areas of operation: Active in western, southwestern, northern and eastern Burkina Faso, in particular at border areas with Mali and Niger.

Leadership: Capt. Ibrahim Traoré and Col.-Maj. David Kabre (chief of staff).

Structure: Comprised of the army, the air force, the gendarmerie and paramilitary forces.

History: Reached its current form in 1985 with the inauguration of the air force.

Objectives: Maintain national security and territorial integrity and counter jihadist groups.

Opponents: Ansarul Islam, ISSP and JNIM.

Affiliates/allies: Benin, Côte d'Ivoire, G5 Sahel Joint Force (FC-G5S), Ghana, Mali, Niger and self-defence groups.

Resources/capabilities: Burkina Faso's defence budget for 2022 was US$467 million (2.4% of GDP), compared to US$813m (3.9% of GDP) for 2023. Each new recruit must undergo an initial training of 18 months.[8]

Volunteers for the Defense of the Homeland (VDP)

Strength: A recruitment campaign launched in October 2022 resulted in 90,000 applications. By December 2022, 50,000 volunteers had been selected.[9] In May 2023, Prime Minister Apollinaire Kyélem of Tambèla announced the government's intention to double the number of VDP volunteers to 100,000.[10]

Areas of operation: Country-wide.

Leadership: Col. Boukaré Zoungrana is the de facto commander of the Brigade of Vigilance and Patriotic Defense (BVDP).

Structure: Comprised of volunteers; 35,000 remain in their residential communities and 15,000 are assigned alongside the FABF across the country.[11] The VDP is a constituent of

Volunteers for the Defense of the Homeland (VDP)

the BVDP, which also includes FABF reserve forces. It is organised under the regiments present in each of the six regions.

History: Roch Kaboré, president between 2015 and 2022, created the VDP on the back of existing self-defence groups such as the Koglweogo and the Dozo. The government presented the VDP as an inclusive force for each 'region, ethnicity, political opinion and religious denomination'.[12] Since the VDP's creation in January 2020, however, the fighters have regularly faced accusations of discriminatory attacks against pastoralist Fulani communities.

Objectives: Support the FABF in fighting armed groups and protecting Burkina Faso's territorial integrity through local security operations.

Opponents: JNIM and ISSP.

Affiliates/allies: FABF.

Resources/capabilities: Light weaponry. Each volunteer is trained over two weeks to learn to handle weapons and integrate the code of conduct. A Patriotic Support Fund was set up in January 2023 to facilitate the mobilisation of resources.

Group to Support Islam and Muslims (JNIM)

Strength: Unknown.

Areas of operation: Northern, eastern and, to a lesser extent, southern Burkina Faso.

Leadership: Iyad Ag Ghaly, a long-time Tuareg militant who is also the leader of Ansar Dine, one of the main groups constituting JNIM.

Structure: Created as an alliance of equals.

History: JNIM was created in 2017 as a coalition between al-Qaeda-affiliated groups such as Ansar Dine, al-Mourabitoun, al-Qaeda in the Islamic Maghreb–Sahel, Katibat Macina and other smaller factions.

Objectives: Establish an Islamic caliphate in the Sahel, replacing existing state structures and expelling foreign forces.

Opponents: FABF, foreign forces, Russian private military contractors and ISSP.

Affiliates/allies: Al-Qaeda, al-Qaeda in the Islamic Maghreb–North Africa, Katibat Macina and Katibat Serma. Cooperates with Ansarul Islam, though their relationship is ambiguous.

Resources/capabilities: Heavy weaponry and improvised explosive devices (IEDs), including vehicle-borne IEDs and suicide-vehicle-borne IEDs.

Islamic State Sahel Province (ISSP)

Strength: Unknown.

Areas of operation: Sahel, Centre-Nord, Est, Boucle du Mouhoun, Sud-Ouest, Centre-Sud and Cascades.

Leadership: Abdul Bara al-Sahrawi (also known as al-Ansari) and a cadre of local commanders.

Structure: Unknown.

History: ISSP emerged from a split within al-Mourabitoun in 2015 and was originally known as the Islamic State in the Greater Sahara (ISGS). ISGS pledged allegiance to the Islamic State (ISIS) in 2015, and in 2019 it became part of the Islamic

State West Africa Province (ISWAP). ISIS recognised the group as an independent *wilayat* (province) in March 2022 under the name ISSP.

Objectives: Establish an Islamic caliphate based on strict interpretation of the Koran and adherence to ISIS ideology.

Opponents: JNIM, UN Multidimensional Integrated Stabilization Mission in Mali (MINUSMA) and FABF.

Affiliates/allies: Katibat Salaheddine, ISIS, ISWAP and other smaller militias.

Resources/capabilities: IEDs and light weaponry.

G5 Sahel Joint Force (FC-G5S)

Strength: Between 5,000 and 10,000 troops provided by the four remaining member countries (Burkina Faso, Chad, Mauritania and Niger).[13]

Areas of operation: Border regions between Mali and Mauritania, between Niger and Chad and in the Liptako-Gourma tri-border area.

Leadership: Eric Yemdaogo Tiare (executive secretary).

Structure: In January 2023, the defence ministers of the four member countries announced the operationalisation of 14 new battalions, including five in Burkina Faso, two in Chad, two in Mauritania and five in Niger.[14] However, as of 30 April 2023, the task force was still in the process of developing a new concept of operations.

History: While the G5 Sahel as an organisation was established in 2014 (comprising members Burkina Faso, Chad, Mali, Mauritania and Niger), the joint force was created in February 2017 with the support of France and the United Nations to address threats across the Sahel, such as terrorism and transnational organised crime, including the smuggling of goods and human trafficking. Mali withdrew from FC-G5S in May 2022.

Objectives: Strengthen security along the borders of member states through intelligence sharing and the deployment of joint patrols.

Opponents: JNIM and ISSP.

G5 Sahel Joint Force (FC-G5S)

Affiliates/allies: Foreign and regional armed forces and MINUSMA.

Resources/capabilities: Suffers from underfunding and unpredictable financing. Troop deployment is slow due to a lack of logistical capacity and equipment.

Notes

[1]   Institute for Economics and Peace, 'Global Terrorism Index 2023: Measuring the Impact of Terrorism', March 2023, p. 22.

[2]   'Burkina Faso Increases Defense Budget by Nearly 50 Percent for 2023', *North Africa Post*, 6 April 2023.

[3]   AFP, 'Jihadist-hit Burkina Extends State of Emergency by 6 Months', *Barron's*, 13 May 2023.

[4]   Rédaction Africanews, 'Burkina PM Vows No Deal with Jihadists, Hints at Election Delay', Africa News, 31 May 2023.

[5]   Ravina Shamdasani, 'Burkina Faso: Killing of Civilians', UN Human Rights Office of the High Comissioner, 25 April 2023.

[6]   Agnès Faivre, 'Au moins 150 civils massacrés dans le nord du Burkina Faso' [At Least 150 Civilians Massacred in Northern Burkina Faso], *Libération*, 23 April 2023.

[7]   'Forced to Eat Leaves: Hungry and Besieged in Burkina Faso', Al-Jazeera, 12 December 2022.

[8]   'Pourquoi des activistes sont-ils enrôlés de force comme auxiliaires de l'armée au Burkina Faso?' [Why Are Activists Forcibly Recruited as Army Auxiliaries in Burkina Faso?], BBC News, 30 March 2023.

[9]   'L'armée au Burkina mise sur les civils contre le terrorisme' [The Army in Burkina Counts on Civilians to Fight Terrorism], DW, 30 December 2022.

[10]   Rédaction Africanews, 'Burkina PM Vows No Deal with Jihadists, Hints at Election Delay'.

[11]   'L'armée au Burkina mise sur les civils contre le terrorisme' [The Army in Burkina Counts on Civilians to Fight Terrorism].

[12]   Anna Schmauder and Annabelle Willeme, 'The Volunteers for the Defense of the Homeland', Clingendael Institute, 9 March 2021.

[13]   UN Security Council, 'Peace and Security in Africa', S/2022/838, 16 November 2022.

[14]   A. Y. Barma, 'G5 Sahel: l'Etat-major de la Force conjointe ramené à Niamey, 14 bataillons bientôt opérationnels (Ministres de la Défense)' [G5 Sahel: Joint Force Headquarters Brought Back to Niamey, 14 Battalions Soon to Be Operational (Ministers of Defence)], ActuNiger, 12 January 2023.

Sub-Saharan Africa

NIGER

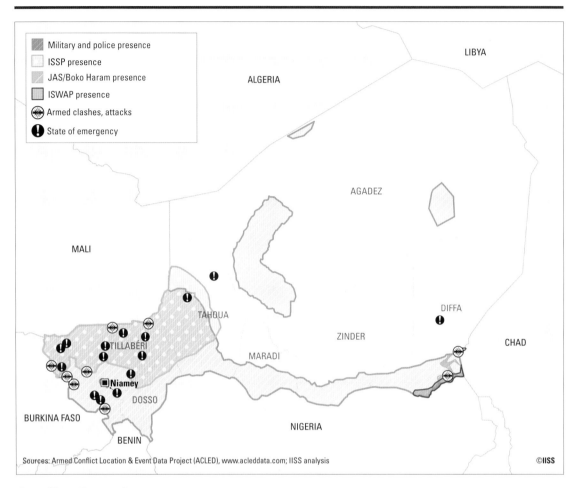

Legend:
- Military and police presence
- ISSP presence
- JAS/Boko Haram presence
- ISWAP presence
- Armed clashes, attacks
- State of emergency

Sources: Armed Conflict Location & Event Data Project (ACLED), www.acleddata.com; IISS analysis   ©IISS

Conflict Overview

Niger is located within the Sahelo-Saharan strip, where growing cross-border security threats in the last decade have undermined the country's fragile political and economic stability, as well as eroded its social cohesion. The conflicts in Niger are multidimensional, with various groups challenging the state's authority and criminal networks exploiting prevailing insecurity. Intensifying cycles of violence, deteriorating governance conditions and a growing humanitarian crisis all shape the conflict environment.

Niger has long been known for providing a highly active transit route that enables circular migratory flows for those travelling across the region. Yet, as of 2023, six of the seven countries bordering it face a crisis of one degree or another. As a result, Niger's border areas are most affected by conflict. Porous borders have enabled an influx of violent extremist organisations (VEOs) from Burkina Faso, Libya, Mali and Nigeria into Niger. Historically, northern Nigeria-based Jama'atu Ahlis Sunna Lidda'awati wal-Jihad (JAS, popularly known as Boko Haram) and its splinter group the Islamic State West Africa Province (ISWAP) were the most dominant actors contesting state power in the south and east of Niger. In the past couple of years, however, they have been outpaced by the Group to Support Islam and Muslims (JNIM) and the Islamic State Sahel Province (ISSP), which are increasingly operating in the western border areas of Niger's Tahoua and Tillabéri regions, adjacent to Burkina Faso and Mali.

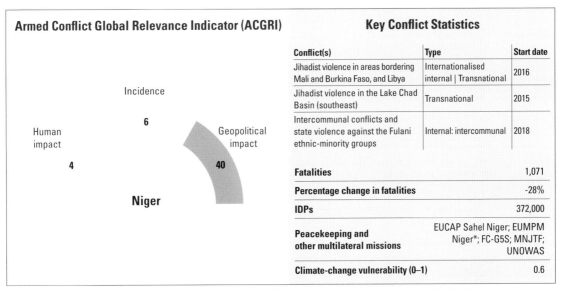

Armed Conflict Global Relevance Indicator (ACGRI)

Incidence

6

Human impact

4

Geopolitical impact

40

Niger

Key Conflict Statistics

Conflict(s)	Type	Start date
Jihadist violence in areas bordering Mali and Burkina Faso, and Libya	Internationalised internal | Transnational	2016
Jihadist violence in the Lake Chad Basin (southeast)	Transnational	2015
Intercommunal conflicts and state violence against the Fulani ethnic-minority groups	Internal: intercommunal	2018
Fatalities		1,071
Percentage change in fatalities		-28%
IDPs		372,000
Peacekeeping and other multilateral missions		EUCAP Sahel Niger; EUMPM Niger*; FC-G5S; MNJTF; UNOWAS
Climate-change vulnerability (0–1)		0.6

ACGRI pillars: IISS calculation based on multiple sources for 2022 and 2023 (scale: 0–100), except for some cases according to data availability. See Notes on Methodology and Data Appendix for all variables and further details on Key Conflict Statistics. *Launched in February 2023. However, all security cooperation between the EU and Niger was suspended after the military coup in July 2023.

Meanwhile, cross-border banditry is increasing in the Lake Chad Basin along Niger's southeastern border with Nigeria.

Insecurity has disrupted the local economy, leaving the country more vulnerable to criminality and compounding issues of poverty, food insecurity, unemployment and weak governance. Intercommunal conflict has accelerated since 2018, as groups compete for control over land, resources and political power. The Tuareg and Fulani communities, in particular, have been involved in clashes over grazing rights, access to water and political representation. High levels of poverty and a lack of livelihood opportunities all fuel local grievances and exacerbate conflict dynamics. At the same time, the heavy-handed (and, at times, abusive) approach of the Niger Armed Forces (FAN) deployed to respond to the violence has undermined their legitimacy and ability to operate effectively.

Conflict Update

Niger has taken steps to position itself as a vanguard in the fight against terrorism, and it has committed significant national resources to tackling the ensuing crisis. As of June 2023, however, the situation remained highly volatile. Furthermore, after the end of the reporting period, a *coup d'état* on 26 July 2023 removed from power the legitimate president, Mohamed Bazoum, fuelling a domestic and regional crisis that is highly unpredictable. In August 2023, the regional body Economic Community of West African States threatened military intervention, but this did not result in the coup leaders ceding power and reinstating Bazoum.

Throughout the reporting period, in Niger's southwest areas, rival groups fought for control over the Liptako-Gourma tri-border area, claiming the lives of dozens of soldiers and civilians.[1] Particularly in Tahoua and Tillabéri, both ISSP and JNIM conducted several armed operations, intimidated local authorities and targeted civilians. Towards the southeast, in the Lake Chad Basin and along the border with Nigeria, JAS/Boko Haram and ISWAP played a destabilising role, stoking intercommunal tensions and exploiting grievances around access to resources.[2] These groups all openly contest the state and propose alternative orders.

Before being overthrown in July 2023, Bazoum pursued his campaign slogan 'consolidate and move ahead' by prioritising national security, strengthening military capacity and improving intelligence gathering to combat violent extremism.[3] His efforts may have yielded some results, as conflict-related deaths decreased in 2022 compared to previous years.[4] One contributing factor to this trend was the state's commitment to local dialogues. Talks with non-state armed groups, facilitated by the government's High

Sub-Saharan Africa

Authority for the Consolidation of Peace, increased community-level peace prospects.

Another contributing factor was the reinforcement of the FAN across the country, as evidenced by the large-scale operations in border areas in early 2023, as well as the government's efforts to strengthen international partnerships. In March 2023, Niger committed to separate security-cooperation agreements with Benin and Mali. Furthermore, a number of its ongoing bilateral partnerships and public commitments to multilateral operations – including the G5 Sahel and the Multinational Joint Task Force (MNJTF) – aim to address the underlying grievances fuelling conflict in the country. Thus, as neighbouring countries have turned away from cooperation with traditional security actors, Niger's geopolitical influence has grown. From 2022–23, the country engaged in close economic and military cooperation with the European Union, France and the United States, indicating that it is positioning itself as an ally to Western forces in their fight against violent extremism in the Sahel. Bazoum's removal from office in July, however, threatens Niger's partnership with the West.

Attacks by the FAN against civilians – mostly ethnic Fulanis due to their perceived over-representation within jihadist groups, a trend that is common in Mali and Burkina Faso as well – exacerbated communal tensions and contributed to Niger's humanitarian crisis in the reporting period. In January 2023, for instance, at least 11 Fulani civilians were killed by the FAN and buried in a mass grave near the border with Burkina Faso. Three months earlier, in the same area, an attack on a mine killed 11 workers.[5] The FAN and its partners' efforts to combat VEOs left communities vulnerable to criminality and banditry. Likewise, kidnapping and other illicit activities became increasingly common in areas where the state had almost no presence. Niger's focus on securitisation therefore did not address the root of the country's multidimensional crisis – as evidenced by the way drivers of instability resurfaced elsewhere.

A number of challenges such as poverty, food insecurity, criminality and corruption continued to affect the country across the reporting period. Niger remained among the world's poorest nations in 2022, and 4.4 million people faced food insecurity in the same year, according to the European Commission.[6] Acute food insecurity in 2023 is predicted to reach a ten-year high.[7] Amidst important geopolitical shifts in the Sahel, finding ways to address these structural challenges will be pivotal in determining Niger's trajectory towards peace and stability.

Conflict Parties

Niger Armed Forces (FAN)

Strength: 33,100 active military personnel (army: 33,000; air force: 100) and 24,500 active gendarmerie and paramilitary personnel (gendarmerie: 7,000; republican guard: 9,000; national police: 8,500).

Areas of operation: Regions of Tahoua and Tillabéri in western Niger, the northern region of Agadez, as well as the southern and southeastern regions of Maradi and Diffa.

Leadership: President Mohamed Bazoum (until July 2023), Alkassoum Indatou (defence minister) and Gen. Salifou Mody (chief of staff).

Structure: Consists of the army, the air force, the gendarmerie, the republican guard and the national police.

History: Founded upon Niger's independence in 1961 and officered by the French Colonial Forces, the FAN was reorganised following a 1974 military coup. In 2003, an air-force component was created.

Objectives: Maintain internal and border security against jihadist groups and protect territorial integrity.

Opponents: Ansarul Islam, ISSP, JNIM, ISWAP and JAS/Boko Haram.

Affiliates/allies: Benin, Burkina Faso, France, G5 Sahel Joint Force (FC-G5S), Mali, United Nations Multidimensional Integrated Stabilization Mission in Mali (MINUSMA) and the US.

Resources/capabilities: Niger's defence budget was US$243m (1.6% of GDP) for 2022 and is US$326m (2.0% of GDP) for 2023.

Group to Support Islam and Muslims (JNIM)

Strength: Unknown.

Areas of operation: Limited presence in western Niger.

Leadership: Iyad Ag Ghaly, a long-time Tuareg militant who is also the leader of Ansar Dine, one of the main groups constituting JNIM.

Structure: Created as an alliance of equals.

History: JNIM was created in 2017 as a coalition between al-Qaeda-affiliated groups such as Ansar Dine, al-Mourabitoun, al-Qaeda in the Islamic Maghreb–Sahel, Katibat Macina and other smaller factions.

Group to Support Islam and Muslims (JNIM)

Objectives: Establish an Islamic state in the Sahel, replacing existing state structures and expelling foreign forces.

Opponents: FAN, foreign forces, Russian private military contractors and ISSP.

Affiliates/allies: Al-Qaeda, al-Qaeda in the Islamic Maghreb–North Africa, Katibat Macina and Katibat Serma. Cooperates with Ansarul Islam, though their relationship is ambiguous.

Resources/capabilities: Heavy weaponry and improvised explosive devices (IEDs), including vehicle-borne IEDs and suicide-vehicle-borne IEDs.

Islamic State Sahel Province (ISSP)

Strength: Unknown.

Areas of operation: Western Niger (Dosso, Tahoua and Tillabéri regions).

Leadership: Abdul Bara al-Sahrawi (also known as al-Ansari) and a cadre of local commanders.

Structure: Unknown.

History: ISSP emerged from a split within al-Mourabitoun in 2015 and was originally known as the Islamic State in the Greater Sahara (ISGS). ISGS pledged allegiance to the Islamic

State (ISIS) in 2015, and in 2019 it became part of ISWAP. ISIS recognised the group as an independent *wilayat* (province) in March 2022 under the name ISSP.

Objectives: Establish an Islamic caliphate based on strict interpretation of the Koran and adherence to ISIS ideology.

Opponents: JNIM, MINUSMA and FAN.

Affiliates/allies: Katibat Salaheddine, ISIS, ISWAP and other smaller militias.

Resources/capabilities: IEDs and light weaponry.

French armed forces

Strength: Approximately 1,500 troops in Niger.[8]

Areas of operation: Border areas in the Nigerien part of the Liptako-Gourma area, including Inates, Ti-n-Gara and Tongo Tongo.

Leadership: Sébastien Lecornu (French minister of defence).

Structure: Consists of French military personnel formerly operating in Mali and Burkina Faso as part of *Operation Barkhane*.

History: In January 2021, former president Mahamadou Issoufou ordered the immediate deployment of special forces in *Operation Almahaou*, which has been supported by the French armed forces. Later, following the withdrawal of the

French Army from Mali in February 2022 and Burkina Faso in February 2023, and the end of *Operation Barkhane*, French authorities announced that a section of the army's troops would be redeployed to military bases in Niger.

Objectives: Assist the FAN in the fight against VEOs; protect local communities from attacks; and free villages and towns from insurgent control.

Opponents: ISSP and JNIM.

Affiliates/allies: FAN and FC-G5S.

Resources/capabilities: Heavy weaponry.

G5 Sahel Joint Force (FC-G5S)

Strength: Between 5,000 and 10,000 troops provided by the four remaining member countries (Burkina Faso, Chad, Mauritania and Niger).[9]

Areas of operation: Border regions between Mali and Mauritania, between Niger and Chad and in the Liptako-Gourma tri-border area.

Leadership: Eric Yemdaogo Tiare (executive secretary).

Structure: In January 2023, the defence ministers of the four member countries announced the operationalisation of 14 new battalions, including five in Burkina Faso, two in Chad, two in Mauritania and five in Niger.[10] However, as of 30 April 2023, the task force was still in the process of developing a new concept of operations.

History: While the G5 Sahel as an organisation was established in 2014 (comprising members Burkina Faso, Chad,

Mali, Mauritania and Niger), the joint force was created in February 2017 with the support of France and the UN to address threats across the Sahel, such as terrorism and transnational organised crime, including the smuggling of goods and human trafficking. Mali withdrew from FC-G5S in May 2022.

Objectives: Strengthen security along the borders of member states through intelligence sharing and the deployment of joint patrols.

Opponents: JNIM and ISSP.

Affiliates/allies: Foreign and regional armed forces and MINUSMA.

Resources/capabilities: Suffers from underfunding and unpredictable financing. Troop deployment is slow due to a lack of logistical capacity and equipment.

Multinational Joint Task Force (MNJTF)

Strength: Approximately 13,000 troops from the armed forces of Benin, Cameroon, Chad, Niger and Nigeria.[11]

Areas of operation: Lake Chad Basin.

Leadership: Maj.-Gen. Gold Chibuisi (force commander).

Multinational Joint Task Force (MNJTF)

Structure: Headquartered in N'Djamena (Chad), the MNJTF comprises four geographical sectors, with their own headquarters in Monguno (Nigeria), Baga Sola (Chad), Diffa (Niger) and Mora (Cameroon). Each sector is led by a commander with wide autonomy, while the MNJTF force commander has coordination powers.

History: The MNJTF evolved from a Nigerian initiative in 1994 to a multinational force in 1998 to tackle cross-border crimes and banditry affecting the Lake Chad Basin. After years of inactivity, the Peace and Security Council of the African Union (AU) agreed to revive the MNJTF in 2015 to counter JAS/Boko Haram's growing activity.

Objectives: Coordinate regional counter-insurgency efforts and restore security in areas affected by JAS/Boko Haram

and ISWAP in the Lake Chad Basin. The MNJTF also helps support stabilisation programmes, humanitarian-assistance efforts and the return of forcibly displaced people.

Opponents: JAS/Boko Haram and ISWAP.

Affiliates/allies: The national armies of Benin, Cameroon, Chad, Niger and Nigeria; international partners (the AU, Burkina Faso, the EU, France, Mali, the United Kingdom and the US); FC-G5S; and MINUSMA.

Resources/capabilities: Estimated initial operational budget of US$700m. Th EU is the force's main contributor, channelling its funds through the AU. Bureaucratic delays and lack of adequate resources have hampered the MNJTF's ability to fulfil its mandate.

Other relevant parties

JAS/Boko Haram and ISWAP are both present in Diffa region in southeastern Niger as part of the transnational Lake Chad Basin conflict involving primarily Nigeria and Cameroon, as well as Chad.

Notes

1   Armed Conflict Location & Event Data Project (ACLED), www. acleddata.com.

2   International Crisis Group, 'Niger and Boko Haram: Beyond Counter-insurgency', Report no. 245, 27 February 2017.

3   Seidik Abba, 'Sahel: What's the Secret to Niger's Security Resilience?', 30 June 2022.

4   Institute for Economics and Peace, 'Global Terrorism Index: Measuring the Impact of Terrorism', March 2023, p. 14.

5   Armed Conflict Location & Event Data Project (ACLED), www. acleddata.com.

6   European Commission, European Civil Protection and Humanitarian Aid Operations, 'Niger Factsheet'.

7   World Food Programme, 'Food Insecurity and Malnutrition in West and Central Africa at 10-year High as Crisis Spreads to Coastal Countries', 18 April 2023.

8   French Ministry of Armed Forces, 'NIGER – Operation conjointe pour la sécurisation du Liptako nigèrien' [NIGER – Joint Operation to Promote Security in the Nigerien Liptako], 25 April 2023.

9   UN Security Council, 'Peace and Security in Africa', S/2022/838, 16 November 2022.

10   A. Y. Barma, 'G5 Sahel: l'Etat-major de la Force conjointe ramené à Niamey, 14 bataillons bientôt opérationnels (Ministres de la Défense)' [G5 Sahel: Joint Force Headquarters Brought Back to Niamey, 14 Battalions Soon to Be Operational (Ministers of Defence)], ActuNiger, 12 January 2023.

11   Freedom Chukwudi Onuoha, Andrew E. Yaw Tchie and Mariana Llorens Zabala, *A Quest to Win the Hearts and Minds: Assessing the Effectiveness of the Multinational Joint Task Force* (Oslo: Norwegian Institute of International Affairs, 2023), p. 37. The MNJTF website puts this number at around 10,000 troops.

NIGERIA

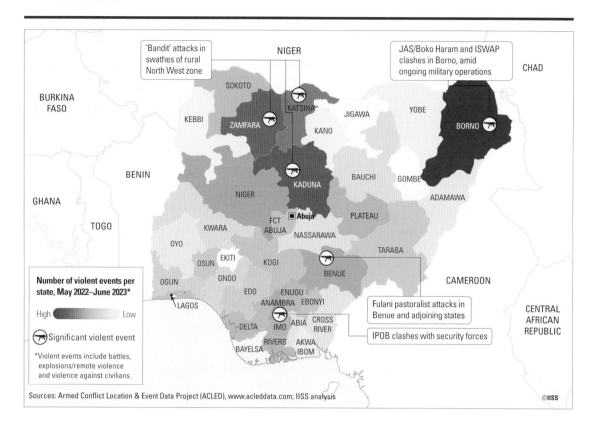

'Bandit' attacks in swathes of rural North West zone

NIGER

JAS/Boko Haram and ISWAP clashes in Borno, amid ongoing military operations

CHAD

BURKINA FASO

SOKOTO

KATSINA

JIGAWA

YOBE

KEBBI

ZAMFARA

KANO

BORNO

BENIN

NIGER

KADUNA

BAUCHI

GOMBE

ADAMAWA

GHANA

FCT ■Abuja

PLATEAU

TOGO

KWARA

ABUJA

NASSARAWA

OYO

EKITI

OSUN   KOGI

TARABA

BENUE

CAMEROON

Number of violent events per state, May 2022–June 2023*

OGUN   ONDO

EDO

ENUGU

ANAMBRA   EBONYI

Fulani pastoralist attacks in Benue and adjoining states

CENTRAL AFRICAN REPUBLIC

High ▬▬▬ Low

LAGOS

DELTA   IMO   ABIA   CROSS RIVER

IPOB clashes with security forces

Significant violent event

RIVERS   AKWA

BAYELSA   IBOM

*Violent events include battles, explosions/remote violence and violence against civilians.

Sources: Armed Conflict Location & Event Data Project (ACLED), www.acleddata.com; IISS analysis

©IISS

Conflict Overview

Since its uneasy transition from military rule in 1999, Nigeria has experienced multiple political and security crises. Elite competition, cronyism and security forces' counterproductive tendency to militarise political and social disputes have all endured across the military and civilian eras. Under former president Muhammadu Buhari, economic turbulence (including rising debt, unemployment and inflation) has added to concerns about the permanence of the Nigerian state, which has already been weakened by multiplying armed conflicts, festering ethno-religious tensions and mounting youth discontent with the status quo.[1]

Nigeria's political culture is heavily cartelised, being characterised by both backroom dealing among political elites and substantial overlaps between these elites and their commercial counterparts, especially those in the oil sector that stiches Nigeria's unwieldy federal system together. The centrality of oil in Nigeria's economy and political system has deleterious effects on the functioning of government institutions and distribution of economic resources. Repeated rounds of administrative decentralisation since the military era have only served to further concentrate power at the federal level, with most of Nigeria's 36 states dependent on centrally distributed oil revenues. This system is overlaid atop a complex ethnic terrain, characterised by religious friction between the largely Christian south and Muslim north and mutual suspicion between Nigeria's primary ethnic blocs (the southwestern Yoruba, the southeastern Igbo, and the northern Hausa and Fulani), which have dominated post-colonial politics at the expense of over 200 smaller ethnic groups.

Such friction has increased during election years, as gangs or armed groups hired by contending politicians have the potential to exacerbate

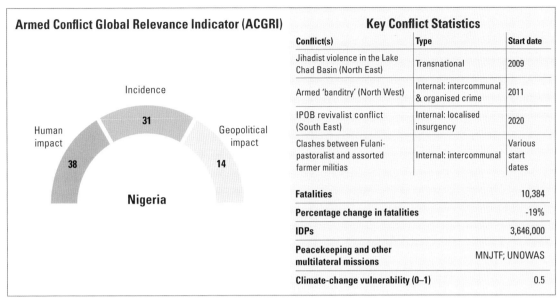

Armed Conflict Global Relevance Indicator (ACGRI)

Incidence

31

Human impact

38

Geopolitical impact

14

Nigeria

Key Conflict Statistics

Conflict(s)	Type	Start date
Jihadist violence in the Lake Chad Basin (North East)	Transnational	2009
Armed 'banditry' (North West)	Internal: intercommunal & organised crime	2011
IPOB revivalist conflict (South East)	Internal: localised insurgency	2020
Clashes between Fulani-pastoralist and assorted farmer militias	Internal: intercommunal	Various start dates

Fatalities	10,384
Percentage change in fatalities	-19%
IDPs	3,646,000
Peacekeeping and other multilateral missions	MNJTF; UNOWAS
Climate-change vulnerability (0–1)	0.5

ACGRI pillars: IISS calculation based on multiple sources for 2022 and 2023 (scale: 0–100), except for some cases according to data availability. See Notes on Methodology and Data Appendix for all variables and further details on Key Conflict Statistics.

Nigeria's wider security crisis. Although violence in the oil-producing Niger Delta has declined in recent years, conflict has become entrenched in northern Nigeria. From 2009 onwards, Jama'atu Ahlis Sunna Lidda'awati wal-Jihad (JAS, popularly known as Boko Haram) jihadists increased their presence from small pockets of Nigeria's North East geopolitical zone (and adjoining areas of Cameroon) to southwestern Chad and southeastern Niger. As the insurgency expanded, so too did its tendency to fragment, further complicating strategies for combating it. The ensuing regional security crisis in the Lake Chad Basin saw the revival of the Western- and African Union (AU)-backed Multinational Joint Task Force (MNJTF) in 2015, with the Nigerian armed forces making increasing (if qualified) gains against jihadist factions in the North East. More recently, the North West has been convulsed by nebulous 'bandit' (criminal-gang) violence, in which political grievances have become subsumed within economic motivations and warlordism.

Conflict Update

The presidential elections on 25 February 2023 and state elections in mid-March dominated the reporting period. Unlike previous elections, which took the form of tense contests between two contenders backed by their respective party machines, the 2023 elections featured three serious challengers, and the candidate running on the incumbent party ticket – Bola Ahmed Tinubu – did not enjoy the support of the outgoing president. Tinubu, the wealthy former governor of Lagos State and political 'godfather' of the South West zone, won the election on the All Progressives Congress ticket. His rivals were long-term presidential aspirant Atiku Abubakar of the Peoples Democratic Party and outsider businessman Peter Obi of the Labour Party.

With turnout for the presidential elections at an all-time low of 25.7%, and multiple reports of irregularities and intimidation, concerns about diminishing public enthusiasm for the electoral process appeared to be well founded.[2] Expectations that Obi would capture the youth vote only partially materialised, with initial indications suggesting that ethnic alignment remained an important factor among young people who voted. Obi was, however, able to make inroads in parts of the south, which may assist him in the 2027 elections. The elections took place amid inter-party violence, with attacks on electoral-commission offices and threats against politicians being particularly prevalent in the

South East and parts of the North East zones, as well as in Kaduna State in the North West.[3]

As the electoral drama unfolded, multi-sided violence involving jihadist insurgencies persisted across northern Nigeria.[4] The fragmentation of JAS/Boko Haram continued in the aftermath of the death of its leader, Abubakar Shekau, in 2021. Deadly clashes between the remnants of JAS/ Boko Haram and the significantly more powerful Islamic State West Africa Province (ISWAP) escalated after September 2022, whilst internal clashes within ISWAP resumed.[5] Despite Nigerian military gains (often accomplished through airstrikes) against the contending jihadist factions in the Lake Chad Basin, ISWAP and Ansaru (a JAS/Boko Haram offshoot) were able to capitalise on insecurity and disaffection in the North West and North Central regions to establish a presence there, as Nigeria's overstretched security forces struggled to contain the multiplying threats. Notably, an audacious ISWAP raid on a prison in Nigeria's capital, Abuja, released dozens of jihadist prisoners in July 2022.[6]

Violence continued in the Middle Belt and North West regions, with established conflicts (comprising overlapping ethno-political and pastoralist–farmer disputes) becoming enmeshed with militarised responses to lawlessness and banditry. As in the North East, security forces have made gains in dismantling several powerful bandit groups, but without necessarily converting these military gains into efforts to extend state authority and address the underlying causes of instability and political discontent. Reliance on airstrikes to neutralise security threats has resulted in heavy civilian casualties.[7] Furthermore, security forces have suffered significant setbacks, as in Niger State, where dozens of personnel were killed as they attempted to intervene in a bandit attack on a Chinese-run mine.[8]

Finally, the IPOB (a Biafran-revivalist group) and its armed wing, the Eastern Security Network (ESN), continued to destabilise the South East. Separatist forces were linked to numerous attacks against electoral-commission offices and local politicians and administrators in 2023.[9] Meanwhile, violence between vigilantes and Fulani pastoralists (some of whom were displaced from more northerly regions) has continued in the South East, further hardening ethno-political divisions.

Thus, despite state forces making some progress in suppressing threats from jihadist and bandit gangs during the reporting period, security remains precarious in much of Nigeria. The state's dependence on paramilitary and vigilante groups to uphold a degree of security in rural areas – amid growing political polarisation – indicates that deeper problems concerning the capabilities and legitimacy of the Nigerian state have gone largely unaddressed.

Conflict Parties

Nigerian armed forces	
Strength: 143,000 military personnel, including 100,000 army personnel. Paramilitary forces (known as the Nigeria Security and Civil Defence Corps) number approximately 80,000 troops.	further degraded the institution. In 2021, then-president Buhari oversaw a reorganisation of senior military personnel. In June 2023, President Tinubu replaced all senior staff.
Areas of operation: Across Nigeria.	**Objectives:** Establish and maintain security across Nigeria.
Leadership: President Bola Ahmed Tinubu (commander-in-chief of the armed forces) and Maj.-Gen. Christopher Musa (chief of defence staff).	**Opponents:** JAS/Boko Haram, ISWAP, Ansaru, ESN, armed bandits and pastoralist militias.
Structure: The Nigerian armed forces comprise the army, the air force and the navy. The army is organised into eight divisions, with the 7th Division being responsible for counter-insurgency operations in the North East.	**Affiliates/allies:** Vigilante groups, Civilian Joint Task Force (CJTF), MNJTF, the United Kingdom and the United States.
History: Nigeria has the largest army in West Africa, and it has played a dominant role in Nigeria's politics since 1966. Poor performance, morale and equipment have damaged its reputation, while corruption and human-rights abuses have	**Resources/capabilities:** Heavy and light weaponry in the land, air, sea and cyber spheres. Resources and capabilities have significantly improved in recent years, though poor equipment and training remain areas of concern. Despite military spending amounting to US$2.8 billion in 2022 and a defence budget of US$2.7bn for 2023, this represents just 0.6% and 0.5% of Nigeria's GDP respectively (one of the lowest rates in West Africa).

Jama'atu Ahlis Sunna Lidda'awati wal-Jihad (JAS)/Boko Haram

Strength: Prior to Abubakar Shekau's death in May 2021, JAS/Boko Haram was estimated to have about 1,500–3,000 fighters.[10] However, around 2,000 fighters have demobilised and surrendered to Borno State authorities since Shekau's death, whilst others have been absorbed into ISWAP.[11]

Areas of operation: Adamawa and southern areas of Borno and Yobe states. The breakaway Bakura faction retains a presence on the shores of Lake Chad. Ansaru (an al-Qaeda-affiliated splinter group) has expanded its presence in the North Central and North West zones after years of inactivity.

Leadership: Led by Shekau from 2010 until his death in 2021 and now highly factionalised. Notable factional leaders include Bakura Doron (the political leader of the Bakura faction) and Bakura Shalaba Modu (the religious leader of the Bakura faction). Some reports indicate Modu was killed by Doron in 2022.[12]

Structure: Highly decentralised structure with a weak chain of command, various offshoots and cells that act independently. Several of these offshoots have been absorbed into ISWAP since 2021, with others (notably the Bakura faction) resisting ISWAP.

History: JAS/Boko Haram was established in 2002 by Mohammad Yusuf. Following Yusuf's death in 2009, Shekau increased the group's territorial control, though predation and indiscriminate violence eroded legitimacy. JAS/Boko Haram pledged allegiance to the Islamic State (ISIS) in 2015, operating under the name of ISWAP. In 2016, Shekau split with ISWAP, and in 2021, he killed himself to avoid capture by ISWAP.

Objectives: Establish an Islamic caliphate in the North East of Nigeria and neighbouring regions.

Opponents: Nigerian armed forces, CJTF, MNJTF and ISWAP.

Affiliates/allies: The Ansaru faction maintains links to al-Qaeda.

Resources/capabilities: Stolen weaponry from military bases and black-market acquisitions, including rocket-propelled grenades, improvised bombs, mortars, assault rifles, tanks and armoured personnel carriers (APCs). The group has a limited anti-aircraft capability and reportedly has been using uninhabited aerial vehicles since 2018. The group funds itself through looting and kidnapping for ransom.

Islamic State West Africa Province (ISWAP)

Strength: 4,000–5,000 fighters.[13]

Areas of operation: Within Nigeria, the core areas of territorial control are the forests of northern Borno State and northeastern Yobe State, extending into Lake Chad and adjoining areas of Cameroon, Chad and Niger.

Leadership: Unclear. Following the death of Abu Musab al-Barnawi (the son of Mohammad Yusuf) in 2021, a succession of ISWAP senior commanders, some of whom were (inconsistently) reported to be the leader of the insurgency, have been killed in military operations and airstrikes.

Structure: ISWAP retains elements of the fragmented leadership structure and volatile factionalism of JAS/Boko Haram, though it has established a more coherent and organised approach to governing its territory. The leadership of ISWAP responds to instructions from ISIS and has refined its practices and strategy via this relationship.

History: JAS/Boko Haram became known as ISWAP in 2015, but the two groups split in 2016. ISWAP distinguished itself from JAS/Boko Haram by prioritising military over civilian targets and providing a degree of order in the regions in which it operates. Power struggles among ISWAP commanders have resulted in leadership changes since 2015. In 2021, ISWAP attacked JAS/Boko Haram, and JAS/Boko Haram's Bakura faction retaliated against ISWAP.[14]

Objectives: Establish an Islamic caliphate in northeast Nigeria and neighbouring regions.

Opponents: Nigerian armed forces, CJTF, MNJTF and JAS/Boko Haram.

Affiliates/allies: ISIS and Islamic State in the Greater Sahara.

Resources/capabilities: ISWAP has obtained most of its weaponry – including APCs, assault rifles, rocket-propelled grenades and mortars – by raiding military bases and attacking troops. It also used financial assistance from ISIS to acquire looted military equipment from its own fighters.[15] Further income is generated via taxes collected from local populations.

Armed bandits (criminal gangs)

Strength: Unclear. There are allegedly over 100 bandit gangs in the North West, with the largest groups believed to have around 2,000 members. Estimates for the total number of bandits range from 10,000–30,000.[16]

Areas of operation: North West and North Central zones (particularly Kaduna, Katsina, Kebbi, Niger and Zamfara states, as well as, to a lesser extent, Sokoto State).

Leadership: There are multiple prominent bandit leaders in control of larger bandit groups, though none command widespread allegiance. Major gang leaders include Bello Turji

Kachalla and Dogo Gide, whilst Adamu Aliero Yankuzo was controversially made a customary chief in Zamfara State in 2022 as part of a de facto peace deal.

Structure: Most gangs do not have a formal structure and are prone to splitting (sometimes violently).

History: There has been only limited research into the phenomenon of banditry in northwestern Nigeria, though most accounts suggest that the current iteration of banditry emerged in 2011, with at least some groups being hired by politicians as security during the 2011 general elections. The

Armed bandits (criminal gangs)

attacks and abductions have since escalated and spread from Zamfara State to adjoining states. Most gang members are ethnic Fulani, though some gangs are ethnically mixed.[17]

Objectives: Although most groups have a clear criminal motivation, this is interwoven with overt and covert political elements. This includes the reassertion of an 'authentic' Fulani pastoralist identity against ruling elites and security services; grievances surrounding the confiscation of grazing areas; and reprisals against vigilante actions (often by Hausa vigilantes) that have targeted the bandits or the wider Fulani community.[18]

Opponents: Hausa sedentary farmers, vigilante groups and Nigerian armed forces.

Affiliates/allies: Links with some (though not all) Fulani pastoralist militias, including those in Niger and Mali. Limited tactical cooperation with ISWAP.

Resources/capabilities: Small arms and light weapons. Bandits often use motorcycles to carry out their attacks. There are some indications of bandits receiving training from (former) JAS/Boko Haram members on the use of improvised explosive devises and anti-aircraft guns.

Fulani pastoralist militias

Strength: Unknown.

Areas of operation: Active in Fulani-inhabited areas of northern Nigeria (especially the North West zone) and parts of the Middle Belt. Due to the presence of armed bandits, some of whom have engaged in looting or attacks on elements of the Fulani community, there are increased reports of Fulani pastoralists being displaced to southern areas of the country.

Leadership: No formal leadership.

Structure: Fulani groups include both semi-nomadic pastoralists and settled communities in urban and rural areas. Pastoralist communities are highly decentralised, as they are divided into clans (*lenyi*) and sub-clans. Individuals have significant autonomy over whether to fight or retaliate for

perceived wrongs; decisions such as these may be made without community leaders' knowledge or approval. For some conflicts, mobilisation occurs along ethnic and kinship lines.

History: Pastoralist–farmer conflicts have a long history in Nigeria, but they have become deadlier in recent years, with the Fulani pastoralist militias acquiring more sophisticated weaponry and cooperating with armed bandits in northern Nigeria.

Objectives: Protecting traditional 'cattle culture', securing pasture for grazing, and countering vigilantism and cattle raids.

Opponents: Hausa sedentary farmers, vigilante groups, Nigerian armed forces and ESN in the South East.

Affiliates/allies: Some cooperation with armed bandits.

Resources/capabilities: Small arms, including locally made guns.

Farmer militias and vigilante groups

Strength: Unclear.

Areas of operation: Middle Belt, South West and South East, as well as some Hausa areas of the North West zone.

Leadership: Within several communities in the conflict areas, active mobilisations are primarily driven by traditional community leaders.

Structure: Militias from agriculturalist communities mobilise on an ethnic basis, sometimes leveraging a Christian identity. Militias are recruited predominantly from the Adara, Berom, Tarok and Tiv ethnic groups, while parts of the (Muslim) Hausa have formed vigilante groups against banditry. Larger ethnic groups also maintain self-defence militias with the backing of regional political elites.

History: Pastoralist–farmer conflicts have a long history in Nigeria, though they have become deadlier in recent years. Land encroachment by farmers, disputes over 'indigenous' status and elite meddling have exacerbated conflicts, turning them into ethnic and religious ones. Due to security weaknesses, the Nigerian state has become increasingly reliant on paramilitary and vigilante forces.

Objectives: Protect against raids by Fulani pastoralists and bandits. Prevail in local political disputes.

Opponents: Bandits and Fulani pastoralists.

Affiliates/allies: Nigerian armed forces, CJTF and ESN in the South East.

Resources/capabilities: Small arms, including locally made guns.

Indigenous People of Biafra (IPOB)/Eastern Security Network (ESN)

Strength: Unclear.

Areas of operation: South East.

Leadership: Nnamdi Kanu, founder and leader of the IPOB.

Structure: The ESN is the armed wing of the separatist IPOB, though details of its internal structures are unclear.

History: The IPOB emerged in 2012, promoting an ethnic Igbo separatist agenda. IPOB established the ESN in December 2020 to protect Igbo communities from Fulani pastoralists, some of whom were displaced due to rising insecurity in the

North West. A security crisis escalated in January 2021 after the Nigerian armed forces raided the town of Orlu in Imo State in search of ESN militants. Violence, including attacks on security infrastructure, has continued since then. As of 2022, IPOB has reportedly split into three factions, though the consequences for the ESN are unclear.

Objectives: Protect rural communities from armed Fulani pastoralists and achieve the secession of southeastern Nigeria from the rest of the country.

Opponents: Nigerian security forces and Fulani pastoralists.

Indigenous People of Biafra (IPOB)/Eastern Security Network (ESN)

Affiliates/allies: Ambazonia Governing Council, a Cameroonian separatist group.	**Resources/capabilities:** Weaponry includes small arms and locally made weapons. There are reports of arms smuggling from Cameroon.

Multinational Joint Task Force (MNJTF)

Strength: Approximately 13,000 troops from the armed forces of Benin, Cameroon, Chad, Niger and Nigeria.[19]	**Objectives:** Coordinate regional counter-insurgency efforts and restore security in areas affected by JAS/Boko Haram and ISWAP in the Lake Chad Basin. The MNJTF also helps support stabilisation programmes, humanitarian-assistance efforts and the return of forcibly displaced people.
Areas of operation: Lake Chad Basin.	
Leadership: Maj.-Gen. Gold Chibuisi (force commander).	
Structure: Headquartered in N'Djamena (Chad), the MNJTF comprises four geographical sectors, with their own headquarters in Monguno (Nigeria), Baga Sola (Chad), Diffa (Niger) and Mora (Cameroon). Each sector is led by a commander with wide autonomy, while the MNJTF force commander has coordination powers.	**Opponents:** JAS/Boko Haram and ISWAP.
	Affiliates/allies: The national armies of Benin, Cameroon, Chad, Niger and Nigeria; international partners (the AU, Burkina Faso, the European Union, France, Mali, the UK and the US); G5 Sahel Joint Force; and the United Nations Multidimensional Integrated Stabilization Mission in Mali.
History: The MNJTF evolved from a Nigerian initiative in 1994 to a multinational force in 1998 to tackle cross-border crimes and banditry affecting the Lake Chad Basin. After years of inactivity, the Peace and Security Council of the AU agreed to revive the MNJTF in 2015 to counter JAS/Boko Haram's growing activity.	**Resources/capabilities:** Estimated initial operational budget of US$700 million. The EU is the force's main contributor, channelling its funds through the AU. Bureaucratic delays and a lack of adequate resources have hampered the MNJTF's ability to fulfil its mandate.

Notes

1   The deteriorating economic situation is in part attributable to the collapse of oil prices due to the coronavirus pandemic and subsequent borrowing by the federal government.

2   Chatham House, 'Nigeria's Election Results Put Disenfranchisement in the Spotlight', 1 March 2023.

3   International Crisis Group, 'Mitigating Risks of Violence in Nigeria's 2023 Elections', Report no. 311, 10 February 2023; and Beacon Consulting Limited, 'December 2022: Nigeria Security Report', December 2022.

4   Armed Conflict Location & Event Data Project (ACLED), www.acleddata.com. In total, 4,173 people were reported to have been killed in 596 events involving jihadist groups (including airstrikes, clashes between jihadist groups and/or security forces, and attacks on civilians) across the reporting period, with the vast majority of such events being clustered in Borno State. This represents a slight increase in the lethality of violence involving jihadist groups, up from 3,781 fatalities across a similar number of events between May 2021 and June 2022.

5   Beacon Consulting Limited, 'July 2022: Nigeria Security Report', July 2022; and Armed Conflict Location & Event Data Project (ACLED), www.acleddata.com.

6   Beacon Consulting Limited, 'May 2022: Nigeria Security Report', May 2022; and Malik Samuel, 'Kuje Prison Break: Is Nigeria Out of Security Options?', Institute for Security Studies, 11 July 2022.

7   'Death Toll from Nigerian Air Force's Accidental Bombing in Nasarawa State Rises to 56', Sahara Reporters, 28 January 2023; 'Military Airstrikes Neutralise 82 Terrorists in Zamfara', Daily Trust, 30 June 2022; and Abubakar Ahmadu Maishanu, 'Death Toll Rises in Zamfara Attack', Premium Times, 21 December 2022.

8   Beacon Consulting Limited, 'June 2022: Nigeria Security Report', June 2022.

9   International Crisis Group, 'Mitigating Risks of Violence in Nigeria's 2023 Elections', p. 7.

10 Stig Jarle Hansen, 'The Fractious Future of the Islamic State in West Africa', War on the Rocks, 3 November 2021.

11 International Crisis Group, 'After Shekau: Confronting Jihadists in Nigeria's North East', Briefing no. 180, 29 March 2022.

12 Maman Inoua Elhadji Mahamadou Amadou and Vincent Foucher, 'Boko Haram in the Lake Chad Basin: The Bakura Faction and Its Resistance to the Rationalisation of Jihad', German Institute for International and Security Affairs (SWP), German Institute of Development and Sustainability, and Kiel Institute for the World Economy, 8 December 2022; and Richard Assheton, 'Boko Haram Chief "Killed for Trying to Defect"', The Times, 7 April 2022.

13 Tomás F. Husted, 'Boko Haram and the Islamic State West Africa Province', IF10173, Congressional Research Service, 24 February 2022.

14 International Crisis Group, 'After Shekau: Confronting Jihadists in Nigeria's North East'.

15   Vincent Foucher, 'The Islamic State Franchises in Africa: Lessons from Lake Chad', International Crisis Group, 29 October 2020.

16   James Barnett and Murtala Rufai, 'The Other Insurgency: Northwest Nigeria's Worsening Bandit Crisis', War on the Rocks, 16 November 2021; 'Matawalle: There Are Over 30,000 Bandits in the North', *Cable*, 2 April 2021; and James Barnett, Murtala Ahmed Rufa'i and Abdulaziz Abdulaziz, 'Northwestern Nigeria: A Jihadization of Banditry, or a "Banditization" of Jihad?', *CTC Sentinel*, vol. 15, no. 1, January 2022, p. 50.

17   International Crisis Group, 'Violence in Nigeria's North West: Rolling Back the Mayhem', Report no. 288, 18 May 2020.

18   'How Banditry Started in Zamfara', *Daily Trust*, 10 September 2021; and Barnett, Ahmed Rufa'i and Abdulaziz, 'Northwestern Nigeria: A Jihadization of Banditry, or a "Banditization" of Jihad?'.

19   Freedom Chukwudi Onuoha, Andrew E. Yaw Tchie and Mariana Llorens Zabala, *A Quest to Win the Hearts and Minds: Assessing the Effectiveness of the Multinational Joint Task Force* (Olso: Norwegian Institute of International Affairs, 2023), p. 37. The MNJTF website puts this number at around 10,000 troops.

CAMEROON

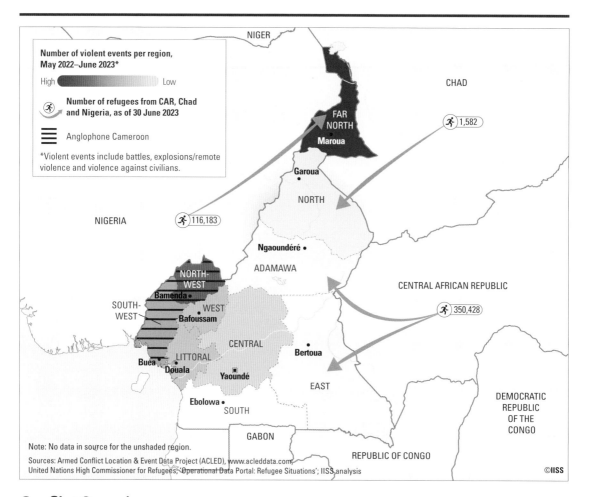

Number of violent events per region, May 2022–June 2023*

High ▬▬▬▬▬▬▬▬ Low

Number of refugees from CAR, Chad and Nigeria, as of 30 June 2023

≡ Anglophone Cameroon

*Violent events include battles, explosions/remote violence and violence against civilians.

NIGER

CHAD

FAR NORTH
Maroua

🏃 1,582

Garoua

NORTH

NIGERIA   🏃 116,183

Ngaoundéré •

ADAMAWA

CENTRAL AFRICAN REPUBLIC

NORTH-WEST
Bamenda •

SOUTH-WEST   WEST
Bafoussam

🏃 350,428

CENTRAL

Bertoua •

Buea   LITTORAL
Douala

Yaoundé

EAST

DEMOCRATIC REPUBLIC OF THE CONGO

Ebolowa •
SOUTH

GABON

REPUBLIC OF CONGO

Note: No data in source for the unshaded region.

Sources: Armed Conflict Location & Event Data Project (ACLED), www.acleddata.com; United Nations High Commissioner for Refugees, 'Operational Data Portal: Refugee Situations'; IISS analysis

©IISS

Conflict Overview

Cameroon faces several multidimensional security challenges. However, the country's stability is primarily threatened by an intra-state conflict stemming from separatist claims made by members of its anglophone minority, who have long denounced their political and economic marginalisation and cultural assimilation by the francophone majority, in Cameroon's Southwest and Northwest regions. This crisis dates back to the colonial period, when Southern Cameroons under British rule voted in 1961 to join French Cameroon, with the promise that Southern Cameroons would keep its autonomy under a federal system. However, in 1972 this system was abolished, leading to the centralisation of government in francophone Cameroon.

The current conflict began with peaceful protests in 2016. Following the government's early militarised response, the protests quickly escalated into a full-scale armed conflict and culminated in 2017 in the launch of the secessionist movement for the independence of 'Ambazonia'. Anglophone politics have become increasingly fragmented since then and two major competing actors have emerged: the Interim Government of Ambazonia (IG) and the Ambazonia Governing Council (AGC or AGovC). Both groups have military wings: the IG created the Ambazonia Self-Defence Council (ASDC) and the AGC created the Ambazonia Defence Forces (ADF).

Cameroon is also affected by intercommunal violence, mainly in the Northwest region, with

Armed Conflict Global Relevance Indicator (ACGRI)

Incidence

7

Human
impact

Geopolitical
impact

8

7

Cameroon

Key Conflict Statistics

Conflict(s)	Type	Start date
Anglophone minority separatist conflict	Internal: localised insurgency	2017
Jihadist violence in the Lake Chad Basin (North and Far North)	Transnational	2014
Communal conflicts (Northwest and Far North)	Internal: intercommunal	1960s
Fatalities		1,150
Percentage change in fatalities		-16%
IDPs		987,000
Peacekeeping and other multilateral missions		MNJTF; UNOCA
Climate-change vulnerability (0–1)		0.5

ACGRI pillars: IISS calculation based on multiple sources for 2022 and 2023 (scale: 0–100), except for some cases according to data availability. See Notes on Methodology and Data Appendix for all variables and further details on Key Conflict Statistics.

tensions arising between Mbororo Fulani herders and indigenous farming communities, and in the Far North region, with conflict between Choa Arab herders and Musgum fishers and farmers. Since 2017, agropastoral conflicts in the Northwest region have become progressively linked to the anglophone crisis, as the Mbororo have aligned with the government to gain legitimacy and limit the extortion practices against them.[1]

Meanwhile, Cameroon's Far North and North regions are affected by the ongoing insurgency of Jama'atu Ahlis Sunna Lidda'awati wal-Jihad (JAS, popularly known as Boko Haram), Islamic State in West Africa Province (ISWAP) and other jihadist groups in the Lake Chad Basin. Porous borders with Nigeria and Chad have enabled these groups to conduct cross-border attacks and recruit fighters. The crucial role played by the Cameroonian army in the anti-jihadist Multinational Joint Task Force (MNJTF) has reinforced the francophone ruling elite's political position, reducing the international pressure for diplomatic solutions to the anglophone crisis.

Cameroon also continues to be challenged by a refugee crisis, with displaced people predominantly coming from the Central African Republic and Nigeria. The country's conflict proclivity is further exacerbated by institutional weakness and a growing perception of entrenched corruption.

Conflict Update

Between May 2022 and June 2023, fighting continued between armed anglophone separatists and the Cameroonian armed forces, resulting in fatalities on both sides and a large number of civilian casualties. Compared to 2021, the number of violent events reduced in the Southwest and Northwest regions: in the reporting period, 344 violent events with 584 fatalities were registered, against the 469 violent events and 768 fatalities reported between May 2021 and June 2022.[2] While violence decreased in the anglophone regions, however, separatist groups progressively increased attacks in francophone zones, especially during the summer of 2022. This trend seems to have slowed since November 2022, but it is unclear whether anglophone separatists will regain the capacity to attack francophone areas or will focus on increasing attacks in the anglophone regions in the second half of 2023.

At the same time, diplomatic negotiations reached a deadlock. Although the international community scaled up its efforts to reach a diplomatic solution to the anglophone crisis, no significant advancement was made. In July 2022, during his visit to Cameroon, France's President Emmanuel Macron declared that the conflict could be solved by fostering decentralisation and promoting dialogue

Sub-Saharan Africa

between parties, but no channel for mediation was opened in the aftermath. The Cameroonian government also rejected, in September 2022, mediation by Switzerland and, in January 2023, a negotiation process led by Canada, which had succeeded in organising pre-talks between the government and separatist groups from November–December 2022. Furthermore, in December 2022, the Ministry of Defence announced the creation of a committee to identify and prosecute anglophone separatist sponsors living abroad, particularly in the United States.

The intensity of the conflict has been further exacerbated by institutional weakness, embodied by the precarious health of President Paul Biya, who celebrated his 90th birthday and over 40 years in power in 2023. Indeed, Biya has made progressively fewer public appearances, which have been largely limited to pre-recorded speeches, over the last several years. The current leadership's fragility was exemplified by the murder in February 2023 of investigative journalist Martinez Zogo, for which several intelligence officials and the powerful businessman Jean-Pierre Amougou-Belinga were detained, prompting allegations that it was a state crime. Some factions of the current elite may have tried to use this episode to oust their rivals and gain greater influence in the power struggle over who will become Biya's successor. The murder thus raises concerns that internal political competition could generate a new wave of violence.[3]

Cameroon's security has also continued to be jeopardised by violence in its Far North and North regions, perpetrated by the Lake Chad Basin factions of JAS/Boko Haram and ISWAP. In the reporting period, 430 violent events were registered in these two regions, with 484 fatalities.[4] Militants' main targets were civilians, Cameroonian army personnel and MNJTF forces; violence against civilians caused almost half of the total fatalities in the two regions. ISWAP and JAS/Boko Haram fighters also reportedly attacked villages, killing civilians and burning houses, as well as abducted women, fishermen and farmers. While Cameroon's Rapid Response Brigade (BIR) and the MNJTF continued to carry out anti-insurgent activities, ambushing suspected militants, the security situation remains critical given the high adaptability and mobility of the terrorists.

Cameroon has been further destabilised by intercommunal clashes, especially in the Northwest region. In the reporting period, 33 fatalities were reported as a result of violence between civilians and Fulani militia.[5] Such conflicts mainly replicate long-standing agropastoral tensions, with Fulani competing with farmers over disputed land and accusing locals of burning pastures needed to feed their cattle. Intercommunal violence revolving around natural-resource access has been compounded by the fact that Cameroon is also highly exposed to pandemics and climate hazards. Since August 2022, several divisions of the Far North region have experienced flooding. Meanwhile, cholera and monkeypox epidemics have been particularly severe in the Far North, Southwest, Northwest and Littoral regions. Altogether, these elements have created an extremely fragile environment, putting additional pressure on the government's already weak response capacity amid growing security concerns.

Conflict Parties

Cameroonian armed forces

Strength: Approximately 25,400 regular military personnel and 9,000 paramilitaries. The scale of deployment in anglophone Cameroon is unclear but consists of elements of the military police (the gendarmerie) and the elite military force (the BIR).

Areas of operation: Northwest and Southwest regions, in a military region designated RMIA 5. RMIA 5 has its headquarters in Bamenda, the capital of the Northwest region.

Leadership: RMIA 5 is led by Gen. Agha Robinson Ndong, but the president is commander of the armed forces.

Structure: The BIR has no general staff and is under the authority of the chief of staff of the army. The gendarmerie is under the authority of the secretary of state in the Ministry of Defence.

History: The BIR was created in 2001 to combat banditry along Cameroon's frontiers but has been used since then as an elite intervention force. The gendarmerie was created in the early 1960s as a direct descendant of the French colonial-era force.

Objectives: Counter-insurgency against separatist groups in the Northwest and Southwest regions and restoration of the regular flow of commerce disrupted by separatist groups.

Cameroonian armed forces

Opponents: IG and ASDC; AGC and ADF; various smaller militias; and JAS/Boko Haram, ISWAP and other jihadist groups.

Affiliates/allies: Receives military assistance from France, Israel and the US. Cameroon also has military-cooperation agreements with China and Russia, the latter signed in April 2022.

Resources/capabilities: Much of the equipment inventory is ageing but infantry fighting vehicles and protected patrol vehicles have been acquired from China, France and South Africa and gifted by the US. The armed forces are improving their intelligence, surveillance and reconnaissance capabilities with fixed-wing aircraft and small uninhabited aerial vehicles.

Interim Government of Ambazonia (IG)/Ambazonia Self-Defence Council (ASDC)

Strength: The ASDC consists of several local self-defence groups, including the Seven Karta Militia, the Ambazonia Restoration Army (ARA), the Tigers of Ambazonia, the Southern Cameroons Defence Forces (SOCADEF), the Manyu Ghost Warriors and possibly the Red Dragons. Collectively the ASDC can draw on an estimated 1,000–1,500 fighters.[6] The largest group is the ARA.

Areas of operation: The ASDC operates throughout the Northwest and Southwest regions. The ARA and SOCADEF operate there too. The Seven Karta is primarily present in Mezam division, the Tigers in Manyu and Meme divisions, the Ghost Warriors in Manyu division and the Red Dragons in Lebialem division.

Leadership: Current elected leader is Iya Marianta Njomia. Before Njomia's appointment, the IG leadership was fractured between Sisiku Julius Ayuk Tabe and Samuel Ikome Sako. The links between the IG and the various groups within the ASDC are often tenuous. Leadership of many of the individual groups is also unknown.

Structure: The IG operates a government structure that includes an executive and a legislative body. The ASDC lacks a centralised command structure. The structure of the several localised self-defence organisations that compose it is unclear, yet many leaders are titled 'general'.

History: The IG emerged from the Southern Cameroons Ambazonia Consortium United Front and declared Ambazonia's independence on 1 October 2017. The ASDC was created in March 2018 as a coordinating mechanism following a call for collective self-defence from the IG.

Objectives: Ambazonia's independence through a strategy of armed insurgency, increased international pressure on the Cameroonian government and disruption of commerce.

Opponents: Cameroonian armed forces.

Affiliates/allies: The IG coordinates with other groups through the Southern Cameroons Liberation Council (SCLC), and at times coordinates with the AGC/ADF.

Resources/capabilities: The IG and ASDC rely on makeshift weaponry and some imports of small arms from neighbouring Nigeria. Financing for the IG comes primarily from donors in the Cameroonian diaspora, while affiliates of the ASDC have been implicated in kidnapping for ransom to fund their operations.

Ambazonia Governing Council (AGC)/Ambazonia Defence Forces (ADF)

Strength: Estimated 200–500 fighters.[7]

Areas of operation: Throughout Northwest and Southwest regions, parts of Littoral region.

Leadership: The AGC is led by Lucas Cho Ayaba (based in Norway), while the chairman of the ADF council is Benedict Kuah.

Structure: The AGC operates a government structure that includes an executive and a legislative branch. Various leaders in the ADF have a 'general' title.

History: The AGC was created in 2013 as a merger of several other self-determination movements and remains outside the IG. In September 2017, the AGC declared a war of independence against the Cameroonian government and the ADF was deployed as its official armed wing.

Objectives: Ambazonia's independence through a strategy of insurgency and disruption of commerce. The AGC's goal is to make the anglophone territory ungovernable and thus compel the Cameroonian government to concede.

Opponents: Cameroonian armed forces.

Affiliates/allies: At times interacts with groups in the ASDC and coordinates with SOCADEF. It has a loose relationship with the IG.

Resources/capabilities: The ADF relies on makeshift weaponry and some imports of small arms from neighbouring Nigeria. Financing for the ADF comes primarily from donors in the Cameroonian diaspora, while some members have been implicated in kidnapping for ransom to fund their operations.

Southern Cameroons Defence Forces (SOCADEF)

Strength: Approximately 400 members.[8]

Areas of operation: Meme division, Southwest region.

Leadership: Led in exile from the US by Ebenezer Derek Mbongo Akwanga.

Structure: While SOCADEF is ostensibly the armed wing of the African People's Liberation Movement (APLM), the degree of coordination between the two is unclear. SOCADEF's organisation on the ground is unknown.

History: SOCADEF is an independent armed secessionist group that grew out of the APLM and the Southern Cameroons Youth League.

Objectives: Ambazonia's independence through a strategy of insurgency and disruption of commerce.

Sub-Saharan Africa

Southern Cameroons Defence Forces (SOCADEF)

Opponents: Cameroonian armed forces.

Affiliates/allies: SOCADEF maintains a loose alliance with the AGC/ADF. In March 2019, its parent organisation, the APLM, joined the SCLC.

Resources/capabilities: Makeshift weaponry and some imports of small arms from neighbouring Nigeria.

Jama'atu Ahlis Sunna Lidda'awati wal-Jihad (JAS)/Boko Haram

Strength: Prior to Abubakar Shekau's death in May 2021, JAS/Boko Haram was estimated to have about 1,500–3,000 fighters in Nigeria. The number of fighters in Cameroon is unclear.[9]

Areas of operation: North and Far North regions.

Leadership: Led by Shekau from 2010 until his death in 2021 and now highly factionalised. Notable factional leaders include Bakura Doron (the political leader of the Bakura faction) and Bakura Shalaba Modu (the religious leader of the Bakura faction). Some reports indicate Modu was killed by Doron in 2022.[10]

Structure: Highly decentralised structure with a weak chain of command, various offshoots and cells that act independently. Several of these offshoots have been absorbed into ISWAP since 2021, with others (notably the Bakura faction) resisting ISWAP.

History: JAS/Boko Haram was established in 2002 by Mohammad Yusuf. Following Yusuf's death in 2009, Shekau increased the group's territorial control, though predation and indiscriminate violence eroded legitimacy. JAS/Boko Haram pledged allegiance to the Islamic State (ISIS) in 2015, operating under the name of ISWAP. In 2016, Shekau split with ISWAP, and in 2021, Shekau killed himself to avoid capture by ISWAP.

Objectives: Establish an Islamic caliphate in northern Cameroon and neighbouring regions.

Opponents: Cameroonian armed forces, MNJTF and ISWAP.

Affiliates/allies: No clear affiliation in Cameroon.

Resources/capabilities: Stolen weaponry from military bases and black-market acquisitions, including rocket-propelled grenades, improvised bombs, mortars, assault rifles, tanks and armoured personnel carriers (APCs). The group has a limited anti-aircraft capability and reportedly has been using uninhabited aerial vehicles since 2018. The group funds itself through looting and kidnapping for ransom.

Islamic State West Africa Province (ISWAP)

Strength: 4,000–5,000 fighters.[11]

Areas of operation: North and Far North regions.

Leadership: Unclear. Following the death of Abu Musab al-Barnawi (the son of Mohammad Yusuf) in 2021, a succession of ISWAP senior commanders, some of whom were (inconsistently) reported to be the leader of the insurgency, have been killed in military operations and airstrikes.

Structure: ISWAP retains elements of the fragmented leadership structure and volatile factionalism of JAS/Boko Haram, though it has established a more coherent and organised approach to governing its territory. The leadership of ISWAP responds to instructions from ISIS and has refined its practices and strategy via this relationship.

History: JAS/Boko Haram became known as ISWAP in 2015, but the two groups split in 2016. ISWAP distinguished itself from JAS/Boko Haram by prioritising military over civilian targets and providing a degree of order in the regions in which it operates. Power struggles among ISWAP commanders have resulted in leadership changes since 2015. In 2021, ISWAP attacked JAS/Boko Haram, and JAS/Boko Haram's Bakura faction retaliated against ISWAP.[12]

Objectives: Establish an Islamic caliphate in northern Cameroon and neighbouring regions.

Opponents: Cameroonian armed forces, MNJTF and JAS/Boko Haram.

Affiliates/allies: ISIS and Islamic State in the Greater Sahara.

Resources/capabilities: ISWAP has obtained most of its weaponry – including APCs, assault rifles, rocket-propelled grenades and mortars – by raiding military bases and attacking troops. It also used financial assistance from ISIS to acquire looted military equipment from its own fighters.[13] Further income is generated via taxes collected from local populations.

Various small militias

Strength: Unclear, but approximately 100–150 members in total across nearly a dozen militias, including the Vipers, often going under the generic term 'Amba Boys'.

Areas of operation: Northwest and Southwest regions.

Leadership: Unknown.

Structure: Unknown.

History: Various small militias emerged following the conflict's beginnings in October 2017; their operations blur the line between insurgency and crime.

Objectives: Ambazonia's independence through insurgency, but many groups also seem to seek short-term material gains from the conflict and are responsible for many of the kidnappings for ransom in the region.

Opponents: Cameroonian armed forces.

Affiliates/allies: The Vipers coordinate with the ADF and SOCADEF on an ad hoc basis.

Resources/capabilities: Makeshift weaponry and small arms imported from Nigeria.

Notes

1   Fanta Dada Petel and Thierry Vircoulon, 'Les Peuls Mbororo dans le conflit anglophone: des luttes foncières locales au conflit régional' [The Fulani Mbororo in the Anglophone Conflict: From Local Land Struggles to Regional Conflict], Institut français des relations internationales, June 2022.

2   Armed Conflict Location & Event Data Project (ACLED), www.acleddata.com. Violent events include battles, explosions/remote violence and violence against civilians.

3   Michelle Gavin, 'From Bad to Worse in Cameroon?', Council on Foreign Relations, 13 February 2023.

4   Armed Conflict Location & Event Data Project (ACLED), www.acleddata.com.

5   *Ibid*. Fatalities refer to battles, violence against civilians and explosions/violence.

6   Institute for Peace and Security Studies, 'Cameroon Conflict Insight', Peace and Security Report, vol. 1, March 2020, p. 8.

7   International Crisis Group, 'Cameroon's Anglophone Crisis: How to Get to Talks?', Report no. 272, 2 May 2019, p. 32.

8   *Ibid*.

9   Stig Jarle Hansen, 'The Fractious Future of the Islamic State in West Africa', War on the Rocks, 3 November 2021.

10   Maman Inoua Elhadji Mahamadou Amadou and Vincent Foucher, 'Boko Haram in the Lake Chad Basin: The Bakura Faction and Its Resistance to the Rationalisation of Jihad', German Institute for International and Security Affairs (SWP), German Institute of Development and Sustainability, and Kiel Institute for the World Economy, 8 December 2022; and Richard Assheton, 'Boko Haram Chief "Killed for Trying to Defect"', *The Times*, 7 April 2022.

11   Tomás F. Husted, 'Boko Haram and the Islamic State West Africa Province', IF10173, Congressional Research Service, 24 February 2022.

12   International Crisis Group, 'After Shekau: Confronting Jihadists in Nigeria's North East', Briefing no. 180, 29 March 2022.

13   Vincent Foucher, 'The Islamic State Franchises in Africa: Lessons from Lake Chad', International Crisis Group, 29 October 2020.

CHAD

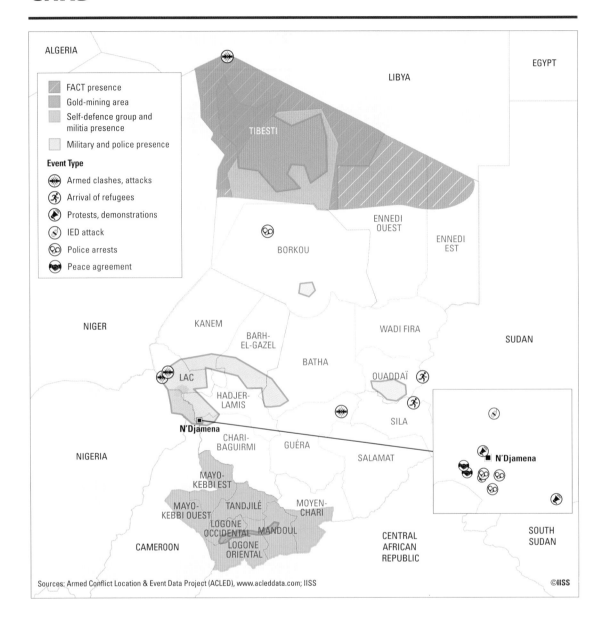

Sources: Armed Conflict Location & Event Data Project (ACLED), www.acleddata.com; IISS   ©IISS

Conflict Overview

A landlocked country spanning the Sahel and Central Africa, Chad has experienced continued instability since its independence from France in 1960. Enduring grievances over ethnically motivated political exclusion and poor governance of the country's natural resources, including oil and minerals, have fuelled political instability,

powered by generations of armed groups. Multiple military coups have further exposed the fragility of Chad's political system, which remains largely predicated on military might, ethnic divisions and patrimonial government practices.

From 1965–90, the Chadian Civilian War – a complex and protracted conflict – played a critical

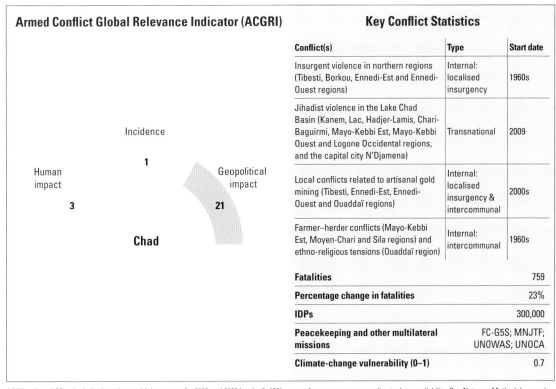

Armed Conflict Global Relevance Indicator (ACGRI)

Incidence

1

Human impact

3

Geopolitical impact

21

Chad

Key Conflict Statistics

Conflict(s)	Type	Start date
Insurgent violence in northern regions (Tibesti, Borkou, Ennedi-Est and Ennedi-Ouest regions)	Internal: localised insurgency	1960s
Jihadist violence in the Lake Chad Basin (Kanem, Lac, Hadjer-Lamis, Chari-Baguirmi, Mayo-Kebbi Est, Mayo-Kebbi Ouest and Logone Occidental regions, and the capital city N'Djamena)	Transnational	2009
Local conflicts related to artisanal gold mining (Tibesti, Ennedi-Est, Ennedi-Ouest and Ouaddaï regions)	Internal: localised insurgency & intercommunal	2000s
Farmer–herder conflicts (Mayo-Kebbi Est, Moyen-Chari and Sila regions) and ethno-religious tensions (Ouaddaï region)	Internal: intercommunal	1960s

Fatalities	759
Percentage change in fatalities	23%
IDPs	300,000
Peacekeeping and other multilateral missions	FC-G5S; MNJTF; UNOWAS; UNOCA
Climate-change vulnerability (0–1)	0.7

ACGRI pillars: IISS calculation based on multiple sources for 2022 and 2023 (scale: 0–100), except for some cases according to data availability. See Notes on Methodology and Data Appendix for all variables and further details on Key Conflict Statistics.

role in shaping the country's political and military landscape. It was characterised by shifting alliances, multiple phases and the involvement of a variety of internal and external actors. In 1990, Idriss Déby Itno, then a young military officer, overthrew the dictator Hissène Habré, but internal divisions persisted. New armed groups formed in the following decades, which continue to fight the government over grievances related to power and resource sharing.

In April 2021, long-term president Déby died while at the front line in the battle against the Fighters of the Front for Change and Concord in Chad (FACT) rebellion. He was unconstitutionally succeeded by his son Mahamat Idriss Déby Itno, who installed a transitional military council (CMT), initially for 18 months. The authoritarian transition regime has since struggled to contain northern rebellions, quell further uprisings in the south, tackle residual violence by Jama'atu Ahlis Sunna Lidda'awati wal-Jihad (JAS, commonly known as Boko Haram) in the Lake Chad Basin and address persistent communal violence all at once.

Chad's geographic positioning has historically been an additional cause of its fragility, with Libya and the Central African Republic (CAR) affected

by civil war to its north and south, Sudan facing instability to its east, and JAS/Boko Haram continuing to challenge its southwest borders with Niger, Nigeria and Cameroon. A continuous flow of arms and skilled fighters from these neighbouring countries provides a significant pool of resources for Chadian rebel groups. Such rebellions stem from a long history of civil wars and domestic insurgencies, and they continue to form a major conflict system in the country's north, especially along its porous borders with Libya and Sudan.

A member both of the G5 Sahel, fighting against al-Qaeda's and the Islamic State's presence in the central Sahel, and of the Multinational Joint Task Force (MNJTF), combating JAS/Boko Haram and the Islamic State West Africa Province (ISWAP) in the Lake Chad Basin, Chad also contributes a great number of troops to the United Nations Multidimensional Integrated Stabilization Mission in Mali (MINUSMA). Chad's long-standing close cooperation with France (its main military partner) and other foreign forces has earned it the reputation of being a reliable military partner for the West in a troubled region, despite its poor democratic track record.

Sub-Saharan Africa

Conflict Update

Over the reporting period, Chad's political transition under Mahamat Déby's CMT became increasingly undemocratic. The military transitional government went back on its initial commitment to hand over power to civilians within 18 months, instead extending its rule for another two years.

In October 2022, a popular protest organised by opposition movement Wakit Tama was violently repressed by state security forces, leaving at least 50 to potentially over 300 people dead in the capital city N'Djamena.[1] The crackdown was reminiscent of Chad's history of authoritarian rule and state-led abuse of political critics. France's failure to condemn the security sector's brutality further fuelled popular opposition to French involvement in the country – a trend that is ongoing in other Sahelian countries. Meanwhile, the CMT has made little progress on its agenda to reform the constitution and electoral system, suggesting that the country may not return to a constitutional order even in the 24-month extended time frame (by October 2024).

In 2022, the government organised the Inclusive and Sovereign National Dialogue with Qatar's mediation support. The dialogue lasted several months and was supposed to offer a framework for the consensual resolution of long-standing political divides between the military, ruling elite, political and civil-society movements, and non-state armed groups (NSAGs). However, the dialogue did not produce the desired outcomes, primarily because some armed groups were excluded and multiple leading NSAGs, including the FACT, the Union of Resistance Forces (UFR) and the Military Command Council for the Salvation of the Republic (CCMSR), either declined to partake in or withdrew from the process.

Meanwhile, tensions endured throughout the country. The FACT continued its push (begun in 2021) from southern Libya towards N'Djamena and clashed with the Chadian army. Rumours of a new rebellion forming on the Chad–CAR border in 2022, with alleged support from the CAR, strained diplomatic relations between the two countries. And in April 2023, conflict breaking out in Sudan created an additional risk factor in Chad's volatile surrounding regions.

Against this backdrop, Chad signed a defence-cooperation agreement with Saudi Arabia in January 2023 and increased defence and security allocations by 20% in its 2023 national budget, suggesting that the government is preparing for war.[2] The country also opened an embassy in Israel in early 2023, a further indication of the government's resolve to tighten ties with countries that have the technical capacity to act as critical security partners and have a track record of supporting authoritarian African states.

Although several rebel NSAGs, including those that boycotted the Inclusive and Sovereign National Dialogue, remain active, direct clashes with government forces slowed down in 2022 and early 2023. The threat they pose to the capital city N'Djamena seems more distant than a year earlier. However, the fact that Chadian forces are overstretched across multiple fronts and enjoy limited popular support suggests that these trends could easily be reversed.

Beyond political rebel groups, Chad also continues to face extensive communal violence, mostly powered by a combination of ethnic rivalries and opposing economic interests. In the country's north, an ill-regulated artisanal-gold-mining industry and the widespread use of uncontrolled drugs such as tramadol have led to frequent deadly clashes and fuelled a criminal economy that partly relies on human trafficking and slavery. Elsewhere, especially but not limited to the regions of Sila, Ouaddaï and Wadi Fira, long-standing farmer–herder competition regularly results in violent clashes with high civilian death tolls.

Conflict Parties

Chadian armed forces

Strength: 33,250 active military personnel (air force: 350; army: approximately 27,500; state security service: 5,400), as well as 11,900 active gendarmerie and paramilitary personnel.

Areas of operation: Primarily active in counter-insurgency efforts in the Lake Chad Basin but also involved in nationwide securitisation operations.

Chadian armed forces

Leadership: President Mahamat Idriss Déby Itno, Bichara Issa Djadallah (minister of defence) and Azem Bermendoa Agouna (chief of the general staff).

Structure: Comprised of the army, the air force, the state security service, and gendarmerie and paramilitary forces.

History: Founded in 1960, following the country's independence from France. Throughout the 1960s and 1970s, Chad's military was heavily influenced by France, which continued to provide training, equipment and military advisers. In the 1980s, the armed forces were reorganised and re-equipped with support from the United States, which sought to counter Libyan influence in the region. The armed forces have a long history of being politicised, with most presidents since independence coming from a military background.

Objectives: Maintain national security and territorial integrity and counter violent extremism.

Opponents: FACT, UFR, CCMSR, other NSAGs, JAS/Boko Haram and ISWAP.

Affiliates/allies: French armed forces, MNJTF, G5 Sahel Joint Force (FC-G5S).

Resources/capabilities: Chad's defence budget for 2022 was US$319 million (2.7% of GDP) and is US$339m (2.8% of GDP) for 2023.

Front for Change and Concord in Chad (FACT)

Strength: 1,000–1,500 fighters in 2021 (most recent data available).[3]

Areas of operation: Primarily in northern Chad and southern Libya.

Leadership: Mahamat Mahadi Ali.

Structure: Unknown.

History: Founded by Mahamat Mahadi Ali, FACT emerged in 2016 as a splinter group from the Union of Forces for Democracy and Development rebel group. Since Idriss Déby's death in 2021, FACT has gained increasing popular support among smaller rebel factions and local ethnic groups such as the Goran (of which Mahadi is a member), Zaghawa and Tebu.

Objectives: Overthrow the Chadian government, deemed illegitimate by FACT.

Opponents: Chadian armed forces.

Affiliates/allies: Unclear.

Resources/capabilities: Light and heavy weaponry, armed vehicles and improvised explosive devices (IEDs).

Union of Resistance Forces (UFR)

Strength: Unclear.

Areas of operation: Northern regions of Chad.

Leadership: Timane Erdimi.

Structure: UFR is an alliance of eight separate Chadian rebel groups.

History: Established in 2009, the main goal of the coalition was initially to overthrow the regime of Idriss Déby. Erdimi, a relative of Idriss Déby, was allegedly picked to lead the insurgency the same year.

Objectives: Overthrow the Chadian government and 'liberate' the Chadian people.

Opponents: Chadian armed forces and France.

Affiliates/allies: Unclear.

Resources/capabilities: Light weaponry and IEDs.

Military Command Council for the Salvation of the Republic (CCMSR)

Strength: Unclear.

Areas of operation: Operates primarily in the northern Chadian region of Tibesti but originated in southern Libya. CCMSR is marginally active in eastern Niger and western Sudan.

Leadership: Rachid Mahamat Tahir.

Structure: Unknown.

History: In 2016, following a dispute among members of the FACT coalition, a faction of primarily Kreda clansmen decided to split from the group and form the CCMSR.

Objectives: Overthrow the Chadian government.

Opponents: Chadian armed forces.

Affiliates/allies: Libyan defence brigades and armed groups.

Resources/capabilities: Light weaponry.

Multinational Joint Task Force (MNJTF)

Strength: Approximately 13,000 troops from the armed forces of Benin, Cameroon, Chad, Niger and Nigeria.[4]

Areas of operation: Lake Chad Basin.

Leadership: Maj.-Gen. Gold Chibuisi (force commander).

Structure: Headquartered in N'Djamena (Chad), the MNJTF comprises four geographical sectors, with their own headquarters in Monguno (Nigeria), Baga Sola (Chad), Diffa (Niger) and Mora (Cameroon). Each sector is led by a commander with wide autonomy, while the MNJTF force commander has coordination powers.

History: The MNJTF evolved from a Nigerian initiative in 1994 to a multinational force in 1998 to tackle cross-border crimes and banditry affecting the Lake Chad Basin. After years of inactivity, the Peace and Security Council of the African Union (AU) agreed to revive the MNJTF in 2015 to counter JAS/Boko Haram's growing activity.

Sub-Saharan Africa

Multinational Joint Task Force (MNJTF)

Objectives: Coordinate regional counter-insurgency efforts and restore security in areas affected by JAS/Boko Haram and ISWAP in the Lake Chad Basin. The MNJTF also helps support stabilisation programmes, humanitarian-assistance efforts and the return of forcibly displaced people.

Opponents: JAS/Boko Haram and ISWAP.

Affiliates/allies: The national armies of Benin, Cameroon, Chad, Niger and Nigeria; international partners (the AU, Burkina Faso, the European Union, France, Mali, the United Kingdom and the US); FC-G5S; and MINUSMA.

Resources/capabilities: Estimated initial operational budget of US$700m. The EU is the force's main contributor, channelling its funds through the AU. Bureaucratic delays and lack of adequate resources have hampered the MNJTF's ability to fulfil its mandate.

French armed forces

Strength: 1,500 military personnel in Chad.[5]

Areas of operation: N/A.

Leadership: Sébastien Lecornu (French minister of defence).

Structure: Consists of French military personnel stationed in Chad, primarily in the N'Djamena French military base and the Chadian military bases of Faya and Abéché.

History: France has provided military assistance to Chadian authorities since Chad's independence in the name of safeguarding the political stability of the region. Between 1986 and 2014, the French military was involved in the Chadian–Libyan conflict through *Operation Épervier*. The Chadian capital of N'Djamena then hosted the headquarters of French-led *Operation Barkhane* (2014–22), along with a major air-force military base still in use today.

Objectives: Assist the Chadian armed forces, MNJTF and FC-G5S in the fight against violent extremism; protect local communities from attacks; and free villages and towns from insurgent control.

Opponents: JAS/Boko Haram, CCMSR, FACT and UFR.

Affiliates/allies: Chadian armed forces, MNJTF and FC-G5S.

Resources/capabilities: Heavy weaponry.

Notes

1   Human Rights Watch, 'Chad: Scores of Protesters Shot Dead, Wounded', 26 October 2022; and 'Manifestations du 20 octobre au Tchad: la CNDH a rendu son rapport sur le «jeudi noir»' [20 October Protests in Chad: CNDH Delivers Its Report on 'Black Thursday'], Radio France Internationale (RFI), 24 February 2023.

2   Remadji Hoinathy, 'Do Those Seeking Peace in Chad Need to Prepare for War?', Institute for Security Studies, 27 March 2023.

3   Thomas Howes-Ward, 'Libya's Foreign Militias', Carnegie Endowment for International Peace, 10 April 2018.

4   Freedom Chukwudi Onuoha, Andrew E. Yaw Tchie and Mariana Llorens Zabala, *A Quest to Win the Hearts and Minds: Assessing the Effectiveness of the Multinational Joint Task Force* (Oslo: Norwegian Institute of International Affairs, 2023), p. 37. The MNJTF website puts this number at around 10,000 troops.

5   IISS, *The Military Balance 2023* (Abingdon: Routledge for the IISS, 2023), p. 443.

Sub-Saharan Africa

CENTRAL AFRICAN REPUBLIC

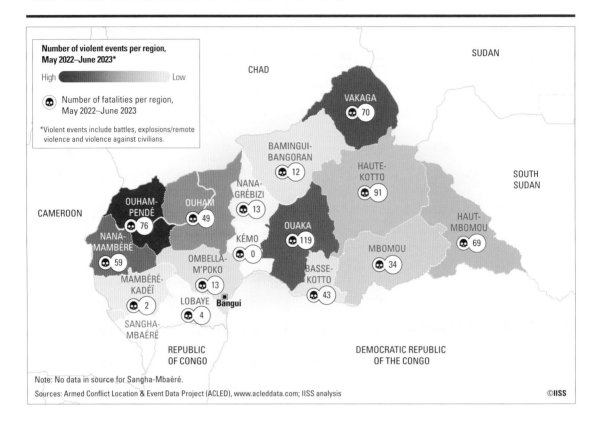

Number of violent events per region, May 2022–June 2023*

High ◁▬▬▬▬▬▷ Low

⊙ Number of fatalities per region, May 2022–June 2023

*Violent events include battles, explosions/remote violence and violence against civilians.

CHAD

SUDAN

VAKAGA ⊙ 70

BAMINGUI-BANGORAN ⊙ 12

HAUTE-KOTTO ⊙ 91

SOUTH SUDAN

NANA-GRÉBIZI ⊙ 13

OUHAM-PENDÉ ⊙ 76

OUHAM ⊙ 49

CAMEROON

OUAKA ⊙ 119

HAUT-MBOMOU ⊙ 69

NANA-MAMBÉRÉ ⊙ 59

KÉMO ⊙ 0

MBOMOU ⊙ 34

OMBELLA-M'POKO ⊙ 13

BASSE-KOTTO ⊙ 43

MAMBÉRÉ-KADÉÏ ⊙ 2

LOBAYE ⊙ 4   Bangui

SANGHA-MBAÉRÉ

REPUBLIC OF CONGO

DEMOCRATIC REPUBLIC OF THE CONGO

Note: No data in source for Sangha-Mbaéré.

Sources: Armed Conflict Location & Event Data Project (ACLED), www.acleddata.com; IISS analysis   ©IISS

Conflict Overview

The Central African Republic (CAR) has been plagued by violence for decades, rooted in deep and widespread poverty and perpetuated by the absence of the state and its security forces. The country's natural-resource wealth, instead of being a source of development, has worsened grievances and fuelled the struggle for the resources' control. Additionally, the structural weakness of its army and the porosity of its borders have made the country prone to the interference of external actors, especially Chad and Sudan in the last decade and more recently Rwanda and Russia.

The onset of the current crisis dates to 2012, when Séléka, a coalition of primarily Muslim armed groups, launched an offensive against then-president François Bozizé. He was replaced in March 2013 by Michel Djotodia, who briefly became president of the republic. In response to the brutality of Séléka forces, self-defence militias (known as 'anti-balaka' groups) consisting predominantly of

Christian fighters emerged and carried out reprisal violence against Séléka. When regional pressure forced Djotodia to step down, Séléka withdrew to the country's north. To stabilise the CAR, France deployed *Operation Sangaris* between 2013 and 2016 and the United Nations has deployed the UN Multidimensional Integrated Stabilization Mission in the Central African Republic (MINUSCA) since 2014. Notwithstanding these efforts, the country continues to experience insecurity and violence.

In March 2016, Faustin-Archange Touadéra, Bozizé's former prime minister, was elected president. Several rounds of peace negotiations and agreements followed, but armed confrontation did not stop. Struggling with a weak and unprofessional army and a push by Russia to exclude France from the country, Touadéra turned in 2017 to the Russian private military company Wagner Group for assistance. In exchange for their support, the government

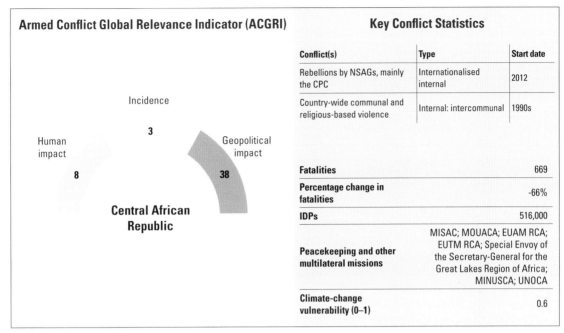

Armed Conflict Global Relevance Indicator (ACGRI)

Incidence

3

Human
impact

8

Geopolitical
impact

38

**Central African
Republic**

Key Conflict Statistics

Conflict(s)	Type	Start date
Rebellions by NSAGs, mainly the CPC	Internationalised internal	2012
Country-wide communal and religious-based violence	Internal: intercommunal	1990s

Fatalities	669
Percentage change in fatalities	-66%
IDPs	516,000
Peacekeeping and other multilateral missions	MISAC; MOUACA; EUAM RCA; EUTM RCA; Special Envoy of the Secretary-General for the Great Lakes Region of Africa; MINUSCA; UNOCA
Climate-change vulnerability (0–1)	0.6

ACGRI pillars: IISS calculation based on multiple sources for 2022 and 2023 (scale: 0–100), except for some cases according to data availability. See Notes on Methodology and Data Appendix for all variables and further details on Key Conflict Statistics.

has allegedly compensated Wagner with control of mining areas.[1] The political situation deteriorated in 2020 when the Constitutional Court rejected Bozizé's presidential candidacy. Major rebel groups created the Coalition of Patriots for Change (CPC) to disrupt the elections. The groups included the Union for Peace in the Central African Republic (UPC); the Popular Front for the Renaissance of Central Africa (FPRC); Return, Reclamation, Rehabilitation (3R); the Central African Patriotic Movement (MPC); and some anti-balaka groups. In December 2020, Rwandan troops were deployed under a bilateral security agreement to help the government safeguard the elections. Even after Touadéra won a second five-year term in 2020, the security outlook remained extremely fragile.

Conflict Update

The intensity of armed conflict decreased in the reporting period compared with 2021, but violence continued to be pervasive across the country. This included deadly confrontations between non-state armed groups (NSAGs, mainly those belonging to the CPC) and Central African Armed Forces (FACA) supported by Wagner and Rwanda's military. Between May 2022 and June 2023, slightly fewer than 670 fatalities were registered, against more than 1,900 reported between May 2021 and June 2022.[2] Although Wagner continued to play a fundamental role in supporting the government's fight against CPC armed groups, it increasingly operated independently of the FACA during the reporting period. This took a heavy toll on civilians and confirmed a trend that has been reported since mid-2021.[3] On some occasions, Wagner even attacked FACA soldiers, mirroring the growing tensions between the two groups. Amid persisting security concerns, the UN Security Council renewed in November 2022 the MINUSCA mandate until 15 November 2023, with China, Gabon and Russia abstaining. Due to increasing security challenges, the CAR and Sudan closed their shared border between January and March 2023. Additionally, Touadéra met in February 2023 with Chadian Transitional President Idriss Déby to discuss how to tackle armed groups along their border. Due to border porosity, the ongoing conflict in Sudan is likely to further deteriorate security in northern CAR.

Sub-Saharan Africa

On the domestic side, the government is seeking to remove a constitutional two-term limit, which would allow Touadéra to run for president again in 2025. But the proposed constitutional amendment faces opposition and, if approved, is likely to further fuel the cycle of violence, replicating the 2020 election campaign and putting at risk the already fragile democratic framework.

Against this backdrop, the growing role of competing external actors has contributed to a more complex geopolitical environment, which has not been conducive to stability and peace. On the one hand, the central government has continued to be extremely dependent on Wagner's security assistance to maintain power, especially regarding control of strategic mining areas. On the other hand, due to Russia's influence, relations between the CAR and its main donors, notably the European Union, France and the United States, have become more complicated. The flow of financial assistance has dropped due to the fear that the subsidies could be directed to Wagner. This has tightened an already constrained CAR state budget, which used to depend on foreign allocations for almost 45% of its total funds.[4] In particular, Paris faced increasing friction with the government during the last months of 2022, with CAR authorities and their Russian allies carrying out a media campaign against the former colonial power. In addition to cuts in financial assistance, Paris progressively withdrew its advisers and troops from the country. The worsening relations with France are symbolised by the government's decision in July 2022 to launch Sango, the first CAR cryptocurrency. Considering the low level of access to the internet and electricity in the country, not to mention the problems related to the high costs of bitcoin mining, it seems unlikely that locals will be able to use this new cryptocurrency. For these reasons, Sango is far from being a tool capable of mitigating the country's economic hardship. It is rather a way for Bangui to challenge the influence exercised by France in the region through the franc of the Financial Community of Africa.

At the same time, it seems that Western countries, mainly the US and France, have scaled up diplomatic efforts to remove Wagner from the country. As part of this strategy to counter Russian influence on the continent, in January 2023 the US Treasury Department designated the Wagner Group as a 'transnational criminal organisation'. Although denied by the CAR's foreign minister, Sylvie Baïpo-Temon, rumours persist about ongoing negotiations between Touadéra and the US for the withdrawal of Wagner forces from the country in return for increased humanitarian aid and financial and military assistance.[5] Against this backdrop, Touadéra faces the difficult task of balancing the benefits of Wagner's support with the need to secure international financial assistance; mitigate growing frustration within the FACA with the unconstrained and unaccountable role of Russian paramilitaries; and appease neighbouring Chad and Sudan, which both depend on Western support and consider Wagner a threat to their stability.[6]

Conflict Parties

Central African Armed Forces (FACA)

Strength: 9,150 active military, as well as 1,000 gendarmerie and paramilitary.

Areas of operation: Main cities.

Leadership: Claude Rameaux Bireau (defence minister) and Gen. Zéphirin Mamadou (chief of staff).

Structure: The army is structurally weak, and effective military and security organisation remain largely absent. A lack of financial resources and defence-industrial capacity makes equipment maintenance difficult. The presidential guard is the best trained and equipped unit.

History: Experienced mutinies in 1996 and 1997. Having been involved in many coups since independence, the army evaporated when the Séléka took power in 2013, with many soldiers joining the anti-balaka groups. The army-reconstruction process started gradually in 2014, supported by the EU, Russia and the UN. Since then, the reconstruction process has been slow.

Objectives: Protecting the Touadéra regime and securing CAR territory from external threats and attacks.

Opponents: NSAGs, including UPC, FPRC, 3R, MPC and anti-balaka groups.

Affiliates/allies: MINUSCA, Rwandan troops deployed in the CAR and Wagner Group.

Resources/capabilities: Insufficient budget, limited military equipment and mobility. Wages are often unpaid.

Union for Peace in the Central African Republic (UPC)

Strength: Unclear.

Areas of operation: Central and southeastern CAR (Haute-Kotto, Haut-Mbomou, Mbomou and Ouaka provinces).

Leadership: Ali Darassa, a long-standing Fulani rebel and bandit, formerly a commander of the Baba Laddé militia. The UPC leadership is made up of professional bandits and regional mercenaries.

Structure: Unknown.

History: The first group to split from the Séléka coalition in 2014, the UPC has strategically enlarged its territory since then and is widely considered the most powerful armed group currently in the CAR.

Objectives: Officially, the UPC protects Fulani communities, but its main objective is to control natural resources and trade routes between the CAR and some of its neighbours.

Opponents: Government forces and some anti-balaka groups.

Affiliates/allies: 3R and possibly MPC. The UPC is a member of the CPC but has kept a low profile within the coalition. In some locations, the UPC has also been cooperating with the FPRC.

Resources/capabilities: Involved in the cattle and gold trade and weapons trafficking between Chad, the Democratic Republic of the Congo and South Sudan.

Popular Front for the Renaissance of Central Africa (FPRC)

Strength: Unclear.

Areas of operation: Haute-Kotto province.

Leadership: Abdoulaye Hissène (military leader) and Noureddine Adam (political leader).

Structure: Originally composed of Rounga, Goula, Chadian and Sudanese fighters. Most of the Goula elements left the movement in 2017 and 2018, joining the Patriotic Rally for the Renewal of Central Africa.

History: Emerged after the fall of the Séléka coalition in 2014. Leading Séléka members Hissène and Adam created FPRC to maintain control of the northeast. In 2019, they fought against the Movement of Central African Liberators for Justice (MLCJ) but lost and were pushed out of Birao, the main city in Vakaga province.

Objectives: The FPRC's political agenda focuses on protecting Muslim communities and partitioning the country. In 2015, Adam proclaimed the creation of a short-lived independent state, the Logone Republic, and has subsequently tried unsuccessfully to reunite the former Séléka groups.

Opponents: MLCJ and government forces.

Affiliates/allies: Member of the CPC.

Resources/capabilities: The FPRC controls some of the weapons trafficking, trade and cattle routes between the CAR, Chad and Sudan and thus can count on significant financial resources. It is well connected to the Chadian and Sudanese security services, from which it receives mercenaries as well as military equipment.

Return, Reclamation, Rehabilitation (3R)

Strength: Unclear.

Areas of operation: Ouham-Pendé and Nana-Mambéré provinces, with headquarters in De Gaulle town.

Leadership: Bi Sidi Souleman (alias Sidiki Abass), a Fulani warlord. Abass was sanctioned by the UN in 2020. His death has been falsely reported several times, including in December 2020.

Structure: Unclear.

History: 3R emerged in late 2015 at the northwest border between the CAR and Cameroon and was mandated by Fulani

cattle owners based in Cameroon to protect their cattle during the transhumance. Its recruitment is Fulani-based.

Objectives: Protect Fulani cattle and economically exploit pastoralists.

Opponents: MINUSCA, government forces and anti-balaka groups.

Affiliates/allies: UPC, and it is a member of the CPC.

Resources/capabilities: 3R's main sources of revenue are the taxation of Fulani pastoralists and gold and weapons smuggling between Chad and Cameroon. Most of its military equipment comes from Chad.

Central African Patriotic Movement (MPC)

Strength: Unclear.

Areas of operation: Mainly Ouham and Nana-Grébizi provinces, with a stronghold in Kaga-Bandoro.

Leadership: Mahamat Al-Khatim, a Chadian whose family has settled in the CAR. He was appointed special adviser to the prime minister after the 2019 Khartoum agreement but resigned in August 2019. Leaders are all Chadian fighters.

Structure: Mostly composed of Chadian fighters from the Salamat region. The Salamat leaders have a strong influence over Khatim.

History: The MPC was initially a splinter group of the FPRC, created by Khatim in mid-2015. The MPC is the strongest armed group in Ouham province. In July 2020, Khatim unsuccessfully attempted to form the 'Markounda coalition' under his leadership.

Objectives: Secure the interests of the Salamat communities in Ouham and Nana-Grebizi provinces (cattle migration, access to land and markets).

Opponents: Anti-balaka groups.

Affiliates/allies: Chadian security forces, and it is a member of the CPC.

Sub-Saharan Africa

Central African Patriotic Movement (MPC)

Resources/capabilities: The main sources of revenue are weapons smuggling between Chad and the CAR, the taxation of pastoralists from Chad, and the taxation of trade and artisanal gold mining in the CAR provinces under its control.

Anti-balaka groups

Strength: Unclear.

Areas of operation: Activity is sporadic, concentrated in Basse-Kotto, Kémo, Ombella-M'Poko and Ouaka provinces.

Leadership: No central leadership or chain of command but Bozizé has some political influence over the movement. Two coordination branches (run by Maxime Mokom and by Sébastien Wenezoui and Patrice-Edouard Ngaissona, respectively) present themselves as interlocutors for the movement and have signed the Khartoum agreement. Suspected of war crimes, Ngaissona was arrested in France in 2018 and handed over to the International Criminal Court. The trial opened in February 2021.

Structure: No structure.

History: A loose network of anti-Muslim local militias, which initially emerged as a self-defence movement against the Séléka in Bozizé's ethnic stronghold and spread to western CAR in late 2013. In 2017, the movement's territorial reach expanded to southeastern CAR. At present the active anti-balaka groups focus on banditry and extortion.

Objectives: No clear agenda. The initial goal to drive Muslims out of the CAR quickly morphed into violent economic predation (looting and extortion). Despite their initial anti-Séléka motive, some have allied with Muslim armed groups. In December 2020, two anti-balaka factions close to Bozizé (the Ndomaté and Mokom branches) joined the CPC.

Opponents: Competing anti-balaka groups and some Muslim armed groups.

Affiliates/allies: Some anti-balaka groups are part of the CPC.

Resources/capabilities: Artisanal weaponry, very few automatic weapons. No organised control of natural resources and trade routes.

Rwanda Defence Force (RDF)

Strength: Deployment estimated to be around 1,000.[7]

Areas of operation: Throughout the CAR.

Leadership: Maj.-Gen. Eugene Nkubito.

Structure: Unknown.

History: On 21 December 2020, the Rwandan defence ministry confirmed that it had deployed troops to the CAR under a bilateral security agreement with the CAR government. Rwandan forces participated in the protection of Bangui in December 2020 and in the counter-offensive led by Russian contractors and the FACA against the CPC that started in January 2021. Bilateral agreements allow Rwandan troops to operate largely beyond the rules of engagement of MINUSCA, with greater autonomy of action and discretion in the use of force.

Objectives: Support stabilisation and protect the contingent of Rwandan troops within MINUSCA against CPC rebels.

Opponents: CPC forces.

Affiliates/allies: MINUSCA, the FACA and Wagner Group.

Resources/capabilities: Unknown.

Wagner Group

Strength: 1,000–1,500 (estimates).[8]

Areas of operation: Central and eastern provinces and Vakaga province.

Leadership: Unclear after the group's chief Yevgeny Prigozhin and commander Dmitry Utkin were killed in an aeroplane crash on 23 August 2023.

Structure: The company was established by businessman Yevgeny Prigozhin. Its structure is not well documented.

History: The Wagner Group is a Russian security organisation closely linked to the Kremlin, Russian military intelligence and Russia's Ministry of Defence. It is used by Russia to carry out a range of officially deniable military and intelligence operations and commercial activities. Reports about the presence of the group in the CAR first emerged in 2018, when Russian instructors were sent to train the CAR army at the Berengo base. The group was established in 2014, and it and other private military companies proliferated following Russia's involvement in the 2015 war in Syria, where they played an active role. The Wagner Group also operates extensively in Africa, where it is contracted to provide security for governments and is involved in profitable resource extraction. It took a leading role in the siege of Bakhmut in Donetsk region from August 2022–May 2023, which raised its public profile significantly in Russia. However, its status is currently in limbo. Following an abortive mutiny led by Prigozhin on 23–24 June 2023, a major part of the Wagner Group's forces was deployed in Belarus. The death of Prigozhin and other senior Wagner Group figures in August 2023 has deepened uncertainty about the group's future. After the mutiny, Putin acknowledged that the group was directly funded by the Russian state and noted the lack of any Russian legislation allowing such private military groups. At the end of July, Russia advanced legislation enabling regional governors to create military companies, and this could lead to further significant changes in their form and function.

Objectives: Initially, provide close protection for Touadéra, train the CAR army and set up two bases: Berengo for military training (Lobaye province) and Bria for medical facilities

Wagner Group

(Haute-Kotto province). Since December 2020 and the CPC attacks, protect Bangui and organise a counter-offensive with the FACA and Rwandan troops. Since mid-2021, it has increasingly operated independently from the FACA.	**Opponents:** CPC forces.
	Affiliates/allies: FACA and Rwandan troops.
	Resources/capabilities: Unknown.

United Nations Multidimensional Integrated Stabilization Mission in the Central African Republic (MINUSCA)

Strength: 18,486 personnel.[9]	**Objectives:** MINUSCA's highest priority is the protection of civilians. Other tasks include supporting the transition process, facilitating humanitarian assistance, promoting and protecting human rights, supporting justice and the rule of law, and supporting disarmament, demobilisation, reintegration and repatriation.
Areas of operation: Throughout the CAR.	
Leadership: Valentine Rugwabiza (special representative of the secretary-general for the CAR and head of MINUSCA).	
Structure: MINUSCA comprises 13,396 military personnel, 3,000 police, 1,230 civilian personnel, 418 chief-of-staff officers, 152 experts and 290 UN volunteers.[10]	**Opponents:** Various armed groups.
	Affiliates/allies: FACA.
History: MINUSCA was authorised by the UN Security Council on 10 April 2014. In November 2022, its mandate was extended until 15 November 2023.	**Resources/capabilities:** Approved budget for 1 July 2022–30 June 2023: approximately US$1.2 billion.[11]

Notes

1 Pauline Bax, 'Russia's Influence in the Central African Republic', International Crisis Group, 3 December 2021.

2 Armed Conflict Location & Event Data Project (ACLED), www.acleddata.com. These figures refer to battles, violence against civilians and explosions/violence.

3 ACLED, 'Wagner Group Operations in Africa: Civilian Targeting Trends in the Central African Republic and Mali', 30 August 2022.

4 'Seeking a Way Out of Kremlin's Embrace', *Africa Confidential*, vol. 64, no. 7, 30 March 2023.

5 Cyril Bensimon, 'Les Etats-Unis engagent une stratégie pour évincer d'Afrique les mercenaires du Groupe Wagner' [US Embarks on a Strategy to Oust the Mercenaries of the Wagner Group from Africa], *Le Monde*, 20 February 2023.

6 Enrica Picco, 'Ten Years After the Coup, Is the Central African Republic Facing Another Major Crisis?', International Crisis Group, 22 March 2023; and Declan Walsh, 'A "New Cold War" Looms in Africa as U.S. Pushes Against Russian Gains', *New York Times*, 19 March, 2023.

7 Based on author's interview with country's analysts, April 2023.

8 *Ibid.*

9 As of February 2023. UN Peacekeeping, 'MINUSCA Fact Sheet'.

10 *Ibid.*

11 UN General Assembly, 'Seventy-sixth Session, Agenda Item 152, Financing of the United Nations Multidimensional Integrated Stabilization Mission in the Central African Republic', A/RES/76/282, 29 June 2022.

Sub-Saharan Africa

SOUTH SUDAN

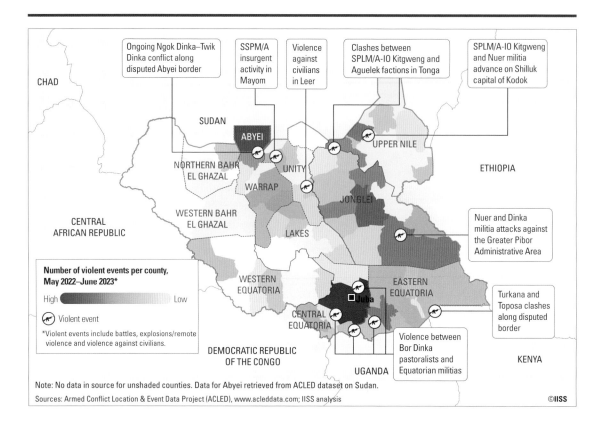

Ongoing Ngok Dinka–Twik Dinka conflict along disputed Abyei border

SSPM/A insurgent activity in Mayom

Violence against civilians in Leer

Clashes between SPLM/A-IO Kitgweng and Aguelek factions in Tonga

SPLM/A-IO Kitgweng and Nuer militia advance on Shilluk capital of Kodok

CHAD

SUDAN

ABYEI

NORTHERN BAHR EL GHAZAL

UNITY

UPPER NILE

WARRAP

ETHIOPIA

JONGLEI

WESTERN BAHR EL GHAZAL

CENTRAL AFRICAN REPUBLIC

LAKES

Nuer and Dinka militia attacks against the Greater Pibor Administrative Area

Number of violent events per county, May 2022–June 2023*

High ▬▬▬▬▬ Low

🔫 Violent event

*Violent events include battles, explosions/remote violence and violence against civilians.

WESTERN EQUATORIA

Juba

EASTERN EQUATORIA

Turkana and Toposa clashes along disputed border

CENTRAL EQUATORIA

DEMOCRATIC REPUBLIC OF THE CONGO

UGANDA

Violence between Bor Dinka pastoralists and Equatorian militias

KENYA

Note: No data in source for unshaded counties. Data for Abyei retrieved from ACLED dataset on Sudan.

Sources: Armed Conflict Location & Event Data Project (ACLED), www.acleddata.com; IISS analysis   ©IISS

Conflict Overview

Following two lengthy civil wars (1955–72 and 1983–2005), South Sudan formally separated from Sudan in July 2011, taking three-quarters of Sudan's oil with it. In 2005, the Sudan People's Liberation Movement/Army (SPLM/A), the largest rebel force in the Second Sudanese Civil War, split into two wings: a political wing (the SPLM), which has ruled the country since its independence in 2011, and a military wing (the SPLA), with many militia and rebel splinter groups absorbed into the new army. The military ruptured in December 2013 amid heightened tensions among South Sudan's fractious elite, instigating a protracted civil war. Massacres of ethnic Nuer civilians by security forces and ethnic Dinka paramilitary soldiers in the capital city, Juba, led to the disintegration of the military, unleashing waves of retaliatory violence against government strongholds in Jonglei, Unity and Upper Nile states.[1] Military defectors combined into the SPLM/A–In Opposition (SPLM/A–IO) rebellion and initially made gains against the government, which relied on Ugandan military support to secure Juba.

In August 2015, the government reluctantly signed the Agreement on the Resolution of the Conflict in the Republic of South Sudan (ARCSS) with the splintering SPLM/A–IO. The power-sharing agreement collapsed in mid-2016, instigating a more complex wave of conflict in the southern and western regions. As the SPLM/A–IO continued to fragment, new rebel groups emerged, notably the National Salvation Front in the southern Equatoria region.

The Revitalised ARCSS (R-ARCSS) was brokered by Uganda and Sudan and was signed in September 2018 by an increasingly confident government and desperate opposition. The R-ARCSS reshaped rather than resolved the conflict, with the government exploiting divisions in the SPLM/A–IO to encourage defections to the military (renamed the South Sudan People's Defence Forces), while counter-insurgency operations against smaller rebel groups continued. Meanwhile,

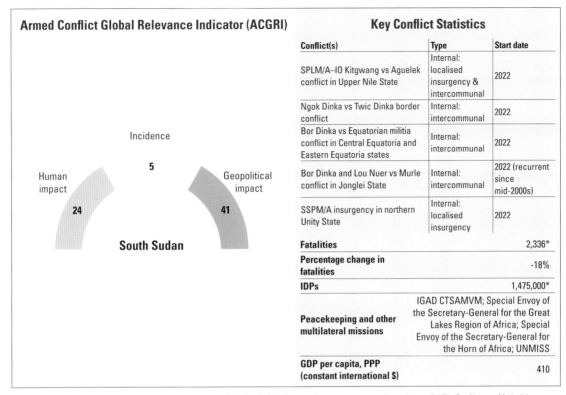

Armed Conflict Global Relevance Indicator (ACGRI)

Incidence

5

Human impact   24

Geopolitical impact   41

South Sudan

Key Conflict Statistics

Conflict(s)	Type	Start date
SPLM/A–IO Kitgwang vs Aguelek conflict in Upper Nile State	Internal: localised insurgency & intercommunal	2022
Ngok Dinka vs Twic Dinka border conflict	Internal: intercommunal	2022
Bor Dinka vs Equatorian militia conflict in Central Equatoria and Eastern Equatoria states	Internal: intercommunal	2022
Bor Dinka and Lou Nuer vs Murle conflict in Jonglei State	Internal: intercommunal	2022 (recurrent since mid-2000s)
SSPM/A insurgency in northern Unity State	Internal: localised insurgency	2022
Fatalities		2,336*
Percentage change in fatalities		-18%
IDPs		1,475,000*
Peacekeeping and other multilateral missions		IGAD CTSAMVM; Special Envoy of the Secretary-General for the Great Lakes Region of Africa; Special Envoy of the Secretary-General for the Horn of Africa; UNMISS
GDP per capita, PPP (constant international $)		410

ACGRI pillars: IISS calculation based on multiple sources for 2022 and 2023 (scale: 0–100), except for some cases according to data availability. See Notes on Methodology and Data Appendix for all variables and further details on Key Conflict Statistics. *The Abyei area is not included in sources for South Sudan: ACLED (fatalities) and Internal Displacement Monitoring Centre (IDPs).

soaring localised violence (often organised by political and military players) has followed the flagging implementation of the agreement, as South Sudan continues its tumultuous transition towards a post-oil economy and instability deters the investment needed to establish oilfields to offset declining production.[2]

Across decades of war, the causes and dynamics of the overarching conflict have remained similar, even as smaller conflicts involving an array of militias and splinter groups have further complicated the picture. The centre–periphery tensions and marginalisation of South Sudanese peoples in Sudan have been reproduced within the new country, while contending elites have sought to augment their financial and political power through engineering subnational conflict and exploiting regional turbulence in the Horn of Africa.

Conflict Update

Across the reporting period, the security situation continued to deteriorate in much of South Sudan, driven in part by the 2021 split in the SPLM/A–IO. The divide saw two senior commanders – Simon Gatwech Dual (an ethnic Lou Nuer) and Johnson Olonyi Thabo (an ethnic Shilluk) – establishing a breakaway group known as the Kitgwang faction in an effort to unseat the SPLM/A–IO's leader, Riek Machar. In January 2022, the two Kitgwang leaders signed separate peace agreements with the government. However, violence increased in parts of Unity and Upper Nile states over the following months, as some SPLM/A–IO loyalists defected to the Kitgwang faction, hoping to use the military-integration provisions of the agreements to bolster their power.

Following gains against remaining SPLM/A–IO loyalists in February and April 2022, amidst a brewing rivalry between the two Kitgwang commanders, Gatwech became increasingly dissatisfied with the terms of the peace agreement he had signed.[3] By August, the Kitgwang faction had fractured in two, with ethnic Nuer troops aligning with Gatwech

Sub-Saharan Africa

and ethnic Shilluk troops remaining loyal to Olonyi's Aguelek forces, who received backing from the government. This schism incited further violence in Upper Nile State, which had been an epicentre of the 2013–18 civil war. In November, thousands of Nuer militiamen advanced on the Shilluk capital of Kodok in Fashoda county, killing 180 Shilluk internally displaced persons at Aburoc camp and re-displacing thousands to Kodok.[4] The government belatedly deployed forces to Kodok, stalling the militia advance.

Escalating insecurity has not threatened President Salva Kiir's regime and may have even helped it further consolidate control in advance of general elections that were postponed to December 2024. Emboldened by the continued fragmentation of the SPLM/A–IO, which is the only signatory to the R-ARCSS that is capable of challenging the ruling SPLM party, the regime has taken steps to further marginalise Machar. In October 2022, Machar was formally expelled from the ruling party, and in March 2023, Kiir fired the SPLM/A–IO's defence minister, Angelina Teny (who is Machar's senior wife), and unilaterally removed control of the powerful defence ministry from the SPLM/A–IO.

In South Sudan's northwest, intense violence continued in Warrap State and the disputed Abyei area. In late June 2022, clashes between the military and a Rek Dinka militia killed 232 people (including 165 soldiers) in the Rualbet area of Tonj North county, with dozens more civilians killed or sexually abused during a subsequent military deployment to the area.[5] This violence represents a continuation of tensions between residents of Warrap State and South Sudanese authorities that have grown in the shadow of rivalries between powerful military and political elites in the state. Meanwhile, clashes between Twic Dinka and Ngok Dinka militias that began in February 2022 over control of the border town of Agok reignited in October, with an ensuing cease-fire agreement collapsing amid renewed violence in January.[6] The South Sudan People's Movement/Army (SSPM/A) rebel group also launched an audacious attack in nearby Mayom county in July 2022, killing the county commissioner, who was the brother of the powerful presidential security adviser Tut Gatluak.[7] Counter-insurgency operations were launched immediately following the attack, while four rebel commanders were executed by security services.[8]

Finally, in the southeast, Pibor county was attacked by a large number of ethnic Bor Dinka and Lou Nuer militiamen (the latter reportedly supported by Nuer militiamen from Ethiopia's Gambella region) in December 2022 and January 2023, with alleged reprisal attacks by ethnic Murle militias reported in parts of northern Jonglei State.[9] These mark the latest episode of ethnically organised violence in Jonglei State, which has been escalating since the mid-2000s, fuelled by elite agendas, ethnic polarisation and the erosion of livelihoods and customary justice mechanisms.

Conflict Parties

South Sudan People's Defence Forces (SSPDF), formerly Sudan People's Liberation Movement/Army (SPLM/A)/ Transitional Government of National Unity (TGoNU)/South Sudan armed forces	
Strength: The SSPDF's precise size is unclear. Official payroll figures state that over 330,000 people are employed by the defence ministry as a whole, though informal figures suggest the SSPDF comprises at most 90,000 soldiers.[10]	**History:** The SPLM/A was founded in 1983 to fight for South Sudan's autonomy. The army fractured at the outset of South Sudan's civil war in 2013. In 2018, the SPLA was renamed the SSPDF, and it has since embarked on a slow integration process with demobilised armed groups that signed the R-ARCSS.
Areas of operation: Uneven presence throughout the country, with control of several areas outsourced to ex-militia commanders (including in Unity and Upper Nile states).	**Objectives:** Defend the sovereignty and territorial integrity of South Sudan.
Leadership: Salva Kiir (commander-in-chief) and Gen. Santino Deng Wol (chief of defence forces).	**Opponents:** National Salvation Front–Thomas Cirillo (NAS–TC), SSPM/A and South Sudan United Front/Army (SSUF/A).
Structure: 11 divisions, including Presidential Guard (Division 9), Mechanised (Division 10) and a Division 11 based in Warrap State in breach of the 2018 R-ARCSS. There are three services (ground force, air force and defence, and riverine forces), in addition to military intelligence.	**Affiliates/allies:** National Security Service (NSS) and SPLM/A–IO Aguelek faction in Upper Nile State. SSPDF elements have links to ethnic militias in several areas on an ad hoc basis. Regionally, the army has close connections to the Ugandan and Sudanese armies and maintains links to several Sudanese rebel groups.

South Sudan People's Defence Forces (SSPDF), formerly Sudan People's Liberation Movement/Army (SPLM/A)/ Transitional Government of National Unity (TGoNU)/South Sudan armed forces

Resources/capabilities: Predominantly an infantry force equipped with heavy artillery, tanks, armoured fighting vehicles and supported by some attack helicopters and amphibious vehicles, some of which are grounded. Significant off-budget security spending is believed to occur, much of which is routed through the Office of the President.

National Security Service (NSS)

Strength: At least 15,000.

Areas of operation: Nationwide, with a strong presence in Juba.

Leadership: Akol Koor (director-general, Internal Security Bureau, ISB) and Simon Yien (director-general, General Intelligence Bureau, GIB).

Structure: The ISB is responsible for internal security and maintains a sizeable Operations Division and a Protection Division, which serve as elite military units to secure critical infrastructure. The GIB is tasked with external affairs and has a presence in several neighbouring countries. Both branches appear to maintain small death squads.

History: The NSS was established in 2011, though several prototype intelligence units emerged within the SPLM/A during the 1990s, which were expanded and trained with assistance from Sudan's notorious National Intelligence and Security Service (NISS) after 2005.[11] Over the course of the war, the NSS became increasingly powerful and militarised.

Objectives: Regime security, intelligence and counter-intelligence.

Opponents: Though tasked with protecting the regime, concerns about Koor's growing power led President Kiir to augment SSPDF Military Intelligence as a counterweight to the NSS. This resulted in a proxy war between the two in Warrap State in 2020 that was won by Koor.

Affiliates/allies: The NSS has organised pro-government militias during the civil war, though it demonstrates a capacity to subvert the actions of rivals within the government and military through sponsoring militias. Koor revived links with Ethiopian security services in 2021.

Resources/capabilities: Small arms and light weapons. The NSS is better resourced and equipped than other parts of the security sector, possibly due to its significance to regime security, as well as its connections to business – especially the oil sector.

Sudan People's Liberation Movement/Army–In Opposition (SPLM/A–IO)

Strength: Unclear. At the outset of the civil war, the SPLM/A–IO had around 40,000 fighters. Following the R-ARCSS, SPLM/A–IO forces likely comprised at most 35,000, but the 2021 split and recent defections will have reduced this number considerably.

Areas of operation: Following defections beginning mid-2019, the SPLM/A–IO's territorial scope was reduced to several non-contiguous pockets. Current areas occupied include Leer county in Unity State; Maban county in Upper Nile State; parts of Western Bahr el Ghazal, Jonglei and Western Equatoria states; and limited parts of Central and Eastern Equatoria states.

Leadership: Riek Machar.

Structure: SPLM/A–IO administrative and geographical structures mostly mirror those of the SPLA at the onset of the 2013 civil war. These structures have been undermined by Machar's efforts to personalise power and his rivalries with military commanders, as well as the uneasy integration of new factions into the rebellion after 2015.

History: The SPLM/A–IO emerged from mass defections in the security sector in 2013. It was initially dominated by ethnic Nuers, who were supplanted by non-Nuer forces after 2015. Since mid-2019, the group has lost several senior commanders and military units, who have defected to or aligned themselves with the government.

Objectives: Prior to the R-ARCSS: remove Kiir from power and govern South Sudan. After the R-ARCSS: secure a favourable position in the new government and the new unified army.

Opponents: SPLM/A–IO Kitgwang (Gatwech faction), SPLM/A–IO Aguelek and NAS–TC.

Affiliates/allies: Nuer militias in parts of Jonglei, Unity and Upper Nile states.

Resources/capabilities: Small arms and light weapons, often taken from government supplies. The SPLM/A–IO has experienced difficulties procuring weapons and ammunition, though it received limited supplies from Sudan during the civil war.[12] The group is likely financed through taxation of trade routes and smuggling.

SPLM/A–IO Kitgwang (Simon Gatwech Dual faction) (also known as Kit-Gwang, Kitgweng)

Strength: Unclear.

Areas of operation: Panyikang county in Upper Nile State, central and southern Unity State, and northern Jonglei State.

Leadership: Simon Gatwech Dual.

Structure: Hybrid military–militia structure. Dispersed ethnic Nuer SPLM/A–IO Kitgwang forces are under the overall command of Gatwech, though, in practice, units operate under local commanders who have ties with specific Nuer clan or sectional militia forces and increasingly fight alongside these militias.

History: In August 2021, senior SPLM/A–IO commanders Gatwech and Olonyi signed the Kitgwang Declaration, announcing the removal of Machar. In January 2022, the

SPLM/A–IO Kitgwang (Simon Gatwech Dual faction) (also known as Kit-Gwang, Kitgweng)

Kitgwang leadership signed two separate peace agreements with the government. In late July 2022, fighting broke out between forces loyal to Gatwech and Olonyi.

Objectives: Reverse the political and military marginalisation of senior commanders and secure Nuer interests.

Opponents: SPLM/A–IO, SSPDF and SPLM/A–IO Aguelek.

Affiliates/allies: Assorted Nuer militias, particularly in northern Jonglei State. Although opposed to the SPLM/A–IO, there has been tactical collaboration between the two forces when fighting Aguelek forces in Upper Nile State.

Resources/capabilities: Small arms and light weapons.

SPLM/A–IO Aguelek faction (also known as Agwelek)

Strength: Unclear.

Areas of operation: Northwestern Upper Nile State.

Leadership: Johnson Olonyi Thabo.

Structure: Hybrid military–militia structure. The Aguelek is in effect a personalised Shilluk militia formed around Olonyi, which has entered into a series of partnerships with the government and rebel factions. Since being pushed out of Panyikang county by Gatwech's forces in 2022, Olonyi has sought to mobilise parts of the Shilluk population.

History: Several Shilluk commanders (including Olonyi) rebelled following the 2010 elections. Olonyi joined South Sudan's military under a 2013 amnesty but rebelled in 2015,

loosely integrating his forces into the SPLM/A–IO. Olonyi signed the Kitgwang Declaration in 2021 and later signed a peace agreement on behalf of the Aguelek faction with the government in 2022.

Objectives: Reverse the political and military marginalisation of senior commanders and secure Shilluk interests.

Opponents: SPLM/A–IO and SPLM/A–IO Kitgwang (Gatwech faction).

Affiliates/allies: SSPDF and Shilluk militia.

Resources/capabilities: Small arms and light weapons, with some material provided by the government.[13]

National Salvation Front–Thomas Cirillo (NAS–TC)

Strength: Unclear.

Areas of operation: Parts of Central and Western Equatoria states, especially around border areas with Uganda and the Democratic Republic of the Congo.

Leadership: Thomas Cirillo Swaka.

Structure: A guerrilla force, which recruits (often forcibly) from southern Equatorian communities. The group was joined initially by some SPLM/A–IO officials who accused Machar of disenfranchising non-Nuers, though several commanders have since established new splinter factions, which are increasingly inactive.

History: Formed in 2017 by Swaka, who defected from the SPLA in February 2017. After rejecting the R-ARCSS in 2018, the NAS–TC became the main active armed opposition to the

government. Since early 2019, intensive counter-insurgency operations by government and SPLM/A–IO forces have weakened the group.

Objectives: Replacement of centralised system of rule under President Kiir with a federal system that allows for greater autonomy of traditionally marginalised groups, particularly in Equatoria.

Opponents: SSPDF and SPLM/A–IO.

Affiliates/allies: Cirillo is chair of the South Sudan Opposition Movements Alliance, and the NAS–TC is the only significant armed group within the alliance. He is based in Addis Ababa, Ethiopia, though Ethiopia does not provide the group with any open support.

Resources/capabilities: Small arms and equipment looted from the SSPDF, mainly during ambushes.

South Sudan People's Movement/Army (SSPM/A)

Strength: Unclear.

Areas of operation: As of mid-2022, the border region between Mayom county in Unity State and Twic county in Warrap State, with a presence in West Kordofan State in Sudan. Following counter-insurgency operations, the current location(s) of the group is unknown.

Leadership: Stephen Buay Rolnyang.

Structure: Hybrid military–militia structure, comprising Bul Nuer militiamen (who are among the most militarised of South Sudan's Nuer clans) under the command of Buay and his deputies.

History: Buay was arrested in 2018 and expelled from the army for alleged plans to defect. Buay rebelled in May 2021,

aligning himself with ex-army chief Paul Malong Awan before splitting from Malong. The SSPM/A was involved in a string of attacks in July 2022, before being subject to counter-insurgency operations.

Objectives: Unclear. Buay appears to be motivated by personal grievances, which are equivalated with grievances against the Unity State authorities and President Kiir's regime.

Opponents: SSPDF.

Affiliates/allies: Buay made overtures in October 2022 to Malong, Cirillo and Gatwech in a bid to construct an anti-government alliance. This was provisionally accepted by Malong but rejected by Cirillo.

Resources/capabilities: Small arms and light weapons.

United Nations Mission in the Republic of South Sudan (UNMISS)

Strength: 17,954 total personnel, including 13,221 peacekeepers and 1,468 police (as of June 2022).[14]

Areas of operation: Across the country.

Leadership: Nicholas Haysom (special representative of the secretary-general for South Sudan and head of UNMISS).

Structure: UNMISS comprises a sizeable military, a smaller police contingent and civilian components.

History: Established upon South Sudan's independence in 2011. Under SRSG Hilde Johnson, the mission was primarily tasked with preventing and resolving violence and supporting the government's state-building efforts. During the civil war, the mission oversaw Protection of Civilians sites in cities that experienced heavy fighting and ethnic killings.

Objectives: After the war began in 2013, the UNMISS mandate shifted towards civilian protection, human-rights monitoring and supporting humanitarian aid. Since the 2018 R-ARCSS, UNMISS has reoriented its political activities to focus on implementing the agreement, with a new emphasis on upcoming elections as of 2022.

Opponents: While neutral, UNMISS has experienced numerous violations of its status-of-forces agreement with the South Sudanese government, including attacks against its personnel and frequent denial-of-access incidents. These incidents have occurred to a lesser extent with SPLM/A–IO rebels.

Affiliates/allies: N/A.

Resources/capabilities: Approved budget (July 2021–June 2022): US$1.2 billion.[15]

Notes

1   John Young, 'A Fractious Rebellion: Inside the SPLM–IO', Small Arms Survey, September 2015.

2   Joshua Craze, 'Making Markets: South Sudan's War Economy in the 21st Century', World Peace Foundation, United States Institute of Peace, February 2023; and Dan Watson, 'Surface Tension: "Communal" Violence and Elite Ambitions in South Sudan', ACLED, 19 August 2021.

3   Joshua Craze, 'The Periphery Cannot Hold: Upper Nile Since the Signing of the R-ARCSS', Small Arms Survey, November 2022.

4   UN Security Council, 'Situation in South Sudan: Report of the Secretary-General', S/2023/135, 22 February 2023, p. 3.

5   UN General Assembly, 'Technical Assistance and Capacity-building for South Sudan', A/HRC/52/82, 7 February 2023, p. 4.

6   'Twic, Ngok Dinka Agree to Cease Hostilities', Radio Tamazuj, 1 November 2022; and Alhadi Hawari, 'Gov't Urged to Deploy Troops to Abyei–Warrap Border After Killings', Eye Radio, 4 January 2023.

7   'South Sudan Rebels Kill Mayom County Commissioner', *Sudan Tribune*, 22 July 2022.

8   'U.N. Condemns Execution of Four South Sudan Rebels', Reuters, 10 August 2022.

9   Wol Mapal, '56 Killed in Ethnic Violence in Pibor Administrative Area', Eye Radio, 27 December 2022; 'Villages Destroyed as Fighting Intensifies in Pibor', Radio Tamazuj, 26 December 2022; and 'Attack on Civilians at Akobo–Ulang Border Leaves 15 Dead', Radio Tamazuj, 19 March 2023.

10 Republic of South Sudan Ministry of Finance and Planning, 'Approved Budget Fiscal Year 2022–23', p. 15; and Flora McCrone, 'Hollow Promises: The Risks of Military Integration in Western Equatoria', Small Arms Survey, June 2020.

11 Brian Adeba, 'Oversight Mechanisms, Regime Security, and Intelligence Service Autonomy in South Sudan', *Intelligence and National Security*, vol. 35, no. 6, 2020.

12 Conflict Armament Research, 'Weapon Supplies into South Sudan's Civil War: Regional Re-transfers and International Intermediaries', November 2018, pp. 30–3.

13 Joshua Craze, 'Upper Nile Prepares to Return to War', Small Arms Survey, March 2023.

14 'Facts and Figures', UNMISS website.

15 *Ibid.*

Sub-Saharan Africa

ETHIOPIA

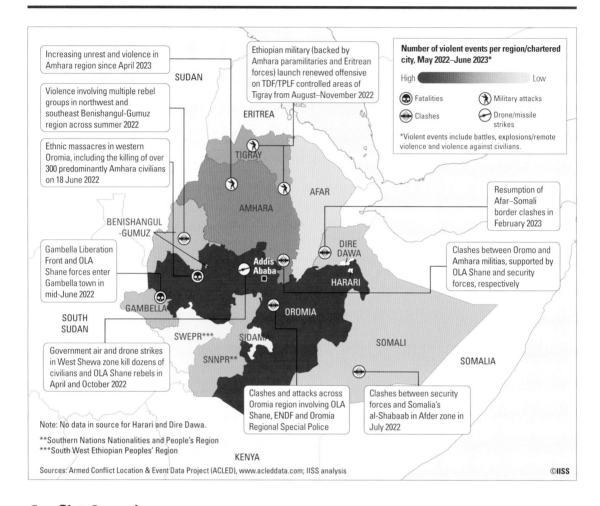

Increasing unrest and violence in Amhara region since April 2023

Violence involving multiple rebel groups in northwest and southeast Benishangul-Gumuz region across summer 2022

Ethnic massacres in western Oromia, including the killing of over 300 predominantly Amhara civilians on 18 June 2022

Ethiopian military (backed by Amhara paramilitaries and Eritrean forces) launch renewed offensive on TDF/TPLF controlled areas of Tigray from August–November 2022

Number of violent events per region/chartered city, May 2022–June 2023*

High ━━━━━━━━━━━━ Low

⊙ Fatalities   ⚔ Military attacks

⊛ Clashes   ⟍ Drone/missile strikes

*Violent events include battles, explosions/remote violence and violence against civilians.

Resumption of Afar–Somali border clashes in February 2023

Gambella Liberation Front and OLA Shane forces enter Gambella town in mid-June 2022

Clashes between Oromo and Amhara militias, supported by OLA Shane and security forces, respectively

Government air and drone strikes in West Shewa zone kill dozens of civilians and OLA Shane rebels in April and October 2022

Clashes and attacks across Oromia region involving OLA Shane, ENDF and Oromia Regional Special Police

Clashes between security forces and Somalia's al-Shabaab in Afder zone in July 2022

Note: No data in source for Harari and Dire Dawa.

**Southern Nations Nationalities and People's Region
***South West Ethiopian Peoples' Region

Sources: Armed Conflict Location & Event Data Project (ACLED), www.acleddata.com; IISS analysis   ©IISS

Conflict Overview

Multiple axes of violent conflict cut across contemporary Ethiopia and have played out at an increasingly dangerous scale during Ethiopia's modern history. Localised grievances – sometimes resulting from historical disenfranchisement and at other times from a selective politicisation of history – have metastasised into ethnically charged border or land disputes, escalating into insurgency during times of national turbulence.[1] Conversely, contestations over control of the state (and its constitutional form) have inflamed provincial disputes, turning subnational flashpoints into national crises (e.g., regarding the expansion of Addis Ababa into Oromia region and the contested borders of Tigray

region). Such conflicts are part of a long-running cycle in which the state experiences phases of dismantlement and (eventual) reassembly. These phases have occurred in parallel with a growing ethnic consciousness among marginalised groups, which has rubbed against attempts at promoting a singular Ethiopian national identity.

Ethiopia's current turmoil stems from the transition from the previous order led by the Tigray People's Liberation Front (TPLF) since 1991 to the rule of Prime Minister Abiy Ahmed, who came to power as a reformist in 2018. Under Tigrayan Prime Minister Meles Zenawi (1995–2012), the TPLF oversaw the establishment of a federal system organised around

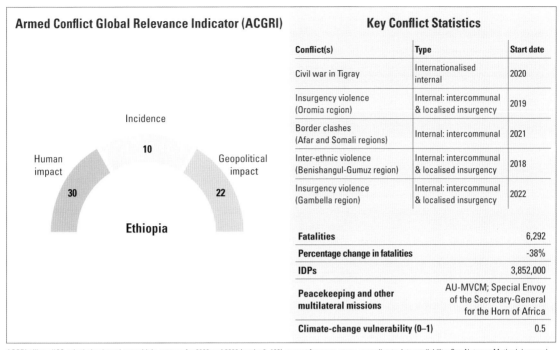

Armed Conflict Global Relevance Indicator (ACGRI)

Incidence
10
Human impact
30
Geopolitical impact
22

Ethiopia

Key Conflict Statistics

Conflict(s)	Type	Start date
Civil war in Tigray	Internationalised internal	2020
Insurgency violence (Oromia region)	Internal: intercommunal & localised insurgency	2019
Border clashes (Afar and Somali regions)	Internal: intercommunal	2021
Inter-ethnic violence (Benishangul-Gumuz region)	Internal: intercommunal & localised insurgency	2018
Insurgency violence (Gambella region)	Internal: intercommunal & localised insurgency	2022

Fatalities	6,292
Percentage change in fatalities	-38%
IDPs	3,852,000
Peacekeeping and other multilateral missions	AU-MVCM; Special Envoy of the Secretary-General for the Horn of Africa
Climate-change vulnerability (0–1)	0.5

ACGRI pillars: IISS calculation based on multiple sources for 2022 and 2023 (scale: 0–100), except for some cases according to data availability. See Notes on Methodology and Data Appendix for all variables and further details on Key Conflict Statistics.

ethnicity, onto which a corresponding party system (the Ethiopian People's Revolutionary Democratic Front, EPRDF) was grafted. The EPRDF system was gradually wrenched apart as the federal government intensified its efforts to control restive regions that were gravitating away from the centre. The TPLF's dominance within the EPRDF diminished with the death of Zenawi in 2012. What followed were a series of violently suppressed protest movements in Amhara and Oromia regions in 2015–16 and 2018, amid political manoeuvring by ethnic Amhara and Oromo elites.

In April 2018, Abiy – an Oromo politician and former military-intelligence officer – was installed as prime minister and set about liberalising Ethiopia's politics and economy while promoting a homogeneous pan-Ethiopian identity. Most significantly, Abiy signed a peace agreement with Eritrea in 2018, officially ending the frozen conflict between the two countries since 2000, but heightening tensions with the ousted TPLF in the process. In late 2019, Abiy dismantled the EPRDF, replacing it with the Prosperity Party, which the TPLF declined to join. In November 2020, amid worsening subnational violence and a brewing constitutional crisis, the TPLF attacked the Ethiopian National Defence Force's (ENDF) Northern Command, leading to war, widespread starvation and serious human-rights abuses (notably mass rape and displacement) in northern Ethiopia.[2]

Conflict Update

During the reporting period, hostilities re-escalated in Tigray from August–October 2022, until an agreement between the two conflict parties ended the civil war in November. The TPLF armed forces (also known as the Tigray Defence Force, TDF) withstood initial advances by the ENDF and its Amhara paramilitary allies but gradually lost control of critical positions, particularly against Eritrean forces. Ultimately, the ENDF succeeded in exhausting the TDF's capacity for resistance, though it and its allies likely sustained heavy losses.[3] Total civilian casualties in the two years of war remain unclear but are estimated in the hundreds of thousands when indirect deaths are taken into account.[4]

By late October 2022, the military situation had become bleak for the TDF. In an unexpected move, the federal government and the TPLF signed the

Agreement for Lasting Peace Through a Permanent Cessation of Hostilities on 2 November, following African Union-led talks in Pretoria.[5] The agreement envisages the disarmament and demobilisation of the TDF in exchange for the restoration of basic services to Tigray and resumption of humanitarian aid. The TPLF's designation as a terrorist group was lifted in March 2023, paving the way for participation in an interim Tigrayan regional government, which was inaugurated under the leadership of Getachew Reda.[6]

Considerable opacity surrounded the Pretoria talks. The Abiy regime had appeared intent on pursuing a military victory and it seemed to be caught off guard by the rapid progress made in Pretoria and the concessions made by TPLF negotiators. The result has been an incomplete and vague peace process – lacking detailed provisions on matters such as transitional justice and reconciliation – that has nevertheless largely halted violent conflict in Tigray.

However disadvantageous the Pretoria agreement may be to the TPLF, it provides routes through which the TPLF can reconstitute itself as a political force over time. Conversely, the agreement relieves immediate pressures on the Abiy government but exacerbates longer-term problems involving influential constituencies opposed to the agreement, namely Eritrea and Amhara nationalists, whose interests are converging. For instance, in April 2023, growing friction between Amhara region and the federal government was exemplified by demonstrations and (limited) clashes in Amhara after the government announced that regional Special Police forces were to be absorbed into federal security structures.[7] Low-level clashes involving the *fano* and local militias continued the following month and escalated significantly by late July. In early August, the *fano* briefly occupied the regional capital of Bahir Dar and the city of Gondar, with clashes reported across numerous rural and urban areas in Amhara region, including towns on the main highway between Addis Ababa and Tigray. The Abiy regime currently operates in

survival mode, continually revising political alliances to stay afloat, and it will need to engage in a careful rebalancing of its relationships with ethno-political blocs in the wake of the peace agreement.

From a security standpoint, the diversion of military forces to Tigray contributed to a security vacuum elsewhere in Ethiopia, compounding the multi-layered conflict in Oromia. This vacuum was exploited by the Oromo Liberation Army (OLA) insurgency, amid incursions by armed groups from neighbouring regions (including the Amhara *fano* militia).[8] This resulted in escalating violence in parts of Oromia and adjacent areas of Amhara, including a number of high-profile massacres and deadly ENDF airstrikes in West Shewa zone in Oromia.[9] On 25 April 2023, peace talks between the federal government and OLA began in Tanzania, though they ended several days later without an agreement. Fighting between the OLA and government intensified in parts of Oromia in the wake of the talks.

Concurrently, Ethiopia's peripheries experienced shifts in control between insurgents and security forces. In the southwest, Gambella town was attacked and briefly occupied by the recently formed Gambella Liberation Front (GLF, operating alongside the OLA). Dozens of people died during the fighting, with at least 50 civilians killed by government forces after the rebels withdrew.[10] In Benishangul-Gumuz, OLA and ethnic Gumuz militias gained ground in April and May 2022, though they were dislodged from several villages during a government counter-offensive in June.[11]

Finally, in late July 2022, serious clashes between security forces and al-Shabaab insurgents from Somalia were reported in the eastern Somali region, with authorities claiming to have killed upwards of 200 insurgents.[12] Fighting occurred along the Somalia border and deep into Afder zone in Somali region (approximately 150 kilometres into Ethiopia), raising concerns regarding the ability of the fragmenting Ethiopian security system to contain al-Shabaab.

Conflict Parties

Ethiopian National Defence Force (ENDF)	
Strength: Rapid expansion from 135,000 in mid-2020 to approximately 503,000.[13] However, there are no comprehensive and reliable casualty figures for the August–	November 2022 fighting in Tigray, where it is likely the military sustained significant casualties.
	Areas of operation: Uneven presence across the country.

Ethiopian National Defence Force (ENDF)

Leadership: Prime Minister Abiy Ahmed (commander-in-chief) and Gen. Berhanu Jula (chief of general staff).

Structure: The ENDF is designed to conduct both conventional war and counter-insurgency missions. It is organised into six regional commands (two of which were established in 2020, reflecting the increasing internal focus and activities of the ENDF). Additionally, there is a Special Forces and Presidential Guard division.

History: Grew out of a coalition of rebels spearheaded by the TPLF, which removed the Derg regime in 1991. The ENDF underwent a lengthy defence-transformation process following the 1998–2000 war with Eritrea. Once a major contributing country to United Nations peacekeeping missions, numbers of ENDF peacekeepers have declined sharply since 2021.

Objectives: Maintain Ethiopia's territorial integrity and fight armed opposition/secessionist movements inside the country.

Opponents: OLA, *fano* and minor regional separatist movements. A permanent cessation-of-hostilities agreement was reached with the TPLF/TDF in November 2022, effectively bringing an end to the two-year civil war.

Affiliates/allies: China, Eritrea, Iran, Russia, Somalia, Turkiye and the United Arab Emirates (UAE).

Resources/capabilities: Around 220 Soviet-era tanks, 20 attack aircraft, 18 attack helicopters and a small number of uninhabited aerial vehicles. Ethiopia's defence budget more than tripled from US$430 million in 2022 to US$1.5 billion in 2023 as a result of the Tigrayan war and the deteriorating security situation.

Tigray People's Liberation Front (TPLF)/Tigray Defence Force (TDF)

Strength: Unclear. At the outset of conflict, the TPLF commanded around 30,000 Special Police paramilitaries and was supported by tens of thousands of village-militia members and a small number of ENDF soldiers. These numbers will have been affected by attrition during various rounds of combat, as well as recruitment and conscription.[14]

Areas of operation: Central and eastern areas of Tigray region, with previous incursions into Amhara and Afar regions.

Leadership: Getachew Reda (president of the Interim Regional Administration of Tigray) and Gen. Tadesse Werede Tesfay (TDF commander-in-chief).

Structure: The TDF is the armed wing of the TPLF and comprises the Tigray Regional Special Police (paramilitary forces organised in a conventional military structure); local militias (organised into groups of 30–50 at village level under locally elected leadership); and Tigrayan ENDF defectors.

History: The TDF emerged from the build-up of forces in Tigray prior to the conflict in 2020. After initial losses, the TDF regained control of much of Tigray region in 2021, advancing into Amhara and Afar regions. After signing the Agreement for Lasting Peace Through a Permanent Cessation of Hostilities, the TDF relinquished heavy weaponry in January 2023 and began demobilising in May.

Objectives: During the conflict, the TPLF/TDF sought to defend the Tigray regional government. Since November 2022, the TPLF has sought to secure Tigray's interests in an agreement with the federal government.

Opponents: ENDF (prior to November 2022), Eritrean Defence Forces (EDF), Amhara militia and Amhara Regional Special Police.

Affiliates/allies: Established an office in the Sudanese capital of Khartoum in late February 2021. In mid-2021, the TDF and the OLA signed a military-cooperation deal, though this alliance appears to have been suspended.

Resources/capabilities: The TDF seized significant amounts of ENDF equipment (including tanks, artillery and long-range rockets) at the outset of the conflict, and it has replenished its military equipment and ammunition through attacks on opposing forces and seizures of weapons caches.

Regional Special Police (Liyu Police, also referred to as 'Liyu Haile' or 'Special Force')

Strength: As of 2021, by region: Addis Ababa (numbers unknown; formed in late 2019), Afar (2,000–3,000), Amhara (5,000), Benishangul-Gumuz (3,000–4,000), Dire Dawa (2,000–3,000), Gambella (2,000–3,000), Oromia (9,000–10,000), Sidama (numbers unknown), Southern Nations Nationalities and People's Region (SNNPR) (4,000–5,000), Somali (15,000) and Tigray (27,000–28,000).[15]

Areas of operation: Special Police forces have been formed in almost all regions, although the scale of recruitment varies by region.

Leadership: Special Police are under the control of regional presidents.

Structure: Formed into paramilitary units, which at times work alongside federal or volunteer *kebele* (village) militia. Despite being colloquially referred to as the 'Special Force', the Special Police are not elite commando units (which are instead part of the ENDF).

History: Somali region formed a Special Police force in 2007, with other regions gradually following suit.[16] After 2019, force numbers increased in areas where neighbouring regions posed a threat (specifically Amhara, Oromia and Tigray regions). In April 2023, federal authorities announced the Special Police would be disbanded and absorbed into federal security forces.

Objectives: Preserve public order and peace within the region, as constitutionally mandated.

Opponents: Armed political opposition, local *shifta* (armed bandits) and neighbouring regional Special Police and militia.

Affiliates/allies: Varies by region.

Resources/capabilities: Funded from regional police budgets; equipped with small arms and transport vehicles (and, in some circumstances, riot gear).

Oromo Liberation Army (OLA), previously the Oromo Liberation Front (OLF)

Strength: Over 2,000 estimated OLA fighters in 2020. This number may have increased significantly since then, but new estimates are not official.[17]

Areas of operation: Oromia region (particularly in the west, as well as parts of the south and centre) and some adjoining areas of Amhara region. OLA activity has also been intermittently reported in parts of Benishangul-Gumuz region and SNNPR.

Leadership: The OLA no longer comes under Dawud Ibsa's political leadership of the OLF and has split into several armed factions under local leadership. The Western Command is led by Kumsa Diriba (also known as Jaal Maaro), the Southern Command by Gemechu Aboye and the Central Command by Sagni Negassa.[18]

Structure: Locally organised into loose groupings of fighters, spread across at least seven commands. An OLF–OLA High Command ostensibly exists to coordinate the commands, though in practice each command is largely autonomous.

History: The OLF was established in 1973 by Oromo nationalists. In mid-2018, the OLF signed a peace agreement with the government. The OLA officially split from the OLF political party in April 2019, amid deteriorating security in Oromia and concerns over demobilisation. The government refers to the OLA as OLA Shane/Shene ('the five').

Objectives: Oromo self-determination.

Opponents: ENDF and regional Special Police.

Affiliates/allies: Until 2018, Eritrea. Following the rapprochement between Eritrea and Ethiopia this support ceased and the OLA in Oromia survived on local support and resources. The OLA entered into a formal alliance with the TPLF (alongside several smaller movements) in late 2021, which is now defunct.

Resources/capabilities: The OLA acts clandestinely and is weak in military terms. It is equipped with small arms.

Fano

Strength: Unclear.

Areas of operation: Amhara region; Metekel zone in Benishangul-Gumuz region; and Horo Guduru Welega, East Welega and North Shewa zones of Oromia region. The *fano* is also present in parts of Tigray region that are disputed with Amhara region.

Leadership: Unclear local leadership, with the group possessing no formal command structure.

Structure: Locally organised into loose groupings of fighters with no coherent structure, comprising ethnic Amhara militias and former members of the Amhara Regional Special Police (which was disbanded in April 2023).

History: Historically, *fano* has referred both to nineteenth-century free peasants and to 1930s-era nationalist forces fighting Italian occupation. The term was revived by Amhara youth during anti-TPLF protests and post-2018 by ethno-nationalist militias. The *fano* supported the government during the 2020–22 Tigray War, though it was the subject of a May 2022 crackdown by authorities.

Objectives: Promote ethnic Amhara interests, including the territorial expansion of Amhara region and the safety of Amhara settlers across Ethiopia.

Opponents: ENDF, TPLF/TDF, and Oromo and Gumuz militias.

Affiliates/allies: Former Amhara Regional Special Police.

Resources/capabilities: Unknown.

Gambella Liberation Front (GLF)

Strength: Unclear.

Areas of operation: Gambella region.

Leadership: Gatluak Buom Pal.

Structure: Recruited mainly from the ethnic Nuer community of Gambella, with possible links to the co-ethnic eastern Jikany Nuer clan on the South Sudanese side of the common border. Organised into a loose band of young people, whose only major operation has been conducted in conjunction with the OLA.

History: The group emerged following the 2021 Gambella regional elections, citing irregularities, malpractice and grievances against the leadership in Gambella. It also highlighted localised insecurity (specifically regarding ethnic

Murle raids). In June 2022, the group attacked and briefly occupied Gambella town, with assistance from OLA fighters.

Objectives: Replacing the Gambella regional leadership, reversing the marginalisation and underdevelopment of the region.

Opponents: ENDF and regional Special Police.

Affiliates/allies: OLA. Gatluak Buom is based in the Sudanese capital of Khartoum, but it is not clear whether this necessarily indicates Sudanese support for the GLF, given that many co-ethnic rebel or militia leaders from the South Sudanese side of the border also reside in Khartoum.

Resources/capabilities: Unclear, though likely small arms, alongside any weapons that may have been captured during the June 2022 raid on Gambella town.

Eritrean Defence Forces (EDF)

Strength: Increased from an estimated 201,750 active personnel in 2021–22 to 301,750 in 2022–23, most likely due to

a general mobilisation that accompanied the resumption of hostilities in Tigray during the reporting period.

Eritrean Defence Forces (EDF)

Areas of operation: Since November 2020, the EDF has been present across Tigray, though it has made partial withdrawals (usually to border areas) at several stages of the conflict. The EDF is reported to still be present in Tigray since the November 2022 Agreement for Lasting Peace Through a Permanent Cessation of Hostilities, though in smaller numbers.

Leadership: President Isaias Afwerki (commander-in-chief) and Maj.-Gen. Filipos Weldeyohanes (chief of staff).

Structure: The EDF comprises mostly conscripts. Reservists were called up in 2020 and 2022, during EDF operations in Tigray. The army is made up of approximately 41 divisions (up to 20 of which have been present in Tigray) and divided between five military zones, largely covering the border with Ethiopia.

History: The EDF was formed after Eritrea's separation from Ethiopia in 1993 but has its roots in the former Eritrean People's

Liberation Front rebellion. The EDF has since engaged in two full-scale wars (the 1998–2000 Ethiopian–Eritrean War and the 2020–22 Tigray War) and various border conflicts.

Objectives: Maintain Eritrea's territorial integrity and fight armed opposition/secessionist movements inside the country.

Opponents: Complex relationship with Sudan.

Affiliates/allies: Ethiopia (since 2018), Saudi Arabia, Somalia and the UAE.

Resources/capabilities: The scale of the Eritrean defence budget is unknown. Due to prolonged UN sanctions (lifted in November 2018), much of Eritrea's military equipment still comprises outdated Soviet-era systems, which will have resulted in serviceability issues. The navy remains capable of only limited coastal-patrol and interception operations.

Notes

[1] For instance, in Benishangul-Gumuz region and along the border between Afar and Somali regions.

[2] UN Human Rights Council, 'Report of the International Commission of Human Rights Experts on Ethiopia', A/HRC/51/46, 19 September 2022.

[3] Gerrit Kurtz, 'Sustaining Peace in Ethiopia', German Institute for International and Security Affairs (SWP), 14 March 2023; and Alex de Waal, 'Facing Famine, Tigray Concedes to Ethiopian Government, and Abiy', Responsible Statecraft, 16 November 2022.

[4] 'Tigray Death Toll Could Be as High as 600,000, African Union Envoy Says', The National, 16 January 2023.

[5] Owiso Owiso, 'The Ethiopia–Tigray Permanent Cessation of Hostilities Agreement and the Question of Accountability for International Crimes', Just Security, 28 November 2022.

[6] African Union, 'Agreement for Lasting Peace Through a Permanent Cessation of Hostilities Between the Government of the Federal Democratic Republic of Ethiopia and the Tigray People's Liberation Front (TPLF)', 2 November 2022; and African Union, 'Declaration of the Senior Commanders on the Modalities for the Implementation of the Agreement for Lasting Peace Through a Permanent Cessation of Hostilities Between the Government of the Federal Democratic Republic of Ethiopia (FDRE) and the Tigray People's Liberation Front (TPLF)', 12 November 2022.

[7] 'Abiy Disarms Regional Forces and Riles His Old Backers', Africa Confidential, vol. 64, no. 9, 20 April 2023.

[8] Damena Abebe, 'Conflict Trend Analysis: Western Oromia: March 2023', Rift Valley Institute, 2023.

[9] Amnesty International, 'Ethiopia: Authorities Must Investigate Massacre of Ethnic Amhara in Tole', 21 July 2022.

[10] 'Gov't Forces Engaged With Gambella, Oromo Armed Groups in Ongoing Exchange of Gunfire in Gambella City; Gunshots Heard in Two Towns in Western Oromia', Addis Standard, 14 June 2022; 'At Least 50 Civilians Killed in Extra-judicial Execution by Security Forces, Armed Groups in Gambella: New Report', Addis Standard, 29 September 2022; and Henry Wilkins, 'What's Behind Violence in Ethiopia's "Other" Conflict?', VOA, 2 September 2022.

[11] Tsegaye Birhanu, 'Conflict Trend Analysis: Benishangul-Gumuz Regional State: May–November 2022', Rift Valley Institute, 2022.

[12] 'Ethiopia Says Military Action Against Al-Shabaab Continued "Accompanied by Victory", Hundreds Killed, Weapons Seized', Addis Standard, 28 July 2022; and Caleb Weiss and Ryan O'Farrell, 'Puzzles Deepen in the Context of Shabaab's Attempted Ethiopian Invasion', Long War Journal, 28 July 2022.

[13] IISS, The Military Balance 2023 (Abingdon: Routledge for the IISS, 2023), pp. 420, 424.

[14] Author interviews, 2023.

[15] IISS, The Armed Conflict Survey 2021 (Abingdon: Routledge for the IISS, 2021), p. 238.

[16] European Institute of Peace, 'The Special Police in Ethiopia', October 2021.

[17] IISS, The Armed Conflict Survey 2021, p. 238.

[18] Abebe, 'Conflict Trend Analysis: Western Oromia: March 2023', p. 7.

SOMALIA

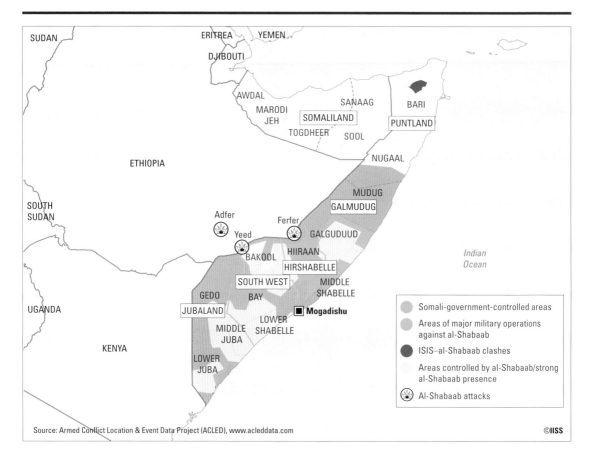

Source: Armed Conflict Location & Event Data Project (ACLED), www.acleddata.com   ©IISS

Conflict Overview

Since 1991, Somalia has been affected by a pro-longed civil war, resulting in continued instability and insecurity. The conflict started after the collapse of Siad Barre's regime, when Islamist forces began expanding across the country, mainly via the Islamic Courts Union (ICU), which established sharia-based courts and controlled territory with its militias. In 2006, the ICU took control of Mogadishu, establishing itself as the de facto ruling authority of Somalia, despite the existence of the internationally supported Transitional Federal Government (TFG). With Mogadishu's fall, the TFG's leadership requested military support from Ethiopia to help regain control of the country, which became a turning point in the conflict.

While the Ethiopian–TFG military campaign made rapid progress and quickly dismantled the

ICU, it also inadvertently radicalised large sections of Somali society, leading to the rise of the Islamic insurgent group al-Shabaab. Al-Shabaab's successful military counter-offensives against the Ethiopian–TFG coalition and its growing alignment with al-Qaeda's ideology eventually resulted in the group consolidating its presence in Somalia and formalising its allegiance to al-Qaeda in 2012. Since then, international concerns regarding al-Shabaab's expansion have made Somalia a focus for country- and multinational-led counter-terrorism and stabilisation initiatives.

In March 2007, the African Union (AU) deployed a peacekeeping mission to Somalia (AU Mission in Somalia, AMISOM) to support the development of the TFG's institutional infrastructure, train Somali military forces and facilitate the delivery of

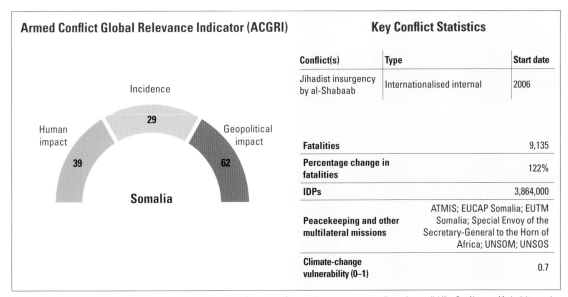

Armed Conflict Global Relevance Indicator (ACGRI)

Incidence

29

Human impact

Geopolitical impact

39   62

Somalia

Key Conflict Statistics

Conflict(s)	Type	Start date
Jihadist insurgency by al-Shabaab	Internationalised internal	2006
Fatalities		9,135
Percentage change in fatalities		122%
IDPs		3,864,000
Peacekeeping and other multilateral missions		ATMIS; EUCAP Somalia; EUTM Somalia; Special Envoy of the Secretary-General to the Horn of Africa; UNSOM; UNSOS
Climate-change vulnerability (0–1)		0.7

ACGRI pillars: IISS calculation based on multiple sources for 2022 and 2023 (scale: 0–100), except for some cases according to data availability. See Notes on Methodology and Data Appendix for all variables and further details on Key Conflict Statistics.

humanitarian aid to the local population. AMISOM initially operated under a six-month mandate, but it was continuously renewed over the course of 15 years until its substitution with a different mission was agreed in March 2022. In April 2022, AMISOM became the AU Transition Mission in Somalia (ATMIS), a lighter and scalable mission that aims for a full withdraw from Somalia by the end of 2024.

Conflict Update

The presidential transition that resulted in Hassan Sheikh Mohamud's return to power in May 2022 has brought new momentum for the fight against al-Shabaab and Somalia's engagement with international partners. Al-Shabaab has found itself on the back foot from both a governance and a security perspective. However, while these factors paint a positive picture overall, the Federal Government of Somalia (FGS, which supplanted the TFG in 2012) now faces key challenges in addressing the extremely dire humanitarian context in which it operates, and consolidating and maintaining control of areas where al-Shabaab was dominant until recently.

In a major shift from its recent past, al-Shabaab launched an offensive outside Somalia's borders, striking several villages and military facilities on the other side of the Somali–Ethiopian border for two weeks in late July and early August 2022. As the offensive failed to achieve any kind of success, it is uncertain what motivated al-Shabaab to reach into Ethiopia.[1] The most likely explanation seems to be linked to the same anti-Ethiopian and nationalist sentiments that were a major driving force behind al-Shabaab's establishment in the early 2000s: baiting Ethiopia into a counter-attack on Somali soil or triggering public Ethiopian involvement in Somali domestic affairs would be a major propaganda victory for al-Shabaab and a significant driver for pro-al-Shabaab radicalisation. Besides a localised military response from Ethiopian forces, however, the operation did not elicit any major response. This constituted a significant strategic setback for al-Shabaab, at a time when the group has been rapidly losing influence and status, mainly due to grievances that have emerged in al-Shabaab-controlled areas as the humanitarian situation continues to degrade.

Following four consecutive missed rainy seasons and the worst drought of the past 40 years, the UN Office for the Coordination of Humanitarian Affairs reported that 6.7 million people were expected to be directly affected by acute food insecurity in late 2022 – almost half of Somalia's population.[2] Al-Shabaab-controlled areas have also experienced drought, and the group has struggled significantly to retain control and keep extorting resources from the local population. A fifth missed rainy season, between October and December 2022, further weakened al-Shabaab's grip over its controlled territories, as various local clan militias mounted armed uprisings against the group and its increasingly demanding and unsustainable levels of resource extortion.

Violence increased significantly in the second half of 2022, as clan militias' and governmental security forces' efforts converged into an all-out military offensive against al-Shabaab across Somalia. A major terrorist attack against a hotel in Mogadishu that killed at least 21 people became the catalyst for President Mohamud to call for a 'total war' against al-Shabaab, together with a plea for clan militias to cooperate with security forces to eradicate al-Shabaab once and for all.[3]

The combined offensive of Somali security forces and clan militias made significant progress throughout 2022 and the first half of 2023, with major breakthroughs in several al-Shabaab strongholds in the Bakool, Bay, Galgaduud, Hiran and Middle Shabelle regions.[4] The main challenge, however, will be to retain control of these areas, as the ongoing offensive is stretching Somali forces thin.

ATMIS also stands as a key player in the fight against al-Shabaab, and a successful reconfiguration of its tasks is central to Somalia's prospects for success. Departing from AMISOM's traditional configuration, Mogadishu expects ATMIS involvement to be lighter and more mobile, which, however, would increase the mission's risk profile by having ATMIS forces more frequently involved in clashes with al-Shabaab. This requires a complex balancing act, as this expectation clashes with ATMIS's goal of progressively reducing its presence until its full withdraw from Somalia by the end of 2024. Delays in Somalia's ability to generate and maintain effective and autonomous military units are hindering progress on both fronts, as ATMIS has yet to achieve a full reconfiguration, and the initial drawdown of 2,000 personnel planned for December 2022 was extended until the end of June 2023.[5]

President Mohamud is also grappling with the Islamic State's (ISIS) growing presence in Somalia's Puntland region. The killing of Bilal al-Sudani, one of the group's key financial orchestrators, in a United States special-forces operation carried out in January 2023 in northern Somalia shows that ISIS considers Somalia an important hub for its operations in the Horn of Africa and across the African continent.[6]

Conflict Parties

Somali National Army (SNA)

Strength: 13,900 active military personnel, as well as 3,000 troops under the Puntland government and an unspecified number of militias.

Areas of operation: Galmudug, Hirshabelle, Jubaland, Puntland and South West states (excluding self-declared independent Somaliland).

Leadership: Gen. Odowaa Yusuf Rageh (chief of defence forces).

Structure: Divided into four command divisions and spread across Somalia's operational sectors. The SNA has associated special-forces units such as the US-trained Danaab.

History: Efforts to build the SNA began in 2008. After two decades of state collapse, the SNA had to be built through both new recruitment and the incorporation of existing armed actors, such as clan militias. These efforts were challenged by the lack of coordination among international partners, internecine clan fighting and the ongoing al-Shabaab insurgency. As a result, the SNA continues to suffer from deep-seated internal cleavages and cohesion problems.

Objectives: Secure the territorial authority of the FGS, primarily through the defeat of al-Shabaab.

Opponents: Al-Shabaab, the Islamic State in Somalia (ISS), militias and criminal actors.

Affiliates/allies: ATMIS, Ethiopia, the European Union, Türkiye, the United Kingdom and the US.

Resources/capabilities: Suffers from severe shortages of resources – particularly of small arms – amid widespread internal corruption. This includes soldiers selling their arms (even to al-Shabaab) to make up for irregular and low salaries.

Harakat al-Shabaab al-Mujahideen ('al-Shabaab')

Strength: Active fighting force of an estimated 7,000 militants.[7]

Areas of operation: Strongest in southern Somalia (Hirshabelle, Jubaland and South West). Presence is more limited in Galmudug and Puntland.

Leadership: Ahmad Umar Diriye, better known as Abu Ubaidah, is the current leader, or emir.

Structure: A consultative council (*majlis al-shura*) is the group's central decision-making body, although regional political and military authorities enjoy considerable autonomy. Al-Shabaab's military wing is divided into six regional fighting units. An intelligence wing with a transnational reach (*Amniyat*) oversees a large security apparatus through which the group curtails dissent and maintains internal cohesion.

Harakat al-Shabaab al-Mujahideen ('al-Shabaab')

History: Al-Shabaab emerged in December 2006 after breaking away from the ICU, which had offered little resistance against the Ethiopian invasion of Somalia. Over a decade later, al-Shabaab has evolved into a highly effective insurgent group, which appeals to nationalist sentiments to boost recruitment and can challenge the authority of the federal government.

Objectives: Defeat the federal government and establish Islamist rule in Somalia.

Opponents: Federal government, SNA and ISS.

Affiliates/allies: Opportunistic alliances with militias and organised-crime syndicates.

Resources/capabilities: Al-Shabaab has benefitted from access to several sources of income, including checkpoint taxation, extortion, kidnappings, illicit trade, revenues from piracy and funding from transnational Islamist groups.

Islamic State in Somalia (ISS)

Strength: Between 250 and 300 fighters.[8]

Areas of operation: Based in the Galgala mountain region of Puntland, but periodically conducts targeted attacks in Bosaso and Mogadishu.

Leadership: Abd al-Qadir Mumin.

Structure: Little is known about its internal structure but given the group's small size and the regular targeting of senior figures by both Somali and US forces, it is likely to be relatively decentralised.

History: Mumin broke away from al-Shabaab with a small group of fighters in October 2015 and pledged allegiance to ISIS. Al-Shabaab has vowed to eliminate the rival group.

Objectives: Expand its influence by spreading ISIS's ideology within Somalia and neighbouring countries, such as Ethiopia, and to attract broader support.

Opponents: Al-Shabaab, and Somali and Puntland security forces.

Affiliates/allies: Believed to have connections with other Islamic State affiliates in Yemen and Central Africa.

Resources/capabilities: Small arms.

African Union Transition Mission to Somalia (ATMIS)

Strength: Approximately 20,000 troops.

Areas of operation: The five troop-contributing countries are Burundi, Djibouti, Ethiopia, Kenya and Uganda. Their forces are each responsible for a sector in central and southern Somalia, including Middle Shabelle (Burundi); Galguduud and Hiiraan (Djibouti); Bay, Bakool and Gedo (Ethiopia); Gedo, Lower Juba, Lower Shabelle and Middle Juba (Kenya); and Banadir and Lower Shabelle (Uganda).

Leadership: Ambassador Mohammed El-Amine Souef and Maj.-Gen. Marius Ngendabanka (acting ATMIS force commander).

Structure: The ATMIS contingent functions like a conventional military.

History: The United Nations authorised the AU to deploy the peacekeeping mission AMISOM in February 2007 to support the TFG. The mission had a six-month mandate and was allowed to use force only in self-defence. In the following years, the situation failed to stabilise, and the UN agreed to boost AMISOM troops and extend the mission's mandate and scope. The recent transition into ATMIS reflected the willingness of former president Mohamed Abdullahi 'Farmaajo' Mohamed (2017–22) to take full responsibility for the country's security situation, as well as a shared international willingness to enable Somalia's security forces to reach acceptable capability and autonomy levels.

Objectives: Defeat al-Shabaab, retake its territory and protect the FGS.

Opponents: Al-Shabaab.

Affiliates/allies: Supported by numerous international governments and periodically by military contingents from allied countries who deliver training, including the EU, Turkiye, the UK and the US.

Resources/capabilities: Draws from the military contingents of contributing countries and is occasionally supported by other international partners.

Sub-Saharan Africa

Notes

1   Sunguta West, 'Al-Shabaab's Attack in Ethiopia: One-off Incursion or Persistent Threat?', Jamestown Foundation *Terrorism Monitor*, vol. 20, no.17, 9 September 2022.

2   UN Office for the Coordination of Humanitarian Affairs, 'Somalia: The Cost of Inaction', October 2022.

3   Mohamed Dhaysane, 'Somalia's President Vows "Total War" Against al-Shabab', VOA, 24 August 2022.

4   Samira Gaid, 'The 2022 Somali Offensive Against al-Shabaab: Making Enduring Gains Will Require Learning from Previous Failures', *CTC Sentinel*, vol. 15, no. 11, November/December 2022, pp. 31–8.

5   UN Security Council, 'Security Council Extends Drawdown of African Union Transition Mission in Somalia by Six Months, Unanimously Adopting Resolution 2670 (2022)', 21 December 2022.

6   'Islamic State Terror Banker Bilal al-Sudani Killed by US Special Forces in Somalia Mountain Cave Hideout', Sky News, 27 January 2023.

7   Soufan Center, 'IntelBrief: Somalia Continues to Deteriorate as al-Shabaab Gains Ground', 18 March 2022.

8   European Institute of Peace, 'The Islamic State in East Africa', September 2018.

DEMOCRATIC REPUBLIC OF THE CONGO

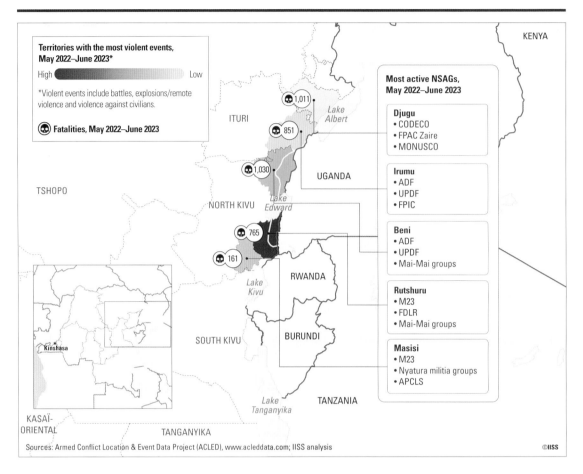

Sources: Armed Conflict Location & Event Data Project (ACLED), www.acleddata.com; IISS analysis   ©IISS

Conflict Overview

Armed conflict in the Democratic Republic of the Congo (DRC) has long been concentrated in the country's eastern provinces, namely Ituri, North Kivu and South Kivu. Much of this unrest stems from the fallout of the First (1996–97) and Second (1998–2003) Congo wars, which themselves were fuelled by the region's colonial history, long-held intercommunal and anti-governmental grievances, and the 1994 genocide against the Tutsis in Rwanda. Weak governance, corruption, underdevelopment, conflict over land and resources, and regional interests remain some of the main drivers of conflict in the DRC. Rebel groups from neighbouring countries, such as the Democratic Forces for the Liberation of Rwanda (FDLR), the Ugandan Allied Democratic Forces (ADF) and the Resistance for the

Rule of Law in Burundi (RED Tabara), have also found refuge in eastern DRC, effectively turning the area into a battleground for external actors.

Instability is further fuelled by tensions between different ethnic groups and between ethnic groups and the government. For instance, claims over belonging and 'Congolité' identity are at the heart of the March 23 Movement (M23), a Tutsi-led rebellion which, after an eight-year dormancy, resumed its activities in November 2021 in North Kivu province. The group has accused the Congolese government of not upholding its commitments agreed in the peace deal signed after M23's last insurrection, of preventing former combatants from reintegrating, and of refusing political dialogue. Mai-Mai

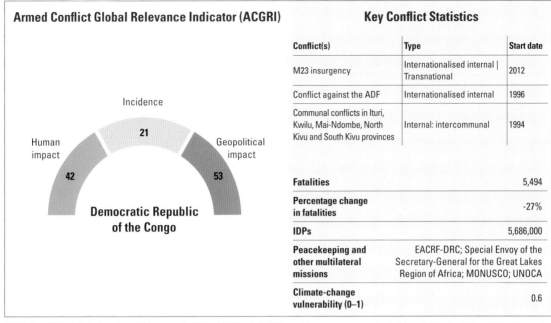

Conflict(s)	Type	Start date
M23 insurgency	Internationalised internal | Transnational	2012
Conflict against the ADF	Internationalised internal	1996
Communal conflicts in Ituri, Kwilu, Mai-Ndombe, North Kivu and South Kivu provinces	Internal: intercommunal	1994
Fatalities		5,494
Percentage change in fatalities		-27%
IDPs		5,686,000
Peacekeeping and other multilateral missions		EACRF-DRC; Special Envoy of the Secretary-General for the Great Lakes Region of Africa; MONUSCO; UNOCA
Climate-change vulnerability (0–1)		0.6

ACGRI pillars: IISS calculation based on multiple sources for 2022 and 2023 (scale: 0–100), except for some cases according to data availability. See Notes on Methodology and Data Appendix for all variables and further details on Key Conflict Statistics.

groups, formed as community-based self-defence militias during the Second Congo War, have also continued to proliferate, with over 220 factions.[1] These militias often target civilians perceived to be 'outsiders', such as the Banyamulenge and Kinyarwanda-speaking populations. Finally, in Ituri province, competition over political power and control of mineral resources, particularly gold, has been at the core of a deadly conflict between Lendu and Hema communities, whose interests are represented by the Cooperative for the Development of the Congo (CODECO) and the Ituri Self-Defense Popular Front Zaire (FPAC Zaire) armed groups, respectively.

Conflict Update

In the reporting period, there were nearly 120 non-state armed groups (NSAGs) active in the DRC, showcasing the country's complex, highly fragmented and diffuse conflict landscape.[2] The ongoing 'state of siege' (state of emergency) in North Kivu and Ituri provinces, imposed by President Félix Tshisekedi in May 2021, achieved few results in terms of security.

The most significant development of the reporting period was the resurgence of the M23 rebellion, which started seizing territory in April–May 2022. The capture of the town of Bunagana at the border with Uganda in June 2022 marked a turning point in the conflict, as it became apparent that M23 had the upper hand over the Armed Forces of the Democratic Republic of the Congo (FARDC).

As the Congolese government's accusation that Rwanda was supporting M23 and the Rwandan government's accusation that the FARDC was collaborating with Hutu militias (including the FDLR) were confirmed, diplomatic relations between the countries further deteriorated.[3] In October 2022, the Rwandan ambassador to the DRC was expelled from the country, diminishing hopes for any further diplomatic dialogue between Tshisekedi and Rwandan President Paul Kagame.

In response to the crisis, the East African Community (EAC), which the DRC joined in May 2022, deployed a regional force to eastern DRC, a first for the bloc. Troops from Burundi, Kenya, South Sudan and Uganda were progressively deployed from August 2022 onwards in North Kivu. The force acts as a 'buffer' between M23 and the FARDC, retaking the territories surrendered by the rebellion. However, civil society has decried the force's lack of an offensive mandate and denounced it as yet another foreign intervention weakening Congolese sovereignty.[4]

The expansion of M23 also caused great civil unrest among civilians who deplored Rwandan support to the group, the inefficiency of the long-standing United Nations Organization Stabilization Mission in the DRC (MONUSCO) and the perceived 'complicity' of international actors who did not sanction Kigali.[5] Violent protests took place across the country, peaking in the period July–September 2022 and leading to dozens of deaths, sometimes at the hands of peacekeepers.[6]

Further north, the Ugandan ADF continued looting and attacking civilians, despite the Congolese and Ugandan armed forces' joint operation, *Operation Shujaa*, which began in November 2021. Though the operation registered some successes in early 2023, its destruction of ADF camps had the adverse effect of further dispersing and fragmenting the group, which fled to new territories and reinforced its ranks. The ADF remained the deadliest armed group in the DRC, followed by CODECO militias, active in Ituri province.[7]

In South Kivu, violent conflict generally decreased in the reporting period thanks to the demobilisation of many Mai-Mai and Twirwaneho militants, though some militias remained active in Mwenga, Uvira and Fizi territories. Furthermore, Burundian armed forces, including the Imbonerakure (the Burundian ruling party's youth militia), who have been covertly deployed in the area since December 2021, continued clashing with Burundian rebel groups RED Tabara and the National Liberation Front, with the support of the FARDC.

In the usually calm western provinces of Mai-Ndombe (particularly Kwamouth Territory) and Kwilu, intercommunal violence primarily between the Teke and Yaka ethnic groups over customary power and land tenure led to a deadly conflict that resulted in nearly 400 direct fatalities in 2022, with violence peaking in August 2022.[8] Violence decreased significantly by early 2023, although isolated attacks have continued.

Peace efforts, particularly in relation to the M23 crisis, have multiplied at the regional level. Kenya has taken the lead on commanding the EAC Regional Force (EACRF) and hosted a series of peace talks in Nairobi. Likewise, Angolan president João Lourenço has hosted summits and talks between Tshisekedi and Kagame, with support from Qatar. Internationally, partners such as the United States, the European Union and France have condemned M23 and Rwanda, although non-governmental organisations (NGOs) and watchdogs have criticised the lack of sanctions from such partners.

In January 2023, M23 started withdrawing from its occupied territories, markedly accelerating this process in April. Ceasefires were brokered by the EAC in Nairobi and Luanda. However, M23 refuses to demobilise until it has had dialogue with Kinshasa, which would come at great political cost for Tshisekedi, as the overwhelming majority of Congolese people are opposed to any negotiations with the group and want to see it defeated militarily.

Upcoming presidential and parliamentarian elections, scheduled for 20 December 2023, are also driving violence. There have been many instances of armed groups raiding voter-registration centres and attacking Banyamulenge and Kinyarwanda-speaking aspiring voters, due to their purported association with Rwanda.

Conflict Parties

Armed Forces of the Democratic Republic of the Congo (FARDC)	
Strength: About 134,250 active personnel.	The power structure is unclear; many soldiers and battalions operate semi-independently, and the army is generally considered to be ill-disciplined and lacking in accountability.
Areas of operation: Countrywide, but mainly deployed to North Kivu and Ituri provinces.	
Leadership: President Felix Tshisekedi (commander-in-chief) and Célestin Mbala (chief of staff). Tshisekedi appointed Jean-Pierre Bemba as defence minister in March 2023. Bemba is a former warlord who led the Movement for the Liberation of the Congo.	**History:** Born out of an international effort to restructure the Congolese army at the end of the Second Congo War through the incorporation of former rebel groups. Since then, it has continuously integrated demobilised combatants from rebel groups and other conflict parties.
Structure: Comprises land forces, a navy, air forces and a republican guard. Each province has a military governor.	**Objectives:** Formally, to defend the country's borders, protect civilians and neutralise rebel armed groups. In reality, many

Armed Forces of the Democratic Republic of the Congo (FARDC)

officers and soldiers form allegiances with rebel groups to pursue their own agendas (whether community defence, wealth accumulation or power grabbing – or often a combination of all three).

Opponents: NSAGs in the DRC (except those with which the FARDC has an ideological alliance, such as Hutu militias against M23) and the Rwanda Defence Force (RDF).

Affiliates/allies: The Ugandan People's Defence Force (UPDF), with which it has been carrying out joint operations

against the ADF since November 2021. It is also supported by MONUSCO and, since August 2022, the EACRF in eastern DRC.

Resources/capabilities: Despite its size, the Congolese army has been largely unable to exert control over the national territory. It is poorly trained, underfunded, undisciplined and relies mainly on light weapons, although it also has artillery, over 400 armoured vehicles, anti-aircraft guns and surface-to-air missiles.

March 23 Movement (M23)

Strength: The group probably resumed operations with approximately 400 fighters in November 2021.[9] Voluntary and forced recruitment and Rwandan support have most likely increased combatant numbers to approximately 3,000.[10]

Areas of operation: The southern area of North Kivu province, particularly Rutshuru, Nyiragongo and Masisi territories, surrounding the strategic border town of Goma.

Leadership: The leadership of M23 is exclusively made up of Congolese Tutsis. Sultani Makenga is the group's military leader, and Bertrand Bisimwa is its current president. Willy Ngoma and Lawrence Kanyuka are the military and political spokespeople, respectively. The group has installed a parallel civil administration in the territory it occupies, from April 2022 onwards.

Structure: The group has two factions. The faction that has resumed fighting in the DRC is made up of previously demobilised combatants in Uganda, led by Makenga. The faction of combatants that was demobilised in Rwanda under the leadership of Jean-Marie Runiga Lugerero has remained inactive.

History: On 23 March 2009, members of the Rwanda-backed and Tutsi-led National Congress for the Defence of the People

signed a peace treaty with the Congolese government and integrated into the FARDC. In 2012, around 300 of them defected and created the M23 insurgency, accusing the government of failing to uphold its end of the peace deal. It waged a 19-month rebellion and was eventually defeated in November 2013. It took up arms again in November 2021.

Objectives: Officially, to force the Congolese government to uphold its commitments from the 2013 peace deal and subsequent 2019 road map, regarding the reintegration of ex-combatants into civilian life. M23 also presents itself as a guardian of Tutsi rights in the DRC.

Opponents: FARDC, MONUSCO and Hutu militias. The group has also made a point of not clashing with the EACRF.

Affiliates/allies: M23 benefits from political, military and on-the-ground troop support from the RDF, although Kigali denies such allegations. The UN Group of Experts and other NGOs have proven Rwandan support to the group.

Resources/capabilities: Supported by Rwanda, M23 has highly sophisticated equipment. Bintou Keita, the head of MONUSCO, said in June 2022 that M23 has increasingly behaved like 'a conventional army rather than an armed group'.[11]

Allied Democratic Forces (ADF)

Strength: Estimates ranged from 1,000–1,500 in mid-June 2022, but joint FARDC and UPDF operations might have decreased those numbers, especially as the ADF has increased abductions in early 2023, presumably to reinforce its ranks.[12]

Areas of operation: Active in the border zone between North Kivu and Ituri provinces, especially in Beni, Irumu and Mambasa territories, in an area ranging from Butembo in the south to Komanda in the north.

Leadership: Leadership is predominantly Ugandan. Musa Baluku is the leader of the ADF's biggest (and only active) faction.

Structure: Operates in small, highly mobile groups out of camps. The ADF recruits new members from Burundi, Kenya, South Africa and Tanzania.

History: Born out of a 1995 merger between Ugandan rebel factions that shared the goal of overthrowing the government of Ugandan President Yoweri Museveni and expanding Salafism in Ugandan politics. The group fled Uganda and found a foothold in North Kivu in the mid-1990s, and it

benefitted from the support of Mobutu Sese Seko during the First Congo War. Following a decade of low-level fighting during the 2000s, it re-emerged as a pre-eminent actor in 2013.

Objectives: Establish an Islamic caliphate in Central Africa.

Opponents: The group targets so-called 'Christian villages'. It has also targeted Hutu civilians (specifically Banyabwisha) due to their purported collaboration with the FARDC. It regularly clashes with the FARDC, UPDF and MONUSCO.

Affiliates/allies: The ADF pledged allegiance to the Islamic State (ISIS) in 2017. ISIS started claiming ADF attacks and recognised the group as its Central Africa Province in 2019. Though there is no direct chain of command between ISIS leadership and the ADF, ISIS has boosted the group's visibility, attracted foreign recruits, helped finance it and enhanced its technical skills.

Resources/capabilities: The group is said to have been severely weakened by joint FARDC and UPDF operations, particularly in late 2022 and early 2023. However, it has also ramped up its use of improvised explosive devices in urban settings.

Cooperative for the Development of Congo (CODECO)

Strength: 2,000–2,500.[13]

Areas of operation: Ituri province, mainly Djugu Territory, with occasional activity in Mahagi Territory.

Leadership: Each faction is headed by a different leader.

Structure: Seven different factions: Congo Liberation Army (ALC), Army of Revolutionaries for the Defence of Congolese People, Bon Temple, Force for the Defence against the Balkanisation of Congo, Gutsi, Islamic, and Union of Revolutionaries for the Defence of the Congolese People (URDPC), each with its own interests and areas of operations. The URDPC has consolidated its influence over the other factions, with the exception of the ALC.

History: Rooted in the Lendu ethnolinguistic group, which is traditionally agriculturalist and in conflict with the pastoralist Hema people. Created as an agricultural cooperative in the 1970s, CODECO became an armed group in 2017.

Objectives: Its political and ideological objectives (if any) are unclear. The group mainly targets Hema civilians and seems driven by economic considerations as it fights for control over and exploits the gold mines in Ituri.

Opponents: FARDC and Hema self-defence groups, especially the FPAC Zaire. CODECO members routinely target civilians, especially internally displaced persons, on whom they often inflict sexual violence. CODECO factions periodically clash with one another.

Affiliates/allies: Sometimes associates with the Patriotic and Integrationist Force of Congo (FPIC), a group composed mainly of ethnic Biras who want to 'reclaim' land 'occupied' by the Hema in Irumu Territory.

Resources/capabilities: Financial resources derived from the gold mines it has control over, especially in the area surrounding Mongbwalu.

Anti-M23 coalition

Strength: At least 600 combatants, potentially thousands.[14]

Areas of operation: North Kivu province in areas where M23 is active.

Leadership: The various armed groups recruit, train and arm their fighters, and they generally obey the command of FARDC military authorities in the fight against M23.

Structure: The coalition brought together rival armed groups (some of whom were initially self-defence militias), including the FDLR, Nduma Defence of Congo–Renovated, Alliance of Patriots for a Free and Sovereign Congo (APCLS), Nyatura Collective of Movements for Change–People's Defence Forces, Nyatura Abazungu, People's Defence Forces (Kabido) and Patriotic Self-Defence Movement.

History: The groups gathered in May 2022 as M23 was seizing territory in Rutshuru Territory (North Kivu province) and formed a coalition to join the FARDC in the fight against M23.

They also agreed to a truce between them. The FDLR is a remnant of the *génocidaires* (perpetrators of the Rwandan genocide) who fled to Zaire (present-day DRC) when the Rwandan Patriotic Army seized power in Kigali in 1994, and most of these militias draw their support from Hutu and Hunde ethnic groups.

Objectives: Defeat M23. The ideology of the coalition members is founded on opposition to Tutsi ethnic groups.

Opponents: M23 and RDF. The coalition has also clashed with the EACRF and attacked civilians.

Affiliates/allies: The coalition groups fight on behalf of the FARDC and have received weapons and ammunition from FARDC members on several occasions.

Resources/capabilities: Small arms that were previously in their possession and provided by the FARDC.

Mai-Mai (Mayi-Mayi) groups

Strength: Nearly 50 different Mai-Mai groups were active in the reporting period.[15] Some have formed large coalitions of several hundred fighters, but most comprise fewer than 200.

Areas of operation: Most of North and South Kivu, as well as part of Ituri, Maniema, Haut-Katanga and Tanganyika provinces.

Leadership: Mai-Mai groups operate independently, each having its own leadership structure. Some, such as the Raia Mutomboki, are divided into subgroups that each respond to a particular commander.

Structure: Mai-Mai militias are largely informal and non-hierarchical, though some have notorious commanders.

History: Mai-Mai groups mostly formed as community-based self-defence militias during the Second Congo War. A majority have anti-Tutsi and anti-Banyamulenge sentiments and see themselves as indigenous defenders against 'Rwandan' foreigners.

Objectives: Officially, community self-defence. In reality, most Mai-Mai militias fight for territorial control and self-enrichment, which they pursue through illegal taxation and looting.

Opponents: Mostly Banyamulenge ethnic militias, such as the Ngumino and Twirwaneho. They have also joined the fight against M23, with some travelling from South Kivu and more distant provinces. Mai-Mai groups regularly clash against the FARDC and each other, and target civilians.

Affiliates/allies: Mai-Mai militias have allied with the FARDC in the fight against M23 in North Kivu. Some militias also form alliances of convenience with each other.

Resources/capabilities: Armed almost exclusively with machetes and other bladed weapons, though some groups have small arms as well.

Ugandan People's Defence Force (UPDF)

Strength: About 40,000–45,000 active military personnel, with an estimated 5,000 deployed in the DRC, split between a bilateral deployment as part of an ongoing operation against the ADF and a contingent deployed with the EACRF.[16]

Areas of operation: North Kivu (Beni Territory) and Ituri (Irumu Territory) provinces as part of *Operation Shujaa*, as well as North Kivu province (Rutshuru Territory) as a contingent of the EACRF.

Leadership: Ugandan President Yoweri Museveni (commander-in-chief) and Wilson Mbadi (chief of defence forces).

Structure: Deployed in the DRC since November 2021 as part of the bilateral *Operation Shujaa* against the ADF and since April 2023 as part of the multilateral EACRF.

History: Originated from the National Resistance Army, a rebel movement led by Museveni that waged a guerrilla war against Milton Obote's regime and took power in 1986.

Objectives: In the DRC, its objective is to defeat the ADF, though there is speculation that it is also largely motivated by economic interests.[17]

Opponents: ADF (in the context of *Operation Shujaa*).

Affiliates/allies: FARDC and other contingents of EACRF.

Resources/capabilities: The UPDF is a well-trained, efficient army, which has received support and training from the US and France, among others, in part due to its involvement in the fight against al-Shabaab in the Horn of Africa. It possesses mostly light weapons, but also armoured fighting vehicles, artillery and missiles. It is known to be more effective and better disciplined than the FARDC.

Burundi National Defence Force (FDNB)

Strength: 30,050 active military personnel, with an estimated 2,000 deployed with the EACRF in the DRC.[18]

Areas of operation: Bilaterally in South Kivu (Fizi, Mwenga and Uvira territories) and as part of the EACRF in North Kivu (mainly in Masisi Territory).

Leadership: President Evariste Ndayishimiye (commander-in-chief) and Emmanuel Ntahomvukiye (defence minister).

Structure: Land and air forces. The FDNB forcibly recruits the Imbonerakure to fight in the DRC.

History: Its origins, unlike those of the Ugandan and Rwandan armed forces, lie in the colonial-era national guard. Some of the army's units supported the failed coup attempt in 2015.

Objectives: Defend Burundi's national integrity and defeat rebel groups.

Opponents: RED Tabara, National Liberation Front and two Burundian rebel groups that operate in South Kivu province.

Affiliates/allies: In South Kivu, the FDNB collaborates with the FARDC and local groups such as the Mai-Mai Kijangala, Mai-Mai Kashumba and Gumino to fight against RED Tabara.

Resources/capabilities: Mostly small arms and light weapons. The army is generally considered to lack discipline.

East African Community Regional Force (EACRF)

Strength: At least 2,050 soldiers, with the following contingents: Uganda (1,000), Kenya (900), Burundi (100) and South Sudan (50).[19]

Areas of operation: North Kivu province in areas where M23 operates. South Sudanese forces have also been deployed at the border with South Sudan in Haut-Uélé province.

Leadership: Under Kenyan command.

Structure: The force comprises a Kenyan contingent, a Ugandan contingent, a Burundian contingent and a South Sudanese contingent. This is the first international deployment of South Sudanese troops. Rwandan intelligence officers are supposedly part of the force as well. Each contingent operates independently.

History: After the DRC joined the EAC in 2022, the EAC heads of state decided to deploy regional troops to assist Kinshasa against NSAGs in August 2022. This is the bloc's first-ever troop deployment.

Objectives: Oversee M23's withdrawal from occupied areas. One of the conditions for the withdrawal is that the FARDC will not enter M23-occupied territories while the withdrawal is ongoing.

Opponents: M23 and other NSAGs, though the force has stated that it will not fight against M23 or adopt an offensive mandate.

Affiliates/allies: Supports the FARDC but does not fight alongside them.

Resources/capabilities: As each contingent operates independently, capabilities reflect those of the national army of the troops in question.

United Nations Organization Stabilization Mission in the DRC (MONUSCO)

Strength: 12,878 military personnel and an extra 4,875 personnel (military observers, police and civilians).[20] This is the maximum authorised strength in accordance with UN Security Council Resolution 2556 (2020).

Areas of operation: North Kivu province, with some activity in Ituri province. It is scaling down its operations in South Kivu

province and has even withdrawn from some of the province's territories.

Leadership: Bintou Keita (Guinea) (special representative of the secretary-general in the DRC and head of MONUSCO). Lt-Gen. Otávio Rodrigues de Miranda Filho (Brazil) (force commander).

Sub-Saharan Africa

United Nations Organization Stabilization Mission in the DRC (MONUSCO)

Structure: In addition to its military personnel, MONUSCO comprises police, military observers and a Force Intervention Brigade, which is authorised to act offensively against armed actors. MONUSCO's largest troop contributors are Bangladesh, India and Pakistan.

History: In 2010, MONUSCO replaced the UN Organization Mission in DRC, established in 1999 to oversee the implementation of the Lusaka Ceasefire Agreement. Resolution 2556 plans for a gradual withdrawal of the mission from the DRC, although an exact timeline has yet to be determined.

Objectives: Protect civilians, and support efforts towards stabilisation, the strengthening of public institutions and the reform of governance and security.

Opponents: NSAGs.

Affiliates/allies: Periodically conducts joint operations with the FARDC, though relations are often tense.

Resources/capabilities: MONUSCO's 2022–23 budget is estimated to be US$1.1 billion based on the approved budget for 1 July 2021–30 June 2022, making it by far the best-funded (and equipped) conflict party in the DRC.[21]

Other relevant parties

The above list contains only the most notorious of the estimated 120 armed groups active in the DRC in the reporting period.[22] Other particularly active armed groups include the FPAC Zaire (in Ituri province), Banyamulenge ethnic militias (in South Kivu province) and the Yaka ethnic militia (in the western provinces of Kwilu and Mai-Ndombe). In the northern provinces of Haut-Uélé and Bas-Uélé, NSAGs from the Central African Republic and South Sudan sporadically attack and/or abduct civilians.

Notes

1   Armed Conflict Location & Event Data Project (ACLED), www.acleddata.com.

2   *Ibid*. Data retrieved 19 July 2023.

3   For more information on the nature and extent of Rwandan involvement in the DRC, see the 'Rwanda' chapter.

4   Congo Research Group and Ebuteli, 'Majority of Congolese Reject East African Community Regional Force', February 2023.

5   Oliver Liffran et al., 'Diplomatic Cat and Mouse from New York to Paris over Rwanda's Alleged Support for M23 Rebels', Africa Intelligence, 1 July 2022; and Fred Bauma and Jason Stearns, 'DRC: "We Know the M23 Is Backed by Rwanda, but France Has Looked the Other Way"', *Le Monde*, 16 December 2022.

6   'Bilan revu des manifestations anti-MONUSCO en RDC : 36 morts' [Revised Death Toll of Anti-MONUSCO Protests in DRC: 36 Dead], Radio Okapi, 2 August 2022.

7   In the reporting period, the ADF killed over 1,310 civilians and CODECO killed over 659 civilians. Armed Conflict Location & Event Data Project (ACLED), www.acleddata.com. Data retrieved 19 July 2023.

8   Armed Conflict Location & Event Data Project (ACLED), www.acleddata.com; and 'DR Congo: Rampant Intercommunal Violence in West', Human Rights Watch, 30 March 2023. ACLED data retrieved 19 July 2023.

9   UN Security Council (UNSC), 'Final Report of the Group of Experts on the Democratic Republic of the Congo', S/2022/479, 14 June 2022.

10   UNSC, 'Final Report of the Group of Experts on the Democratic Republic of the Congo', S/2023/431, 13 June 2023, p. 15.

11   Edith M. Lederer, 'UN Envoy Warns Congo's M23 Rebels Are Acting Like an Army', AP News, 30 June 2022.

12   International Crisis Group, 'A Perilous Free-for-all in the Eastern DR Congo?', Hold Your Fire!, 13 May 2022; and UNSC, 'Final Report of the Group of Experts on the Democratic Republic of the Congo', S/2023/431, 13 June 2023.

13   Adolphe Agenonga Chober and Georges Berghezan, 'La CODECO, au coeur de l'insécurité en Ituri' [CODECO, At the Heart of Insecurity in Ituri], Group for Research and Information on Peace and Security, 2 June 2021.

14   UNSC, 'Midterm Report of the Group of Experts on the Democratic Republic of the Congo', S/2022/967, 16 December 2022.

15   Armed Conflict Location & Event Data Project (ACLED), www.acleddata.com. Data retrieved 19 July 2023.

16   Andrew Bagala, 'UPDF Soldiers Abroad Surge Beyond 12,000', *Daily Monitor*, 11 April 2023.

17   Congo Research Group and Ebuteli, 'Uganda's Operation Shujaa in the DRC: Fighting the ADF or Securing Economic Interests?', June 2022.

18   'RDC : une compagnie de soldats burundais attendue au Nord-Kivu' [DRC: A Contingent of Burundian Soldiers Expected in North Kivu], Radio France Internationale, 3 March 2023.

19   Estimate. See Armed Conflict Location & Event Data Project (ACLED), www.acleddata.com.

20   UN Peacekeeping, 'MONUSCO Fact Sheet'. Numbers as of February 2023.

21   UN General Assembly, 'Resolution Adopted by the General Assembly on 30 June 2021', A/RES/75/300, 8 July 2021.

22   Armed Conflict Location & Event Data Project (ACLED), www.acleddata.com. Data retrieved 19 July 2023.

RWANDA

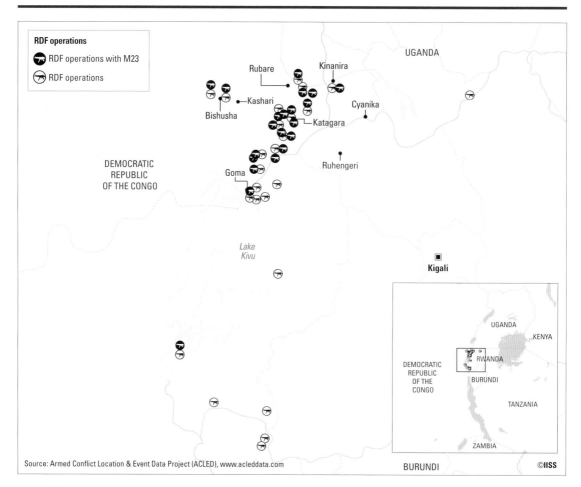

RDF operations

RDF operations with M23

RDF operations

Rubare

Kinanira

UGANDA

Kashari

Bishusha

Cyanika

Katagara

DEMOCRATIC
REPUBLIC
OF THE CONGO

Goma

Ruhengeri

Lake
Kivu

Kigali

UGANDA

KENYA

DEMOCRATIC
REPUBLIC
OF THE
CONGO

RWANDA

BURUNDI

TANZANIA

ZAMBIA

BURUNDI

Source: Armed Conflict Location & Event Data Project (ACLED), www.acleddata.com

©IISS

Conflict Overview

Since the 1994 genocide against the Tutsis in Rwanda, the Rwandan army – under the leadership of President Paul Kagame's Rwandan Patriotic Front (RPF) party – has been militarily involved in the Democratic Republic of the Congo (DRC). Pursuing former *génocidaires* (perpetrators of the Rwandan genocide), it triggered regime change to ensure Kinshasa would remain sympathetic to its political and economic interests, leading to the First (1996–97) and Second (1998–2003) Congo wars. During the Second Congo War, Kigali supported the creation of the Congolese Tutsi-led Rally for Congolese Democracy (RCD), which later became the National Congress for the Defence of the People (CNDP). In March 2009, the CNDP signed a

peace treaty and integrated into the Armed Forces of the DRC (FARDC). Three years later, some former CNDP soldiers mutinied and created the March 23 Movement (M23). It launched an offensive against the Congolese forces but was defeated by the United Nations Organization Stabilization Mission in the DRC (MONUSCO) in November 2013. In November 2021, M23 resumed its activities, calling attention yet again to Rwanda's role in regional conflict.

At the same time, Kigali has been fighting against Rwandan rebel groups formed in exile and operating from the DRC and Burundi, namely the Democratic Forces for the Liberation of Rwanda (FDLR) and the National Liberation

Armed Conflict Global Relevance Indicator (ACGRI)		Key Conflict Statistics		
		Conflict(s)	**Type**	**Start date**
		Support to M23 insurgency in the eastern DRC	Transnational	2021
Incidence		Conflict against the FDLR in the DRC and the FLN in Burundi	Internationalised internal	1994
0				
Human impact Geopolitical impact		**Fatalities**		14
1 **6**		**Percentage change in fatalities**		-26%
		Refugees		249,685
Rwanda		**Peacekeeping and other multilateral missions**		Special Envoy of the Secretary-General for the Great Lakes Region of Africa; UNOCA
		Climate-change vulnerability (0–1)		0.5

ACGRI pillars: IISS calculation based on multiple sources for 2022 and 2023 (scale: 0–100), except for some cases according to data availability. See Notes on Methodology and Data Appendix for all variables and further details on Key Conflict Statistics.

Front (FLN). Though their tactics are different, both groups fight for regime change in Kigali. Overall, the different conflict theatres significantly overlap, rendering the Great Lakes Region a complex conflict system in which elements of intra-state and inter-state conflict converge.

In the last few years, Rwanda has also been playing an important role as a security provider beyond the confines of its neighbouring region. It is the largest contributor of troops per capita to UN peacekeeping missions globally, and it increasingly provides bilateral security support. For instance, Rwandan troops have been deployed in the Central African Republic (CAR) since December 2020 and in Mozambique since July 2021.[1]

Conflict Update

In December 2022, the UN Group of Experts on the DRC confirmed Rwandan support to M23 in the form of weapons provision, troop reinforcement, military intelligence and political support. In the DRC, the Rwanda Defence Force (RDF) has acted jointly with M23 but also independently, especially against the FDLR.[2]

The M23 resurgence explicitly became a diplomatic stand-off between Kinshasa and Kigali in May and June 2022, when the first reports of Rwandan troops entering the DRC materialised. Tensions grew, with several instances of cross-border shelling and mutual accusations of airspace violations. Clashes between the militaries of the two countries at their land borders became commonplace. On 30 October 2022, the Congolese government expelled the Rwandan ambassador to the DRC, curtailing any remaining hopes for diplomatic dialogue.

Meanwhile, Kigali has continuously denied any wrongdoing, instead referring to the DRC's failure to control its territory as the root cause of instability, and it has repeatedly denounced the collaboration between the FARDC and Hutu rebel groups such as the FDLR and Nyatura militia groups.[3] Kagame has made it abundantly clear that he will not ask for permission to intervene militarily in the DRC in the name of defeating the former *genocidaires*.[4] Kigali has also accused Kinshasa of fuelling anti-Tutsi and anti-Rwandan sentiment at large in the DRC. These groups have increasingly been targets of xenophobia and hate speech in the DRC, prompting Kigali and international observers to warn against a possible escalation of tensions along ethnic lines.

During the reporting period, there were no relevant developments in the Rwandan conflict against the FLN in Burundi, except for an FLN attack in June 2022, which killed two people in southwestern Rwanda.[5]

Sub-Saharan Africa

Conflict Parties

Rwanda Defence Force (RDF)

Strength: 33,000 active military personnel.

Areas of operation: Rwanda, eastern DRC and Burundi (though it is not deployed in any capacity in Burundi, but rather intervenes as the need arises), and bilaterally deployed in the CAR and Mozambique. Rwanda also contributes troops to two UN peacekeeping missions: the UN Multidimensional Integrated Stabilization Mission in the CAR (2,110 troops) and the UN Mission in the Republic of South Sudan (2,581 troops).[6] In both cases it is the main contributor to the mission.

Leadership: President Paul Kagame (commander-in-chief), Maj.-Gen. Albert Murasira (minister of defence) and Gen. Jean Bosco Kazura (chief of defence staff).

Structure: Includes land forces, a unit of marines and an air force.

History: The RDF's predecessor, the Rwandan Patriotic Army, was made up of Rwandan Tutsis exiled in Uganda who fought alongside the National Resistance Army during the Ugandan civil war and went on to overthrow the Hutu regime in Rwanda during the 1994 genocide.

Objectives: Defend Rwanda's territorial integrity and national sovereignty. Bilateral troop deployment signals Rwanda's will to become a key actor in crisis response on the continent.

Opponents: In the DRC: FARDC and their allies, mostly Hutu self-defence militias. In Burundi: FLN.

Affiliates/allies: The RDF provides military support to and fights alongside M23 in the DRC.

Resources/capabilities: Although smaller than its Congolese counterpart, the RDF is well trained, disciplined and effective. It is also well equipped, with armoured fighting vehicles, artillery, missiles, transport aircraft and attack helicopters. It is regarded as one of the best militaries in Africa.

Democratic Forces for the Liberation of Rwanda (FDLR)

Strength: 500–1,000 combatants (2020 estimates, but likely fewer now). The group was significantly weakened over the last decade.[7]

Areas of operation: Controls the area of the DRC's Virunga National Park. Localities of Kibumba, Kazaroho and Tongo in North Kivu province's Rutshuru Territory are the FDLR's strongholds.

Leadership: Pacifique Ntawunguka (alias 'Omega', commander) and Gen. Gaston Iyamuremye (alias 'Rumuli', 'Victor Byiringiro' or variations thereof, president).[8]

Structure: Direct military command. Some commentators say that its chain of command is intertwined with that of the FARDC.[9] Some splinter groups have been created, although they have seldom been active in recent years.

History: Formed in 2000 from a merger of several Rwandan rebel groups in eastern DRC, all opposed to the Kagame regime. Many of the original FDLR members were members of the Interahamwe (the militia that carried out much of the 1994 genocide) and many of its leaders (current and previous) were convicted of genocide. The group is under UN sanctions and on the United States' list of terrorist organisations.

Objectives: Overthrow the Kagame regime and regain power in Rwanda.

Opponents: M23 and RDF. The FDLR sometimes targets civilians it accuses of being sympathetic to M23. Prior to the coalition being formed in May 2022 (see below), the FDLR would also routinely clash with the FARDC and other Congolese armed groups.

Affiliates/allies: In May 2022, the FDLR joined an 'anti-M23' coalition that fights alongside the FARDC and brings together the Nduma Defence of Congo–Renovated, Alliance of Patriots for a Free and Sovereign Congo, Nyatura Collective of Movements for Change–People's Defence Forces, Nyatura Abazungu, People's Defence Forces (Kabido), Patriotic Self-Defence Movement and various Mai-Mai militias.

Resources/capabilities: The FARDC provides the FDLR with ammunition. The group also generates revenue through coal and charcoal trading. Its exact capabilities are unknown. However, it is likely that it does not pose a real threat to Rwanda's territorial sovereignty, but rather an 'ideological threat' (in the words of Rwandan senior security adviser Gen. James Kabarebe).[10]

National Liberation Front (FLN)

Strength: Unknown, but in the hundreds.

Areas of operation: Operates from Kibira National Park in northern Burundi and occasionally launches attacks in Rwanda.

Leadership: Paul Rusesabagina. Following FLN-claimed attacks in Rwanda in 2018, Rwandan security services captured Rusesabagina and put him on trial in Kigali in 2021, where he was sentenced to 25 years in prison. His sentence was commuted in March 2023.

Structure: The FLN is the armed wing of the Party of Democracy in Rwanda (PDR)–Ihumure, a Rwandan opposition party (primarily Hutu) which operates mainly from Europe and the US and is part of the Rwandan Movement for Democratic Change coalition.

History: Rusesabagina founded PDR-Ihumure and the FLN in 2006. The FLN initially mainly operated from the DRC before moving to Burundi, where it benefitted from the support of

National Liberation Front (FLN)

Burundian troops under late Burundian president Pierre Nkurunziza. Current President Évariste Ndayishimiye has adopted an offensive mandate against the group as part of a normalisation effort with Rwanda.

Objectives: Seize power from the RPF.

Opponents: Military forces of Burundi and Rwanda.

Affiliates/allies: Despite Ndayishimiye's efforts against the group, it has been known to collaborate with the Imbonerakure. The US was a driving force in facilitating the early release of Rusesabagina.

Resources/capabilities: Small arms and light weapons exclusively. The FLN is financed by opponents in the diaspora and in exile (mainly in Belgium and the US).

March 23 Movement (M23)

Strength: The group probably resumed operations with approximately 400 fighters in November 2021.[11] Voluntary and forced recruitment and Rwandan support have most likely increased combatant numbers to approximately 3,000.[12]

Areas of operation: The southern area of North Kivu province in the DRC, particularly Rutshuru, Nyiragongo and Masisi territories, surrounding the strategic border town of Goma.

Leadership: The leadership of M23 is exclusively made up of Congolese Tutsis. Sultani Makenga is the group's military leader, and Bertrand Bisimwa is its current president. Willy Ngoma and Lawrence Kanyuka are the military and political spokespeople, respectively. The group has installed a parallel civil administration in the territory it occupies, from April 2022 onwards.

Structure: The group has two factions. The faction that has resumed fighting in the DRC is made up of previously demobilised combatants in Uganda, led by Makenga. The faction of combatants that was demobilised in Rwanda under the leadership of Jean-Marie Runiga Lugerero has remained inactive.

History: On 23 March 2009, members of the Rwanda-backed and Tutsi-led National Congress for the Defence of the People signed a peace treaty with the Congolese government and

integrated into the FARDC. In 2012, around 300 of them defected and created the M23 insurgency, accusing the government of failing to uphold its end of the peace deal. It waged a 19-month rebellion and was eventually defeated in November 2013. It took up arms again in November 2021.

Objectives: Officially, to force the Congolese government to uphold its commitments from the 2013 peace deal and subsequent 2019 road map, regarding the reintegration of ex-combatants into civilian life. M23 also presents itself as a guardian of Tutsi rights in the DRC.

Opponents: FARDC, MONUSCO and Hutu militias. The group has also made a point of not clashing with the East African Community Regional Force.

Affiliates/allies: M23 benefits from political, military and on-the-ground troop support from the RDF, although Kigali denies such allegations. The UN Group of Experts and other non-governmental organisations have proven Rwandan support to the group.

Resources/capabilities: Supported by Rwanda, M23 has highly sophisticated equipment. Bintou Keita, the head of MONUSCO, said in June 2022 that M23 has increasingly behaved like 'a conventional army rather than an armed group'.[13]

Sub-Saharan Africa

Notes

1. For an overview of and update on the conflicts in the Central African Republic and Mozambique, see their respective chapters in this book.
2. UN Security Council (UNSC), 'Midterm Report of the Group of Experts on the Democratic Republic of the Congo', S/22/967, 16 December 2022; and Armed Conflict Location & Event Data Project (ACLED), www.acleddata.com.
3. Human Rights Watch, 'DR Congo: Army Units Aided Abusive Armed Groups', 18 October 2022.
4. Rwanda TV, '"What Have We Done?" – President Kagame Talking About the Accusations of the DRC Against Rwanda', YouTube, 9 January 2023.
5. 'Suspected Militants Shoot at Bus in Southwestern Rwanda, Kill Two', Reuters, 20 June 2022.
6. UN Peacekeeping, 'Contribution of Uniformed Personnel to UN by Mission, Country, and Personnel Type', May 2023. Numbers as of 31 May 2023.
7. Congo Research Group, 'Should We Talk About the FDLR Every Time We Talk About the M23?', 18 August 2022.
8. UNSC, 'Final Report of the Group of Experts on the Democratic Republic of the Congo', S/2022/479, 14 June 2022.
9. Olivier Liffran and Joan Tilouine, 'As Fight Against M23 Continues, Kigali and Kinshasa Wage War of Intelligence', Africa Intelligence, 13 March 2023.
10. Rwanda Government Communications (@RwandaOGS), tweet, 9 March 2023.
11. UNSC, 'Final Report of the Group of Experts on the Democratic Republic of the Congo', S/2022/479, 14 June 2022.
12. UNSC, 'Final Report of the Group of Experts on the Democratic Republic of the Congo', S/2023/431, 13 June 2023, p. 15.
13. Edith M. Lederer, 'UN Envoy Warns Congo's M23 Rebels Are Acting Like an Army', AP News, 30 June 2022.

UGANDA

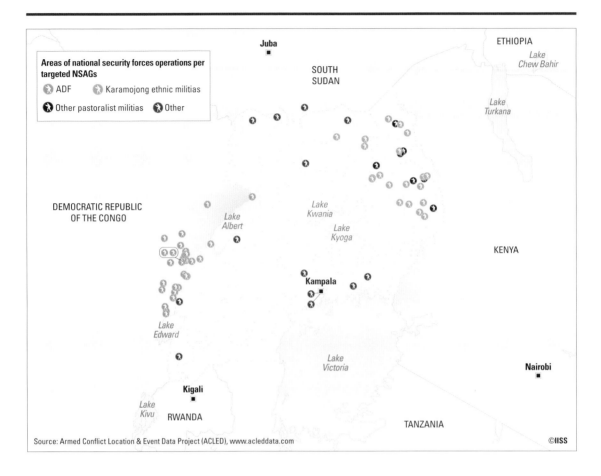

Source: Armed Conflict Location & Event Data Project (ACLED), www.acleddata.com   ©IISS

Conflict Overview

Since 2012, when the Ugandan army defeated Joseph Kony's Lord's Resistance Army and its remnants fled to the neighbouring Central African Republic (CAR) and Democratic Republic of the Congo (DRC), Uganda has experienced relative peace. The country was successful in deterring Somalia-based al-Shabaab following the July 2010 bombing that killed 76 people who were watching the FIFA World Cup final.[1] However, the threat of Salafi-jihadist terrorism returned in late 2021, when Islamic State Central Africa Province (ISCAP) claimed that it had detonated an improvised explosive device at a police station in Kampala.[2] In the following month, the Allied Democratic Forces (ADF), a Ugandan-born rebel group affiliated with the Islamic State (ISIS) that has been operating in the DRC since the 1990s, carried out three separate attacks in the capital

and its surrounding area.[3] In response, the Ugandan People's Defence Force (UPDF) launched a joint operation (*Operation Shujaa*) with the Congolese forces against the ADF in the DRC in November 2021. This remains ongoing as of June 2023.

Within Uganda, insecurity has returned in recent years to the northeastern region of Karamoja, where pastoralism is prevalent. The area, known as the 'northern cattle corridor', is at the border between Kenya, South Sudan and Uganda and has been marginalised by the state since colonial times. It experiences acute communal conflict, mainly in the form of violent cattle raids. Peace had returned to the region following two disarmament campaigns in 2001 and 2006. However, the failed reintegration of combatants and new hardships led to the resumption of the conflict in 2019.[4]

Armed Conflict Global Relevance Indicator (ACGRI)

Incidence

2

Human
impact

0

Geopolitical
impact

7

Uganda

Key Conflict Statistics

Conflict(s)	Type	Start date
Conflict in Karamoja	Internal: intercommunal	Predates colonisation
ADF insurrection in eastern DRC	Internationalised internal	1996
Fatalities		255
Percentage change in fatalities		-31%
IDPs		4,800
Peacekeeping and other multilateral missions		Special Envoy of the Secretary-General for the Great Lakes Region of Africa; Special Envoy of the Secretary-General for the Horn of Africa
Climate-change vulnerability (0–1)		0.4

ACGRI pillars: IISS calculation based on multiple sources for 2022 and 2023 (scale: 0–100), except for some cases according to data availability. See Notes on Methodology and Data Appendix for all variables and further details on Key Conflict Statistics.

Conflict Update

Throughout the reporting period, Ugandan security forces arrested dozens of suspected ADF members and funders within Uganda and clashed with the group near the Congolese border on a number of occasions.[5] In June 2023, the ADF killed at least 40 people, mostly students, in western Uganda – the group's deadliest attack ever in the country.[6] ADF recruitment was ongoing in several areas of the country, and police reported that they foiled multiple attacks. In the DRC, beyond its involvement in *Operation Shujaa*, the Ugandan army joined the East African Community Regional Force (EACRF) as part of the regional response against the March 23 Movement (M23) insurrection.[7] Ugandan contingents of the EACRF were deployed in April 2023 in Bunagana, Kiwanja and Rutshuru (all in Rutshuru

Territory, North Kivu province) to oversee M23 withdrawal in those localities, although the UPDF has made it clear that it will not fight M23.[8]

Insecurity in Karamoja has mainly taken the form of intercommunal fighting between various pastoralist militias, some of which cross the border from neighbouring Kenya. In response, the UPDF launched *Operation Usalama Kwa Wote* (Peace for All) in July 2021, combining voluntary and forceful disarmament. From July 2021–September 2022, it arrested over 11,600 people, over 9,000 of whom were released.[9] In August and November 2022, the Jie, Karamojong and Turkana communities also signed peace agreements, promising to cease hostilities and to support the UPDF in its disarmament campaign.

Conflict Parties

Ugandan People's Defence Force (UPDF)

Strength: About 40,000–45,000 active military personnel.

Areas of operation: Countrywide in Uganda (with extensive deployment in Karamoja), the DRC (5,000 troops, split between a bilateral deployment as part of an ongoing operation against the ADF and a contingent deployed with the EACRF) and Somalia (3,000 troops, as part of the African Union Transition Mission in Somalia).[10]

Leadership: President Yoweri Museveni (commander-in-chief) and Wilson Mbadi (chief of defence forces).

Structure: Comprises land and air forces. It has a rigid vertical structure, and the army is well disciplined.

History: Originated from the National Resistance Army, a rebel movement led by Museveni that waged a guerrilla war against Milton Obote's regime and took power in 1986.

Objectives: Protect Uganda's interests domestically and abroad, and defend the country's sovereignty and territorial integrity. In the DRC, its objective is to defeat the ADF, though there is speculation that it is also largely motivated by economic interests.[11]

Sub-Saharan Africa

Ugandan People's Defence Force (UPDF)

Opponents: Domestically, pastoralist militias in northeast Uganda. In both Uganda and the DRC, the ADF.

Affiliates/allies: Armed Forces of the Democratic Republic of the Congo (FARDC) in the DRC since the beginning of *Operation Shujaa*, and EACRF in the context of overseeing M23's withdrawal.

Resources/capabilities: The UPDF is a well-trained, efficient army, which has received support and training from the United States and France, among others, in part due to its involvement in the fight against al-Shabaab in the Horn of Africa. It possesses mostly light weapons, but also armoured fighting vehicles, artillery and missiles. It is known to be more effective and better disciplined than the FARDC.

Allied Democratic Forces (ADF)

Strength: Estimates ranged from 1,000–1,500 in mid-June 2022, but joint FARDC and UPDF operations might have decreased those numbers, especially as the ADF has increased abductions in early 2023, presumably to reinforce its ranks.[12]

Areas of operation: Traditionally present in the Rwenzori border region between Uganda and the DRC. The ADF carried out attacks in the Kampala metropolitan area in late 2021 and in western Uganda (Kasese district) in June 2023.

Leadership: Leadership is predominantly Ugandan. Musa Baluku is the leader of the ADF's biggest (and only active) faction.

Structure: Operates in small, highly mobile groups out of camps. The ADF recruits new members from Burundi, Kenya, South Africa and Tanzania.

History: Born out of a 1995 merger between Ugandan rebel factions that shared the goal of overthrowing the government of Ugandan President Yoweri Museveni and expanding Salafism in Ugandan politics. The group fled Uganda and found a foothold in North Kivu in the mid-1990s, and it benefitted from the support of Mobutu Sese Seko during the First Congo War.

Following a decade of low-level fighting during the 2000s, it re-emerged as a pre-eminent actor in 2013.

Objectives: Establish an Islamic caliphate in Central Africa.

Opponents: The group targets so-called 'Christian villages'. It has also targeted Hutu civilians (specifically Banyabwisha) due to their purported collaboration with the FARDC. It regularly clashes with the FARDC, UPDF and UN Organization Stabilization Mission in the DRC.

Affiliates/allies: The ADF pledged allegiance to ISIS in 2017. ISIS started claiming ADF attacks and recognised the group as its Central Africa Province (ISCAP) in 2019. Though there is no direct chain of command between the ISIS leadership and the ADF, ISIS has boosted the group's visibility, attracted foreign recruits, helped finance it and enhanced its technical skills.

Resources/capabilities: The group is said to have been severely weakened by joint FARDC and UPDF operations, particularly in late 2022 and early 2023. However, it has also ramped up its use of improvised explosive devices in urban settings.

Karamojong ethnic militias

Strength: Unknown, though reportedly thousands of fighters have been arrested.[13]

Areas of operation: Northern region (Abim, Agago, Amudat, Gulu, Kaabong, Karenga, Kitgum, Kotido, Moroto, Nabilatuk, Nakapiripirit, Napak and Otuke districts) and Eastern region (Bulambuli and Kween districts), with a concentration of activity in Kotido and Moroto districts.[14]

Leadership: No formal leadership.

Structure: 'Karamojong' is a loose term for various ethnic groups living in Karamoja, where the militias are divided along ethnic (predominantly Jie, Karimojong and Pokot) and local lines.

History: Karamojong people have a cultural tradition of cattle rustling (as in other pastoralist societies) as a means of redistributing resources, but traditional weapons (spears, bows and arrows) were replaced with small arms in the 1980s. The raids in Karamoja became particularly violent between the late 1980s and the early 2000s.[15]

Objectives: Raid cattle and challenge central state authority.

Opponents: UPDF and police. The militias also routinely clash with each other.

Affiliates/allies: The militias sometimes support each other when clashing with the UPDF.

Resources/capabilities: Small arms and light weapons (often coming from outside Uganda), and arrows.

Turkana ethnic militias

Strength: Unknown, but between hundreds and thousands in Uganda, with higher numbers during the dry season as pastoralists cross over from Kenya into Uganda looking for water and pasture.[16]

Areas of operation: Northwestern Kenya and northeastern Uganda.

Leadership: No formal leadership.

Structure: No formal structure.

History: A memorandum of understanding (MoU) was signed in 2019 between Kenya and Uganda to improve coexistence between communities on both sides of the border. The agreement allowed the Turkana to graze their cattle in Uganda. However, poor implementation of the MoU has been cited as a reason for the return of the conflict, as Turkanas

Turkana ethnic militias	
have mostly refused to disarm, instead fleeing back to Kenya when disarmament campaigns take place and crossing back into Uganda with their weapons.[17]	**Affiliates/allies:** The Turkana have joined forces with resurgent local raiders from certain communities such as the Matheniko to raid other communities.[18]
Objectives: Grazing on Karimojong land and cattle rustling.	**Resources/capabilities:** Small arms and light weapons.
Opponents: UPDF (in Uganda), Kenya Defence Forces (in Kenya) and other ethnic militias, particularly the Jie (in Uganda).	

Notes

1 Chris Harnisch, 'Al Shabaab's First International Strike: Analysis of the July 22 Uganda Bombings', Critical Threats, 14 July 2010.

2 Max Security, 'Uganda Alert: Islamic State Claims IED Attack Against Police Post in Kampala's Kawempe Division on October 8; First Ever Attack Claimed in Country', 10 October 2021.

3 Dino Mahtani, 'The Kampala Attacks and Their Regional Implications', International Crisis Group, 19 November 2021. For more information on ADF activity in the DRC, see the DRC chapter.

4 Liam Taylor, 'In Uganda's Karamoja, Rampant Rustling and a Militarised Response as Violence Returns', *New Humanitarian*, 26 January 2022.

5 Armed Conflict Location & Event Data Project (ACLED), www.acleddata.com.

6 'Uganda School Attack: Dozens of Pupils Killed by Militants Linked to Islamic State Group', BBC, 17 June 2023.

7 For more information on M23, see the DRC and Rwanda chapters in this book.

8 Defence Spokesperson (@UPDFspokespersn), tweet, 3 April 2023.

9 Liam Taylor, '"Hell Is Coming": The Ugandan Army's Heavy-handed Crackdown in Karamoja', *New Humanitarian*, 1 December 2022.

10 Andrew Bagala, 'UPDF Soldiers Abroad Surge Beyond 12,000', *Daily Monitor*, 11 April 2023.

11 Congo Research Group and Ebuteli, 'Uganda's Operation Shujaa in the DRC: Fighting the ADF or Securing Economic Interests?', June 2022.

12 International Crisis Group, 'A Perilous Free-for-all in the Eastern DR Congo?', Hold Your Fire!, 13 May 2022; and United Nations Security Council, 'Final Report of the Group of Experts on the Democratic Republic of the Congo', S/2023/431, 13 June 2023.

13 Taylor, '"Hell Is Coming": The Ugandan Army's Heavy-handed Crackdown in Karamoja'.

14 Armed Conflict Location & Event Data Project (ACLED), www.acleddata.com.

15 Elizabeth Stites, 'Conflict in Karamoja: A Synthesis of Historical and Current Perspectives, 1920–2022', Karamoja Resilience Support Unit, October 2022.

16 Hesborn Etyang, 'Governor Wants Turkana Herders Jailed in Uganda for Illegal Weapons Released', *Star*, 14 May 2023; and International Crisis Group, 'CrisisWatch: Tracking Conflict Worldwide', May 2023.

17 Raphael Lotira Arasio and Elizabeth Stites, 'The Return of Conflict in Karamoja, Uganda: Community Perspectives', Karamoja Resilience Support Unit, October 2022.

18 'Karamoja: UPDF Warns Turkana Pastoralists Against Supplying Guns', *Independent*, 9 April 2022.

Sub-Saharan Africa

MOZAMBIQUE

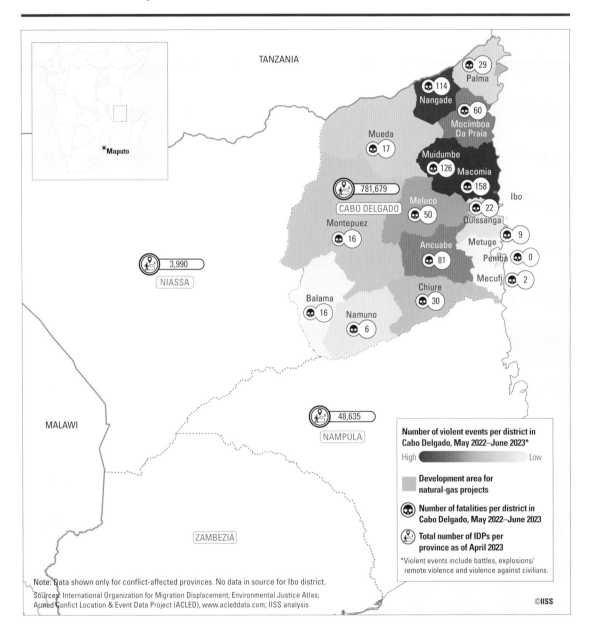

Conflict Overview

Since 2017, Mozambique has been facing an insurgency in its northeastern, gas-rich and majority Muslim Cabo Delgado province, which has spilled over into the neighbouring Nampula and Niassa provinces. The insurgency has resulted in a humanitarian crisis and has delayed the implementation of large liquefied natural gas (LNG) projects. Attacks are allegedly linked to Ahlu al-Sunnah wal-Jamaah (ASJ, locally known as 'al-Shabaab'), and the Islamic State (ISIS) announced in 2019 that the insurgency is part of its Central Africa Province (ISCAP).

Armed Conflict Global Relevance Indicator (ACGRI)		

Incidence

4

Human impact   Geopolitical impact

6   17

Mozambique

Key Conflict Statistics

Conflict(s)	Type	Start date
Islamist insurgency in Cabo Delgado	Internationalised internal	2017
Fatalities		766
Percentage change in fatalities		-41%
IDPs		1,030,000
Peacekeeping and other multilateral missions		EUTM Mozambique; Personal Envoy of the Secretary-General for Mozambique; SAMIM
Climate-change vulnerability (0–1)		0.5

ACGRI pillars: IISS calculation based on multiple sources for 2022 and 2023 (scale: 0–100), except for some cases according to data availability. See Notes on Methodology and Data Appendix for all variables and further details on Key Conflict Statistics.

The conflict is the result of historic disenfranchisement and political marginalisation, especially of the Mwani people.[1] This, alongside widespread poverty, north–south disparities and a lack of job opportunities, has generated favourable grounds for Islamist insurgencies to promote their propaganda and radicalise youth who are seeking an escape from socio-economic exclusion and a sense of belonging. As elsewhere on the continent, Mozambique has seen an overlap between local grievances and transnational Salafi jihadist ideology.

Additionally, the discovery of resources such as natural gas and rubies has not benefited local populations, thus increasing resentment towards the ruling Frelimo party and contributing to escalating terrorism in the region. Frelimo has dominated Mozambique's political space since the country's independence from Portugal in 1975, and especially

after the end of the civil war in 1992. Its grip on power has raised allegations of electoral fraud and corruption, which have undermined the government's domestic legitimacy, as well as reinforced Mozambicans' perception that natural-resource revenues are managed to the exclusive benefit of elites.[2] Conflict proclivity is also exacerbated by Mozambique's tight fiscal situation and weak state capacity, especially in peripheral regions.

From 2019 to early 2021, ASJ's range and capabilities steadily increased. Its high-profile assault on Palma in March 2021 resulted in many deaths and halted regional LNG projects. Following these events, upon Mozambique's invitation, the Rwandan military was deployed in the area; the Southern African Development Community (SADC) put in place its Standby Force Mission in Mozambique (SAMIM); and the European Union launched an EU Training Mission (EUTM).

Conflict Update

Overall, Mozambique's armed forces have benefited from the regional military support provided by Rwanda, SAMIM and EUTM, which has helped prevent further violent escalation – though operational coordination is still limited, with Rwandan forces preferring to act unilaterally rather than coordinate with Mozambique's military and police. A remarkable achievement for the government was

the reopening in November 2022 of the key port of Mocímboa da Praia, which had been seized by rebels in August 2020 and consequently all port activities had been halted.

However, the number of violent events registered in Cabo Delgado remained significant (430 episodes in the reporting period versus 508 from May 2021–June 2022), with ISIS-affiliated insurgents

Sub-Saharan Africa

continuing to carry out attacks in the province.[3] Violent extremists have demonstrated a strong capacity to adapt to the evolving scenario and have increasingly abused civilians; targeted security and defence forces; and seized weapons and ammunition. Throughout the reporting period, ASJ typically attacked security forces and remote towns through road ambushes and armed assaults, but attacks against larger targets also occurred. While central and northern districts of Cabo Delgado continued to experience violence, insurgents also started launching attacks in southern areas previously not affected by the conflict. For instance, in July 2022, a ruby mine near Montepuez in southern Cabo Delgado was attacked, resulting in the decision to temporarily stop operations in the region. Concerns about potential violence also led the graphite industry in Cabo Delgado's southern Balama district to halt its activities. This expansion of armed attacks into new areas could represent a strategic shift for the militants – an attempt to stretch security forces and their allies, while increasing the threat on key gemstone- and graphite-exploitation sites in southern districts.

Against this backdrop, in August 2022, the SADC decided to renew the SAMIM mandate, while transitioning from operating under 'Scenario 6', which focused on military operations, to 'Scenario 5', which signifies a multidimensional peacekeeping mission combining operations with military, civilian, police and correctional-services components. In the same period, Italy, Lithuania and Sweden joined the EUTM, which now comprises 118 military and civilian personnel from a dozen EU member states.[4] Additionally, Rwanda decided to expand its area of operations to southern Cabo Delgado. By the end of 2022, the number of Rwandan soldiers in Cabo Delgado was 2,500, compared to the initial 1,000 units deployed in 2021. While SAMIM forces were sent to zones with no ongoing extractive industries, Rwanda's additional troops were assigned specifically to protect ruby and graphite assets in southern districts.[5]

The southward expansion of the conflict into mineral-rich areas risks replicating what happened with gas enterprises in the northernmost district of Palma, where operations were halted in 2021 due to the deteriorating security outlook. In this regard, however, there are recent signs that gas operations are likely to resume. For instance, in November 2022, Mozambique successfully exported its first LNG shipment out of Cabo Delgado. Likewise, in February 2023, the CEO of TotalEnergies visited the LNG site on the Afungi peninsula, and in May 2023 TotalEnergies published a report on Cabo Delgado, as part of the process to restart LNG activities. In the wake of growing international support, and in an effort to capitalise on recent (though scattered) successes and attract foreign gas investments, in August 2022 Maputo launched a new multidimensional strategy, the Integrated Development and Resilience Program for the North (PREDIN), to restore peace and promote sustainable socio-economic development in northern Mozambique. With a budget of around US$2 billion, PREDIN represents a step forward in the government's response to the conflict, as it recognises internal socio-economic inequalities and grievances as conflict drivers and proposes solutions to local problems.[6] The government has thus expanded the scope of its commitment to combine socio-economic measures and political changes with the military action carried out on the ground.

Altogether, despite recent advancements and the enhanced commitments made by the government and its regional partners, the security situation in Cabo Delgado remains extremely uncertain, with persisting humanitarian concerns regarding food insecurity and internally displaced people. In the Cabo Delgado, Niassa and Nampula provinces, over one million people experience acute food insecurity, and around 834,304 people are internally displaced in northern Mozambique, of which 781,679 are displaced in Cabo Delgado.[7]

Conflict Parties

The Mozambican Defence Armed Forces (FADM)

Strength: 11,200 active military personnel (air force: 1,000; army: 9,000–10,000; navy: approximately 200).

Leadership: Cristóvão Artur Chume (defence minister) and Joaquim Rivas Mangrasse (chief of staff).

Areas of operation: Northern (Cabo Delgado, Nampula and Niassa) and north-central (Manica, Sofala, Tete and Zambezia) Mozambique.

Structure: Consists of infantry forces, a navy and an air force. Together with the Police of the Republic of Mozambique (PRM) they form the Defence and Security Forces (FDS).

The Mozambican Defence Armed Forces (FADM)

History: Created following Mozambique's independence in 1975 but reached its current form after the civil war (1977–92) between Frelimo and the Mozambican National Resistance (Renamo). Former Renamo fighters were integrated into the FADM as part of the 1992 Rome General Peace Accords; this process was then accelerated by a further peace agreement between the government and Renamo in 2019.

Objectives: Protect Mozambique's territory against domestic and foreign enemies. Provide assistance during periods of high insecurity and civil unrest, such as during states of emergency.

Opponents: ASJ and the Renamo Military Junta (RMJ).

Affiliates/allies: SAMIM, the Rwanda Defence Force (RDF), EUTM, local self-defence militias and PRM.

Resources/capabilities: Mozambique's defence budget was US$162m (0.9% of GDP) for 2022 and is US$193m (1.0% of GDP) for 2023.

Police of the Republic of Mozambique (PRM)

Strength: Unclear.

Areas of operation: Nationwide.

Leadership: Bernardino Rafael (commander-general).

Structure: Operates under the Ministry of Interior and consists of multi-level police units, including special-operations units that the government relies on for internal security. Counter-insurgency efforts in Cabo Delgado were initially led by the PRM, with support from foreign-owned private military companies to ensure security. Then, in January 2021, Mozambican President Filipe Nyusi turned counter-insurgency leadership over to the FADM. Together with the FADM they form the FDS.

History: Replaced the People's Police of Mozambique in 1992.

Objectives: Enforce laws and regulations, as well as ensure public security.

Opponents: ASJ and RMJ.

Affiliates/allies: FADM, SAMIM, local self-defence militias and RDF.

Resources/capabilities: Unknown.

Ahlu al-Sunnah wal-Jamaah (ASJ), also known as al-Shabaab

Strength: Estimated around 1,000 fighters.[8]

Areas of operation: Cabo Delgado (particularly the districts of Macomia, Meluco, Mocímboa da Praia, Mueda, Muidumbe, Nangade, Palma and Quissanga) and Niassa (particularly the district of Mecula), as well as border areas of Mtwara Region in Tanzania. In June 2022, Nampula province experienced its first conflict event.

Leadership: Abu Yasir Hassan, also known as Abu Qassim.

Structure: Unknown.

History: Formed between 2015 and 2017 and launched its first attack in 2017. ISIS formally recognised it as part of ISCAP in 2019.

Objectives: No specific manifesto, but the group's public statements indicate that it aims to separate Cabo Delgado residents from the Mozambican state and establish a new state in at least part of Cabo Delgado, drawing on its interpretation of Islamic legal structures. The control of mineral-rich areas is also at stake in the conflict.

Opponents: FDS, SAMIM, RDF, local self-defence militias and Mozambican government officials.

Affiliates/allies: ISIS and ISCAP.

Resources/capabilities: Unclear, but weapons and personnel appear to be locally sourced.

Rwanda Defence Force (RDF)

Strength: 2,500 troops deployed in Mozambique.[9]

Areas of operation: Palma and Mocímboa da Praia districts, as well as segments of Macomia district, in Cabo Delgado. In early 2023, troops were placed in the southern district of Ancuabe.

Leadership: Maj.-Gen. Eugene Nkubito.

Structure: Unknown, though there are both military and police personnel deployed in Mozambique.

History: Deployment began in July 2021, and the commitment scaled up during 2022, reaching around 2,500 personnel.

Objectives: Officially, it aims to defeat ASJ and train Mozambican forces to maintain peace in Cabo Delgado. In practice, it has moved to secure those areas most necessary for work on major natural-gas and mineral projects in Cabo Delgado to resume.

Opponents: ASJ.

Affiliates/allies: FDS, SAMIM and local self-defence militias.

Resources/capabilities: Funded by the government of Rwanda, according to both the Rwandan and Mozambican governments.

Southern African Development Community Standby Force Mission in Mozambique (SAMIM)

Strength: Estimated 2,100.[10]

Areas of operation: Macomia, Muidumbe, Mueda, Nangade and Quissanga districts in Cabo Delgado.

Leadership: Xolani Mankayi (maj.-gen.).

Structure: National contingents from Angola, Botswana, Democratic Republic of the Congo, Lesotho, Malawi, South Africa, Tanzania and Zambia. Personnel from these states and other SADC members provide logistical support.

Sub-Saharan Africa

Southern African Development Community Standby Force Mission in Mozambique (SAMIM)

History: Established in June 2021 and first deployed the following month. In August 2022, the SAMIM mandate was renewed.

Objectives: Officially, it has moved from operating under SADC's 'Scenario 6' (an intervention to end violent conflict) to 'Scenario 5' (a peacekeeping mission).

Opponents: ASJ.

Affiliates/allies: FDS, RDF and local self-defence militias.

Resources/capabilities: Funding has been difficult to acquire; SADC has largely relied on funds and in-kind contributions from member governments.

Notes

1   Giovanni Faleg, 'Conflict Prevention in Mozambique', European Union Institute for Security Studies (EUISS), Brief no. 5, April 2019.

2   Emilia Columbo, 'Stabilizing Mozambique', Council on Foreign Relations, 29 August 2022.

3   Armed Conflict Location & Event Data Project (ACLED), www.acleddata.com.

4   Club of Mozambique, 'Mozambique: More Countries Join Training Mission Against Terrorism', 27 May 2022; and EUTM Mozambique – Press and information team, 'EUTM MOZ Hosts the Portuguese Defense Policy Deputy Director', European Union Training Mission in Mozambique, 24 March 2023.

5   Borges Nhamirre, 'Rwanda Expands Its Protection of Mozambique's Natural Resources', Institute for Security Studies, 1 February 2023.

6   Republic of Mozambique, 'Programa de Resiliência e Desenvolvimento Integrado do Norte de Moçambique' [Integrated Development and Resilience Program for the North of Mozambique], 3 August 2022.

7   Integrated Food Security Phase Classification, 'Mozambique: Acute Food Insecurity Situation November 2022–March 2023', 28 March 2023. Numbers refer to phases three and four, as of March 2023. International Organization for Migration, 'Northern Mozambique Crisis: Mobility Tracking Assessment', May 2023. Numbers for internally displaced people are as of April 2023, taken from data-collection round 18.

8   'The Islamist Insurgency in Mozambique', IISS *Strategic Comments*, vol. 27, no. 22, August 2021.

9   Nhamirre, 'Rwanda Expands Its Protection of Mozambique's Natural Resources'.

10   'The Islamist Insurgency in Mozambique'.

SUDAN

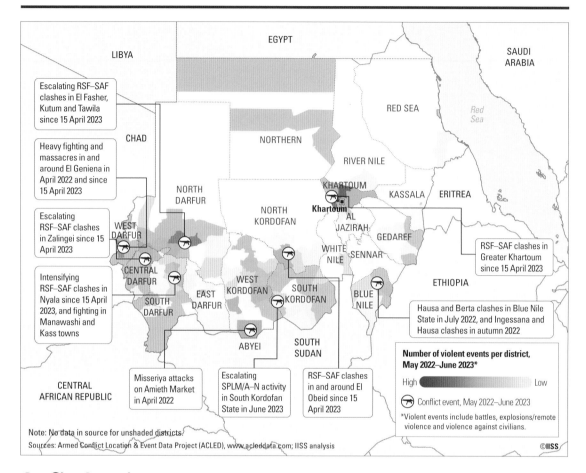

Escalating RSF–SAF clashes in El Fasher, Kutum and Tawila since 15 April 2023

Heavy fighting and massacres in and around El Geniena in April 2022 and since 15 April 2023

Escalating RSF–SAF clashes in Zalingei since 15 April 2023

Intensifying RSF–SAF clashes in Nyala since 15 April 2023, and fighting in Manawashi and Kass towns

Misseriya attacks on Amieth Market in April 2022

Escalating SPLM/A–N activity in South Kordofan State in June 2023

RSF–SAF clashes in and around El Obeid since 15 April 2023

RSF–SAF clashes in Greater Khartoum since 15 April 2023

Hausa and Berta clashes in Blue Nile State in July 2022, and Ingessana and Hausa clashes in autumn 2022

Number of violent events per district, May 2022–June 2023*

High — Low

Conflict event, May 2022–June 2023

*Violent events include battles, explosions/remote violence and violence against civilians.

Note: No data in source for unshaded districts.

Sources: Armed Conflict Location & Event Data Project (ACLED), www.acleddata.com; IISS analysis

©IISS

Conflict Overview

Across its multiple wars and military governments, Sudan established a system of rule that embraced perpetual crisis. Civil wars in southern Sudan (1955–72 and 1983–2005) spread to the Two Areas (Blue Nile and South Kordofan states) in 1987, with the state outsourcing counter-insurgency operations to militias. After Omar al-Bashir seized power in 1989, Sudan's deinstitutionalisation accelerated, with tracts of the country abandoned to local power brokers, paramilitaries and rebellions. The remnants of the state clustered around a shadow economy anchored in Khartoum, as factions of the ruling Islamist party and a burgeoning security cabal competed for resources and positions.

These central characteristics of power competition and factionalism within this system were amplified once oil production began in 1999, financing a peace agreement signed in 2005 with the principal rebel movement in southern Sudan, the Sudan People's Liberation Movement/Army (SPLM/A). Meanwhile, conflict in Darfur intensified in 2003, with the regime's counter-insurgency strategy catalysing a humanitarian disaster. In the following decade, President Bashir navigated international opprobrium and a fraught power-sharing arrangement with southern rebels, characterised by accusations of mutual destabilisation and acrimonious disputes, notably over the status of the long-contested Abyei area.

When South Sudan seceded in 2011, Sudan lost three-quarters of its oil reserves, which led to the removal of Bashir in April 2019 amid widespread

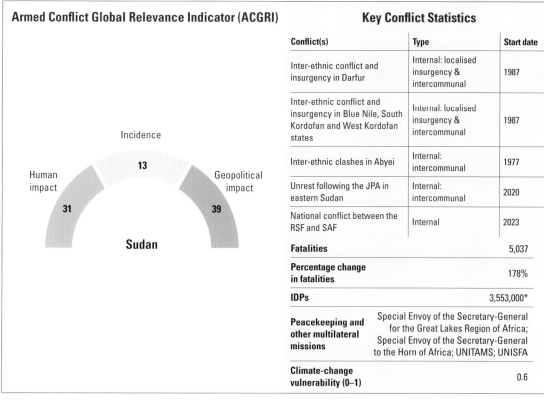

Armed Conflict Global Relevance Indicator (ACGRI)

Incidence **13**

Human impact **31**

Geopolitical impact **39**

Sudan

Key Conflict Statistics

Conflict(s)	Type	Start date
Inter-ethnic conflict and insurgency in Darfur	Internal: localised insurgency & intercommunal	1987
Inter-ethnic conflict and insurgency in Blue Nile, South Kordofan and West Kordofan states	Internal: localised insurgency & intercommunal	1987
Inter-ethnic clashes in Abyei	Internal: intercommunal	1977
Unrest following the JPA in eastern Sudan	Internal: intercommunal	2020
National conflict between the RSF and SAF	Internal	2023
Fatalities		5,037
Percentage change in fatalities		178%
IDPs		3,553,000*
Peacekeeping and other multilateral missions		Special Envoy of the Secretary-General for the Great Lakes Region of Africa; Special Envoy of the Secretary-General to the Horn of Africa; UNITAMS; UNISFA
Climate-change vulnerability (0–1)		0.6

ACGRI pillars: IISS calculation based on multiple sources for 2022 and 2023 (scale: 0–100), except for some cases according to data availability. See Notes on Methodology and Data Appendix for all variables and further details on Key Conflict Statistics. *The Abyei area is not included in the source.

demonstrations against worsening economic conditions and misgovernment. Hopes that a fully civilian government would steer Sudan out of its intersecting crises were dashed in June 2019, when the paramilitary Rapid Support Forces (RSF, which emerged from the war in Darfur) massacred civilians at the main protest camp in Khartoum. Two months later, a power-sharing agreement was reached between the military bloc and an unwieldy alliance of opposition parties, trade unionists and resistance committee activists (who were at the forefront of the demonstrations), known as the Forces for Freedom and Change (FFC).

Divisions soon emerged within the FFC, amid signs that a strategic alignment between rebel groups and the military was forming during the negotiations that resulted in the Juba Peace Agreement (JPA) of October 2020. The JPA ultimately enlarged the military bloc – whilst exacerbating violence in the provincial areas from which most of its signatories originated – and revived a dormant conflict in eastern Sudan. A coup initiated by the military bloc in October 2021 generated further turmoil, paving the way for tensions to escalate within the bloc.

Conflict Update

On 15 April 2023, fighting between the Sudan Armed Forces (SAF) and the RSF erupted in Khartoum and major cities across Sudan (particularly in Darfur), creating a humanitarian crisis which repeated ceasefire agreements failed to abate. The violence followed a brewing power struggle between the two dominant military figures – General Abdel Fattah al-Burhan (the leader of the SAF) and his former deputy, General Mohamed Hamdan Dagalo (the head of the RSF, popularly known as 'Hemeti').

The national-level conflict was foreshadowed by a series of contentious negotiations to address the fallout of the 2021 coup. The most significant development took place on 5 December 2022, when a framework agreement was unexpectedly reached between the military bloc and several political parties. This deal envisaged a return to the pre-coup status quo, with a new two-year transition period under civilian control, during which the military would detach itself from political and economic activity. The RSF would be integrated into the SAF, and the JPA would be placed under 'review'.[1]

Subsequently, public brinkmanship between Burhan and Hemeti over the proposed RSF integration heightened tensions, as did militia recruitment by both parties. Meanwhile, the JPA review sparked an outcry from JPA signatories who worried that they would lose political power and influence, with many signatories attaching themselves to a separate negotiation track sponsored by Egypt.

At the outset of the fighting, the SAF swiftly secured most southern and eastern cities, as the RSF dug into residential and industrial areas of the capital to mitigate shelling and airstrikes by the SAF. Heavy fighting continued in towns and cities in Darfur and in El Obeid along the main road between Darfur and Khartoum.[2] In El Geneina in West Darfur State, clashes between the belligerents soon became enmeshed with violence involving ethnically organised militias. The RSF reportedly executed the governor of West Darfur after he claimed that the RSF was conducting a genocide in El Geneina. Importantly, the powerful Abdelaziz al-Hilu faction of the SPLM/A–North (SPLM/A–N) engaged the SAF in South Kordofan and Blue Nile states throughout June, capturing several settlements. Meanwhile, JPA signatory groups largely abstained from the fighting in much of Darfur, as did several Arab-identifying clans.

Numerous ceasefire agreements were brokered after the fighting began, largely through indirect talks between the SAF and RSF in Jeddah, Saudi Arabia, with the United States' backing. These agreements resulted in short periods during which evacuations of foreign nationals and some humanitarian-aid deliveries could take place, though they were repeatedly broken by both sides. As of mid-August 2023, conservative estimates indicated that at least 4,000 people had been killed, with 3.4 million people internally displaced and over 900,000 people fleeing to neighbouring countries.[3]

A protracted national conflict will further imperil Sudan's troubled peripheries. Prior to the conflict between the RSF and SAF, over 200 people were killed in fighting between ethnic Rizeigat and Masalit militias in West Darfur in April 2022, whilst over 120 were killed during clashes between the Rizeigat and Gimir in Kulbus locality, West Darfur, in June 2022. Meanwhile, ethnic clashes in Lagawa town in West Kordofan State morphed into serious fighting between security forces and the SPLM/A–N (Abdelaziz al-Hilu faction) in October 2022, killing dozens.[4] Finally, in Blue Nile State, hostilities involving the Hausa and Fulani (who migrated from West Africa generations ago) and a number of smaller ethnic groups (who regard themselves as indigenous) resulted in hundreds of deaths in June and October 2022.[5] These subnational flashpoints may become entangled in the national conflict (as has already happened in West Darfur), and their location along volatile international borders increases the chance that violence will spill over into adjoining countries.

Conflict Parties

Sudan Armed Forces (SAF)	
Strength: About 104,300 active personnel, with higher estimates in the range of 120,000–200,000.[6]	the Bashir regime. In 2020, the Popular Defence Forces militia was disbanded, becoming 'Reservists'.
Areas of operation: Uneven presence across Sudan.	**History:** Established in 1925, the military has become a major political player in post-colonial Sudan and has gradually lost its reputation as a professional force. Under presidents Jaafar Nimeiri and Bashir, the SAF's capacity was degraded as part of a coup-proofing strategy, with security outsourced to intelligence agencies and militias.
Leadership: Gen. Abdel Fattah al-Burhan (commander-in-chief and chairman of the governing Sovereignty Council).	
Structure: Has a conventional command and ground-force structure and a separate military-intelligence branch, which pursues its goals autonomously. The SAF was responsible for overseeing parts of the militia network that proliferated under	**Objectives:** Uphold the territorial integrity of Sudan and check the power of rival state and non-state forces.

Sudan Armed Forces (SAF)

Opponents: RSF, Sudan Liberation Movement/Army–Abdel Wahid al-Nur (SLM/A–AW) and SPLM/A–N (Abdelaziz al-Hilu faction).

Affiliates/allies: Maintains links with Egypt and various regional powers (notably South Sudan and Chad), and has strengthened ties to Saudi Arabia and Israel. It also has links to Russia. The SAF has relationships with various armed groups in Darfur and eastern Sudan, as well as the Malik Agar faction of the SPLM/A–N.

Resources/capabilities: Acquires its military equipment – including ammunition, small arms and armoured vehicles – from a mix of domestic and international manufacturers, financed by the state. This is in addition to Soviet-era tanks and transport planes. The SAF also allegedly controls a vast number of commercial companies in several sectors.

Rapid Support Forces (RSF)

Strength: About 40,000 active personnel, with higher estimates in the range of 75,000–100,000.[7]

Areas of operation: Uneven presence across Sudan, though particularly concentrated in Darfur and Khartoum.

Leadership: Gen. Mohamed Hamdan Dagalo, commonly known as 'Hemeti'. Burhan dismissed him from his role as deputy chairman of the Sovereign Council on 19 May 2023.

Structure: Unclear, though the force likely functions as a hybrid military–militia, with weak formal structures and relatively autonomous commanders who have links to co-ethnic communities and irregular militias. Its geographical command sectors appear to mirror those of the SAF.

History: Established in 2013 from a faction of the Border Guards paramilitary group, the RSF was initially controlled by the notorious National Intelligence and Security Service (now known as the General Intelligence Service). As the RSF's power has increased, efforts have been made to diversify its ethnic base (which is mostly comprised of Arab-identifying groups in western Sudan).

Objectives: The RSF's original purpose was to provide security for the Bashir regime, whilst also supporting the SAF in counter-insurgency activities, notably in Darfur, and Blue Nile and South Kordofan states. Since the 2019 coup, it has increasingly served as a platform for Hemeti's personal ambitions and family interests.

Opponents: SAF, SLM/A–AW and SPLM/A–N (Abdelaziz al-Hilu faction).

Affiliates/allies: The RSF pursues a personalised approach to foreign relations under Hemeti, who has ties to regional leaders, Russia and the United Arab Emirates (UAE). Previously close relations with Saudi Arabia, however, have become more distant. The RSF also has connections to various militias in Darfur.

Resources/capabilities: Financed through Hemeti's extensive involvement in gold production in various parts of Sudan, as well as the taxation of commercial and agricultural trade in Darfur and commercial interests in Khartoum. The RSF has 20 armoured personnel carriers, seven infantry fighting vehicles and a large number of land-cruiser-type vehicles.[8]

Sudan Liberation Movement/Army–Abdel Wahid al-Nur (SLM/A–AW)

Strength: It is unclear how many fighters the group has in its Jebel Marra Mountains stronghold, though it has recently increased recruitment activity. The group has 200–700 personnel based in South Sudan and had at least 100 based in Libya in 2019.[9]

Areas of operation: Jebel Marra in central Darfur, parts of Libya and South Sudan. The group also has a presence in ethnic Fur internally displaced persons (IDP) camps in Darfur.

Leadership: Abdel Wahid al-Nur (leader) and Abdullah Haran (deputy chair). Abdelgadir Abdelrahman Ibrahim (alias 'Gaddura'), the group's long-standing military commander, defected to the RSF during the reporting period. Mubarak Aldouk leads the main splinter faction.

Structure: Fragmented structure, with Nur at times bypassing the official chain of command to manage an array of semi-autonomous commanders directly. Several factions have defected to the SAF and/or the RSF, with some continuing to engage in hostilities and violent competition over gold mines with loyalist factions.

History: Emerged in 2001 (as the Darfur Liberation Front) out of Fur, Zaghawa and Masalit self-defence militias. The group's

insurgency began in 2003 under the SLM/A name, with support from Eritrea, the SPLM/A, and the Justice and Equality Movement. In 2004, it split into two (predominantly Fur and Zaghawa) factions. During Nur's long exile in Paris, the group has experienced further splintering and instability.

Objectives: The group's goals have shifted over time, though they have centred around reversing Darfur's subordinate position in Sudan since 2003. With the subsequent fragmentation of the group, these goals have become more parochial and multi-layered. Nur did not participate in the JPA, and he denounced the 2021 coup.

Opponents: SAF, RSF and SLM/A–AW splinter factions.

Affiliates/allies: The UAE and some qualified support from South Sudan. Splinter factions often receive support from the SAF or the RSF.

Resources/capabilities: Factions of the SLM/A–AW generate income based on opportunities in their geographical area (e.g., gold in Jebel Marra, taxation in IDP camps, smuggling in Libya, and commercial and cross-border trade, as well as limited agricultural activities, in South Sudan).

Sudan People's Liberation Movement/Army–North (SPLM/A–N) (Abdelaziz al-Hilu faction)

Strength: Unknown.

Areas of operation: Southern areas of Blue Nile State and the Nuba Mountains of South Kordofan State.

Sudan People's Liberation Movement/Army–North (SPLM/A–N) (Abdelaziz al-Hilu faction)

Leadership: Abdelaziz al-Hilu (commander) and Joseph Tuka (deputy commander).

Structure: Headquartered in Kauda, the SPLM/A–N has a relatively centralised senior command structure under Hilu, which gives way to a more autonomous tier of commanders at the middle ranks. Tuka commands the Blue Nile division, which mainly comprises non-Ingessana ethnic groups.

History: Emerged from the SPLM/A's campaigns in the Two Areas in 1987. The group's respected former commander, Yousif Kuwa, led forces in the Nuba Mountains until his death in 2001. In 2011, following the secession of South Sudan, SPLA forces marooned in Sudan formed the SPLM/A–N under the leadership of Malik Agar. In 2017, the group split, with the majority of forces siding with Hilu.

Objectives: Restructure power relations in Khartoum, in order to grant autonomy to marginalised or oppressed provinces, and flatten Sudan's ethnic and religious hierarchies.

Opponents: SAF, RSF and SPLM/A–N (Malik Agar faction).

Affiliates/allies: South Sudan.

Resources/capabilities: Unknown.

Notes

1   International Crisis Group, 'A Critical Window to Bolster Sudan's Next Government', 23 January 2023; and 'History Won't Repeat Itself, *Africa Confidential*, vol. 64, no. 2, 19 January 2023.

2   United Nations Office for the Coordination of Humanitarian Affairs (UNOCHA), 'Sudan: Clashes Between SAF and RSF: Flash Update No. 6', 24 April 2023; and Ayin Network, 'The Sudan Conflict Observer – May 10 Update', 10 May 2023.

3   UN Office of the High Commissioner for Human Rights, 'Sudan: Türk Decries "Disastrous" Impact of War, Urges Accountability', 15 August 2023; and UNOCHA, 'Sudan Situation Report: 17 Aug 2023', 17 August 2023.

4   Armed Conflict Location & Event Data Project (ACLED), www.acleddata.com.

5   Rift Valley Institute and Cross-Border Conflict Evidence, Policy and Trends, 'One Year After the Coup: What Next for Sudan's Juba Peace Agreement?', Sudan Rapid Response Update 5, November 2022; and Zeinab Mohammed Salih, 'At Least 230 Sudanese Villagers Killed in Tribal Attacks over Disputed Land', *Guardian*, 26 October 2022.

6   Jérôme Tubiana, 'Darfur After Bashir: Implications for Sudan's Transition and for the Region', no. 508, United States Institute of Peace, April 2022.

7   *Ibid*.

8   UN Security Council (UNSC), 'Final Report of the Panel of Experts on the Sudan', S/2023/93, 7 February 2023, p. 27; and Richard Kent, Mohamed Aboelgheit and Nick Donovan, 'How the RSF Got Their 4x4 Technicals: The Open Source Intelligence Techniques Behind Our Sudan Exposé', Global Witness, 5 April 2020.

9   *Ibid.*, p. 12; and UNSC, 'Final Report of the Panel of Experts on the Sudan Established Pursuant to Resolution 1591 (2005)', S/2019/34, 10 January 2019, p. 30.

Sub-Saharan Africa

5 Asia

Taliban security personnel walk along a road after gunfire erupted between Afghanistan and Pakistan border forces, 20 February 2023

Overview

South and Southeast Asia host a number of long-standing armed conflicts. Three of them – the war in Afghanistan, Pakistan's struggle with ethnic insurgency and anti-state terrorist groups, and the dispute over Kashmir – have a significant impact on regional and global security. This is primarily due to the transnational actors involved in these conflicts and the potential of the Kashmir dispute to escalate into a conventional war between nuclear powers India and Pakistan. Meanwhile, the conflict in Myanmar is comparatively more localised in nature but has continued to intensify, raising concerns among Myanmar's neighbours and the international community.

The intensity of two of these conflicts – the dispute over Kashmir and especially the war in Afghanistan – has significantly reduced in terms of violence over

the last two reporting periods (including violence against civilians, see Figure 1). Tensions along the Line of Control (LoC) between India and Pakistan have abated since a ceasefire took effect in February 2021, leading to a 38% decline in conflict-related fatalities during May 2022–June 2023 compared to May 2021–June 2022.[1] Likewise, while the number of incidents was 47 in 2020, this dropped to 23 in 2022.[2] This relative calm has allowed Indian forces to upgrade their border defences and surveillance, which has led to a decline in border crossings and violence by militants in Indian-administered Jammu and Kashmir (J&K).[3]

The Afghan Taliban has continued to consolidate power and has maintained control over nearly all of Afghanistan's territory since its August 2021 takeover of the country. Some armed groups have

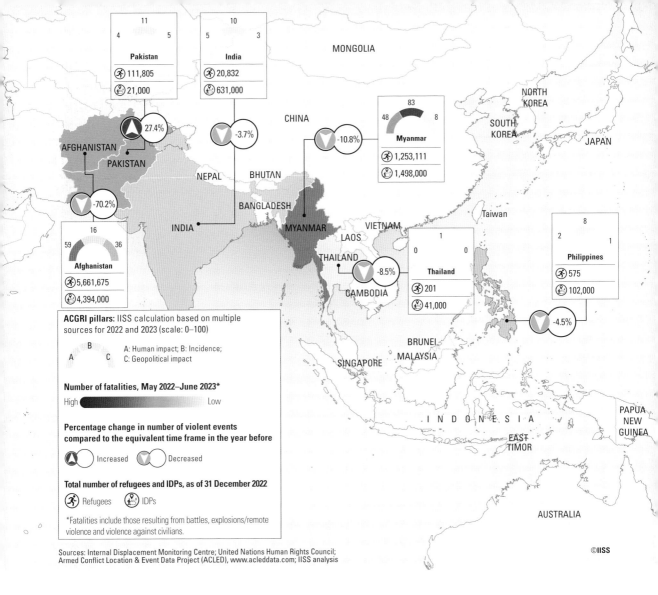

Sources: Internal Displacement Monitoring Centre; United Nations Human Rights Council;
Armed Conflict Location & Event Data Project (ACLED), www.acleddata.com; IISS analysis

sought to challenge the Taliban's rule, but none have managed to gather enough support, either domestically or internationally, to pose a significant threat. Notably, despite continuing to carry out attacks on Taliban security forces, foreign diplomats and civilians, Islamic State Khorasan Province (ISKP) has been unable to maintain control over territory or meaningfully challenge the Taliban's authority. Furthermore, the Taliban's security forces successfully killed high-profile ISKP leaders during the reporting period. The desire of regional and international powers to maintain stability in Afghanistan so that it does not serve as a staging ground for transnational terrorist groups has led to a flurry of diplomacy. Even New Delhi has managed to establish inroads with the Taliban through aid and limited diplomacy.

Meanwhile, the conflict in Myanmar between the military junta and a loose coalition of pro-democracy forces and ethnic armed organisations (EAOs), following the military coup by the State Administration Council (SAC, also known as Myanmar armed forces or the Tatmadaw) in February 2021, has continued to escalate despite sanctions imposed by the United States, United Kingdom and European Union and the suspension of aid. During the reporting period, the SAC (Tatmadaw) heightened its campaign against EAOs through airstrikes; disqualified 40 political parties, including Aung San Suu Kyi's National League for Democracy (NLD); and declared martial law in dozens of townships.[4] Notably, it also carried out massacres, beheadings and violence in areas, including the central plains region where the Bamar ethnic majority primarily

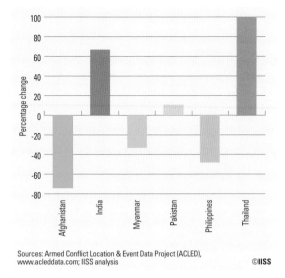

Sources: Armed Conflict Location & Event Data Project (ACLED),
www.acleddata.com; IISS analysis   ©IISS

Figure 1: Percentage change in violent events involving violence against civilians, May 2022–June 2023

and Tehrik-e-Taliban Pakistan (TTP) fighters, who benefited from safe havens provided by the Taliban in Afghanistan. The TTP agreed to 'unilateral' short-term ceasefires with Pakistan's security forces while still carrying out attacks, often unclaimed. It then launched a deadly campaign of violence against the security forces in November 2022. While most attacks have taken place in Khyber Pakhtunkhwa (KP), the TTP has also conducted attacks in major cities like Karachi.

The region's other conflicts, which are more localised and have a lesser impact on regional dynamics, remained relatively stable in the reporting period. This includes the Malay Muslim ethno-nationalist autonomy movement and insurgency in Thailand; the Philippines' two conflicts, the Moro insurgency in Mindanao and the nationwide Maoist insurgency; and India's Maoist insurgency. Peace deals between the Indian government and insurgent groups further reduced the intensity of the small-scale conflict in northeast India, except in Manipur, where ethnic clashes caused over a hundred fatalities at the very end of the reporting period.[5]

lives, which had not seen organised violence for decades prior to the coup.

The reporting period also saw an intensification in confrontations between Pakistan's security forces

Conflict Drivers

Political and institutional
Post-colonial arrangements
The most active conflicts in the region are rooted in the ethnic, religious, irredentist and centre–province tensions that emerged in newly formed, post-colonial states. The decision of the last Hindu ruler of Jammu and Kashmir (princely state) to join India in 1947, for instance, created a conflict that divided Kashmir between India and Pakistan. In Pakistan, the Baloch insurgency and insecurity in the Pashtun tribal areas are partly fuelled by questions over the legitimacy of the Durand Line as the Afghanistan–Pakistan border. The post-colonial order that divided Pakistan into west and east wings, culminating in the secession of East Pakistan to form Bangladesh, also led to ethnic resentment and tensions within the country. Likewise, the division of the historical Islamic sultanate of Patani by the Anglo-Siamese Treaty in 1909 laid the groundwork for the Malay Muslim autonomy movement and insurgency in southern Thailand.

Similarly, the conflicts in Myanmar stem from the Bamar majority's attempt to control ethnic minority groups following the country's independence

from British rule in 1948, which triggered struggles for autonomy among these minority groups. Thus, many of Myanmar's internal armed conflicts arise from EAOs vying for autonomy in remote borderlands, which the military junta has responded to with concerted military campaigns and indiscriminate violence, disproportionately affecting civilian populations with affiliations to these groups.

Socio-economic
Socio-economic divides
Socio-economic inequalities are one of the main causes of the insurgencies in India, Pakistan and the Philippines. Poverty and a lack of economic opportunities in parts of the Philippines continue to fuel recruitment for both Moro Muslim rebel groups and the New People's Army (NPA). India's Communist Party of India–Maoist has long tapped into sentiments of disenfranchisement among rural, impoverished populations. Similarly, the conflict between Pakistan and Baloch insurgents is partially fuelled by economic inequality, including most recently the distribution of economic benefits

derived from natural-resource extraction and the China–Pakistan Economic Corridor (CPEC) traversing Balochistan.

Marginalisation of majority-minority groups
In Myanmar, Pakistan and the Philippines, insurgents have cited internal migration of majority ethnic and religious groups to minority areas or the entry of multinational (especially Chinese) firms as key motivators for continued fighting. These movements are viewed as attempts to subjugate 'majority-minority' groups in their provincial homelands.[6] Projects like CPEC and the China–Myanmar Economic Corridor simultaneously motivate resistance and incentivise groups to consolidate control over future development zones so that they can engage in rent seeking.

Illicit economies
Illicit trade and informal taxation are also powerful economic drivers of conflict. The cultivation and export of illicit narcotics play a central role in Afghanistan, while illicit trade in narcotics, gems, timber and people fuels the conflict in Myanmar. In April 2022, the Taliban banned the cultivation of poppy, which is used to produce opium. By 2023, satellite imagery revealed a 99% decrease in poppy cultivation in Helmand province, the main poppy-growing region of Afghanistan, a development which was met with a rare statement of praise from US Special Representative for Afghanistan Thomas West.[7] While the ban may slightly improve the Taliban's standing with the West, others argue that it risks plunging the economy further into crisis and fuelling external migration.

Climate vulnerability and water governance
Massive floods in the summer of 2022 submerged one-third of Pakistan, affecting at least 33 million people.[8] This could exacerbate conflict drivers, through mass migration from KP, interior Sindh, rural Punjab and parts of Balochistan into major Pakistani cities. Not only could this alter local voter counts and electoral politics, but it could also lead to disenfranchised populations living in urban peripheries.

Disputes over drinkable water also aggravate conflict in the region. In late May 2023, at least two Iranian border guards and one Taliban fighter were killed in an exchange of gunfire surrounding a disagreement over how much the Taliban can restrict the flow of the Helmand River into Iran. A long-standing diplomatic dispute over the use of the Indus, Chenab and Jhelum rivers is also one of the drivers of the conflict between Pakistan and India over Kashmir.

Geopolitical
International interventions
The conflicts in Afghanistan, Kashmir and Pakistan have strong international drivers that often perpetuate violence by altering power dynamics on the ground. For decades, the continued intervention of US and NATO troops, regional support for the Taliban and other forms of covert and overt intervention were key drivers of the conflict in Afghanistan, making it the most internationalised of internal conflicts in Asia. India has long opposed the internationalisation of the Kashmir conflict, especially since the 2019 revocation of Articles 370 (1949) and 35A (1954, a provision of Article 370) of the Indian constitution, which had provided special status to J&K, and the division of the region into two separate union territories.

China's involvement
Beijing has shown a moderate but growing level of interest in conflicts that impact security on its periphery and its economic interests. It has mostly articulated this through bilateral diplomatic ties, but it has also increasingly spearheaded regional diplomacy regarding Afghanistan, be it through minilateral formats such as a trilateral dialogue with Afghanistan and Pakistan or through the Shanghai Cooperation Organisation (SCO) with Russia. These interests are evident as well in China's engagement with both Myanmar and Pakistan, which are key recipients of investment through the Belt and Road Initiative (BRI). China has played a role in facilitating peace negotiations between Myanmar's military and EAOs, and has also encouraged Pakistan's government to prioritise security and political stability. China maintains an embassy in Afghanistan, primarily because of its desire to contain the East Turkestan Islamic Movement and to take advantage of future investment opportunities for the BRI and the oil and mining industries.

Transnational jihadism
The spread of transnational jihadism in South and Southeast Asia has traditionally raised concerns among regional and Western governments. Since 2014, various groups in the area have pledged allegiance to the Islamic State (ISIS). More recently, the Taliban's takeover of Afghanistan in 2021 has contributed to the resurgence of the TTP in Pakistan (see the Asia Regional

Spotlight chapter), with important repercussions for regional security. The domestic threat mounted by ISKP in Afghanistan also has transnational implications for Western and global security.

Conflict Parties

Coalitions

In certain conflicts, coalitions have been formed between political entities and non-state actors. In Myanmar, EAOs, which are often viewed as independent militias, have organised themselves into coalitions. During the reporting period, some of these groups collaborated with the Bamar-majority National Unity Government (NUG) and its armed wing, the People's Defence Force, to establish regional command centres in opposition to the military junta. Certain EAOs possess greater strength and autonomy compared to others. This is particularly true for groups situated along the China–Myanmar border, such as the United Wa State Army and the Kachin Independence Army. In contrast, EAOs like the Karen National Union and the Chin National Front (CNF) have fewer military capabilities and are more likely to rely on coalition dynamics.

Meanwhile, the rise of the Taliban in Afghanistan has strengthened the TTP's position. The TTP itself operates somewhat as an umbrella group and frequently loses splinter groups only to reabsorb them later. With the Afghan Taliban now firmly in control, the emboldened TTP has refocused its strategy on targeting the Pakistani state, with the double benefit of a safe haven across the border and inspiration from the success of its Afghan associates. The Taliban is unlikely to try to exert control over the TTP due to the latter's past assistance and the familial, tribal and ideological ties between the two groups.

Non-state armed groups

Ongoing conflicts in Asia involve multiple non-state armed groups (NSAGs). These groups are predominantly organised around ethnic or religious affiliations, although some, like the Maoist groups in northeastern India or the NPA in the Philippines, are also driven by secular ideologies. Certain groups, such as militant

Kashmiri Muslim groups in J&K or the Patani Malay National Revolutionary Front (or Barisan Revolusi Nasional, BRN) in southern Thailand, operate along both ethnic and religious lines. Other groups, like the various EAOs in Myanmar or Baloch separatist movements in Pakistan, are primarily organised along ethnic and subregional divisions.

The majority of the NSAGs active in the region have localised objectives that do not extend beyond the borders of the countries in which they operate, and in some cases, they even remain within specific subregions of those countries. The kinship ties and personal experiences of local or more prominent leaders also matter, as does groups' proximity to criminal practices such as kidnapping for ransom or arms and narcotics smuggling. It is important to note that ISKP and al-Qaeda stand out as exceptions, as their stated goals are above all transnational, and both have a history of carrying out international terrorist attacks.

Third-party interventions

Peacekeeping missions and intergovernmental organisations have been largely ineffective at reducing conflict in the region. The United Nations Military Observer Group in India and Pakistan is headquartered in Islamabad and Srinagar. While the mission plays a crucial role in monitoring developments pertaining to the ceasefire of 17 December 1971 and reporting them to the UN secretary-general, as an observer mission it lacks the authority to enforce peace or deter potential hostilities effectively. The Association of Southeast Asian Nations (ASEAN) is similarly inconsequential in the conflict in Myanmar, although it did exclude Myanmar's generals from its meetings. The military junta has largely ignored ASEAN's five-point peace plan, and ASEAN's involvement in addressing the crisis has been criticised by the US-based Council on Foreign Relations as a 'complete failure'.[9]

Regional and International Dimensions

The conflicts of greatest consequence for regional and global security are India and Pakistan's dispute over Kashmir; the threat of transnational terrorism emanating from Afghanistan and Pakistan; and the raging conflict between Myanmar's military junta and a loose coalition of armed resistance groups. Afghanistan's importance to international actors is otherwise motivated by previous investment into the country and large outflows of refugees. The conflicts in northeastern India, southern Thailand and the Philippines, on the other hand, have received limited regional and international attention primarily because they are localised in nature.

Besides ASEAN's five-point peace plan, Beijing has also taken an interest in mediating aspects of the conflict in Myanmar, due to its desire to limit instability along the China–Myanmar border and other geostrategic and economic interests. Compared to many other regional conflicts, the international community is more deeply engaged in the situation in Myanmar due to two factors. Firstly, the ongoing persecution against the Rohingya minority in Myanmar has drawn global condemnation. Secondly, the military coup that deposed the democratically elected and internationally popular leader Aung San Suu Kyi reversed a democratic rebound in Myanmar and captured global attention.

The Taliban's consolidation of power in Afghanistan, meanwhile, has sparked significant interest from neighbouring countries, including China and Pakistan. These nations are worried that the Taliban may create a safe haven for militant groups, allowing them to launch attacks outside the country. Afghanistan also remains a point of interest for lawmakers and civil society in the US and Europe. This heightened attention compared to other countries facing humanitarian crises and security threats can be attributed to various factors. The two-decade presence of US and NATO troops in Afghanistan required the long-term commitment of elected officials and civil society. When the Taliban assumed power, US and UN sanctions, which had been imposed on the group and its leaders as non-state actors,

shifted overnight to become sanctions on the de facto leaders of Afghanistan, a development that further internationalised the situation. Although the US Department of the Treasury created exemptions to these sanctions that technically exclude Afghanistan as a territory, the chilling effect on investment, trade and everyday banking transactions was immediate and remains in place. Most importantly, concerns over terrorism and the Taliban's flagrant disregard for human rights have also raised interest from voters, the Afghan diaspora, and members of the US Congress and parliaments in Europe.

Nevertheless, several factors have diminished the international relevance of the conflicts in Afghanistan and Pakistan. The withdrawal of US and NATO forces from Afghanistan in 2021 was a deliberate decision to de-prioritise the region and the potential terrorist threat it posed amid growing intervention fatigue at home and Washington's desire to shift its focus to peer-to-peer competition, particularly with China. The Russian invasion of Ukraine and heightened tensions between the US and China have also diverted attention away from the region for Washington and its closest partners. Successful 'over-the-horizon' counter-terrorism strikes, such as the one that killed al-Qaeda chief Ayman al-Zawahiri on 31 July 2022, and the Taliban's demonstrated capability to target ISKP leaders have reinforced the belief that terrorism threats can be effectively managed from outside the region.[10] Although terrorist attacks within Pakistan have increased, they have not yet reached a level that would destabilise the state. However, a convergence of violence from the TTP, ISKP and Baloch separatist groups in Pakistan poses a threat to foreign investments, particularly from China. In this regard, the TTP and certain Baloch separatist groups share a common enemy in Pakistan's security forces, despite having different objectives.

Outlook

Prospects for peace

Progress has been made towards peace in certain conflict regions, while others have regressed. Along the LoC in Kashmir, a fragile ceasefire reaffirmed in 2021 but still to be formalised between India and Pakistan is likely to remain in place as India focuses

on China and Pakistan contends with an acute economic and political crisis. Yet upcoming general elections in both countries could lead to border posturing and provocations. In India's northeast, the central and state governments signed peace deals with eight Assam-based tribal armed groups, the

Naga faction Zeliangrong United Front (ZUF) and the National Socialist Council of Nagalim–Isak Muivah (NSCN–IM).[11] Likewise, in September 2022, the Working Committee, an umbrella organisation comprising seven Naga armed groups, signed a 'Joint Concordant' to work together in their respective peace processes. Despite some ongoing insurgent activity, the prospects for achieving a broader peace in Thailand have also improved. The BRN, in its sixth round of dialogue with the Thai government, has taken a positive step by agreeing to include other armed groups in future negotiations aimed at reducing violence under a Joint Comprehensive Plan Towards Peace. The conflict in the Philippines between separatist movements and the government is likely to remain highly localised and contained.

The Taliban has continued to consolidate its control over the majority of Afghanistan, two years after assuming power. Outside powers have largely refrained from direct intervention in Afghanistan, and no armed group, including ISKP, has been able to mount a meaningful challenge to the Taliban's dominance. It is unlikely that Afghanistan will descend into civil war or the Taliban will face a significant threat to its rule in the near future.

Escalation potential and regional spillovers

During the reporting period, the conflict between Myanmar's armed forces and the various EAOs intensified. It expanded to include pro-democracy movements following the coup in February 2021. Despite some mediation efforts by China, there do not appear to be any significant prospects for de-escalation in the near future.

Compared to pre-August 2021 levels, overall violence in Afghanistan has decreased significantly. However, the Taliban's governance decisions, such as banning girls and women from secondary education, higher education and the workplace, have alienated the international community and many Afghans. This has led to diplomatic and economic isolation, which puts a strain on Afghanistan's population and makes it difficult for the Taliban to provide the minimum services expected of a government. The Taliban's enabling of safe havens for the TTP has also strained its relationship with Pakistan. There is a real risk that terrorist attacks by the TTP in Pakistan might be traced back to operatives in Afghanistan and could lead to border escalation between the Taliban and Pakistan's security forces, including artillery cross-border fire or even airstrikes by Pakistan. The Taliban may engage in diplomatic efforts to gain greater recognition from the international community, but it is unlikely to make significant policy reversals or respond positively to demands. There is the potential for pockets of resistance within Afghanistan, but a major escalation in the conflict is unlikely in the near term. The ability of Taliban leader Mullah Haibatullah Akhundzada and his powerbrokers in Kandahar to keep different Taliban factions together under their leadership will be key.

In Pakistan, both the TTP and ISKP have become emboldened, and ceasefires between the former and Pakistan's security forces have broken down. Within the reporting period, Pakistan faced the possibility of defaulting on its loans and significant political unrest, although a US$3 billion staff-level agreement reached with the IMF in June 2023 offered temporary economic relief.[12] Under these circumstances, groups like the TTP could take advantage of the instability.

Strategic implications and global influences

Three potential conflicts in the region have the capacity to escalate into major conventional wars with nuclear implications. These include one between the US and China in the Taiwan Strait; one between Pakistan and India along the LoC; and one between China and India along the Line of Actual Control (LAC). The first two carry the highest risk of escalation. By contrast, the strategic implications of the low-intensity insurgencies in India, the Philippines and Thailand are minimal for their host states, regions and the international community. These insurgencies could extract some concessions from their respective central governments and may cause casualties and political or economic disruption at a localised level, but they are not capable of challenging the existing political order of their countries at the provincial, state or federal level. The conflict in Myanmar is more internationalised in that it has attracted US sanctions and Chinese efforts at mediation. Furthermore, Myanmar's military junta views the tacit alliance between the NUG and certain EAOs as a moderate threat to its rule, as evidenced by its harsh military response. The threat of transnational terrorist groups in Afghanistan and Pakistan, meanwhile, will have greater strategic implications if these groups attack targets outside of the region. So far this has not been the case, although their propaganda has continued to fuel a radicalisation risk in South Asia and beyond.

In recent years, the most significant instance in which China has approached engaging in an armed conflict is along the LAC with India. It separates contested regions like Aksai Chin, claimed by India as part of Ladakh, and Arunachal Pradesh, claimed by China as South Tibet. Ladakh's new administrative status as a union territory is, according to India, an internal matter with 'no implication for either the external boundaries of India or the ... [LAC] with China'.[13] Yet, on 6 August 2019, China strongly opposed this as being 'unacceptable' and as 'undermining its territorial sovereignty'.[14] In May 2020, Chinese and Indian soldiers clashed in the Galwan Valley, and in December 2022, there was another clash between hundreds of Chinese and Indian soldiers along the LAC.

Efforts to de-escalate and initiate dialogue through the Five-Point Consensus and talks between the People's Liberation Army and Indian Army at the corps-commander level have led to a limited reduction in tensions, but both sides remain entrenched in their positions. India, lifting some of its focus from the LoC with Pakistan, is increasing its attention on the LAC. The combination of a more assertive Chinese foreign policy under President Xi Jinping and India's growing hawkishness while also selectively aligning with the Unites States' Indo-Pacific strategy to contain China has made it challenging to separate tensions along the LAC from the broader context of great-power competition. The separate visits to India of China's foreign and defence ministers as part of India's hosting of the G20 and SCO leaders' summits in 2023 has created an opportunity for limited re-engagement between India and China, if outstanding points of tension regarding borders are resolved.

Russia's invasion of Ukraine has raised concerns that China might take similar actions in Taiwan, although some aver that the example of Moscow's troubles could deter China. It is unclear whether Washington would respond to Chinese military actions against Taiwan. Historically, the US has maintained a position of 'strategic ambiguity' toward Taiwan, which neither promises nor rejects the defence of Taiwan. The US Congress's increasing hawkishness and occasional statements by President Joe Biden endorsing defence commitments to Taiwan has placed this ambiguity into question, although these statements have been quickly walked back in official diplomatic communications. This raises questions about Washington's commitment to the '"One China" policy, which recognises the People's Republic of China as the only legitimate government of China' in exchange for Beijing's purported commitment to peaceful unification, rather than use of force.[15]

Tensions between Washington and China continued to harden during the reporting period. In August 2022, then-house speaker Nancy Pelosi travelled to Taiwan on an official visit. Beijing was outraged and shortly after conducted a large military exercise around Taiwan. Chinese fighter aircraft have been regularly entering Taiwan's air defence identification zone, with a significant increase in 2022 that continued in 2023. The election of a hawkish or right-wing Republican candidate like Donald Trump as US president could further escalate tensions with China, especially regarding Taiwan, given his past policy positions and choice of advisers. The outcome of Taiwan's 2024 presidential elections may also influence China's responses, particularly if the China-friendly opposition Kuomintang party comes into power.

REGIONAL KEY EVENTS

POLITICAL EVENTS

 PAKISTAN

August 2022

Severe flooding submerges one-third of Pakistan for weeks, affecting 33m people.

MILITARY/VIOLENT EVENTS

 AFGHANISTAN

31 July 2022

A US drone strike kills Ayman al-Zawahiri, the head of al-Qaeda, in Kabul.

KASHMIR

17 August

The J&K Chief Electoral Officer announces the addition of 2–2.5m new registrants for elections, potentially bolstering voters by a third, including many non-Kashmiris.

 INDIA

14 September

The NSCN–IM and Working Committee sign a 'Joint Concordant' to work together in their respective peace processes.

 INDIA

15 September

The Indian central and state governments sign peace deals with eight Assam-based tribal armed groups.

 AFGHANISTAN

December

The Taliban extends its education ban to include women attending university and orders all non-governmental organisations and the UN operating in Afghanistan to stop employing women.

 KASHMIR

December

State authorities seize more than 20 homes associated with the banned Islamist movement Jamaat-e-Islami.

 AFGHANISTAN

2 September

An unclaimed terrorist attack targets the Guzargah mosque in Herat, killing at least 18 people.

 AFGHANISTAN

5 September

ISKP uses a suicide bomber to kill six people outside the Russian Embassy in Kabul, including two Russian embassy staff.

 AFGHANISTAN

30 September

A bombing at the Kaaj tuition centre in a predominantly Hazara neighbourhood in Kabul kills at least 35 people. It is widely believed that ISKP is responsible.

 MYANMAR

23 October

The SAC (Tatmadaw) conducts an airstrike on the Kachin Independence Organisation as it celebrates its 62nd anniversary, killing over 50 people.

 PAKISTAN

28 November

The TTP ends a ceasefire and calls for its fighters to resume attacks against Pakistan's armed forces and police.

 AFGHANISTAN

2 December

ISKP attacks the Pakistani embassy in Kabul, injuring the mission chief's personal guard.

 CHINA, INDIA

9 December

Hundreds of Chinese and Indian soldiers clash along the LAC using blunt weapons but no firearms. No deaths are reported.

INDIA

27 December

India's central and state governments sign a peace agreement with the ZUF.

 MYANMAR

February 2023

The SAC (Tatmadaw) extends martial law orders for 40 townships.

 THAILAND

21–22 February

In a sixth round of peace talks with the Thai government, the BRN agrees to allow other armed groups to join further negotiations.

  KASHMIR

20 March

Dubai's Emaar Properties announces J&K's first foreign investment, a US$60m shopping and office complex in Srinagar.

 MYANMAR

28 March

The SAC (Tatmadaw) announces that the NLD party is among 40 political parties that will be dissolved.

 PAKISTAN

9 May

Former prime minister Imran Khan is briefly arrested, unleashing mass street protests and rioting followed by a military crackdown.

 MYANMAR

10 January 2023

The SAC (Tatmadaw) bombs the headquarters of the CNF.

 PAKISTAN

30 January

A TTP suicide bomber targets a mosque in Peshawar that is primarily attended by police officers, resulting in the deaths of about 100 people.

 KASHMIR

February

Reports emerge that Indian authorities have sanctioned the return of armed civilian militias in Hindu-majority areas of J&K.

 PAKISTAN

17 February

TTP militants attack the Karachi police chief's headquarters, resulting in the deaths of two police officers, a Sindh Ranger and a civilian.

 MYANMAR

1 March

A task force calling itself the 'Ogre Column' carries out massacres and beheadings in one of Myanmar's resistance hotspots.

 AFGHANISTAN

April

The Taliban's General Directorate of Intelligence kills the head of an ISKP cell in Kabul, who was responsible for the bombing at Kabul's airport in August 2021.

 MYANMAR

11 April

The SAC (Tatmadaw) kills over 170 people, mostly civilians, during airstrikes on the opening ceremony of a local office run by the NUG.

 INDIA

3 May

Ongoing violent clashes erupt between the (mostly Hindu) Meitei community and the (predominantly Christian) Nagas and Kukis, resulting in over 100 deaths.

Asia

KASHMIR

22–24 May

The Indian government hosts the Third G20 Tourism Working Group Meeting in Srinagar to support the perception of normalcy in J&K.

 MYANMAR

1–2 June

China's Yunnan provincial government facilitates talks between Myanmar's military junta and the Brotherhood Alliance.

 PAKISTAN

5 August

Khan is arrested and sentenced to three years in prison for corrupt practices.

Notes

1   'Yearly Fatalities', Datasheet – Jammu & Kashmir, South Asia Terrorism Portal.

2   *Ibid.*

3   When referring to developments before 15 August 2019, the acronym 'J&K' refers to the state of Jammu and Kashmir (including Kashmir, Jammu and Ladakh regions, which India controls). For developments after the abrogation of Article 370 and the bifurcation of J&K in 2019, J&K refers to the Union Territory of Jammu and Kashmir (including Jammu and Kashmir regions, which India controls).

4   Manny Maung, 'Myanmar Junta Dissolves Political Parties', Human Rights Watch, 29 March 2023; and 'Myanmar Junta Extends Martial Law in Resistance Stronghold Sagaing Region', *Irrawaddy*, 23 February 2023.

5   John Reed and Jyotsna Singh, 'India's Manipur State Riven by Ethnic Violence', *Financial Times*, 15 June 2023.

6   'Majority-minority' groups refers to ethnic and religious groups that are a minority relative to the national population but make up the majority in a particular province or area.

7   Alcis, 'Unprecedented Reduction of Opium Production in Afghanistan', 2023.

8   Leo Sands, 'Pakistan Floods: One Third of Country Is Under Water – Minister', BBC, 30 August 2022.

9   Joshua Kurlantzick, 'ASEAN's Complete Failure on Myanmar: A Short Overview', Council on Foreign Relations, 29 August 2022.

10 Jim Garamone, 'U.S. Drone Strike Kills al-Qaida Leader in Kabul', US Department of Defense, 2 August 2022.

11 Bharti Jain, 'Assam Government Signs Peace Agreement with Insurgents', *Times of India*, 15 September 2022; and K. Sarojkumar Sharma, 'Centre, Manipur Rebel Outfit Sign Peace Pact', *Times of India*, 28 December 2022.

12 Ariba Shahid, 'Pakistan, IMD Reach $3 Billion Staff-level Agreement', Reuters, 30 June 2023; and IMF, 'IMF Reaches Staff-level Agreement with Pakistan on a US$3 Billion Stand-by Arrangement', Press Release no. 23/251, 29 June 2023.

13 The Wire Staff, 'India Tells China: No Change in LaC or LoC After Recent Moves', Wire, 12 August 2019.

14 Bloomberg News, 'China Says India's Kashmir Move "Unacceptable", Undermines Its Territorial Sovereignty', *Print*, 6 August 2019.

15 UNI, 'In Response to US, PLA Conducts Military Exercises Off Taiwan', The North-East Affairs, 25 May 2022.

The Re-emergence of the Tehrik-e-Taliban Pakistan and Implications for Regional Security

The Tehrik-e-Taliban Pakistan (TTP) was originally formed in 2007 in Pakistan as an umbrella organisation of Sunni Muslim Deobandi armed groups, targeting the state and its institutions. It has recently undergone a revival, principally due to the Afghan Taliban's takeover of Afghanistan in August 2021 and the latter's little intent or capacity to control, let alone degrade, the TTP's presence on its side of the border. The TTP represents, once again, a clear security threat to Pakistan's military and political leadership.[1] This threat has become the most central issue in Pakistan–Afghanistan relations, given its significance for regional stability and the challenge it represents for trade, Afghan refugees, and people-to-people and infrastructure connectivity for land-locked Afghanistan. Pakistan's 2023 general electoral season will likely further complicate consensus-building on how to strategically manage the TTP and its activities.

Staying power

Between 2007 and 2015, despite a formal 2008 ban, the TTP rose to prominence under founder Baitullah Mehsud and his successors, assuming the de facto leadership of Pakistan-based terrorist groups. Aside from targeting the state, the TTP directed its violence against Western soldiers and officials in the hope that it would hasten their departure from Afghanistan and Pakistan. After absorbing fighters from Pakistan's notorious Lashkar-e-Jhangvi group and disgruntled Kashmir-focused fighters from South Punjab province, the TTP also led sectarian attacks against Pakistani Shias, worsening Pakistan's relations with Iran. The TTP's actions were thus neither parochial nor fully internationalised: the TTP operated largely separately from al-Qaeda and later the Islamic State (ISIS), despite likely sharing some operational links and foot soldiers. The group primarily generated insecurity by targeting security forces through a relentless succession of small-scale attacks, but it also executed high-profile ones. For instance, the TTP's leader from 2013–18, Fazal Hayat (also known as 'Mullah Fazlullah'), claimed the attempted and failed killing of prominent girls' education campaigner Malala Yousafzai in 2012. He also directed a suicide gun and bomb assault on the Peshawar Army Public School (APS) in December 2014, which killed 151 people.[2]

The TTP's rise was initially the product of its leadership, tactics and safe havens, which expanded to Pakistan's former North-West Frontier Province (NWFP) and parts of the former Federally Administered Tribal Areas (FATA). Early on, the TTP's propaganda relied on emerging and initially unregulated social-media platforms. From its Swat district stronghold, the TTP secured support within and beyond local tribes (which spanned both sides of the Pakistan–Afghanistan border) to expand its territorial control south of Pakistan's tribal belt, particularly to North Waziristan. Its foot soldiers were groups of mostly young, koranic-school-educated Pashtun men recruited through coercion, kinship, tribal ties and shared grievances against the state and Pakistan's military. 2014 was the peak of the TTP's influence on Pakistan's security dynamics.

Following the APS attack, the army launched *Operation Zarb-e-Azb* in June 2015, the largest counter-terrorist and counter-insurgency operation in the then FATA in a decade, designed to both degrade and interdict the TTP. In practice, although over 3,500 TTP fighters were officially killed in Pakistan by the military, the operation also pushed hundreds if not thousands of TTP and other Pakistan-based fighters into eastern Afghanistan, across what neither the group, nor successive Afghan governments, have recognised as an international border – contrary to Pakistan's position.[3] The TTP leadership was therefore able to escape the reach of Pakistani forces and continued to orchestrate attacks in Pakistan from Afghanistan. At the time, Pakistan criticised the unwillingness of NATO forces to force Kabul to deny sanctuary to the TTP.

The military achievements of the Afghan Taliban (which Pakistan often refers to as the Tehrik-e-Taliban Afghanistan or TTA) in the latter part of the decade, culminating with its seizure of Kabul in 2021, overshadowed the TTP's momentum, as the former further entrenched its militant leadership credentials by appearing far more successful than the latter. The follow-on Pakistani *Operation Raad-ul-Fasaad* and the construction of a fence along critical parts of the contested border also ensured the continuity of Pakistan's purpose in 2013–22, with the latter claiming not just to have 'turned the tide' against terrorism but (at least once) to have 'defeated' it.[4] The TTP nevertheless kept a permanent presence on Afghan soil – comprising over 3,500 men according to a June 2019 United Nations report.[5]

From 2019–21, Pakistan's then-prime minister Imran Khan, who had risen to national prominence from the tribal Khyber Pakhtunkhwa (KP) region (a new province comprising NWFP and FATA), signalled a softer approach to the TTP, as he blamed the military for rising insecurity and civil–military tensions. But the Financial Action Task Force's adoption of sanctions on Pakistan for abetting terrorist financing gave the Pakistan military the upper hand and kept the TTP, among other groups, under pressure. At the same time, however, the agreement between the United States and the Afghan Taliban in February 2020 attenuated some of this pressure, as it did not explicitly require the Afghan Taliban to interdict the TTP, unlike other terrorist groups threatening the US and its allies.

Renewed ascendency after 2021

The Afghan Taliban's seizure of Kabul in 2021 was the single-most impactful factor which contributed to reversing the TTP's languishing fortunes, allowing it to extend its influence as a fighting force in Pakistan while remaining below the threshold of terrorism that would draw international concern. Immediately lauding Kabul's new 'emirate', the TTP drew inspiration from the Afghan Taliban and, under Mufti Noor Wali Mehsud (the group's current leader appointed in 2018), renewed its allegiance to Afghan Taliban leader Mullah Haibatullah Akhundzada. In return, the Afghan Taliban largely shielded the TTP from Pakistani government demands. It is unclear if the Afghan Taliban expected and obtained TTP support in fighting Islamic State Khorasan Province (ISKP), Kabul's main security concern.

Pakistan's response to this was hampered by domestic politics. In January 2022, Pakistan's first national-security policy committed resolutely to combatting terrorism, but this document did not bind opposition parties. Khan himself had appeared to praise publicly the Taliban's Kabul takeover in August 2021. Civil–military tensions, which peaked with Khan's removal from office in April 2022 and his replacement with Shehbaz Sharif, prevented any strong and widespread consensus on counter-terrorism from emerging. A notable exception to this situation was the resolve exhibited in the alleged cross-border airstrikes by the Pakistan military, targeting the TTP in Afghanistan's Khost and Kunar provinces, in April 2022. By summer 2022, a 'unilateral' ceasefire was brokered with the TTP under the leadership of Sharif, whose Pakistan Muslim League–Nawaz party had historically been among those more amenable to talks with the group. This was retrospectively seen as ill-conceived as it allowed the TTP to regroup, recruit and rearm.

Within three months of the first anniversary of the Taliban's seizure of Kabul, the TTP denounced the ceasefire, having been able to rebuild itself amid the benign neglect, if not active support, of its hosts in Kabul. It quickly resumed attacks in Pakistan, executing over 100 by April 2023.[6] On 30 January 2023, an attack on a mosque in Peshawar, which is primarily attended by police officers, killed over 100 people, making it the single-worst TTP attack in terms of fatalities since the 2014 APS assault.[7] The event also suggested the possibility of insider assistance, given that the attacker wore a police uniform and passed multiple checkpoints. The violence rekindled a long-standing public debate in Pakistan on the division of labour between federal and local law-enforcement agencies as well as respective priorities. That same month, the TTP also claimed the assassination of a senior Inter-Services Intelligence (ISI) counter-terrorism officer near Multan.

The renewed ascendency of the TTP (see Figure 1) and its growing territorial implantation in Pakistan was also fostered by its absorption of over 20 smaller groups which had demobilised by the end of the war in Afghanistan in August 2021.[8] In 2021, the TTP appointed shadow governors to some of Pakistan's Pashtun-dominated areas, including Balochistan, replicating the Afghan Taliban's pre-2021 practice. Moreover, the group specifically targeted its decade-old social-media propaganda (from when Fazal was leader in 2013–18) towards new audiences, such as women. It also supported the reversal of the 2018 constitutional amendment 'mainstreaming' the FATA into KP, therefore extending the authority of

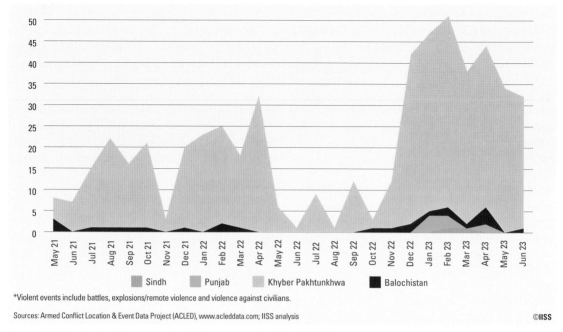

*Violent events include battles, explosions/remote violence and violence against civilians.

Sources: Armed Conflict Location & Event Data Project (ACLED), www.acleddata.com; IISS analysis   ©IISS

Figure 1: TTP-related violent events in Pakistan per region, May 2021–June 2023*

Pakistan's authorities into the traditionally autonomous tribal belt. Pakistan's security establishment denied a TTP re-entrenchment, arguing that the group retained only an 'organic' presence in the country, citing contested evidence that its suicide bombers were Afghans.

Despite the TTP's classification as a terrorist group by the US, countries other than Pakistan and Afghanistan have recently paid comparatively little attention to the TTP. While the group's attack on a Pakistan Navy ship and maritime-patrol aircraft in the Port of Karachi in 2011 had prompted foreign concern and support to ensure the physical security of Pakistan's military and nuclear infrastructure, foreign prioritisation of the TTP has since consistently waned. Concomitantly, China has emerged as a privileged partner for Pakistan due to a shared interest in regional stability and counter-terrorism, as well as a desire to prevent the TTP from targeting Chinese nationals and the China–Pakistan Economic Corridor, where Baloch insurgents and other terrorists already pose a threat. In May 2023, following a trilateral meeting, the foreign ministers of Afghanistan, China and Pakistan made a joint statement asserting that the TTP would no longer be allowed to use Afghanistan to destabilise the region.

Capturing and retaining momentum

The TTP's ability to retain momentum as a top-tier armed group in Afghanistan and Pakistan will depend on whether Afghanistan continues to provide a safe haven for the group, as well as TPP and army dynamics in Pakistan. In Afghanistan, the Taliban would probably only confront the group if it thought that stabilising ties with Pakistan would benefit the regime or if China forced its hand. The likelihood of this happening would increase if the Haqqani network, a major faction of the Taliban regime with ties to Pakistan, grew in influence. It would instead decrease if the TTP helped the supreme leader Akhundzada build up his own reportedly nascent armed faction within the Taliban or, given that TTP members identify strongly with Pashtuns, if the Taliban leant more on Pashtuns as a power base.

Post-2021, Kabul is less reliant on ties with Pakistan, having developed relations with China, Pakistan's strategic partner, as well as Iran, Qatar and Turkiye. An indication of the strength of bilateral strategic ties between Afghanistan and Pakistan could be the Afghan Taliban's persistence, over time, in relocating significant numbers of TTP fighters away from the border to lessen the threat to Pakistan. On a separate note, as long as US and Western counter-terrorism efforts concentrate on the threats from al-Qaeda and ISKP, it will be less likely that the TTP will become a security focus for the Afghan Taliban. Any evidence of collusion between the TTP and al-Qaeda or ISKP would strengthen Pakistan's case for international support fighting the group. Evidence of this happening is increasing: UN reports note that the TTP went from 'collaborat[ing]' with ISKP in 2022, to selling weapons to the group in 2023. The report from 2023 also states that al-Qaeda is seeking to infiltrate the TTP, and its local affiliate is helping the TTP work around Afghan Taliban restrictions.[9]

In Pakistan, the TTP's resurgence seemed to have plateaued as of June 2023, with its pattern of neither escalating nor de-escalating its overall activities appearing increasingly vulnerable. Firstly, the TTP did not react to the mass political protests and localised violence (including against symbols of the military) which broke out after Khan's arrest by security forces in May 2023. This was despite Prime Minister Sharif drawing a derogatory parallel between Khan's party and the TTP. Secondly, as Pakistan's summer and autumn general election season loomed, the group had yet to threaten campaigning candidates, as it had in 2008, 2013 and 2018, or voters, an action which could distort polling turnout or outcome. Thirdly, the TTP did not seek to opportunistically target successive protests in KP in early 2023, which criticised the return of militants and terrorism to the region, or to capitalise on a civil-society movement opposed to military operations in KP. Together these developments underscore the extent to which the TTP and Pakistan's political class have taken a selective and calculated approach to each other, in a long-standing, latent co-dependency between domestic politics and militancy.

The TTP's ability to keep momentum on its side and grow its influence is ultimately limited by the Pakistan military's objective to stabilise the country. In March 2023, Chief of Army Staff General Syed Asim Munir presided over a rare moment of civil–military communion after the killing of a serving ISI brigadier in South Waziristan, allegedly by TTP militants. In May, after a fatal attack on Iranian border guards, Iran called on Pakistan to do more against militants on its side of the border. Even though it was unclear if the TTP was involved in the attack or coordinating with an Iran-based outfit called Jaish ul-Adl, Iran's call resonated with the military, which has often struggled to stabilise ties with Iran. Pakistan's military also retains both a willingness to confront the TTP and the ability to escalate its decade-old 'intelligence-based' counter-terrorism operations to reverse the TTP's recent gains and, if need be, to secure the 2023 election cycle or prevent security concerns from worsening Pakistan's ongoing economic turmoil.[10] Suppressing the TTP altogether would require sustained and targeted counter-extremism, de-radicalisation, and disarmament, demobilisation and reintegration policies. The need to focus on Pakistan's twin political and economic crises currently puts this objective out of reach, but Pakistan's military appears both willing and able to combat and actively manage the TTP's resurgence.

Notes

1   A 2022 UN report called the TTP 'the largest component of foreign terrorist fighters in Afghanistan'. UN Security Council (UNSC), 'Thirtieth Report of the Analytical Support and Sanctions Monitoring Team Submitted Pursuant to Resolution 2610 (2021) Concerning ISIL (Da'esh), Al-Qaida and Associated Individuals and Entities', S/2022/547, 15 July 2022, p. 17. 2023 estimates of the group's strength range from 4,000–6,000 fighters in Afghanistan. The group's strength in Pakistan is unknown, though there may be several thousand fighters in the country. UNSC, 'Fourteenth Report of the Analytical Support and Sanctions Monitoring Team Submitted Pursuant to Resolution 2665 (2022) Concerning the Taliban and Other Associated Individuals and Entities Constituting a Threat to the Peace Stability and Security of Afghanistan', S/2023/370, 1 June 2023, p. 17.

2   Inter-Services Public Relations (ISPR), 'No PR-246/2015-ISPR', 13 August 2015.

3   '490 Soldiers, 3,500 Militants Killed in Operation Zarb-e-Azb So Far: DG ISPR', *Express Tribune*, 15 June 2016; and UNSC, 'Seventh Report of the Analytical Support and Sanctions Monitoring Team Submitted Pursuant to Resolution 2255 (2015) Concerning the Taliban and Other Associated Individuals and Entities Constituting a Threat to the Peace, Stability and Security of Afghanistan', S/2016/842, 5 October 2016, p. 13.

4   ISPR, 'General Qamar Javed Bajwa, Chief of Army Staff (COAS) Along with Federal Interior Minister, CM and Home Minister Balochistan, Commander Southern Command Met Representatives of Hazara Community at Quetta', No PR-154/2018-ISPR, 2 May 2018; and ISPR, 'No PR-507/2016-ISPR', 29 December 2016.

5   UNSC, 'Tenth Report of the Analytical Support and Sanctions Monitoring Team Submitted Pursuant to Resolution 2255 (2015) Concerning the Taliban and Other Associated Individuals and Entities Constituting a Threat to the Peace, Stability and Security of Afghanistan', S/2019/481, 13 June 2019, p. 18.

6   UNSC, 'Fourteenth Report of the Analytical Support and Sanctions Monitoring Team Submitted Pursuant to Resolution 2665 (2022) Concerning the Taliban and Other Associated Individuals and Entities Constituting a Threat to the Peace Stability and Security of Afghanistan', p. 17.

7   'Death Toll from Peshawar Mosque Bombing Rises to 101 as Police Say "Major Arrests" Made', *Dawn*, 1 February 2023.

8   Abdul Sayed and Tore Hamming, 'The Tehrik-i-Taliban Pakistan After the Taliban's Afghanistan Takeover', CTC *Sentinel*, vol. 18, no. 5, May 2023.

9   UNSC, 'Thirteenth Report of the Analytical Support and Sanctions Monitoring Team Submitted Pursuant to Resolution 2611 (2021) Concerning the Taliban and Other Associated Individuals and Entities Constituting a Threat to the Peace Stability and Security of Afghanistan', S/2022/419, 26 May 2022, p. 21; and UNSC, 'Fourteenth Report of the Analytical Support and Sanctions Monitoring Team Submitted Pursuant to Resolution 2665 (2022) Concerning the Taliban and Other Associated Individuals and Entities Constituting a Threat to the Peace Stability and Security of Afghanistan', pp. 13–14, 20.

10   See, for example, ISPR, 'On 20 May 23, Security Forces Conducted an Intelligence Based Operation in General Area Tank, on Reported Presence of Terrorists', No PR-63/2023-ISPR, 20 May 2023.

AFGHANISTAN

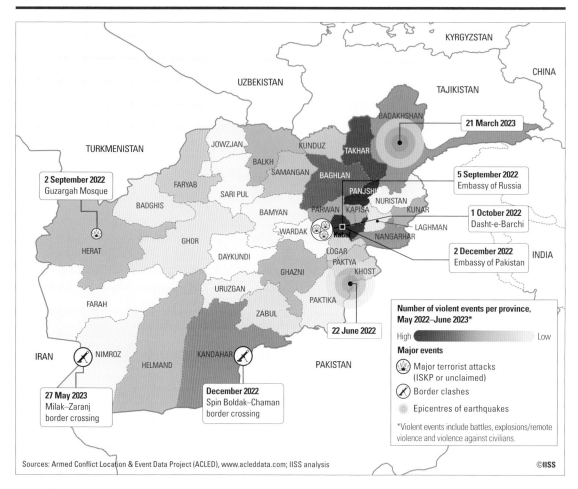

Sources: Armed Conflict Location & Event Data Project (ACLED), www.acleddata.com; IISS analysis   ©IISS

Conflict Overview

Afghanistan has experienced multiple wars across the last four decades, including the 1979–89 Soviet–Afghan War and 1992–96 Afghan Civil War, during which the Taliban consolidated its power. The most recent conflict began with the United States' invasion in October 2001, which initiated two decades of fighting between the Taliban, Afghan security forces and a US-led international coalition.

The original aim of the US invasion was to destroy al-Qaeda, but this later expanded to overthrowing the entire Taliban regime. The Bonn Conference in December 2001 laid the groundwork for a new Afghan government and led to the creation of the International Security Assistance Force to support the newly formed Afghan National Defence

and Security Forces (ANDSF). The ensuing US-led counter-insurgency peaked in 2010–11, and in 2014 foreign forces' offensive combat operations ostensibly concluded. The ANDSF took control, but it remained dependent on US air support, funding and technical expertise, and the Taliban gradually contested more districts.

Former US president Donald Trump (2017–21) appointed Zalmay Khalilzad as the US Special Representative for Afghanistan Reconciliation in September 2018 to negotiate an agreement with the Taliban for an acceptable US military withdrawal. The resulting agreement signed on 29 February 2020 called for a prisoner release, the gradual reduction of US forces and the removal of US and United

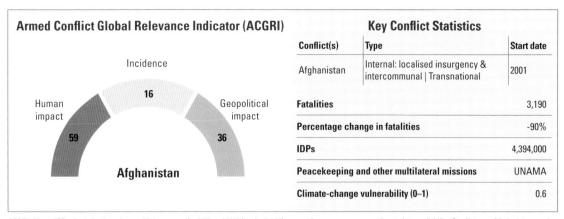

Armed Conflict Global Relevance Indicator (ACGRI)

Incidence

16

Human impact

59

Geopolitical impact

36

Afghanistan

Key Conflict Statistics

Conflict(s)	Type	Start date
Afghanistan	Internal: localised insurgency & intercommunal | Transnational	2001
Fatalities		3,190
Percentage change in fatalities		-90%
IDPs		4,394,000
Peacekeeping and other multilateral missions		UNAMA
Climate-change vulnerability (0–1)		0.6

ACGRI pillars: IISS calculation based on multiple sources for 2022 and 2023 (scale: 0–100), except for some cases according to data availability. See Notes on Methodology and Data Appendix for further details on Key Conflict Statistics.

Nations sanctions. In exchange, the Taliban agreed to participate in intra-Afghan negotiations, work towards a ceasefire and prevent any group from using Afghanistan to threaten the US or its allies; but the negotiations produced no results. The Taliban made rapid gains throughout the summer as US troops withdrew, and on 15 August 2021, the Taliban entered Kabul without any armed resistance. The last US soldier left Afghanistan on 30 August 2021, after a two-week evacuation effort.

Since August 2021, when the Afghan government collapsed and the Taliban consolidated power for the second time, the scale of the conflict has decreased significantly. However, a localised insurgency continues in the form of Islamic State Khorasan Province (ISKP) and anti-Taliban resistance groups. Furthermore, the conflict continues to feature international aspects due to cross-border attacks between Afghanistan and Pakistan and the threat of terrorist groups using Afghanistan as a staging ground.

Conflict Update

There was a noticeable reduction in violence across the reporting period compared to previous years. The Taliban maintained a firm hold on the government, and although both ISKP and anti-Taliban resistance groups, such as the National Resistance Front (NRF), were able to inflict occasional casualties on the Taliban, neither were able to take control of any territory. However, ISKP remained a major threat to the Taliban and continued to carry out attacks on Taliban members and terrorise civilians in Afghanistan, particularly the Hazara people, as it had done during the previous government. One such attack took place on 30 September 2022, when a blast at the Kaaj tuition centre in the predominantly Hazara neighbourhood of Dasht-e-Barchi in Kabul killed at least 35 people.[1] Another attack on 2 September 2022 targeted the Guzargah mosque in Herat, killing at least 18 people.[2] ISKP also targeted foreign diplomatic missions and used a suicide bomber to kill six people, including two Russian embassy staff, on 5 September 2022.[3] In December 2022, ISKP claimed responsibility for

an attack on the Pakistani embassy in Kabul, which injured the head of the mission's personal guard.[4]

In April 2023, the Taliban's General Directorate of Intelligence increased its frequency of raids against alleged ISKP members. These operations led to the killing of the head of an ISKP cell in Kabul, who was responsible for the tragic bombing at Kabul's airport during the US evacuation in August 2021.[5] Human-rights organisations have accused the Taliban of using indiscriminate tactics and of 'disappearing' alleged ISKP members.[6] ISKP is a common enemy for both the Taliban and Western countries, but US officials, at least publicly, have indicated that the Taliban does not want the United States' help in combating ISKP.

During the reporting period, the Tehrik-e-Taliban Pakistan (TTP), also commonly known as the Pakistani Taliban, found refuge in Afghanistan while escalating its campaign against Pakistan's security forces, particularly the police. The Pakistani government holds the Afghan Taliban partly responsible for this increase in violence, due to its ideological influence over the TTP and the sanctuary it has provided. Pakistan has sent senior diplomatic, military and religious delegations to Afghanistan to persuade the group to adopt more moderate social policies and to curb the TTP, but these efforts have been unsuccessful. Cross-border skirmishes between Pakistan's security forces and the Afghan Taliban have been frequent, resulting in casualties on both sides and the periodic closure of the border for trade and movement. For instance, in mid-December 2022, there was a skirmish along the Chaman border crossing which included artillery exchanges. The Torkham border was also temporarily closed in late February 2023 due to an exchange of gunfire between Pakistan's security forces and the Taliban.

Taliban officials continued to engage with the international community but did not receive formal recognition. Cabinet-level officials increasingly have been viewed as messengers between Taliban leader Mullah Haibatullah Akhundzada and the outside world, rather than decision-makers. Most countries closed their Afghan embassies following the fall of the previous Afghan government and have not reopened them. Exceptions to this include China, Iran, Pakistan, Qatar, Russia, Turkiye, Turkmenistan and the United Arab Emirates.

In September 2021, the Taliban effectively banned girls from attending secondary school. The Taliban regularly denies that this ban is permanent, but has not taken any steps to reverse it. The ban was also extended to all women attending university in December 2022 and, in the same month, the Taliban ordered all non-governmental organisations (NGOs) and the UN operating in Afghanistan to stop employing women. The Taliban's draconian stance on women in education and the workplace has sabotaged its own efforts towards normalisation with the West and reduced the amount of diplomatic engagement from Western countries, particularly the US. The NGO ban has led organisations ranging from the Norwegian Refugee Council to the UN Assistance Mission in Afghanistan to threaten to cease operations in the country.

Nevertheless, during the reporting period, various officials from the United Kingdom, the European Union, the Gulf, Japan and the UN visited Kabul to meet with Taliban leaders. However, no country recognised the Taliban as the legitimate government of Afghanistan. Russia had previously considered recognition, but in April 2023, Russian Minister of Foreign Affairs Sergey Lavrov stated that Russia 'will not recognize the Taliban government de-jure unless it fulfils its internationally recognized obligations'.[7]

Conflict Parties

The Taliban (Islamic Emirate of Afghanistan or de facto government of Afghanistan post-August 2021)

Strength: Approximately 150,000 active military personnel. The Taliban has announced plans to expand its regular armed forces to 200,000 personnel.

Areas of operation: Deployed throughout Afghanistan with activity concentrated in Baghlan, Kabul, Nangarhar, Panjshir and along the border with Pakistan.

Leadership: Mullah Haibatullah Akhundzada (emir), Mohammad Yaqoob (defence minister), Mullah Fazal Mazloom (deputy defence minister), Qari Fasihuddin (chief of staff of the armed forces), Haji Mali Khan (deputy chief of staff of the armed forces), Amanuddin Mansour (commander of the air force) and Abdul Haq Wasiq (intelligence director). Sirajuddin Haqqani (interior minister) maintains significant influence over security matters and effectively controls security in Kabul.

Structure: A mix of formal ministries and informal insurgency-era units in the process of shifting towards a formal military structure. The organisation is historically polycentric, but power is increasingly concentrated in the hands of Mullah Haibatullah Akhundzada and his inner circle in Kandahar.

History: The Taliban (translated as 'the students') movement began in the Afghan refugee camps of Pakistan following the 1979 Soviet invasion and occupation of Afghanistan. Under Mullah Mohammad Omar, the group entered the Afghan Civil War in 1994 and captured Kandahar city. Taliban fighters quickly conquered other areas of Afghanistan and the group officially ruled as an Islamic emirate from 1996–2001, though it never controlled the whole country. The Taliban seized control over the entire country in August 2021 following a 20-year insurgency.

Objectives: Maintain territorial control and security, disarm all non-Taliban citizens, stifle any dissent and fight ISKP.

Opponents: ISKP and various anti-Taliban resistance groups that are typically organised along ethnic lines.

Affiliates/allies: Has connections of varying formality with non-state armed groups in South Asia, including al-Qaeda, the Islamic Movement of Uzbekistan, the Turkistan Islamic Party and the TTP.

Resources/capabilities: Estimated US$1.2–1.5 billion annually.[8]

Islamic State Khorasan Province (ISKP)

Strength: 1,000–3,000 primarily in Afghanistan and Pakistan (estimate).[9]

Areas of operation: Primarily confined to Nangarhar province in eastern Afghanistan but able to carry out complex attacks in Kabul and present in nearly all provinces.

Leadership: Led by Sanaullah Ghafari (alias 'Shahab al-Muhajir'). The original leader, Hafiz Saeed Khan (previously head of the TTP Orakzai faction), was killed in a US drone strike in July 2016. Successive leaders were also either killed in US strikes or arrested.

Structure: An Islamist militant organisation, formally affiliated with the larger Islamic State (ISIS), of which it is the Central and South Asia branch.

History: Formed and pledged loyalty to then-ISIS leader Abu Bakr al-Baghdadi in October 2014. The initial membership primarily comprised disgruntled and estranged TTP members.

Objectives: Similar to ISIS, ISKP maintains both local and global ambitions to establish a caliphate in Central and South Asia to be governed under a strict Islamic system, modelled after the group's own interpretation of a caliphate.

Opponents: Mainly focuses on fighting the de facto Taliban government, attacking the Hazara ethnic minority which is also primarily Shia, and targeting foreign diplomats and officials.

Affiliates/allies: ISIS.

Resources/capabilities: Since its founding in 2014, ISIS has invested in improving ISKP's organisation and capabilities. However, with the decline of its territory in Iraq and Syria, ISIS has fewer resources to invest in foreign networks and therefore its investment in the group has declined. ISKP relies on small arms, improvised explosive devices (IEDs) and vehicle-borne IEDs.

Al-Qaeda

Strength: Several dozen to 400 fighters.[10]

Areas of operation: The mountainous region between Afghanistan and Pakistan, and potentially Kabul. Al-Qaeda is resident in at least 15 Afghan provinces, primarily in the eastern, southern and southeastern regions.[11]

Leadership: Saif al-Adel assumed leadership of al-Qaeda following the July 2022 drone strike that killed Ayman al-Zawahiri. He is believed to be based in Iran.

Structure: Below Adel and his immediate advisers, the group maintains a *shura* (consultation) council and committees for communications, finance and military operations.

History: Created as a broad alliance structure by Arab fighters who travelled to Afghanistan and Pakistan to fight against the Soviet invasion in the 1980s. The organisation (officially formed in 1988) was initially led by Osama bin Laden, who envisioned it as a base for a global jihadist movement to train operatives and to support other jihadist organisations. The group was responsible for several high-profile terrorist attacks against the US, including the 9/11 attacks. Bin Laden was killed in a US special-operations raid in Abbottabad,

Pakistan in 2011. Zawahiri, who had led the group since 2011, was killed in an apartment in Kabul by a US drone strike on 31 July 2022.

Objectives: Focus has always been to fight the 'far enemy' (the West), particularly the US, which supports current Middle Eastern regimes, and bring about Islamist governance in the Muslim world. Its affiliate groups often pursue local objectives independent of the goals and strategy of the central organisation.

Opponents: US and other Western and regional countries supporting non-Islamic regimes.

Affiliates/allies: Currently maintains an affiliation with five groups: al-Qaeda in the Islamic Maghreb in North Africa, al-Qaeda in the Arabian Peninsula in Yemen, al-Qaeda in the Indian Subcontinent in South Asia, Jabhat al-Nusra in Syria and al-Shabaab in Somalia. As of early 2022, it maintains a strong relationship with the Afghan Taliban.

Resources/capabilities: Capable of engaging in complex terrorist attacks on hard and soft targets. It has also provided military advice to the Afghan Taliban.

Anti-Taliban resistance groups

Strength: Unclear.

Areas of operation: Primarily in Panjshir province and Andarab district, Baghlan province. The senior leadership is primarily located outside of Afghanistan.

Leadership: Ahmad Massoud, Amrullah Saleh and others.

Structure: Militia, including former ANDSF soldiers.

History: After the collapse of the ANDSF in August 2021 and the flight of most prominent anti-Taliban warlords, a group of former Afghan commandos retreated to Panjshir to continue fighting. The Taliban ultimately took control of Panjshir, but resistance groups began to coalesce and reorganise inside Afghanistan and abroad, including the NRF organised by

Massoud and Saleh, the Afghanistan Freedom Front, the Afghanistan Islamist National and Liberation Movement, and the Unknown Soldiers of Hazaristan. On 11 April 2023, the Taliban reportedly killed eight members of the NRF, including a prominent commander, Akmal Amir.[12]

Objectives: Liberate key areas of Afghanistan and ultimately remove the Taliban from power in Afghanistan.

Opponents: Taliban.

Affiliates/allies: Unclear, but seeking support from the US, European countries and some regional countries.

Resources/capabilities: Unknown.

Asia

Other relevant parties

During the reporting period, the Pakistan Armed Forces exchanged small-arms fire and artillery with the TPP along the border between Pakistan and Afghanistan, amid increasingly strained relations with the Taliban due to its support of the TPP.

Notes

1   'Kabul Attack: Death Toll Rises to 35 Mostly "Girls, Young Women"', Al-Jazeera, 1 October 2022.

2   UN Security Council (UNSC), 'Security Council Press Statement on Attack in Herat', 3 September 2022.

3   Mohammad Yunus Yawar, 'Two Russian Embassy Staff Dead, Four Others Killed in Suicide Bomb Blast in Kabul', Reuters, 5 September 2022.

4   Munir Ahmed, 'IS Claims Attack at Pakistan Embassy That Wounded Guard', AP News, 4 December 2022.

5   Nadine Yousif, 'Taliban Kill IS Leader Behind Kabul Airport Bombing', BBC, 26 April 2023.

6   Human Rights Watch, 'Afghanistan: Taliban Execute, "Disappear" Alleged Militants', 7 July 2022.

7   'Russia Assumes That Taliban Is a Reality, and Talks with Them Are Necessary – Lavrov', TAAS, 26 April 2023.

8   William Byrd, 'Taliban Are Collecting Revenue – But How Are They Spending It?', United States Institute of Peace, 2 February 2022.

9   UNSC, 'Sixteenth Report of the Secretary-General on the Threat Posed by ISIL (Da'esh) to International Peace and Security and the Range of United Nations Efforts in Support of Member States in Countering the Threat', S/2023/76, 1 February 2023, p. 8.

10 UNSC, 'Fourteenth Report of the Analytical Support and Sanctions Monitoring Team Submitted Pursuant to Resolution 2665 (2022) Concerning the Taliban and Other Associated Individuals and Entities Constituting a Threat to the Peace Stability and Security of Afghanistan', S/2023/370, 1 June 2023, p. 14.

11 UNSC, 'Twelfth Report of the Analytical Support and Sanctions Monitoring Team Submitted Pursuant to Resolution 2557 (2020) Concerning the Taliban and Other Associated Individuals and Entities Constituting a Threat to the Peace Stability and Security of Afghanistan', S/2021/486, 1 June 2021, p. 12.

12 Ayaz Gul, 'Taliban Raid Kills 8 Afghan Opposition Fighters', VOA, 11 April 2023.

PAKISTAN

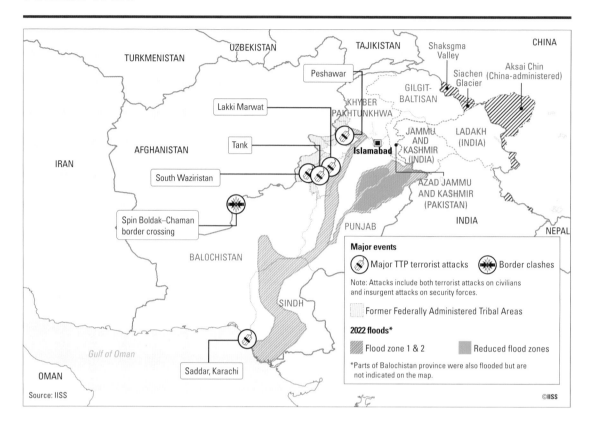

Source: IISS   ©IISS

Conflict Overview

Pakistan has experienced ethnic and centre–province tensions resulting from the perceived marginalisation of the Baloch, Pashtuns and Sindhis by the Punjabi majority since gaining independence in 1947. The 1971 secession of East Pakistan to form Bangladesh made Punjab the country's majority province in terms of population and increased these tensions.[1] The mass migrations that followed British India's partition also enflamed ethnic unrest as Urdu-speaking migrants, or Mohajirs, emigrated from contemporary northern India to Sindh province in Pakistan. This means that conflicts in Pakistan sometimes conflate demands for increased civil liberties and provincial autonomy with violent separatist insurgent movements, primarily in Balochistan and Khyber Pakhtunkhwa (KP). Terrorist groups and violent separatist and insurgent movements capitalise on underlying ethnic and economic agitation (and the repressive state crackdowns that follow terrorist attacks) to stoke tensions.

The Baloch insurgency has fought the state for greater autonomy or the secession of Balochistan by waging campaigns in 1948, 1958, 1962 and 1973. The return to violence in 2003 launched the phase of the insurgency that continues today. Baloch armed groups have fragmented on several occasions and some splinter organisations have demobilised. Several of these groups set aside some of their differences in 2018 to form a coalition with the Baloch Republican Army (BRA) under the banner of the Baloch Raaji Ajoi Sangar (BRAS). The BRAS split in late April 2023, however, after the leader of one of its factions was arrested. Another BRAS member, the Baloch Liberation Army (BLA), continues to pose the most significant threat to the Pakistani state in Balochistan and Karachi, which is in Sindh province and is Pakistan's financial capital and most populous city.

Groups originating in KP and Pashtun tribal areas (formerly known as the Federally

Armed Conflict Global Relevance Indicator (ACGRI)

Incidence

11

Human
impact

Geopolitical
impact

4   5

Pakistan

Key Conflict Statistics

Conflict(s)	Type	Start date
Baloch insurgency in Balochistan and Karachi	Internal: localised insurgency	Restarted in 2003
Islamist insurgency in KP and the former FATA	Internal: localised insurgency & intercommunal | Transnational	2001

Fatalities	1,874
Percentage change in fatalities	6%
IDPs	21,000
Peacekeeping and other multilateral missions	UNMOGIP
Climate-change vulnerability (0–1)	0.5

ACGRI pillars: IISS calculation based on multiple sources for 2022 and 2023 (scale: 0–100), except for some cases according to data availability. See Notes on Methodology and Data Appendix for further details on Key Conflict Statistics.

Administered Tribal Areas, or FATA) have also fought against the state and the Shia religious minority. Increased Pakistani incursions into the then-FATA targeting al-Qaeda members raised tensions following the 9/11 terrorist attacks. Militant groups coalesced to form what is often referred to as the Pakistani Taliban. This group eventually became the Tehrik-e-Taliban Pakistan (TTP).

The TTP's attack on the Army Public School in Peshawar in December 2014 marked an inflection point. It also led the government to formulate the National Action Plan, its first counter-terrorism policy. *Operation Zarb-e-Azb*, launched in 2014, and *Operation Raad-ul-Fasaad*, begun in 2017, led to a noticeable decline in insurgent attacks, but TTP attacks have increased significantly since 2021.

Conflict Update

Pakistan's security situation worsened significantly during 2022–23. The Afghan Taliban's triumph over the internationally backed government in Afghanistan in August 2021 galvanised the TTP, and it increased its attacks against Pakistani security forces during the reporting period. Additionally, Baloch separatist groups and Islamic State Khorasan Province (ISKP) carried out acts of terrorism in the country. However, tensions along the Line of Control (LoC) with India remained relatively calm due to a ceasefire that took effect from midnight on 24–25 February 2021.

After a short-lived ceasefire agreed in November 2021 and several months of fighting, the TTP announced a new ten-day ceasefire on 29 April 2022 to celebrate Eid al-Fitr, which marks the end of Ramadan.[2] The ceasefire was later extended indefinitely, but on 28 November 2022 the TTP called for its fighters to resume attacks. Assaults on Pakistan's security forces continued throughout both ceasefires, which may have allowed TTP fighters to move more easily from their safe havens in Afghanistan to Pakistan. Following the end of the latest ceasefire, the Pakistani military took a harder line against the TTP. Pakistan's attempts to convince the Afghan Taliban to control the TTP have been unsuccessful, likely due to the close historical, ideological and familial connections between the two groups, as well as the TTP's pledge of loyalty to the Afghan Taliban.

The TTP has focused its attacks on Pakistan's police force. On 30 January 2023, a TTP suicide bomber targeted a mosque in Peshawar that was primarily attended by police, resulting in the deaths of approximately 100 people.[3] On 17 February 2023, TTP militants attacked the headquarters of the Karachi police chief in the busiest commercial area of the city. The attack resulted in the deaths of two police officers, a Sindh Ranger and a civilian.[4] Targeting police officers is attractive to the TTP because they represent the state and are ill-equipped to handle such threats, and the attacks erode confidence in the state.

Asia

The increasing violence took place against the backdrop of a political deadlock. Imran Khan was removed from the position of prime minister on 10 April 2022 through a vote of no confidence in the National Assembly. Some analysis claims that the opposition parties were emboldened to initiate the motion due to strained relations between Khan and the powerful security establishment. A coalition government consisting of two of the country's major parties and several smaller ones assumed power and functioned as a lame-duck administration. Khan's Pakistan Tehreek-e-Insaf party, however, achieved a resounding victory in a July 2022 by-election in Punjab, which has historically been dominated by the Pakistan Muslim League–Nawaz party, and continued to hold large street rallies. On 29 November 2022, General Syed Asim Munir took over from General Qamar Javed Bajwa as Pakistan's army chief. It is not certain whether general elections will take place by autumn 2023 as scheduled. If they do not occur, civil unrest is a significant possibility.

Pakistan is also facing a major economic crisis exacerbated by severe flooding in August 2022 that submerged one-third of the country for weeks, affecting 33 million people.[5] In 2022, the country's current-account deficit was 4.6% of GDP. Inflation is forecast to rise to 27.4% in 2023 from 9.7% in 2021.[6] The Pakistani rupee also hit an all-time low during this period.[7] In mid-April 2023, the State Bank of Pakistan's foreign-exchange reserves could cover only one month of imports.[8] Within the reporting period, Pakistan faced the possibility of defaulting on its loans and significant political unrest, although commitments from friendly countries and a US$3 billion staff-level agreement reached with the IMF in June 2023 offered temporary economic relief.

Conflict Parties

Pakistan Armed Forces (PAF)

Strength: 651,800 active military and 291,000 active paramilitary personnel.

Areas of operation: Deployed throughout Pakistan (particularly along the LoC with India) and in Balochistan and KP, including the former FATA, along the border with Afghanistan.

Leadership: President Arif Alvi (commander-in-chief), Gen. Sahir Shamshad Mirza (chairman of the joint chiefs of staff committee), Gen. Syed Asim Munir (chief of army staff), Adm. Muhammad Amjad Khan Niazi (chief of naval staff), Air Chief Marshal Zaheer Ahmed Baber Sidhu (chief of air staff) and Lt-Gen. Nadeem Anjum (director general, Inter-Services Intelligence, or ISI). ISI falls outside the military command structure, but its leaders are drawn from the military and have significant oversight over some operations.

Structure: The PAF consists of nine 'Corps' commands, an Air Defence Command and a Strategic Forces Command. *Operation Raad-ul-Fasaad* involves an array of PAF units that support the police and the Pakistani Civil Armed Forces (PCAF) in counter-terrorism operations.

History: The ongoing *Operation Raad-ul-Fasaad* succeeded the 2014–17 *Operation Zarb-e-Azb*. It was launched in response to a resurgence in attacks by TTP splinter group Jamaat-ul-Ahrar. *Operation Khyber-4* was launched in 2017 under *Operation Raad-ul-Fasaad* to eliminate terrorists in what is now Rajgal valley, Khyber district.

Objectives: Eliminate insurgent groups that threaten the Pakistani state, control or eliminate the TTP, ensure border security with Afghanistan, and guard the LoC and the China–Pakistan Economic Corridor.

Opponents: TTP, BLA and other Baloch separatist groups, ISKP, and Indian Armed Forces. The PAF's relationship with the Afghan Taliban is increasingly strained due to the group's support of the TTP.

Affiliates/allies: PCAF, Pakistani police and anti-India armed groups based in Pakistani-administered Azad Jammu and Kashmir.

Resources/capabilities: Well resourced with an array of weapons systems and equipment. The defence budget for 2022 was US$9.8bn, and it is US$11.1bn for 2023.

Pakistani Civil Armed Forces (PCAF)

Strength: Unclear.

Areas of operation: Throughout Pakistan, but most active fighting is against insurgent groups in Balochistan and KP.

Leadership: Various. Founded by the Interior Ministry, although most divisions are commanded by officers seconded from the PAF.

Structure: The main divisions of the PCAF involved in conflict with insurgent groups and participating in the PAF-led *Operation Raad-ul-Fasaad* are the Frontier Corps (Frontier Corps KP and Frontier Corps Balochistan), the Frontier Constabulary, the Sindh Rangers and the Punjab Rangers. Each group's authority is limited to its respective geographic area.

Pakistani Civil Armed Forces (PCAF)

History: Contributed to *Operation Raad-ul-Fasaad* since its commencement in 2017 and to the army's 34th Light Infantry Division (Special Security Division) since 2016.

Objectives: Eliminate insurgent groups that threaten the Pakistani state, provide additional security in tribal areas and major urban areas.

Opponents: TTP, BLA and other Baloch separatist groups, and ISKP.

Affiliates/allies: PAF and Pakistani police.

Resources/capabilities: Primarily equipped with small arms and light weapons, with some shorter-range artillery and mortars.

Tehrik-e-Taliban Pakistan (TTP)

Strength: Circa 4,000–6,000 in Afghanistan, where the majority of TTP fighters are currently based.[9] Strength in Pakistan is unknown, although recent analysis suggests there may be several thousand fighters in the country.

Areas of operation: Balochistan and KP.

Leadership: Mufti Noor Wali Mehsud (emir and overarching leader), supported by a central *shura* (consultation) council.

Structure: Divided by locality into factions, or constituencies, each of which is led by a local emir and supported by a local *shura* council, which report to the central *shura* council. Each faction has a *qazi* (judge) to adjudicate local disputes.

History: In 2007, some factions of militant groups in Pakistan's tribal areas unified as the TTP under the leadership of Baitullah Mehsud, who was killed in a US airstrike in 2009. A TTP *shura* council elected Hakimullah Mehsud as the organisation's second emir, but internal divisions grew under his leadership over legitimate targets for attacks and peace talks with the government. The divisions later worsened under Fazal Hayat (Mullah Fazlullah) and caused several factions to

break away, including leaders who formed ISKP in 2014. The 2014 TTP attack on the Army Public School in Peshawar triggered a debilitating PAF counter-offensive. Following Hayat's death in 2018, the leadership reverted to the Mehsud clan under Mufti Noor Wali Mehsud, who sought to reunite and rebuild the group. In 2020, this process culminated with the reintegration of the Hizb-ul-Ahrar, Jamaat-ul-Ahrar and Amjad Farouqi groups and the Hakimullah Mehsud faction into the TTP fold. TTP leader Mufti Noor Wali Mehsud reiterated his allegiance to the Afghan Taliban's leadership following the latter's takeover of Afghanistan. On 2 April 2022, the TTP launched its al-Badr spring offensive and began to target Pakistani soldiers and police. A ceasefire was announced at the end of April 2022, but on 28 November 2022 the TTP called for its fighters to resume attacks.

Objectives: To defend and promote a rigid Islamist ideology in KP, including in the former FATA.

Opponents: PAF and PCAF.

Affiliates/allies: Afghan Taliban, al-Qaeda and occasionally ISKP.

Resources/capabilities: Has access to small arms and improvised explosive devices (IEDs).

Baloch Raaji Ajoi Sangar (BRAS, an alliance that includes the Balochistan Liberation Army, BLA; the Baloch Republican Army, BRA; and the Baloch Liberation Front, BLF)

Strength: Unclear.

Areas of operation: Balochistan and Karachi.

Leadership: BLA: leadership contested between Hyrbyair Marri and Bashar Zaib. BRA: Brahumdagh Bugti. BLF: Allah Nazar Baloch.

Structure: The BRAS is an alliance of the BLA, BRA and BLF. The BLA is divided into different factions. Pakistan's government alleges that several factions of the BLA exist and are led by different individuals. The insurgency is deeply divided, with different groups, infighting and fragmentation. The BRAS reportedly began to splinter in April 2023 due to the arrest of Baloch Nationalist Army (BNA) senior leader Gulzar Imam Shambay.

History: The alliance was formed in 2018. The BLA is the largest group and was formed in 2000 under the leadership of Afghanistan-based Balach Marri, who was subsequently

killed in an airstrike in Helmand in 2007. Its leadership since then has been subject to additional deaths and significant internal contestation. In July 2019, the US State Department listed the BLA as a Specially Designated Global Terrorist.

Objectives: Seeks independence for the region of Balochistan as a solution to perceived discrimination against the Baloch people. Opposes the extraction of natural resources in Balochistan by Pakistani and foreign actors, especially China, due to the implications of the China–Pakistan Economic Corridor for Baloch aspirations.

Opponents: PAF and PCAF.

Affiliates/allies: None formally, but the Pakistani state has accused it of periodically working with Indian intelligence and the TTP.

Resources/capabilities: Attacks by BRAS members have involved small arms and IEDs, including suicide vests and car bombs.

Islamic State Khorasan Province (ISKP)

Strength: 1,000–3,000 primarily in Afghanistan and Pakistan (estimate).[10]

Areas of operation: Balochistan, KP and Afghanistan.

Leadership: Led by Sanaullah Ghafari (alias 'Shahab al-Muhajir'). The original leader, Hafiz Saeed Khan (previously head of the TTP Orakzai faction), was killed in a US drone strike in July 2016. Successive leaders were also either killed in US strikes or arrested.

Asia

Islamic State Khorasan Province (ISKP)

Structure: An Islamist militant organisation, formally affiliated with the larger Islamic State (ISIS), of which it is the Central and South Asia branch.

History: Formed and pledged loyalty to then-ISIS leader Abu Bakr al-Baghdadi in October 2014. The initial membership primarily comprised disgruntled and estranged TTP members.

Objectives: Similar to ISIS, ISKP maintains both local and global ambitions to establish a caliphate in Central and South Asia to be governed under a strict Islamic system, modelled after the group's own interpretation of a caliphate.

Opponents: Mainly focuses on fighting the PAF and PCAF in Pakistan, but also targets Shia religious sites.

Affiliates/allies: ISIS.

Resources/capabilities: Since its founding in 2014, ISIS has invested in improving ISKP's organisation and capabilities. However, with the decline of its territory in Iraq and Syria, ISIS has fewer resources to invest in foreign networks and therefore its investment in the group has declined. ISKP relies on small arms, IEDs and vehicle-borne IEDs.

Al-Qaeda

Strength: Several dozen to 400 fighters.[11]

Areas of operation: The mountainous region between Afghanistan and Pakistan, and potentially Kabul.

Leadership: Saif al-Adel assumed leadership of al-Qaeda following the July 2022 drone strike that killed Ayman al-Zawahiri. He is believed to be based in Iran.

Structure: Below Adel and his immediate advisers, the group maintains a *shura* council and committees for communications, finance and military operations.

History: Created as a broad alliance structure by Arab fighters who travelled to Afghanistan and Pakistan to fight against the Soviet invasion in the 1980s. The organisation (officially formed in 1988) was initially led by Osama bin Laden, who envisioned it as a base for a global jihadist movement to train operatives and to support other jihadist organisations. The group was responsible for several high-profile terrorist attacks against the US, including the 9/11 attacks. Bin Laden was killed in a US special-operations raid in Abbottabad, Pakistan, in 2011. Zawahiri, who had led the group since 2011,

was killed in an apartment in Kabul by a US drone strike on 31 July 2022.

Objectives: Focus has always been to fight the 'far enemy' (the West), particularly the United States, which supports current Middle Eastern regimes, and bring about Islamist governance in the Muslim world. Its affiliate groups often pursue local objectives independent of the goals and strategy of the central organisation.

Opponents: US and other Western and regional countries supporting non-Islamic regimes.

Affiliates/allies: Currently maintains an affiliation with five groups: al-Qaeda in the Islamic Maghreb in North Africa, al-Qaeda in the Arabian Peninsula in Yemen, al-Qaeda in the Indian Subcontinent in South Asia, Jabhat al-Nusra in Syria and al-Shabaab in Somalia. As of early 2022, it maintains a strong relationship with the Afghan Taliban.

Resources/capabilities: Capable of engaging in complex terrorist attacks on hard and soft targets.

Other relevant parties

Multiple instances of artillery and small-arms fire occurred between the Afghan Taliban and Pakistani troops during the reporting period. The TTP has pledged allegiance to the Afghan Taliban's emir and has links to the group through ideology, family ties and resources.

Notes

1   Michael Kugelman and Adam Weinstein, 'In Pakistan, a Tale of Two Very Different Political Movements', *Lawfare*, 4 January 2021.

2   SAMRI (@SAMRIReports), tweet, 29 April 2022.

3   'Death Toll from Peshawar Mosque Bombing Rises to 101 as Police Say "Major Arrests" Made', *Dawn*, 1 February 2023.

4   Imtiaz Ali, 'Security Forces Clear Karachi Police Chief's Office on Sharea Faisal, 3 Terrorists Killed', *Dawn*, 17 February 2023.

5   Leo Sands, 'Pakistan Floods: One Third of Country Is Under Water – Minister', BBC, 30 August 2022.

6   Refers to 'inflation rate, end of period consumer prices'. International Monetary Fund, World Economic Outlook Database, April 2023.

7   Irshad Ansari, 'Rupee Downfall: Pakistani Currency Endured Historic Lows in 2022', *Tribune*, 27 December 2022.

8   'SBP's Foreign Reserves Up After $300 Million Loan', Geo News, 20 April 2023.

9   United Nations Security Council (UNSC), 'Fourteenth Report of the Analytical Support and Sanctions Monitoring Team Submitted Pursuant to Resolution 2665 (2022) Concerning the Taliban and Other Associated Individuals and Entities Constituting a Threat to the Peace Stability and Security of Afghanistan', S/2023/370, 1 June 2023, p. 17; Asfandyar Mir, 'Afghanistan's Terrorism Challenge: The Political Trajectories of Al-Qaeda, the Afghan Taliban, and the Islamic State', Middle

East Institute, 20 October 2020; US Department of Defense Office of Inspector General, 'Operation Freedom's Sentinel: Lead Inspector General Report to the United States Congress', 21 May 2019, p. 25; and Daud Khattak, 'The Pakistan Taliban Is Back', *Diplomat*, 9 March 2021.

10 UNSC, 'Sixteenth Report of the Secretary-General on the Threat Posed by ISIL (Da'esh) to International Peace and Security and the Range of United Nations Efforts in Support of Member States in Countering the Threat', S/2023/76, 1 February 2023, p. 8.

11 UNSC, 'Fourteenth Report of the Analytical Support and Sanctions Monitoring Team Submitted Pursuant to Resolution 2665 (2022) Concerning the Taliban and Other Associated Individuals and Entities Constituting a Threat to the Peace Stability and Security of Afghanistan', S/2023/370, 1 June 2023, p. 14.

Asia

KASHMIR

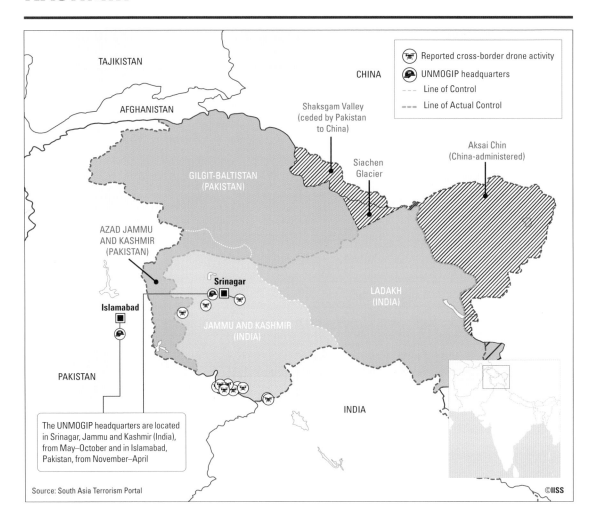

TAJIKISTAN

CHINA

AFGHANISTAN

Shaksgam Valley
(ceded by Pakistan
to China)

Siachen
Glacier

Aksai Chin
(China-administered)

GILGIT-BALTISTAN
(PAKISTAN)

AZAD JAMMU
AND KASHMIR
(PAKISTAN)

Srinagar

Islamabad

LADAKH
(INDIA)

JAMMU AND KASHMIR
(INDIA)

PAKISTAN

INDIA

> Reported cross-border drone activity
> UNMOGIP headquarters
> Line of Control
> Line of Actual Control

The UNMOGIP headquarters are located
in Srinagar, Jammu and Kashmir (India),
from May–October and in Islamabad,
Pakistan, from November–April

Source: South Asia Terrorism Portal

©IISS

Conflict Overview

The Kashmir conflict erupted in the former, Muslim-majority, princely state of Jammu and Kashmir following the partition of India in 1947. In August that year, Muslim rebels seized Poonch in Jammu province and declared an 'Azad' (free) government, while thousands of Pakistani militants crossed the border to remove Jammu and Kashmir's Hindu Maharaja. Amid this uprising and invasion, the Maharaja provisionally acceded to the Indian Union, sparking the Indo-Pakistani War of 1947–48 over Kashmir. A United Nations-brokered cease-fire in January 1949 divided Jammu and Kashmir into Indian-administered Jammu and Kashmir

(J&K) and Pakistani-administered Azad Jammu and Kashmir (AJ&K), effectively freezing the conflict until the Indo-Pakistani War of 1965, which resulted in a stalemate.

In the late 1980s, a controversial election sparked a mass mobilisation against the Indian government. The initially indigenous movement was led by the Jammu Kashmir Liberation Front (JKLF), but it was gradually supplanted by pro-Pakistani factions such as the Hizbul Mujahideen (HM) and absorbed greater numbers of foreign fighters into the insurgency. In 1990, the Indian state imposed direct rule over the region, blanketed the region with

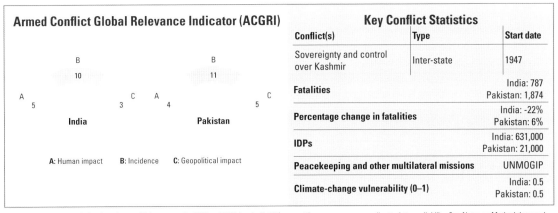

Armed Conflict Global Relevance Indicator (ACGRI)		

Key Conflict Statistics

Conflict(s)	Type	Start date
Sovereignty and control over Kashmir	Inter-state	1947
Fatalities		India: 787 Pakistan: 1,874
Percentage change in fatalities		India: -22% Pakistan: 6%
IDPs		India: 631,000 Pakistan: 21,000
Peacekeeping and other multilateral missions		UNMOGIP
Climate-change vulnerability (0–1)		India: 0.5 Pakistan: 0.5

ACGRI pillars: IISS calculation based on multiple sources for 2022 and 2023 (scale: 0–100), except for some cases according to data availability. See Notes on Methodology and Data Appendix for further details on Key Conflict Statistics.

security forces and introduced the Armed Forces Special Powers Act, leading to aggressive counter-insurgency operations throughout the 1990s. Talks between India and Pakistan between 1997 and 2008 reduced violence levels within Indian-administered Kashmir and along the Line of Control (LoC) separating the Indian and Pakistani regions, but they did not achieve a breakthrough on core political issues. Between 2008 and 2016, three large uprisings took place in the Kashmir Valley, boosted by social media and combining elements of civil unrest and low-level insurgency.[1] In August 2019, India's ruling Bharatiya Janata Party (BJP) revoked Article 370 of the Indian constitution, which guaranteed J&K's special autonomous status.[2] This split the region into centrally controlled 'Union Territories' of Jammu and Kashmir, and Ladakh. Since 2020, the BJP has started to loosen residency, employment and voting restrictions that previously favoured indigenous Kashmiris. Following growing exchanges of fire across the LoC in 2019–20, India and Pakistan signed a ceasefire agreement in February 2021.

Conflict Update

At the international level, India has sought to cultivate an image of stability to boost Kashmir's attractiveness for tourism and external investment, as well as to bolster the legitimacy of the BJP administration's actions in the region since 2019. In March 2023, the J&K administration announced a US$60 million investment from Dubai's Emaar Properties to build a shopping and office complex in Srinagar.[3] Having attracted over 16m tourists to J&K in 2022, India leveraged its G20 presidency by hosting a May 2023 working-group meeting in Srinagar on tourism to further bolster the image of normalcy.[4]

At the same time, the BJP has used its decision to impose central rule and create 'Union Territories' to consolidate its local influence. Its 2020 redefinition of domicile rules in J&K has empowered previously disenfranchised 'non-indigenous' elements of the population, with reports in January 2023 that up to a million voters could potentially vote for the first time in any upcoming elections.[5] Combined with the creation of six new districts in Jammu, these measures appear likely to strengthen the BJP's electoral clout and raise the prospect of BJP electoral success in any future Union Territory Assembly elections.[6] In April 2023, the Jammu and Kashmir Union Territory government began a widespread campaign to enrol Kashmiri Pandits – a community expelled from Kashmir during violence in the 1990s – in electoral lists and, in doing so, further strengthen the BJP. Elections are expected to be held during 2023, the first since 2014. The elections are likely to be contested by the BJP and the People's Alliance for Gupkar Declaration, a political union between major local parties campaigning for the restoration of J&K's autonomous status. The exact timing of the elections, however, is likely to depend on the BJP's confidence in its ability to win them.

These political dynamics during the reporting period have shaped a growing trend of armed-group attacks against both non-local labourers and long-time residents applying for the new domicile status. In one

Asia

example, on 27 February 2023, a smaller armed group – the Kashmir Freedom Fighters – killed a Kashmiri Pandit, labelling the community 'pawns of occupation'.[7] Indeed, during 2022, there were 17 attacks against non-locals compared to six in 2021, indicating growing attempts to deter non-locals from settling and claiming domicile status in J&K.[8] This trend is likely to increase with the announcement of the assembly elections.

That being said, conflict-related fatalities during May 2022–June 2023 decreased by 38% compared with May 2021–June 2022, as the February 2021 agreement regarding the LoC held.[9] While the number of incidents reached 47 in 2020, this dropped to 23 in 2022. Incidents of cross-border militant incursions also declined, from 99 in 2020 and 77 in 2021 to 27 in 2022, as Indian forces have used the ceasefire agreement to build and upgrade border-defence and surveillance infrastructure along the LoC.[10] An inability to infiltrate appears to have hurt armed groups' capacity to initiate violent incidents; the number of militant grenade and improvised-explosive-device (IED) attacks declined from 180 (May 2021–June 2022) to 42 (May 2022–June 2023).[11]

In the face of growing constraints along the LoC, Pakistani AJ&K-based militants have appeared to shift towards employing drones to move arms across the LoC. While these incidents peaked at 47 reported occurrences in 2021, there were at least 15 reported incidents of drone incursions in May 2022–June 2023, with most of these clustered around the Jammu and Samba districts of J&K.[12] During 2023, Indian security forces began testing and developing counter-drone spoofing and jamming devices.

Pakistan's strategy of supporting Kashmiri insurgents seems to have increasingly focused on sponsoring 'indigenous' Kashmiri armed groups, such as The Resistance Front (TRF), formed after the abrogation of Article 370 in 2019. This likely reflects the severe constraints faced by the Pakistani state during the reporting period. Firstly, Pakistan was under pressure to act against armed groups and their sources of finance since being placed on the Financial Action Task Force 'grey list' in 2018, which forced it to adopt a less explicit approach to supporting cross-border infiltration. Secondly, it faced instability on multiple fronts, including economic crises, massive flooding, political turmoil, deteriorating relations with the Afghan Taliban and a resurgence of internal Tehrik-e-Taliban Pakistan activity. These overlapping crises are likely to contain Pakistani efforts to support militant infiltrations.

Conflict Parties

Indian Armed Forces

Strength: Approximately 330,000–350,000 Indian security personnel in J&K. This includes approximately 130,000 army soldiers; 45,000 infantry troops within the Rashtriya Rifles (RR), the special counter-insurgency unit; 60,000 paramilitary personnel of the Central Reserve Police Force (CRPF), as well as battalions of the Border Security Force, Indo-Tibetan Border Police, Sashastra Seema Bal and Central Industrial Security Force; and around 83,000 personnel from the J&K Police (JKP). There are also about 100,000–120,000 Indian security personnel in Ladakh.[13]

Areas of operation: All districts of J&K and along the LoC. The CRPF's Jammu and Kashmir Zone Srinagar Sector covers Budgam, Ganderbal and Srinagar districts; its Kashmir Operations Sector covers Anantnag, Awantipora and Baramulla districts; and its Jammu Sector covers the Jammu region.

Leadership: Indian army troops in the region are primarily under the Northern Command based in Udhampur (J&K) and led by Lt-Gen. Upendra Dwivedi. The CRPF, the primary paramilitary force, is under the Ministry of Home Affairs. A special director general has overall command of the CRPF in J&K, while inspectors general command the respective sectors.

Structure: The Northern Command has four assigned corps headquarters, controlling nine infantry divisions and a number of independent brigades. The XV Corps, with its headquarters in Srinagar, has operational command of the Kashmir Valley. The RR is organised into five division-sized counter-insurgency forces, with four deployed in J&K and one deployed in Ladakh.

History: A heavy troop presence has been maintained along the LoC since 1949. Thousands of troops were used to crush an anti-India armed rebellion in the late 1980s. Initially, paramilitary and regular army troops fought the Pakistan-backed insurgents. The RR was introduced in 1994 and coordinates with other security agencies including the Special Operations Group, a JKP counter-insurgency unit.

Objectives: Border defence and counter-insurgency.

Opponents: HM, Lashkar-e-Taiba (LeT), Jaysh-e-Mohammad (JeM), TRF, Ansar Ghazwat-ul-Hind, Al-Badr, Pakistan Armed Forces (PAF) and Chinese People's Liberation Army (in Ladakh).

Affiliates/allies: Village Defence Guards, volunteer state-armed groups concentrated in hilly and border areas with sizeable Hindu populations (Doda, Kathua, Kishtwar, Poonch, Rajouri, Ramban and Reasi districts).

Resources/capabilities: Ministry of Defence and Ministry of Home Affairs budgetary funds; voluntary donations through

Indian Armed Forces

the National Defence Fund, the Army Central Welfare Fund and the Armed Forces Battle Casualties Welfare Fund; voluntary web-based public donations through portals such as 'Bharat Ke Veer' (India's Bravehearts); and government contracts under *Operation Sadbhavana*.

Pakistan Armed Forces (PAF)

Strength: In total, the PAF has 651,800 active military personnel and 291,000 active paramilitary personnel. Elements of the Rawalpindi-based X Corps as well as paramilitary and local forces are deployed in AJ&K; their total strength is believed to be approximately 125,000.

Areas of operation: All districts of AJ&K and along the LoC.

Leadership: Pakistani troops in the region are under the I and X Corps of the Pakistan Army. The I Corps headquarters is based in Mangla Cantonment (Pakistan) and the X Corps headquarters is based in Rawalpindi (Pakistan). The Mujahid Force, a paramilitary unit, is headquartered in Bhimber (AJ&K) and works under the National Guard of Pakistan, which is controlled and commanded by the chief of army staff based in General Headquarters in Rawalpindi.

Structure: The X Corps consists of four infantry divisions, attached independent brigades and the division-sized Force Command Northern Areas, which operates in the Gilgit-Baltistan area. The I Corps is composed of two infantry divisions, an armoured division and attached independent brigades.

History: Pakistan has maintained a heavy troop presence along the LoC since 1949. The Azad Army, an anti-Maharaja militia composed of ex-servicemen of the British Indian Army, captured the main districts of Muzaffarabad and Mirpur before the Pakistan Army officially entered Jammu and Kashmir in May 1948 to take control and consolidate the territorial gains. The Pakistan Army has not faced any insurgency within AJ&K. Its operations are directed at Indian forces and the LoC.

Objectives: Guard the LoC and China–Pakistan Economic Corridor.

Opponents: Indian Armed Forces.

Affiliates/allies: Anti-India armed groups based in AJ&K.

Resources/capabilities: Ministry of Defence budgetary funds, arms exports, government contracts and commercial ventures under army-controlled charitable foundations, such as Fauji Foundation, Army Welfare Trust, Shaheen Foundation and Bahria Foundation.

Hizbul Mujahideen (HM)

Strength: Fewer than 100 members in J&K and over 1,000 in AJ&K. A broader network of supporters and sympathisers also assist the main organisation on both sides of the LoC.

Areas of operation: Concentrated in Anantnag, Kulgam, Pulwama and Shopian districts, with a marginal presence in northern Kashmir districts.

Leadership: Mohammad Yusuf Shah (alias Syed Salahuddin). Farooq Ahmad Bhat (alias Farooq Nali) is the chief commander in the Kashmir Valley – the epicentre of the low-intensity armed conflict – and oversees area commanders for each district.

Structure: Headquarters in Muzaffarabad, AJ&K. Cadres comprise mostly local Kashmiris who receive rudimentary arms training from senior members. Divisional commanders work under a semi-autonomous structure but also receive instructions on both sides of the LoC via satellite communication and encrypted messaging apps.

History: An indigenous armed group with a pro-Pakistan ideology, HM was founded in September 1989 by Mohammad Ahsan Dar, a former member of the pro-independence

organisation JKLF. (The JKLF was an affiliate of Jamaat-e-Islami, a pro-Pakistan religio-political organisation in J&K). Many JKLF members joined HM after 1994, when the former suffered heavy losses and voluntarily quit the armed conflict to pursue non-violent means. HM recruitment of local Kashmiri youth also surged after the death of its young commander Burhan Muzaffar Wani in July 2016. Despite suffering heavy losses between 2017 and 2020, HM survived by procuring funds and weapons locally.

Objectives: Dislodge Indian rule in Kashmir and merge the region with Pakistan through a war of attrition. The group has stated that it would support negotiated settlement through dialogue under certain circumstances.

Opponents: Indian government and security forces.

Affiliates/allies: LeT, JeM and TRF.

Resources/capabilities: Resources, including weapons and IEDs, are procured locally by associates and sympathisers. Funding is provided by charities, mosque-based donations across Pakistan and the Pakistani military establishment.

Lashkar-e-Taiba (LeT)

Strength: Largest armed group in Kashmir in early 2022.

Areas of operation: Across the Kashmir Valley, mostly active in the northern districts of Baramulla, Bandipora and Kupwara.

Leadership: Hafiz Muhammad Saeed. Overall command is in the hands of a divisional commander, who is often a non-

Kashmiri. Mohammad Yusuf Dar (alias Yusuf Kantroo), killed in 2022, was the last 'operational head' of the group in the Kashmir Valley.

Structure: Headquarters in Muridke, Punjab province, Pakistan. Valley-based cadres are mostly Pakistani nationals working under district commanders and trained in camps.

Lashkar-e-Taiba (LeT)

History: Pakistan-based cleric Saeed, who also heads the missionary organisation Jamaat-ud-Dawa (JuD), founded LeT in the late 1980s. Since LeT entered Kashmir in the early 1990s, it has carried out several deadly attacks against Indian Armed Forces and political workers. Despite losing its commanders in quick succession since the 2017 launch of the Indian army's *Operation All Out*, the group has survived and has recruited increasing numbers of local youth, particularly in the last three years.

Objectives: Merge Kashmir with Pakistan. The group has supported efforts to achieve a peaceful resolution to the conflict.

Opponents: Indian government and security forces.

Affiliates/allies: HM, JeM, TRF and Al-Badr. Though banned by the Pakistani government in 2002, LeT is believed to maintain connections to Pakistani intelligence agencies.

Resources/capabilities: Fundraising through charities in Pakistan (e.g., JuD and Falah-e-Insaniyat), which receive government and public contributions, and social networks in Pakistan and Afghanistan. Funds are also raised through the collection and selling of sacrificial-animal skins on Eid.

Jaysh-e-Mohammad (JeM)

Strength: Second-largest group in Kashmir in 2022.

Areas of operation: Southern Kashmir.

Leadership: Maulana Mohammad Masood Azhar Alvi is the group's founder and leader.

Structure: Headquartered in Bahawalpur, Punjab province, Pakistan, its members are mostly Pakistanis. Divisional commanders work under the chief operational commander based in Kashmir.

History: Founded by Pakistani Masood Azhar in 2000, JeM entered Kashmir in the early 2000s and introduced suicide attacks. The Pakistani government banned the group in 2002. After a period of dormancy, JeM re-emerged in 2017 with an attack on a paramilitary camp in Pulwama.

Objectives: Merge Kashmir with Pakistan.

Opponents: Indian government and security forces.

Affiliates/allies: HM and LeT. Believed to have ties to the Taliban in Afghanistan.

Resources/capabilities: The most powerful insurgent group in Kashmir, with highly trained cadres and better resources than other groups. Fundraising is done through seminaries, mosques (e.g., Binori Town Mosque) and charities in Pakistan (e.g., Al Rashid Trust), and donation appeals published in magazines and pamphlets. Money is also raised through legal businesses operating in Pakistan and funds allegedly received from political (e.g., Jamiat Ulema-e-Islam) and other militant organisations in Pakistan.

The Resistance Front (TRF)

Strength: Largest recruiter in 2020 after HM, LeT and JeM.

Areas of operation: Has carried out attacks in northern, central and southern districts of Kashmir Valley.

Leadership: No central leadership. Mohammad Abbas Sheikh, who was killed in August 2021, was the last leader of the group.

Structure: Composite organisation without defined structure. JKP claims that the TRF is a hybrid militant outfit composed of cadres from existing armed groups such as LeT and HM. TRF militants killed by Indian security forces and arrested TRF sympathisers have been identified as native Kashmiris.

History: Founded after the abrogation of Article 370 in August 2019, the TRF started by lobbing grenades in Srinagar in late 2019. The group has used social media to publish statements and claim attacks. The Indian government declared it a terrorist organisation in January 2023.

Objectives: Dislodge Indian rule in Kashmir and violently deter settlers from mainland India and security forces.

Opponents: Indian government.

Affiliates/allies: India in January 2023 declared it a 'proxy' of LeT and banned it along with LeT.

Resources/capabilities: JKP claims that the TRF uses a broader network of supporters and sympathisers who are not formally part of the group – and do not feature in police records – to carry out some targeted killings. These are called 'hybrid militants' in Indian security forces parlance.

United Nations Military Observer Group in India and Pakistan (UNMOGIP)

Strength: 42 experts on mission from several countries including Croatia, South Korea, Thailand, Argentina, the Philippines, Sweden, Switzerland, Italy, Romania and Uruguay (in descending order of troop numbers), as well as 68 civilian staff.[14]

Areas of operation: UN field stations: six based in AJ&K and four based in J&K. The Sialkot field station in Pakistan monitors the working boundary, which is the international border between Punjab province, Pakistan, and the disputed territory of Jammu and Kashmir.

Leadership: Maj.-Gen. José Alcaín from Uruguay (chief military observer and head of mission); Nester Odaga-Jalomayo from Uganda (chief of mission support).

Structure: UNMOGIP is mandated by UN Security Council (UNSC) Resolution 91. Headquarters alternates between Islamabad in November–April and Srinagar in May–October.

History: The UN Commission for India and Pakistan (UNCIP) was created under UNSC Resolution 39 in 1948. In January 1949, the first team of unarmed military observers arrived to supervise the ceasefire between India and Pakistan. UNMOGIP replaced UNCIP under Resolution 91 of March 1951. After Resolution 307 in 1971, India and Pakistan made minor adjustments to the ceasefire line and in 1972 established the LoC to be supervised by UN military observers.

United Nations Military Observer Group in India and Pakistan (UNMOGIP)	
Objectives: Monitor, investigate and report ceasefire violations as a neutral observer along the 770-kilometre LoC and working boundary between India and Pakistan. It also receives petitions from political groups within Kashmir on the situation at the LoC and submits findings to India, Pakistan and the UN secretary-general.	**Opponents:** N/A.
	Affiliates/allies: UN departments of peace operations and operational support.
	Resources/capabilities: Funding through UN regular budget: estimated $10.52m.[15]

Notes

1   Sameer P. Lalwani and Gillian Gayner, 'India's Kashmir Conundrum: Before and After the Abrogation of Article 370', Special Report no. 473, United States Institute of Peace, August 2020, p. 6.

2   When referring to developments before 15 August 2019, the acronym 'J&K' refers to the state of Jammu and Kashmir (including Kashmir, Jammu and Ladakh regions, which India controls). For developments after the abrogation of Article 370 and the bifurcation of J&K in 2019, J&K refers to the Union Territory of Jammu and Kashmir (including Jammu and Kashmir regions, which India controls).

3   Fayaz Bukhari, 'India's Jammu and Kashmir Gets First Foreign Investment from Dubai's Emaar', Reuters, 20 March 2023.

4   Michael Kugelman, 'India Projects Image of Normalcy from Kashmir', *Foreign Policy*, 13 April 2023.

5   Rupam Jain and Kanupriya Kapoor, 'How India's Ruling Party Is Tightening Its Grip on Kashmir', Reuters, 12 January 2023.

6   'Jammu Gets 6 New Assembly Constituencies, 12 Segments Reserved for STs, SCs', *Print*, 5 May 2022.May 5 (PTI

7   Peerzada Ashiq, 'Militants Gun Down Kashmiri Pandit, New Terror Outfit Claims Hand in Killing', *Hindu*, 26 February 2023.

8   'Jammu & Kashmir; Assessment – 2023', South Asia Terrorism Portal.

9   'Yearly Fatalities', Datasheet – Jammu & Kashmir, South Asia Terrorism Portal.

10 Ajit Kumar Singh, 'Jammu and Kashmir: Tense Peace', *South Asia Intelligence Review*, vol. 21, no. 40, 27 March 2023.

11 'Yearly Explosions', Datasheet – Jammu & Kashmir, South Asia Terrorism Portal.

12 Jammu & Kashmir: Timeline (Terrorist Activities) – 2022, South Asia Terrorism Portal; and Jammu & Kashmir: Timeline (Terrorist Activities) – 2023, South Asia Terrorism Portal.

13 Estimates. See Anushka Vats, 'Cenre Plans to Replace Indian Army with CRPF in Kashmir Valley; Withdrawl to be Done in Phased Manner', English Jagran, 20 February 2023; Zulfikar Majid, 'No Final Call by Centre on Removal of Army from Kashmir Valley', *Deccan Herald*, 23 February 2023; Snehesh Alex Philip, 'What Imran Khan Says Is 9 Lakh Soldiers in Kashmir Is Actually 3.43 Lakh Only', *Print*, 12 November 2019; and Manjeet Negi, '60,000 Chinese Troops Deployed Near Indian Border, Indian Army Also Enhances Troops in Ladakh', *India Today*, 3 January 2022.

14 Numbers as of February 2023. UN Peacekeeping, 'UNMOGIP Fact Sheet'.

15 Estimated from the January 2021–December 2021 approved budget. *Ibid.*

MYANMAR

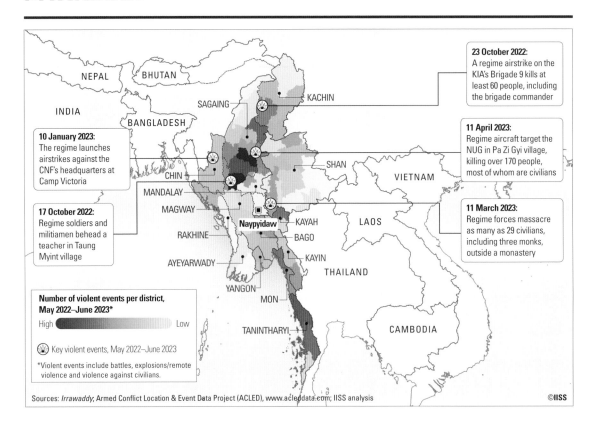

23 October 2022:
A regime airstrike on the KIA's Brigade 9 kills at least 60 people, including the brigade commander

11 April 2023:
Regime aircraft target the NUG in Pa Zi Gyi village, killing over 170 people, most of whom are civilians

10 January 2023:
The regime launches airstrikes against the CNF's headquarters at Camp Victoria

17 October 2022:
Regime soldiers and militiamen behead a teacher in Taung Myint village

11 March 2023:
Regime forces massacre as many as 29 civilians, including three monks, outside a monastery

Number of violent events per district, May 2022–June 2023*

High ▬▬▬▬▬ Low

Key violent events, May 2022–June 2023

*Violent events include battles, explosions/remote violence and violence against civilians.

Sources: *Irrawaddy*, Armed Conflict Location & Event Data Project (ACLED), www.acleddata.com; IISS analysis   ©IISS

Conflict Overview

Myanmar has suffered from a multitude of related, yet distinct, internal conflicts since gaining independence from British India in 1948. War in post-colonial Myanmar, formerly known as Burma, is historically linked to successive governments' efforts to consolidate control over the country's peripheries, where a diverse array of ethnic minorities reside. The post-independence era has witnessed the rise and fall of numerous ethnic-based movements fighting for greater autonomy and self-determination, as well as a communist insurgency that lasted until 1989.

The country is also marked by a perennial struggle between democratic forces and a military that has ruled under various guises since General Ne Win staged a *coup d'état* in 1962. A popular uprising against the military in 1988 saw the emergence of a non-violent opposition movement led by Aung San Suu Kyi and her National League for Democracy (NLD). A new junta-drafted constitution in 2008 eventually allowed for a quasi-democratic transition predicated on a tenuous power-sharing agreement between the military and elected NLD government. However, the reform period between 2011 and 2021 was marred by continued civil–military contest, a non-inclusive peace process and an ethnic-cleansing campaign against the Rohingya.

Then, on 1 February 2021, the military reversed its own reform process by staging another *coup d'état* after the NLD won a second landslide victory in the 2020 general elections. Accustomed to new freedoms, the population refused to acquiesce after the military launched a violent crackdown on anti-coup protests. A grassroots armed movement emerged among the Bamar majority population, leading to conflict in central lowland areas where violence had been absent for decades. The nascent People's Defence Force (PDF) soon joined several pre-existing ethnic armed organisations (EAOs)

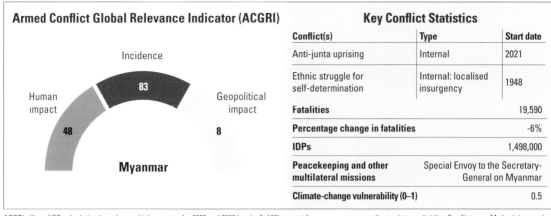

Armed Conflict Global Relevance Indicator (ACGRI)

Incidence

83

Human impact

Geopolitical impact

48

8

Myanmar

Key Conflict Statistics

Conflict(s)	Type	Start date
Anti-junta uprising	Internal	2021
Ethnic struggle for self-determination	Internal: localised insurgency	1948
Fatalities		19,590
Percentage change in fatalities		-6%
IDPs		1,498,000
Peacekeeping and other multilateral missions		Special Envoy to the Secretary-General on Myanmar
Climate-change vulnerability (0–1)		0.5

ACGRI pillars: IISS calculation based on multiple sources for 2022 and 2023 (scale: 0–100), except for some cases according to data availability. See Notes on Methodology and Data Appendix for further details on Key Conflict Statistics.

to wage a new, widespread insurgency against the regime. Under existential threat, the military responded with fanatic attacks on its opponents and their civilian supporters, thrusting Myanmar into an era of violent destruction unseen since the Second World War.

Conflict Update

Both the regime and its opponents launched increased attacks on one another in the reporting period, leading to a further deterioration of security as extreme forms of violence spread across the country and resentment between the military and general population deepened. Revolutionary forces under the National Unity Government (NUG) and allied EAOs continued to expand their fighting capacity and reach into areas previously dominated by the regime, allowing for increasingly sophisticated attacks on assorted military, administrative and infrastructure targets. Violent events occurred in nearly 300 of Myanmar's 330 townships, making it difficult for the regime to administer the country and protect its economic interests.[1] Resistance forces' gains, however, were tempered by a severe arms shortage, with less than a quarter of PDF fighters in possession of assault rifles or other battlefield weapons.

The regime also departed from its earlier strategy, which focused on containing the growth of the post-coup armed movement, and launched more direct and intense attacks on resistance actors and their supporters. Though it had previously upheld a policy not to target EAO leaders, the regime bombed the headquarters of the Chin National Front (CNF) and decimated the leadership of the Kachin Independence Army's (KIA) Brigade 9 with an airstrike that killed more than 60 people.[2]

In February 2022, the regime extended martial law to 40 townships with a strong PDF presence.[3] Many of these townships have been subjected to scorched-earth tactics predicated on the robust use of heavy aerial firepower and the perpetration of atrocities. In March 2023, a task force calling itself the 'Ogre Column' carried out a spree of massacres and beheadings after being airdropped into a resistance hotspot.[4] Then, on 11 April 2023, regime aircraft killed over 170 people, the vast majority of them civilians, during repeated strikes on an opening ceremony for a local office run by the NUG.[5] As of 31 May 2023, security forces had also burned down a total of 70,324 civilian homes across areas with resistance activity.[6] In total, approximately 1.5 million people have been internally displaced by the violence since the coup.[7] Systematic attacks on civilians continue to accelerate as the regime attempts to crush the population's will to resist.

Long considered an internal conflict, the war in Myanmar saw the increased involvement of Russia and China through arms transfers and support during the reporting period. This substantially reinforced the latter's capabilities, including in conducting airstrikes, which have now become a daily occurrence

Asia

in the country. Political intervention by China has also propped up the junta. In February 2022, China's new special envoy to Myanmar told members of the Federal Political Negotiation and Consultative Committee (FPNCC), the most powerful bloc of EAOs, not to wage offensives along the Myanmar–China border. On 2 May, China's foreign minister travelled to Naypyidaw, becoming the highest-ranking Chinese official to meet with the regime since the coup. China's diplomatic intervention is helping the regime negotiate with its most powerful opponents. In early June 2023, the Yunnan provincial government facilitated talks between the regime and three FPNCC groups (the Brotherhood Alliance) that had been reluctant to meet publicly.[8]

Western efforts to support the pro-democratic movement appeared less impactful across the reporting period. In December 2022, the United States government authorised non-lethal assistance to the resistance movement as a part of the Burma Unified through Rigorous Military Accountability Act. However, none of the promised aid had reached the opposition by mid-2023 amid bureaucratic complexities.

Association of Southeast Asian Nations (ASEAN) members also struggled to mediate the conflict or convince the junta to implement the Five Point Consensus, a road-map resolution agreed to by the bloc in April 2021 that calls for dialogue amongst all parties. As the 2023 ASEAN chair, Indonesia has been attempting 'quiet diplomacy' with more stakeholders, but ASEAN's leadership was cast into doubt after Myanmar's neighbours launched their own 'Track 1.5' initiative in early 2023.[9]

In February 2023, the regime extended the state of emergency for another six months, indicating that it would not hold the elections ostensibly slated for later in the year.[10] Then, one month later, junta officials dissolved the NLD and 39 other parties that together had won 88.5% of the union parliament seats in the 2020 elections.[11] With few signs of a potential route or political settlement to end the crisis, Myanmar continues down a path towards ever-worsening violence.

Conflict Parties

State Administration Council (SAC) (Myanmar armed forces or Tatmadaw)

Strength: Public estimates of the current size of Myanmar's armed forces range from 100,000–300,000 active military personnel, in addition to around 100,000 active paramilitary personnel (numbers are disputed), with increasing deployment of auxiliary and non-combat forces to fight the growing resistance movement.

Areas of operation: Operates nationwide, with headquarters in Naypyidaw.

Leadership: Senior-General Min Aung Hlaing (commander-in-chief of defence services and SAC chairperson) and Vice Senior-General Soe Win (vice commander-in-chief of defence services and SAC vice chairperson).

Structure: The armed forces include three service branches: the army, navy and air force. The army is divided into six Bureaus of Special Operations controlling 14 regional military commands.

History: The military seized power in 1962 and ruled via several successive regimes for the next five decades. It then rewrote the constitution in 2008 to initiate a partial democratic transition, retaining 25% of the seats in parliament for itself.

In 2016, it entered into a power-sharing agreement with the NLD before seizing back state power in another coup on 1 February 2021.

Objectives: Preserve the union, quell ethnic and political dissent, maintain political power, conduct Bamar-centric state-building, modernise the military and secure international legitimacy.

Opponents: More than 20 EAOs, NUG/PDF, dozens of localised resistance groups and the general population.

Affiliates/allies: Various People's Militia Forces and Border Guard Forces (BGFs) integrated into the command structure. The SAC supports irregular forces including local independent militias and partisan village-defence units. It also enjoys growing military and political support from Russia and China.

Resources/capabilities: The SAC is largely self-sufficient in the production of small arms and light weapons. It has also improved its technical capacity for domestic production (including naval patrol boats and small drones), and it has a notable surveillance and intelligence capacity, especially in urban areas. The air force is equipped with Russian and Chinese aircraft capable of night-time operations.

National Unity Government/People's Defence Force (NUG/PDF)

Strength: 300 PDF battalions of 200–500 troops each, estimated at 65,000 personnel, as well as approximately 400 autonomous resistance outfits known as the Local People's Defence Forces (LPDFs), estimated at 30,000 personnel.[12]

Areas of operation: Armed resistance is nationwide, with strongest presence in Sagaing and Magway regions and Kayin and Kayah states. The NUG and PDF have a growing presence in Mandalay and Bago regions, as well as in

National Unity Government/People's Defence Force (NUG/PDF)

northern Shan State. Political and bureaucratic elements are active in Thailand, the US and Europe.

Leadership: Aung San Suu Kyi (state counsellor), U Win Myint (president), Duwa Lashi La (acting president), Mahn Winn Khaing Thann (prime minister), U Yee Mon (defence minister) and Zin Mar Aung (foreign minister).

Structure: The NUG operates 17 ministries, with the Ministry of Defence responsible for the PDF. Its military command structure is not yet consolidated, with many units operating independently. Integrated units operate under two joint structures with EAO allies, or under one of three semi-autonomous military division commands.

History: The NUG was founded in April 2021. It formed the PDF under its command in May 2021, and localised groups proliferated rapidly after the NUG called for a nationwide uprising in September that year.

Objectives: National liberation via the overthrow and dismantling of the SAC (Tatmadaw) (to be replaced by a federal army) and the creation of a democratic federal union.

Opponents: SAC (Tatmadaw) and its proxy militias.

Affiliates/allies: Closest military partners include the KIA, Karen National Union (KNU), Karenni Army (KA), CNF and All Burma Students' Democratic Front (ABSDF). Limited support is also provided by the Brotherhood Alliance. Political coordination is undertaken through the National Unity Consultative Council (NUCC), which includes ethnic-based consultative councils, political parties, civil-society organisations and civil strike groups.

Resources/capabilities: The NUG claims that it has a budget of US$100m, 60% of which is for purchasing arms.[13] Only about 20% of PDF fighters carry automatic rifles, while almost all LPDF fighters rely on home-made weapons.[14] PDFs operating under EAOs are the best equipped, with access to rockets, mortars and limited quantities of other light weapons.

Karen National Liberation Army/Karen National Union (KNLA/KNU)

Strength: Between 4,000 and 6,000 regular fighters, up to 2,000 home-guard fighters organised as the Karen National Defence Organisation (KNDO), and control over multiple PDF units.[15]

Areas of operation: Military operations in Bago Region, Kayin State, Mon State and Tanintharyi Region. Political elements are active in Thailand.

Leadership: Gen. Saw Kwe Htoo Win (chairperson), Padoh Saw Hser Gay (vice chairperson) and Padoh Saw Tahdoh Moo (general secretary).

Structure: The KNLA comprises seven brigades that operate with varying degrees of autonomy. Its political wing (the KNU) operates 14 administrative departments.

History: The KNU was established in 1947 and, that same year, it formed the KNDO, a collection of local armed units that later evolved into the KNLA. It is one of the most influential armed groups in Myanmar. It fought fierce battles with the military in

the 1950s and 1960s, reaching the peak of its power in the early 1990s, after which it suffered numerous splits. It agreed to a ceasefire in 2012 before signing the Nationwide Ceasefire Agreement (NCA) in 2015. Some brigades, but not all, resumed heavy fighting after the 2021 coup.

Objectives: Seek Karen self-determination within a federal democratic union, oppose military rule through either peaceful or revolutionary means, and reunite Karen factions.

Opponents: SAC (Tatmadaw) and some BGFs.

Affiliates/allies: Allied with the NUG via the Joint Command and Coordination structure and is also a participant in the NUCC.

Resources/capabilities: Primarily fields small arms and light weapons. The KNLA is capable of overrunning fixed positions and disrupting logistics. It is funded through various business endeavours and donations from the diaspora, and it possesses a sophisticated capacity for international public relations.

Karenni Army (KA) and Karenni Nationalities Defence Force (KNDF)

Strength: Up to 3,000 troops from the KA and 8,800 personnel among the KNDF, about 2,200 of whom are armed.[16]

Areas of operation: Kayah State and the area around Pekon, southern Shan State.

Leadership: The KNDF was formed under the tutelage of the KA but over the last year has become increasingly independent. The KA is led by Khu Oo Reh (chairperson), Abel Tweed (vice chairperson) and Khu Plureh (general secretary). The KNDF is led by Khun Bi Htoo (chief of staff) and Mar Wi (deputy commander).

Structure: The KA is organised into five battalions. The KNDF began as an umbrella network of Karenni PDFs but is now comprised of 22 battalions under a strengthened chain of command.

History: The KA was founded in Kayah State in 1957. It signed a state- and union-level ceasefire in 2012 but never signed the NCA despite encouragement from the military and fellow EAOs. The KNDF was formed on 31 May 2021 to consolidate and coordinate the various ethnic Karenni resistance outfits that emerged following the 2021 coup.

Objectives: Reverse the 2021 coup, overthrow the SAC (Tatmadaw) and achieve ethnic and national liberation.

Opponents: SAC (Tatmadaw) and Pa-O National Army (PNA).

Affiliates/allies: KA and KNDF forces fight alongside allied PDF units under the Central Command and Coordination Committee (C3C) organised by the NUG. Political coordination is carried out by the Karenni State Consultative Council and the NUCC.

Asia

Karenni Army (KA) and Karenni Nationalities Defence Force (KNDF)

Resources/capabilities: Capable of disrupting logistics, assaulting fixed positions and waging urban combat. The KA and KNDF fight with automatic rifles, launchers, mines and homemade weapons, including commercial drones armed with improvised explosive devices (IEDs).

Chinland Joint Defence Committee (CJDC)

Strength: Approximately 10,000 fighters across Chin State.[17]

Areas of operation: Chin State and the adjacent areas along the border with Magway and Sagaing regions.

Leadership: Salai Timmy Htut serves as the general secretary of the CJDC alliance. The CNF is led by Pu Zing Cung (chairperson).

Structure: The CJDC is an alliance of 18 Chin resistance outfits. These include the CNF, Chin National Defence Force and township-based chapters of the Chinland Defence Forces (CDF).

History: The CNF was founded in 1988 in Mizoram, India. It agreed to a ceasefire in 2012 and signed the NCA in 2015 but quickly rearmed following the 2021 coup. It then helped train and equip new Chin resistance forces, especially those under the CDF. The CJDC alliance was formed in August–September 2021.

Objectives: Overthrow the military junta and achieve greater ethnic autonomy for Chin people.

Opponents: SAC (Tatmadaw).

Affiliates/allies: The CNF is militarily allied with the NUG under the C3C joint structure. Political coordination is carried out at the Interim Chin National Consultative Committee. Chin groups are also party to the NUCC.

Resources/capabilities: Adept mountain guerrillas capable of impeding logistics and blocking enemy movements across the state with roadside ambushes. Chin resistance forces dominate rural areas but struggle to contest major towns. Most fighters are equipped with homemade single-shot rifles, but armament is steadily improving. CNF fighters used drones, as well as landmines and an anti-tank mine, to disable two armoured vehicles in April 2023.[18]

Kachin Independence Army/Kachin Independence Organisation (KIA/KIO)

Strength: Up to 10,000 regulars with several thousand more PDF fighters under its command.

Areas of operation: Historical operations in Kachin State and northern Shan State, with static control of some areas along the border with China. Expanded operations allowed the KIA/KIO to gain new footholds in Sagaing and Mandalay regions following the 2021 coup.

Leadership: Gen. N'Ban La heads the KIO and is the senior commander of the KIA.

Structure: Divided into ten brigades, with control over multiple subordinate PDF units.

History: Formed in 1961 and signed a ceasefire agreement in 1994 that broke down in 2011. The KIA/KIO founded the Northern Alliance in 2016 before launching a major joint offensive against the SAC (Tatmadaw). A new, de facto ceasefire lasted from 2018 to the 2021 coup, after which the group launched renewed offensives.

Objectives: Seek Kachin autonomy within a federal democratic union and overthrow the military junta.

Opponents: SAC (Tatmadaw), Shanni Nationalities Army (SNA) and some local ethnic militias.

Affiliates/allies: Member of the FPNCC and leader of the defunct Northern Alliance. The KIA/KIO has a military alliance with the NUG via the C3C. Political coordination is through the Kachin National Consultative Assembly and the NUCC.

Resources/capabilities: Generates income through taxation and various activities including mining and hydropower. The KIA/KIO enjoys a large and active diaspora support. It manufactures or assembles small arms and ammunition in its area of control and possesses light weapons. It is able to capture territory, down helicopters and raise proxy forces.

Brotherhood Alliance

Strength: Arakan Army (AA): estimates vary from 15,000–30,000 fighters; Ta'ang National Liberation Army (TNLA): 8,000–10,000 fighters, including irregulars; and Myanmar National Democratic Alliance Army (MNDAA): 4,000–5,000 fighters.

Areas of operation: The AA operates primarily in northern Rakhine State and Paletwa Township, Chin State. The MNDAA and TNLA operate mainly in northern Shan State.

Leadership: Twan Mrat Naing (AA commander-in-chief), Tar Aik Bong (TNLA chairperson) and Peng Deren (MNDAA commander-in-chief).

Structure: All three groups operate with complete autonomy but often coordinate political stances on national issues. The groups are known to sometimes operate in combined units in Shan State. Major past offensives were led by the TNLA. All three groups operate political wings and local administrations as well.

History: The AA and TNLA were founded in 2009, while a ceasefire with the MNDAA broke down that same year. All three groups received significant support from the KIA under the banner of the Northern Alliance. After growing increasingly powerful, the three groups split from the KIA to form their own alliance in 2019 before launching fresh offensives against the military.

Brotherhood Alliance

Objectives: Ethnic autonomy and self-determination and an end to military dictatorship.

Opponents: SAC (Tatmadaw) and its proxy forces.

Affiliates/allies: All three groups are formal members of the FPNCC. They also provide limited arms and training to some PDFs.

Resources/capabilities: Capable of mobilising large contingents of fighters to stage coordinated frontal assaults on military and police positions, fielding small arms, mortars, IEDs, 107-millimetre surface-to-surface rockets and satellite-communications equipment. The three groups are also able to capture territory, disrupt logistics and civilian commerce, and raise proxy forces.

United Wa State Army/United Wa State Party (UWSA/UWSP)

Strength: 20,000–30,000 regular fighters.[19]

Areas of operation: Wa State, a de facto autonomous enclave with two non-contiguous territories in eastern Shan State.

Leadership: Currently undergoing a generational leadership change, with Bao Youxiang (chairperson) expected to hand power to his son, Bao Ai Kham.

Structure: Nine brigades deployed across two separate regions.[20]

History: Arose from the Communist Party of Burma in 1989 and immediately signed a ceasefire with the government which it maintains today. The UWSA/UWSP captured additional territory along the Thai border in the 1990s and built a large drug empire to fund its operations. Its status as the most powerful EAO and greatest potential source of weapons for anti-junta groups gives it substantial influence over the nation's conflicts. It operates an autonomous statelet with a fully functioning administration and local economy.

Objectives: Preservation of autonomy over Wa State and maintenance of buffer forces through proxy allies, as well as economic development.

Opponents: SAC (Tatmadaw).

Affiliates/allies: The UWSA/UWSP is the leader of the FPNCC. Its closest allies are the National Democratic Alliance Army (NDAA) and Shan State Progress Party (SSPP), but it also has considerable influence over the Brotherhood Alliance. It maintains close ties with the Yunnan provincial government.

Resources/capabilities: Fields advanced equipment such as Chinese-made drones, armoured vehicles, anti-aircraft guns and FN-6 point-defence man-portable air-defence systems. The UWSA/UWSP also manufactures small arms like the Type-81 assault rifle.

Other relevant parties

The ABSDF, Arakan Liberation Party, Burma People's Liberation Army, Democratic Karen Benevolent Army, KNU–Peace Council, Kawthoolei Army, NDAA, New Mon State Party, PNA, Pa-O National Liberation Army, Restoration Council of Shan State, SNA, SSPP, various urban guerrilla groups and independent local resistance outfits.

Notes

1   Armed Conflict Location & Event Data Project (ACLED), www. acleddata.com.

2   'Five Killed in Junta Airstrike on Chin Resistance Force Headquarters Near Myanmar–India Border', Myanmar Now, 12 January 2023; and Nyein Swe and Aung Naing, 'Two Months After Deadly Air Raid, Hpakant Remains on High Alert', Myanmar Now, 29 December 2022.

3   'Myanmar Junta Extends Martial Law in Resistance Stronghold Sagaing Region', Irrawaddy, 23 February 2023.

4   Maung Shwe Wah, 'In Myanmar's Heartland, New Horrors from a Junta Struggling for Control', Myanmar Now, 11 March 2023.

5   News Wires, 'Death Toll Climbs to at Least 170 in Myanmar Junta Air Strike on Village', France 24, 14 April 2023.

6   Data for Myanmar, Facebook post, 13 June 2023. The data covers 1 May 2021–31 May 2023.

7   UN Children's Fund, 'Myanmar Country Office: Humanitarian Situation Report No. 4', June 2023.

8   Ingyin Naing, 'Peace Talks in Myanmar Highlight China's Increasing Influence', VOA, 4 June 2023.

9   Gwen Robinson, 'Myanmar Tests Indonesia's Resolve as ASEAN Fissures Deepen', Nikkei Asia, 19 April 2023.

10 Agence France-Presse in Yangon, 'Myanmar Junta Extends State of Emergency, Delaying Promised Elections', Guardian, 2 February 2023.

11 Manny Maung, 'Myanmar Junta Dissolves Political Parties', Human Rights Watch, 29 March 2023; and Ye Myo Hein (@ YeMyoHein5), tweet, 29 March 2023.

12 Ye Myo Hein, 'Understanding the People's Defence Forces in Myanmar', United States Institute of Peace, 3 November 2023.

13 'The Ministry of Defence Under the National Unity Government Announced on 16 April That People's Defence Forces Will Be Equipped with More Arms', BNI, 21 April 2023.

14 Ye Myo Hein, 'Understanding the People's Defence Forces in Myanmar'.

15 Strength numbers for the KNLA/KNU, KIA/KIO and the Brotherhood Alliance are the author's own estimates. For further information see Stein Tønnesson, Min Zaw Oo and Ne Lynn Aung, 'Pretending to Be States: The Use of Facebook by Armed Groups in Myanmar', *Journal of Contemporary Asia*, vol. 52, no. 2, May 2021; and Bertil Lintner, 'Rebel Yell: Arakan Army Leader Speaks to Asia Times', *Asia Times*, 18 January 2022.

16 See Antonio Graceffo, 'How China Prolongs Myanmar's Endless Internal Conflicts', Jamestown Foundation *China Brief*, vol. 23, no. 5; and Morgan Michaels, 'Battle for Kayah Is Key for Myanmar Junta and Its Opponents', IISS Myanmar Conflict Map, June 2023.

17 Ye Myo Hein, 'One Year On: The Momentum of Myanmar's Armed Rebellion', Wilson Center, May 2022.

18 Khin Yi Yi Zaw, 'Chin Armed Group Attacks, Disables Junta Vehicles on Road to Hakha', Myanmar Now, 14 April 2023.

19 Bertil Lintner, 'Silence on Coup Makes Strategic Sense for Myanmar's Wa', *Irrawaddy*, 12 July 2021.

20 Anthony Davis, 'Wa an Early Winner of Myanmar's Post-coup War', *Asia Times*, 22 February 2022.

INDIA

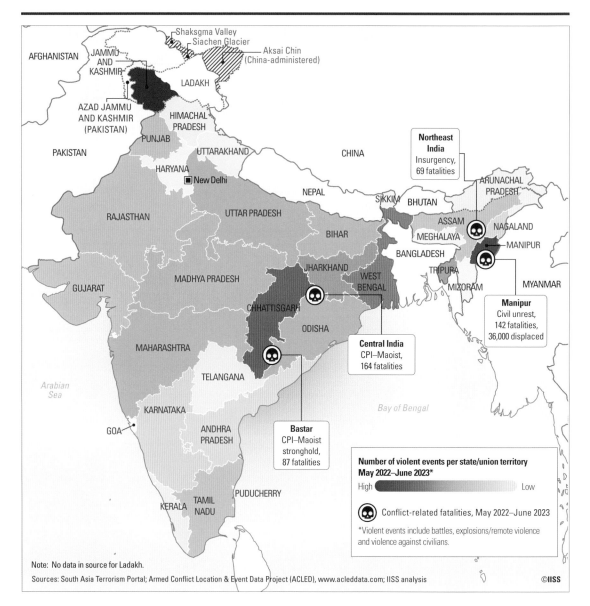

Sources: South Asia Terrorism Portal; Armed Conflict Location & Event Data Project (ACLED), www.acleddata.com; IISS analysis

Conflict Overview

For New Delhi, the conflicts in India's central heartlands and northeastern peripheries are a lesser priority than the politically and strategically more important Kashmir conflict. Thus, both the central and the northeastern conflicts have simmered for several decades, marked by an Indian state approach of containing rather than defeating the insurgencies. Both conflicts are the result of

perceived neglect or a fear of assimilation or exploitation, either by the 'mainland' or by a class-based or ethnic 'other'.

Conflict in these regions began in the northeast in the 1950s, when the Naga National Council (NNC) mobilised due to fears that the Nagas would be forcibly assimilated into India. Failed peace agreements led to the proliferation of numerous

Armed Conflict Global Relevance Indicator (ACGRI)

Incidence

10

Human
impact

Geopolitical
impact

5

3

India

Key Conflict Statistics

Conflict(s)	Type	Start date
Ethnic conflicts in the northeast	Internal: localised insurgency & intercommunal	1955
Maoist insurgency in central India	Internal: localised insurgency	2004

Fatalities	787
Percentage change in fatalities	-22%
IDPs	631,000
Peacekeeping and other multilateral missions	UNMOGIP
Climate-change vulnerability (0–1)	0.5

ACGRI pillars: IISS calculation based on multiple sources for 2022 and 2023 (scale: 0–100), except for some cases according to data availability. See Notes on Methodology and Data Appendix for further details on Key Conflict Statistics.

Naga factions. Though many of these factions have coexisted with New Delhi through a series of prolonged ceasefires since 1997, peace negotiations remain gridlocked over unresolved issues. A peace agreement was reached with Mizoram-based insurgents in 1986, while a host of other ethno-separatist conflicts in Assam, Manipur, Meghalaya and Tripura, driven by a fusion of anti-centre sentiment, local ethnic rivalries and extremely porous international borders, peaked in the 1990s and have steadily declined since.

The Maoist insurgency in central India is comparatively more insulated from geopolitical dynamics. It emerged in 1967 with a peasant revolt at Naxalbari that gave rise to the 'Naxalite' movement, which sought to overthrow feudal structures and impose a new economic order. The insurgency peaked in 2009–10 when the Communist Party of India–Maoist (CPI–Maoist) occupied a 'Red Corridor' spanning much of Bihar, Chhattisgarh, Jharkhand, Maharashtra and West Bengal states. Since 2014, security forces' successes have rolled back CPI–Maoist influence.

Conflict Update

The Naga peace talks remained gridlocked throughout the reporting period, with the National Socialist Council of Nagalim–Isak Muivah (NSCN–IM) continuing to demand a separate flag and constitution for the Naga people. The Indian central and state governments signed peace deals with eight Assam-based tribal armed groups and the Naga Zeliangrong United Front (ZUF) in September and December 2022, respectively.[1] However, in March 2023 the Manipur government withdrew from its ceasefire with two Kuki militant groups – the Kuki National Army (KNA) and the Zomi Revolutionary Army (ZRA) – following tensions between the state's majority Meitei and minority Kuki communities.[2]

In May 2023, these tensions erupted into communal violence, resulting in 137 deaths and internally displacing 50,698 people.[3] Concentrated in the Kuki-dominated Churachandpur and

Meitei-dominated Imphal West districts, the violence occurred following the Manipur High Court's recommendation that the majority Meitei community be granted Sixth Schedule status (offering special constitutional protections), which was perceived as a threat to Kuki communities. While the clashes were primarily communal in nature, a cluster of Kuki armed groups under a ceasefire with the Indian government became increasingly involved. There were 84 battles in Manipur during May (36) and June (48) alone, with each month witnessing more battles than any one year in Manipur since 2016.[4] Despite government curfews and the increased deployment of security forces, as of June 2023, the situation remains volatile.

The Maoist conflict accounted for 164 conflict-related fatalities in May 2022–June 2023 but also registered a 25.5% decline in fatalities compared with May 2021–June 2022.[5] This reflected a continued trend of shrinking Maoist influence across the former Red Corridor, with particularly high levels of surrenders in states such as Odisha. Despite this decline, the CPI–Maoist has retained strongholds in Chhattisgarh's Bastar region (which includes Bastar, Bijapur, Dantewada, Kanker, Kondagaon, Narayanpur and Sukma districts) and has continued to attack security forces. In April 2023, for example, an improvised explosive device (IED) killed ten police officers and a driver in Dantewada.[6]

Conflict Parties

Indian Armed Forces

Strength: 1,463,700 active military personnel.

Areas of operation: Northeast (III Corps and IV Corps). The army does not play a direct role in anti-CPI–Maoist operations in central India.

Leadership: Lt.-Gen. H.S. Sahi (III Corps commander) and Lt.-Gen. Dinesh Singh Rana (IV Corps commander). The III Corps and IV Corps are both subordinate to the army's Eastern Command, led by Lt-Gen. Rana Pratap Kalita.

Structure: Zonal command structure subdivided into corps commands.

History: The Indian Army was formed as a direct successor to the British Indian Army after independence in 1947. The army, navy and air force are primarily responsible for external defence, but the army and air force have played a pivotal role in Indian counter-insurgency operations since the 1950s.

Objectives: Counter-insurgency and border defence.

Opponents: Non-state armed groups (NSAGs).

Affiliates/allies: Other state forces, although coordination challenges exist.

Resources/capabilities: Most suitably equipped and trained to operate in the difficult, rugged terrain of northeast India, drawing upon logistics and airpower to supply distant outposts. Heavy weaponry is rarely deployed to counter-insurgency operations, though there have been exceptions.

Assam Rifles

Strength: 65,150.

Areas of operation: Northeast India (Nagaland and Manipur).

Leadership: Lt.-Gen. Pradeep Chandran Nair (director general).

Structure: Organised into 46 battalions officered by army personnel. It is under the jurisdiction of the Ministry of Defence, but as a central paramilitary force it is answerable to the Ministry of Home Affairs.

History: Originally formed as the Cachar Levy in 1835, the Assam Rifles plays a central role in counter-insurgency operations in northeast India.

Objectives: Counter-insurgency and border defence.

Opponents: Naga armed groups, Manipur valley-based insurgent groups and other armed groups in the hills of Manipur.

Affiliates/allies: Cooperates with other state forces, although challenges exist around intelligence sharing, overlapping jurisdictions and operational coordination.

Resources/capabilities: Battalions are typically equipped to the same standard as an Indian Army infantry battalion, with small arms and mortar capabilities.

Central Reserve Police Force (CRPF)

Strength: 324,800.

Areas of operation: Northeastern, central and eastern India. It takes a leading role in central India, in states such as Andhra Pradesh, Bihar, Chhattisgarh, Jharkhand, Maharashtra and Odisha.

Leadership: Sujoy Lal Thaosen (director general).

Structure: CRPF battalions are central-government forces but are deployed to state governments to assist in law-and-order activities. CRPF forces are designed to augment existing state police forces to combat CPI–Maoist insurgents across the Red Corridor. The central government is responsible for deploying CRPF forces and for coordinating with individual state governments.

History: Originally founded as the Crown Representative Police Force in 1939 before being rechristened after independence. The force has evolved into one of the largest of the central police forces and has the broadest remit of supporting state governments in law-and-order duties, as well as a limited counter-insurgency remit.

Objectives: Support state-level law enforcement in counter-insurgency duties.

Opponents: CPI–Maoist in central India and an array of armed groups in northeastern India.

Affiliates/allies: Cooperates with other state forces, although challenges exist around intelligence sharing, overlapping jurisdictions and operational coordination.

Resources/capabilities: CRPF battalions vary in degrees of modernisation. While special units such as the CRPF's 'Commando Battalions for Resolute Action' are equipped with modern INSAS rifles and AK-series rifles, this varies across units. Some units have mine-protected vehicles; however, these are rare and CRPF units are thus often vulnerable to IED attacks.

State Police Forces

Strength: 450,000.

Areas of operation: Varied.

Leadership: Led by a state-level director general of the police, answerable to state-government political leadership.

Structure: Typically organised into zones and ranges, with supplementary armed police battalions for counter-insurgency support.

History: Varied according to the formation of individual states.

Objectives: Law-and-order and counter-insurgency duties.

Opponents: NSAGs.

Affiliates/allies: Cooperates with other state forces, although challenges exist around intelligence sharing, overlapping jurisdictions and operational coordination.

Resources/capabilities: While special armed police units are better equipped and have undergone modernisation, the bulk of state police forces face logistical challenges in navigating treacherous terrain and fair-weather roads, as well as deficiencies in firearms, including reliance on old, colonial-era rifles.

National Socialist Council of Nagalim–Isak Muivah (NSCN–IM)

Strength: 5,000.

Areas of operation: Naga-inhabited northeast India: Arunachal Pradesh, Assam, Manipur and Nagaland.

Leadership: Thuingaleng Muivah (general secretary).

Structure: The group is organised centrally but is demographically dominated by the Tangkhul tribe of Manipur.

History: After splitting from the original NSCN in 1988, the NSCN–IM has since emerged as one of the most powerful NSAGs in northeast India. Observing a ceasefire limited to the territorial jurisdiction of Nagaland with the Indian government since 1997, the group continues to recruit; clashes with rivals and occasionally Indian security forces in non-ceasefire areas; and runs its own parallel government from its 'capital'

in Camp Hebron, on the outskirts of Dimapur. In 2015 it signed a Framework Agreement with the government of India, with the view to concluding a comprehensive settlement, but the group's ethnic composition remains a bone of contention.

Objectives: Gain hybrid 'sovereignty' over Nagaland, incorporating Nagas under one territorial entity with a separate flag and constitution.

Opponents: State forces, National Socialist Council of Nagaland–Khaplang (NSCN–K), ZUF and Kuki armed groups.

Affiliates/allies: Naga civil society.

Resources/capabilities: The best equipped of northeast India-based insurgents with connections to the Southeast Asia regional arms market.

Working Committee (WC)

Strength: Umbrella organisation of seven armed groups.[7]

Areas of operation: Arunachal Pradesh, Manipur and Nagaland.

Leadership: N. Kitovi Zhimomi (convenor).

Structure: A conglomerate of smaller armed groups.

History: Formed as the Working Group in 2016, the WC is an umbrella organisation now consisting of seven separate armed groups, often referred to as 'Naga political groups', which joined together to increase their political clout in the peace process. The WC signed its own Framework Agreement with the central government on 17 November 2017, forming a basis for future negotiations.

Objectives: Secure a peace deal granting the Naga autonomy within the Indian constitution.

Opponents: Its main opponent is the NSCN–IM. However, in September 2022 and January 2023, the group signed a series of agreements committing to cooperate with the NSCN–IM.

Affiliates/allies: Fellow Working Committee members.

Resources/capabilities: Varied across membership. The NSCN–Reformation (NSCN–R) is the most operationally competent faction, followed by the NSCN–Kitovi-Neokpao/Unification.

Kuki armed groups under Suspension of Operations (SoO) agreements

Strength: 25 Kuki militant groups, most of which are broadly organised under two umbrella fronts, the Kuki National Organisation (KNO) and the United People's Front (UPF). As of 2021, there were 1,207 KNO militants and 1,059 militants affiliated with the UPF. The KNO is comprised of 17 armed groups, and the UPF is comprised of eight.[8]

Areas of operation: Kuki-inhabited areas of Manipur and Assam.

Leadership: In the February 2023 renewal of the SoO ceasefire agreements, the UPF was represented by Ketheos Zomi and Joshua Thadou and the KNO was represented by Seilen Haokip.

Structure: Loosely organised umbrella organisations.

History: SoO agreements were initially signed by the central government, the Manipur government and Kuki groups in 2008. In March 2023, the Manipur government withdrew from SoO agreements with the ZRA (a member of the UPF) and the KNA (a member of the KNO). However, the central government is unlikely to withdraw from these agreements.

Objectives: Gain statehood for Kuki-inhabited areas of Manipur.

Opponents: State forces, NSCN–IM and Meitei activists. There are numerous rivalries between Kuki factions which have led to inter-factional violence.

Asia

Kuki armed groups under Suspension of Operations (SoO) agreements

Affiliates/allies: NSCN–Khaplang/Yung Aung (NSCN–K/YA) and Coordination Committee (CorCom, Manipur) member groups.

Resources/capabilities: Weapons are stored in KNO and UPF designated camps.

Communist Party of India–Maoist (CPI–Maoist)

Strength: Around 2,500 members in the Chhattisgarh–Maharashtra region, with up to 40% of members being women (police estimate, 2021).[9]

Areas of operation: Andhra Pradesh, Bihar, Chhattisgarh, Jharkhand, Kerala, Madhya Pradesh, Maharashtra, Odisha, Telangana and West Bengal. Hotspot of CPI–Maoist activity in the Bastar region of Chhattisgarh.

Leadership: Comprised of a central committee made up of representatives from the various states. The committee is led by Nambala Keshava Rao (general secretary, alias Basavraj).

Structure: Local command structures include 'zonal' commanders (zones roughly correspond to Indian districts) and local 'area' commanders under sub-committees.

History: Formed in 2004 following the merger of the Communist Party of India (Marxist–Leninist), People's War (People's War Group) and the Maoist Communist Centre of India. The organisation peaked in its control of territory in approximately

2009, leading then-prime minister Manmohan Singh to label the insurgency the country's single-largest security challenge. Since 2014, counter-insurgency operations and organisational splits have led to the group's gradual decline.

Objectives: Overthrow Indian parliamentary democracy in favour of a communist regime through rural insurgency. Mobilise a power base by tapping into marginalised communities in India's hinterlands. Deploys hit-and-run attacks against Indian security forces.

Opponents: Indian security forces, civilians suspected of collaboration and smaller splinter factions such as the People's Liberation Front of India.

Affiliates/allies: Seeks to cultivate alliances with disempowered local civilians.

Resources/capabilities: Primarily arms itself with home-made firearms, although its elite fighting units wield AK-47s and semi-automatic weapons seized from police. The group also makes frequent use of IEDs.

National Socialist Council of Nagaland–Khaplang/Yung Aung (NSCN–K/YA)

Strength: Unclear.

Areas of operation: Myanmar (Sagaing), as well as Arunachal Pradesh, Manipur and Nagaland.

Leadership: Burmese Naga Yung Aung after death of S.S. Khaplang in 2017.

Structure: Various factions have split from the NSCN–K, including the pro-talks NSCN–R in 2016, the pro-talks NSCN–Khango-Konyak (NSCN–KK) in 2018 and the anti-talks NSCN–Nyemlang Konyak (which has since been renamed as the NSCN–K/Niki Sumi) in 2020.

History: Formed as a splinter group of the original NSCN in 1988, the NSCN–K drew particular recruitment strength from the Konyaks of eastern Nagaland and Myanmar. Although it

signed a ceasefire with the government in 2001, it rescinded this in April 2015 and began conducting operations against security forces in cooperation with other NSAGs in Manipur and Assam. Since the departure of the NSCN–KK faction from the NSCN–K in the summer of 2018, the group has been led by Myanmar-born Yung Aung.

Objectives: Gain sovereignty over an independent Nagaland through armed struggle; cross-border strikes.

Opponents: State forces, NSCN–IM and other rival NSCN factions.

Affiliates/allies: Leading member of the United National Liberation Front of Western South East Asia, and allied with CorCom.

Resources/capabilities: Unknown.

Coordination Committee (CorCom)

Strength: Umbrella organisation of six anti-talk armed groups.[10]

Areas of operation: Arunachal Pradesh, Manipur and Myanmar.

Leadership: Formed by the leader of the People's Liberation Army of Manipur (PLAM).

Structure: CorCom's organisational structure is best described as a framework for cooperation between its member armed groups.

History: When formed in 2011, CorCom included a seventh armed group, the United People's Party of Kangleipak (UPPK). However, the UPPK was expelled from the group in 2013 after it began responding to peace overtures from the Indian government.

Objectives: Gain sovereignty over Manipur.

Opponents: State forces, rival anti- and pro-talks Manipuri armed groups.

Affiliates/allies: Some of its constituent organisations have aligned with the Myanmar military as of 2021.

Resources/capabilities: Significant variation in capabilities. Whereas the PLAM and United National Liberation Front are well-trained, disciplined and cohesive outfits, the Kangleipak Communist Party is a series of small, fragmented factions.

Other relevant parties

Other relevant groups include the ZUF, a small organisation based in the tri-junction area bordering Assam, Manipur and Nagaland, which signed a peace agreement in 2022, as well as a cluster of eight Assam-based Adivasi (or tribal) militant groups which also signed a peace accord in September 2022. The Kuki Independent Army – one of the few Kuki armed groups not in a ceasefire with the government – was also reported to have looted weapons from the camps of ceasefire signatory groups in April 2023.

Notes

1   Bharti Jain, 'Assam Government Signs Peace Agreement with Insurgents', *Times of India*, 15 September 2022; and K. Sarojkumar Sharma, 'Centre, Manipur Rebel Outfit Sign Peace Pact', *Times of India*, 28 December 2022.

2   K. Sarojkumar Sharma, 'Manipur Pulls Out of Ceasefire Pact with 2 Kuki Militant Groups', *Times of India*, 12 March 2023.

3   Numbers are as of 3 July 2023 and 11 June 2023, respectively. Umang Sharma, 'Manipur Violence: One Beheaded, Three Shot Dead', Firstpost, 3 July 2023; and 'Manipur Violence: Over 50,000 Displaced People Staying in 349 Relief Camps', *Economic Times*, 11 June 2023.

4   Armed Conflict Location & Event Data Project (ACLED), www.acleddata.com. ACLED data collection for Manipur began in 2016.

5   See 'Yearly Fatalities', Datasheet – Maoist Insurgency, South Asia Terrorism Portal.

6   Anurag Dwary and Divyanshu Dutta Roy, '10 Cops, Driver Killed in Blast by Maoists in Chhattisgarh's Dantewada', NDTV, 26 April 2023.

7   Including the NSCN–Kitovi-Neokpao/Unification, NSCN–R, NNC/Federal Government of Nagaland, NNC–Parent, National People's Government of Nagaland/Naga National Council–Non-Accord, Government of the Democratic Republic of Nagaland/Naga National Council–Non-Accord and the NSCN–KK.

8   K.S. Vangamla Salle, 'Manipur: Suspension of Operation with Kuki Groups Extended for Six Months', EastMojo, 27 February 2021.

9   '"40% of Armed Maoists in Chhattisgarh, Maharashtra Region Are Women"', *Hindustan Times*, 15 August 2021.

10 Including the PLAM, People's Revolutionary Party of Kangleipak (PREPAK), PREPAK–Progressive, United National Liberation Front, Kanglei Yawol Kanna Lup and the Kangleipak Communist Party.

Asia

THAILAND

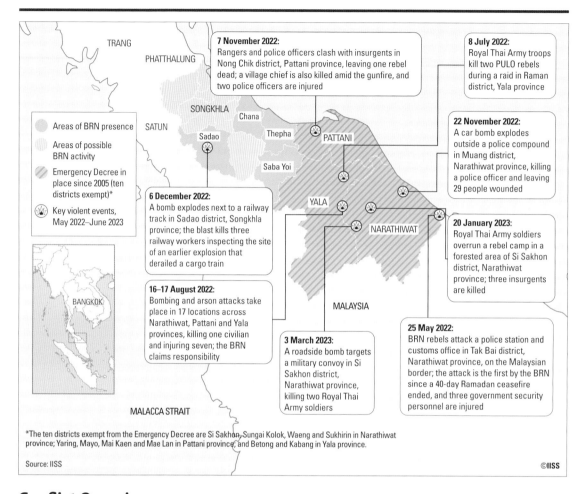

7 November 2022:
Rangers and police officers clash with insurgents in Nong Chik district, Pattani province, leaving one rebel dead; a village chief is also killed amid the gunfire, and two police officers are injured

8 July 2022:
Royal Thai Army troops kill two PULO rebels during a raid in Raman district, Yala province

22 November 2022:
A car bomb explodes outside a police compound in Muang district, Narathiwat province, killing a police officer and leaving 29 people wounded

6 December 2022:
A bomb explodes next to a railway track in Sadao district, Songkhla province; the blast kills three railway workers inspecting the site of an earlier explosion that derailed a cargo train

20 January 2023:
Royal Thai Army soldiers overrun a rebel camp in a forested area of Si Sakhon district, Narathiwat province; three insurgents are killed

16–17 August 2022:
Bombing and arson attacks take place in 17 locations across Narathiwat, Pattani and Yala provinces, killing one civilian and injuring seven; the BRN claims responsibility

3 March 2023:
A roadside bomb targets a military convoy in Si Sakhon district, Narathiwat province, killing two Royal Thai Army soldiers

25 May 2022:
BRN rebels attack a police station and customs office in Tak Bai district, Narathiwat province, on the Malaysian border; the attack is the first by the BRN since a 40-day Ramadan ceasefire ended, and three government security personnel are injured

Areas of BRN presence
Areas of possible BRN activity
Emergency Decree in place since 2005 (ten districts exempt)*
Key violent events, May 2022–June 2023

*The ten districts exempt from the Emergency Decree are Si Sakhon, Sungai Kolok, Waeng and Sukhirin in Narathiwat province; Yaring, Mayo, Mai Kaen and Mae Lan in Pattani province; and Betong and Kabang in Yala province.

Source: IISS

©IISS

Conflict Overview

Malay Muslim separatists have fought the Thai state for independence since the late 1950s in the southern provinces of Narathiwat, Pattani and Yala, and in four districts of Songkhla province. The conflict originated in the early twentieth century, when the 1909 Anglo-Siamese Treaty divided the territory of the historical Islamic sultanate of Patani, separating the area from Muslim-majority Malaysia. The southern provinces have failed to assimilate with Buddhist-dominated Thailand, and Muslim residents – representing 85% of the region's population – largely reject Bangkok's authority.[1]

The uprising was led by the Patani United Liberation Organisation (PULO) until the late 1990s, when it was weakened by counter-insurgency operations. Rebel attacks in 2001 reignited the conflict, which intensified in 2004 after then-prime minister Thaksin Shinawatra ordered a security crackdown. The south has been governed under an Emergency Decree since 2005, creating a militarised climate in which authorities man roadside checkpoints and detain suspected rebels for up to 30 days without charge. The alleged torture of detainees has reinforced Malay grievances in the south, where high poverty rates of 24.7% in Narathiwat and 44.4% in Pattani, compared to 6.8% nationally in 2020, further fuel rebel recruitment.[2]

The Patani Malay National Revolutionary Front (or Barisan Revolusi Nasional, BRN) has emerged as the predominant conflict actor, launching ambushes and bombings targeting the Royal Thai Army and local

Armed Conflict Global Relevance Indicator (ACGRI)			

Armed Conflict Global Relevance Indicator (ACGRI)

Incidence

1

Human impact — Geopolitical impact

0 — 0

Thailand

Key Conflict Statistics		
Conflict(s)	**Type**	**Start date**
Southern Thailand separatist conflict	Internal: localised insurgency	2001
Fatalities		50
Percentage change in fatalities		-11%
IDPs		41,000
Functioning of government (0–10)		6.1
Climate-change vulnerability (0–1)		0.4

ACGRI pillars: IISS calculation based on multiple sources for 2022 and 2023 (scale: 0–100), except for some cases according to data availability. See Notes on Methodology and Data Appendix for further details on Key Conflict Statistics.

paramilitaries. Sporadic violence has persisted in rural areas as peace initiatives have stalled. From 2014–19, the umbrella rebel group Mara Patani engaged in dialogue with the Thai government, but it proved unable to stem attacks by BRN forces. The BRN finally entered direct talks, mediated by Malaysia, in 2020. The two sides negotiated a 40-day Ramadan ceasefire in 2022 and agreed to discuss political solutions.[3]

Conflict Update

A fifth round of formal peace negotiations between the Thai government and the BRN took place in early August 2022, but ended without any concrete results. The election of Anwar Ibrahim as Malaysian prime minister that November injected new momentum into the peace process. Anwar appointed Zulkifli Zainal Abidin as facilitator to replace Abdul Rahim Noor and pledged that Malaysia would continue in its role as mediator to reduce the 'trust deficit' between the two sides.[4]

In a sixth round of dialogue, held in February 2023, the BRN agreed to invite other insurgent groups such as the PULO to join future talks. The head of the Thai delegation, Gen. Wanlop Rugsanaoh, and BRN chief negotiator Anas Abdulrahman also agreed to hold discussions on violence reduction, public engagement and political solutions over a two-year period, under a Joint Comprehensive Plan Towards Peace. Despite this commitment, talks with the BRN are still at an exploratory stage (as of June 2023) and the path to a future territorial or political settlement remains uncertain.

The BRN and PULO remained active in Narathiwat, Pattani, Yala and southern districts of Songkhla during the reporting period. Bombings targeted convenience stores, gas stations and infrastructure including railway tracks and electricity pylons. These attacks were intended to be disruptive rather than inflict civilian casualties. Assaults on security installations and roadside ambushes targeting troops, police officers and paramilitary forces were more deadly. Law-enforcement raids on rebel hideouts often ended in shoot-outs.

While some insurgent attacks were claimed by the BRN or PULO, other incidents occurred without any claim of responsibility. Separatist rebels in the south, even those affiliated with the two main groups, operate locally and largely autonomously in small units. This means that attacks may persist even if PULO leaders join the BRN in future peace talks, and dissatisfied factions could escalate their activities.

Conflict Parties

Royal Thai Army

Strength: 245,000 active military personnel (including about 115,000 conscripts).

Areas of operation: The Fourth Area Army of the Royal Thai Army, headquartered in Nakhon Si Thammarat, operates

Asia

Royal Thai Army

across the four insurgency-affected provinces of Narathiwat, Pattani, Songkhla and Yala.

Leadership: Lt-Gen. Santi Sakuntanark (appointed in October 2022) commands the Fourth Area Army, operating under Royal Thai Army Commander-in-Chief Gen. Narongpan Jitkaewthae.

Structure: Coordinates operations with the Internal Security Operations Command (ISOC). The Royal Thai Army has ten infantry divisions, three mechanised/armoured cavalry divisions, an artillery division and a division-sized special-operations command. Two infantry divisions are assigned to the Fourth Area Army.

History: Formed in 1874 and shaped by nationwide counter-insurgency campaigns starting in the 1960s. Since 1932, the armed forces have carried out 13 successful coups, the most recent in 2014.[5]

Objectives: Defend the monarchy and protect the political order enshrined in the 2017 military-backed constitution,

introduced by the National Council for Peace and Order regime. In southern Thailand, the Royal Thai Army aims to pacify the Malay Muslim population and prevent the insurgency from spreading to provinces further north.

Opponents: BRN, PULO and other separatist groups.

Affiliates/allies: Thai monarchy, Palang Pracharath Party and United Thai Nation Party. The Royal Thai Army is supported in operations against rebels by the Royal Thai Police and paramilitary forces, including Village Defence Volunteers.

Resources/capabilities: The Fourth Area Army is primarily equipped with small arms, light weapons and field artillery. The divisional cavalry squadrons operate some older armoured-vehicle types. The Royal Thai Army also possesses tanks, modern armoured vehicles, self-propelled artillery and attack helicopters. Equipment is purchased primarily from China and the United States.

Thai paramilitary and militia forces

Strength: 79,000 (estimate) across the southern provinces of Narathiwat, Pattani, Songkhla and Yala.[6]

Areas of operation: Paramilitary forces provide security along the border with Malaysia, while local recruits serve in their communities and at road checkpoints across the four southern provinces.

Leadership: Paramilitary forces are coordinated by the Royal Thai Army, ISOC and the Royal Thai Police.

Structure: Paramilitary forces active across the south include the Rangers, Border Patrol Police (BPP) and the Volunteer Defence Corps (VDC). At the local level, Village Defence Volunteers (*Chor ror bor*) and Village Protection Volunteers (*Or ror bor*) defend communities.

History: Paramilitary forces were created to aid the Royal Thai Army in counter-insurgency operations and border protection. The BPP was formed in 1951, the VDC in 1954 and the Rangers in 1978, initially to fight communist rebels. Village-level

volunteer units were formed in 2004 as the southern conflict intensified.

Objectives: The Rangers, BPP and VDC have a more conventional security role, serving alongside the Royal Thai Army and Royal Thai Police to limit the activity of insurgents, through manning security posts and conducting regular patrols. Village volunteers serve to protect Buddhist communities in the south and provide local surveillance and intelligence support to the military.

Opponents: BRN, PULO and other separatist groups in the south.

Affiliates/allies: Formally allied to the Royal Thai Army and the Royal Thai Police.

Resources/capabilities: Paramilitary forces are typically more lightly armed than the military. Village forces are provided with rifles and shotguns, receive a monthly stipend and undergo 10–15 days' training.[7]

Patani Malay National Revolutionary Front (Barisan Revolusi Nasional, BRN)

Strength: Approximately 3,000 fighters.[8]

Areas of operation: Narathiwat, Pattani and Yala provinces. The BRN also operates in at least four southern districts of Songkhla province (Chana, Saba Yoi, Sadao and Thepha). Infrequent bomb attacks have targeted tourist areas and Bangkok, though the BRN has no firm presence there.

Leadership: Led by an executive council, the Dewan Pimpinan Parti, under Secretary-General Sama-ae Kho Zari. Anas Abdulrahman has served as the lead negotiator in peace talks with the Thai government since January 2020.

Structure: Five organisational units cover politics, economic and financial affairs, women's affairs, youth and armed forces. BRN fighters operate in a loose, cell-like structure. Religious teachers play a central role in recruitment from Islamic schools.

History: Founded in the early 1960s by religious teacher Haji Abdul Karim Hassan. By 1984, the group had split into three

factions: BRN-Coordinate (BRN-C), BRN-Congress and BRN-Ulama. BRN-C became dominant and constitutes the BRN today. A separate, 500-strong armed wing, the Runda Kumpulan Kecil, emerged in 2000 but is now integrated within the main organisation.

Objectives: Initially established to fight for independence in the former territory of the historical Patani sultanate, which existed from the 1400s until it was conquered by the kingdom of Siam in 1786 and later absorbed into the Thai state. The BRN is now open to negotiating for autonomy or self-rule, while continuing attacks aimed at making the region ungovernable in the short term.

Opponents: Royal Thai Army and Thai paramilitary forces in the south. The BRN is also opposed to local civilians whom it perceives to be collaborating with the Thai state, including village headmen and teachers.

Patani Malay National Revolutionary Front (Barisan Revolusi Nasional, BRN)

Affiliates/allies: PULO remnants and other Malay separatist rebel groups.

Resources/capabilities: Firearms including M-16, AK-47 and AK-102 assault rifles. The BRN uses pipe bombs and retains the capability to construct low-grade improvised explosive devices (IEDs).

Patani United Liberation Organisation (PULO)

Strength: 100 fighters (estimate).[9]

Areas of operation: Narathiwat, Pattani and Yala provinces. The PULO may also be operational in southern districts of Songkhla province.

Leadership: Kasturi Mahkota serves as the head of the PULO–MKP (Majlis Kepimpinan Pertubuhan, or Party Leadership Council) and leads the main PULO faction.

Structure: The PULO is split into three factions under its current iteration, which is also known as 'PULO-G5' (fifth generation). The Kasturi-led faction has five operational units. PULO fighters operate in small cells, in a similar fashion to the BRN.

History: Founded in Saudi Arabia in 1968 by Patani Malay scholar Kabir Abdul Rahman, who served as PULO chairman until his death in 2008. The PULO was the most powerful rebel group in southern Thailand until the 1990s, when its strength declined as the BRN grew in prominence. The PULO was

dormant from 2016 until it launched bomb attacks in Pattani province in April 2022.

Objectives: Fought for decades for an independent state encompassing areas governed by the historical sultanate of Patani. In April 2022, Kasturi rejected peace talks under the framework of the Thai constitution (which would rule out independence for the south) but has since indicated that the PULO may join the existing dialogue between the government and the BRN.

Opponents: Royal Thai Army and Thai paramilitary forces in the south.

Affiliates/allies: Ideologically allied to the BRN but has no known operational ties. The PULO may have ties to remnants of smaller southern rebel groups.

Resources/capabilities: Firearms including AK-47 and M-1 carbine rifles, and handguns. The PULO retains the capability to construct IEDs using basic materials.

Notes

1   Matthew Wheeler, 'Behind the Insurgent Attack in Southern Thailand', International Crisis Group, 8 November 2019.

2   Figures are for 2020. World Bank, 'Thailand Rural Income Diagnostic: Challenges and Opportunities for Rural Farmers', October 2022.

3   Michael Hart, 'Despite Recent Attacks, Southern Thailand's Peace Talks Are Making Progress', World Politics Review, 21 June 2022.

4   Tassanee Vejpongsa, 'Malaysian PM Vows to Help Thailand Solve Southern Violence', AP News, 9 February 2023.

5   'Grading Thailand's 13 Successful Coups', Thai Enquirer, 22 May 2020.

6   The estimated 79,000 paramilitary and militia personnel in southern Thailand comprise 8,000 VDC members, 59,000 Village Defence Volunteers, 4,000 Village Protection Volunteers and an estimated 8,000 Rangers. It is unknown how many BPP officers are in the south. See Paul Chambers, 'Irregular and Inappropriate: Thailand's Paramilitaries and Pro-government Militias', Fulcrum, ISEAS – Yusof Ishak Institute, 12 April 2021.

7   Pro-government Militias Guidebook, 'Village Protection Volunteers (Or Ror Bor) (Thailand)'.

8   Srisompob Jitpiromsri, Napisa Waitoolkiat and Paul Chambers, 'Special Issue: Quagmire of Violence in Thailand's Southern Borderlands Chapter 1: Introduction', Asian Affairs: An American Review, vol. 45, no. 2, 28 April 2019.

9   Mariyam Ahmad, Muzliza Mustafa and Nisha David, 'In Thai Deep South, Another Rebel Group Wants Role in Peace Talks', Benar News, 24 June 2022.

Asia

PHILIPPINES

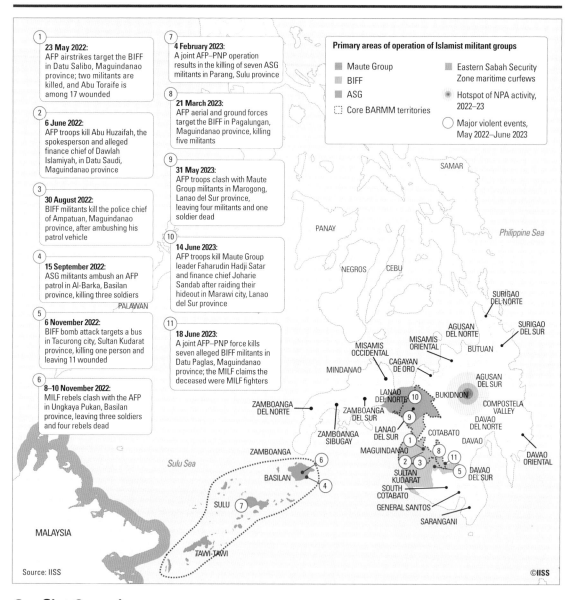

1. **23 May 2022:** AFP airstrikes target the BIFF in Datu Salibo, Maguindanao province; two militants are killed, and Abu Toraife is among 17 wounded

2. **6 June 2022:** AFP troops kill Abu Huzaifah, the spokesperson and alleged finance chief of Dawlah Islamiyah, in Datu Saudi, Maguindanao province

3. **30 August 2022:** BIFF militants kill the police chief of Ampatuan, Maguindanao province, after ambushing his patrol vehicle

4. **15 September 2022:** ASG militants ambush an AFP patrol in Al-Barka, Basilan province, killing three soldiers

5. **6 November 2022:** BIFF bomb attack targets a bus in Tacurong city, Sultan Kudarat province, killing one person and leaving 11 wounded

6. **8–10 November 2022:** MILF rebels clash with the AFP in Ungkaya Pukan, Basilan province, leaving three soldiers and four rebels dead

7. **4 February 2023:** A joint AFP–PNP operation results in the killing of seven ASG militants in Parang, Sulu province

8. **21 March 2023:** AFP aerial and ground forces target the BIFF in Pagalungan, Maguindanao province, killing five militants

9. **31 May 2023:** AFP troops clash with Maute Group militants in Marogong, Lanao del Sur province, leaving four militants and one soldier dead

10. **14 June 2023:** AFP troops kill Maute Group leader Faharudin Hadji Satar and finance chief Joharie Sandab after raiding their hideout in Marawi city, Lanao del Sur province

11. **18 June 2023:** A joint AFP–PNP force kills seven alleged BIFF militants in Datu Paglas, Maguindanao province; the MILF claims the deceased were MILF fighters

Primary areas of operation of Islamist militant groups

- Maute Group
- BIFF
- ASG
- Core BARMM territories
- Eastern Sabah Security Zone maritime curfews
- Hotspot of NPA activity, 2022–23
- Major violent events, May 2022–June 2023

Source: IISS   ©IISS

Conflict Overview

The Philippine government has fought Moro separatists in western Mindanao since 1972. After earlier uprisings against colonial authorities, the March 1968 Jabidah massacre of Moro army recruits by Philippine soldiers ignited revived secessionism. Driven by the political, cultural and religious oppression of Moro Muslims, the Moro National Liberation Front (MNLF) and later the Moro Islamic Liberation Front (MILF) waged an armed campaign for independence. Both groups eventually signed final peace deals with Manila (the MNLF in 1996 and the MILF in 2014), which included provisions for disarmament and self-rule.

Since 2019, MILF chairman Al Haj Murad Ebrahim has led a transitional government in the Bangsamoro Autonomous Region in Muslim

Armed Conflict Global Relevance Indicator (ACGRI)			Key Conflict Statistics			
	Incidence		Conflict(s)	Type		Start date
	8		Moro insurgency in Mindanao	Internal: localised insurgency		1972
Human impact		Geopolitical impact	Nationwide Maoist insurgency	Internal		1969
2		**1**	**Fatalities**			1,035
			Percentage change in fatalities			-6%
Philippines			**IDPs**			102,000
			Functioning of government (0–10)			5
			Climate-change vulnerability (0–1)			0.5

ACGRI pillars: IISS calculation based on multiple sources for 2022 and 2023 (scale: 0–100), except for some cases according to data availability. See Notes on Methodology and Data Appendix for further details on Key Conflict Statistics.

Mindanao (BARMM), which will govern until the planned elections in 2025. However, several radical Islamist militant groups remain active and continue to fight for either an independent Moro homeland or a local caliphate. Despite laying siege to Marawi city in 2017 and conducting a string of bombings, these groups – the Abu Sayyaf Group (ASG), the Maute Group and the Bangsamoro Islamic Freedom Fighters (BIFF) – have been weakened by the army and are largely restricted to remote areas.[1] Alongside ideology, high poverty and joblessness rates in the BARMM are key drivers for rebel recruitment.

Similar factors have fuelled a nationwide Maoist insurgency by the New People's Army (NPA) in rural areas since 1969. Fighting spiked during the dictatorship of Ferdinand Marcos but has died down in recent decades, with the NPA retaining a foothold in eastern Mindanao. Peace talks with the NPA's political wing, the Communist Party of the Philippines (CPP), have failed under six presidents in the post-1986 democratic era. The mountainous and forested terrain on which both Maoist rebels and Islamist militants strategically operate has hindered attempts by the military to defeat them.

Conflict Update

The political climate in the BARMM continued to stabilise in the reporting period. Philippine President Ferdinand Marcos Jr appointed Ebrahim for a second term as chief minister and the MILF retained majority control of the BARMM regional parliament.[2] MNLF founder Nur Misuari lent his support to the MILF-led transitional government, reducing tensions between the powerful Moro fronts. Marcos assured BARMM leaders of his support for the peace process, signalling continuity with the policy of former president Rodrigo Duterte (2016–22).

MILF rebel disarmament continued. However, BARMM provincial governors called for the process to intensify amid insecurity in areas still controlled by the MILF, whose fighters occasionally skirmished with rival MNLF factions and Armed Forces of the Philippines (AFP) troops.[3] There are concerns that these localised AFP–MILF encounters could continue to increase in the absence of the Malaysian-led

International Monitoring Team, which departed Mindanao upon the expiry of its mandate in June 2022. Fears are also rising over the proliferation of firearms and private militias in the BARMM, where personal rivalries and clan politics drive violence that threatens to outlast the Moro uprising.

Meanwhile, Islamist militant groups showed signs of further decline. The ASG remained present in Basilan and Sulu, but its ability to launch maritime kidnappings was eroded.[4] The Maute Group was dealt a major blow when its leader Faharudin Hadji Satar was killed by government forces in Marawi, stymying recruitment efforts. In Maguindanao and Cotabato, the AFP engaged BIFF rebels who increasingly turned to banditry. This shift signalled that the group was struggling to finance its militant activities, which were limited to roadside bomb blasts and ambushes.

The NPA found itself in similarly dire straits, with the death of its exiled founder Jose Maria Sison in

December 2022 compounding battlefield losses. Marcos has refused to enter into peace talks with the NPA and has persisted with Duterte's strategy of encouraging rebels to surrender in return for livelihood aid, while launching military offensives. The NPA's campaign of guerrilla attacks lost momentum in the reporting period, although it could rebound in rural regions of eastern Mindanao where it has deeper historical roots.

Conflict Parties

Armed Forces of the Philippines (AFP)

Strength: 145,300 regular combatants across the army, navy and air force. Reserve force of 131,000, as well as 50,000 reservists serving in Citizen Armed Forces Geographical Units.

Areas of operation: Operates nationwide. Its headquarters, Camp Aguinaldo, is in Quezon city, Metro Manila.

Leadership: Led by Lt-Gen. Andres Centino (chief of staff), appointed in January 2023.

Structure: Divided into six area unified commands. The Western Mindanao Command, with three assigned infantry divisions, is tasked with tackling Islamist groups, while the Eastern Mindanao Command, with two assigned infantry divisions, is primarily tasked with fighting the NPA. AFP infantry battalions are comprised of 300–500 soldiers.[5]

History: Established by the 1935 National Defense Act under the United States' colonial rule. The AFP passed to Philippine control upon the country's independence in 1946.

Objectives: Defeat the NPA nationwide and defeat Islamist militant groups active in western Mindanao. To this effect, the AFP launches targeted raids and air/ground offensives and conducts routine patrols in areas of militant activity, often over difficult terrain.

Opponents: ASG, BIFF, Maute Group and NPA.

Affiliates/allies: The MILF and MNLF, which provide intelligence support in operations against Islamist militants. The AFP is supported by the Philippine National Police (PNP) in gun battles and law-enforcement raids.

Resources/capabilities: The army primarily uses small arms and artillery in operations against rebels and is assisted by air-force light-attack aircraft and helicopters. Naval assets are deployed in the Sulu Sea to prevent the transit of militants.

Abu Sayyaf Group (ASG)

Strength: 130 active members (AFP estimate).[6]

Areas of operation: Active presence in the maritime provinces of Basilan and Sulu. The group is now inactive in Tawi-Tawi province and the Zamboanga peninsula, as well as in Malaysia's Sabah State, which it previously used as a hideout. Its presence in the Sulu and Celebes seas is restricted by naval patrols.

Leadership: Mundi Sawadjaan commands the main ASG faction in Sulu province. The leaders in Basilan are unknown; the ASG has had no centralised command structure in Basilan since the death of Furuji Indama in a military operation in September 2020.

Structure: Operates as a loose network of affiliated factions and sub-factions arranged along clan and family lines.

History: Formed in 1991 by radical Islamist preacher Abdurajak Abubakar Janjalani. In the 2000s, the group became notorious for hostage-taking in the Sulu Sea. The ASG temporarily joined forces with the BIFF and the Maute

Group in 2017 to lay siege to Marawi city. It has since retreated to outlying islands.

Objectives: Sustain itself through criminal enterprise and re-establish an Islamic sultanate in the Sulu archipelago. In 2014, then-leader Isnilon Hapilon (now deceased) declared allegiance to the Islamic State (ISIS) and sought the creation of a regional caliphate in Southeast Asia.

Opponents: AFP, MILF and an MNLF faction led by Muslimin Sema. MNLF fighters based in Sulu under Nur Misuari have traditionally been tolerant of the ASG, but in 2022 the MNLF vowed to assist the AFP in anti-ASG operations.

Affiliates/allies: Allied ideologically with ISIS, the BIFF and the Maute Group but has no known operational ties.

Resources/capabilities: Uses high-powered firearms and improvised explosive devices (IEDs) to attack AFP troops, and its fighters retain bomb-making skills. The ASG's capacity to conduct high-risk maritime kidnappings has reduced substantially in recent years.

Bangsamoro Islamic Freedom Fighters (BIFF)

Strength: 100–200 active fighters (estimate).

Areas of operation: Most active in Liguasan Marsh and an area of Maguindanao province known as the 'SPMS box' (encompassing the towns of Shariff Aguak, Pagatin, Mamasapano and Datu Salibo). The BIFF is also known to operate in North Cotabato and Sultan Kudarat provinces.

Leadership: Divided into three factions, led by Esmael Abdulmalik (alias 'Abu Toraife'), Ismael Abubakar (alias 'Imam Bongos') and Ustadz Karialan (alias 'Imam Minimbang').

Structure: No centralised leadership, though its three factions cooperate in a tactical alliance against the AFP.

Bangsamoro Islamic Freedom Fighters (BIFF)

History: Formed as a splinter of the MILF in 2010 when its founder, Ameril Umbra Kato, grew frustrated with the MILF's decision to drop demands for independence in favour of autonomy and self-governance. The BIFF fought in the 2017 siege of Marawi and has since clashed with the AFP in Maguindanao province.

Objectives: Establish an independent homeland for the Moro people. The BIFF pledged allegiance to ISIS in 2014 and fought to establish a regional caliphate. Only the most extreme BIFF faction, commanded by Abu Toraife, still holds this ambition.

Opponents: AFP, MILF and MNLF. Despite being its parent group, the MILF is opposed to the BIFF and has cooperated with the AFP in recent years in attacks against BIFF militants.

Affiliates/allies: Nominally allied to the ASG and the Maute Group but has no operational ties.

Resources/capabilities: Uses high-powered rifles in battles with AFP troops and retains the ability to construct IEDs. The BIFF occasionally launches IED attacks or ambushes on AFP, PNP and civilian targets but is now mostly on the defensive, engaging AFP troops when attacked.

Maute Group

Strength: 30–40 active fighters (AFP estimate).[7] The Maute Group previously comprised up to 1,000 members but most were killed by AFP troops during the 2017 siege of Marawi.

Areas of operation: Active in Lanao del Norte and Lanao del Sur provinces. It operates primarily in forested and mountainous areas.

Leadership: Unknown. The Maute Group's leader Faharudin Hadji Satar (aliases 'Abu Bakar' and 'Abu Zacaria') was killed by AFP troops in June 2023. He was also the 'emir' of the Islamic State in Southeast Asia.

Structure: Since founders Abdullah Maute and Omar Maute were killed during the 2017 Marawi siege, the group has lacked a defined structure.

History: Founded in 2010–11 and espouses an extreme form of Salafi-Wahhabi ideology more often associated with jihadist groups in the Middle East. The Maute Group led the 2017

Marawi siege, in which its senior leaders were killed and capabilities damaged. It has since retreated to remote hideouts.

Objectives: Through seizing and holding territory in Marawi, the Maute Group aimed to forge a regional Islamic caliphate in Southeast Asia, centred on Mindanao. Despite its defeat in Marawi, the group still claims to represent the East Asian *wilayat* (province) of the Islamic State.

Opponents: AFP, MILF and MNLF.

Affiliates/allies: The Maute Group repeated its pledge of allegiance to ISIS in a 2022 video recording, though any operational ties are uncertain. The group is ideologically allied to the ASG and the BIFF faction led by Abu Toraife.

Resources/capabilities: Possesses a limited cache of rifles and retains the ability to construct low-grade IEDs. Materials seized in late 2022 by the AFP from a Maute Group training camp indicated plans to manufacture homemade grenades and rocket-propelled grenade launchers.

Moro Islamic Liberation Front (MILF)

Strength: 15,156 active fighters serving in its Bangsamoro Islamic Armed Forces (BIAF), down from 40,000 in 2019 as 24,844 have since been demobilised.[8] The remainder of the BIAF force is set to be decommissioned under the terms of the Comprehensive Agreement on the Bangsamoro (CAB), signed in 2014.

Areas of operation: Western Mindanao. Most fighters remain encamped in a network of MILF bases and no longer fight AFP forces. Up to 3,000 demobilised MILF rebels will be trained to serve alongside the AFP and PNP in Joint Peace and Security Teams across the BARMM.[9] The MILF's headquarters, Camp Darapanan, is in Maguindanao province.

Leadership: Led by chairman Al Haj Murad Ebrahim, who serves as chief minister of the BARMM.

Structure: Operates similarly to a regular army, with battalions and a centralised leadership body. The MILF is in the process of decommissioning and has formed a political party – the United Bangsamoro Justice Party – to contest future BARMM elections.

History: Founded in 1977 by Hashim Salamat after breaking away from the MNLF. The MILF fought the AFP for decades to secure independence for Moro Muslims in western Mindanao.

Objectives: Initially advocated for an independent Moro state and targeted the AFP in ambushes and bomb attacks. In the late 1990s the MILF began peace talks with Manila, seeking autonomy. After signing the CAB in 2014, the MILF committed to peace and now aims to become the leading political force in the BARMM.

Opponents: ASG, BIFF and Maute Group. MILF members still clash intermittently with rival MNLF factions at the local level, but fighting is short-lived and often related to clan disputes.

Affiliates/allies: Formally allied to the AFP. Both main factions of the rival MNLF, under Muslimin Sema and Nur Misuari, have expressed support for MILF-led governance of the BARMM.

Resources/capabilities: Access to high-powered rifles, grenade launchers and other conventional weapons. These are all set to be decommissioned under the CAB, with the process expected to be complete by the end of 2024.

Asia

Moro National Liberation Front (MNLF)

Strength: Fewer than 10,000 active fighters. The MNLF's strength has declined since the 1970s, when it had around 30,000 members.

Areas of operation: Western Mindanao and the Sulu archipelago. Most fighters are encamped and rarely engage in combat, aside from local inter-factional and clan disputes with the MILF or other MNLF members.

Leadership: Led by chairman Muslimin Sema. MNLF founder Nur Misuari remains an influential figure and leads a 3,000-strong faction in Sulu.

Structure: Initially a centralised organisation, the MNLF splintered into two after signing a peace agreement with the government in 1996. Both factions are now broadly aligned.

History: Formed as a splinter of the now-defunct Muslim Independence Movement (MIM) in 1972 and fought the AFP with the aim of forging an independent Moro state in western Mindanao.

Objectives: No longer advocates for Moro independence and has formed a political party, the Bangsamoro Party, to contest future BARMM elections. The Muslimin Sema faction has consistently supported the Manila–MILF peace process. The Nur Misuari faction had previously criticised the process, but in 2022 it publicly backed the MILF-led interim authority, indicating its support for peace.

Opponents: BIFF and Maute Group. The main MNLF faction led by Muslimin Sema is opposed to the ASG, while the Nur Misuari faction is rhetorically opposed but retains kinship ties. The MILF is a historical rival of the MNLF, but the two sides rarely resort to violence.

Affiliates/allies: The AFP since a 1996 peace deal, but violence has occasionally broken out – most notoriously in the 2013 siege of Zamboanga.

Resources/capabilities: The MNLF no longer fights the AFP but retains access to a wide network of bases and high-powered rifles. The Nur Misuari faction remains a powerful but dormant actor in the conflict.

New People's Army (NPA)

Strength: 2,112 fighters (AFP estimate) spread across at least 24 guerrilla fronts nationwide.[10] This includes at least four active fronts in eastern Mindanao.[11] The NPA's estimated strength has fallen from its historical 3,000–4,000 fighters (consistent over the past decade) due to sustained military operations and a high surrender rate.

Areas of operation: Most active in its traditional strongholds of eastern Mindanao and Mindoro, Samar and Negros. NPA rebels are also present in northern Luzon and other rural communities nationwide.

Leadership: NPA founder and CPP chairman Jose Maria Sison died in self-imposed exile in the Netherlands in 2022, aged 83.[12] It is unknown who will replace him as overall leader. Day-to-day conflict is overseen by a network of NPA ground commanders.

Structure: Rebels operate in small, closely knit units in the countryside, while hit squads operate in Special Partisan Units in urban areas. The NPA is the armed wing of the CPP, which is represented in peace talks by the National Democratic Front of the Philippines (NDFP). Sison's widow, Julie de Lima, serves as interim chairperson of the NDFP peace-negotiation panel.

History: The NPA was formed in 1969 by the CPP, which was established in 1968. It has battled government troops for more than 50 years, with fighting centred on rural areas. NDFP-led peace talks have failed under six presidents in the post-1986 democratic era.

Objectives: Ideology has remained unchanged since the 1960s. The NPA is fighting what it labels a 'protracted people's war' to overthrow the Manila government and replace it with a socialist system.[13] It does not seize and hold territory but exercises de facto control in its rural strongholds via extortion and intimidation. It also launches ambushes targeting AFP troops, with the aim of weakening AFP morale.

Opponents: AFP and PNP. The NPA does not engage in conflict with Moro or Islamist rebel groups in western Mindanao and largely avoids operating in their areas of influence.

Affiliates/allies: Has no known affiliates, though in its early years it received funds and weapons from China and like-minded Maoist rebel groups based abroad.

Resources/capabilities: High-powered rifles looted from AFP and PNP bases, and other firearms seized from private security guards during armed raids on businesses. The NPA also deploys IEDs and rudimentary explosives.

Other relevant parties

Philippine authorities often use the term Dawlah Islamiyah (Islamic State) to refer to the BIFF and the Maute Group, drawing little distinction. A smaller ISIS-aligned group, Ansar Khalifah Philippines (AKP) – which had in recent years carried out IED attacks and engaged in criminal activity in the southern Mindanao provinces of Sarangani and South Cotabato – was also considered part of Dawlah Islamiyah. AKP is now considered inactive as a distinct group and its remnants have effectively been subsumed into the BIFF further north in Maguindanao and North Cotabato provinces, while retaining a limited presence in its past strongholds in the south. ASG rebels in Sulu province under Mundi Sawadjaan are also sometimes referred to as members of Dawlah Islamiyah.

Notes

1   See Amnesty International, 'Philippines: "Battle of Marawi" Leaves Trail of Death and Destruction', 17 November 2017.

2   Riyaz ul Khaliq, 'Bangsamoro Administration Reappointed, Elections in 2025', Anadolu Agency, 19 August 2022.

3   Ferdinandh B. Cabrera, '4 BARMM Governors Ask Palace to Hasten Decommissioning of MILF', Minda News, 24 February 2023.

4   Frencie Carreon, 'Abu Sayyaf Becoming a Thing of the Past, Wesmincom Chief Claims', Rappler, 4 January 2023.

5   Julie S. Alipala, 'AFP Reduces Troop Presence in Sulu; Improved Security Status Cited', *Inquirer*, 3 September 2022.

6   BenarNews Staff, '"Tired" Abu Sayyaf Members Surrender to Philippine Military', Benar News, 8 November 2022.

7   Edwin Fernandez, 'Marines Capture DI-MG Lair in Lanao Sur', Philippine News Agency, 13 December 2022.

8   Llanesca T. Panti, 'Basilan Rep. Hataman Sees Flaws in MILF Decommissioning Process', GMA News, 14 November 2022.

9   Priam Nepomuceno, 'Joint Peace Security Team Activated in Lanao Norte Town', Philippine News Agency, 12 December 2022.

10 Jojo Riñoza and Richel V. Umel, 'Philippine Military Chief: Communist Guerrillas Down to 24 Fronts Nationwide', Benar News, 3 November 2022.

11 Carina Cayon, 'End of Communist Terrorism in Eastern Mindanao Nears as 18 NPA Units Dismantled in 2022', Philippine Information Agency, 3 January 2023.

12 Reuters, 'Self-exiled Philippine Communist Leader Sison Dies at 83', VOA, 17 December 2022.

13 Stanford University, Center for International Security and Cooperation, 'Communist Party of the Philippines – New People's Army'.

Data Appendix

Number of violent events, by country, 1 May 2022–30 June 2023

Number of violent events (defined by the Armed Conflict Location & Event Data Project (ACLED) as battles, explosion/remote violence or violence against civilians) from 1 May 2022–30 June 2023. Data collected on 11 July 2023.

Source: IISS calculation based on ACLED data, www.acleddata.com.

	Violent events
Russia–Ukraine*	51,564
Syria	11,789
Brazil	10,580
Myanmar	9,767
Mexico	7,778
Iraq	6,533
Yemen	5,691
Nigeria	3,657
Somalia	3,373
Colombia	2,513
Democratic Republic of the Congo	2,500
Burkina Faso	1,920
Afghanistan	1,900
Israel–Palestinian Territories**	1,726
Mali	1,694
Sudan***	1,494
Pakistan	1,259
India	1,204
Ethiopia	1,201
Philippines	960
Cameroon	859
Haiti	779

	Violent events
Nagorno-Karabakh**	754
Honduras	726
Niger	694
South Sudan****	572
Mozambique	430
Turkiye	366
Central African Republic	315
Uganda	243
El Salvador	147
Chad	135
Thailand	130
Egypt	96
Libya	96
Rwanda	25

*Refers to Ukraine data only as it is the theatre of conflict.
**The figure represents the sum of events for the two parties involved in the conflict. For the Nagorno-Karabakh conflict it represents the sum of fatalities for Armenia and Azerbaijan.
***Includes the Abyei area per the source classification.
****Does not include the Abyei area per the source classification.

Number of fatalities due to violent events, by country, 1 May 2022–30 June 2023
Number of reported fatalities due to violent events (defined by ACLED as battles, explosion/remote violence or violence against civilians) from 1 May 2022–30 June 2023. Data collected on 11 July 2023.
Source: IISS calculation based on ACLED data, www.acleddata.com.

	Number of fatalities
Russia–Ukraine*	78,451
Myanmar	19,590
Nigeria	10,384
Somalia	9,135
Mexico	8,810
Brazil	8,312
Burkina Faso	7,541
Syria	6,834
Ethiopia	6,292
Democratic Republic of the Congo	5,494
Sudan**	5,037
Mali	4,661
Yemen	3,792
Iraq	3,606
Afghanistan	3,190
South Sudan***	2,336
Colombia	2,128
Pakistan	1,874
Haiti	1,728
Cameroon	1,150
Niger	1,071
Philippines	1,035
Honduras	894

	Number of fatalities
India	787
Mozambique	766
Chad	759
Central African Republic	669
Israel–Palestinian Territories****	357
Nagorno-Karabakh****	303
Turkiye	300
Uganda	255
Egypt	138
El Salvador	135
Libya	127
Thailand	50
Rwanda	14

*Refers to Ukraine data only as it is the theatre of conflict.
**Includes the Abyei area per the source classification.
***Does not include the Abyei area per the source classification.
****The figure represents the sum of fatalities for the two parties involved in the conflict. For the Nagorno-Karabakh conflict it represents the sum of fatalities for Armenia and Azerbaijan.

Number of refugees (total), counted by country of origin, as of 31 December 2022

Number of refugees, specifically those in a refugee-like situation under the mandate of the United Nations High Commissioner for Refugees (UNHCR), and Palestinian refugees recorded by the UN Relief and Works Agency for Palestine Refugees in the Near East (UNRWA).

A refugee is someone who is unable or unwilling to return to their country of origin owing to a well-founded fear of being persecuted for reasons of race, religion, nationality, membership of a particular social group or political opinion (as per the UNHCR 1951 Refugee Convention). In the case of Palestinian refugees, these are persons whose normal place of residence was Palestine during the period 1 June 1946–15 May 1948, and who lost both their home and means of livelihood as a result of the 1948 conflict.

Data from UNHCR and UNRWA is updated to 31 December 2022 and was collected on 16 June 2023. **Sources:** UNHCR, www.unhcr.org/refugee-statistics/download; and UNRWA, 'Refugee Data Finder', www.unhcr.org/refugee-statistics/download/?url=p7aBkY.

	Number of refugees
Syria	6,547,818
Israel–Palestinian Territories*	5,888,253
Russia–Ukraine**	5,679,880
Afghanistan	5,661,675
South Sudan	2,294,983
Myanmar	1,253,111
Democratic Republic of the Congo	931,903
Sudan	836,756
Somalia	790,513
Central African Republic	748,327
Nigeria	391,074
Iraq	288,261
Rwanda	249,685
Mali	226,720
Ethiopia	149,245
Cameroon	147,359
Pakistan	111,805
Colombia	109,135
Turkiye	92,198
Honduras	64,976
El Salvador	58,637

	Number of refugees
Nagorno-Karabakh*	56,857
Yemen	38,627
Burkina Faso	33,318
Haiti	30,304
Egypt	24,327
Niger	21,947
India	20,832
Libya	17,854
Mexico	17,642
Chad	12,810
Uganda	7,510
Brazil	2,744
Philippines	575
Thailand	201
Mozambique	104

*The figure represents the sum of refugees for the two parties involved in the conflict. For the Nagorno-Karabakh conflict it represents the sum of refugees from Armenia and Azerbaijan.
**Refers to Ukraine data only as it is the theatre of conflict.

Number of internally displaced persons (total), by country, as of 31 December 2022

Total number of internally displaced persons (IDPs) due to conflict and violence recorded by the Internal Displacement Monitoring Centre (IDMC).

IDPs are persons or groups of persons who have been forced or obliged to flee or to leave their homes or places of habitual residence, in particular as a result of or in order to avoid the effects of armed conflict, situations of generalised violence, violations of human rights or natural or human-made disasters, and who have not crossed an internationally recognised state border (as per 1998 UN Guiding Principles on Internal Displacement).

Data from the IDMC is as of 31 December 2022 for all countries except Egypt, for which the data is as of 31 December 2020, collected on 27 July 2023.

Source: IDMC, www.internal-displacement.org/database/displacement-data.

	Number of IDPs (conflict and violence)
Syria	6,865,000
Democratic Republic of the Congo	5,686,000
Russia–Ukraine*	5,914,000
Colombia	4,766,000
Yemen	4,523,000
Afghanistan	4,394,000
Somalia	3,864,000
Ethiopia	3,852,000
Nigeria	3,646,000
Sudan**	3,553,000
Burkina Faso	1,882,000
Myanmar	1,498,000
South Sudan**	1,475,000
Iraq	1,169,000
Turkiye	1,099,000
Mozambique	1,030,000
Cameroon	987,000
Nagorno-Karabakh***	667,400
India	631,000
Central African Republic	516,000
Mexico	386,000
Mali	380,000

	Number of IDPs (conflict and violence)
Niger	372,000
Chad	300,000
Honduras	247,000
Haiti	171,000
Libya	135,000
Philippines	102,000
El Salvador	52,000
Thailand	41,000
Pakistan	21,000
Israel–Palestinian Territories***	12,000
Brazil	5,600
Uganda	4,800
Egypt	3,200
Rwanda	N/A

*Refers to Ukraine data only as it is the theatre of conflict.

**Does not include 150,000 IDPs in the Abyei area.

***The figure represents the sum of IDPs for the two parties involved in the conflict. For the Nagorno-Karabakh conflict it represents the sum of IDPs for Armenia and Azerbaijan. For the conflict in Israel–Palestinian Territories, it only includes Palestinian IDPs since there is no data available for Israel.

Number of foreign countries 'involved' in the conflict, by country, as of 30 June 2023

Number of foreign countries deemed to be involved in the conflict.

For *internal conflicts*: foreign countries are considered 'involved' if they are either present through the deployment of military capabilities (outside of a multilateral mission as defined in the Armed Conflict Global Relevance Indicator (ACGRI)) or they meet all the following criteria: presence of intelligence assets; provision of military financial support; role in an advisory or operational command-and-control capacity; and sale or transfer of military equipment.

For *inter-state conflicts*: foreign countries are considered 'involved' if they are either present through the deployment of military capabilities (outside of a multilateral mission as defined in the ACGRI) or they meet two or more of the following criteria: presence of intelligence assets; provision of military financial support; role in an advisory or operational command-and-control capacity; and sale or transfer of military equipment.* Data collected on 26 June 2023 from the Military Balance+. Military-aid data for Ukraine is from 31 May 2023, collected on 30 June 2023 from the Ukraine Support Tracker by the Kiel Institute for the World Economy, and covers the time period from 24 January 2022–31 May 2023.

Sources: IISS calculation based on the Military Balance+, milbalplus.iiss.org; and Christoph Trebesch et al., 'The Ukraine Support Tracker: Which Countries Help Ukraine and How?', KIEL *Working Paper*, no. 2218, 2023.

	Foreign countries 'involved' in the conflict	Number of countries 'involved' in the conflict
Russia–Ukraine**	Belarus	9
	Canada	
	Germany	
	Netherlands	
	Norway	
	Poland	
	Sweden	
	United Kingdom	
	United States	
Syria	Iran	5
	Israel	
	Russia	
	Turkiye	
	United States	
Iraq	Iran	4
	Operation Inherent Resolve (United States)***	
	Turkiye	
Niger	France	4
	Germany	
	Italy	
	United States	
Yemen	Iran	4
	Operation Restoring Hope (Saudi Arabia)***	
	United Arab Emirates	

	Foreign countries 'involved' in the conflict	Number of countries 'involved' in the conflict
Democratic Republic of the Congo	Burundi	3
	Rwanda	
	Uganda	
Somalia	Turkiye	3
	United Kingdom	
	United States	
Central African Republic	Russia	2
	Rwanda	
Nagorno-Karabakh	Russia	2
	Turkiye	
Chad	France	1
Ethiopia	Eritrea	1
Israel–Palestinian Territories	Iran	1
Libya	Turkiye	1
Mali	Russia	1
Mozambique	Rwanda	1
Nigeria	United Kingdom	1
Afghanistan	None	0
Brazil	None	0
Burkina Faso	None	0
Cameroon	None	0
Colombia	None	0
Egypt	None	0

	Foreign countries 'involved' in the conflict	Number of countries 'involved' in the conflict
El Salvador	None	0
Haiti	None	0
Honduras	None	0
India	None	0
Mexico	None	0
Myanmar	None	0
Pakistan	None	0
Philippines	None	0
Rwanda	None	0
South Sudan	None	0
Sudan	None	0
Thailand	None	0
Turkiye	None	0

	Foreign countries 'involved' in the conflict	Number of countries 'involved' in the conflict
Uganda	None	0

*The involvement of the Russian paramilitary Wagner Group is not included as part of Russia's involvement and is not considered for the purpose of the ACGRI calculation.

**Refers to Ukraine data only as it is the theatre of conflict. Support includes the provision of weapons, equipment and financial aid with military purposes as per the Ukraine Support Tracker by the Kiel Institute for the World Economy.

***In the case of involvement of coalitions of countries, the name of the coalition and the country leading it are displayed. Each coalition is assigned a score of two for the purposes of the ACGRI calculation.

Number of UNSC resolutions concerning conflicts under review, by country, 1 May 2022–30 June 2023

Number of resolutions announced by the UN Security Council (UNSC) between 1 May 2022 and 30 June 2023 concerning the country and conflict under review. Countries for which no resolution was announced receive a value of 0.

Source: IISS calculation based on UNSC, www.un.org/securitycouncil/content/resolutions-0.

	Number of resolutions		Number of resolutions
Libya	6	Egypt	0
Somalia	6	El Salvador	0
Sudan	6	Ethiopia	0
Afghanistan	4	Honduras	0
Democratic Republic of the Congo	4	India	0
Mali	4	Israel–Palestinian Territories	0
South Sudan	4	Mexico	0
Iraq	3	Mozambique	0
Syria	3	Nagorno-Karabakh	0
Central African Republic	2	Niger	0
Colombia	2	Nigeria	0
Haiti	2	Pakistan	0
Yemen	2	Philippines	0
Myanmar	1	Russia–Ukraine	0
Brazil	0	Rwanda	0
Burkina Faso	0	Thailand	0
Cameroon	0	Turkiye	0
Chad	0	Uganda	0

Number of military personnel deployed by major geopolitical powers in conflict-affected countries, by country, as of 30 June 2023*

Total number of military personnel deployed into conflict-affected countries by geopolitical powers within the G20 group (including unilaterally, as part of a combat coalition or a mission under the aegis of an international organisation and excluding deployments which are not conflict related). Data collected on 30 June 2023, except for the data for Ukraine, which was collected on 1 September 2023.

Source: IISS calculation based on Military Balance+, milbalplus.iiss.org.

	Number of personnel deployed			Number of personnel deployed
Russia–Ukraine**	175,000		Brazil	0
Syria	8,135		Burkina Faso	0
Iraq	7,607		Cameroon	0
Nagorno-Karabakh***	5,630		Ethiopia	0
Democratic Republic of the Congo	4,284		Haiti	0
South Sudan	3,803		Mexico	0
Niger	3,095		Myanmar	0
Yemen	2,500		Rwanda	0
Chad	1,500		Thailand	0
Mozambique	1,221		Turkiye	0
Mali	1,170		Uganda	0
Sudan	748			
Libya	661			
Egypt	616			
Somalia	528			
Honduras	400			
Philippines	300			
Central African Republic	293			
El Salvador	100			
Israel–Palestinian Territories***	100			
Nigeria	80			
Colombia	70			
India****	13			
Pakistan****	13			
Afghanistan	0			

*The variable covers only deployments related to the specific conflict. This means that either the deployed military forces are conflict parties or that the deployment has an explicit mandate to assist the conflict parties with training and capability building. The US deployments in Thailand and Turkiye are not considered conflict related and are not included in the variable calculation for either country.

**Refers to Russian deployments in Ukraine.

***The figure represents the sum of deployments in the two parties involved in the conflict. For the Nagorno-Karabakh conflict it represents the sum of deployments for Armenia and Azerbaijan.

****The personnel deployed as part of the UN Military Observer Group in India and Pakistan are attributed to both India and Pakistan.

Number of operational peacekeeping, special political and military missions, and other multilateral missions concerning conflicts in countries under review, as of 30 June 2023

Number of multilateral peacekeeping operations, special political and military missions, and other multilateral presences under the aegis of international organisations present in a country. These include missions undertaken by the UN, regional organisations or ad hoc groups related to UN sanctions/UNSC resolutions or endorsed by the UN and other international organisations. Data refers to active missions as of 30 June 2023 that fulfil the two following criteria: 1) objective (relating to multidimensional peace and conflict resolution) and 2) geographical scope (relating to the analysed conflicts in the countries under review).

Data collected on 26 August 2023 from the Military Balance+, Stockholm International Peace Research Institute's (SIPRI) Map of Multilateral Peace Operations 2023 published in May 2023 and the UN Special Political Missions and Other Political Presences 2023 published in July 2023.

Sources: IISS calculations based on Military Balance+, milbalplus.iiss.org; SIPRI, www.sipri.org/publications/2023/other-publications/sipri-map-multilateral-peace-operations-2023; UN Political and Peacebuilding Affairs, www.dppa.un.org/en/dppa-around-world; and the official websites of the UN, European Union, regional organisations and ad hoc coalitions.

	Names of missions	Number of missions
Central African Republic	AU Mission for the Central African Republic and Central Africa (MISAC)	7
	AU Observer Mission to the Central African Republic (MOUACA)	
	EU Advisory Mission in the Central African Republic (EUAM RCA)	
	EU Training Mission in the Central African Republic (EUTM RCA)	
	Special Envoy of the Secretary-General for the Great Lakes Region of Africa	
	UN Multidimensional Integrated Stabilization Mission in the Central African Republic (MINUSCA)	
	UN Regional Office for Central Africa (UNOCA)	
Somalia	AU Transition Mission in Somalia (ATMIS)	6
	EU Capacity Building Mission in Somalia (EUCAP Somalia)	
	EU Training Mission Somalia (EUTM Somalia)	
	Special Envoy of the Secretary-General to the Horn of Africa	
	UN Assistance Mission in Somalia (UNSOM)	
	UN Support Office in Somalia (UNSOS)	
Mali	AU Mission for Mali and the Sahel (MISAHEL)	5
	EU Capacity Building Mission Sahel Mali (EUCAP Sahel Mali)	
	EU Training Mission Mali (EUTM Mali)	
	UN Multidimensional Integrated Stabilization Mission in Mali (MINUSMA)	
	UN Office for West Africa and the Sahel (UNOWAS)	
Niger	EU Capacity Building Mission Sahel Niger (EUCAP Sahel Niger)	5
	EU Military Partnership Mission in Niger (EUMPM Niger)*	
	G5 Sahel Joint Force (FC-G5S)	
	Multinational Joint Task Force (MNJTF)	
	UN Office for West Africa and the Sahel (UNOWAS)	
Chad	G5 Sahel Joint Force (FC-G5S)	4
	Multinational Joint Task Force (MNJTF)	
	UN Office for West Africa and the Sahel (UNOWAS)	
	UN Regional Office for Central Africa (UNOCA)	

Data Appendix

	Names of missions	Number of missions
Democratic Republic of Congo	East African Community Regional Force in the Democratic Republic of the Congo (EACRF-DRC)	4
	Special Envoy of the Secretary-General for the Great Lakes Region of Africa	
	UN Organization Stabilization Mission in the Democratic Republic of the Congo (MONUSCO)	
	UN Regional Office for Central Africa (UNOCA)	
Israel–Palestinian Territories	EU Border Assistance Mission for the Rafah Crossing Point (EUBAM Rafah)	4
	EU Police and Rule of Law Mission for the Palestinian Territory, EU Coordinating Office for Palestinian Police Support (EUPOL COPPS)	
	UN Special Coordinator for the Middle East Peace Process (UNSCO)	
	UN Truce Supervision Organization (UNTSO)	
South Sudan	Intergovernmental Authority on Development (IGAD) Ceasefire and Transitional Security Arrangements Monitoring and Verification Mechanism (CTSAMVM)	4
	Special Envoy of the Secretary-General for the Great Lakes Region of Africa	
	Special Envoy of the Secretary-General for the Horn of Africa	
	UN Mission in the Republic of South Sudan (UNMISS)	
Sudan	Special Envoy of the Secretary-General for the Great Lakes Region of Africa	4
	Special Envoy of the Secretary-General to the Horn of Africa	
	UN Integrated Transitional Assistance Mission in Sudan (UNITAMS)	
	UN Interim Security Force for Abyei (UNISFA)	
Burkina Faso	G5 Sahel Joint Force (FC-G5S)	3
	Multinational Joint Task Force/Accra Initiative (MNJTF/AI)	
	UN Office for West Africa and the Sahel (UNOWAS)	
Iraq	EU Advisory Mission in support of Security Sector Reform in Iraq (EUAM Iraq)	3
	NATO Mission Iraq (NMI)	
	UN Assistance Mission for Iraq (UNAMI)	
Libya	AU Mission in Libya	3
	EU Border Assistance Mission in Libya (EUBAM Libya)	
	UN Support Mission in Libya (UNSMIL)	
Mozambique	EU Training Mission in Mozambique (EUTM Mozambique)	3
	Personal Envoy of the Secretary-General for Mozambique	
	Southern African Development Community Mission in Mozambique (SAMIM)	
Nagorno-Karabakh	EU Mission in Armenia (EUMA)	3
	Personal Representative of the Chairperson-in-Office on the conflict dealt with by the Organization for Security and Co-operation in Europe (OSCE) Minsk Conference	
	Russian–Turkish Joint Monitoring Centre (RTJMC)	
Cameroon	Multinational Joint Task Force (MNJTF)	2
	UN Regional Office for Central Africa (UNOCA)	
Colombia	Organization of American States (OAS) Mission to Support the Peace Process in Colombia (MAPP/OEA)	2
	UN Verification Mission in Colombia (UNVMC)	
Ethiopia	AU Monitoring, Verification and Compliance Mission (AU-MVCM)	2
	Special Envoy of the Secretary-General for the Horn of Africa	
Nigeria	Multinational Joint Task Force (MNJTF)	2
	UN Office for West Africa and the Sahel (UNOWAS)	

	Names of missions	Number of missions
Russia–Ukraine**	EU Advisory Mission Ukraine (EUAM Ukraine) EU Military Assistance Mission in support of Ukraine (EUMAM Ukraine)	2
Rwanda	Special Envoy of the Secretary-General for the Great Lakes Region of Africa UN Regional Office for Central Africa (UNOCA)	2
Uganda	Special Envoy of the Secretary-General for the Great Lakes Region of Africa Special Envoy of the Secretary-General for the Horn of Africa	2
Yemen	Special Envoy of the Secretary-General for Yemen UN Mission to Support the Hudaydah Agreement (UNMHA)	2
Afghanistan	UN Assistance Mission in Afghanistan (UNAMA)	1
Haiti	UN Integrated Office in Haiti (BINUH)	1
India	UN Military Observer Group in India and Pakistan (UNMOGIP)	1
Myanmar	Special Envoy of the Secretary-General on Myanmar	1
Pakistan	UN Military Observer Group in India and Pakistan (UNMOGIP)	1
Syria	Special Envoy of the Secretary-General for Syria	1
Brazil	0	0
Egypt	0	0
El Salvador	0	0
Honduras	0	0
Mexico	0	0
Philippines	0	0
Thailand	0	0
Turkiye	0	0

*Launched in February 2023. However, all security cooperation between the EU and Niger was suspended after the military coup in July 2023.
**Refers to Ukraine data only as it is the theatre of conflict.

Data Appendix

Humanitarian funding (in US$), by recipient country, as of 31 December 2022

Total reported incoming funding from governments and multilateral organisations, by recipient country, in 2022. This includes financial funding received by local governments, multilateral organisations, non-governmental organisations, pooled funds, private organisations and Red Cross and Red Crescent organisations operating in the country under review. Data collected on 26 July 2023.

Source: UN Office for the Coordination of Humanitarian Affairs, Financial Tracking Service, fts.unocha.org.

	Total incoming funding (US$ millions)
Russia–Ukraine*	3,803.3
Afghanistan	3,631.1
Yemen	2,541.2
Syria	2,468.0
Ethiopia	2,169.3
Somalia	2,131.8
South Sudan	1,298.3
Sudan	1,064.7
Democratic Republic of the Congo	975.7
Nigeria	773.9
Turkiye	708.4
Israel–Palestinian Territories**	528.0
Iraq	496.9
Colombia	463.6
Central African Republic	461.5
Pakistan	456.8
Niger	444.6
Burkina Faso	388.7
Myanmar	365.4
Mali	352.9

	Total incoming funding (US$ millions)
Chad	337.9
Mozambique	320.5
Uganda	298.1
Cameroon	232.3
Haiti	197.9
Egypt	162.6
Libya	141.8
Honduras	130.4
Mexico	103.0
Philippines	84.2
Rwanda	49.7
El Salvador	43.7
Thailand	38.9
Brazil	33.5
Nagorno-Karabakh**	14.5
India	11.0

*Refers to Ukraine data only as it is the theatre of conflict.
**The figure represents the sum of funding for the two countries involved in the conflict. For the Nagorno-Karabakh conflict it represents the sum of funding for Armenia and Azerbaijan.

Gini index, by country, latest available data

The Gini index measures the extent to which the distribution of income (or, in some cases, consumption expenditure) among individuals or households within an economy deviates from a perfectly equal distribution. A Lorenz curve plots the cumulative percentages of total income received against the cumulative number of recipients, starting with the poorest individual or household. The Gini index measures the area between the Lorenz curve and a hypothetical line of absolute equality, expressed as a percentage of the maximum area under the line. Thus, a Gini index of 0 represents perfect equality, whilst an index of 100 implies perfect inequality.

Source: World Bank, data.worldbank.org/indicator/ SI.POV.GINI?most_recent_year_desc=true.

	Gini index	Year
Central African Republic	56.2	2008
Mozambique	54.0	2014
Brazil	52.9	2021
Colombia	51.5	2021
Honduras	48.2	2019
Burkina Faso	47.3	2018
Cameroon	46.6	2014
Mexico	45.4	2020
South Sudan	44.1	2016
Rwanda	43.7	2016
Uganda	42.7	2019
Democratic Republic of the Congo	42.1	2012
Turkiye	41.9	2019
Haiti	41.1	2012
Philippines	40.7	2021
El Salvador	39.0	2021
Israel	38.6	2018
Chad	37.5	2018
Syria	37.5	2003
Niger	37.3	2018

	Gini index	Year
Yemen	36.7	2014
Mali	36.1	2018
India	35.7	2019
Nigeria	35.1	2018
Thailand	35.1	2021
Ethiopia	35.0	2015
Sudan	34.2	2014
Palestinian Territories*	33.7	2016
Egypt	31.9	2019
Myanmar	30.7	2017
Pakistan	29.6	2018
Iraq	29.5	2012
Armenia	27.9	2021
Azerbaijan	26.6	2005
Ukraine	25.6	2020
Afghanistan	N/A	N/A
Libya	N/A	N/A
Somalia	N/A	N/A

*Refers to the West Bank and Gaza.

GDP per capita, constant prices, purchasing power parity (international dollars), per country, 2022
GDP per capita represents the constant price purchasing-power-parity terms of final goods and services produced within a country during a specified time period divided by the total population.

It is expressed in 2017 international dollars. Data collected on 30 July 2023 from the World Economic Outlook (April 2023) by the International Monetary Fund (IMF).

Source: IMF, www.imf.org/en/Publications/WEO/weo-database/2023/April.

	GDP per capita
Israel	44,336
Turkiye	33,284
Mexico	19,247
Thailand	17,915
Libya	17,242
Colombia	15,890
Brazil	15,192
Armenia	15,071
Azerbaijan	14,963
Egypt	13,619
Ukraine	10,722
Iraq	10,436
El Salvador	9,307
Philippines	8,890
India	7,054
Honduras	5,786
Pakistan	5,662
Palestinian Territories*	5,394
Nigeria	5,004
Myanmar	4,105

	GDP per capita
Cameroon	3,739
Sudan	3,698
Ethiopia	2,909
Haiti	2,677
Uganda	2,563
Rwanda	2,428
Afghanistan**	2,329
Burkina Faso	2,180
Mali	2,130
Yemen	1,712
Chad	1,449
Niger	1,277
Mozambique	1,243
Democratic Republic of the Congo	1,168
Somalia	1,121
Central African Republic	915
South Sudan	410
Syria	N/A

*Refers to the West Bank and Gaza.
**As of 2020.

Functioning of government, by country, 2022

The functioning of government, a pillar of the Economist Intelligence Unit (EIU) Democracy Index, assesses the effectiveness of the system of checks and balances on the exercise of government authority as well as elements such as openness and transparency of government, public access to information, government accountability, pervasiveness of corruption, public confidence in government and political parties. The functioning of government is scored on a 0–10 scale. Data collected on 30 June 2023 from the EIU Democracy Index 2022. **Source:** EIU, www.eiu.com/n/campaigns/democracy-index-2022/.

	Functioning of government
Israel	7.9
India	7.5
Colombia	6.1
Thailand	6.1
Armenia	5.7
Brazil	5.0
Pakistan	5.0
Philippines	5.0
Turkiye	5.0
Mexico	4.6
Rwanda	4.3
Honduras	3.9
Nigeria	3.9
Uganda	3.9
El Salvador	3.6
Egypt	3.2
Azerbaijan	2.9
Ethiopia	2.9
Ukraine	2.7

	Functioning of government
Burkina Faso	2.5
Cameroon	2.1
Niger	1.5
Mozambique	1.4
Sudan	1.4
Afghanistan	0.1
Palestinian Territories	0.1
Central African Republic	0.0
Chad	0.0
Democratic Republic of the Congo	0.0
Haiti	0.0
Iraq	0.0
Libya	0.0
Mali	0.0
Myanmar	0.0
Syria	0.0
Yemen	0.0
Somalia	N/A
South Sudan	N/A

Data Appendix

Climate-change vulnerability score, by country, 2021
The Notre Dame Global Adaptation Initiative (ND-GAIN) vulnerability score summarises a country's exposure, sensitivity and capacity to adapt to the negative externalities of climate change across six sectors: food, water, health, ecosystems, habitats and infrastructure. It is scored on a 0–1 scale. Data collected on 26 July 2023.

Source: ND-GAIN, gain.nd.edu/our-work/country-index/.

Country	ND-GAIN vulnerability score
Chad	0.7
Somalia	0.7
Afghanistan	0.6
Central African Republic	0.6
Democratic Republic of the Congo	0.6
Mali	0.6
Niger	0.6
Sudan	0.6
Burkina Faso	0.5
Cameroon	0.5
Ethiopia	0.5
Haiti	0.5
Honduras	0.5
India	0.5
Mozambique	0.5
Myanmar	0.5
Nigeria	0.5
Pakistan	0.5
Philippines	0.5

Country	ND-GAIN vulnerability score
Rwanda	0.5
Syria	0.5
Yemen	0.5
Armenia	0.4
Azerbaijan	0.4
Brazil	0.4
Colombia	0.4
Egypt	0.4
El Salvador	0.4
Iraq	0.4
Libya	0.4
Mexico	0.4
Thailand	0.4
Turkiye	0.4
Uganda	0.4
Ukraine	0.4
Israel	0.3
Palestinian Territories	N/A
South Sudan	N/A

Armed groups, by region, as of 30 June 2023*
Number of armed groups by region. This data is drawn from the International Committee of the Red Cross' (ICRC) annual survey on armed groups conducted in June 2023.

Region**	Number of armed groups
Americas	68
Middle East and North Africa	150
Africa	145
Eurasia	13
Asia and the Pacific	83

*The ICRC uses the generic term 'armed group' for a group that is not a state but has the capacity to cause violence that is of humanitarian concern. Armed groups also include those groups that qualify as conflict parties to a non-international armed conflict according to the Geneva Conventions, which the ICRC defines as 'non-state armed groups'.

**The regional figure refers to the sum of armed groups active in the countries covered by the ICRC survey in each region. Data collected by the following ICRC offices (as listed by the ICRC): Brazil, Colombia, El Salvador, Guatemala, Haiti, Honduras, Mexico, Nicaragua, Paraguay, Peru and Venezuela

Source: Matthew Bamber-Zryd, 'ICRC Engagement with Armed Groups in 2023', ICRC Humanitarian Law & Policy, 20 October 2023, https://blogs.icrc.org/law-and-policy/2023/10/10/icrc-engagement-with-armed-groups-in-2023/.

for the Americas; Egypt, Iraq, Islamic Republic of Iran, Israel and the Occupied Territories, Jordan, Kuwait (regional), Lebanon, Libya, Syrian Arab Republic, Turkiye and Yemen for the Middle East and North Africa; Abidjan (regional), African Union, Algeria, Burkina Faso, Central African Republic, Chad, Dakar (regional), Democratic Republic of the Congo, Eritrea, Ethiopia, Kampala (regional), Mali, Mauritania, Mozambique, Nairobi (regional), Niger, Nigeria, Pretoria (regional), Somalia, South Sudan, Sudan, Tunis (regional) and Yaoundé (regional) for Africa; Armenia, Azerbaijan, Balkans (regional), Brussels, Budapest (regional), Central Tracing Agency Bureau for the International Armed Conflict Between the Russian Federation and Ukraine, Georgia, Greece, London (regional), Moscow (regional), Paris (regional), Republic of Moldova Tashkent (regional) and Ukraine for Eurasia; and Afghanistan, Bangkok (regional), Bangladesh, Beijing (regional), Jakarta (regional), Kuala Lumpur (regional), Myanmar, New Delhi (regional), Pakistan, Philippines, Sri Lanka and Suva (regional) for Asia and the Pacific.

Population living under either the full or fluid control of armed groups, in millions, by region, as of 30 June 2023*

People living in areas fully or fluidly controlled by armed groups, in millions. This data is drawn from the ICRC's annual survey on armed groups conducted in June 2023.

Region**	Population under the full or fluid control of armed groups (millions)
Americas	33.6
Middle East and North Africa	45.5
Africa	79
Eurasia	0.9
Asia and the Pacific	35.5

*The ICRC uses the generic term 'armed group' for a group that is not a state but has the capacity to cause violence that is of humanitarian concern. Armed groups also include those groups that qualify as conflict parties to a non-international armed conflict according to the Geneva Conventions, which the ICRC defines as 'non-state armed groups'.

**The regional figure refers to the sum of armed groups active in the countries covered by the ICRC survey in each region.

Data collected by the following ICRC offices (as listed by the ICRC): Brazil, Colombia, El Salvador, Guatemala, Haiti, Honduras,

Source: Matthew Bamber-Zryd, 'ICRC Engagement with Armed Groups in 2023', ICRC Humanitarian Law & Policy, 20 October 2023, https://blogs.icrc.org/law-and-policy/2023/10/10/icrc-engagement-with-armed-groups-in-2023/.

Mexico, Nicaragua, Paraguay, Peru and Venezuela for the Americas; Egypt, Iraq, Islamic Republic of Iran, Israel and the Occupied Territories, Jordan, Kuwait (regional), Lebanon, Libya, Syrian Arab Republic, Turkiye and Yemen for the Middle East and North Africa; Abidjan (regional), African Union, Algeria, Burkina Faso, Central African Republic, Chad, Dakar (regional), Democratic Republic of the Congo, Eritrea, Ethiopia, Kampala (regional), Mali, Mauritania, Mozambique, Nairobi (regional), Niger, Nigeria, Pretoria (regional), Somalia, South Sudan, Sudan, Tunis (regional) and Yaoundé (regional) for Africa; Armenia, Azerbaijan, Balkans (regional), Brussels, Budapest (regional), Central Tracing Agency Bureau for the International Armed Conflict Between the Russian Federation and Ukraine, Georgia, Greece, London (regional), Moscow (regional), Paris (regional), Republic of Moldova Tashkent (regional) and Ukraine for Eurasia; and Afghanistan, Bangkok (regional), Bangladesh, Beijing (regional), Jakarta (regional), Kuala Lumpur (regional), Myanmar, New Delhi (regional), Pakistan, Philippines, Sri Lanka and Suva (regional) for Asia and the Pacific.

Number of armed groups providing public services and/or extracting taxes from the population under their control, by region, as of 30 June 2023* Number of armed groups providing public services or extracting taxes, by region. This data is drawn from the ICRC's annual survey on armed groups conducted in June 2023.

Region**	Number of armed groups
Americas	64
Middle East and North Africa	108
Africa	120
Eurasia	13
Asia and the Pacific	58

*The ICRC uses the generic term 'armed group' for a group that is not a state but has the capacity to cause violence that is of humanitarian concern. Armed groups also include those groups that qualify as conflict parties to a non-international armed conflict according to the Geneva Conventions, which the ICRC defines as 'non-state armed groups'.

**The regional figure refers to the sum of armed groups active in the countries covered by the ICRC survey in each region.
Data collected by the following ICRC offices (as listed by the ICRC): Brazil, Colombia, El Salvador, Guatemala, Haiti, Honduras,

Source: Matthew   Bamber-Zryd,   'ICRC Engagement   with   Armed   Groups   in   2023', ICRC Humanitarian Law & Policy, 20 October 2023, https://blogs.icrc.org/law-and-policy/2023/10/10/ icrc-engagement-with-armed-groups-in-2023/.

Mexico, Nicaragua, Paraguay, Peru and Venezuela for the Americas; Egypt, Iraq, Islamic Republic of Iran, Israel and the Occupied Territories, Jordan, Kuwait (regional), Lebanon, Libya, Syrian Arab Republic, Turkiye and Yemen for the Middle East and North Africa; Abidjan (regional), African Union, Algeria, Burkina Faso, Central African Republic, Chad, Dakar (regional), Democratic Republic of the Congo, Eritrea, Ethiopia, Kampala (regional), Mali, Mauritania, Mozambique, Nairobi (regional), Niger, Nigeria, Pretoria (regional), Somalia, South Sudan, Sudan, Tunis (regional) and Yaoundé (regional) for Africa; Armenia, Azerbaijan, Balkans (regional), Brussels, Budapest (regional), Central Tracing Agency Bureau for the International Armed Conflict Between the Russian Federation and Ukraine, Georgia, Greece, London (regional), Moscow (regional), Paris (regional), Republic of Moldova Tashkent (regional) and Ukraine for Eurasia; and Afghanistan, Bangkok (regional), Bangladesh, Beijing (regional), Jakarta (regional), Kuala Lumpur (regional), Myanmar, New Delhi (regional), Pakistan, Philippines, Sri Lanka and Suva (regional) for Asia and the Pacific.

Index